D0406688

Professional
Visual C++ 5 ActiveX/COM
Control Programming

Sing Li
Panos Economopoulos

Wrox Press Ltd.®

Professional Visual C++ 5
ActiveX/COM Control Programming

© 1997 Wrox Press

Published by Wrox Press Ltd. 30 Lincoln Road, Olton, Birmingham, B27 6PA
Printed in Canada

ISBN 1-861000-37-5

Trademark Acknowledgements

Wrox has endeavored to provide trademark information about all the companies and products mentioned in this book by the appropriate use of capitals. However, Wrox cannot guarantee the accuracy of this information.

Credits

Authors
Sing Li
Panos Economopoulos

Technical Editors
Julian Dobson

Technical Reviewers
David Gardner
Zor Gorelov
Christian Gross
Richard Harrison
Matt Telles

Development Editor
John Franklin

Cover/Design/Layout
Andrew Guillaume
Graham Butler

Copy Edit/Index
Simon Gilks
Dominic Shakeshaft

Author Biographies

Bitten by the microcomputer bug since 1978, Sing has grown up with the microprocessor age. His first personal computer was a $99 do-it-yourself Netronics COSMIC ELF computer with 256 bytes of memory, mail ordered from the back pages of Popular Electronics magazine. Currently, Sing is an active author, consultant, and entrepreneur. He has written for popular technical journals and is the creator of the "Internet Global Phone", one of the very first Internet phones available. His wide-ranging consulting expertise spans Internet and Intranet systems design, distributed architectures, digital convergence, embedded systems, real-time technologies, and cross platform software design.

Recently, he has completed an assignment with Nortel Multimedia Labs working in Computer Telephony Integration, and Advanced Callcenter Management products. Sing is a founder of microWonders, an emerging company specializing in products to fulfill the ubiquitous "computing anywhere" vision.

Sing can be reached at singli@microwonders.com

Panos Economopoulos has been the architect, designer and leader for implementations of a number of complex and successful distributed computer systems. Currently, he is Manager of Research and Development at Telesis North. Here, he designed the OnAir series of mobile client-server products that provide efficient and robust remote access to BackOffice servers over a variety of satellite and other wireless networks. He has extensive experience as a consultant to the Industry and has developed, and taught, a variety of courses both at University undergrad level and for mature developers. He's also carried out advanced research at the University of Toronto - results of which have been published in several research journals.

Panos can be reached at epanos@interlog.com

Dedications

The first and foremost thank you goes to my lovely wife, Kim, who stood by me throughout the roller-coaster ride. Thanks also goes to David and Meion Li for making everything in this life possible. A round of gratitude is due for the great 'gang' at Nortel Labs, in particular to Rosanne Allen, Felix Lee, Andy Ng, Michael Hung, Florin Chiperi, Wei Cui, Janet Ho, Bryce Lee, Ravindra Conway, Mara Miezitis, Henry Raud, and Shaun Griffin for their confidence in me and endless encouragement. Special thanks goes to Allen Lee, who graciously acted as the bouncing board for ideas throughout the project; and to Dr. Robert Lieberman for being my spiritual guiding light. Kudos to Mr. Baris Dortok, whose indomitable determination is a source of inspiration for me; and to Dr. Merv England, Dr. John Carter, and Mr. Peter Woo who collectively "turned on" the hidden computer beast inside me almost two decades ago.

Sing Li

To all my teachers; past, future, and present; whether they know it or not...
To my family; who did not start a revolution when they should...

Panos Economopoulos

& Thanks

We would both like to thank the super-duper team at Wrox; in particular John Franklin, Julian Dobson, David Maclean plus the Wrox Press operations and production staff. Thanks also goes to Richard Harrison, Christian Gross, Viagnehy Fernandez, Dave Gardner, Zor Gorelov and Matt Telles, whose collective wisdom and expertise had contributed to everything of substance contained within the following pages.

Sing & Panos

Table of Contents

CONTENTS

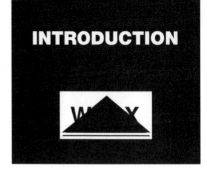

"Long Live the Information Superhighway!"

Wait a minute. I heard some loud heckling from the back row:

"I thought this is a 'Microsoft ActiveX' technical programming book?"

It is.

The point is, there are two ways you can show a technology: either in dry, boring isolation, talking about the nuances without reference to the problems that the technology is supposed to solve, or, as we've attempted to do, applying the technology to a real-world situation. We've decided to show you ActiveX programming by applying this technology to a large growth area: intranets.

As you'll soon see, the ActiveX family of technologies is a very broad family, covering the gamut of Internet-intranet, client-server and distributing computing solutions. It has to be this way, since ActiveX represents Microsoft's entire investment in the Internet-intranet (and object based distributed computing) race.

Within this book, ActiveX will be used as a vehicle to explore many of the concepts and techniques involved in intranet construction. In many cases, the concepts and approaches explored are generally applicable to your practice, whether it's Microsoft-, UNIX-, or even Netscape-centric.

What's Covered in this Book

Just before the technical reader who is fluent in Visual C++ decides to return this book for a refund, I must say that this is by no means a 'lame theoretical treatise'. We turn on the power-throttle, and shine our high beams on the core ActiveX technologies once we've reached Chapter 2. In fact, a discussion of what intranets are about has been relegated to Appendix A, simply because you don't actually need to know about them to gain an understanding of ActiveX.

From there we dive into the depths of the Microsoft's Component Object Model (COM) which is fundamental to all of Microsoft's ActiveX technology. Covering the basics, we'll be taking a view that reduces this complex topic to simple programming practices that we're fully familiar with. From there, we examine the concept of COM aggregation and show how it further enhances code reuse and provides a powerful mechanism for COM.

In Chapter 3, we take our understanding of COM and put it into practice by writing an ActiveX control from scratch, using just raw C++. Here, we'll become intimate with the complete anatomy of a simple ActiveX control. When we move on to more powerful libraries and code generation wizards, this basic understanding will enable us to adapt and troubleshoot more effectively. In this chapter, we encounter many essential COM interfaces through actual hands-on programming; we'll also get acquainted with some indispensable COM programming tools such as the MIDL compiler and the Object Viewer utility.

To handle some more complex problems without coding forever, we'll take a look at programming libraries to simplify the COM object programming task (ActiveX controls, to be precise). We'll explore how to code powerful, yet super efficient and tiny COM objects using the Active Template Library (ATL) 2.1, and we'll spend some time explaining many of the new COM interfaces. We'll show how ATL makes everything simple. Also in this chapter, we'll be learning about the threading models supported by COM objects and the different types of COM servers that can be created. Using ATL to create ActiveX controls is the focus of Chapter 4.

Chapters 2, 3 and 4 give us enough background to understand what ActiveX provides for the intranet development environment. We'll understand how ActiveX controls can be fundamental building blocks (actually software components) in both client- and server-based programming.

We'll make excursions into the ActiveX controls (OCX) specifications in Chapter 5, covering the differences between the OLE Control specification (for Visual controls) and the new OC96 specification (for ActiveX controls). We'll actually be designing an Events Calendar control. This control will display currently active events (for the month) from different company departments for easy and straightforward access. The distributed 'live update' nature of this control eliminates the need for consolidating events information in a centralized database.

In Chapters 6 and 7 we put our design into code. Using Visual C++ 5.0 and MFC 4.21, we'll be building the actual Events Calendar intranet control. The control class and custom wizard provided by MFC greatly simplify much of the development. We'll also be building two additional 'back-end' ActiveX controls using ATL 2.1 to do data processing for the Visual Calendar control. Finally, we'll test the controls and show that the Calendar control is a bona fide ActiveX control which can be hosted within containers such as Visual Basic 5.0, Internet Explorer 3.0, and FrontPage 97.

In Chapter 8, we shift into the highest gear and attempt to put the Calendar control through its paces by using DCOM to run the front-end and back-end ActiveX controls across three separate machines. Along the way, we'll learn a lot about DCOM and how it enables true distributed computing. We'll also be examining the difficult problem of ActiveX control code installation and revision control, and see how the Internet Explorer 3.0 provides us with a ready-made solution to the problem. As part of the installation solution, we'll develop a small program to download controls from remote sites.

After the intensive programming in Chapter 8, we shift our focus to a hot intranet issue in Chapter 9: security. We'll examine the topic by drawing a parallel to the Windows NT security model which is fundamental to all other security mechanisms built upon it. We'll learn about the various security, authentication and encryption APIs and COM interfaces available to intranet application developers. Special attention will be paid to DCOM-related security issues and how arbitrary distributed objects may be prevented or allowed to execute on certain machines.

We conclude our coverage in Chapter 10 by examining some real, and hard-to-tackle, ActiveX and intranet deployment issues; suggesting potential solutions wherever they're available.

We'll cover a lot of ground in the book. I hope your journey into the exciting world of ActiveX will be as pleasant, productive, and profitable for you as it has been for us.

What You Need to Use This Book

To use this book you need Visual C++ 5.0, the latest version of Microsoft's best-selling C++ compiler and development environment. This version is 32-bit only, so you'll need to install it on Windows 95, Windows NT 3.51 or NT 4, which means a 486 CPU or better and a minimum 16Mb of memory.

For Visual C++, you'll need quite a lot of hard disk space–a typical installation is 170 Mbytes. You can do a minimal installation which takes up around 40 Mbytes, but this will mean longer compile times as the CD-Rom will be utilized more often.

Some of the later chapters require you to have access to a network and a second computer to test the code correctly. You'll also need to have DCOM for Windows 95 (information on obtaining this is given in Chapter 8) or Windows NT 4.0.

Conventions Used

We use a number of different styles of text and layout in the book to help differentiate between the different kinds of information. Here are examples of the styles we use and an explanation of what they mean:

> **These boxes hold important, not-to-be forgotten, mission critical details which are directly relevant to the surrounding text.**

Background information, asides and references appear in text like this.

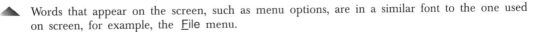 **Important Words** are in a bold font.

Words that appear on the screen, such as menu options, are in a similar font to the one used on screen, for example, the File menu.

Keys that you press on the keyboard, like *Ctrl* and *Enter*, are in italics.

All filenames are in this style: **Videos.mdb**.

Function names look like this: **sizeof()**.

Code which is new, important or relevant to the current discussion will be presented like this:

```
void main()
{
    cout << "Beginning Visual C++";
}
```

whereas code you've seen before, or which has little to do with the matter at hand, looks like this:

```
void main()
{
    cout << "Beginning Visual C++";
}
```

The Wrox Press Web Site

Once you've purchased a book from Wrox Press, the support doesn't stop there. We believe that you've entered into a partnership with us, and as such, it's our responsibility to provide you with the latest information available to us.

The Wrox Press web site is the medium we use to provide this information to you. Although it is a sales tool, providing information on our latest titles, it's actually much more than that. We have a wealth of links to relevant web sites around the world, errata sheets for current Wrox Press titles, useful tools and add-ins we've found. Sometimes, there are even extra chapters that were removed if they didn't quite fit the book in its final form.

If you have any suggestions regarding the Wrox Press web site, then please email the Webmaster at **webmaster@wrox.com**. The web site is as much your resource as it is ours.

Finally, we have two identical sites:

For Europe, on a 64K line: **http://www.wrox.co.uk/**
For the US, on a 256K line: **http://www.wrox.com/**

We recommend that you use a version 3.0 web browser.

Tell Us What You Think

We've tried to make this book as accurate and enjoyable for you as possible, but what really matters is what the book actually does for you. Please let us know your views, whether positive or negative, either by returning the reply card in the back of the book or by contacting us at Wrox Press using either of the following methods:

email:	**feedback@wrox.com**
Internet:	**http://www.wrox.com/contact.stm**
	http://www.wrox.co.uk/contact.stm

Source Code

The decision was taken not to put the source code for the book on a CD-Rom or disk, as there's little benefit to you, the reader. All the programs in the book are shown in full, or rather, the additions to the AppWizard generated code are shown in full. However, for those who have better things to do than type in code, the full programs are available from our web sites:

```
http://www.wrox.com/scripts/bookcode.idc?Code=0375
http://www.wrox.co.uk/scripts/bookcode.idc?Code=0375
```

Errors

While we have made every effort to make sure the information contained within this book is accurate, we're only human. If you're having difficulty with some aspect of the book, or have found an actual error, then please check our errata sheet for this book on our web site:

```
http://www.wrox.com/scripts/errata.idc?Code=0375
http://www.wrox.co.uk/scripts/errata.idc?Code=0375
```

If the answer to your problem isn't there, then please feel free to fill out the form at the bottom of the page with your question or, an answer if you have one.

Building An Intranet : A Case Study

Let's start by showing the case study of the intranet site we'll be partially solving through our ActiveX journey.

We're a consultant team and have been asked to evaluate the applicability of an intranet for a fictitious company called Aberdeen & Wilshire International. Aberdeen & Wilshire is a San Francisco based company with branches in Dallas, New York, Washington D.C., Vancouver, Toronto, and London. The headquarters is in San Francisco, with a sales office at every region, though assembly and manufacturing is done mostly in Dallas. The company employs around 500 people.

The Requirement Analysis

In the first consultation session, we met with the Chief Information Officer, and representatives from the Human Resources department, Sales, Logistics, and Manufacturing. During our meeting, we understood the following requirements:

- Want to take 'least risk' approach to 'phase-in' an intranet. Ideally, the system should be implemented for the headquarters and sales staff first.

- Want to get the intranet up and running within three months and need to obtain immediate results to allay the anxieties expressed by the CEO and Board of Directors; the longer term strategic value of such a system must be clearly visible after the first phase of implementation.

- Must be able to set metrics to measure success.

- Staging must ensure that full-scale corporate-wide deployment would be possible.

- Need to minimize expenditure.

Existing Network Topology

The CIO has explained that the shop has achieved its 'PC on every desk goal' throughout the corporate offices (except for manufacturing). The hardware configurations are non-uniform: some of the office PCs are 486s with 8 MB of memory while those in the corporate headquarters are Pentium Pro 200 MHz. Every PC is networked within the department via Ethernet. Most departments operate on Novell 2.x or 3.x file servers, with an occasional Microsoft based peer-to-peer workgroup LAN. Most desktops are running either Windows for Workgroup 3.11 or Windows 95. There are 200 PCs in San Francisco, and about 50 Macintoshes. Most PCs in San Francisco are running Windows 95 or Windows NT Workstation as the desktop environment. There are about 20 PCs in Toronto running a mixture of OS/2 Warp and Merlin. 15 workstations in Dallas are UNIX based. In Washington DC, Vancouver, and London, there are approximately 50 networked computers at each site consisting of 45% PCs running Windows 3.11 and Windows 95–the rest being Macintoshes. All departments are internetworked through routers and leased lines. Servicing the backbone are a series of HP UNIX Servers. They act mainly as the conduit for email, ftp, telnet, networked FAX and remote printing services. San Francisco, New York, and Toronto have their own Windows NT departmental servers running the Microsoft BackOffice suite. All access to the corporate backbone is via TCP/IP based clients or utilities. Their corporate email is serviced through a UNIX backbone server running a proprietary, in-house developed, email system.

Identified Problematic Areas

The value of an intranet and what it can do for Aberdeen & Wilshire, prompts the group to identify the following areas which will lend themselves to almost immediate intranet application:

The AW Personnel Directory

It is currently being administered at the San Francisco headquarters. The cost of maintenance is high. A full time staff member is responsible for the coordination, update, production, planning, layout and distribution of the directory. Unfortunately, with the high turnover experienced within the recent years, it has become increasingly difficult to keep the information up-to-date. The directory is published twice a year and, often not all printed copies are completely distributed before the information becomes outdated.

Distribution of Memos Regarding Corporate and Departmental Events

The conventional paper circulation is expensive, wasteful, and inefficient, especially when using couriers to the Canadian and UK offices. An attempt has been made to use email for this purpose. Unfortunately, higher level management and directors who are invited to many of the departmental events often missed them because they received a mailbox full of such announcements. People working across departments or disciplines are often bombarded with a barrage of 'junk announcements'. Maintenance and update of mailing lists for distribution of event notices is also a significant chore.

This is the area we'll be looking at during the course of the book.

Automation in Human Resources

The Human Resources department is swamped with forms. Company policies and government regulations have forced the department into keeping both current and historical employee records. With the recent resource cuts, the department is under heavy pressure to provide improved services with significantly less personnel. Under this situation, the head of Human Resources is looking to automation in order to alleviate the most voluminous and common Human Resource interactions. The two most common areas requiring human interactions or paper form processing are:

Inquiries about policies, procedures, and processes

Change of personal employee information

Our Proposal

While the above company and situation is hypothetical, you're likely to find similar (if not identical) requirements and situations in most modern corporations. It serves as a good basis for the rationale of introducing an intranet, which can address many of these requirements almost immediately.

In order to guide Aberdeen & Wilshire into an intranet that they can operate and maintain over the long term, we realize that the project must be implemented in a phased approach. Many of the staff members that will be responsible for the upkeep of the intranet lack the expertise necessary and will require extensive training. However, the team's unusually high enthusiasm for this intranet effort should mean that the smoothing out of the rough spots is an easy process.

Also, to address the CIO's comment on risk and immediate results, we must make the first phase of the project simple, quick, and effective.

To this end, we've planned the project as two phases:

Phase I: Proof of Concept

Create a web using static web pages, standard HTML forms provision, and standard CGI handlers covering all the required functional areas.

Phase II: ActiveX Deployment

Activate the web by gradually introducing ActiveX technology on the web pages and server, explaining and discussing the changes with the personnel involved in the various portions of the project.

The intranet we design will cover the following areas:

- The Aberdeen & Wilshire Events Calendar announcing corporate-wide and departmental events.

- The Employee Directory, maintaining an up-to-date directory for employee names, departments, email addresses and phone numbers.

- Human Resources will pilot the replacement of forms for changing of employee's personal information including address and phone numbers; it will also require that the system can be administered *securely* over the intranet.

- A hard look at how a Microsoft-centric ActiveX solution may or may not work with the mixed constituents within the corporation.

One week after presenting this proposal to the Aberdeen & Wilshire intranet team, the proposal received the team's unanimous approval. Our consultancy asked to assist in the planning, design and coordination during the two phases of the project. Within two weeks, higher level management commitment was obtained and funding was available for beginning the project.

Summary

We've laid out the framework for a hypothetical intranet consultancy assignment and we're going to use that fabrication as a vehicle through the COM, ATL and ActiveX jungle.

ActiveX Technology and Tools

ActiveX is a combination of software components and technologies, both existing and new, which together represents Microsoft's foray into the component bases programming market place. The exact definition and composition that constitutes ActiveX is changing as we speak, however the core technology is well established.

In this chapter, we begin with a discussion of what makes up ActiveX today. We'll learn about ActiveX as an evolution of the client-server technology, and examine both the client- and the server-side compositions. We'll also be looking at the high level intercomponent (object) communications facility which makes all this ActiveX magic possible.

At the end of this chapter, you should understand what ActiveX is.

Fundamental Technologies (ActiveX Protocols)

Let's start by looking at the technology called COM. What exactly is it, and how has it established such an important role in the ActiveX architecture?

COM/ActiveX

COM is important, very important. There's no doubt about it. It is, unfortunately, not quite as intuitive as you might like it to be. We'll be spending a good part of a chapter trying to grasp the idiosyncrasies of its techniques later on. For now, though, let's get to grips with what it actually is.

Binary Interoperability

Simply put, COM is a binary interoperability specification and communication convention for software components.

Since most independent software components are also self contained (i.e. have enough functionality to manage their own data, either globally or per instance), they are frequently called objects or servers as well. This is the reason why COM is frequently being compared to other interoperability mechanisms for software in general.

Being a binary specification, COM is inherently programming language independent. Unlike software libraries or DLLs which are compiled to specific language or linkage conventions, COM based software component interfaces are created ready to work with any COM client. For example, this allows a Visual C++ application to use COM objects created in Visual Basic, or a VBScript within an intranet web page to control a COM object written in MicroFocus COBOL.

A World of Interfaces

Under COM, client applications interact with software components through a set of well defined interfaces. A significant portion of the effort involved in creating a COM based software component is spent on the implementation of these interfaces. A software component must provide means for the client to discover or learn about its interfaces. For example, Microsoft provides documentation for many interfaces which its operating system components exposes. The Mail Application Programming Interface standard (MAPI) is a good example of a mostly COM-based way of interacting with the operating system. In addition to providing explicit documentation, it's also possible for a component to build a 'type library' which will describe all the interfaces it provides and the calling conventions, together will either some help text and/ or help files to describe how the component and its interfaces may be used.

The behavior of present day COM software component is very close to the Utopian ideal of writing code once, and reusing it forever and ever. In fact, this is achievable in COM. It's possible to write completely generic software components which can be reused indefinitely by any future client. The mechanism enabling this, which we've eluded to before, is forcing the client and server to agree on a 'binding contract' known as an **interface**. Any particular software component can expose one or more of these interfaces. As in any other contract, any interface is cast in stone once specified–there can be no changes to it.

Each and every interface ever defined by anyone for any purpose at any time can be uniquely identified through an Interface ID. An interface consists of a set of methods; each method within an interface has specific parameters and return values. The following is an example of a very common interface:

Interface Name   `IUnknown`
Methods   `ULONG QueryInterface(IID, IPointer)`
                   `HRESULT AddRef()`
                   `HRESULT Release()`
Interface ID   `{00000000-0000-0000-C000-000000000046}`

The `IUnknown` interface is the cornerstone of COM, and is implemented by every COM based software component. The contract being specified by this interface is that:

- The interface is uniquely identified by `{00000000-0000-0000-C000-000000000046}` on every machine.

- The interface is guaranteed to have three methods: `AddRef()`, `Release()` and `QueryInterface()`.

- The methods are to be in the order of `QueryInterface()`, `AddRef()`, and `Release()`.

- The parameters and return value of each method are guaranteed to match those specified.

- The operation and calling procedures for these methods are specified (and frozen) in written form.

The actual COM specification goes one step further and specifies how these interfaces must be laid out in a binary fashion. The `IUnknown` interface is very common. In fact, every single ActiveX component or control must implement these three methods. We'll discuss in depth what these methods do in the next chapter.

Readers familiar with data communications will recognize that defining interfaces in COM is very similar to defining communications protocols. In fact, COM can be viewed as a communications protocol between software components (objects) within a machine. In this analogy, the messages allowed in the protocol are defined by the interface description, while the proper sequencing of these messages is defined by the written description of how to use the interface. As in the case of communications protocols, the protocol specification can't be changed once it is defined. For an analogy of how reusability may be achieved forever, witness how a 57.6Kbps PC modem still maintains compatibility with 110, 300, 1200, 2400, 9600, 14.4k, 28.8k, 33.6k modems by continuing to honor the communications protocol standards associated with these modes of communication.

Operation Through Discovery

During actual operation, a client using a COM component first obtains the class ID (CLSID) of the component. This can be done in many ways, typically for intranet web sites, the CLSID is embedded in a web page. Given the CLSID, the client can create an instance of the COM component. This will give the component its own private data space. At this point, the client can find out what interfaces the component supports. In practice, a client always knows how to use a fixed set of interfaces, and it will probe the component to see if it supports them. Once a component is determined to support a desired interface, the client can make a call into the interface's method to perform the desired operation.

The ability to discover interfaces that a component offers is vital to backward compatibility and code reuse. For example, a new version of a client can scour the system for a component which would support a newer version of an interface (note that each version of an interface still has a different unique ID); failing this, it can use an older component which support the compatible older version of the interface.

Prevalent Throughout ActiveX

Realizing that COM is the basis for component based computing from Microsoft, it's easy to see why it's pervasive in the ActiveX architecture. COM is at every single component boundary. It is how **Iexplore.exe** invokes **Shdocvw.dll** which in turn invokes **Mshtml.dll** (again through COM). It is how the Internet Explorer makes use of ActiveX controls (say, to display a video clip). It is how an ActiveX Scripting Host, such as **Mshtml.dll** interacts with a scripting engine, such as **Vbscript.dll**. It is the *selected* way for one software component to communicate with another. When we create our intranet example later, we'll create a COM interface time and time again to communicate with the client application, other components, and the operating system.

With time, more and more of the operating system services and monolithic applications (such as the applications within the Office 97 suite) will be componentized through COM.

Ready for the Networked World

By design, COM is extensible to network based operation without having to recompile the software components. What this says, essentially, is that any COM component can participate in **distributed** computing. For example, once you've finished your mortgage calculation ActiveX control and hooked it up the your local system, it can immediately be used corporate-wide by anyone over the intranet. Furthermore, the user will have a choice of running the component on their own computer, or on *your* computer utilizing *your* CPU resources. In reality, of course, there are security measures, bounds and checks that will make this more complicated. However, with the right configuration in place, this is indeed a possible scenario. The extension to COM which makes all this possible is called the Distributed Component Object Model or DCOM.

DCOM

Under DCOM, any COM objects may be remoted (thrown over to the server side) without changing internal code. This means that we can write server COM objects which can be called by client ActiveX controls.

Since COM (and therefore DCOM) offers an interface discovery capability, it is possible for the client to dynamically discover the interfaces necessary to communicate with the remote object. This opens up the possibility for an amazing variety of innovative and new applications. During the operation, the client ActiveX control simply creates the remote server object, and starts invoking remote COM methods supplied by the COM interfaces supported by the server object.

While totally transparent to the client (an application or ActiveX control), and the remote object (the remote DCOM server object), DCOM actually carries out its work through a variant of the standard DCE Remote Procedure Call mechanism which Microsoft has named Object RPC.

It's easy to see how, with the combination of ActiveX and DCOM, one can create truly distributed applications. While this may sound like science fiction, the infrastructure required to support Distributed COM is actually included with Windows NT 4.0. It's also available for Windows 95 in the form of 'DCOM for Windows 95'. This operating system enhancement can be downloaded over the Internet from Microsoft, and it will come as a standard feature in the Windows 97 operating system.

DCOM maintained the 'binary' nature of its standalone cousin. Binary interoperability between components over a network presents significant new opportunities. This means that even machines with dissimilar architectures and processors can work together in a distributed computing environment enabled by DCOM. For example, our Windows 95 machine can be solving a mathematical problem using the resources of a DCOM object executing on a Windows NT server, another one executing on an UNIX workstation, and a third one running on a Power Macintosh computer.

Where Is DCOM Taking Us

The full power of distributed computing will be realized in the future when the 'fixed' nature of the relationship between the client DCOM object and the server DCOM object is severed. In this case, a 'server object location service' or 'object request broker' will be responsible for locating an appropriate server object, based on a set of specified criteria or runtime conditions, in a network to service the request. In the world of distributed object based computing, your computing problem is solved cooperatively by a network of computers–the exact location and configuration of any particular computing resource becomes a non-issue. Microsoft is currently working on technology which will enable this, and we may be able to get a glimpse of it in a future version of Windows NT. We'll take a further look at distributed computing later when we take an in-depth look at DCOM.

> *There are significant developments in distributed object standards put forth by organizations such as the Object Management Group (OMG). Microsoft neither endorses or condones these standardization efforts. If history is any indication (witness how Microsoft has led the industry to true office applications integration through DDE followed by 3 generations of OLE), Microsoft will continue to evolve towards the common vision via incremental yet profitable steps, endorsing and deploying whatever technology is necessary and commercially beneficial at the time.*

Security

With DCOM opening up the possibility of software components interoperating over a network, suddenly security becomes an even more important issue. After all, nobody would want their computer 'hijacked' through DCOM by remote clients. We also do not want unauthorized individuals from starting remote processes on important servers. Unavoidably, we must examine the issue of security.

In order to operate securely over the network successfully:

▲ Internal security arrangements must not be compromised when allowing access to/from the network

▲ Confidential information must not be revealed when transferred over the network

▲ Control of who can access protected resources through the network must be in place

These requirements can be distilled into the following principles:

▲ Authentication–means verification of identity. It goes hand in hand with integrity which, for transmitted resources implies they have not been tampered with.

▲ Authorization–specifying who has access rights to access what. Authentication must have preceded this so that the access check is meaningful.

▲ Privacy–disallowing unauthorized access to private information, regardless of potential attempts to the contrary.

A number of technologies that deal with these issues are available. The problems and the potential solutions are very different on the closed LAN to the open Internet. The challenge when the LAN becomes an intranet that eventually gets connected to the Internet is to find a way to deploy the right solutions for each domain.

Monikers

We'll now touch on one new set of system service software components which has been introduced for network operation, and one which you may frequently hear about.

A Moniker object is essentially a 'name' which can be used to obtain the actual object through a 'binding' process. The 'binding' of a Moniker will resolve the name and make the actual object referred to available. For example, a Moniker object representing an linked Excel spreadsheet can be put through the binding process to make the actual spreadsheet available.

For intranet/Internet use, Microsoft needed to modify the basic Moniker concept and introduced the Asynchronous Moniker. The difference between a regular Moniker and an asynchronous one is that the binding for an Asynchronous Moniker is assumed to be slow. While the binding method for a regular Moniker object is blocking until the operation completes, the binding method for an Asynchronous Moniker returns immediately without waiting for the actual binding operation to finish. The completion of the actual binding operation is signified through a callback function.

The URL Moniker is an instance of an Asynchronous Moniker. URL Monikers are used to encapsulate URLs. The 'binding' operation of a URL Moniker typically brings the 'object' across the net or from the cache.

A URL Moniker is a protocol independent entity, and though Gopher, FTP, and HTTP are natively supported, you can extend this by implementing new kinds of protocols and supporting Monikers. Implementing a custom protocol at this level will make it available to Internet Explorer 3.0 and any other COM objects/controls/applications which make use of URL Monikers.

Code/Object Downloading

Now that we know that ActiveX controls need not reside on the computer when an application starts, a question comes to mind: how does the ActiveX control get installed and registered on the user's system in the first place?

The answer is quite complex, there are at least three ways. It can be:

- Installed with the application installation
- Explicitly downloaded and/or installed by the user
- Automatically downloaded and installed when the application requires it

In any case, once an ActiveX control is installed into a user's system, it will stay there until it's physically deleted by the user or a newer version of the control is detected. In the latter case, the new version of the ActiveX control may be downloaded and installed automatically.

Obviously, this isn't a desirable long term solution, since both the user's hard disk and registry will become unbearably bloated. Microsoft is planning to fix this solution with an update which will maintain objects for a reasonable 'life-time'. Until then, keep buying larger hard disks.

Since every ActiveX control is also a COM object, the system support for COM objects in both Windows 95 or Windows NT is used to locate, create, and activate ActiveX Controls. It also means that each and every ActiveX control is uniquely identified by a UUID and version numbers, and that the interfaces that they support are identified by a universally unique ID (IID).

The 'ActiveX controls download on demand' is a built-in feature of Internet Explorer 3.0. More specifically, it's a feature of the HTML extension dialect supported by Internet Explorer 3.0. When a web page containing an ActiveX control is created, the **CODEBASE** tag can be used to specify the source URL for the ActiveX control. Once this is specified, IE 3.0 will take care of the download should it be necessary.

If you code your own COM objects and would like to take advantage of the ActiveX Internet Component Download service just like IE 3.0, you can make a call to the new `CoGetClassObjectFromURL()` API. We'll cover the syntax and usage of this call in a later chapter.

Since we're downloading binary code for execution in these cases, how can we ensure that the code wouldn't do damage to the user's system when executed? The answer is simply: we can't. What can be done, though, is to guarantee that the code has come from a reputable or trusted source and that it has not been modified during transit. This is the purpose of the Microsoft Authenticode technology. Authenticode uses digital signature technology to ensure authenticity of origin and integrity of the transmitted module.

The Tools of the Trade

On a very high level, the 'users' of ActiveX technologies can be pigeon-holed into two general categories:

- Creator of ActiveX components
- Consumers of ActiveX components

Creators of ActiveX components are independent software vendors who sell OCXs and in-house developers who may create reusable OCXs for consumption within a corporate environment. They typically do hard-core programming with languages such as C or C++. Since the actual task of creating ActiveX components from scratch isn't a trivial exercise, creators of ActiveX components will typically take advantage of existing software libraries, or code generation facilities provided by a programming tool, which may significantly reduce the development effort. The main thrust of this book, covering the application of Visual C++ 5.0, is targeted directly to this group of users. Given the ever increasing popularity and sophistication of rapid development environments, it's also possible that these developers may be building components using Visual Basic, Java, or Delphi.

Consumers of ActiveX components are applications designers and programmers who may use these ActiveX components in building their applications. Moreover, ActiveX components consumers refers to intranet designer/developers who may be using ActiveX controls within their intranet web pages, and/or their Active Server Pages. Regardless of subcategory, the consumers of ActiveX components tend to keep their focus more on the application design. Most consumers of ActiveX components work within 'authoring environments' where they may visually lay out and configure ActiveX controls. For intranet designers, the top authoring environments include FrontPage 97 and Visual Interdev. The programming languages used by ActiveX components consumers are usually script based (VBScript, JavaScript, Perl, etc.) or interpreted (Visual Basic, Visual J++, etc).

In real life, the classification for any particular user may not be completely black or white. It's likely that an intranet designer/developer will take on tasks reflecting both creators and consumers. However, to simplify product design and marketing, one will see complete product lines catering for each of these categories.

As in any other trade, using the right tool for the job can make a tremendous difference in terms of required effort or perceived difficulty. We'll now commence a concise coverage of the currently available tools. This coverage is aimed to provide understanding of what is available, how and when they may be useful, and a discussion of their strengths and weaknesses. Though our descriptions will be brief, we'll focus on the applicability to creation and maintenance of intranets.

Development Tools

Development tools are tools for creating standalone applications and ActiveX controls. Our survey for development tools will cover the Visual Studio 97 suite and the Visual C++ 5.0 compiler. Visual C++ 5 is the tool with which we'll be building the ActiveX samples within this book.

Obviously, development tools like Visual C++ 5 are definitely created for the component builders rather than the component users. Nevertheless, even component users will benefit from knowing the capability of a tool like Visual C++ 5.0 in order to gain an appreciation for the types of custom ActiveX Controls which can be created quickly.

Visual Studio 97

The Visual Studio 97 product is a super-set product suite produced by Microsoft. Leveraging their success with the Office 97 Suite and BackOffice Suite of applications, this is the latest in a series of marketing attempts to increase overall sales and revenue. Office 97 bundles together the most popular Microsoft desktop applications; BackOffice bundles together the major Microsoft servers; Visual Studio 97 bundles together the most popular intranet and ActiveX component design and creation tools. This impressive bundle includes Visual C++ 5.0, Visual Basic 5.0, Visual Interdev 1.0, Visual J++, Visual FoxPro, and MSDN Library edition.

The piece which unifies all the individual products is the IDE (Interactive Development Environment). Basically, all of the included tools can work out of the same environment. Simply by selecting different files to edit, or different project target types, the appropriate compiler or operating modules will be activated.

Currently, the developer group that works with all of C++, Basic, Java, and FoxPro is a very small group. However, having all the tools at your disposal with a price tag much less than purchasing each one individually may make the suite justifiable.

Of worthy mention here is Visual Basic 5.0's ability to create fully functional visual ActiveX controls within its interactive environment. This significantly lowers the entry barrier for programmers who want to create ActiveX controls, but who don't want to spend the time climbing the steep C++ and COM learning curves.

The inclusion of Visual J++ also provides a multiplatform alternative to creating ActiveX controls (i.e. creation of Java applets).

Visual C++ Version 5.0

The long-awaited annual update of the popular production grade C++ compiler. This new version provides many features which will please ActiveX programmers. Let's take a look at some of more significant:

Native Compiler Support for COM

When coding COM object clients, it's no longer necessary to include a mountain of hopelessly nested include files, or to repeatedly code tedious wrapper classes; this new feature of Visual C++ will save thousands of hours of programmer's time and many, many trees for code printouts. What's more, the implementation is simple! The **#import** directive can be used to import complete type library definitions and cause the compiler to automatically generate wrapper classes in hidden files. The COM object and interfaces exposed can then be accessed through a series of new 'smart pointer' types. As long as you work within the smart pointer system, these new types will take care of all the reference counting and lifetime management for you. The result is a tremendous saving in code 'surface area'. It's now possible to write C++ code which accesses multiple COM objects all in less than one single page of code!

New and Improved ActiveX Code Generation Wizards

These generate ActiveX controls, Active Document Servers, ActiveX Control containers, add-ins for Developer Studio, Active Server Components, Internet Explorer Controls, Property Pages, etc.

New Version of MFC and ATL Libraries

We'll have much more to say about these in the next two sections.

Leaner Compiled Executables

A new optimization switch in the linker will now create executables that are leaner than those of the earlier 4.2 release compiler.

Higher Performance Runtime

The **memmove()** and **memcopy()** routines have been turbo charged, and the performance of many transcendental functions has been improved; finally, integer to string conversion from and to 64-bit integers are now available.

Automating the Development Environment via Scripting

It's now possible to automate and drive the environment using VBScript macro built into the Developer Studio environment. It's also possible to write custom add-ins in C++ which can perform custom functions based on certain events in the build process or when the user manually clicks a button on the toolbar.

ClassView Now Knows About COM Interfaces

The class pane now knows about COM interfaces, and will automatically update the IDL file and associated source and header files when you add or modify a method (but not delete) in an interface.

ANSI C++ Conformance (X3J16)

bool, **true**, and **false** are now native; you no longer have to wonder if they are **INT** or **SHORT**, **SIGNED** or **UNSIGNED**. Also of significance is the incorporation of the entire Standard Template Library (STL) as part of the C++ runtime. This inclusion will make coding of algorithms and management of lists and dynamic elements much simpler.

Choice of Class Libraries

Continuing its tradition, Visual C++ 5.0 includes the famous Microsoft Foundation Classes library. Version 4.21 of the MFC library is shipped, which reflects the relatively little change that has occurred in this library since the last release: version 4.2. With the MFC library and its associated wizards, an ActiveX developer can quickly create:

- Visual ActiveX controls
- Applications or controls which use other COM objects
- Applications which can serve as Active Document Servers
- ISAPI extensions: either filters or applications
- Automation objects which can be used as Active Server components
- Applications which can embed ActiveX controls

Wizards Galore

Visual C++ 5.0 comes with wizards to create:

- ATL based COM objects
- DevStudio Add-ins
- MFC ActiveX Controls
- MFC DLLs
- MFC EXEs
- ISAPI Extensions
- Custom AppWizards
- Databases (Enterprise Edition Only)

Both the AppWizard and the MFC ActiveX ControlWizards have been updated to provide new functionality provided by the libraries in this release. (see description of the libraries in the following sections). The Custom AppWizard is a new addition which allows a user to create customized AppWizards which can be based on existing projects or one of the standard AppWizards.

Class Libraries

Development tools In this day and age of high productivity and object-oriented design/programming, a good C++ compiler without a decent class library is quite useless. Thankfully, Visual C++ 5.0 comes with not one, but two excellent class libraries which can be put to immediate use for building ActiveX controls, components, and applications. We'll take a look at them in this section. In later chapters, we'll be working with each library in depth when we create our applications.

Microsoft Foundation Classes 4.21

MFC 4.21 is a tried and true C++ class library which has evolved over the last five years. MFC provides a set of solid utility classes to deal with common data types, and data structures. It also provides class wrappers for most aspects of Windows based programming, including many of the custom defined types. The accompanying AppWizard can be used to generate Windows applications which conform to the Multiple Document Interface, or the Single Document Interface specification. These applications can also be configured to act as ActiveX control containers, as well as Active Document servers. There's also a wizard which can be used in generating ActiveX controls

Besides support for utility classes and Windows programming, MFC 4.21 also offers significant support for database access, this is performed primarily through:

- ODBC 3.0 (thread-safe) Classes
- RDO (Remote Data Object) Classes
- DAO 3.5 (Data Access Object) Classes

More recently, new classes were added to handle ActiveX control programming and Internet programming. These classes cover the following areas:

- ISAPI Classes for programming ISAPI extensions
- Windows Socket Classes for programming on the Winsock level
- Win32 Internet API Wrapper Classes for programming on the Win32 extension level
- OLE Control Classes for programming (visual) ActiveX Controls
- Active Document Classes for programming Active Document Servers
- Asynchronous Moniker Classes for support of downloads over slow-links
- Ability to create Data-Bound ActiveX Controls

The actual class library code can be linked into the executable or DLL as a static library, or a DLL version of the class library may be used. Linking with the DLL version will reduce the executable size, but the DLL must be distributed with any applications or controls. Apart from Microsoft, MFC is currently licensed by several competing compiler vendors including Watcom and Symantec.

When creating ActiveX controls with visual elements, the use of MFC significantly reduces the number of COM interfaces which you have to code (from 20+ down to about 3), thus simplifying the process.

ActiveX Template Library 2.1

While MFC has experienced relatively little change between Visual C++ 4.2 and Visual C++ 5.0, the ATL 2.1 library has a whole lot more features than its former 1.1 incarnation. As a newcomer to libraries for creating ActiveX applications and controls, ATL 2.1 has achieved tremendous popularity in a very short lifetime. This isn't surprising, given the power of templates for relieving the tedium of everyday repetitious programming.

While not as mature as the Microsoft Foundation Classes, ATL is every bit as versatile as MFC for creating ActiveX controls and components. You can easily create the following components using ATL 2.1:

- Nonvisual, minimal ActiveX controls (the only one supported in ATL 1.1)
- Full, visual ActiveX controls
- Internet Explorer ActiveX controls
- Internet Explorer ActiveX components for scripting
- Property Pages
- Dialog Boxes
- ActiveX Server components
- Microsoft Transaction Server components

Unlike MFC, ATL is a code generating technology. A template library promotes reuse through the compile time dynamic configuration of generated code based on template definitions. This is why there are fine distinctions between the different types of ActiveX controls. The goal of ATL is to generate 'just enough' code for the application. It doesn't require the linking of any static libraries, and it doesn't require any DLLs during runtime. However, since an Internet Explorer ActiveX control that is visible has different mandatory COM interfaces that it must implement when compared to an ActiveX component that is used by a script, there are two wizards generating different template definitions.

Underneath the wizard, ATL has core template implementations corresponding to the required COM interfaces for the above listed classes of ActiveX objects. It also knows about its default characteristics (i.e. whether delegation is allowed or not during object creation) so that the generated code is 'ready for action'. Other utility classes provided by ATL include classes which deal with **Variant** data types (frequently encountered when dealing with automation or dual interface implementations), classes wrapping the **Bstr** data type, and classes implementing connection points for handling incoming events.

Using ATL to create ActiveX components will give the leanest (and usually highest performance) ActiveX control possible. However, it's also deemed as the most difficult way to build an ActiveX control. We'll show in later chapters that using ATL 2.1 to program an ActiveX control is not only simple, but also the most fun. We'll build several of our controls using ATL 2.1.

Moving Ahead

The key enabling technology which makes the ActiveX possible is the 'glue' that holds all these software components together. This led us to an examination of COM. This fundamental layer of 'intercomponent control/communications infrastructure' allows for a new way of designing applications which focuses on reuse and scalability.

Great applications and system architectures are useless, unless we have ways of harnessing these powers for customized uses. To address custom development, Microsoft has substantially beefed up the conventional development tools such as Visual C++ 5.0, Visual Basic 5.0, as well as the new entry to the family, Visual J++. Realizing that component users are considerably more in number (and therefore importance) than component creators, Microsoft has introduced multiple 'authoring tools' to fulfill the requirement of this market. In the meantime, it has attempted to try the same scheme, which made Office and BackOffice successful, on their software developers. This resulted in the introduction of an all-in-one suite of development tools called the Visual Studio 97.

With an understanding of the underpinning of ActiveX technology, and knowing what tools are available, we are now ready to re-examine the task of deploying ActiveX controls on our Intranet. As we proceed in this book and actually apply some of these ActiveX technologies to our Aberdeen and Wilshire intranet, it's important to keep two guiding (technology independent) thoughts in mind:

- There is always more than one way to solve a problem–choosing the appropriate tools and components available is half the battle. We hope that our survey of the currently available ActiveX tools will help you in this area.

- In this young intranet industry, the only constant is change. Don't be afraid to try something new or experiment with a new alternative. We live in a world where improved techniques and products often make obsolete old solutions. Our plans for developing controls must take this flux into account.

An Unusual Introduction to COM

For readers who are intimately familiar with basic COM principles, feel free to skip to Chapter 3, where we start designing and building ActiveX components for our intranet application. For those who want to brush up on the basics, or explore an alternative view of what COM is all about, or indeed those who have no prior COM knowledge, please read on.

It is most important to lay down a solid foundation before constructing a skyscraper. In this chapter, we'll send home the (thankfully simple) concepts underlying COM, upon which the amazing skyscraper known as ActiveX is built. It will be a fascinating journey behind this utility 'object model' as we learn about the various types of COM objects. There'll be ground rules governing the interactions that these objects can have, and we'll take time out to explain each one and why they are there.

On the Windows platforms, specifically Win32 based systems, COM objects are built in very particular ways–and we'll find out how they are built. The system provides many services and APIs that support the model, and we'll be taking a look at lots of these. We'll discover how the system manages information concerning COM objects in the registry. We'll also learn how to use a powerful professional tool, called Object Viewer, which we'll use throughout the book.

In the last portion of the chapter, we'll take a look at a several advanced COM concepts which enable 'component computing', another cornerstone of the ActiveX movement. These concepts include Automation, Containment, Delegation, and Aggregation. When you've completed this chapter, you'll be familiar with all the conceptual pieces that are required to really make sense of the intense technical material presented in the rest of the book. Bear with us as we go through this chapter–you won't see any code until the next chapter, but I sure hope you'll agree with me that the journey is well worth your time.

COM, the Component Object Model, as specified by Microsoft, is a binary object interoperability standard. COM tries to solve the object reuse problem, on a large scale, allowing for the independent and uncoordinated evolution of the interacting objects. The word **binary**, here, is especially significant because it represents the lowest possible level of information/data/code exchange. For example, when we transfer files from Internet file archives to our computer, the files arrive as a binary stream over the 'wire'. By specifying the COM standard on a binary level, one can attempt to arrive at a standard that's independent of the hardware platform, the transmission medium, and the computer language used for implementation.

Instead of adopting an entirely 'how to program' point of view, we're going to look at how COM achieves some of its magic, and why it was designed in a particular way. Hopefully, this will help to make the concepts 'stick'. In reality, there's nothing particularly difficult about COM once you understand why it was developed in the first place. It is true that, in order to achieve its stated goals, COM does impose a set of design restrictions. However, the initial difficulty of adhering to the rules is far outweighed by the 'binary level, cross platform, code reuse' benefit that it offers.

Binary Large Objects

A Binary Large Object, or BLOB, is simply a sequence of binary numbers stored in the memory and/or disk of a computer. In this way, any piece of data, graphic or program can be viewed as a BLOB.

In terms of achieving binary interoperability (as opposed to language dependent or source level interoperability), the primary problem which COM addresses is this: given a BLOB on a machine, which we know to be a software component (through some other mechanism, such as calling a 'blob-dispensing' system API), how can we make use of it?

For example, the following diagram depicts one such BLOB in memory, occupying memory addresses from **$000000A0** to **$00001FA0**.

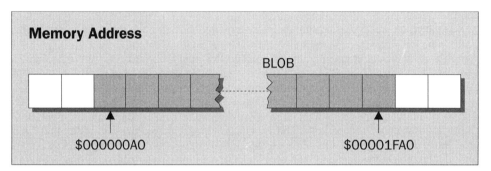

One immediate answer may be to jump to the first memory location (**$000000A0**) and start executing. This is a **convention** used frequently in operating systems for execution of programs and is, in fact, how dynamically linked libraries (DLLs) work. The COM specification consists of a set of conventions very similar in nature to this illustration.

The real-world problem, though, is often more complicated. Most software components residing on a system don't simply 'execute', but provide many functions or services for other components or programs. Therefore, it's also necessary for a calling program to find out what a BLOB can do, and find some way to execute these individual pieces of functionality.

One way to accomplish this is to mark a specific offset into the BLOB, and specify that it must be the entry point to a function which will tell the calling program what the BLOB can do. We can get the specific offset from the dispenser API when we obtain the BLOB, or it could be a convention that all BLOBs have the same special offset. The following diagram illustrates this:

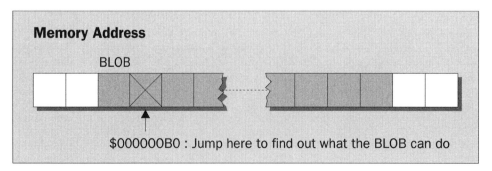

Now, any calling program or component which wants to take advantage of the services provided by the BLOB can call the function at the specified offset to find out its capabilities. This is fine for an operating system like DOS, where there's only ever one executing program. However, in multitasking operating systems, it isn't uncommon for the BLOB components to be used by multiple calling programs/components at the same time. Each 'client' may require the BLOB to allocate and manage certain system resources on its behalf. In order for the BLOB to properly handle these 'clients' and maintain a consistent state for each one, a convention has to be specified as to how the calling program can let the BLOB know that:

- It will be using the services of the BLOB
- It has finished using the services of the BLOB

To accomplish this, two more special offset locations into the BLOB are marked. When a calling program/component calls into offset #1, the BLOB will register that the component wants to use the services of the BLOB; if offset #2 is called, the BLOB will assume the caller has finished using the services of the BLOB. Now, our 'marked' BLOB looks like this:

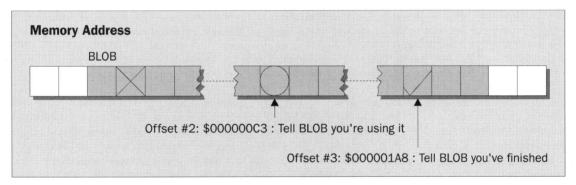

Memory Address

BLOB

Offset #2: $000000C3 : Tell BLOB you're using it

Offset #3: $000001A8 : Tell BLOB you've finished

Since the three marked offsets on the BLOB are so very fundamental to the usability of the BLOB as a component on the system, you can group them together. By grouping a set of pointers to these offsets together, and specifying (and dictating) that this group must be consecutively located within the BLOB, we have to specify only **one** single offset instead of the three offsets. For example, in our case, simply specifying that memory **$000000A6** is the offset is enough for the calling program:

Address	Meaning
$000000A6	Read the pointer at this location and jump there (**$000000B0**) to find out what the BLOB does.
$000000AA	Read the pointer at this location and jump there (**$000000C3**) to let the BLOB know that you're using it.
$000000AE	Read the pointer at this location and jump there (**$000001A8**) to let the BLOB know that you've finished using it.

Notice that, up to this point, our discussion has remained totally generic. We've specified a way of dealing with components that are represented by BLOBs that can be applicable to any computing machine with the Von-Neumann architecture (i.e. it stores program and data in memory locations during execution).

It may surprise you to find that what we've just covered represents a good portion of what COM fundamentals are all about. Even though there's no Microsoft-specific jargon, no 'WINTEL' influences, no language specific constructs, it represents the heart and soul of COM and ActiveX. As a matter of fact, if you've created a BLOB according to the above specification, then you've officially created an ActiveX control (according to the definition of an ActiveX control from Microsoft's OC96 specifications–which we'll cover in detail later).

This, hopefully, will strengthen your faith that this material can be applied generically to any new system that you may encounter–that you are not forever doomed to be Microsoft's harbinger. The message is further fortified by Microsoft's ongoing effort in making COM/ActiveX a publicly administered standard.

Back to our discussion of the BLOB. It turns out that, despite repeated efforts by various groups of experts, it seems that the characteristics of a 'BLOB' representing a software component (i.e. a piece of self-contained, reusable software) can't be further agreed upon (in general) beyond the simple offset scheme illustrated above. Other standards (such as DSOM from IBM), which try to deal with component BLOBs on a higher level, are less popular. This is mainly because other additions beyond the 'bare essentials' are often inapplicable in other problem domains, machine architecture, or computing languages.

Let's translate the scenarios so far into COM-talk. The 'offset to find out what the BLOB does' is called the **QueryInterface()** method. The 'offset to let the BLOB know you're going to be using it' is called the **AddRef()** method. The 'offset to let the BLOB know you've finished using it' is called the **Release()** method. Together, when we combine them into consecutive memory locations, they become the **IUnknown interface**. It's now clear that a method is akin to a function, and an interface is simply a table of functions identified by its address, expressible as a C++ pointer. Just to confuse the issue a little bit, you typically deal with a pointer to an interface rather than the interface itself: this translates to a pointer to a table of functions, or a pointer to a pointer in C++.

In other words, the **IUnknown** interface consists of the **QueryInterface()**, **AddRef()**, and **Release()** methods. We'll describe them below in the 'official' format:

The IUnknown Interface

Consider the BLOB discussed above. It's a BLOB and it has a way of letting others know what it can do through the use of interfaces. The most basic interface is **IUnknown** and is called this because it defines an interface that all others can talk to without having to know the exact workings of the object. The **IUnknown** interface contains three methods and is the 'base' interface for **all** other COM interfaces. This means that if you implement any other interface, you must implement the methods of the **IUnknown** interface as a subset. How is this possible? Well, if we go back to our original description of the interface mechanism, you'll see that C++ automatically creates a virtual function table (vtable) with the first three methods from the **IUnknown** interface. It also means that if you've obtained a pointer to any interface from an object, you can count on the methods of the **IUnknown** interface to be available from the interface pointer.

All this emphasizes how important and fundamental **IUnknown** really is. Except for the unfortunate name, which seems to tone down its importance, **IUnknown** is vital to even the most trivial operations using COM.

Recall our BLOB and the table of offsets. The existence of **IUnknown** within every interface implies that the first three offsets in any offset tables must be pointing to the following functions:

```
IUnknown::QueryInterface()
IUnknown::AddRef()
IUnknown::Release()
```

The double colons (**::**) notation is used to indicate the constituent methods in an interface, in a way similar to member functions of a C++ class. But we must be very careful not to draw too many analogies between C++ conventions and COM, since they are entirely different beasts. Again, COM is a binary object interoperation specification, and the **IUnknown** requirements simply specify a convention for creating these tables of offsets into functions within the object.

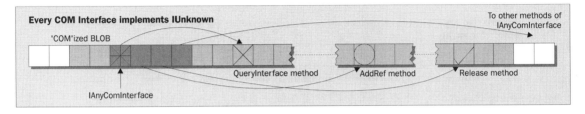

Tuning in on the COM terminology, these tables of offsets themselves (darkly shaded memory regions in the above figure) are frequently called **vtables**. They are named after a compiler generated structure in the code image produced by the linker. More precisely, it is the way that Microsoft C++ compilers create and handle tables of virtual functions for abstract classes in C++. The original rationale for choosing this format probably has to do with making implementation of COM objects simple for Microsoft C/C++ compiler users. This makes very good sense if you consider that:

- C++ is the most widespread object-oriented language to date

- The main development languages on the Windows platforms are C/C++

It's important to understand, though, that this is just a convenient implementation choice. Throughout its evolution, the vtable format has taken on a life of its own. With the appropriate programming, one can generate code images containing these vtable structures from almost any language from any vendor. In particular, there's ample coverage in popular programmer's magazines (Dr Dobb's Journal, Microsoft Developer's Journal, etc.) on how to create COM objects using C, Visual Basic, Java, and even COBOL. Nevertheless, since this book is addressed to C++ developers and you'll use C++ to create and use COM interfaces and objects, we'll soon make the complete connection between COM and C++. In the next chapter, where we actually create a COM object server using raw C++, you'll get a clear idea of how to map C++ classes to COM interfaces and objects.

Typically, the **AddRef()** and **Release()** methods will only increment or decrement a reference counter within the object to let it know when it is the best time to free the resources that it holds (i.e. when no more users are using it). **QueryInterface()**, on the other hand, will return an interface pointer (a pointer to another table of predefined functions), corresponding to the interface ID passed in, provided that the object supports the interface. Otherwise, **E_NOINTERFACE** will be returned. As a matter of fact, any calling program or component **must** interact with an object through its interfaces (obtained from **QueryInterface()**). There's no other way to exercise the services provided by an object except through the interfaces. For example, if I know that an interface exists for checking for the validity of an employee ID called **IDCheck**, I can call **QueryInterface()** requesting **IID_IDCheck**, and if **QueryInterface()** does not return **E_NOINTERFACE**, I can use the returned interface pointer to call on the methods provided by the object through the **IIDCheck** interface.

Every COM object must then implement the **IUnknown** interface, and every COM object which implements the **IUnknown** interface is considered an ActiveX control (actually, the object also needs to be 'self-registering', but we'll cover this later).

Let's take a quick look at the members of the **IUnknown** interface.

IUnknown::QueryInterface()

This method is prototyped as:

```
HRESULT QueryInterface( REFIID iid,
                        void ** ppvObject );
```

Parameters

Parameter	Meaning
iid	Identifier of the interface being requested. We'll be taking a look at where this identifier comes from in the section called *The Chicken and Egg Problem* later on.
ppvObject	This is the returned pointer to the interface requested. If the operation failed or the interface requested isn't supported by the object, this pointer will be pointing to **NULL** upon return. Use the **HRESULT** return value to determine the actual situation.

Return Value

Value	Explanation
S_OK	The requested interface is supported and a pointer is returned in the **ppvObject** argument.
E_NOINTERFACE	This object doesn't support the requested interface.

Comments

QueryInterface() is used to obtain any interface that an object may support, given a pointer to any of the object's interfaces. Since we know that **QueryInterface()** is part of every COM interface, it follows that we can get any interface that an object provides, as long as we have a single interface pointer to the object. We'll examine the implications of **QueryInterface()** later on, in the section entitled *A Few Golden Rules*.

When an interface is returned by a call to **QueryInterface()**, it's assumed by the client that the object has already performed an **AddRef()** to the interface pointer before returning it, incrementing its reference count. The caller of **QueryInterface()** must remember to call **Release()** on the interface pointer when it has finished with it. Be very careful with this convention. Many of the most difficult-to-debug situations in COM stem from unmatched **AddRef()** and **Release()** calls. We'll have more words on this later.

A note on returned values: COM allows an interface member function to return any necessary error codes. Consequently, we must be prepared to receive error codes beyond the expected ones in production code.

HRESULT is a 32-bit code that is a compromise between the ability to efficiently transfer error codes and allowing a reasonably large range that can be partitioned. Let's take a quick look at how **HRESULT** accomplishes this.

The following is how the bits in an **HRESULT** are partitioned:

Severity			
1	2 bits	13 bits	16 bits
	Reserved	Facility	Code

The Severity field (1 bit) can be either **0** for **SUCCESS** or **1** for **ERROR**. This bit is used to determine if the method call has succeeded in performing its intended task. Note that we can actually differentiate between 'level of success' by combining this field with the rest of the **HRESULT**. The Reserved field (2 bits) must be zero, and not be used. The Facility (13 bits) is pre-assigned to different 'groups' of related codes. Some common Facilities include **FACILITY_RPC** for RPC related codes and **FACILITY_DISPATCH** for **IDispatch** (discussed later in this chapter) related codes. The only facility that's usable freely, without first coordinating with Microsoft, is **FACILITY_ITF** (**ITF** is interface). This allows for definition of code specific to any interface. Within the Code field (16 bits), COM will be defining its code with the range of **0x0000** to **0x01FF**, leaving **0x2000** to **0xFFFF** for the programmer.

IUnknown::AddRef()

AddRef(), together with **Release()**, is fundamental to the object lifetime management scheme in COM. See the section on 'Object Lifetime Management' later on in this chapter. Essentially, an internal counter holds the number of users referencing this object. Once this counter reaches zero, the instance of the object is free to dispose of itself and release any resources that it may be holding. **AddRef()** is prototyped as:

```
ULONG AddRef(void);
```

Return Value

Usually returns a value between **1** and x, where x is the number of times that the interface has been referenced. However, program logic should never depend on the validity of this value. It isn't guaranteed by COM to return a valid value. However, certain interface implementations, in DEBUG mode, do guarantee the return value corresponds to the newly incremented reference count.

Comments

Since the count maintained by **AddRef()** tracks the number of references to an interface pointer currently active, one must be very careful when making copies, passing interface pointers as argument to functions, or returning interface pointers from functions. All these actions essentially make an additional reference to the same interface, and the client must remember to call the **AddRef()** method on the interface. When the desired operation is finished, the holder of the interface pointer must remember to call the interface's **Release()** function.

> *Note that **AddRef()**, along with its counterpart, **Release()**, are the only standard COM interface methods that do not return an **HRESULT**.*

IUnknown::Release()

This is the 'partner in crime' method to **AddRef()**. Each call to this function decreases the reference count to the interface/object. When the count reaches zero, it's okay to free the interface/object and all its currently allocated resources from memory. Specific implementations of certain interfaces and objects, though, may not directly follow this convention. It's just a way to let the object/BLOB know that it's no longer wanted; however, what it wants to do with itself is up to the implementer of the object. The prototype for **Release()** is very similar to that for **AddRef()**.

```
ULONG Release(void);
```

Return Value

Again, most of the time the returned value is the reference count to the interface/object, but **do not** depend on this for proper operation. Similarly to **AddRef()**, certain implementations may guarantee the return value in DEBUG mode to be the newly decremented reference count.

Comments

Every interface pointer starts its life (returning from **QueryInterface()**) with a reference count of **1**. Every time the interface pointer is copied, the reference count should be increased by 1 through calls to **AddRef()**. Every time a client is through using it, or is about to wipe out its value, **Release()** should be called on it.

When the reference count of all interfaces on the object reaches zero, the object is expected to free itself from memory and free all the resources it owns. As mentioned previously, however, this isn't an absolute requirement.

The Chicken and Egg Problem

Okay, okay, now we know that there are special spots in the object (in our core memory) that make it usable as a component by other code or components (via the COM **IUnknown** mechanism). But how does the component get into the computer memory in the first place?

That's a very good question. Here's where the real generic stuff starts to lose its flavor. While the concept of object 'instantiation' or creation is generic, the actual implementation of this 'object creation process' is both platform and operating system dependent.

The idea is to bring alive a copy of an object that we want to use as a component. In object design or COM terms, this action is called creating an 'instance' of the object. Why are we creating an 'instance'? Is there another running copy of the object (i.e. another instance) somewhere else?

Yes, the point is that there *could* already be another copy of the running object in the system. Since most modern operating systems are multitasking, it's possible that the component you want to use has already been 'instantiated' by another running program. Furthermore, when getting an instance of the object, we don't know (and shouldn't care, if the object is designed properly) whether it's serving us alone, or if it's also being used by other clients.

Back to the 'how' of creating an instance of an object. First, we definitely need a way to uniquely identify the object we want to create. We need to be able to name our objects so that we (or our clients) can find it again. With you, me, my friend, his Aunt Martha, and Aunt Martha's friends all creating ActiveX objects, how do we cope with the assignment of names? If we give it text-based names, one can easily get into a situation where multiple people assign the same name to different objects. If two different objects with the same name get installed into the same system, one can imagine the disastrous effect. One potential solution is to coordinate the assignment of names through some sort of centralized authority, in a scheme similar to the assignment of IP addresses for the Internet.

Microsoft's solution, and the solution in the industry in general, is to avoid dealing with complex coordination issues altogether. Instead, for naming an object, one can use an *almost* randomly generated extremely large number. The algorithm used to generate such a number will ensure the possibility of generating the same number twice in the entire universe within several lifetimes is effectively nil. Wow! It turns out that one can generate a 16-byte (128-bit) number satisfying this property based on the current date and time, some id (i.e. network MAC address) on the machine generating the number, and a random seed. The number thus created is called a Universally Unique Identifier (UUID), or a Globally Unique Identifier (GUID), which is a slightly less ambitious name. You've seen these beasts before, probably without realizing what they were. A UUID typically looks like this:

```
{5CA735E0-2819-11D0-8DCF-000000000000}
```

or this:

```
static const GUID myID = { 0x5ca735e0, 0x2819, 0x11d0, { 0x8d, 0xcf, 0x0, 0x0, 0x0,
0x0, 0x0, 0x0 } };
```

Now, armed with a way to absolutely and uniquely identify something in the entire universe, one may be tempted to start naming everything else (that needs a name) using the same mechanism. Well, Microsoft did exactly that. As a matter of fact, UUIDs are currently used to name COM objects, interfaces, type information libraries, and categories of COM objects. UUIDs for object naming are called CLSIDs (Class IDs); for interfaces, they're called IIDs (Interface IDs); for type information libraries, they're called LIBIDs (Library IDs); and for categories of COM objects, they're called CATIDs (Category IDs). We'll take a look at some of these other named items later on. One can easily extend this mechanism to name every fragment of code, every window instance, every breath of air we breath and every moment of life we live… since all these entities are unique in time. For now, it suffices to say that we can create an instance of an object provided we know its class ID (CLSID).

A Few Golden Rules

Earlier, when we examined the COM BLOB, we ended up with a discussion of the **IUnknown** interface and its three methods. We've been dealing with these interface pointers, or 'pointers to pointers to a table of function pointers'. We can see the services provided by the BLOB can be exercised purely through these interface points using a generic mechanism. Notice that at no time did we actually deal with a pointer to the BLOB itself. This is not an oversight, but a fundamental feature/rule of COM itself:

> **The client of a COM object shall interact with the object only via its interfaces.**

As a matter of fact, even if we **do** have a pointer to the BLOB itself, there's very little we can do with it. For one thing, it may not be implemented in any language that we know or care about (remember that COM is implementation-language neutral). At least with an interface, we have a well-documented way of getting the BLOB to do something useful for us. This brings up a second fundamental COM rule:

> Each interface is a documented, binding contract between the COM object client
> and the object offering the interface. It is not subject to change, ever!

The keywords here are, as COM pundits proudly reiterate, 'contract' and 'binding'. A contract, once specified, should never change. No minor revisions, no rethinking, no assorted excuses should ever change the terms of the contract. This means that the documentation to an interface is invaluable, and should be planned and worded very carefully (remember that you're drafting up a contract).

Notice, however, that while the rules say that the 'contract' shall not change, they do not state that the ways in which we fulfill the contract can't change. This means that while the interface itself can't change (i.e. the number of methods, the parameters of the methods, what each method in an interface does, etc.), the implementation of the interface can change freely—as long as the contract is honored word-for-word.

This, in fact, is one of the powers of a COM interface. Once specified, it gives a true 'plug-in replaceable' fitting point for components. Imagine the following scenario, where our 'Electronic Desktop Banking Machine' object is using a Bank-of-America-provided COM object through the **IGetBankUserInfo** interface (the '**I**' before an interface name is convention). Since the **IGetBankUserInfo** interface is a well-defined contract, the Banking Machine object could easily connect to the **IGetBankUserInfo** interface of an object from the Wells Fargo Bank.

This may sound like something standard subroutine libraries or DLLs can do, but upon deeper reflection, you'll see that the run-time-connection, language-neutral, operating-system-neutral, and location-neutral nature of COM object interaction goes far beyond the capabilities of conventional subroutine libraries.

Each and every interface provided by a COM object is given an interface ID, and that ID is a UUID. For example, the only standard COM interface that we've covered so far, **IUnknown**, has an IID of:

{00000000-0000-0000-C000-000000000046}

All standard COM and OLE interfaces have UUIDs that have been set aside and are of the following type:

{ dw-w1-w2-C000-000000000046}

where **dw** is a double word and **w1**, **w2** are words. However, the UUIDs that are generated for the objects that you and I create (we'll shortly see how) look definitely more random than that!

Since interfaces are done deals as soon as they're specified and published, how do we cope with the changing environments of real-world applications?

Like any other contractual situation, you draft up another one! Examining the COM and OLE documentation from Microsoft, you'll find many situations where this happens. For example, there exists an **IClassFactory** interface (which we'll cover later, so don't worry about what it does), and an **IClassFactory2** interface that is an enhancement of the original. It isn't uncommon to see an interface named **Ixxxx**, **Ixxxx2**, **Ixxxx3**, **Ixxxx4**,... in the specification of a COM object which has 'served its time'. The bottom line is that an interface, once specified and documented, must never change.

As we've already discovered, our beloved **IUnknown** has a very special property in COM: every other COM interface implemented must include **IUnknown** as a subset. The object-oriented crowd sometimes says 'all COM interfaces must inherit from **IUnknown**'. What this means, if we go back to our BLOB, is that the first three functions in the function pointer table that's pointed to by the interface must be `QueryInterface()`, `AddRef()`, and `Release()`. Every interface must implement these three functions, with no exceptions.

> **Every COM interface must implement the methods of `IUnknown` as its first three methods.**

A unique corollary to this rule is:

> **Given any interface pointer to an object instance, you can get the pointer to any other interface implemented by the object via the `QueryInterface()` method.**

This is vital, since what it's saying is that once you have any interface pointer to an object (including the trivial `IUnknown`), you can get the object to do anything that the object is capable of doing!

Often in COM programming, we may need to deal with multiple instances of an object. Since we never have a pointer to an object itself (and we surmised that we really have no need for such a pointer), how do we determine if two of the instances we hold refer to the same object? Enter another special property of the magical `IUnknown` interface:

> **A COM object instance must return the *same* `IUnknown` pointer any time the `IUnknown` interface is explicitly requested from the object via the `QueryInterface()` method of any of the object interfaces.**

This property is called the 'identity', and is used exclusively to compare COM object instances. There exists no other reliable way to determine if two object instances are the same. However, not having an absolute way of addressing an object instance does have its drawbacks, especially in the distributed computing case. One can't easily manage a large set of 'worker' object instances, or temporarily 'disconnect' from an object instance and then resume interactions sometime later. This is one widely criticized weakness of the COM model.

Creating an Object Instance

Finally, we have all the background to create our object instance. We do this by calling:

```
CoCreateInstance( CLSID rclsid,
                  LPUNKNOWN pUnkOuter,
                  DWORD dwClsContext,
                  REFIID riid,
                  LPVOID* ppvObj);
```

The **CLSID** is the class ID of the object you're creating.

Wait a minute, there seems to be something very non-COM about this **CoCreateInstance()** function. It isn't a method of an interface! (Don't worry, we'll get to the other parameters in a moment.)

That's correct, it's an API function, provided by your friendly COM support system residing in your local operating system. The implementation of this function, though, is *mostly* operating system-, platform-, or programming-language-independent (although the C/C++ language is used in the reference implementation). And, believe it or not, your object *is* actually created by a method of a well-defined interface obtained from an object! Bear with me for a moment, and we'll examine how this actually happens under the hood.

Curious? Here's a simple-minded abstraction of an implementation for the `CoCreateInstance()` call.

```
HRESULT CoCreateInstance(CLSID rclsid, LPUKNOWN pUknOuter, DWORD dwClsContext, REFIID
riid, LPVIOD* ppvObj)
{
   HRESULT hresult;
   IClassFactory *pCF;
   CoGetClassObject(rclsid, dwClsContext, NULL, IID_IClassFactory, &pCF);
   hresult = pCF->CreateInstance(pUnkOuter, riid, ppvObj)
   pCF->Release();
   return hresult;

}
```

Notice what happens in the code above. `CoGetClassObject()`is called to somehow (magically) obtain a pointer to an interface, indicated by `IID_IClassFactory`, from somewhere.

I am purposely being vague here because this is where generality breaks. The implementation of `CoGetClassObject()` is absolutely platform and OS dependent. Yes, from a COM point of view it does happen somehow magically.

On Win32 based systems, the following is what actually happens.

Based on the CLSID passed in the `rclsid` parameter, the function goes to the system registry and looks up the object there. Residing in the system registry, there's a registration database of all the objects currently available on the system. Also available from the database are specific attributes and information regarding the objects installed on the system. One of these attributes indicates the type of module the component is actually in. Such a module is called an 'object server'. Under Win32, COM supports a 'DLL', an 'EXE', or a remote server. In more abstract COM terms, they are called an In-process server (DLL), a Local server (EXE), and a Remote server. Before we proceed, we need to define certain terms we're going to use:

DCOM: DCOM stands for Distributed COM, frequently called 'COM with a longer wire'. This is an extension to COM. With DCOM, you can take two COM objects, place them on separate machines over the network, and have them interoperating together across the network as if they're still on the same machine. All without recompilation of the code. We'll have much more to say about DCOM in Chapter 7.

Marshaling: When accessing an interface of an object running in another process, COM has to use an interprocess communications (IPC) mechanism. The actual mechanism used by COM is a lightweight form of a 'Remote Procedure Call' (RPC). Marshaling refers to the action of packing and unpacking of the data passed during this IPC operation. We'll have more coverage of RPC and marshaling in the next chapter.

Proxy Object: When a 'client' makes a call to the interface of an object running in another process/thread, the object that intercepts the call within the client process is called the Proxy Object. This is a COM object which will take the parameters and 'marshal' it across the process boundary to a corresponding Stub Object in the process hosting the service object for our interface method. More coverage of this sequence of action can be found in the next chapter.

Stub Object: As explained in the Proxy Object definition above. It's a COM object within a COM server which unmarshals data passed into the process by a corresponding Proxy Object. The Stub Object is the COM object that actually makes the interface call on behalf of a calling 'client' object in another process (or thread in certain cases). More coverage in the next chapter.

We're now ready to summarize the different types of servers in the following table.

COM Server Type	Win32 Implementation	Comments
In-Proc (or In-Process) Server	A DLL containing the implementation of one or more COM objects.	An In-Proc server, as its name indicates, runs within the same process as the client using it. In-Proc servers provide the highest performance of the three types of server.
Local Server	An EXE containing the implementation of one or more COM objects.	A local server runs in its own process, but is executing on the same machine as the client. Communications between the client and the server (component) are performed through local remote procedure call (RPC). Interprocess communications between the client and the local server require marshaling code and stub.
Remote Server	An EXE running on a remote computer implementing one or more COM objects. Or a 'surrogate' EXE and associated In-Proc server running on the remote computer implementing one or more COM objects. Or a Windows NT service running on a Windows NT server implementing one or more COM objects.	Enabled by DCOM. This extends the local server model to go across machine boundaries. Standard DCE RPC is used underneath to communicate between client and servers on different machines. The same marshaling code and stub can be used as with the local server.

The **dwClsContext** specifies what type of server the client will accept. It can be any of the following values:

Value	Explanation
CLSCTX_INPROC_SERVER	Client accepts only in-proc server. Under Win32, the implementation is expected to reside in a DLL, and be executed in the same process as the client.
CLSCTX_LOCAL_SERVER	Client accepts only local server. Under Win32, the implementation is expected to be in its own EXE file. The marshaling proxy/stub code is assumed to be already registered with the system. The server will be running in a separate process from the client.

Table Continued on Following Page

Value	Explanation
CLSCTX_REMOTE_SERVER	Client accepts only remote server. The server providing the service resides on another machine over the network. The marshaling proxy/stub code is assumed to be already registered with the system. The server and client are expected to be running on separate machines (may be the same machine with a loop-back setup).
CLSCTX_ALL	The client will accept service of this object from any type of server. If the server is a local server or remote server, the marshaling proxy/stub code must be registered with the system for the interfaces used by the client.

If a match for the object and **dwClsContext** can be found in the registry, the actual location (on disk) of where the object server resides will be noted (path name of the DLL or EXE, or Network Machine Name for a remote object server).

If the object to be created is serviced by a remote server, a rather complex sequence of events will occur, but I'll defer discussion to Chapter 8 when we discuss DCOM.

If the object to be created is serviced by a local server (EXE), the EXE will be loaded and executed if it isn't already running on the system. Following this, some magic 'marshaling' code will be called to obtain an **IClassFactory** interface from a class factory object within the executable. Since this process is very similar between local and remote servers, we'll examine this case in more detail in the DCOM chapter.

The most interesting case for us right now is the case of an in-proc server. For an in-proc server, the system code implementing **CoGetClassObject()** will now load the DLL and call a function which an in-proc server *must* export. This function is called **GetObjectFactory()**. This 'magic' function creates a 'class factory' object and returns an interface called **IClassFactory** from a class factory object.

Building Class Factories and Manufacturing Objects

This is where the magic stops. Once we've instantiated and obtained an interface from a 'class factory' object instance, we're ready to manufacture classes (unfortunate terminology shift, but we're actually making object instances) using regular COM means!

As the name implies, the class factory object has knowledge on how to manufacture classes (really object instances), and you can control it through the **IClassFactory** interface. In fact, since it came from the object server DLL, it knows how to manufacture one corresponding type of object instance, but it can create as many of them as you want. Useful little BLOBs!

To implement **CoGetClassObject()** on other systems where DLLs may not be supported, say some older variant of UNIX, this may be handled differently; but the bottom line is that a class factory object is created, and we have a pointer to the **IClassFactory** interface from it. This is the only system-specific part of the object instance creation process.

You may wonder why we need an extra 'factory' object in order to create an object instance. Couldn't we just invoke a magic function to directly instantiate our object? The answer is that if there's to be a general mechanism which allows the creation of any COM object, then this mechanism must invoke some 'creator' function that is supplied with the object we want to create. This is necessary since object creation may require acquisition of system resources, coordination among objects, etc. What better way to make this functionality available but through COM: by introducing the **IClassFactory** interface all details about the creation of a particular object can be hidden in the implementation of the corresponding factory object. Now it's only the factory object that has to be explicitly created by the COM subsystem.

If your application needs to create many instances of the same class, it would be a smart idea to call **CoGetClassObject()** yourself, instead of calling **CoCreateInstance()**, and store the **IClassFactory** interface pointer for future use.

In reality, an object may support the **IClassFactory2** interface instead of **IClassFactory**. (Remember that an interface never changes? Well, Microsoft had to create a new one here.) **IClassFactory2** supports licensing, which wasn't a concern addressed by the original **IClassFactory** interface. We won't be discussing licensing, since it generally doesn't apply to intranet development projects. The interested reader can consult the description of **IClassFactory2** in the Win32 SDK for more information. For our discussions, we'll assume that the in-proc object server which we're dealing with provides the **IClassFactory** for the class factory object.

To actually create an object instance using a class factory object, we call the **CreateInstance()** method of the **IClassFactory** interface. This confirms that, except for the magical creation of the class factory object itself, everything else in the object creation process follows the standard COM convention and rules.

The **IClassFactory** interface, the second COM interface we'll examine, is defined as follows.

IClassFactory Interface

The **IClassFactory** interface is typically the only interface exposed by a class factory object. The class factory object can be used to create multiple instances of the corresponding class of object. Creation of objects is through the **IClassFactory::CreateInstance()** method. A second **IClassFactory::LockServer()** method is provided for a client to maintain the class factory object in memory if needed. This is useful when you require quick, repeated object instance creation.

There should be a class factory object for each and every one of the objects registered on a system. Each creatable object class will have its CLSID registered in the system registry. Implementation to create the initial class factory object may be system dependent.

We already know that **CoCreateInstance()** uses **IClassFactory** internally to create the object. This suggests that often, we could bypass using **IClassFactory** directly, and just let a helper function like **CoCreateInstance()** do the hard work. It turns out that there are various other helper functions simpler than **CoCreateInstance()** in software layers above COM (namely OLE, which ActiveX replaces) which also cover object creation. We won't cover them in this book, as our focus will be mainly on ActiveX object creation, and they aren't so useful to us in that sense.

Since **IClassFactory** is a COM interface, it inherits from **IUnknown** and implements **QueryInterface()**, **AddRef()** and **Release()**. The following are all the methods implemented by **IClassFactory**:

Method Name	Base Interface	Description
`QueryInterface()`	`IUnknown`	Gets pointer to a supported interface.
`AddRef()`	`IUnknown`	Increments reference count.
`Release()`	`IUnknown`	Decrements reference count.
`CreateInstance()`		Creates an uninitialized object.
`LockServer()`		Locks the class factory object in memory, and doesn't allow it to be released.

The two interesting new methods are `IClassFactory::CreateInstance()` and `IClassFactory::LockServer()`. Here are their definitions.

IClassFactory::CreateInstance()

```
HRESULT CreateInstance( IUnknown * pUnkOuter,
                        REFIID riid,
                        void ** ppvObject );
```

Parameters

Parameter	Meaning
`pUnkOuter`	A pointer to an outer `IUnknown` (which, contrary to basic COM rules, is not `AddRef()`'ed) or `NULL`. An `IUnknown` is passed only if the client object wants to 'aggregate' the newly created object. The Aggregation mechanism is a powerful COM mechanism enabling object reuse, and it will be covered in a later section.
`riid`	An Interface ID (IID) indicating the interface desired from the newly created object. Since we never hold any pointer to the object itself when working with COM, we always have to specify an interface ID in order to get hold of the new object.
	In the case of aggregation (i.e. the `pUnkOuter` parameter is not `NULL`), there's no choice. The parameter must ask for the `IUnknown` interface via `IID_IUnknown`, otherwise reference counting during aggregation may not work properly.
	When not aggregating (`pUnkOuter = NULL`), the interface for initializing the object is frequently requested here. This is because `CreateInstance()` simply creates the object but doesn't take any parameter to pass initialization data for the new object. Exactly what interface is responsible for initialization of an object is entirely dependent on the object itself; COM places no rules in this area.
`ppvObject`	A pointer to the requested interface if successful. Otherwise, it will be set to `NULL` upon return. Check the return value to determine whether there was a failure or if the object doesn't support the requested interface.

Return Values

Value	Reason
S_OK	The method executed successfully.
CLASS_E_NOAGGREGATION	The caller passed in a non-**NULL** outer **IUnknown**, indicating that aggregation was desired. The newly created object, however, doesn't support aggregation.
E_NOINTERFACE	The newly created object doesn't support the interface requested.
E_UNEXPECTED	An unexpected error has occurred.
E_OUTOFMEMORY	The method ran out of memory during execution.
E_INVALIDARG	The method has been called with invalid argument(s).

Comments

We use the **IClassFactory** interface to create COM objects with a registered CLSID. If the object we're creating is to be an inner object in an aggregation, we pass to the class factory the outer **IUnknown** of the aggregation and request the **IUnknown** of the aggregated object. Otherwise, we pass in **NULL** and ask for any interface that we're interested in—typically, an interface which allows us to initialize the object.

There are some legacy objects which support **IClassFactory** but can only create something called a 'single use' object. What this means is that the class factory may be used only to create one instance of the object at any time. If you should ever come across such an object and call **IClassFactory::CreateInstance()** after the object has already been created, you will likely get an **E_UNEXPECTED** error. Fortunately, there should be very few such object classes left around nowadays.

IClassFactory::LockServer()

If you need to create many instances of the same object, you can store away the **IClassFactory** interface pointer from the class factory object, and then lock the class factory object in memory to increase its object creation speed. To do this, we call the **IClassFactory::LockServer()** method.

```
HRESULT LockServer( BOOL fLock );
```

Parameter

Parameter	Meaning
fLock	**TRUE** indicates that you want to lock the server, and **FALSE** that you want to unlock it. Be sure to unlock it after you're finished, or the server may stay around forever.

Table Continued on Following Page

Return Values

Value	Comment
`S_OK`	The lock or unlock operation has been completed successfully.
`E_FAIL`	The operation can't be performed.
`E_OUTOFMEMORY`	The system was out of memory during the operation.
`E_UNEXPECTED`	An unexpected error has occurred.

Comments

Even though you're holding an interface pointer to the `IClassFactory` interface from the class factory object (which you assumed would have been `AddRef()`'ed before it was given to you), you still need to call `IClassFactory::LockServer()` if you want to be guaranteed the best performance possible in creating multiple instances under all circumstances. This is because the `AddRef()` on the `IClassFactory` will maintain the validity of the interface pointer itself, but doesn't semantically guarantee that the actual server is going to remain 'in memory' all the time.

Remember to match the number of `IClassFactory::LockServer(TRUE)` calls with the number of `IClassFactory::LockServer(FALSE)` calls, or else you may have stray servers hanging around. You should not invoke `IClassFactory::Release()` if you still have the server locked. Typical `IClassFactory` implementations will not free the class factory object unless **both** the object reference count and the lock count are `0`.

A Word on Server Types

We've discovered that object servers come in 3 flavors: in-proc, local, and remote. An in-proc server provides objects that run in the same process as the client. On Win32 systems, they're usually created in the form of a DLL. A DLL by definition runs in the same process as the user of the DLL.

Just to give you a feel of how pervasive in-proc servers are, all OCXs are in-proc servers; this includes all OLE controls used in Visual Basic applications as well as the new ActiveX controls used by the Internet Explorer.

A local server provides objects that run in an independent process. On Win32 systems, local servers are usually implemented in the form of an EXE. Depending on the nature of the application the server implements, one single EXE image may be able to manage multiple instances of created objects, or each instance of an object may correspond to a separate running EXE.

The client of the local server communicates with it through proxy code. The proxy is an in-proc object running in the client process exposing the same interfaces as the local server. Internally, however, the proxy implements the interfaces as Remote Procedure Calls (RPC), marshaling the data between the calling client process and a corresponding stub object within the local server. Most of the time, all this activity is transparent to the client and the local server; the client simply makes the interface call, and the server simply services the call. In Chapter 7, we'll discuss situations where this isn't the case.

There's a significant difference between in-proc and local servers, such that the local servers that exist today are typically implemented for the following reasons:

▲ The COM local server implements, or 'front ends' a more traditional server requiring efficient access to shared resources by multiple clients.

▲ A legacy, large, monolithic, non-component based application wants to participate in a COM environment by offering its own subfunctions to external clients (a good example is the set of applications within the Microsoft Office 95 suite, such as Excel, Word, and PowerPoint). This buys the developers some time before componentized versions of the applications can be written.

▲ During development and testing, in order to decouple the client from the server until the server is stable enough to run in-proc within the client process. As a 'beta test' mechanism for DCOM-based remote objects before the DCOM software stabilizes and matures.

This last point is important because, from the client or object server implementer point of view, implementing a local server is almost identical to implementing a remote one. Code written to work with local servers will almost certainly run with very little change when moved to DCOM, since controlling an object and interacting with it across process boundaries is quite similar to interaction across machine boundaries. Therefore, with very little effort, the client and object server implementers can achieve location transparency with a common source base.

This, of course, isn't the case for the poor COM support implementers (i.e. the people writing the DCOM support code—Microsoft for Win32, and Digital for VMS and Software AG for the UNIX implementation). They have to deal with network communications fraught with errors, high latency and failures. As a result, they are faced with the daunting task of providing reliability but also wringing the last ounce of performance out of the transport mechanisms. After all, they're providing support for 'procedure calls' albeit remote. The situation is tremendously simpler when both the caller and the called are on the same machine.

Object Lifetime Management

We've been talking about the **Release()** method of **IUnknown**, and have said that it can be used to free an object. However, we haven't explained in detail under what conditions calling **IUnknown::Release()** will free an object.

To understand this, we need to get deeper into an issue known as 'reference counting'. The premise is quite simple—we need a mechanism through which an entire system of objects could be instantiated on-demand and could be freed as soon as the job has been completed. This frees up resources that other systems of networked objects may be able to make use of.

While very noble, this is also very difficult to implement correctly.

Picture This

Ladies and Gentleman, witness an object proudly exposing itself:

Don't ask me why, or whence it came. It seems that the notation for COM has descended from Microsoft's Ivory Tower research groups and can now commonly be seen in contemporary trade publications, including many non-Microsoft ones. If you can't beat them, join them. The shaded block is an object, and the thing sticking out with a lollipop on top is an interface. When an interface is shown on top, it's usually **IUnknown**, while other less privileged interfaces stick out on the side in whatever space they can find.

Actually, this isn't one of the more functional or particular pretty schemes for diagramming objects and their interconnections, but it is the de facto standard for documenting COM interactions. For example, our former hypothetical automated teller machine example can be diagrammed as:

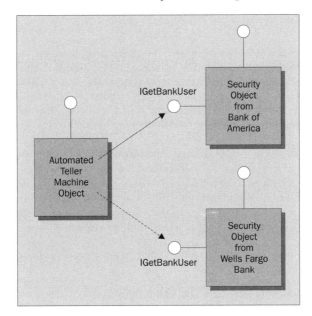

What these diagrams don't convey, however, is quite often the trickiest part of COM programming: the interaction between objects over time across multiple interfaces (or multiple methods in the same interface). This is especially true when objects you're writing are interacting with objects which you didn't write. Typical documentation includes a static description of interface methods with some snippets of ad hoc scenarios of interactions with other objects. What isn't covered, we have to determine through trial and error.

A better diagramming scheme that I'll use throughout this book is the 'stick diagram' or interaction diagrams widely deployed throughout the telecommunications industry for decades. This sort of diagram details the components and the interactions between them over time for a specific operation.

For example, the create object instance scenario described above for an in-proc object server can be presented like this:

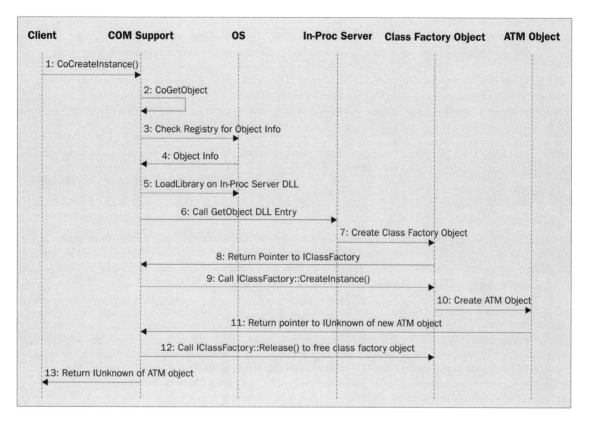

I hope you agree with me that an object interaction diagram definitely speaks louder when you really want to know what's going on under the hood. Typically, the combination of the COM object/interface diagram, with the interface description, and a set of interaction diagrams would represent an acceptable set of design documentations for individual components.

Obviously, to make good and efficient use of COM objects, there are other support pieces that need to be implemented on a system supporting COM. These include object location, object creation, and object management services.

Remember, most objects in the real world require some sort of initialization when instantiated. On a Win32 based system, a function called **CoCreateInstance()** will create such an object. Since we can't deal with the object directly, but only through its interface, we must also pass to **CoCreateInstance()** the IID identifying the interface that we're interested in. How does **CoCreateInstance()** do its job? As we saw before, the secret lies in two Microsoft defined interfaces: **IClassFactory** and **IClassFactory2**. Objects providing these interfaces essentially provide the system with a 'blueprint' on how to create new instances of the objects desired.

The first item we have to deal with is how to positively identify an object.

In addition to a CLSID, a 16-bit major and a 16-bit minor number is provided to identify differing versions of the same object. One can create objects that are 'backward compatible' by recognizing and handling these version numbers.

Interfaces, on the other hand, don't have version numbers. This is because, as we said earlier, in the COM specification an interface forms a contract between the interface provider and the interface user. This contract isn't subject to change. This is so important, that it bears repeating it once more. Once the function of an interface is defined, it shall live forever. The actual implementation or application of the interface may be changing on a case-by-case basis, but the actual contract (interface) itself will never change. In order to modify the 'contract' (interface), a new one must be drawn up (a new interface must be created).

How do you keep track of all the objects available on a system? This is a very interesting question. At the time of writing, the answer is the Windows 95 or Windows NT 4.0 registry. The COM support system manages the object location function. When you make a call to the **CoCreateInstance()**, passing it a valid CLSID, the system support function will find information about the object from the registry and will instantiate the object according to your request.

This simple scheme, however, breaks down when one considers a network of computers all hosting thousands of objects that other computers on the network may want to use. It may surprise you to hear that there's currently no solution for this situation. Although Microsoft is currently designing some new server pieces to address this problem (concrete details aren't available at this time).

When you create an object that you know isn't local to your machine, you must ensure that the registry entry for that object contains the network address of the machine the object is hosted on. Either that, or you can perform the even more undesirable deed of hard-coding the address into your client code. There exists no 'network object manager' or 'network registry manager' which will allow you to create arbitrary objects available over the network. If you or somebody else hasn't done the registration work, you won't be able to access network objects. Each and every network object must be 'wired' this way.

A Quick Tour of the System Registry

Even though we have only examined two COM interfaces in detail, it's clear that the System Registry plays a very important part in the proper functioning of COM. Furthermore, since the system and application configurations, the user preferences, the security database (under NT) are all stored in the registry, the registry is vital to the health and well being of the system as a whole.

In this section, we'll introduce the registry editor, and we'll cover how to use it in order to examine and modify many of the vital entries related to COM object operations.

The registry editor may be used to:

- View registry entries
- Add, delete and modify registry entries
- Backup a portion of or the entire registry
- Batch update the registry through a script file

We won't go into the intricate details of how to use the tool, since you either already know or can learn it quickly. Instead, we'll use the tool immediately, as a viewer, to take a look at how the COM runtime buries away the essential information. In the next chapter, we'll visit the registry editor again when we create custom entries for our very own from-scratch ActiveX control.

Find the registry editor on your system and run it. In Windows 95, it's called `Regedit.exe`; in Windows NT 4.0, it is called `Regedt32.exe`. There are six subtrees that are displayed on the left pane, each of which has associated keys and information.

The one we're most interested in is, not surprisingly, the **HKEY_CLASSES_ROOT** subtree. When we expand this subtree, we'll typically find a very large list of keys. One interesting key is the **CLSID** key. Try expanding this one.

You'll be greeted with a large list of CLSIDs, remember them? These, as we know, are actually 'names' or 'keys' for classes of COM objects. If you expand any one of them, you'll see that they have additional subkeys (attributes) which describe the class further. Typically, you may see a key called **InprocServer32**. This key indicates to the COM runtime that the CLSID represents an in-proc server. The server is a 32-bit implementation (remember there exists still a very large base of 16-bit software out there). The named values under this subkey typically include a **(Default)** and a **ThreadingModel**. The COM runtime looks into the **(Default)** value to find out where the in-proc server implementation DLL is located. The **ThreadingModel** value gives COM an indication of what sort of threading model the server will support; that is, how the object interacts with application threads invoking methods of its exposed interfaces. We'll explore the ramifications of the various **ThreadingModel** choices in a subsequent chapter. For COM objects that are local server based, you'll find a **LocalServer32** key that will provide the COM runtime with a path to find the server EXE. The following table summarizes many of the keys that you'll find under **\HKEY_CLASSES_ROOT\CLSID\{----}**

Key Name	Applies To	Comment
`InprocServer`	16/32-bit servers	Path to 16/32-bit DLL on same machine. Implements an in-proc server.
`InprocServer32`	32-bit servers	Path to 32-bit DLL on same machine. Implements an in-proc server.
`InprocHandler32`	32-bit servers	An object handler is nothing more than a piece of code that implements the interfaces expected by a container when an object is in its loaded state (i.e. it isn't running yet). In other words, it's a glue object that provides the interfaces but doesn't necessarily provide the full function ality. It's typically used in cases where bringing up the local server (where the full functionality is implemented) would be too inefficient.

Table Continued on Following Page

Key Name	Applies To	Comment
LocalServer32	32-bit servers	Path to 32-bit EXE on same machine. Implements a local server running in a separate process.
Insertable	32-bit servers	Indicates that the 32-bit server can be used by existing 16-bit applications.
MiscStatus		Object status information, usually stored in the registry when the object isn't running; that is, at creation, and when loading. Interfaces exist so that interested applications can check on an object's status at all times.
ProgId		A programmatic identifier. The default value of the key is a human readable string uniquely (but not universally) identifying a class that can appear in an Insert Object dialog box. It can also serve as the identifier in a macro programming language to identify the class. APIs are available to convert from/to the corresponding CLSID.
VersionIndependent ProgId		A server must register a second, version-independent programmatic identifier that's guaranteed to remain constant across all versions. A client application accessing the object through this key in, for example, a scripting language, will have access to the current version installed.
Verb	OLE objects	Verbs are specific actions the object can execute that are meaningful to the end user. A container (client app) looks at this key in the registry to find out what verbs the object supports, in order to present them to the user, typically in a pop-up menu.
Control		If the key is present, the object is a control.
Typelib		Type library ID for the object.
MainUserType		The constant name referring to the currently installed version of the server.
AuxUserType		Auxiliary names, for example, a short name for the class, a real-world name for the application when necessary to present to the user, etc.
DataFormat		Lists the default and main data formats supported by the application.
DefaultIcon		Contains icon information for iconic representations of the object. It includes the full path to module (DLL or EXE) where the icon resides and the index of the icon within the executable.

This list is certainly not exhaustive, and any particular pair of COM objects can establish their own private use of keys associated with the CLSID. What we attempt to cover here are the most common ones that we may encounter in our ActiveX programming activities. This explains how COM can know so much about a class given a CLSID. The **ProgId** above is an interesting entry, it gives a human readable string for locating a CLSID. This makes it unnecessary to use and remember CLSIDs in most programming activities. If we know the **ProgID**, we can get the CLSID by invoking the API **CLSIDFromProgID()**. Conversely, from the CLSID, we can get the associated **ProgID** by invoking **ProgIDFromCLSID()**. Given a **ProgID**, it's possible to call **CoCreateInstance()** with the following syntax:

```
CoCreateInstance("ABC.1" )
```

In this case, all we have is a text based name of the class to create. How does **CoCreateInstance()** create the object instance without a CLSID?

The answer, again, lies within the registry. Any COM classes that are registered with a text name are doubly linked back to the CLSID entry with a key right under **HKEY_CLASSES_ROOT**. For example, the **MyObject.1** class with CLSID **{xxxxxxx}** will have the registry entries:

```
\HKEY_CLASSES_ROOT\Myobject.1\CLSID\(Default) = "{xxxxxx}"
```

```
\HKEY_CLASSES_ROOT\CLSID\{xxxxxxx}\ProgID\(Default) = "Myobject.1"
```

```
\HKEY_CLASSES_ROOT\CLSID\{xxxxxxx}\InProcServer32\(Default) =
"C:\DLLDIR\MYOBJECT.DLL"
```

This should completely demystify how the COM runtime does much of its job during object creation. Other keys that are also quite interesting include:

Key Name	Comment
\HKEY_CLASSES_ROOT\TypeLib	All the type libraries registered with the system, ordered by their LIBID.
\HKEY_CLASSES_ROOT\Interface	All the registered interfaces, ordered by their IID. Since you can use **QueryInterface()** during runtime between objects to discover interfaces, this set doesn't cover all the interfaces exposed by all the objects in the system.
	The **(Default)** value contains the text name of the interface (i.e. **"IUnknown"**).
	The **BaseInterface** key contains the IID of the interface from which this interface derives (not directly enforced).
	The **NumMethods** key contains a count of the number of methods contained in this interface.
	The **ProxyStubClsid32** key contains the CLSID of the proxy/stub object used in marshaling parameters and arguments across process or machine boundaries for the local and remote servers.

Bear in mind that what we've examined are very Win32-specific implementation details. COM residing on another non-Win32 platform will have alternative representation and storage for the same object information.

Object Browsing Made Easier: The Object Viewer Tool

After working with the registry editor for a while during COM programming and debugging, you'll wish you had a more intelligent tool available. The problem with the registry editor is that it isn't specific to COM or OLE, and relies on you as the intelligent filter to get to the information you need.

Microsoft has released an excellent tool that practically makes the registry editor obsolete as a viewer. The tool is called the Object Viewer, in the form of Oleview.exe. This tool combs the entire registry, looking up all the OLE objects and controls, stores and sorts all the relevant object information entries, and then presents the compiled information in an easy-to-use format that can be browsed.

> *Oleview.exe is now a standard item including with distributions of Visual C++ 5. However, you can still download the latest version of it from its original home on the Internet. The URL is:*
>
> **http://www.microsoft.com/oledev/olecom/oleview.htm**

Sounds too good to be true? You can try Object Viewer for yourself. Once started, Object Viewer displays all its collected information on two panes.

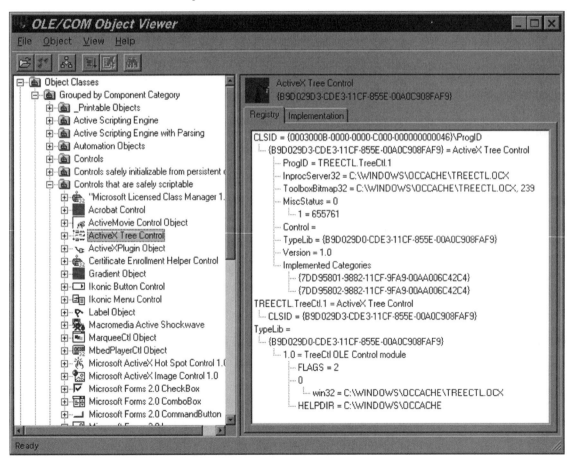

The left pane is a tree view displaying all the various COM objects that are installed on the system. The information available includes:

Information	Comment
ActiveX and OLE Controls by category	The OC96 specification recommended the classification of OCXs (including ActiveX controls) using UUID based component categories (CATIDs). We'll cover this further in Chapter 5. These classifications will allow clients to determine the set of services provided or conventions followed by objects before actually creating them.
COM objects regardless of type	This is a complete list of all the COM objects registered with the system. Different icons represent different types of COM object.
Type Libraries	A type library provides the client with information on the interfaces, methods and parameters that a particular object supports without actually requiring the client to load the object. Originally only used in OLE automation, the type library is now extended to apply to all ActiveX objects regardless of the server characteristics or binding mechanism.
Interfaces	The interfaces registered with the system, including their interface ID, type libraries if available, as well as location of marshaling proxy/stub for local server and DCOM operations.

By expanding any of the information categories, information from individual COM objects can be viewed on the right-hand pane. Furthermore, if you expand any of the individual object entries, the type library information will be displayed. Double-clicking on the object entry will cause Object Viewer to actually create an instance of your object, and to fire `QueryInterface()` calls into your object to determine what sort of known and standard interfaces the selected object supports.

Unfortunately, Object Viewer is just that, a viewer. If you want to adjust and tweak object registry settings directly, you'll still need to use the registry editor. Therefore, you will frequently find instances of Visual (Developer) Studio, Object Viewer, and the registry editor all opened on the typical COM developer's desktop (and the manager asks why COM developers need at least 64MB of memory, and a 21-inch monitor!)

Programmatic Access to the System Registry

It's fine to be able to view the COM related entries of the registry using either the registry editor or the OLE Viewer. COM object servers, however, are required to register themselves with the registry (adding all the relevant entries) under various circumstances. It would be quite an inconvenience to have to spawn `Regedit.exe` every time in order to make the necessary changes.

Instead, Win32 offers a standard set of registry manipulation APIs that the application may use to add, delete, or modify registry entries. These APIs are quite straightforward; the following table summarizes them and provides some usage examples.

Function	Comments
`RegCreateKeyEx()`	Create a new key in the registry (or open an existing one). Specify options for the key as well as the kind of access allowed.
`RegOpenKeyEx()`	Open the specified key. A subkey can be specified as well as options denoting the kind of access the user wants. The key must exist otherwise the call will fail.
`RegCloseKey()`	Release an open key.
`RegDeleteKey()`	Deletes a specified key from the registry.
`RegEnumKeyEx()`	Enumerates subkeys of a given key.
`RegEnumValue()`	Enumerates values of a given key. A key can hold many named values of different data types as well as an unnamed value–the default.
`RegQueryValueEx()`	Retrieve a particular value for a key.
`RegSetValueEx()`	Set a key to a particular value. All types of value are supported.
`RegDeleteValue()`	Deletes a value from a key.

Let's see, now, how we can add the value **"C:\DLLDIR\MYOBJECT.DLL"** of the in-proc server DLL to the key **\HKEY_CLASSES_ROOT\CLSID\{xxxxxxx}\InprocServer32**:

```
HKEY    hKey;
char    *path = "C:\\DLLDIR\\MYOBJECT.DLL";
LONG    rc;

rc = RegOpenKey( HKEY_CLASSES_ROOT, // predefined symbol
                "CLSID\\{xxxxxxx}\\InprocServer32", // sub-key
                &hKey // handle to the key
              );

if ( rc != ERROR_SUCCESS )
   // handle errors

rc = RegSetValueEx( hKey,
                    NULL, // no value name - sets the (Default)
                    0L, // reserved, must be 0
                    REG_SZ, // value type is null-terminated string
                    (CONST BYTE *) path, // address of data
                    lstrlen(path)+1 // size of data
                  );

if ( rc != ERROR_SUCCESS )
   // handle errors

rc = RegCloseKey( hKey );

if ( rc != ERROR_SUCCESS )
   // handle errors
```

Calling into the Object

So, we have instantiated our object, obtained one of its interfaces, and we're ready to party. Now comes another question: how does the user of the object know how to call the methods in the interface?

Of course, an interface is a contract, and therefore the methods in the interface must be documented somewhere. The user of the COM class, having read the documentation or contract, then makes the call according to the documentation.

More practically, the caller must obtain a header file defining the required constants and the prototypes of the functions and parameters in order to use the object. Definitions for many of the standard system classes are available this way. The following is a table of header files that you may want to examine to see some of these classes.

Header File	Description
Atlcom.h	Active Template Library. A template-based framework for the creation of small and fast COM objects and interfaces. ATL is covered in Chapter 4.
Comcat.h	COM category interfaces. This is a generated file, based on a corresponding interface definition file. I'll have quite a lot to say about this later.
Mapix.h, Mapispi.h	MAPI client and service provider interfaces. The MAPI API specifies how electronic mail applications, message store object servers, address book servers and transport servers interact with each other.
D3drmobj.h	Direct 3D interfaces.

According to our discussions so far, in order to invoke the methods of an interface, we instantiate an object and we get a pointer to the interface of interest. In using this approach, the actual pointers into the methods are mapped into offsets into the object (executable image) by the compiler and linker. Calling is extremely efficient, having almost the same overhead as calling a regular C/C++ function. This approach of method invocation is known as 'very early binding' or 'vtable binding'. It's called 'binding' because the user of a COM class essentially 'attaches' or 'binds' to an object instance at runtime. Very early binding allows the compiler to calculate and prepare the most efficient way of 'attachment' to the object and make use of its service. Unlike conventional DLL or library calling, early binding is not sensitive to COM class implementation changes, provided the new class exposes the same set of interfaces. This is, once again, a benefit of the 'immutability' of an interface—once defined it lasts forever.

When We Cannot Bind Early

In real-life programming, there are many situations when a COM class user cannot bind early, or binding early may place too much of a limitation on the application. Good examples can be readily found in interpretive environments such as Visual Basic. In this case, when the client executable is compiled, all the COM classes and interfaces that it would like to work with aren't yet known. Therefore, we really can't bind early. It would be a real pity if Visual Basic could only use early binding, and had to know, at product release time, all the OCXs that it might ever work with. In that case, every time someone else was to write a new OCX (a COM server), Microsoft would have to recompile and redistribute Visual Basic. This simply isn't practical.

If we can't bind early, what can we do? Bind late, of course. What does it mean to bind late? It literally means that the client application will find out at runtime what to do with the object. Since binding late implies that you don't even know the definition of the interfaces until runtime, calling into a 'newly discovered' interface can require a lot of work. Furthermore, unless you have some sort of artificial intelligence built into your client, figuring out the semantics (i.e. what the methods in the interfaces actually do and how they interact) at runtime is almost impossible. Instead of solving this futuristic problem and winning a Turing award in Computing, the COM designers opted for an easier way out.

Again making use of the lifetime consistency inherent in an interface, the COM implementers have specified a special interface that can be used in late binding. This interface is called **IDispatch**. Through the **IDispatch** interface, it's possible for the client to discover at runtime what it can do with the COM object instance. So what we're actually saying is that the client would *early bind* to the COM class's **IDispatch**, and then use it to late-bind to the instantiated object. Okay, this sounds feasible, but it still doesn't solve the semantics and interactions problem!

Solving the problem in generic terms seems impossible until you realize that you can enforce 'object-like' semantics and interaction with the object instance that could be quite usable. The rule we can enforce is:

> COM classes that expose the **IDispatch** interface can implement a group of properties (akin to member variables) that we can **Get** and **Set** through late binding, and they may, also, provide a set of methods (akin to member functions) that we can invoke through late binding via **IDispatch**.

Essentially, we're adding another layer of indirection to drive the object's actual functionality. What we pay for in terms of reduced performance, we gain in terms of tremendous flexibility. Now, any application or development environment which implements capability to drive a COM class through **IDispatch** can freely use any late binding COM classes *during runtime*. Any newly created class, as long as it implements late binding via **IDispatch**, can be immediately used by the existing application. This is quite powerful.

Automation

Hold it! Even though the client can **Get**/**Set** the properties and call methods of the object via **IDispatch**, we still haven't said how the client or calling application knows what to do with these methods or properties. Well, as you may have expected, this is completely problem domain specific. COM doesn't enforce or recommend anything on this level. In reality, however, if a COM class represents an OCX, there are OLE and OCX specifications describing guidelines on the minimal set of properties and methods to be implemented (and this only applies to the category of COM classes representing OCXs, typically used in visual development environments). For other problem domains, it will be up to the group of clients and COM classes to decide what the minimal subset of properties and methods may be.

Late binding works especially well in the visual design or development environment involving the 'user' or 'programmer' in the loop. In this scenario, the 'user' or 'programmer' can actually be shown the textual name of the properties and methods available from the COM class. He or she can then provide the required intelligence, either from pure familiarity or from some sort of documentation, to make good use of the object through these properties or methods.

Due to the overwhelming popularity of the Microsoft's Office suite, its associated Visual Basic for Applications (VBA) language, as well as Visual Basic itself, the late binding mechanism through **IDispatch** has been coined 'Automation'. The term was chosen because the original driving force was the desire to enable writing of macros (scripts) that could drive software components using dialects of Visual Basic, without the presence of the end user (i.e. 'automatic'-ally).

What follows is a fragment of Visual Basic code that uses automation to access a COM object's property and methods.

```
Private Sub Command2_Click()
    Dim a As Long, b As Long, c As Long
    Dim mgr As String
    Dim flag As Boolean

    ' Late Binding Example
    Call CleanForm
    Dim AnObj As Object
    Set AnObj = New Atipblob1
    AnObj.InternalProperty = 3333
    Manager.Text = AnObj.GetManagerName()
    flag = AnObj.OkayToPublishInfo(1990 + Int(Rnd * 100 + 1), Int(Rnd * 12 + 1))
    If flag Then
        Okay.Text = "OKAY"
    Else
        Okay.Text = "NOWAY"
    End If
    Counter1.Text = Str$(AnObj.PeekCounter())
    PropOut.Text = Str$(AnObj.InternalProperty)
    Set AnObj = Nothing
End Sub
```

The object above is of type **Atipblob1** and was created with the following statements:

```
Dim AnObj As Object
Set AnObj = New Atipblob1
```

This object has one property and three methods. The property is called **InternalProperty** and the methods are **GetManagerName()**, **OkayToPublishInfo()**, and **PeekCounter()**. We can see in the above code that a property is used as if it is a data member of a structure, we can use it on both sides of the assignment statement. Method calls, on the other hand, looks exactly like standard C++ member function calls. Note that **Counter1**, **PropOut**, and **Manager** in the above code are edit controls on a form of the Visual Basic application. A statement such as:

```
Manager.Text = AnObj.GetManagerName()
```

will fill the edit control called **Manager** with the value from calling the **GetManagerName()** method of the object. All access to **AnObj**'s methods and property are performed via late binding through the **IDispatch** interface.

Now that we've heard so much about this powerful **IDispatch** interface, let's take a look at its actual definition.

The IDispatch Interface

Except for the **IDispatch::Invoke()** method to perform the actual invocation of the object's methods and properties, the **IDispatch** interface also has a couple of methods that facilitate getting information about the methods to be invoked or properties to be retrieved or set. Let's look in more detail at these:

IDispatch::GetTypeInfo()

Retrieves a description of the object's programmable interface through a 'type information' interface (**ITypeInfo**). (Don't worry too much about this member now, we'll be covering it later in *The Need for Type Libraries*.)

```
HRESULT IDispatch::GetTypeInfo( unsigned int itinfo,
                                LCID lcid,
                                ITypeInfo FAR* FAR* pptinfo );
```

Parameters

Parameter	Meaning
itinfo	The type information to return. Passing **0** asks for **IDispatch** type information.
lcid	The locale ID for the type information. An object may be able to return different type information for different languages (for example, localized member names). We can get the default by passing **LOCALE_USER_DEFAULT**.
pptinfo	Receives a pointer to the requested type information object.

Return Values

The return value obtained from the returned **HRESULT** is one of the following:

Return Value	Meaning
S_OK	Success: the type information exists and was successfully retrieved.
DISP_E_BADINDEX	or
TYPE_E_ELEMENTNOTFOUND	Failure—asked for the wrong type info; **itinfo** argument was not **0**.

Comments

The retrieved type information interface can then be used to get specific information about the methods and properties we want to invoke, **Get** or **Set**. After that, we can invoke the action through the **Invoke()** interface method, as we shall see shortly.

IDispatch::GetIDsOfNames()

Even though an Automation client may use user-readable names for the methods and properties of an Automation server (object), when actually invoking them through **IDispatch::Invoke()**, an ID is used in order to signify exactly which property or method we want. This layer of abstraction allows, for example, methods to have different names-depending on the locality—but just one implementation. The type of the ID is DispID (it's really a **LONG**), and it is called a 'DispID'. The purpose of **IDispatch::GetIDsOfNames()** is to return to the caller an array of DispIDs corresponding to an array of names that were passed in. The array contains either the name of a property, or a method, or the name of a method followed by names of its parameters. Thus, each invocation of **GetIDsOfNames()** refers to one property or one method only....

```
HRESULT IDispatch::GetIDsOfNames( REFIID riid,
                                  OLECHAR FAR* FAR* rgszNames,
                                  unsigned int cNames,
                                  LCID lcid,
                                  DISPID FAR* rgdispid );
```

Parameters

Parameters	Meaning
riid	An historical accident. Must be **IID_NULL**.
rgszNames	Passed-in array of names to be mapped.
cNames	Count of the names to be mapped.
lcid	The locale context in which to interpret the names.
rgdispid	Caller-allocated array, each element of which contains an ID corresponding to one of the names passed in the **rgszNames** array. If **cNames** is **1**, the sole element of the **rgdispid** array corresponds to the method or property name passed in. Otherwise the first element represents the method name, while the subsequent elements represent each of the method's parameters. If any of the names can't be recognized, **DISPID_UNKNOWN** is stored in the corresponding position in the **rgdispid** array and **DISP_E_UNKNOWNNAME** is returned. Thus, the client (controller) knows which of the names weren't recognized.

Return Value

The return value obtained from the returned **HRESULT** is one of the following:

Return value	Meaning
S_OK	Success.
E_OUTOFMEMORY	Out of memory.
DISP_E_UNKNOWNNAME	One or more of the names were not known. The returned array of DispIDs contains **DISPID_UNKNOWN** for each entry that corresponds to an unknown name.
DISP_E_UNKNOWNLCID	The LCID wasn't recognized.

Comments

The member and parameter DispIDs must remain constant for the lifetime of the object instance. This allows a client to obtain the DispIDs once and cache them for later use.

DispIDs are unique only within the same context. The same name may map to different DispIDs, depending on context. For example, a name may have a DispID when it's used as a member name with a particular interface and a different DispID for each time it appears as a parameter. It's worth noting, in passing, the kind of values a DispID may take:

dispID Value	Description
DISPID_VALUE (0)	The default member of the **IDispatch** interface. In other words, if the object is invoked by name, let's say in a client's script, without further specifying a property or method, this member is going to be invoked.
Negative values	Standard DispIDs, already defined by Microsoft. For example, **DISPID_UNKNOWN** (**-1**) returned in the above API call signifies the name requested was not found.
Positive values	These are specified when the interface is defined. As we'll see later, when discussing the Interface Definition Language (IDL), there is a natural place where the DispID for each method or property can be specified. The default member with DispID **DISPID_VALUE** (0) is also specified when defining the Interface.

IDispatch::Invoke()

This is the main method of the **IDispatch** interface. Its invocation results in invoking the requested method of the server interface.

```
HRESULT IDispatch::Invoke( DISPID dispidMember,
                           REFIID riid,
                           LCID lcid,
                           WORD wFlags,
                           DISPPARAMS FAR* pdispparams,
                           VARIANT FAR* pvarResult,
                           EXCEPINFO FAR* pexcepinfo,
                           unsigned int FAR* puArgErr );
```

Parameters

Parameter	Meaning
dispidMember	DispID of the requested member. Most likely, it was obtained by using **GetIDsOfNames()**.
riid	Reserved. Must be **IID_NULL**.
lcid	The locale context. May be necessary in order to interpret arguments. It's also used by the **GetIDsOfNames()** function, and is also passed to **Invoke()** to allow the object to interpret its arguments in a locale-specific way.
wFlags	The flags help clarify how to interpret the requested member DispID. See the table below.
pdispparams	Pointer to a structure containing an array of arguments, an array of argument dispatch IDs for named arguments, and counts for number of elements in the arrays. Dispatch IDs for arguments depend on their position in the method argument list, starting with **0** for the first one. The arguments are read-only except when the **DISPATCH_PROPERTYPUTREF** flag has been set.

Parameter	Meaning
pvarResult	Pointer to where the result is to be stored. Can be **NULL**. Note that the **VARIANT** type is a **union** (in the C++ sense) of, effectively, any kind of value or pointer.
pexcepinfo	Pointer to a structure containing exception information. This structure should be filled in if **DISP_E_EXCEPTION** is returned. Can be **NULL**. In the context of **IDispatch**, an exception is really an error object.
puArgErr	The index within **rgvarg** of the first argument that has an error. May have been set by the caller to indicate missing arguments. The object sets it when arguments of the wrong type have been passed in.

The **wFlags** parameter can be one of the following values:

Value	Description
DISPATCH_METHOD	The member is invoked as a method.
DISPATCH_PROPERTYGET	The member is retrieved as a property or data member.
DISPATCH_PROPERTYPUT	The member is changed as a property or data member.
DISPATCH_PROPERTYPUTREF	The member is changed via a reference assignment, rather than a value assignment. This flag is valid only when the property accepts a reference to an object. This is useful for clients implementing a scripting language that can assign objects by reference.

Return Value

Here are some of the standard values, taken from the returned **HRESULT**:

Return value	Meaning
S_OK	Success.
DISP_E_BADPARAMCOUNT	Wrong number of arguments.
DISP_E_BADVARTYPE	Wrong argument type.
DISP_E_EXCEPTION	An error occurred which should result in an exception. The error information has been filled in **pexcepinfo**.
DISP_E_MEMBERNOTFOUND	The requested member does not exist, or tried to set the value of a read-only property.
DISP_E_NONAMEDARGS	This implementation of **IDispatch** does not support named arguments.

Table Continued on Following Page

Return value	Meaning
`DISP_E_OVERFLOW`	One of the arguments in **rgvarg** could not be coerced to the specified type. Bear in mind that the arguments are passed as **VARIANT** types.
`DISP_E_PARAMNOTFOUND`	One of the parameter dispatch IDs does not correspond to a parameter on the method. In this case **puArgErr** should be set to the first argument that contains the error.
`DISP_E_TYPEMISMATCH`	One or more of the arguments could not be coerced. The index within **rgvarg** of the first parameter with the incorrect type is returned in the **puArgErr** parameter.
`DISP_E_UNKNOWNINTERFACE`	The interface ID passed in **riid** is not **IID_NULL**.
`DISP_E_UNKNOWNLCID`	Wrong locale information.
`DISP_E_PARAMNOTOPTIONAL`	A required parameter was omitted.

More errors, specific to the particular object, may be defined and returned.

Comments

If our COM server supports the **IDispatch** interface, the **Invoke()** method can be quite complicated to implement from scratch. Fortunately, there is significant support in the form of standard Win32 API functions that take care of mundane, repetitive, but also very important tasks like parameter matching, parameter packaging, etc. However, this wouldn't be possible if standard ways of specifying the necessary type information were not available. This brings us right to the next section where this is discussed.

The Need for Type Libraries

Compared to early binding, late binding is extremely inefficient. Imagine having to use the **IDispatch** interface each and every time to discover an object's methods, each and every one of its parameters, and then invoke the method. Picture the number of function calls required between the client and the object. It's quite bad, even when the server is running within the same process. Just imagine what it would be like if the server is a local server running in another process, requiring a context switch for every function call, or across the network requiring network transmission on every call. Definitely less than optimal performance!

A mechanism to easily and quickly find out what properties and methods are supported by an object will really speed things up. If we know what the object can do ahead of time (still at runtime, not as far ahead as early binding), then the only performance hit that we have to take is the unavoidable indirection through **IDispatch**. This will be the best thing that we can do for late binding. Well, the COM folks have done it, and it's called a Type Library.

Type Libraries have existed for a long time internal to COM and the **IDispatch** interface. The **ITypeLib** interface provides access to COM classes managing the type library information. What is added is an easy way for the developer of COM objects to create these type libraries. Instead of making a complicated series of calls into a type library object, one can use a text editor to describe the elements in a text file. Microsoft provides an enhanced version of the Interface Description Language compiler `Midl.exe` that will read the text file (called an IDL file from its file extension) and then call the appropriate API and interfaces on your behalf in order to create the library. We'll talk more about MIDL (and an older variant called `Mktyplib.exe`) in Chapter 3.

Working directly with type libraries is of interest typically only to tools vendors or compiler writers because of the libraries' very low-level nature. For the rest of us, it would suffice to know that the Win32 API's **LoadTypeLib()** and **LoadTypeLibFromResource()** would load a type library file, create the necessary type library objects, and give the caller back an **ITypeLib** interface–ready for further manipulation and querying.

A type library describes comprehensively almost everything contained and used by a particular object server. They may include definitions for:

- COM objects
- COM interfaces
  standard interfaces
  custom interfaces
  dispatch interfaces
  dual interfaces (i.e. both standard and dispatch, covered in a later section)
- **IDispatch** properties
- **IDispatch** methods
- **TYPE** definitions
- **STRUCTURE** definitions

At the time of writing, the format and content of a type library is going through some major revisions. The above list is current as of the beginning of 1997, and may change further. Consult the Win32 SDK or MIDL documentation for the most accurate listing.

Once compiled, a type library becomes a binary resource. It can then be distributed in various forms:

- in its own `.TLB` file
- bound into an EXE file as a resource by invoking the resource compiler
- bound into a DLL file as a resource (via resource compiler in VC5)

The most convenient way for distribution is to include it with the EXE or DLL file. For a COM server supporting **IDispatch** late binding, it's customary to register the type library information at the same time the other registry keys are being added. To register a type library, you can create a new key:

\HKEY_CLASSES_ROOT\Typelib\{------}

where **{-----}** is the CLSID of the type library.

Next, create a subkey with the major revision number:

\HKEY_CLASSES_ROOT\TypeLib\{---}\1.0

Under this, create the minor revision number:

```
\HKEY_CLASSES_ROOT\TypeLib\{----}\1.0\0
```

Under this key, create the keys **Win16** and **Win32**. For each key, set the value to the EXE, TLB, or DLL file that contains the type library. See the figure below for an example of such a registry entry.

Once you've completed this registration, any client or object that would like to access your methods or properties via late binding can do it efficiently by looking up your type library based on the CLSID of the library.

Dual Interfaces

You like the efficiency of early binding, and yet you like the flexibility offered by late binding. Since the code that implements the object's behavior has already been coded, why not make it available to both early and late binders?

This is especially important for certain interpretative development environments which can also compile to more efficient native or optimized runtime code. For example, earlier versions of Visual Basic (prior to 4.0) will use late binding on properties and methods during application design and debug time, but will automatically take advantage of the higher performance early binding if you 'make an EXE' using the compilation facility. Script languages such as VBScript continue to use late binding exclusively, while 'power' languages such as C/C++ work best with early vtable binding.

To mark an interface as supporting both early and late binding, it should be specified to be **dual** when the type library is defined (we'll see how to do this in the next chapter). Note that this is done only to let the client know that the interface or property is accessible both via early and late bindings. It doesn't actually provide any code to implement **IDispatch**.

A dual interface almost always derives from **IDispatch** since all of the **IDispatch** methods must be implemented by a COM class supporting dual interfaces. Note that for the marshaling code that is automatically generated from the interface definition to work properly, a restriction is now imposed in that all member methods of the dual interface must return an **HRESULT**.

Since typical **IDispatch** clients expect properties and methods to be supplied by the COM class, and typical early binding clients may expect direct method calls, the interfaces specified in a class supporting dual interfaces should be defined carefully. For example, a method which sets a property called **HeadCaption** should follow the naming convention of **put_HeadCaption()**. In this way, the early binding client can call **put_HeadCaption()** directly; meanwhile, the late binding client can set the **HeadCaption** property via the **IDispatch::Invoke()** call.

Here's an early binding client. In the following code snippet, **pCustom** is a valid pointer to our custom interface, obtained in the standard way that we have discussed so far:

```
HRESULT    hResult;
BSTR       newTitle = SysAllocString( "New Title"); // allocate new string and copy value

if (newTitle)
   hResult = pCustom->put_HeadCaption( newTitle );

// check for errors
```

In Chapter 5, we'll talk in more details about the relevant data types (i.e. **BSTR**) and helper functions that are related (i.e. **SysAllocString()**). For now, let's consider that we somehow have obtained a pointer to a dispatch interface (i.e. derived from **IDispatch**) called **pDisp**:

```
HRESULT    hResult;
OLECHAR    *szMember = "HeadCaption";
DISPID     dispId;
DISPPARAMS dispParams;

hResult = pDisp->GetIDsOfNames( IID_NULL,
                                &szMember,            // name of the member
                                1,                    // how many passed
                                LOCALE_USER_DEFAULT,  // default locale
                                &dispId               // DISPID of the property
                              );

// check for errors

// strings should be passed in as BSTR. These are
// null-terminated strings that are prefixed
// by their length.  No extra copy is required in order
// to pass them around across process boundaries.
dispParams.rgvarg[0].vt = VT_BSTR;

// allocate new string and copy value
dispParams.rgvarg[0].bstrVal = SysAllocString( "New Title");

// because it is a property put
dispParams.rgdispidNamedArgs = DISPID_PROPERTYPUT;

dispParams.cArgs = 1;
dispParams.cNamedArgs = 1;

hResult = pDisp->Invoke( dispId,                // property DISPID
                         IID_NULL,              // fixed
                         LOCALE_USER_DEFAULT,   // default locale
                         DISPATCH_PROPERTYPUT,  // it is a property put
                         & dispParams,          // the value
```

```
                    NULL,                // no result necessary
                    NULL,                // don't care about exceptions
                    NULL                 // don't care about wrong arguments
              );

// check for errors
```

Object Containment and Delegation

The most powerful thing about the Component Object Model is the ability to use and reuse components dynamically in designing our systems. The idea of being able to encapsulate a concept, business rule, or a logical entity behind a component, and then using and reusing it in systems to solve practical problems is the utopia of software design. Given this, it is entirely foreseeable that in implementing our COM classes, we may like to draw on the services of other predefined COM classes.

This delivers on one of the most promised benefits of object design, allowing us to use our software investment in any future project. How can we accomplish this using COM?

The most obvious way is to simply create other COM object instances during our own operations and make them work for us. Nothing in the COM specification prevents this, and it's a totally legal way of implementing COM classes.

When we create other COM object instances during runtime in order to use their services, this approach is known in COM as **containment**, since in fact, the main object we're creating is seen by the system as containing the worker object.
Containment is easy on the client because the client application or object doesn't even have to know about the existence of the contained object.

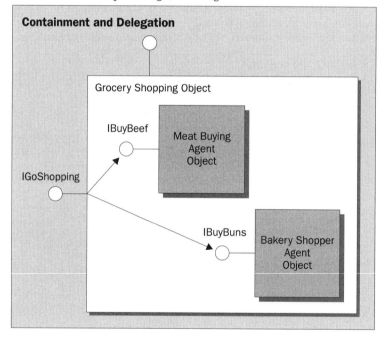

The action of calling a method in the worker object in response to a method call on one of our own interfaces is called **delegation**, since we're delegating the work or a piece of the work to the worker object instance that we've created.

The simplistic example in the figure above shows containment and delegation in action. In this case, we're designing a grocery shopping object for client applications over the Internet. We provide an interface called **IGoShopping** that any client can call to get our COM class to do the shopping for them. In reality, we actually instantiate two worker objects: a Meat Buying Agent object which knows how to get the best quality and prices for all sorts of meat, as well as a Bakery Shopper Agent object which knows about all the finer details of good baking. Our Grocery Shopping object is said to **contain** both the Meat Buying Agent object and the Bakery Shopper Agent object. When our client calls our `IGoShopping::BuyForMeNow()` method, we immediately **delegate** the task to our two worker objects. The Grocery Shopping object calls the methods of the `IBuyMeat` interface from the Meat Buying Agent object as well as the methods of the `IBuyBuns` interface from the Bakery Shopper Agent object to get the hard work done. When the client retires our Grocery Shopping object after shopping concludes, we will, in turn, release our instances of the Meat Buying Agent and the Bakery Shopper Agent objects.

Our Grocery Shopping object adds value to the client by constantly tracking and soliciting the services of the absolutely best meat and bakery buying agents in the entire info-universe. Any client object can reap the fruits of our labor simply by requesting the service of our object.

That's all there is to it. To better visualize the interactions occurring in this particular case of containment and delegation, see the transaction diagram:

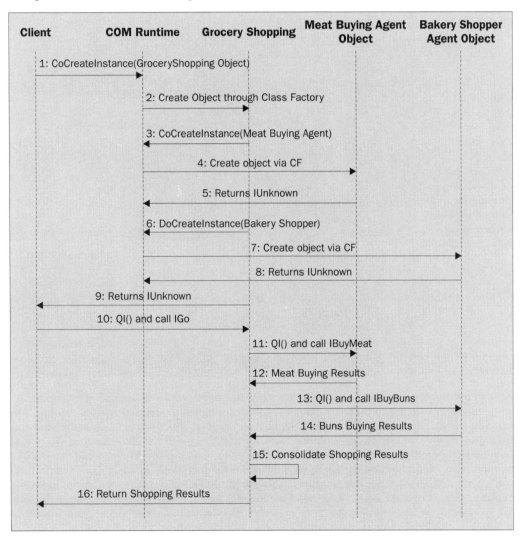

In our example, the worker objects are instantiated when our own object is instantiated, and destroyed when our own object is destroyed. There's nothing in the rule book that says one can't instantiate and destroy worker objects completely within one method call, or between invocation of different methods. However, significantly more attention must be paid in these cases to ensure that the design will have good performance (instantiating an object can be an expensive operation) and that it will be robust. (It's difficult to enforce the calling pattern of methods. Consequently, it can be tricky to ensure the worker objects are created and destroyed properly if they last between multiple method invocations!)

Object Aggregation

In our containment and delegation example, our Grocery Shopping object sits between our client and the actual shopping agent worker objects to provide added value. Frequently in COM programming, we'll find situations where the client of our object may be able to use the interface provided by our worker object directly. In these situations, if we were to use containment and delegation, our delegation code would become a simple wrapper that adds no specific value. The code will immediately call the corresponding method in the worker object.

To cater for these cases, COM provides a mechanism called aggregation, which allows our object (called the aggregator) to expose interfaces of our worker objects (called the aggregates) directly. Schematically, aggregation looks like this:

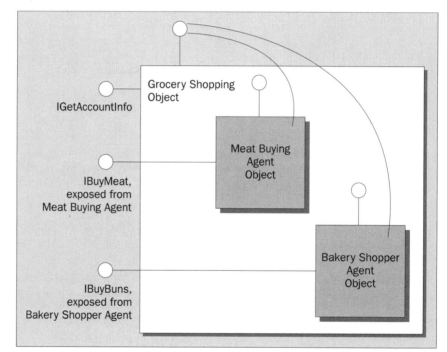

Let's start with our previous example: now suppose that owing to the increased volume of business that our shopping site is receiving, and the fragmentation of our customer's demographics, most customers are demanding that we provide specialized meat buying and bun buying services directly. To accomplish this, we've decided to expose the **IBuyMeat** from the 'Meat Buying Agent' and the **IBuyBuns** interface from the 'Bakery shopping agent' as our own interface. Meanwhile, we've implemented a new interface call **IGetAccountInfo** which the 'Grocery Shopping Object' implements itself. As far as any client of the 'Grocery Shopping Object' (called the aggregator) is concerned, the object implements all of the interfaces **IGetAccountInfo**, **IBuyMeat** and **IBuyBuns**. It does not have to know, or particularly care, that the

'Meat Buying Agent Object' and the 'Bakery Shopping Agent Object' (called the aggregates) are actually working behind the scenes.

In the figure, you may notice that there's a pointer from each of the aggregates to the outside lollipop of the aggregator. Why?

To understand the reason, let's imagine that a client has obtained a pointer to **IBuyMeat**. Now looking at the diagram, the client thinks that the interface belongs to the 'Grocery Shopping Object' and doesn't know about the existence of the 'Meat Buying Agent'. In reality, it's the 'Meat Buying Agent's' interface. What happens now if the client calls the **IUnknown** methods of **IBuyMeat**? What if the client calls **IBuyMeat::QueryInterface()** asking for interface **IGetAccountInfo**?

Of course, since the interface actually belongs to the 'Meat Buying Agent', and the 'Meat Buying Agent' doesn't implement **IGetAccountInfo**, it would return **E_NOINTERFACE**. This is obviously not what we want.

Furthermore, consider the situation when a client holds a pointer to both **IGetAccountInfo** and **IBuyMeat**. Now if the client calls **IGetAccountInfo::QueryInterface()** asking for **IUnknown**, it would get a pointer to the **IUnknown** of the 'Grocery Shopping Object'. This is okay. However, if the client calls **IBuyMeat::QueryInterface()** asking for **IUnknown**, it would get a pointer to the **IUnknown** of the invisible 'Meat Buying Agent Object'. Now if the client compares the two pointers, they would be different! This breaks one of the golden rules of COM that we've already discussed: the rule of **IUnknown** as the identity. I will repeat it here to refresh your memory:

> A COM object instance must return the same **IUnknown** pointer any time the **IUnknown** interface is explicitly requested from the object via the **QueryInterface()** method of any interface.

To fix these problems, COM took a very straightforward approach. As revealed in the above figure, the aggregated objects simply delegates the **IUnknown** methods of its interface to the outer object's **IUnknown**. Note that I did not say the aggregator's **IUnknown**, but rather the outer object's **IUnknown**. Let's try to absorb this for a moment.

Recall that every COM interface must implement the methods of **IUnknown**. Now if a client calls **QueryInterface()**, **AddRef()**, or **Release()** on any aggregated interface (except for the **IUnknown** interface), the corresponding methods of the **IUnknown** interface of the outer object will be called. It's important to realize that aggregation may be nested. In the nested situation, the innermost object's interface may be exposed by the outermost object as one of its interfaces (right 'through' all the intermediate objects in the nesting). In this case, the innermost object must obtain a pointer to the outermost object's **IUnknown** interface so that it may delegate its methods. The reason that we always want the outermost object's **IUnknown** is quite simple: it is **the only object** that is aware of the complete aggregation process, and it alone knows what interfaces it (the outermost object) is supposed to be exposing. Therefore, in our example, we would expect the **IUnknown::QueryInteface()** of the 'Grocery Shopping Object' to be implemented as:

```
// the following declaration assumes that the Grocery Shopping Ojbect
// implements its interfaces
// through multiple inheritance
// (more discussion in Chapter 5)

STDMETHODIMP GroceryShopper::QueryInterface( REFIID riid, LPVOID *ppv )
```

```
{
    if ( riid == IID_IUnknown )
        *ppv = (IUnknown *) this;
    else if ( riid == IID_IGetAccountInfo )
        *ppv = (IGetAccountInfo *) this;
    else if ( riid == IID_IBuyMeat )
        return m_pIUnknownMeatBuyer->QueryInterface( riid, ppv );
    else if ( riid == IID_IBuyBuns )
        return m_pIUnknownBakeryShopper->QueryInterface( riid, ppv );
    else
    {
        // notice that Grocery Shopper ONLY accepts IGetAccountInfo, IBuyMeat and
        // IBuyBuns requests REGARDLESS of the total capabilities of the inner
        // objects the Meat Buying Agent and the Bakery Shopper Agent.  This is
        // because it has to follow its interface contracts with its own clients.
        // It exposes from the aggregates only the functionality that it needs.
        *ppv = NULL;
        return E_NOINTERFACE;
    }
    // AddRef the interface before returning it
    ( (IUnknown *) *ppv )->AddRef();

    return NOERROR;
}
```

Notice how it 'says yes' when asked if it's supporting either interface **IBuyMeat** or **IBuyBuns**; also notice how it actually caches a pointer to the **IUnknown** of each of the aggregates. Without this 'real' **IUnknown** of the aggregate, it won't be able to obtain pointers to **IBuyMeat** and **IBuyBuns**' implementations of the inner objects.

At this point, some of the earlier mysteries should start to clear up. Namely, when we examined **CoCreateInstance()**, there was a parameter called **pUnkOuter** that we said would be used only during aggregation: this is the outer unknown being passed into the aggregate. We also said that if **pUnkOuter** is non-**NULL**, then we must ask for **IUnknown**. This is clearly necessary, as that would be the last chance to get the real **IUnknown** of the aggregate before the inner object delegates its **QueryInterface()** to the outer object.

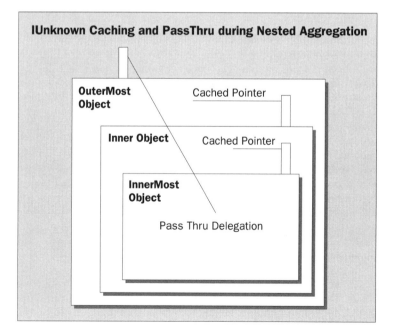

IUnknown Caching and PassThru during Nested Aggregation

OuterMost Object

Cached Pointer

Inner Object

Cached Pointer

InnerMost Object

Pass Thru Delegation

One can also deduce what the inner object should be doing with the **pUnkOuter** passed in. The rules are general, and apply to any object we may want to make 'aggregatable'. So in general, unless you have special reason not to, you should make any COM classes you write aggregatable. This enhances your component's potential usefulness to your users. The rules for the inner object are:

- Store the **pUnkOuter** in a variable within the class.

- When **QueryInterface()**, **AddRef()** or **Release()** is called on any interface (except for **IUnknown**), delegate to **pUnkOuter**.

- If this object aggregates any object, pass the **pUnkOuter** into the inner object as the **pUnkOuter** parameter.

Conceptually, when nested aggregation occurs, the **pUnkOuter** is passed right through to the inner object, while the pointer to the actual **IUnknown** of the each inner object is cached by its immediate aggregator.

That's about as complicated as COM gets. However, reference counting in the above scenario is another can of worms entirely. Notice that when we pass the **pUnkOuter** into the aggregate, the pointer to **IUnknown** is not **AddRef()**'ed. This is the way it's done, and it's an exception to the basic COM rule. In essence, the outer object and the inner objects are all part of one big happy family. Once aggregated, the outer object must be aware that any **AddRef()** and **Release()** done on any of the inner object's interfaces by the outer object (another family member) is actually **AddRef()**'ing its own object! Therefore, it must be careful to 'stabilize' the reference count. For example, if it has finished using an interface from an inner object and wishes to release it, it must first do an **AddRef()** on the interface. This sounds really strange, but you have to do it, because the interface now belongs to the outer object!

There exists a school of thought that suggests aggregation is equivalent to the well-known object-oriented concept of inheritance. In many ways, this is true. One can imagine a situation involving a COM object that aggregates several other COM objects, each, in turn, aggregating other COM objects. In this way, one particular interface can be passed through to the client without any of the intermediate objects actually implementing it. This is certainly similar to the concept of inheriting from a base class that provides an existing set of member functions. Our derived class gains the reuse of these functions with no implementation necessary. The analogy, however, falls apart when one considers overriding any of the base class's implementation.

In classical object-oriented programming, overriding of the base class' method and member variables is allowed freely. It's even possible to selectively override certain members and methods, while inheriting others. As long as the new class is designed carefully and has been fully tested, this is a very good way of reusing existing 'base class' code. Unfortunately, if a base class is used by more than one derived class (i.e. in any reuse situation), and the base class is changed (let's say a series of bug fixes were performed), it's very possible for the derived class to break! This is because the combination of the new base class and the old derived classes has never been tested. Since the derived class has total freedom to override or inherit any element of the base class without restriction, thorough and complete testing of all the permutations and combinations of inheritance and override isn't usually feasible. This is frequently called the 'fragile base class' problem.

The real crux of the problem lies in the lack of a clearly agreed upon responsibility between the base class and the derived class. Inheritance and the ability to selectively override functions leads to this fuzziness. If this sounds like I'm leading on to something, you're absolutely correct. The Interface Contract! That's right, another use of COM's immutable interface.

With aggregation, as we've seen before, we can have interfaces passing through from inner objects to the outer object, providing the benefit of inheritance. Since these interfaces are written to COM specifications, they are contracts with precise, tested behavior. Essentially, they're contracts between the outer object and the inner object. Now, if the outer object decides to override the behavior of an interface, it *must* maintain the terms according to the contract. As a result, in the overriding situation, the onus is on the outer object to ensure its implementation still conforms to the contract expressed by the interface. The COM object doesn't have the luxury of partial overrides: it must override one complete interface at a time; and if it should decide to override, it must ensure that the overridden interface still conforms to the interface specification. COM provides a highly robust reuse mechanism.

Another thing worth noting about aggregation is that it's a purely runtime phenomenon. In fact, there's no indication that a particular COM class uses aggregation to get its job done. For example, examining the type library or registry entry isn't going to give any clue as to whether aggregation is going to take place. Here, again, is a powerful feature in disguise. The implementation of a COM class can use (or not use) aggregation at will, with zero impact on its client or any other tools or utilities which work with the class or object of the class.

Summary

Congratulations, together we've made it through the trenches. COM as a binary interoperability standard is no longer foreign to us. The basic 'BLOB and offsets' features of COM is applicable with any operating system, using any programming language. Yet, with such as simple concept, real component-based software reuse is made possible.

Then, we *really* took a good look at the terminology that COM gives to 'BLOB and offsets' and learned about COM objects and Interfaces. We know now that a COM component can operate 'in-proc', 'local', or remote–meaning it can be a DLL, an EXE, or running on another machine. We found out about the absolutely essential interface, called **IUnknown**, learned about reference counting, and several 'golden rules' of COM programming. We peeked into the system to see how COM objects are created and what information in the registry is maintained by the COM runtime.

Adding icing to the cake, we finished up with a tour of three advanced COM techniques: Automation, Containment and Aggregation. All of these are powerful keys to the reusability and extensibility of COM based software components, yet relatively simple to grasp conceptually.

It's amazing how much complexity (and flexibility) you can build on top of a simple 'BLOB and offsets' binary code reuse scheme. In the next chapter, we'll apply these very principles to construct our first simple ActiveX control. All ActiveX controls are COM objects. And our first control doesn't contain much more than the basic BLOB that we've been examining in this chapter. To hit the ground running, we'll make the control implement an intranet business rule that we'll be able to deploy on our Aberdeen & Wilshire intranet later. To show that what we've covered in this chapter is more than adequate for us to kickstart ActiveX/COM development, we'll build this ActiveX control completely from scratch.

So, sit back and relax or go for a coffee, then come back and join us for an intensive coding session.

Writing An ActiveX Control From Scratch

Hopefully, COM is no longer mysterious to us. We can now proceed to write our first ActiveX control. To get our hands wet, and to make sure that we really understand what was presented in the last chapter, we'll forgo any assistance from Wizards by creating an ActiveX control from scratch. That's right - we'll just use the trusty old Visual C++ 5.0 compiler, without the help of MFC or other class libraries.

Granted, the ActiveX control we create will be very minimal. It just barely passes as an ActiveX control because it implements the **IUnknown** interface. However, in the process of creating this control, we'll gain an appreciation of what's involved, and how most of the tools 'do it' underneath the hood. Again, it will give us more insight into how to take best advantage of what the technology has to offer. As a bonus, it will make our next journey into building ActiveX controls using the Active Template Library 2.1 (ATL 2.1) much easier to follow.

We'll be constructing a hypothetical business rule ActiveX control for the Aberdeen & Wilshire intranet. The control is very simple, but its structure is a good example of how to construct business rule controls which have no user interface. Furthermore, it can be used to encapsulate existing legacy code, making it ActiveX-ready, and easy to use as a client control and/or server-side component. Our control will be used by an event calendar control (which we'll build in Chapter 5) to determine the dynamic status of the department.

The control that we're going to construct has just one late-bound custom interface, with three methods. The first one returns the current department manager's name, or the name of the person in charge at the time. In our implementation, we'll be hard-coding the name. In real life, the control can consult other dynamic sources (e.g. a shift schedule combined with a log from an attendance-tracking punch clock) to provide the necessary information. The second method takes a year and a month, and determines what information should be published to the public for that month. Again, our implementation uses a trivial algorithm to determine if information should be published. In real life, the actual business rule can be more complex. The final method is more of a trace/debug method, which provides a way to peek into the counters being maintained by the object.

In addition to creating and debugging our COM server, we'll also create a client program from scratch to understand how to code client-programs. The client will be used to test our COM server. We'll then develop our client further to really give our COM server a thorough test. The final client program will allow the creation and testing of multiple instances of the COM object.

We'll only create an in-proc server for our object, residing within a DLL. We'll also create the necessary interface description, type library, and registry update code to make it a good, well-behaved COM citizen.

Again, we'll try to do all this without assistance from external libraries or Wizards, just so that we can see how it's really done.

Describing the COM Component

First things first, we need to know what the class that we're creating looks like. From our description above, it is precisely this:

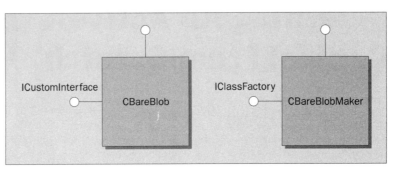

The server will implement two different types of objects. **CBareBlobMaker** is a class factory for the **CBareBlob** class. The **CBareBlob** class will implement a custom interface called **ICustomInterface** which provide the three methods called **GetManagerName()**, **OkayToPublishInfo()**, and **PeekCounters()**.

The first step in creating this BLOB is to describe the object in an IDL file. IDL stands for Interface Description Language, which is something of a misnomer for what it actually does. Historically speaking, objects, libraries, and interfaces were described in a text file called an ODL file or Object Description Language file. As we discovered in the last chapter, the ODL file can be used to generate a type library. The utility that translated the ODL file description into the type library binary resource is a program called **Mktyplib.exe**. However, since both a local server and a remote server need to use RPC (Remote Procedure Calls) to marshal functions and parameters across process or machine boundaries, an additional IDL or interface description file is required to specify the interfaces required to be marshaled. Any COM object that may be used remotely will require the marshaling code; it turns out that, under certain circumstances, even non-remote objects require marshaling code to marshal between process or thread boundaries (see the Threading Model discussion in Chapter 4). So what is this RPC and marshaling all about?

RPC Magic

Now would be an good moment to take a quick digression into explaining RPC. Not invented by Microsoft, RPC has long been used in the UNIX and mini/mainframe world to provide a primitive form of distributed computing between networked computers. The idea behind RPC is quite simple: when an application on the client computer makes a call to a **remote procedure**, that procedure is executed by a remote computer instead of locally. From a programmer's point of view, he or she doesn't even need to *know* whether a particular procedure is local or remote.

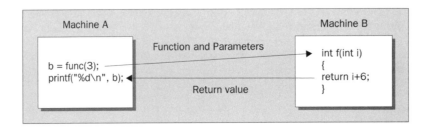

What actually happens, of course, is that there are hidden pieces of code which are activated to handle the communications. On the client side, some code needs to examine the parameters of the function and place them on to the communications medium (e.g. network channel) through a transmission buffer. Once this buffer of data is sent to the site called, another piece of code must examine the buffer, unpackage the parameters, and actually call the implementation of the procedure. If the receiving computer has a different type of CPU or operating system, it must adjust for the potential differences (e.g. big endian versus little endian, CPU word size) when it unpacks the parameters from the buffer.

RPC has specific names for each element:

- ▲ The piece of code on the client side stuffing the parameters into the buffer is called the **proxy**.

- ▲ The piece of code on the server side making the call to the implementation and passing back the return values/parameters is called the **stub**.

- ▲ The action of packing parameters on the proxy, and unpacking them at the stub (also packing of returned value and parameters at the stub) is called **marshaling**.

- ▲ The actual 'bit representation' that's transmitted between the client and the server is a standard agreed upon called the **Network Data Representation** (NDR).

In other words, we have the following scenario:

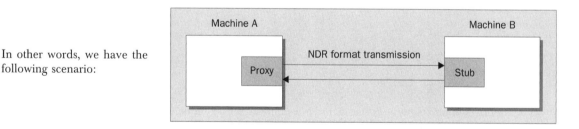

Somebody, or something, must write the proxy and stub code; in real life, most RPC stubs are generated by an IDL (Interface Definition Language) compiler which creates proxy and stub code from an Interface definition file. Under Win32, the Microsoft Interface Description Language compiler, or **Midl.exe**, performs this conversion.

> *It's worth noting here that the MIDL compiler that ships with Visual C++ 4.1 or earlier won't work correctly for our samples. You need Visual C++ 4.2 or later.*

Before the availability of Visual C++ 4.2, you needed to create both an ODL and an IDL file for every COM server that was implemented. Since a typical interface and its methods are described twice (once in each file), it wasn't long before developers (and competitors) started to complain loudly. Microsoft listened, and with Visual C/C++ Version 4.2 and later, combined the two description files into one, and enhanced **Midl.exe** to handle both type library generation and marshaling proxy/stub code generation. Thus, both ODL and the **Mktyplib.exe** utility have become a part of history.

Our object is described in the following IDL file which you can find in the source code, available from the Wrox Press web site (**http://www.wrox.com/scripts/download.idc**):

```
import "oaidl.idl";

[
   uuid(2740CBA0-274C-11d0-8DCF-000000000000),
]
interface ICustomInterface : IUnknown
{
   HRESULT GetManagerName([out, retval] BSTR *lResult);
   HRESULT OkayToPublishInfo([in] long lyear, [in] long lmonth, [out, retval]
VARIANT_BOOL *bResult);
   HRESULT PeekCounters([out] long *lCount1, [out] long *lCount2);}


[
   uuid(0B327BC0-274C-11d0-8DCF-006052008075),
   version(1.0),
]
library BareBlobLib
{
   importlib("stdole32.tlb") ;


   [
      uuid(048E11A0-2754-11d0-8DCF-000000000000)
   ]
   coclass CBareBlob
   {
      [default] interface ICustomInterface ;
   }
} ;
```

One thing that you'll immediately notice is that even though we *are* implementing a class factory class, it is missing in the IDL description. As you may remember from the previous chapter, the class factory class is a special one. It's special in that the creation of the class factory object happens 'by magic' and is both operating system and platform dependent. The way that the class factory object is created under the Win32 system (described in Chapter 1) does not require the specification of the object within an IDL file.

UUIDs Everywhere

Other things you'll notice are the various UUIDs used to identify the interface, the type library, and the COM class. Each of these UUIDs is generated by the **Uuidgen.exe** utility, which ships with your Visual C/C++ compiler. They are 16 bytes or (128 bits) long. A version of **Uuidgen.exe** which has a GUI and works with the Windows clipboard is called **Guidgen**, and is more frequently used in the Windows environment (leaving **Uuidgen.exe** for the people who like to do command line compiles with **NMAKE**). Since **Guidgen.exe** is used very frequently, it's helpful to make sure it is available from the Tools menu of the Developer Studio. Here's what you do to add it:

1 Start Visual C++ 5 or Visual Studio 97.

2 From the Tools menu, select Customize… and go to the Tools tab. In the Menu contents: list you can see all the tools that are currently available to you through the Tools menu.

3 Go to the bottom of the list and double-click on the blank entry. Enter the description **Create a new &UUID**. Press return.

4 In the Command field, click on the ... and locate your **Guidgen.exe** executable under the **\DevStudio\vc\bin** directory. Here, you can also add command line arguments to be passed to your new tool when invoked, and you can specify the initial directory in which to run.

5 Click on the Close button.

6 Now go to the Tools menu and, voilà, the new tool is there!

BSTRs and VARIANT_BOOLs

In the definition of our business rule methods, **GetManagerName()** and **OkayToPublishInfo()**, we've purposely used two COM/OLE specific data types, **BSTR** and **VARIANT_BOOL**. We could have used normal character arrays, such as **LPTSTR** and regular Boolean **BOOL**, but in Chapter 5, we'll learn about Automation, and discover that **BSTR** and **VARIANT_BOOL** are **the only ways** to pass data to certain COM clients. This is important because one of those clients is Internet Explorer 3, which we'll be using heavily as the client on our Intranet!

To avoid questions and headaches later, we've opted to introduce these data types here at this point, making our minimal ActiveX control ready for extension to serve Automation clients later. But what are these data types? **VARIANT_BOOL**, if you look up the definition, is simply a short integer for now. The unique property of **VARIANT_BOOL** is that it will always be compatible with the **VARIANT** data type, which is heavily used in Automation (covered in Chapter 5). Being a fundamental type (**short**), **VARIANT_BOOL** needs no special handling.

BSTR, on the other hand, is a very interesting data type. It is BASICally a string (terrible pun intended). Its origins lie in Visual Basic (the premier Automation client across all Microsoft's product line), and it's used to hold the value of a varying string. With 32-bit COM support, **BSTR** always points to a Unicode string. As a matter of fact, the entire OLE/COM runtime will only deal with strings internally as Unicode. The unique thing about **BSTR** is that the length of the string is pre-calculated and stored in the word immediately **before** the storage of the actual character string (i.e. where **BSTR** actually points to). As with normal character strings, **BSTR** is **NULL**-terminated. Having the string length traveling with the data all the time is extremely useful. Repeated determination of string lengths, accomplished by scanning to the terminating **NULL** character, can waste a lot of computing cycles in a typical application. In the mean time, the **NULL** termination on a **BSTR** makes it compatible with all existing C/C++ string manipulation functions.

The design of **BSTR** turns out to be an excellent way to represent varying strings. So much so, that the MFC's **CString** class was 'revamped' to use a similar algorithm to represent strings in the library.

BSTRs are frequently used as parameters in Automation and other COM interface methods. Since a client and a server are involved in each parameter exchange, and the client and server may be in different processes or on different machines, there needs to be a convention specified with respect to memory allocation for the data holding the characters of the **BSTR**. The convention is simple yet effective:

▲ For **BSTR**s passed by value (an input parameter), the caller has to allocate and free the **BSTR** data.

▲ For **BSTR**s passed by reference (an **[in, out]** parameter), the caller allocates the **BSTR** data, but the party called has the option of returning the same string or a newly allocated one (and freeing the old one); in either case, the caller must free the returned data.

▲ For **BSTR**s passed by reference as an output parameter, the party called allocates the **BSTR** data, and the caller must free it.

Closer examination of the above convention will reveal that it's designed for maximum flexibility, and yet a minimal amount of data is transferred between the caller and party called in a distributed network situation.

Allocation must always be made in guaranteed-sharable memory (since it could be cross-process and/or even cross-machine). The **SysAllocString()** and **SysFreeString()** family of functions in the Win32 APIs are designed to suit this purpose.

The Almighty MIDL

The MIDL compiler is a standard tool for anybody programming RPC on Microsoft platforms. The tool reads an Interface Description Language file, prepared by the programmer, and generates the necessary proxy and stub source files for RPC operations. The MIDL compiler generates code that can be compiled by both the C or C++ compiler.

Midl.exe has a lot of command line options; the following is a brief description of those options that are most important and frequently used during ActiveX development.

Option	Usage
/ms_ext	Microsoft specific extensions. This is the default setting and is the most frequently used.
/I directory list	Specify one or more directories for the include path.
/out directory	Specify the destination directory for output files.
/syntax_check	Check syntax only; do not generate output files.
/D name [=def]	Pass **#define** name and an optional value to the C preprocessor.
/U name	Remove any previous definition (**#undefine**).
/win32	Target environment is Microsoft Windows 32-bit (NT).
/error allocation	Check for out of memory errors.
/error bounds_check	Check size versus transmission length specification.
/error enum	Check **enum** values to be in the allowable range.
/error ref	Check ref pointers to be non-Null.
/error stub_data	Emit additional check for server side stub data validity.

Option	Usage
`/align: {1|2|4|8}`	Designate the packing level of structures. Default is 8, which is the natural alignment for most platforms.
`/Oi`	Generate fully interpreted stubs.
`/Os`	Generate inline stubs.
`@response_file`	Accept input from a response file.
`/?`	Display a list of MIDL compiler switches.
`/confirm`	Display options without compiling MIDL source.
`/o` filename	Redirects output from screen to a file.
`/Wx`	Report warnings at specified level as errors.

Proxy and Stub Generation

To create the type library, proxy and stub code:

1 Open a command line prompt.

2 Make sure that your DOS environment variables are set up; if you're using Windows95, you need to change directory to your **../DevStudio/vc/Bin** directory and run a batch file called **Vcvars32.bat**. Type **Vcvars32 x86** at the command line.

3 Type **MIDL BAREBLOB.IDL**.

If you get a message saying that certain include files can't be found, then you haven't set the environment up correctly.

On your development machine, it's probably worthwhile to set up the default environment to contain all the binary and include paths and variables. This is automatically done with a Windows NT install of Visual C++ 5. On Windows 95 system, you can edit **Autoexec.bat** to include the variables that are found in the **Vcvars32.bat** file.

To make future MIDL compiles easier, you can add the MIDL to your Tools menu in the IDE by following the instructions we gave for UUID generator, except:

1 Modify the Menu text field to **Compile &MIDL**. In the Command field, select the ... button to locate your **Midl.exe** under the **\DevStudio\vc\bin** directory.

2 In the Arguments field, click on the > button and select the filename of the IDL file to compile.

3 In the Initial Directory field, locate the **bin** directory as in step 1.

If you run the tool, a DOS box will be created whenever it runs. If you want the output to go to the Output window of the Developer Studio instead, go back to the Tools tab, select Compile MIDL from the listbox and then check the Use Output Window checkbox. Next time you run the tool, the output will go to a new tab in the Output window.

We can do a bit better than this. You can have the tool take as an argument the current file you're working on. You only need to make sure that the active open window is the IDL file, then just select Tools and then Compile MIDL to get the IDL file compiled. To achieve this, go back to the Tools tab, select Compile MIDL, and click on the right arrow beside the Arguments field. A pop-up menu appears giving you a choice of special arguments. Choose File Path. The string $(FilePath) appears in the Arguments field. This is a Developer Studio macro that takes its value from the current file path. More macros are available. Search the Help Topics with **Argument Macros** to get a description of all available choices.

If you want the compilation of the IDL file to become part of your Visual C++ 5 build process, it's relatively straightforward to add a custom build step to make this happen. Make sure you've added the IDL file to your project using the Project | Add to Project | Files... option. Next, from the file view pane, highlight the IDL file in the list and press the right mouse button. Select Settings.... The Project Settings dialog box will pop up with the IDL file highlighted. Select the Custom Build tab on the right. In the Build Commands list box, double-click on the blank entry, and enter **midl <IDL file name with extension>**. In the Output file(s): list box below, enter **<file name>.tlb**. Add two other entries into the Output file(s) list box: **<file name>.h** and **<file name>_i.c**. For example, the BareBlob project will have BareBlob.tlb, BareBlob.h, and BareBlob_i.c in the list box. This is all that's needed; Visual C++ 5 will manage the dependency for the IDL and output files during build.

When **Midl.exe** is run on an IDL file, the process generates the following files:

File Name	Description
Bareblob.tlb	Binary type library file. The COM runtime can read the type library information directly from this file.
Bareblob.h	Part of the generated proxy/stub code which includes the actual definition of all the interfaces. This is a very handy include file for clients of the object server.
Bareblob_i.c	Part of the generated proxy/stub code which contains all of the interface IDs and class IDs in a C or C++ usable form. This is a very handy include file for clients of the object server.
Bareblob_p.c	Part of the generated proxy/stub code which includes the actual marshaling code for the defined interfaces.
Dlldata.c	Part of the generated proxy/stub code, the DLL glue necessary to create a proxy/stub DLL.

Of these files, the two main ones that we'll be using are **BareBlob.h** and **BareBlob_i.c**. Both of these files need to be included into the source code of the BareBlob control. Specifically, **Bareblob.h** into the control's header file, and **BareBlob_i.c** into the implementation file, as you'll see when we come to write these files. **BareBlob_p.c** and **Dlldata.c** are generated files which can be used to create proxy/stub codes. They're generated each time the IDL is compiled and won't need any manual editing.

Notice that **Bareblob.h** is a MIDL-generated file by default. This means that we can't name our program's header file by the same name. Instead, we'll be naming our actual source code **Bareblob1.cpp** and the header **Bareblob1.h**.

Notice also that in our IDL description, we've defined the interface outside of the COM object and **library** definition. A library, in this case, refers to the type library being generated, and usually corresponds to a binary DLL or EXE which may provide one or more COM object servers. When you declare an interface this way, MIDL will generate the required RPC proxy/stub code for marshaling the interface across machine or process boundaries. The other alternative is to declare the interface within the library description itself:

```
[
   uuid(0B327BC0-274C-11d0-8DCF-006052008075),
   version(1.0),
]
library BareBlobLib
{
   importlib("stdole32.tlb") ;
[
   uuid(2740CBA0-274C-11d0-8DCF-000000000000),
]
interface ICustomInterface : IUnknown
{
      HRESULT GetManagerName([out, retval] BSTR *lResult);
      HRESULT OkayToPublishInfo([in] long lyear, [in] long lmonth, [out, retval]
VARIANT_BOOL *bResult);
      HRESULT PeekCounters([out] long *lCount1, [out] long *lCount2);}

   [
      uuid(048E11A0-2754-11d0-8DCF-000000000000)
   ]
   coclass CBareBlob
   {
      [default] interface ICustomInterface ;
   }
} ;
```

Try it, and run MIDL on it in an empty directory. You'll notice that no proxy/stub code will be generated. An interface that's only used between the COM objects residing entirely within DLL or EXE doesn't need to be accessible outside, and so it doesn't require proxy/stub code to be generated. This style of interface specification is often used in defining 'in-proc only' COM servers. However, even in the 'in-proc only' server case, there may be occasions where interface marshaling may be necessary (see our discussion on COM threading models in Chapter 4).

IDL Syntax

The combined syntax of the former ODL and IDL is a strange blend. While MIDL maintains compatibility with old ODL and IDL 'two files' description, anyone creating new COM servers should really use the new combined IDL syntax that we've described above. After all, it does save you time and headaches by keeping all the definitions in one place. If you work with sample programs or existing code, you may still encounter the ODL and IDL combination once in a while. Let's have a quick rundown of the new syntax. Instead of using the cryptic Backus Naur form, or some parameterized notation, I'm just going to show snippets of IDL declaration for things that ActiveX programmers frequently need to do.

To Define an Interface

```
import "oaidl.idl";
[
    object,
    uuid(00000001-0000-0000-C000-000000000046),
]

interface IClassFactory : IUnknown
{
    typedef [unique] IClassFactory * LPCLASSFACTORY;

    [local]
    HRESULT CreateInstance(
        [in, unique] IUnknown * pUnkOuter,
        [in] REFIID riid,
        [out, iid_is(riid)] void **ppvObject);

    [call_as(CreateInstance)]
    HRESULT RemoteCreateInstance(
        [in] REFIID riid,
        [out, iid_is(riid)] IUnknown ** ppvObject);

    [local]
    HRESULT LockServer(
        [in] BOOL fLock);

    [call_as(LockServer)]
    HRESULT __stdcall RemoteLockServer(
        [in] BOOL fLock);
}
```

The **#import** directive brings in definitions of standard types and interfaces used by COM, such as **IUnknown**, that our interface makes use of. The **object** attribute flags to MIDL that this isn't an RPC interface definition but, instead, a COM interface definition. Interface inheritance (e.g. the above interface inherits from **IUnknown**) is allowed only for COM interfaces. Inheritance in this sense means that the derived interface will implement all the methods of the base interface. Only single inheritance is supported. The UUID following the object attribute is the Interface ID (IID) for this interface. The interface definition follows immediately after. There are also parameter attributes such as **[in]** for input parameters, **[out]** for output parameters, **[in, out]** for parameters which are both input and output, and **[out, retval]** to tag a return value to use in Automation (we'll discuss this in a later chapter). Most of these attributes give MIDL some clues to optimize the proxy and stub code generated. For example, if a parameter is an **[in]** only parameter, the stub won't have to marshal its value back to the proxy. On the other hand, a parameter marked with **[in, out]** will always need to be marshaled both ways.

To Define a Type Library

```
[
    uuid(6384D582-0FDB-11cf-8700-00AA0053006D),
    helpstring("Beeper 1.0 Type Library"),
    version(1.0)
]
library BeeperLib
{
    importlib("stdole32.tlb");
```

```
// Class information
[ uuid(6384D586-0FDB-11cf-8700-00AA0053006D), helpstring("Beeper Object") ]
coclass Beeper
{
    [default] interface IBeeper;
};

};
```

The **importlib** directive makes the standard OLE type definitions (**Stdole32.tlb**) available in this type library. The **Stdole32.tlb** type library includes the definition for some very common interfaces, including **IUnknown**. The **helpstring** attribute may be used to associate a string with the class, library, interface, or methods. This string will be available programmatically when a tool accesses the type library information. For example, the object viewer in Visual Basic 5 will display this **helpstring** to the user when they browse through the type library. The version attribute gives the type library a major (**1**) and minor (**0**) version number; note that versioning of COM interfaces isn't supported by MIDL, since each COM interface is immutable once defined. The **[default]** attribute is used, typically in automation (covered in Chapter 5), to select the default interface to use when there's more than one which may qualify to be a dispatch interface.

To Define a COM Object

In the previous example, the **coclass** is a COM server object definition, bracketing the definition of all the interfaces that this object will support. The UUID provided therein is the CLSID which identifies the class of the COM object. The exported interfaces are specified in the body with the keyword **interface**.

To Define a Type

```
typedef char * CHARPTR;

typedef interface IUnknown *LPUNKNOWN;
```

You can use special keywords to specify the type that forms the base of the **typedef**. In this case, **LPUNKNOWN** is **typedef**'d as a pointer to an interface. The **typedef** capability in MIDL is consistent with the standard C/C++ preprocessor conventions.

To Define a Structure

```
typedef struct tagCLIPDATA {
    ULONG cbSize;      // count that includes sizeof(ulClipFmt)
    long ulClipFmt;    // long to keep alignment
    [size_is(cbSize-4)]
    BYTE * pClipData;  // cbSize-sizeof(ULONG) bytes of data in clipboard format
} CLIPDATA;
```

The declaration is almost like in C++, except that IDL specifiers may appear before the types. The **size_is** attribute is useful for the marshaling proxy/stub. Without the **size_is**, when the structure of **CLIPDATA** is marshaled, there's no way for the proxy/stub code to figure out how many of the bytes pointed to by **pClipData** should be transferred 'across the wire'.

Making Interface Pointers

Defining the IDL file first forced us to consider the interfaces provided by our ActiveX control up front. The output of the MIDL compiles provided us with a binary type library. What's more important, however, is that it also provided us with the **Bareblob.h** file. A lot of the 'dirty work' associated with assembling the required interface vtables (or table of function pointers within the BLOB) is automatically done for us. Let's examine the generated **Bareblob.h** and see how our **ICustomInterface** interface is actually implemented.

Close to the top of **Bareblob.h**, we find the definition for our **ICustomInterface**:

```
interface DECLSPEC_UUID("2740CBA0-274C-11d0-8DCF-000000000000")
    ICustomInterface : public IUnknown
    {
    public:
        virtual HRESULT STDMETHODCALLTYPE GetManagerName(
            /* [retval][out] */ BSTR __RPC_FAR *lResult) = 0;

        virtual HRESULT STDMETHODCALLTYPE OkayToPublishInfo(
            /* [in] */ long lyear,
            /* [in] */ long lmonth,
            /* [retval][out] */ VARIANT_BOOL __RPC_FAR *bResult) = 0;

        virtual HRESULT STDMETHODCALLTYPE PeekCounters(
            /* [out] */ long __RPC_FAR *lCount1,
            /* [out] */ long __RPC_FAR *lCount2) = 0;

    };
```

Notice that it's simply declared as a custom-defined type called **interface**. If we look up the definition of **interface** in **Objbase.h** from the **DevStudio\vc\Include** directory, we'll find that it's defined as a **struct**. This isn't a problem at all, since a **struct** in C++ is exactly the same as a **class**, but with all methods and data members public by default rather than private. In our case, **ICustomInterface** is derived from **IUnknown**, another **struct** defined in .**DevStudio\vc\Include\Unknwn.h** as:

```
interface IUnknown
{
public:
    BEGIN_INTERFACE
    virtual HRESULT STDMETHODCALLTYPE QueryInterface(
        /* [in] */ REFIID riid,
        /* [iid_is][out] */ void __RPC_FAR *__RPC_FAR *ppvObject) = 0;

    virtual ULONG STDMETHODCALLTYPE AddRef( void) = 0;

    virtual ULONG STDMETHODCALLTYPE Release( void) = 0;

    END_INTERFACE
};
```

Under Win32 on Intel platforms, the **BEGIN_INTERFACE** and **END_INTERFACE** macros map to empty strings. What we're left with, essentially is the pure virtual class definition for **QueryInterface()**, **AddRef()**, and **Release()**. Notice that the **Unknwn.h** was created by the MIDL compiler from the **Unknwn.idl** file.

When you create an instance of a pointer to **IUnknown** with the following syntax,

```
IUnknown *MyUnknown;
```

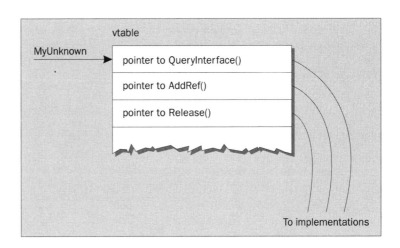

it allows **MyUnknown** to point to structures/classes which have the following in-memory footprint:

Since **ICustomInterface** derives from **IUnknown**, the pure virtual functions defined in **ICustomInterface** will be tagged on right after the **IUnknown** entries, making the pointer good for the following vtable in memory:

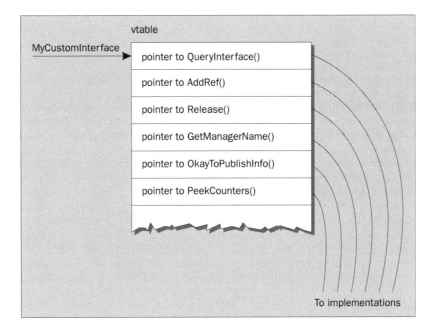

In the next section, we'll actually be creating and populating the vtable that these 'interface pointers' can point to. Basically, to assemble the vtables, you inherit from a base class or structure which has pure virtual functions defined, one for each method that the interface supports, in the order that the methods are defined. To implement the actual methods, though, it boils down to one of two alternative techniques using C++:

▲ Implement the interfaces via Multiple Inheritance

▲ Implement the interfaces via Nested Classes

First, a quick refresher on the basic C++ syntax which corresponds to these two techniques. This refresher will be helpful because both techniques use the more obscure features of C++ that programmers, striving for long term code maintainability, tend to avoid.

Multiple Inheritance

Consider the following code:

```
class base1
{
public:
   virtual int firstFunc(int i)=0;
   virtual int base1Func(int i)=0;
};

class base2
{
public:
   virtual int firstFunc(int i)=0;
   virtual int base2Func(int i)=0;
};

class derived: base1, base2
{
public:
   int firstFunc(int a) { return (a + 1); }
   int base1Func(int a) { return (a + 2); }
   int base2Func(int a) { return (a + 3); }
};
```

The **derived** class inherits from both **base1** and **base2** above. Both base classes are abstract, having two pure virtual member functions. The **base1** class has a vtable consisting of **firstFunc()** and **base1Func()**, while the **base2** class has a vtable consisting of **firstFunc()** and **base2Func()** entries. When **derived** inherits from these classes, it picks up the vtable from both base classes (in COM, it would have picked up two interface definitions). Both **base1** and **base2** have a virtual member called **firstFunc()**, but the **derived** class can only provide one implementation. Therefore, the inherited vtables from both **base1** and **base2** would have their **firstFunc()** function pointing to **derived::firstFunc()**. This is the key to implementation through multiple inheritance. Imagine the **firstFunc()** implementing some interface methods which are common in all the interfaces inherited from, for instance, the **IUnknown** methods. Multiple inheritance implementations are typically very concise and lean, maximize code reuse, but are also relatively hard to maintain. Another obvious shortcoming of these implementations is their inability to handle those situations where the object implements two interfaces that have a method with the same name but which require different implementations.

Nested Classes

Consider the following code:

```
class base1
{
public:
```

```
      virtual int firstFunc(int i)=0;
      virtual int base1Func(int i)=0;
};

class base2
{
public:
      virtual int firstFunc(int i)=0;
      virtual int base2Func(int i)=0;
};

class derived
{
      class inner1: base1
      {
      public:
         int firstFunc(int a) { return(a+1); }
         int base1Func(int a) { return(a+2); }
      };
      class inner2: base2
      {
      public:
         int firstFunc(int a) {return(a+3); }
         int base2Func(int a) { return(a+4); }
      };
public:
   inner1 Abase1;
   inner2 Abase2;
};
```

The abstract base classes (**base1** and **base2**) are exactly the same as in the multiple inheritance case. The **derived** class, however, doesn't inherit from either of them. Instead, two nested class definitions, **inner1** and **inner2**, each derives from the two base classes. These nested classes also implement all the pure virtual functions of the inherited classes (i.e. equivalent to filling in the vtable for the two COM interfaces). Since **inner1** and **inner2** are nothing more than class definitions (i.e. no allocation), we need to create an instance of each as a member of the wrapping **derived** class. These two instances are the **Abase1** and **Abase2** member variable of the **derived** class. Note that, in this case, both **inner1** and **inner2** have an implementation of **firstFunc()**. Unlike the multiple inheritance situation, we can implement the same function **firstFunc()** totally differently for each nested class. Translated, it allows different implementations for methods with the same name across two interfaces. Obviously, if we *do* want the two implementations to be the same, we can create an implementation in the **derived** class, make **inner1** and **inner2** C++ friends of the class, and then call the **derived** implementation from the inner classes.

In our case above, the syntax for calling the methods of the inner classes is:

```
derived a;
a.Abase1.firstFunc(1);
a.Abase2.firstFunc(1);
```

COM Interfaces: vtables in Other Environments

If you examine the source code of the include headers carefully, and follow through the **#ifdef** paths for the C language, you'll find that assembling vtables in C is somewhat more involved. Consequently, if you need to assemble these vtables on another (say, the Macintosh or UNIX) platform, in another programming language (say, COBOL), or with another C++ compiler that doesn't handle vtables in this way (I'd be quite surprised if you find one), creating vtables/interfaces may require more sophisticated coding. The bottom line is that you need to know how code is generated, and you need to create the binary image in the object that represents an interface, as in the figure above.

To date, there are very few computing languages that don't provide some means of accessing memory directly or don't provide pointers of some type. That is, until the advent of Java. The Java language itself doesn't support pointers, so one can't address the process's memory space, and it can run in a 'secure' interpretive environment. In this sort of scenario, creating vtables or implementing COM support within the language would not be possible without some sort of external intervention. There's no need to despair. Seeing that Java without COM can be a very lonely affair, Microsoft has provided this intervention. This extension is realized in their implementation of the Java interpreter (called a Virtual Machine, in Java lingo) which has direct access to all system resources.

Assembling vtables: Implementing IUnknown

Another benefit of declaring the methods in **IUnknown** as pure virtual, besides the fact that an interface pointer can be created for the correctly formatted vtable, is that the end user of the interface is forced to implement it. Since you can't write a C++ program that leaves pure virtual functions in your class or subclass undefined, you're forced to implement the methods of your interface. This is enforced by the compiler during the compilation phase. It's a kind of forced obedience to the terms of the contract. In this case, the side effect is highly desirable.

With no choice left for us, we implement **IUnknown** in **Bareblob1.cpp** (recall that the MIDL generates **Bareblob.h**, so we call our program and headers **Bareblob1** instead) as:

```
STDMETHODIMP    CBareBlob::QueryInterface(REFIID riid, void **ppv)
{
   *ppv = NULL ;

   if (riid == IID_IUnknown)
   {
      *ppv = this ;
   }
   if (riid == IID_ICustomInterface)
   {
      *ppv = &m_CGutsOfBareBlob ;
   }
   if (*ppv == NULL)
   {
      return E_NOINTERFACE ;
   }
   ((IUnknown *) *ppv)->AddRef() ;
   return NOERROR ;
}

STDMETHODIMP_(ULONG)    CBareBlob::AddRef(void)
{
   InterlockedIncrement( (LONG*)&m_cRef ) ;
   return m_cRef ;
}

STDMETHODIMP_(ULONG)    CBareBlob::Release(void)
{
   if (!InterlockedDecrement( (LONG*)&m_cRef ))
```

```
    {
        delete this ;
        return 0 ;
    }

    return m_cRef ;
}
```

The first thing to notice is the use of macros in the definition of these functions. All implementations of the interface methods should use the **STDMETHODIMP** macro to declare the return type. By using the macro, it's guaranteed that the correct signature will be produced on all platforms and languages. These macros essentially add **HRESULT** and **__stdcall** to the function. Taking a look at **Objbase.h** reveals how they're defined for Win32, C++ and Intel platforms:

```
#define STDMETHODCALLTYPE      __stdcall
#define STDMETHODIMP           HRESULT  STDMETHODCALLTYPE
#define STDMETHODIMP_(type) type        STDMETHODCALLTYPE
```

__stdcall is a function-calling convention which is the 'standard' calling convention for 32-bit Windows. Calling conventions affect how the compiler will generate code to implement a function and calls to functions. Under the **__stdcall** convention, the called function is expected to clean up the stack before it returns from a call. This convention is mandatory for the methods of the interfaces implemented by in-proc COM servers. Clients such as Visual Basic 5, Internet Explorer, and Access 97 expect this when accessing an in-proc COM object. By the nature of calling conventions, they are platform specific. There's a good chance that the standard calling convention for another OS or processor won't be the same as **__stdcall**.

HRESULT must be the return type of all interface methods. Only **AddRef()** and **Release()** may return a type other than **HRESULT**. The rest of the interface methods, including all the user defined ones, should always return **HRESULT** and should therefore be defined with **STDMETHODIMP**. The reason for this uniform handling is mainly for the remoting case when a COM server is accessed over a network. In this case, it's necessary for any method call to be able to return RPC or network failure information, which will come through as **RPC_E_xxxx** in the **HRESULT** value (which is essentially a status code).

We should note that similar declaration macros exist for the **.h** file: **STDMETHOD** and **STDMETHOD_(type)**. The methods are declared as **virtual** to ensure that the correct (most derived) method is invoked in the case of class hierarchies.

```
#define STDMETHOD(method)          virtual HRESULT STDMETHODCALLTYPE method
#define STDMETHOD_(type,method)  virtual type STDMETHODCALLTYPE method
```

Notice the implementation of **QueryInterface()**. It's almost as straightforward as pseudocode:

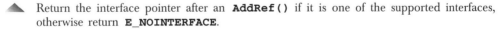 Check the requested IID for either **IUnknown** or **ICustomInterface**.

Return the interface pointer after an **AddRef()** if it is one of the supported interfaces, otherwise return **E_NOINTERFACE**.

With **AddRef()** and **Release()**, we play with a counter of **LONG** type called **m_cRef**. To anticipate multiple simultaneous active users of our server (we'll make this happen later), we use the **InterlockedIncrement()** and **InterlockedDecrement()** Win32 API calls to manage our counter. These APIs ensure that the increment and decrement operation is totally atomic (i.e. complete, without the possibility of another processor or thread messing up the updating of the counter value), giving our **IUnknown** implementation the robustness that it needs. In **Release()** we see how the object will be deallocated in the system, via:

```
if (!InterlockedDecrement( (LONG*)&m_cRef ))
{
    delete this ;
    return 0 ;
}
```

We mentioned, in the last section, that we can either use multiple inheritance or nested classes to assemble the vtable. If you take a look at control creation tools coming out from Microsoft, you'll find that MFC actually uses nested classes to implement the vtables, and that ATL uses the multiple inheritance path. In our case, we'll simply choose one: using nested classes. To ensure that the generated binary code has the vtable and exact ordering of functions that we require, the **CBareBlob** class is defined as follows:

```
class CBareBlob : public IUnknown
{
    //   CGutsOfBareBlob
    ///////////////////////////////////////////
    // Nested class
    class CGutsOfBareBlob : public ICustomInterface
    {
        friend class CBareBlob ;

    public :
        // keep simple constructors or destructors in-line
        CGutsOfBareBlob():m_cRef(0),    m_outRef(0)
        {}


        ~CGutsOfBareBlob()
        {}

        //These are the methods of ICustomInterface
        STDMETHOD(QueryInterface)     (REFIID riid, void **ppv);
        STDMETHOD_(ULONG, AddRef)     (void);
        STDMETHOD_(ULONG, Release)    (void);
        STDMETHOD(GetManagerName)(BSTR *bstrMgr);
        STDMETHOD(OkayToPublishInfo)(long lyear, long lmonth, VARIANT_BOOL *okay);
        STDMETHOD(PeekCounters)(long *lCount1, long *lCount2);    private :

        ULONG       m_cRef ;      // ref count
        ULONG       m_outRef;     // spy on outer Ref
        IUnknown    *m_pUnkOuter ;     // controlling unknown
    }; // end of CGutsOfBareBlob nested class
public:

    //an instance of our nested class
    CGutsOfBareBlob m_CGutsOfBareBlob ;
    CBareBlob(IUnknown *punkOuter);
    ~CBareBlob();

    //These are the methods of IUnknown
    STDMETHOD(QueryInterface)     (REFIID riid, void **ppv);
    STDMETHOD_(ULONG, AddRef)     (void);
```

```
    STDMETHOD_(ULONG, Release)    (void);

  private:

    ULONG      m_cRef ;        // ref count
    IUnknown   *m_pUnkOuter ;      // controlling unknown
  }; // end of CBareBlob class
```

Since **CBareBlob** derives from **IUnknown**, and we know the Microsoft C++ compiler stores the vtable to virtual functions in the very beginning of the object footprint, this makes the **this** pointer of the instantiated **CBareBlob** object the same as an **IUnknown** pointer to the object (this is Microsoft-compiler-specific, and is essential for COM compatibility on x86 architecture platforms). **CBareBlob** also implements all the interfaces required by **IUnknown** (as we've seen earlier in this section), since they were specified to be pure virtual in the base class.

Custom Interface Implemented as a Nested Class

Using the above idea, we can implement the **ICustomInterface** using a class that we've called **CGutsOfBareBlob**. We've nested the class definition to limit its scope (i.e. who it is visible to). It's possible to have many C++ objects within the same compilation unit each, implementing many interfaces. Limiting the scope of these definitions will avoid problems associated with namespace pollution. **CGutsOfBareBlob** inherits directly from **ICustomInterface**, and therefore a pointer to the **m_CGutsOfBareBlob** member of the **CBareBlob** object is an interface pointer to an implemented (by a **CGutsOfBareBlob** object) **ICustomInterface**. As expected, the **CGutsOfBareBlob** class implements all the methods of the **ICustomInterface**, populating the vtable entries with pointers to the actual method implementations.

In our case, having a member variable of **CGutsOfBareBlob** type called **m_CGutsOfBareBlob** within our **CBareBlob** class, means that a **CGutsOfBareBlob** object is instantiated each and every time a **CBareBlob** object is instantiated. We've done this purely for simplicity and convenience. It is, of course, possible to simply have a member pointer to the **CGutsOfBareBlob** class,

```
  CGutsOfBareBlob *m_pCGutsOfBareBlob;
```

and dynamically create an object of the **CGutsOfBareBlob** class, at runtime, when our **CBareBlob** object is instantiated using:

```
  m_pCGutsOfBareBlob = new CGutsOfBareBlob;
```

If **CGutsOfBareBlob** implements a very complicated and large interface, it may even be advantageous not to instantiate it until it's absolutely needed (i.e. when someone calls **QueryInterface()** for the interface that it implements). This type of optimization technique works far better with the nested-classes implementation of COM interfaces. Under the multiple inheritance implementation, interface methods aren't implemented independently on a per-interface basis; this makes the dynamic creation detailed above difficult.

The implementation of the **CGutsOfBareBlob** class can be found in **Bareblob1.cpp**. Recall that **CGutsOfBareBlob** actually implements the methods of the **ICustomInterface**. The first three methods are the obligatory **IUnknown** methods, and they're implemented, almost trivially, in **Bareblob1.cpp**:

```
STDMETHODIMP    CBareBlob::CGutsOfBareBlob::QueryInterface(REFIID riid, void **ppv)
{
   return m_pUnkOuter->QueryInterface(riid,ppv) ;
}


STDMETHODIMP_(ULONG)   CBareBlob::CGutsOfBareBlob::AddRef(void)
{
   return (m_outRef = m_pUnkOuter->AddRef()) ;
}


STDMETHODIMP_(ULONG)   CBareBlob::CGutsOfBareBlob::Release(void)
{
   return (m_outRef = m_pUnkOuter->Release()) ;
}
```

What we're doing here is being a good COM object and making sure we're aggregatable. To do this, remembering our aggregation discussion in Chapter 2, we must cater for a potential 'outer unknown' being passed in from some aggregator. The approach to follow is repeated here for convenience:

> When **QueryInterface()**, **AddRef()** or **Release()** is called on any interface (except for **IUnknown**), delegate to **pUnkOuter**.

Since this is the implementation of the **ICustomInterface**, and not **IUnknown**, we must delegate the call to the **pUnkOuter** as prescribed. Obviously, if the object isn't being aggregated, the outer unknown being passed in would be **NULL**. This case is handled in the constructor of the **CBareBlob** object itself (again found in the **Bareblob1.cpp** file):

```
CBareBlob::CBareBlob(IUnknown *punkOuter)
{
   ObjectCreated() ;

   m_cRef = 0 ;

   // if this is non-null, we're being aggregated
   if (punkOuter)
   {
      m_pUnkOuter = punkOuter ;
      m_CGutsOfBareBlob.m_pUnkOuter = punkOuter ;
   }
   else
   {
      m_pUnkOuter = this ;
      m_CGutsOfBareBlob.m_pUnkOuter = this ;
   }
}
```

If the object is not being aggregated during instantiation, **CBareBlob** will actually set the **m_pUnkOuter** variable to point to the **IUnknown** of the object itself (i.e. **this**). In this case, we're simply reusing the implementations for **QueryInterface()**, **AddRef()**, and **Release()**, which we already have in the **CBareBlob** class (i.e. the implementation for our **IUnknown** interface).

The only other methods that **CGutsOfBareBlob** must implement are the 'real meat' methods of our ActiveX object: **GetManagerName()**, **OkayToPublishInfo()**, and **PeekCounters()**. They are implemented as:

```
STDMETHODIMP CBareBlob::CGutsOfBareBlob::GetManagerName(BSTR * bstrMgrName)
{
   // the real business rule case should do whatever is
   // necessary
   *bstrMgrName = SysAllocString(L"J. Manzini");
   return S_OK;
}

STDMETHODIMP CBareBlob::CGutsOfBareBlob::OkayToPublishInfo(long year, long month,
VARIANT_BOOL *bResult)
{
   // again, do whatever is necessary to implement the business rule
   //
   if (((year + month) % 4) == 0)
      *bResult = FALSE;
   else
      *bResult = TRUE;
   return S_OK ;
}

STDMETHODIMP CBareBlob::CGutsOfBareBlob::PeekCounters(long *lRefCount, long
*lObjCount)
{
   *lRefCount = m_outRef;
   *lObjCount = g_cObject;
   return S_OK ;
}
```

GetManagerName() is a function which will return the name of the person in charge of the department, at the time the method is called. In an actual intranet environment, the code may do whatever is necessary (e.g. check to see which manager has logged on to the system at that time) to determine the name. In our implementation, we've simply hard-coded the name of J. Manzini. Notice that we used **SysAllocString()** to create the **BSTR** variable. The caller will free this **BSTR** just as we described in the earlier **BSTR** discussion.

OkayToPublishInfo() determines, at time of call, whether it is okay to publish any event calendar information. This function can be used to stop external access to data while it's being updated, or to prevent viewing during a certain period of time. Again, the actual implementation can be more involved. Our method, however, takes the year and adds it to the month. If the resulting number is divisible by 4, then the method will return with a status code to prevent the viewing of events.

PeekCounters() acts as a kind of a trace function by returning the value of the internal reference counter, as well as the 'number of objects' counter.

Note that the **g_cObject** counter, which is defined as a global value (in **Bareblob1.cpp**),

```
ULONG   g_cObject = 0 ;
```

is quite different from the **m_outRef** reference counter. To understand this, one must find out where these counters are used. The **g_cObject** counter is incremented in the constructor of **CBareBlob**, and decremented in the destructor of **CBareBlob**.

```
CBareBlob::~CBareBlob()
{
    ObjectDestroyed() ;
}
```

We've used two support functions to increment the global counter, which also need implementing–
`ObjectCreated()` and `ObjectDestroyed()`:

```
VOID ObjectCreated(VOID)
{
    InterlockedIncrement( (LONG*)&g_cObject ) ;
}

VOID ObjectDestroyed(VOID)
{
    InterlockedDecrement( (LONG*)&g_cObject ) ;
}
```

These global functions should be defined at the very top of the source file, or a forward declaration for the functions must be made. As you can see from the above code, these two functions are simply wrappers for the `InterlockedIncrement()` and `InterlockedDecrement()` APIs we've met before.

This corresponds to the number of actual instances of **CBareBlob** objects created. On the other hand, the **m_outRef** counter is incremented in the **IUnknown::AddRef()** or **ICustomInterface::AddRef()**, and decremented in the **IUnknown::Release()** or **ICustomInterface::Release()** functions. This count is the interface reference count for any particular instance of the **CBareBlob** class; it is **not** global. When **m_outRef** reaches zero, that object instance of the **CBareBlob** class can be freed. When **g_cObject** reaches zero, there are no more instances of the **CBareBlob** class around in the system, and the entire server can be freed.

With both **CBareBlob** and **CGutsOfBareBlob** fully coded, we have now implemented both the **IUnknown** and the **ICustomInterface** required by the BareBlob, as specified in our IDL description. From the discussions we had in Chapter 2, you may remember the COM runtime's need for a 'class factory' object in order to figure out how to create our **CBareBlob** object. In the next step, we must now define and create this class factory object.

Implementing a Class Factory

Unlike **CBareBlob**, COM runtime creates a class factory in a system-specific way. This means that it isn't necessary to include the interface specifications of the class factory object in our IDL file. So our IDL file will stay the way it is for now.

The class factory object exposes the **IClassFactory** interface. Thanks again to **Msdev\Include\Objbase.h**, we don't have to assemble our own vtable structure for **IClassFactory**, we simply inherit from it. A lesson can be learnt here. If you're rolling your own ActiveX control and you're implementing some interface already defined by Microsoft or some other third party, it's a good bet that they'll have header files to make your vtable assembly job easy. The easy way to find them is to use the Find in Files feature of Visual C++ 5. Look under the Edit menu for the Find in Files... selection. Point the In Folder field to **DevStudio\vc\include**, and type in the name of the interface you're looking for in the Find what field. Click the Find button and watch the output window.

Our class factory object is implemented by a C++ class named **CBareBlobMaker**. Its source code is found in **Bareblob1.cpp** and **Bareblob1.h** files. The class definition for **CBareBlobMaker** is:

```
class CBareBlobMaker : public IClassFactory
{
public :

    CBareBlobMaker():m_cRef(0)
    {}

    STDMETHOD(CreateInstance)        (IUnknown *punkOuter, REFIID riid, void **ppv);
    STDMETHOD(QueryInterface)        (REFIID iid, void **ppv);
    STDMETHOD_(ULONG, AddRef)        (void);
    STDMETHOD_(ULONG, Release)       (void);
    STDMETHOD(LockServer)            (BOOL bLock);

private:

    ULONG   m_cRef ;        // refcount
} ;
```

As with other interfaces, the **QueryInterface()**, **AddRef()**, and **Release()** methods must be implemented. In addition, the **IClassFactory** interface also has a **CreateInstance()** method, used here to create an instance of **CBareBlob**, as well as a **LockServer()** method to keep the server in memory.

The **QueryInterface()** method of the class factory object will only return pointers to **IUnknown** or **IClassFactory**. Any other interface request will get an **E_NOINTERFACE**.

```
STDMETHODIMP CBareBlobMaker::QueryInterface(REFIID iid, void **ppv)
{
    *ppv = NULL ;

    if (iid == IID_IUnknown || iid == IID_IClassFactory)
        *ppv = this ;
    else
        return E_NOINTERFACE ;

    AddRef() ;

    return S_OK ;
}
```

An interesting observation here is that the **QueryInterface()** call returns the same interface pointer for both **IClassFactory** and **IUnknown**! Why is this legal?

Well it's legal because, if we think about our binary vtable again, the first three entries in the vtable are the same for **IUnknown** as well as **IClassFactory**. The golden rules of COM ensured that. Therefore, passing a pointer to **IClassFactory** as an **IUnknown** pointer is totally legal. Conceptually, it's equivalent to a 'down cast' from a derived class to the base class. In essence, any COM interface pointer can be 'down cast' to an **IUnknown** pointer. So why didn't we also take this real easy way out in our **CBareBlob**?

The answer lies in the requirements of aggregation. If we can do exactly the same thing for the **QueryInterface()**, **AddRef()**, and **Release()** members, then we can do what our class factory class does... make them the same. Unfortunately, for a COM class that supports aggregation, the handling of these members is required, by COM rules, to be different between normal interfaces and **IUnknown**. Because our **CBareBlob** was purposely designed to be aggregatable, we had to implement the **IUnknown** methods separately for each interface. Note that it's still possible–and quite common–for all the non-**IUnknown** interfaces to share an 'inner' set of these methods because, typically, they must all behave in the same general way. This reinforces our previous discussion on multiple inheritance versus nested class implementation of COM interfaces. A pure multiple inheritance implementation can't handle aggregation since all **IUnknown** methods *must* be implemented identically (by one member function of the derived class). However, an external class (outside the multiple inheritance implementation) can be created to remedy the situation.

What I've been saying so far, then, indicates that the class factory object isn't aggregatable. Well, we certainly created the class in a way that is incompatible with aggregation. While COM doesn't explicitly specify that a class factory object is special and may not be aggregated, you're highly unlikely to meet a case where this would happen. At least in the Win32 implementation of COM, you can rest peacefully knowing that you won't be aggregated during class factory object instantiation. Whether this would be different for non-Windows based COM implementation, we'll have to wait and see.

The **AddRef()** and **Release()** methods of **IClassFactory** (and **IUnknown**) for the class factory are implemented as:

```
STDMETHODIMP_(ULONG) CBareBlobMaker::AddRef(void)
{
    return ++m_cRef ;
}

STDMETHODIMP_(ULONG)  CBareBlobMaker::Release(void)
{
    if (--m_cRef == 0)
    {
        delete this ;
        return 0 ;
    }

    return m_cRef ;
}
```

This is almost identical to the **CBareBlob** implementation. Next, we'll look at the most interesting method from **IClassFactory**: the **CreateInstance()** method. Thinking through the process as we've described in Chapter 2, it should be clear that our **CreateInstance()** method can be implemented as follows:

```
STDMETHODIMP CBareBlobMaker::CreateInstance(IUnknown *punkOuter, REFIID riid, void
**ppv)
{
    CBareBlob *cmg ;
    HRESULT hr ;

    *ppv = NULL ;

    if ((punkOuter) && (riid != IID_IUnknown))
```

```
    {
       return CLASS_E_NOAGGREGATION ;
    }

    cmg = new CBareBlob(punkOuter) ;

    hr = cmg->QueryInterface(riid, ppv) ;

    if (FAILED(hr))
    {
       delete cmg ;
       return hr ;
    }

    return S_OK ;
}
```

First, we perform a 'COM rule' consistency check to make sure that the client asks for **IUnknown** if it wants aggregation (**punkOuter != NULL**). Otherwise, we simply instantiate a **CBareBlob** object on the heap with the **new** operator, passing in the **punkOuter** controlling **IUnknown**. Next, we ask the newly instantiated object for the interface ID requested by the client. If the call is successful, we have the interface pointer, all is well, and we return **S_OK**. Otherwise, something is wrong, or the client really doesn't know what it's doing; we simply delete the object and return **E_NOINTERFACE**. Note that we're counting on the **CBareBlob** object to 'do the right thing' with the **punkOuter** passed in, and we also expect the **CBareBlob** to have **AddRef()**'ed any interface returning from a **QueryInterface()** call.

The last method to implement is **LockServer()**. From the client point of view, the semantics of this call are to lock the server in memory so as to improve object creation performance, avoiding the recreation of the class factory object each time the same COM server is instantiated. Wait a minute! Doesn't the class factory object (providing the **IClassFactory** interface) have a reference count? And wouldn't that be enough to hold the class factory in memory? The answer turns out to be **no**! There is a quirk in COM's way of dealing with local servers (not in-proc servers) which would cause deadlocks if we insist that the class factory reference count becomes zero before the DLL is unloaded. To overcome this, the **LockServer()** function must be used to hold the class factory object and its DLL in memory. In our simple in-proc server case, we'll just use the existing global 'object count' variable and increment it for lock, and decrement it for unlock. This is valid in our case because the class factory actually lives in the very same DLL as the implementation of the object that it creates, and we aren't creating objects which require a lot of dynamically created resources.

```
STDMETHODIMP CBareBlobMaker::LockServer(BOOL bLock)
{
    if (bLock)
       ObjectCreated();
    else
       ObjectDestroyed() ;

    return S_OK ;
}
```

Hacking the Registry

That's about it. We've done everything that's required for a simple ActiveX control (or you can call it a COM object server). The last remaining bit of work left to do is creating all the links required for the COM runtime to be able to find and work with our object.

First and foremost, we need to create a few registry entries. We've covered the registration requirements back in Chapter 1. Now we'll actually write code to register the control.

The registry entries that we want to add are:

```
\HKEY_CLASSES_ROOT\CLSID\{048E11A0-2754-11d0-8DCF-000000000000}\(default) =
    "CBareBlob"
\HKEY_CLASSES_ROOT\CLSID\{048E11A0-2754-11d0-8DCF-000000000000}\InProcServer32 =
    "C:\WORK\DEBUG\BAREBLOB.DLL"
\HKEY_CLASSES_ROOT\CLSID\{048E11A0-2754-11d0-8DCF-000000000000}\ThreadingModel =
    "both"

HKEY_CLASSES_ROOT\CBareBlob.1\(default) = "CBareBlob"
HKEY_CLASSES_ROOT\CBareBlob.1\CLSID = {048E11A0-2754-11d0-8DCF-000000000000}
```

We'll be adding these registry entries with the help of some COM requirements. It's actually a requirement of ActiveX controls that they are self-registering (i.e. they're able to add the above registry entries into the registry themselves). We'll implement this self-registration here. Under Win32, the requirements for an in-proc server residing in a DLL are for the DLL to have the following entry point functions exported by name:

Function Name	Purpose
`STDAPI DllRegisterServer(VOID);`	In this routine, an in-proc server is expected to create its registry entries for all classes it supports.
`STDAPI DllUnregisterServer(VOID);`	The in-proc server should remove only those registry entries it created through `DllRegisterServer()`. It should leave alone any entries that currently exist for its object classes which, however, it did not create.

`STDAPI DllGetClassObject(`
`    REFCLSID rclsid,`
`    REFIID riid,`
`    LPVOID FAR *ppv);`
	Normally not invoked directly by client code, but by `CoGetClassObject()` in order to get an interface through which the requested object can get created. `rclsid` is the requested object class id, `riid` is the REFIID of the requested interface and `ppv` returns the interface pointer. Normally used to obtain `IClassFactory` interfaces.

`STDAPI DllCanUnloadNow(void);`	Determines whether the DLL that implements this function is in use. If not, the caller can safely unload the DLL from memory. Care should be taken if the DLL has loaded secondary DLLs.

The `DllRegisterServer()` and `DllUnregisterServer()` entry points are typically used by a utility like `Regsvr32.exe` (which we'll explain and use shortly in this chapter), while `DllGetClassObject()` and `DllCanUnloadNow()` is called directly by the COM runtime support.

In order to make these functions exported in the DLL, we'll create a **Bareblob.def** file. In the file, we explicitly export these functions by name:

```
DESCRIPTION     'a bare blob in a DLL'

EXPORTS         DllGetClassObject  PRIVATE
                DllRegisterServer   PRIVATE
                DllUnregisterServer PRIVATE
                DllCanUnloadNow PRIVATE
```

The **PRIVATE** keyword ensures that another client using the DLL couldn't accidentally import and call one of these functions, and so possibly cause a crash.

We could have used the **_declspec(dllexport)** specifier in the declaration and definition of the functions to get them exported instead of using the **Bareblob.def** file. However, because of the way the COM macros such as **STDAPI** are defined, doing this would require some fairly ugly trickery. Instead, it's far cleaner to include a **.DEF** file. This also eliminates the chance of accidentally exporting mangled C++ function names.

Before we implement the exported functions, we need to have some global strings set up to make life a little easier (try typing in the CLSID several times without getting it wrong once).

```
TCHAR tcSampleDesc[]        = "CBareBlob";
TCHAR tcInprocServer32[]    = "InprocServer32";
TCHAR tcSampleProgID[]      = "CBareBlob";
TCHAR tcProgID[]            = "CBareBlob";
TCHAR tcThreadModel[]       = "ThreadingModel";
TCHAR tcFree[]              = "Both";
TCHAR tcCLSID[]             = "{048E11A0-2754-11d0-8DCF-000000000000}";
```

Note our use of the **TCHAR** type and the **_T()** macro. The **_T()** macro is the same as the **TEXT()** macro. These type and macro definitions originate from the **Tchar.h** header. They're extremely useful for keeping your application character set independent. Using these types and macros, you can write one set of source code for UNICODE, MBCS, or ANSI compilations. Basically, it will make internationalization (adapting your application for another country with another language) of your application simpler in the future. Further discussion of internationalization is beyond the scope of this book, and the reader is encouraged to consult one of the many available books on the subject.

The DllRegisterServer Function

We now implement the **DllRegisterServer()** function for our server. It consist mainly of Win32 based registry manipulation calls.

```
STDAPI DllRegisterServer(VOID)
{
   HKEY    hKey  = NULL;
   HKEY    hKey2 = NULL;
   HKEY    hKey3 = NULL;
   DWORD   result;
   HRESULT hr = SELFREG_E_CLASS;
   TCHAR   cModulePathName[MAX_PATH];
```

```
   // Create HKEY_CLASSES_ROOT\progid\CLSID
   result = RegCreateKey(HKEY_CLASSES_ROOT, tcSampleProgID, &hKey);
   if (result != ERROR_SUCCESS) goto lExit;

   result = RegSetValue(hKey, NULL, REG_SZ, tcSampleDesc, lstrlen(tcSampleDesc));
   if (result != ERROR_SUCCESS) goto lExit;

   result = RegCreateKey(hKey, _T("CLSID"), &hKey2);
   if (result != ERROR_SUCCESS) goto lExit;

   result = RegSetValue(hKey2, NULL, REG_SZ, tcCLSID, lstrlen(tcCLSID));
   if (result != ERROR_SUCCESS) goto lExit;

   RegCloseKey(hKey);
   RegCloseKey(hKey2);
   hKey = NULL;
   hKey2 = NULL;

   // Create HKEY_CLASSES_ROOT\CLSID

   // create CLSID key
   result = RegCreateKey(HKEY_CLASSES_ROOT, _T("CLSID"), &hKey);
   if (result != ERROR_SUCCESS) goto lExit ;

   // create CLSID/GUID key
   result = RegCreateKey(hKey, tcCLSID, &hKey2);
   if (result != ERROR_SUCCESS) goto lExit ;

   // put in sample description value into CLSID\GUID key
   result = RegSetValue(hKey2, NULL, REG_SZ, tcSampleDesc, lstrlen(tcSampleDesc));
   if (result != ERROR_SUCCESS) goto lExit ;

   // get our path ..
   result = GetModuleFileName(g_hDllMain, cModulePathName,
                             sizeof(cModulePathName) /sizeof(TCHAR));
   if (result == 0) goto lExit ;

   // create subkey under CLSID\GUID
   result = RegCreateKey(hKey2, tcInprocServer32, &hKey3);
   if (result != ERROR_SUCCESS) goto lExit ;

   // set key value to the path obtained above
   result = RegSetValue(hKey3, NULL, REG_SZ, cModulePathName,
lstrlen(cModulePathName));
   if (result != ERROR_SUCCESS) goto lExit ;

   // both
   result = RegSetValueEx(hKey3, tcThreadModel, 0, REG_SZ, (BYTE*)tcFree,
sizeof(tcFree));
   if (result != ERROR_SUCCESS) goto lExit;

   RegCloseKey(hKey3);
   hKey3 = NULL;

   // PROGID

   result = RegCreateKey(hKey2, tcProgID, &hKey3);
```

```
        if (result != ERROR_SUCCESS) goto lExit;

        result = RegSetValue(hKey3, NULL, REG_SZ, tcSampleProgID, lstrlen(tcSampleProgID));
        if (result != ERROR_SUCCESS) goto lExit;

        RegCloseKey(hKey3);
        hKey3 = NULL;


        hr = S_OK ;

    lExit:

        // close up
        if (hKey) RegCloseKey(hKey);
        if (hKey2) RegCloseKey(hKey2);
        if (hKey3) RegCloseKey(hKey3);

        return hr;
    }
```

If you look up the header files, you'll find that the **STDAPI** in front of **DllRegisterServer()** is defined to be equivalent to:

```
extern "C" HRESULT __export __stdcall
```

STDAPI takes care of making sure that **DllRegisterServer()** can be called by the client and that the name of the function won't be mangled by C++.

The implementation of **DllRegisterServer()** is quite straightforward, but one can see that this registry manipulation is quite tedious to write and test. The regular nature of it screams out for some sort of automation. In the next chapter, we'll examine an automatic way of doing this based on a script language.

If you've read through the code carefully, then you may have noticed an undeclared identifier creeping in. It occurs when we set the path:

```
        // get our path ..
        result = GetModuleFileName(g_hDllMain, cModulePathName,
                                   sizeof(cModulePathName) /sizeof(TCHAR));
        if (result == 0) goto lExit ;
```

The undeclared identifier is **g_hDllMain**, which is a global handle to the module itself (i.e. the DLL). We've stored this handle in a global variable, which needs to be added to the start of **Bareblob1.cpp** so that it's available. The following line should be at the start of the **Bareblob1.cpp** file.

```
HANDLE g_hDllMain;
```

However, we also have to initialize it. The best way of doing this is in the DLL entry point, namely **DllMain()**:

```
BOOL APIENTRY DllMain(HINSTANCE hDLLInst, DWORD fdwReason, LPVOID lpvReserved)
{
    switch (fdwReason)
    {
```

```
        case DLL_PROCESS_ATTACH :
            g_hDllMain = hDLLInst ;
    }

    return TRUE ;
}
```

The DllUnregisterServer Function

The **DllUnregisterServer()** function is almost a direct reversal of the **DllRegisterServer()** function. It's also rather uninteresting and screams out for some type of automation.

```
STDAPI DllUnregisterServer(VOID)
{
    HKEY    hKey  = NULL;
    HKEY    hKey2 = NULL;
    DWORD   result;
    HRESULT hr = SELFREG_E_CLASS;

    result = RegOpenKey(HKEY_CLASSES_ROOT, tcSampleProgID, &hKey);
    if (result == ERROR_SUCCESS)
    {
        GuardedDeleteKey(hKey, _T("CLSID"));
        RegCloseKey(hKey);
        hKey = NULL;
        GuardedDeleteKey(HKEY_CLASSES_ROOT, tcSampleProgID);
    }

    result = RegOpenKey(HKEY_CLASSES_ROOT, _T("CLSID"), &hKey);
    result = RegOpenKey(hKey, tcCLSID, &hKey2);

    if (result == ERROR_SUCCESS)
    {
        GuardedDeleteKey(hKey2, tcInprocServer32);
        GuardedDeleteKey(hKey2, tcProgID);
        RegCloseKey(hKey2);
        hKey2 = NULL;
        GuardedDeleteKey(hKey, tcCLSID);
    }


    RegCloseKey(hKey);
    hKey = NULL;

    hr = S_OK;

    return hr;
}
```

There's one small but important issue we need to be aware of when working with registry entries during unregistration. If there are unexpected subkeys found under a key that we've created, we should not delete that key, since another object or utility may depend on the value of the key to perform properly. You may have already noticed this behavior, when you've tried to uninstall a program and the uninstaller informs you that it can't remove all entries from the registry. It's reassuring to know that it follows standard procedures! Back to our code: we have a function that makes this kind of check before allowing deletion. The following is the code for **GuardedDeleteKey()** function which wraps the actual **RegDeleteKey()**

Win32 API and allows it to be accessed 'safely'. Another very subtle reason for this function is the difference in implementation of **RegDeleteKey()** under Windows 95 versus Windows NT 4.0. **RegDeleteKey()** will recursively delete a tree of keys and subkeys under Windows 95, while the Windows NT version won't delete a key if it has any subkeys.

If you're following along and entering code, make sure the following function is added at the beginning of the **.cpp** file.

```
LONG GuardedDeleteKey(HKEY hKey, LPCTSTR szSubKey)
{
    // check to see if the key to be deleted still has subkey, if not delete it, other-
wise
    // fail this
    TCHAR cDumHolder[MAX_PATH+1];
    HKEY  hSubkey;

    if (ERROR_SUCCESS != RegOpenKey(hKey, szSubKey, &hSubkey))
        return REGDB_E_INVALIDVALUE;

    if (ERROR_SUCCESS == RegEnumKey(hSubkey, 0, cDumHolder,
                                    sizeof(cDumHolder)/sizeof(TCHAR)))
    {
        RegCloseKey(hSubkey);
        return REGDB_E_INVALIDVALUE;
    }

    RegCloseKey(hSubkey);
    return RegDeleteKey(hKey, szSubKey);
}
```

The DllGetClassObject Function

The **DllGetClassObject()** function provides an entry point for the COM runtime to instantiate an instance of our class factory object, and requests its **IClassFactory** interface at the same time. The three parameters to this function are as follows:

Parameter	Description
REFCLSID rclsid	The class ID (CLSID) of the object that you want a class factory object for.
REFIID riid	The interface to request for from the class factory–typically, either **IClassFactory** or **IClassFactory2**.
LPVOID FAR *ppv	Returns the interface requested if successful; otherwise, it's set to **NULL**.

We implement **DllGetClassObject()** using the following code:

```
STDAPI DllGetClassObject(REFCLSID rclsid, REFIID riid, VOID **ppv)
{
    HRESULT         hr ;
    class CBareBlobMaker *  pcf;

    *ppv = NULL ;
```

```
    if (rclsid != CLSID_CBareBlob)
    {
        return CLASS_E_CLASSNOTAVAILABLE;
    }

    pcf = new CBareBlobMaker() ;

    if (!pcf)
    {
        return CLASS_E_CLASSNOTAVAILABLE;
    }

    hr = pcf->QueryInterface(riid, ppv) ;

    if (FAILED(hr))
    {
        delete pcf ;
        return hr ;
    }

    return S_OK ;
}
```

We first make a check to ensure that the caller (COM runtime) has requested a class factory object able to create **CBareBlob**s (in this case **rclsid == CLSID_CBareBlob**). If not, we return an error since we don't have a class factory class for anything else in this server. If the client did indeed request a **CBareBlob** class factory, we then instantiate a C++ **CBareBlobMaker** object. If this is successful, we then do a **QueryInterface()** on the object for the requested interface. In this case, we're taking advantage of the fact that the **CBareBlobMaker** is actually a C++ class and, therefore, we make a call to its **QueryInterface()** member function directly.

The DllCanUnload Function

The last function we implement, **DllCanUnloadNow()**, is called by the COM runtime from time to time when it wants to determine whether a DLL server can be unloaded. This function is seldom called in older 16-bit COM implementation, but is vital in 32-bit implementation. This function should work in conjunction with **LockServer()**. A DLL can be unloaded if it isn't servicing any object and the server isn't locked. Since both the action of **LockServer()** and the creation of a new instance of **CBareBlob** will call **ObjectCreated()**, which increments the **g_cObject** counter, we can implement this function simply by examining the object count. If the count hasn't reached zero, **DllCanUnloadNow()** returns **S_FALSE**, which won't allow the server DLL to be unloaded.

```
STDAPI DllCanUnloadNow()
{
    return ( g_cObject == 0 ) ? S_OK : S_FALSE;
}
```

This concludes all the coding required by our in-proc COM server servicing **CBareBlob** objects. Now we'll proceed to the compilation and testing of the server.

Finishing up the Source Code

Our source code isn't quite complete yet. There are the **#include**s required to make everything hang together.

We'll start with the header file. Up to now, the header file should contain just the class definitions of **CBareBlob**, **CGutsOfBareBlob** and **CBareBlobMaker**. As these classes are derived from interfaces (**IUnknown**, **ICustomInterface** and **IClassFactory** respectively), we need to tell Visual C++ about them. We do this by adding the following **#include**s to the **Bareblob1.h** file:

```
#include <objbase.h>
#include <initguid.h>
#include "bareblob.h" // this file generated by MIDL
```

Objbase.h defines many COM types, prototypes of COM APIs, and standard interface vtables (pure virtual structures or classes), such as **IClassFactory** and **IUnknown** for us. **Initguid.h** defines the macro which provides the standard way of expressing a GUID when making API calls. **Bareblob.h** was generated by the MIDL when we compiled **Bareblob.idl**, and it contains a declaration for the custom interface **ICustomInterface** that we'll implement.

Moving on to **Bareblob1.cpp** again, we find that we need to **#include** several headers–in particular, the **Bareblob_i.c** file generated for us by MIDL. This file contains all the UUIDs used in our IDL, including the library's UUID, the COM server's CLSID, and the interface's IID. We also include the following: **Windows.h**, to get a basic definition for the Win32 APIs that we call; **Tchar.h**, to get the **_T()** macro; **TCHAR** type, as we've discussed before; and **Olectl.h**, to get the Automation types like **BSTR** and **VARIANT_BOOL**, which we use as parameters for our business rule method implementation.

```
#include <windows.h>
#include "bareblob1.h"
#include <tchar.h>
#include <olectl.h>
#include "bareblob_i.c"  // MIDL generated file,
                         // mainly for the UUID definitions
```

Compiling our Creation

Let's summarize everything we've done so far. We have:

- 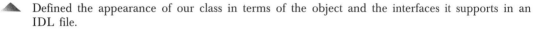 Defined the appearance of our class in terms of the object and the interfaces it supports in an IDL file.

- Run the IDL file through MIDL to generate proxy/stub code, as well as a binary type library.

- Created source files for our project by including some useful output files from MIDL, which provide declarations for interfaces and definitions for IIDs and CLSIDs.

- Coded and implemented the **CBareBlob** class by manually assembling the vtable, and using the nested class **CGutsOfBareBlob**.

- Coded and implemented the **CBareBlobMaker** class which serves as a class factory class for our **CBareBlob** class.

▲   Created a module definition (`.DEF`) file for our COM server, exporting the routines required by the COM runtime.

▲   Coded and implemented four in-proc server support routines for registering and unregistering the server on the system.

Now we're ready to compile our server.

If you like to start from scratch, just for the spirit of it, you can launch AppWizard and select the project type: Dynamic Link Library. After you've created the default workspace, choose Insert | Files into project... and select **Bareblob1.cpp** and **Bareblob.def**. Select Build | Settings..., go to the C/C++ tab, choose Category Code Generation and in the Use run-time library drop-down box make sure that a multithreaded library is selected. On the other hand, if you're feeling lazy, open the project from the downloaded source code.

Either way, select Build | Build Bareblob.dll to build a debug version of your COM server. If everything is okay, you should now have **Bareblob.dll** in your **Debug** directory.

Congratulations, you've just completed the creation of an ActiveX control from scratch!

Knowing this will probably be quite satisfying. However, seeing the object in action will be most gratifying. To do this, we must first register the server. How do we do this?

In the **DevStudio\SharedIDE\bin** directory, you'll find a system utility called **Regsvr32.exe**. This is the utility that we'll use to register the server. On the command line, simply type:

```
REGSVR32 BAREBLOB.DLL
```

A message box will pop up shortly, announcing that the server has registered successfully.

To unregister the server later, you may use:

```
REGSVR32 /u BAREBLOB.DLL
```

Again a message box will notify you of the status of the unregistration.

What happens inside **Regsvr32.exe** is actually quite simple. It calls **LoadLibrary()** on the DLL name that you've specified. If it is a register server request, it will make a call into the **DllRegisterServer()** entry point. If **DllRegisterServer()** returns success, it will report the success of registration; otherwise, the error message will be reported. If you've specified the unregister server operation, it will call the **DllUnregisterServer()** entry point instead. You can see how useful these functions are for COM server self-registration.

Once you've successfully compiled and registered your server, you're ready to instantiate a **CBareBlob**! We can do this even without first writing a client. This is accomplished through the **Oleview.exe** utility that we covered in Chapter 3.

Make sure you have **Oleview.exe** version 2.10.050 or later (check Help | About Oleviewer). If you have the **Oleview.exe** that comes with Visual C++ 5, then you're fine.

Start **Oleview.exe** on your system, and on the left-hand pane, select the All Objects item (you'll have to make sure Expert Mode is turned on in the View menu). Look down the list of objects and find CBareBlob. It is there! You're being recognized by **Oleview.exe**!

Select the **CBareBlob** object on the left pane, and check out the attributes that Object Viewer knows about your class. As you can see, all of it came from the registry entry that you've added in the **DllRegisterServer()** function. Now, let's actually instantiate a copy of **CBareBlob**. You can do this by double-clicking on the **CBareBlob** entry of the left pane. After a quick pause, you can see a list of interfaces showing up. Believe it or not, you've actually instantiated a **CBareBlob** object.

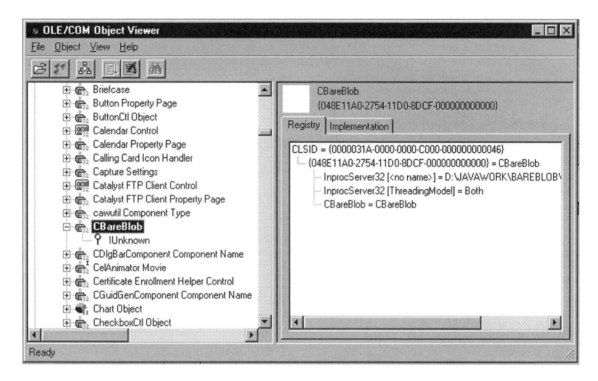

There's no outward sign that the object has been instantiated, because our object provides no user interface. However, **Oleview.exe** obtains the list of interfaces that you see through the following means:

 It creates an object instance of the COM class.

 Next, it obtains a pointer to the **IUnknown** of the object.

 Finally, it goes through the complete list of known interfaces and performs **QueryInterface()** on every one of them, noting which ones are supported.

In other words, not only has your poor object been instantiated, but it has also been interrogated by the system hundreds of times while you're still trying to figure out if object creation actually worked.

Let's prove this. I suppose we could put an infinite loop inside the **QueryInterface()** method of **CBareBlob** and watch Object Viewer choke when it picks on your object, or we could meticulously rig up the debugger and do **TRACE()** inside the **QueryInterface()** implementation. Another less offensive

107

(and easy, no recompile) way to do this is to manually define **ICustomInterface()** in the system registry. This will make the interface 'known' to the system (and Object Viewer), so that the next time your object is interrogated, this interface will be recognized. Sounds better? Let's do it.

Start **Regedit.exe** (or **Regedt32.exe** in Windows NT), expand **HKEY_CLASSES_ROOT** and go to the **Interface** key. Now manually add a subkey in this tree, and label it with the interface ID (IID) of **ICustomInterface**. Add a nameless **(default)** value of **ICustomInterface**. Finally, add a **NumMethods** subkey and set its default value to **6**. The following is a summary of keys to add.

```
\HKEY_CLASSES_ROOT\Interface\{2740CBA0-274C-11d0-8DCF-000000000000}\(default) =
    "ICustomInterface"
\HKEY_CLASSES_ROOT\Interface\{2740CBA0-274C-11d0-8DCF-000000000000}\NumMethods\
    (default) = "6"
```

Now, go back to our friend Object Viewer again (notice how our earlier prophecy has come true: we constantly keep both **Regedit.exe** and **Oleview.exe** open on our development desktop), and double-click on our **CBareBlob** to see its interfaces.

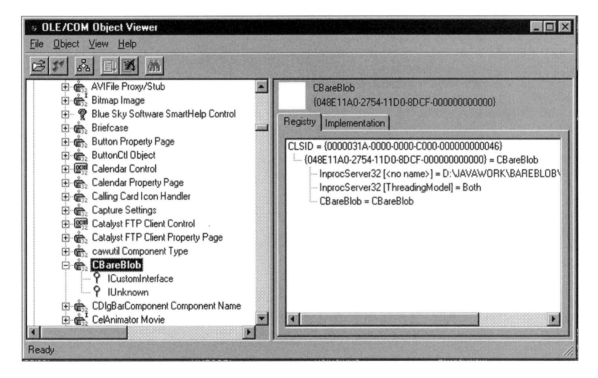

Ta-da! **ICustomInterface** is now recognized by the system! Our faithful object's **QueryInterface()** has returned and proudly announced to the world, 'Elementary, my dear Watson! I do support **ICustomInterface**.'

Before you start to curse me for making such a mountain out of a molehill, let me assure you that we'll spend a good part of the rest of the chapter building much more sophisticated test harnesses for our BLOB object, and for any future ActiveX control that we will be designing.

But seriously, even in this seemingly trivial interaction, Object Viewer has already exercised over 80% of our code. What happened under the hood is this:

1 Object Viewer enumerated the **\HKEY_CLASSES_ROOT\CLSID** keys.

2 It then did a **CoCreateInstance()** on the **CBareBlob** CLSID when we double-clicked on **CBareBlob**, requesting **IUnknown**.

3 The COM runtime loaded our **Bareblob.dll** and made a call into **DllGetClassObject()** to get an **IClassFactory** interface and instantiate a class factory object.

4 Our implementation of the **DllGetClassObject()** instantiated a **CBareBlobMaker** object on the heap and returned a pointer to it to the COM runtime.

5 The COM runtime called **IClassFactory::CreateInstance()**.

6 Our implementation of **CBareBlobMaker::CreateInstance()** created a **CBareBlob** object on the heap, **QueryInterface()**'d it for **IUnknown** and returned the pointer back to the COM runtime.

7 The COM runtime returned the **IUnknown** pointer to Object Viewer.

8 Object Viewer enumerated the **\HKEY_CLASSES_ROOT\Interface** keys.

9 For each IID entry enumerated, **IUnknown::QueryInterface()** of the **CBareBlob** was called to see if the interface is supported.

10 Object Viewer obtained the text representation of all the supported interfaces from **\HKEY_CLASSES_ROOT\Interface** and displayed them.

The following interaction diagram illustrates what went on:

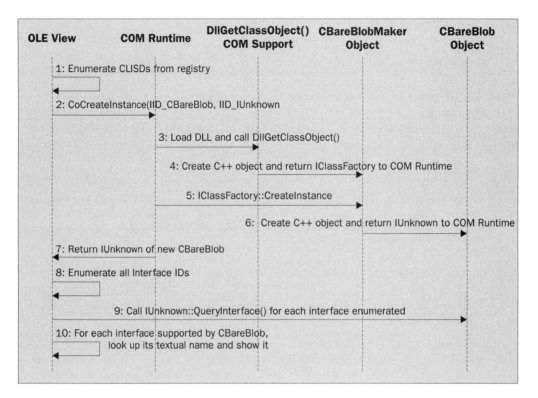

Testing our Object

Having finished writing a component that the system immediately recognizes is very exciting. Using Object Viewer to instantiate and 'test' our object is very easy, but also quite limited. For example, there's no way in Object Viewer to call our custom interfaces.

In order to further test our object (and prove to ourselves that our server is fully working), we now turn to actually writing a simple client. This client should instantiate an object of the **CBareBlob** class through COM, and then make calls into the methods of the **ICustomInterface**.

We'll be constructing the test harness client using straight C for simplicity. If you've followed along this far into the chapter, you're probably tired already. I'll spare you the agony of going through any more complex code. Note that, unlike other ActiveX controls, our object can't be called from Visual Basic or other interpretative environments (like Internet Explorer scripting). This is because we haven't implemented the **IDispatch** interface that's required.

Roughly speaking, we want our client to contain the following pseudo code:

1 Initialize COM subsystem.

2 Call **CoGetClassObject()** on **CBareBlob**'s CLSID to get an **IClassFactory** interface and instantiate a class factory object.

3 Call **IClassFactory::CreateInstance()** to create a **CBareBlob** object and get its **IUnknown** interface.

4 Release the **IClassFactory** interface.

5 Call **IUnknown::QueryInterface()** with the IID of **ICustomInterface** to get the object's **ICustomInterface**.

6 Call **ICustomInterface::GetManagerName()** and print the result.

7 Call **ICustomInterface::OkayToPublishInfo()** and print the result.

8 Call **ICustomInterface::PeekCounters()** and print the result.

9 Release **ICustomInterface**

10 Release **IUnknown**

11 Uninitialize the COM subsystem

Writing a Simple Client Test Harness

For the sake of simplicity, we've opted to create a very simple test-harness client as a console application. We really don't want to mess with GUI code; our focus is on the COM interactions. Doing it as a console application also allows us to keep the code very close to the pseudocode. The following is our coding for the test harness. The file is quite small; I'll try to annotate it as we examine it from the top.

```
#include "precomp.h"
#include "initguid.h"
#include "bareblob.h"

#define IID_DEFINED
#include "bareblob_i.c"
#include "CRTDBG.h"
```

Notice how handy the **BareBlob.h** and **BareBlob_i.c** comes in again. Recall that they were MIDL generated files that include definitions for our custom interfaces, as well as definitions for the IIDs, CLSIDs, etc. These files are indispensable for the client of your COM classes.

The content of **Precomp.h** is:

```
#include <stdio.h>
#include <stdlib.h>
#include <time.h>
#include <objbase.h>
```

We get the **printf()** function from **Stdio.h**. We also include **Stdlib.h** and **Time.h** to use the C++ runtime to generate a random number based on time. The random numbers are used in testing the **OkayToPublishInfo()** function to make it more interesting. **Objbase.h** was included again for the common COM type definitions.

```
main()
{

    IUnknown * pM;
    IClassFactory * pCF;
    ICustomInterface *pCI;
    long localRef, objCount;
    BSTR mgrName;

    srand( (unsigned)time( NULL ) );
```

We declare pointers for the interfaces that we'll be getting from our BLOB and its class factory, and also two variables to hold the values from calls to our custom interface. The **BSTR** is for holding the manager's name that will be returned. We also take this chance to seed the random number generator of the C++ runtime with the current time as a seed.

```
    HRESULT hRes = CoInitialize(NULL);
    _ASSERT(SUCCEEDED(hRes));
```

We initialize the COM subsystem and make sure everything is A-OK.

```
    hRes = CoGetClassObject(CLSID_CBareBlob, CLSCTX_ALL, NULL,
    IID_IClassFactory,  (void **) &pCF);

    if (SUCCEEDED(hRes))
    {
       printf("Got class factory!\n");
    }
    else
    {
       CoUninitialize();
       exit(1);
    }
```

We try to obtain a class factory for **CBareBlob** by calling **CoGetClassObject()**. If we aren't successful, we uninitialize the COM subsystem and exit. Otherwise, we print a message out to the console.

```
    hRes = pCF->CreateInstance(NULL, IID_IUnknown,  (void **) &pM);

    if (pM != NULL)
    {
       printf("Made a bare blob!\n");
    }
    else
    {
       pCF->Release();
       CoUninitialize();
       exit(1);
    }
```

```
      // made one of those blobs, release the class factory
      pCF->Release();
```

With a call to **IClassFactory::CreateInstance()**, we create an instance of our **CBareBlob** object and ask for its **IUnknown**. If successful, we print a message and notify the world. Otherwise, we clean up and exit gracefully. Once we've successfully created the **CBareBlob**, we can release the **IClassFactory** pointer and free the class factory object.

```
      // Get our custom interface!
      hRes = pM->QueryInterface( IID_ICustomInterface, (void **) &pCI);
      if (pCI != NULL)
      {
         printf("Got its custom interface!\n");
      }
      else
      {
         pM->Release();
         CoUninitialize();
         exit(1);
      }
```

Using the **IUnknown** pointer, we **QueryInterface()** for **ICustomInterface**. Thanks to the definition in **Bareblob_i.c**, this is as easy as using the value **IID_ICustomInterface**. If we get the **ICustomInterface** pointer, we print a message and let the world know. Otherwise, we exit gracefully after cleanup.

Now that we have a pointer to **ICustomInterface**, we're ready to call the 'real meat' of the **CBareBlob** object.

```
      hRes = pCI->GetManagerName(&mgrName);
   #ifdef UNICODE
      printf("After calling GetManagerName : = %s\n",
             mgrName);
   #else
      char * tp = new char[50];
      WideCharToMultiByte(CP_ACP,0, mgrName,
         -1, tp, 50, NULL, NULL);
      printf("After calling GetManagerName : = %s\n",
             tp);
      delete [] tp;
   #endif
      SysFreeString(mgrName);
```

We set up the input values and make a call into **ICustomInterface::GetManagerName()**, get the manager name and print it out on the console. It turns out that this is not totally trivial. Recall that **BSTR** type under Win32 is always in Unicode. We need to print out the **BSTR** returned from **GetManagerName()**, and the way we do it will depend on whether the test client is compiled for Unicode or not. The **Tchar.h** header is useless here, since it doesn't know about or work with **BSTR**. Instead, we do our own checking and call the **WideCharToMultiByte()** function to convert the string before printing if necessary. The **WideCharToMultiByte()** function basically converts a Unicode string to a multibyte character set string. The function has many parameters, and there are features catering for characters that can't be converted. We won't cover them at length here, but the Win32 API documentation explains it in detail. The first parameter, though, is used to select the code-page for the multibyte character set; setting this to **CP_ACP** gives us the ANSI character set. Notice that, according to **BSTR** usage conventions, we must call **SysFreeString()** to free the memory allocated.

113

```
long inYear, inMonth;
VARIANT_BOOL flag;
inYear = 1900 + rand() %100;
inMonth = rand() % 13 + 1;
hRes = pCI->OkayToPublishInfo(inYear,
    inMonth, &flag);

printf("Checking for okay to publish info : year = %d, month = %d, status = %s\n",
    inYear, inMonth, (flag == TRUE) ? "OKAY": "NOWAY");
```

For testing the **ICustomInterface::OkayToPublishInfo()** function, we decided to use the **rand()** capability of the C++ runtime to make the test more interesting. The random number is used to enter random Year and Month values for the call. The returned value from the server is decoded, and either OKAY or NOWAY is printed on the console.

```
hRes = pCI->PeekCounters(&localRef, &objCount);
printf("After calling PeekCounters: we now have %d local references and %d"
        "object users.\n", localRef, objCount);
```

The **ICustomInterface::PeekCounters()** testing is straightforward. For each call of **PeekCounters()**, we simply print out the values of the counters from the ActiveX control.

```
pCI->Release();
pM->Release();

printf("Freeing the blob now!\n");


CoUninitialize();
return 0;
}
```

Finally, we release the **IUnknown** pointer to **CBareBlob**, as well as the **ICustomInterface** pointer. We then call **CoUninitialize()** to uninitialize the COM subsystem.

The output you obtain will be similar to this:

```
Got class factory!
Made a bare blob!
Got its custom interface!
After calling GetManagerName : = J. Manzini
Checking for okay to publish info : year = 1927, month = 1, status = NOWAY
After calling PeekCounters: we now have 2 local references and 1 object users.
Freeing the blob now!
```

You may want to run **REGSVR32 /u BAREBLOB.DLL** to unregister your server, and then try running the program again and see what happens.

If we add a loop around the custom interface calls, and run multiple copies of the program, each in its own DOS box, how come the counts from the **ICustomInterface::PeekCounters()** call stay constant (try it if you don't believe me)? This is actually a unique property of in-proc servers. Since the server runs inside the client's process, the copy running in each DOS box has a **CBareBlob** and its object factory all to itself. There's no sharing of any kind in this scenario.

Another good exercise would be to single-step through the program in debug mode and notice when the class factory and the **CBareBlob** objects are actually allocated and freed; and also to experiment with reference counting and object lifetime.

Giving Our BLOB a Workout

The program above is a simple, but quite effective test harness for ActiveX controls that implement only custom interfaces. There are, though, several aspects in the life of an ActiveX object that aren't tested. The most noticeable one being the inability to create multiple instances of **CBareBlob**s.

It turns out that one effective way to give our object a good workout is to write a client test harness which is multithreaded. In this way, each thread in the test harness process can create its own instance of **CBareBlob** and class factory object. It can then test them simultaneously within the same process.

To design such a test harness, we'll start with the source code above and modify it. In particular, we'll make the following modifications:

1 Create a global critical section object to share the console, since each and every print statement should be executed by the reporting thread in an atomic fashion from beginning to end; otherwise, the output will be impossible to read.

2 Define **LOCK** and **UNLOCK** macros to make usage of the critical section easier within the code.

3 Put the **LOCK** and **UNLOCK** macros before and after each and every **printf()** statement.

4 Put a loop around the custom interface calls to repeat them twenty times each.

5 Move all the object creation and testing logic to a thread function.

6 In the main program of the test harness, create up to **MAX_THREAD** number of threads and store their handles in an array, allowing for some delay, say 2 seconds, between the creation of each thread.

7 After the threads have been created, the main program should wait indefinitely for all the started threads to complete their work.

8 After all threads have exited, the main thread should clean up by closing all thread handles and destroying the critical section object.

For readers new to multithreaded programming, please see our *Aside on Threads and Synchronization Objects* section at the end of this chapter for an introduction.

Our main program now becomes:

```
#include "precomp.h"
#include "initguid.h"
#include "bareblob.h"
```

```
#define IID_DEFINED
#include "bareblob_i.c"
#include "CRTDBG.h"
```

```
#include <process.h>
#define MAX_THREAD          10
CRITICAL_SECTION        g_Console;
#define LOCK                EnterCriticalSection(&g_Console);
#define UNLOCK              LeaveCriticalSection(&g_Console);

void AThread(LPVOID lpParam);

main()
{
    HANDLE hThread[MAX_THREAD];
    long Params[MAX_THREAD];
    InitializeCriticalSection(&g_Console);

    for (long i=0; i<MAX_THREAD; i++)
    {
        Params[i] = i;
        hThread[i] = (HANDLE) _beginthread(AThread, NULL, (void *)&Params[i]);

        if (((long)hThread[i]) == -1)
        {
            LOCK
            printf("Main: Thread creation failure!\n");
            UNLOCK
            exit(1);
        }
        else
        {
            LOCK
            printf("Main: Started thread %d!\n",  i);
            UNLOCK
        }
        Sleep(2000); // 2 seconds between each thread
    }

    WaitForMultipleObjects(MAX_THREAD, hThread, TRUE, INFINITE);
    for ( i=0; i<MAX_THREAD; i++)
        CloseHandle(hThread[i]);
    DeleteCriticalSection(&g_Console);

    return 0;
}
```

Notice the declaration of the critical section and its associated macros at the top, and the forward definition of the thread function. Otherwise, the coding of the main thread is very faithful to the pseudocode above.

We needed to add **Process.h** to the include list for the thread related functions, such as **_beginthread()** and **_endthread()**. Also, make sure that you've selected a multithreaded build setting to get the correct compile-symbolic definitions and libraries linked in. This can be done by selecting the Project | Settings... menu. Click on the C/C++ tab. Select Code Generation from the Category drop-down list. In the Use run-time library list, make sure you select Multithreaded.

We've used an array of **long** values called **Params[]** to pass in a unique ID for each thread to identify itself when printing messages to the console. Also, we're using the C++ runtime **_beginthread()** and **_endthread()** instead of the Win32 **CreateThread()** and **ExitThread()**. This is necessary so that we can get the right behavior from C/C++ runtime functions such as **printf()**.

The former object creation and testing portion of the code has now been moved to the thread function. Each thread function does its own **CoInitialize()** at the beginning and **CoUninitialize()** at the end. One's initial reaction is to put **CoInitialize()** and **CoUninitialize()** on the main thread, but it turns out that these functions are designed for apartment model threading, which means it's expected that the same thread which called **CoInitialize()** will call all the COM functions, and will make calls to the interface methods. With Windows NT 4.0 and beyond, there are newer variations of these functions called **CoInitializeEx()**, and **CoUninitializeEx()** which work with free threading (i.e. no expectation of which thread will be calling COM functions). For a discussion of the COM threading models see Chapter 4. For our purposes, having each thread call **CoInitialize()** and **CoUninitialize()** itself works just fine.

```
void AThread(LPVOID lpParam)
{
    long myNumber = *((long *) lpParam);
    IUnknown * pM;
    IClassFactory * pCF;
    ICustomInterface *pCI;
    HRESULT hRes;

    long localRef, objCount, inYear, inMonth;
    VARIANT_BOOL okFlag;
    BSTR mgrName;

    srand( (unsigned)time( NULL ) );
    hRes = CoInitialize(NULL);

    hRes = CoGetClassObject(CLSID_CBareBlob, CLSCTX_ALL, NULL,
                            IID_IClassFactory,(void **) &pCF);

    if (SUCCEEDED(hRes))
    {
        LOCK
        printf("T%d: Got class factory!\n", myNumber);
        UNLOCK
    }
    else
    {
        CoUninitialize();
        _endthread();
    }
    hRes = pCF->CreateInstance(NULL, IID_IUnknown,    (void **) &pM);

    if (pM != NULL)
    {
        LOCK
        printf("T%d: Made a bare blob!\n", myNumber);
        UNLOCK
    }
    else
    {
```

```
        CoUninitialize();
        _endthread();
    }

    // made one of those blobs, release the class factory
    pCF->Release();

    // Get our custom interface!
    hRes = pM->QueryInterface( IID_ICustomInterface, (void **) &pCI);
    if (pCI != NULL)
    {
        LOCK
        printf("T%d: Got its custom interface!\n", myNumber);
        UNLOCK
    }
    else
    {
        pM->Release();
        CoUninitialize();
        _endthread();
    }

    for (long i=0; i< 20; i++)
    {
hRes = pCI->GetManagerName(&mgrName);

    inYear = 1900 + rand() %100;
    inMonth = rand() % 13 + 1;

    hRes = pCI->OkayToPublishInfo(inYear, inMonth, &okFlag);
    hRes = pCI->PeekCounters(&localRef, &objCount);
#ifdef UNICODE
    LOCK
    printf("T%d: After calling GetManagerName : current manager is %s\n",
        myNumber,
         mgrName );
    UNLOCK
#else
    char * tp = new char[50];
     WideCharToMultiByte(CP_ACP,0, mgrName,
       -1, tp, 50, NULL, NULL);
    LOCK
    printf("T%d: After calling GetManagerName : current manager is %s\n",
        myNumber,
          tp);
    UNLOCK
     delete [] tp;
#endif
    SysFreeString(mgrName);

    LOCK

    printf("T%d: After calling OkToPublishInfo : Year = %d, Month = %d Status = %s\n",
         myNumber,
        inYear, inMonth, (okFlag == TRUE) ? "OKAY": "NOWAY");
    UNLOCK
```

```
        LOCK
        printf("T%d: We now have %d local references and %d object users.\n",
            myNumber,
            localRef, objCount);

        UNLOCK
            Sleep(1000);   // sleep for about 1 second
        }

        pCI->Release();
        pM->Release();

        LOCK
        printf("T%d, Freeing the blob now!\n", myNumber);
        UNLOCK

        CoUninitialize();

        _endthread();
    }
```

You'll notice very few differences between our previous **main()** code and the **AThread()** thread function listed above, but the most glaring one is the **LOCK** and **UNLOCK** macros around the **printf()**s, for synchronization, and the fact that a thread cannot simply **exit()** to terminate the program in case of error. Instead, a thread should use **_endthread()** after cleaning up to gracefully exit. Recall that the main thread, which starts all the test threads, will wait for the termination of every single thread before terminating itself.

We've used a pair of **LOCK** and **UNLOCK**s around **each** of the **printf()**s to give another thread a chance to 'sneak in' between the printing of every output line. This gives a somewhat finer-grained shuffle of the threads during execution.

Once you have the debug version compiled, you're ready to party. Execute it from a DOS box, and you'll see output similar to the following:

```
...
Main: Started thread 4!
T2: After calling GetManagerName : current manager is J. Manzini
T2: After calling OkToPublishInfo : Year = 1952, Month = 3 Status = OKAY
T2: We now have 2 local references and 4 object users.
T3: After calling GetManagerName : current manager is J. Manzini
T3: After calling OkToPublishInfo : Year = 1989, Month = 1 Status = OKAY
T3: We now have 2 local references and 4 object users.
T1: After calling GetManagerName : current manager is J. Manzini
T1: After calling OkToPublishInfo : Year = 1914, Month = 10 Status = NOWAY
T1: We now have 2 local references and 4 object users.
T4: Got class factory!
T4: Made a bare blob!
T4: Got its custom interface!
T4: After calling GetManagerName : current manager is J. Manzini
T4: After calling OkToPublishInfo : Year = 1913, Month = 5 Status = OKAY
T4: We now have 2 local references and 5 object users.
T0: After calling GetManagerName : current manager is J. Manzini
```

```
T0: After calling OkToPublishInfo : Year = 1985, Month = 11 Status = NOWAY
T0: We now have 2 local references and 5 object users.
T2: After calling GetManagerName : current manager is J. Manzini
T2: After calling OkToPublishInfo : Year = 1950, Month = 10 Status = NOWAY
T2: We now have 2 local references and 5 object users.
T3: After calling GetManagerName : current manager is J. Manzini
T3: After calling OkToPublishInfo : Year = 1933, Month = 2 Status = OKAY
T3: We now have 2 local references and 5 object users.
...
```

Notice the user count going up from 1 to 10 and then coming back down, while the reference count is the same for all cases. This is exactly what we expect. The user count reflects the number of instances of **CBareBlob** that have been created, and it will increase as the main thread creates more and more threads. The reference count, on the other hand, is per instance. Because the calling sequence for all the interfaces remains the same across all instances (i.e. it is the same code executing), the reference count is the same for all threads. The user count may not hit the maximum because some threads may start exiting before all of them have been created.

Next, try starting multiple DOS windows each running this code. Now try to explain the relationships that you're observing. Recall that each in-proc server actually gets loaded into the process of the client; therefore each DOS window is running a separate copy of the executable and acts as a hard partition. Even though each program creates multiple instances of the **CBareBlob** object, the hard partitioning remains and each DOS box behaves independently from all others.

From an operating system point of view, though, the DLL (in-proc server) is loaded only once in system memory, regardless of how many processes may be using it. It's interesting to imagine what sort of results we would see if **CBareBlob** were implemented via a local server (i.e. running in its own process) instead of in-proc. Hold your curiosity for now, we'll be looking at this scenario in the next chapter.

Even though it's quite simple, the combination of **Bareblob.dll** and our test programs is a potent set of COM server/client driver utilities for playing and experimenting with the various facets of COM or ActiveX programming. We'll be reusing the multithreaded version in later chapters as we build more sophisticated and complex ActiveX components.

An Aside on Threads and Synchronization Objects

Traditional Windows programs (i.e. Windows 3.1 and before) were all single-threaded programs. This was because the underlying operating system, DOS, could only execute one program at a time. The program starts up, executes from beginning to end on the same CPU, and is never interrupted by the operating system. With the advent of Windows 95 and Windows NT, application programs on Windows platforms do not only gain the benefits of multitasking (which means that many programs can be executing on the operating system at the same time), but also multithreading.

A process under a Win32 based operating system can have many threads. The kernel on Windows 95 and Windows NT schedules only threads. This means that each and every thread is conceptually executing simultaneously. In a system with multiple processors, this may actually be true. However, in most cases where the system only has one CPU, the scheduler uses 'time-slicing' to achieve the same effect. Each thread is given a slice of time to execute; it is then preempted, and another thread starts executing. Threads may also give up their right of execution if they're waiting for input/output or the availability of other resources. Since the scheduler works only with threads, a process must have at least one thread in order to be executed. Essentially, then, a process in this sense is a grouping of threads. It goes beyond this, though, since it is the process which gives the threads in its group the resources they need; for example, an address space (in virtual memory) to execute in.

In many ways, the process can be viewed as the set of data structures tracking the utilization of system resources for a group of threads. Threads, on the other hand, can be viewed as a program counter location (the currently executing instruction) and a stack (for storage of temporary or automatic variables). On a system where only one process is running (but with multiple threads executing) the memory space of the process (group of threads) will never be swapped out, and other resources occupied by the process also need not be released. All that's happening in this situation is that each thread gets a chance at execution, with the operating system simply saving and restoring program counters and switching stacks. The registers, stack and other information are called a context. When Windows NT or Windows 95 switches between threads it loads and unloads the thread's context.

When programming in a high level language such as C or C++, multithreading programming is very similar to the multitasking programming of older operating systems (i.e. UNIX), the only difference being the transparency of resource management. For example, when a UNIX process forks, it's assumed that there will be another execution context; but in order to get that other execution context to do something other than what the original process already does, we need to replace its instructions. With multithreaded programming, all of what the threads can do is defined in 'thread functions'. When we create a thread, we give it a thread function. In essence, the behavior of the thread is determined by the code in the thread function. We can create as many threads with as many thread functions (one per thread) as we want within an application, limited only by the system configuration. Even the 'main thread' of a process is simply the C/C++ runtime creating a thread using the operating system **CreateThread()** API, and giving it a thread function equivalent to your **WinMain()** routine. In this way, every thread within a process can be created equally, and the main thread in a process doesn't have any extra visibility or special privileges from the point of view of the operating system or scheduler.

Some aspects of multithreaded programming will take some time to get used to if you come from the single-threaded programming world. The most important of these is the synchronization of shared resources. Since every thread is conceptually executing concurrently, any resource (variables, graphic device context, memory location, disk file, etc.) shared by more than one thread can potentially get corrupted if some form of synchronization isn't implemented. Corruption occurs when two threads try to modify the same item at the same time, or if one thread holds some information about or from the shared resource, and assumes that it's the only one that has access to it.

Win32 offers many synchronization mechanisms for coordinating resource usage between threads and/or processes. The most lightweight and efficient one is a critical section. Once created, any thread can 'enter' a critical section. If a thread tries to 'enter' the same critical section already being 'entered' by another thread, the attempting thread will be 'blocked' and will not be executed until the thread in the critical section 'leaves' it. In this way, sections of code can be bracketed by 'enter' and 'leave' operations on a critical section object. These sections of code, then, are guaranteed to be executed by one thread at a time. We used this technique in our multithreaded client sample to protect the console. Without this protection (you can try it if you like), the output from the threads may merge together, and become almost impossible to read. With the protection of the critical section, any thread entering a **printf()** will complete it before any other thread can enter the same critical section (e.g. get a chance to print to the console).

While efficient, the critical section object has the special property that it can't be owned and it isn't visible outside of the process. Other synchronization objects, including mutexes, semaphores and events, have different properties and are usually accessible from other processes. Interested readers should consult the documentation of the Win32 SDK or other books on advanced Win32 programming.

Another new and yet frequent situation that occurs in multithreaded programming is when a thread wants to wait for and synchronize with another thread. This may be necessary due to the differences in speed of execution or processing between the threads, or the situation may occur by design. In our multithreaded client, the main thread creates many threads with two seconds between each thread creation. After creating them, it has to wait for all of them to finish. Luckily, Win32 provides a way to do just that. The main thread can invoke the `WaitForMultipleObjects()` API call, and pass it an array of thread handles (obtained when the threads are created successfully). A thread is deemed 'signaled' if the thread has finished execution, or has terminated for other reasons. Therefore, by specifying in the `WaitForMultipleObjects()` call that it would like to wait for the entire array of threads to be signaled, the main thread has essentially said that it will wait for all threads to complete. `WaitForMultipleObjects()` is a very powerful call, allowing a thread to wait for a variety of conditions to be triggered before it continues execution. A variant of `WaitForMultipleObjects()`, called `MsgWaitForMultipleObjects()`, allows the application to synchronize with objects such as threads, together with input events (like keyboard or mouse input) and is very useful for multithreaded COM programming.

By design, since there's no endless loop or any hold/wait conditions in our thread function, all threads will eventually finish execution (i.e. will be signaled) and the main thread will then be released from the blocking state and continue on to the cleanup and shutdown activities.

There Must be a Better Way

Working through BareBlob and its drivers gives us a good feel for what raw COM programming is like, and what it involves. While tedious, raw COM programming is actually not as difficult as it may first seem. However, in our commercial world, any mechanism that will allow us to do the job faster, more effectively, or more efficiently, will improve our competitiveness. To this end, as much as we may like to program every ActiveX control from scratch (as we did in this chapter), the fact that there are tools/ libraries out there that make the activity much easier demands our attention.

For the rest of this book, we won't be returning to raw COM programming. There are several choices of tools and libraries that make ActiveX control programming significantly easier. To maintain the competitive edge, you really should be using them. Besides, these tools allow you to focus more on the problem that the actual ActiveX control solves, instead of idiosyncrasies of COM programming or interaction. However, just like COM and DCOM, many of these tools and libraries are in their infancy and have not yet matured. Whenever something doesn't work quite right, or if there are things that the tool or library doesn't handle, raw COM once again becomes the only game in town.

In these dark ages, you'll be glad to have spent the time in these two chapters to understand how to wing-it from scratch, should it ever be necessary in your programming endeavors. In addition, we hope that the focus of COM as a platform, and the operating-system-independent technology will instill in you a sense of the unlimited possibilities that component technology and distributed computing can offer. We hope that the ActiveX components you design will solve your urgent problems of today, and be part of the solution for those (as yet) unknown problems of tomorrow. At a minimum, this should be the goal of every software-component design.

The next chapter covers a library that makes building COM servers substantially easier. We will reconstruct our BareBlob object server in record time, and even add features to it—with almost no work. The new and improved BareBlob ActiveX control that we'll create will be compatible with a large variety of clients, including Visual Basic, Java, and even an ActiveX control container on a web page!

ActiveX Controls The Easy Way: ATL 2.1

You must be wondering, when I'm going to say that MFC will make building these controls much easier. Well, actually, I'm not going to do that. As a matter of fact, using MFC to build the type of ActiveX controls that we need for our intranet project would be quite complicated. MFC provides convenient features for building ActiveX controls, but the generated code tends towards a large footprint. (Of course, in the intranet environment, large controls aren't such a problem and we'll cover using MFC in Chapters 5 and 6.)

For now, we'll cover a new star on the horizon. It's called the ActiveX Template Library 2.1 or (ATL 2.1) and is now supplied as part of Visual C++ 5. As the name suggests, it's a template library, so we'll be taking a workaday C++ stance while using it–don't worry if your template knowledge is a little hazy. Using ATL in this way is the logical next step from the previous chapter: we'll discover how it really simplifies the creation of highly functional ActiveX controls. Our established business rule can now mature so that both Visual Basic 5 and Internet Explorer can use it–we'll be creating test programs to ensure that. Therefore, by the end of the chapter, we'll have created two versions of our ActiveX control: once as an in-proc server supporting both early and late binding, and a second time as a local server that runs in its own processes.

The ease of programming provided by ATL 2.1 will allow us to cover much more ground (compared to the last chapter). We'll understand how ATL 2.1 carries out its magic, and to customize or maintain the generated code. In addition, we'll learn about the brand new 'native COM' support that's an integral part of Visual C++ 5. Using it to rewrite the test harness, we'll see how this support significantly reduces the effort to create COM clients.

By the end of this chapter, you'll be able to build your own reusable nonvisual ActiveX software components, implementing any business rules, using Visual C++ 5 and ATL 2.1. These components can be reused through Visual C++, Visual Basic, VBScript or JAVAScript in Internet Explorer, Visual J++, or any other platform which supports ActiveX controls.

A Template Quickie

If you've been using the new list management classes in MFC 3.x and later, you're probably already familiar with C++ templates and what they can do. For those who haven't, as well as for those who want a quick refresher, we'll breeze right through a quick introduction to templates over the next few pages.

As C/C++ programmers, we're fully familiar with the macro preprocessor's function. The good old **#define** can also be used for parameterized macros, as in:

```
#define GREATER_THAN(x,y)      (x > y)
```

Which allows us to use:

```
if ( GREATER_THAN(my_value,100) )
{
    printf("greater\n");
}
```

Here's the actual code generated after the source has been preprocessed:

```
if ( (my_value > 100) )
{
    printf("greater\n");
}
```

In the past this was the only way one could easily define constants and write inline functions. But today with **const** data types and **inline** qualified functions, there's no excuse for using preprocessor macros for this purpose. The macros perform textual substitution without any knowledge of the underlying language. As a result, nasty side effects are possible and the lack of any type checking makes for some recurring debugging nightmares. In all fairness, however, they are still extremely useful in helping manage the project build process by hiding some system dependencies and facilitating conditional header file inclusion and compilation.

Until a few years ago, macros were the only way one could get the next best thing to something like a 'type variable'. In languages like C/C++ typing is static, that is, the compiler must know the type of an object at compile time. This makes it impossible to write generic pieces of code that would work equally well for a variety of data types. The only way to do this is to create a base class and derive all data types subjected to the generic operation from this base. The old pre-template MFC list management classes are a good example of this approach (the base class is **CObject**, and the generic operations operate on **CObject**). Typical usage of these classes involves a lot of class upcasting (to **CObject** in MFC) and downcasting (from **CObject** in MFC). This isn't exactly a trivial task. Enter templates! The advantage of templates is that they operate at compile time and obey scope, access and type rules. Extending the general concept, one can write C++ classes for generic data types, and then be able to substitute the data type into this class definition 'skeleton' whenever needed. Take the following trivial class example:

```
template <class T >
class ComparableObject
{
public:
    ComparableObject(T aVal): m_var(aVal)
    {}
    BOOL GreaterThan(T comp) { return (m_var > comp); }
    BOOL LessThan(T comp);
```

```
private:
   T m_var;
};


template <class T>
BOOL ComparableObject<T>::LessThan(T comp)
{
   return (m_var < comp);
}
```

Once we have this template class defined, we may use it in the following fashion.

```
ComparableObject<int> aVal(10);


if (aVal.GreaterThan(100))
   printf("greater\n");
```

Instead of working on a text substitution level, templates work via parameterized code generation. Essentially, a new class has been defined for you above, which 'looks like' the **ComparableObject** that you've defined but operates specifically on the **int** data type. Effectively the following code was generated into your executable.

```
class ComparableObjectInt
{
public:
   ComparableObjectInt(int  aVal):m_var(aVal)
   {}
   BOOL  GreaterThan(int comp) { return (m_var > comp); }
   BOOL   LessThan(int comp)  { return (m_var < comp); }

private:
   int m_var;
};

ComparableObjectInt aVal(10);
if (aVal.GreaterThan(100))
   printf("greater\n");
```

Notice how one single instantiation of the template actually caused the creation of new class based on the parameterized type. If we have other lines like:

```
ComparableObject<float> aFloat(3.14195);
ComparableObject<String> aString("starter");
ComparableObject<CMytype> aVal( CMytype());
```

then each instantiation, with a new data type in the parameter, will actually create another class definition for us, as if we'd written the class ourselves for each of the data types. In our case, the only assumption that we make is that our data type will support the less than < and greater than > operators. If the data type that we supplied as an argument to the template instantiation doesn't support the required operator, the linker will complain about undefined function references. This is exactly the same situation as if we'd defined the classes ourselves with a type that doesn't have the required operators.

Template instantiation can be very powerful when used in combination with C++'s inheritance and virtual functions. Note that it's also possible to parameterize a template with multiple class arguments, as well as non-class and default arguments. For example:

```
template < class MappedKey, class MappedItem, long  HashType = 3 >
class MagicList
{
...
};
```

In this case, **MappedKey** and **MappedItem** represents two data types or classes which are parameters to the template class. The class definition itself will make use of these two types, in our example, maybe to create a hash value from arbitrary data type **MappedKey** to another arbitrary data type **MappedItem**. The third value, which should also be used within the template definition, may be used to cause the final instantiated class to behave slightly differently. In our example, the instantiated class may use a different hash algorithm in the lookup depending on the value of **HashType**. If **HashType** isn't supplied, the value of 3 will be assumed.

It's important to realize that every unique parameterization of a template class generates another unique class. This applies to all cases, including:

```
#define HASH_SPARSE    3
#define HASH_DENSE 4

MagicList<String, Mytype, HASH_SPARSE>  FirstMap();
MagicList<String, Mytype, HASH_DENSE>  SecondMap();
```

In this case, even though the class parameterization of **FirstMap** and **SecondMap** is identical, the difference in the non-class argument causes the two signatures (consisting of the template class name and its parameters) to be unique, and two mutually exclusive classes will be generated through the instantiation.

Back in our definition of our **ComparableObject** template class, you should notice the unconventional syntax (repeated below) one has to use in defining the member functions of template classes which aren't defined inline with the class definition (i.e. the member function **LessThan()**).

```
template <class T>
BOOL ComparableObject<T>::LessThan(T comp)
{
    return (m_var < comp);
}
```

To illustrate another important point, let's add one more function declaration to our template. Resulting in the following:

```
template <class T >
class ComparableObject
{
public:
    ComparableObject(T aVal): m_var(aVal)
    {}
    BOOL GreaterThan(T comp) { return (m_var > comp); }
    BOOL LessThan(T comp);
    BOOL SuperOp(T comp);
private:
    T m_var;
};

template <class T>
BOOL ComparableObject<T>::LessThan(T comp)
```

```
    {
        return (m_var < comp);
    }
```

The point to notice here is that even though **SuperOp()** isn't implemented by the template library (let's just say that **ComparableObject** came from some library we've purchased for in-house development), the library is *not* considered incomplete. This is because no problem will arise until someone actually attempts to instantiate the template. Even then, as long as you've defined a **SuperOp()** function for your template instantiation parameter signature, the compiler will be completely happy. For example, if we were to instantiate **ComparableObject** for our own type called **MyType**, we need to have:

```
    BOOL ComparableObject<MyType>::SuperOp(MyType inVal)
    {
        return MyType.CheckValidity();
    }


    ComparableObject<MyType> aValue();
```

Consider the real power here: you've actually augmented the function of the class at design time based on your own requirements. Though object-oriented design purists will frown upon this practice (since the template class definition isn't complete and there's a chance that our last minute supplement may completely break the other behavior of the template class), I've seen this technique used quite successfully in many in-house development projects.

A couple of final points before we release you into the wonderful world of ATL: frequently, a very complex template construct can be lurking behind a simple symbolic representation, courtesy of the friendly **typedef** operator. For example:

```
    typedef   ARealMessgeTemplateClass<int, long, char *,      \
              MyClass, \
              AnotherMessyTemplateClass<long, MyClass>, \
              51123> \
              ReallySimpleType ;

    ReallySimpleType  SoSimple(1, 2, "3");
```

Note that the template class isn't instantiated at **typedef** time (i.e. there's no code generated by the **typedef**, only a new symbol table is created by the compiler), but at the time when the **SoSimple** variable is defined. To decipher the above, note that **ARealMessageTemplateClass<>** is completely and specifically paramaterized by **<int, long, char *, MyClass,...>**; however, actual code generation for the parameterized class doesn't occur until the compiler hits the declaration of **ReallySimpleType**. Note also that the **SoSimple(1,2,"3")** portion isn't template parameterization, but rather a constructor defined for the templated class (which we haven't shown above) which takes **(long, long, char *)** for parameters. I know that the syntax may look quite ugly to you, but it does happen often in real life template coding, and you'll find plenty of examples in the ATL source code.

A template based class becomes an actual data type when instantiated and as such can be used as a class type parameter in another template. Template libraries like ATL do tend to use this construct. Pay particular attention to the extra space between the pair of the closing angle brackets. This space is vital; it's the only thing the compiler has to distinguish the templates from the operator **> >**. Similarly for **< <**.

```
    template < class T >
    class A
    {...};
```

```
template < class S, class A< int > >    // notice the space between > >
class B
{...};
```

That completes our crash-course on templates and the powerful functionality that they can provide. We're now ready to move on and examine the amazing ActiveX Template Library 2.1. We can actually use the library directly without really worrying about how things are done underneath. However, having this background on templates will allow us to confidently dig under the hood should the occasion arise through business requirements.

What's in the Active Template Library

The answer, in a nutshell, is just four C++ implementation files and a whole bunch of header files. That's it.

An optional DLL called **Atl.dll** (20k) is also supplied. It contains many shared routines and can be optionally distributed with your ATL based ActiveX control. However, ATL does **not** depend on it to work properly.

Before moving on, I will assume that you have Visual C++ 5 or later installed, and have selected the ActiveX Template Library install option during installation. If you have an older version of Visual C++ and/or ATL, you may have problems compiling some of the programs since the header files have been changing quite a bit between Windows 95 release and Windows NT 4.0 release. It's also possible to use the Win32 SDK and Active Platform SDK that correspond to the release version of Windows NT 4.0 for development.

If you go to your ATL directory (**DevStudio\Vc\Atl\include** for a typical installation of Visual C++ 5), and look at the content, you'll find practically the entire template library there. The files you'll see are:

File Name	Size	Description
Atlbase.h	29k	Lower level fundamental type and class definitions.
Atlcom.h	57k	Most of the COM object handling.
Atlconv.h	8k	String conversion utility classes from UNICODE and back.
Atlctl.h	71k	NEW: ActiveX control support.
Atliface.h	12k	MIDL generated from **Atliface.idl** below.
Atlwin.h	18k	NEW: basic windows support.
Build_.h	1k	NEW: ATL Build information, check your version here.
Statreg.h	6k	Support file for static linking of registry update code.
Atlconv.cpp	5k	String conversion implementation.
Atlimpl.cpp	67k	Implementation of pieces that won't fit inline.
Atlwin.cpp	18k	NEW: Implementation of windows support.

Table Continued on Following Page

File Name	Size	Description
`Atlctl.cpp`		NEW: Implementation of ActiveX control support.
`Statreg.cpp`	23k	Implementation for static linking of registry update code.
`Atliface.idl`	2k	Interface description for `IRegistrar` (see *Automated Registry Update* section later).

For anyone who may have worked with ATL before version 2.1, the NEW above refers to new features or files.

> *If you have ever had the pleasure of looking at the directory **DevStudio\Vc\Mfc\Src**, which is another library which could help you write ActiveX controls, the reasons should be clear why more and more people will make ATL their preferred choice. The MFC source code collection looks like it is the encoding of the entire New York City white pages in the C++ language! Of course, it does have support for more than controls.*

Let's take the chance here to review the differences between a class library and a template library. This is best illustrated with a diagram:

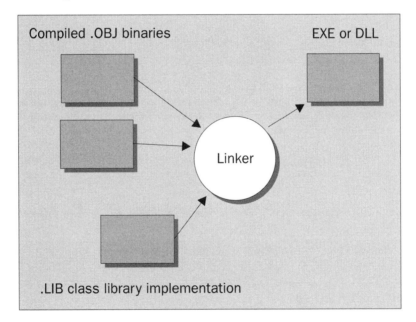

In the picture above, we can see that a class library is typically included at link time, adding binary code to the object that the user creates to provide additional functions. Obviously, it's also possible that the library linked simply points to an external DLL to accomplish its function. The fact remains, though, that most class libraries have a granularity that causes more code than you need to be linked into the final executable.

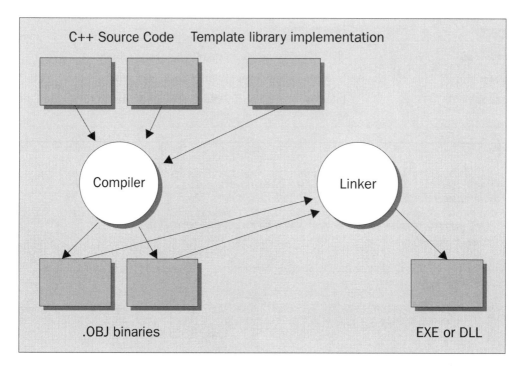

For a template library, the code is generated 'to spec' during compilation time. Essentially, a template library is a highly configurable code generator. A properly designed and written template library ensures that just enough code is generated for each application. Of course, this desirable feature can only be true if the library user uses the library in the intended fashion.

Just because the ATL files are so small, it doesn't mean that they do nothing. The following is ATL's impressive résumé, showing what it can do for you. Don't be alarmed if you don't understand some of the terms used. We'll cover most of them in later sections.

- Creates COM servers that support custom, **IDispatch** based, or dual interfaces quickly and effortlessly.

- Supports creation of in-proc, local, remote, and the new 'NT service' servers (i.e. creating a Windows NT service which acts as a COM object server).

- Supports all COM threading models including single (only one instance, no threading), apartment, and free threading.

- Supports COM aggregation for you with no work from you.

- Supports creation of DCOM (distributed COM) or Remote Automation (older remoting architecture) remote servers.

- Makes implementation of COM object enumeration easy (we cover enumeration later in Chapter 6).

- Makes implementation of connection points easy (again, see Chapter 6).

- Makes support of OLE error (**IErrorInfo**) simple.

Allows you to make 'Oh, so tiny' COM servers by potentially doing away with the C runtime library, as well as removing dependency on any **.LIB** or **.DLL** files.

 Provides many optimization techniques for COM server implementation.

Except for the first four points, the rest of the benefits are probably not evident to you at this point. We'll cover most of these advanced COM concepts in later chapters. For now, the main benefit for us is that ATL allows us to easily design and create ActiveX controls which can be used in C/C++, Visual Basic, Visual J++ (Microsoft's Java), on a web page by Internet Explorer, or over the network. ATL takes care of most of the COM details, so we can concentrate on the actual problem that our component is solving.

Modernizing Our BareBlob with ATL

I hope you haven't forgotten about our business rule control, BareBlob, yet. We'll now recreate our BareBlob with ATL 2.1. In doing so, you'll see how similar the process is to the raw COM coding that we've already done. However, you'll also see how much easier it is with ATL.

As usual, the first step in the process is to define our object in an IDL file. ATL is so helpful that it automatically creates the IDL file of us. And that's not all, it will create all of the required C++ and header files as well. You'll be glad that you've gone through Chapter 3 because these files will be fully recognizable.

Let's (quickly) recreate our BareBlob in ATL. Start Visual Studio and select <u>N</u>ew... from the <u>F</u>ile menu. Then select Project workspace. The New Project Workspace dialog will now pop up.

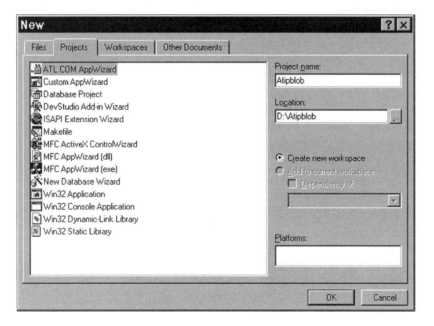

From the selection of wizards, select the ATL COM AppWizard. Give the project a name: use **Atipblob** for this project (ATL in-process BLOB). Make sure the Create new workspace radio button is checked and press the OK button. Next, the wizard will startup and prompt you with its one and only screen:

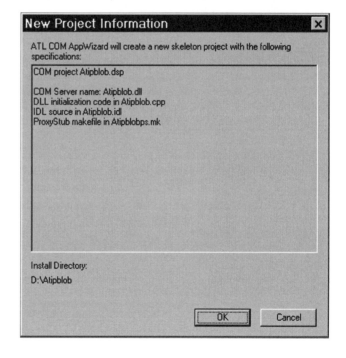

We're going to create only one object in our in-proc server, therefore we select the Dynamic Link Library server type. Merging the proxy/stub code into the DLL will put the proxy and stub code into the same executable image as the server. This is a way to cut down the number of files required for distribution. We won't need this in our case. The Support MFC option will include the appropriate headers if selected. This will allow you to use some of the MFC data classes (i.e. **CString**). The downside of this is that your server will require the MFC runtime DLL, greatly increasing the effective distribution size.

Now click Finish and the wizard will summarize its activities:

Notice how it offers to write both the IDL and the DLL initialization (recall the four required export functions for COM DLL servers) code for us. Click OK to have the code generated, then check the FileView tab of the project to see the files generated.

This is the complete skeleton ATL project, however it doesn't yet contain or support any COM object. To add object support, select Insert | New ATL Object.... The ATL Object Wizard will pop up and offer you a large choice of object types to insert. To implement our business rule control, we need only the Simple Object:

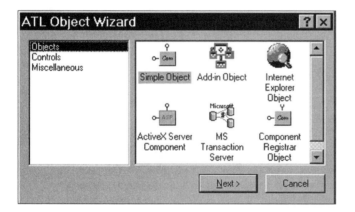

Click Next> to start the wizard on its way. We'll now be prompted with more questions to configure (and generate code for) our object.

Fill in the object information as shown above, to approximately match our initial BareBlob project. We need to change the name of the interface to **ICustomInterface2** and give it a new interface ID because we'll be adding more methods to the interface and modifying one. Recall from Chapter 2 that a COM interface, once specified, can't be changed—this means we must create a new name for our interface.

Note that the name we entered in the CoClass field above will appear in the generated IDL file, the Type field above will actually be inserted into the registry when the generated type library (.TLB file) is registered, the Prog ID will be the string representation of the CLSID which can be used in a client's call to create an object. Now select the Attributes tab to continue the configuration:

Here, we can select the threading model of our object. We'll have a lot more to say about threading models at the end of this chapter (see the section named *COM Threading Models*). For now, we'll select Both which indicates that our object supports both the free threaded and apartment threaded operation. The Single entry essentially says that our object can only serve one client at a time, and is an archaic option provided only for compatibility purposes.

For the type of interface, we'll select Dual. The interface that we've implemented for **BareBlob** was custom, so selecting Dual here gets ATL to help us with implementing an **IDispatch** based interface as well. Our new object will support both early and late binding. This makes it much more popular in the COM world as it will be able to talk to many more potential clients.

We're going to support aggregation with this object, so go ahead and select that check box. The generated ATL code will handle the controlling **IUnknown** appropriately (see Chapter 2 for more details). If an object never needs to support aggregation by design, not checking this box will further optimize object creation handling and also reduce the size of code generated. We will not support the **ISupportError** interface (which provides extended error and context information) or connection points (for firing events from the object back to its client) in this case, deferring discussion for a later chapter dealing with Advanced COM and ATL.

Finally, we'll select the Free Threaded Marshaller option. This option will show us aggregation in action, because our generated object will be soliciting the service of another system helper object called the Free Threaded Marshaller to handle an **IMarshal** interface. The **IMarshal** interface is typically used by the system to marshal interface pointers between threads (called apartments) in a process (again, see the *COM Threading Models* section later on in this chapter).

Now press the OK button to have the wizard generate the code according to your specifications. After code generation (it may take a little while), you'll see the files in your project, as in the screenshot.

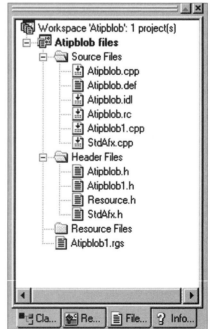

This is beginning to look very much like the 'from scratch' project we did in the last chapter. The only discernible differences are:

- An RC file storing system strings, and registry update information for the ATL library.

- Our **Precomp.h** is replaced by the **StdAfx.h** in ATL.

- An **Atipblob1.rgs** file holding a script for automated registry updates via the **registrar** (see the *Automated Registry Update* section later in this chapter).

Other files you'll recognize from the BareBlob project. The **Atipblob.idl** file is an input for the MIDL compiler. The **Atipblob.h**, and **Atipblob_i.c** (not part of the project) files are generated by MIDL when it is run on the **Atipblob.idl** file. The **Atipblob.def** file lists all the exported routines from the DLL for server registration. The **Atipblob1.h** file contains the declaration of the actual **CAtipblob1** class. Unlike **CBareBlob**, though, it has quite a few ATL macros in there.

You'll also recognize the **Atipblob.cpp** file once you open it. Inside you'll find the implementation of the **DllMain()**, **DllRegisterServer()**, **DllUnregisterServer()**, **DllCanUnloadNow()** and **DLLGetClassObject()** functions.

The **Atipblob1.cpp** file is like our **Bareblob1.cpp** file, where we'll be implementing the methods of **ICustomInterface2**.

The **.RGS** and the **.RC** files didn't exist in the old project. You won't be able to find the registry modification and update routines like those we had to code in the **CBareBlob** case. It turns out that the **.RGS** and the **.RC** files contain the required information regarding the registry keys to be added and deleted during registration/unregistration. ATL will handle this for us, so we don't need to do any explicit coding. We'll cover this at length in a later section.

That accounts for every file that ATL generated for us, and we can see that there's really nothing very mysterious about ATL. It's following very much the same pattern as we did in our raw COM coding example.

To get a different perspective on the same code, click on the ClassView tab, and see which classes have been generated for us:

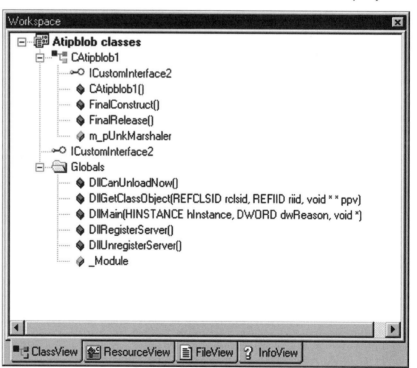

Note that the five required functions, **DllCanUnloadNow()**, **DllGetClassObject()**, **DllMain()**, **DllRegisterServer()**, and **DllUnregisterServer()** are already in place. So is the declaration of the **CAtipblob1** class in the C++ source file and the header file. That wasn't so bad for a few mouse clicks, was it?

Also visible are **FinalConstruct()**, **FinalRelease()**, and the **m_pUnkmarshaler** member variable. These are all used by ATL to implement the free threaded marshaller support that we've asked for.

Spoon Feeding a COM Interface

The little 'spoon like' thing next to **ICustomInterface2** is the new 'visual COM interface' feature of Visual C++ 5.0. We can use this spoon to define our methods and properties for the interface through the GUI. The system will actually update all the relevant files for us! Thank Bill for the spoon.

Let's define the methods and properties of this new interface. Recall our discussion in Chapter 2 about the **IDispatch** interface, and its ability to provide Automation properties which a client like Visual Basic can easily access and configure. We'll add one such property here in our **ICustomInterface2**, it will be named **InternalProperty**. The function of this property is trivial: it will store internally any value that is assigned to it, and will return the stored value if it is queried. Nevertheless, it will demonstrate how to implement a property for Automation clients. Other than that, we'll carry forward our **GetManagerName()** and **OkayToPublishInfo()** business rule implementations. For **PeekCounters()**, we change it to **PeekCounter()** and return only one counter value (the one that changed) since the other one will always stay static as we found out in the last chapter.

To summarize, we have:

Methods and Properties	Description
HRESULT GetManagerName([out, retval] BSTR * pbstrMgrName);	Method to obtain the name of the current manager in charge of the department.
HRESULT OkayToPublishInfo([in] long lYear, [in] long lMonth, [out, retval] VARIANT_BOOL * bOkayFlag);	Method to determine if it's okay to publish Events Calendar information for a particular month in a particular year.
HRESULT PeekCounter([out, retval] long lCounter);	Method used in debugging to show the number of current objects being served (and class factory server locks) by the server.
long InternalProperty;	A property supporting **Get** and **Set** to demonstrate the implementation of an Automation property using ATL 2.1.

To add these definitions to the project, simply highlight the **ICustomInterface2** spoon and press the right mouse button. Select Add Method, and enter the specification for **GetManagerName()**:

Repeat the above procedure to add **OkayToPublishInfo()** and **PeekCounter()**.Finally, select the spoon, right click, and select Add Property to add the **InternalProperty** property:

The **InternalProperty** property, since it supports both **Get** and **Put** operations (i.e. its value can be read-and-change, versus a read-only or write-only property), ends up being implemented by two separate interface methods. These interface methods become **get_InternalProperty()** and **put_InternalProperty()** member functions in the **CAtipblob1** class.

It's a good time to take a look at the ClassView pane again, to see that indeed these new methods and properties are now added to the **ICustomInterface2** definition. Notice also that the **CAtipblob1** class also has skeleton member functions which implement the required functions.

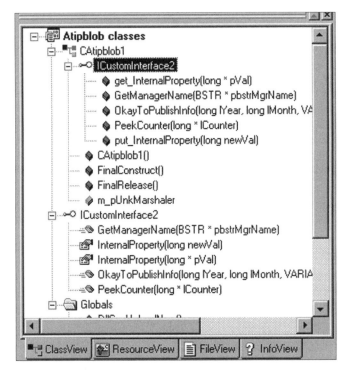

Just in case you may have made some mistakes in data entry while following along, you will (with well-deserved frustration) have found that there's no easy way to delete anything that you've added. The only way to modify or delete the interface method or property definition is to use manual methods. This is when a knowledge of what the IDE actually does for you when you add an element comes in real handy. We know from the last chapter that to define a new method for an interface, we need to:

▲ Add in to the **.IDL** file.

▲ Add the definition to the class definition in the **.H** header file.

▲ Add the implementation to the **.CPP** source file.

This knowledge also allows us to say with confidence that to delete a method or property we need to:

▲ Delete its definition from the **.IDL** file.

▲ Delete the member function(s) declaration in the **.H** header file.

▲ Delete the implementation of the member function(s) in the **.CPP** source file.

To fully implement the **InternalProperty** property, we'll need to create a variable in our object to hold its value. Highlight the **CAtipblob1** class in the ClassView pane, press the right mouse button, and select Add Member Variable. Enter the following:

Add Member Variable `?` `X`

Variable Type:

`long`

Variable Declaration:

`m_lInternalVal`

Access
○ Public   ● Protected   ○ Private

OK

Cancel

Examining the Code

Now, let's see what ATL 2.1 did to handle the **ICustomInterface2**. First, as in **CBareBlob**, we can open and examine the **.IDL** file that ATL had generated for us.

The IDL File

The IDL is called **Atipblob.idl**. Notice where the methods and properties are defined.

```
// Atipblob.idl : IDL source for Atipblob.dll
//

// This file will be processed by the MIDL tool to
// produce the type library (Atipblob.tlb) and marshalling code.

import "oaidl.idl";
import "ocidl.idl";

    [
        object,
        uuid(C98A1A6E-8840-11D0-8DD0-006052008075),
        dual,
        helpstring("ICustomInterface2 Interface"),
        pointer_default(unique)
    ]
    interface ICustomInterface2 : IDispatch
    {
        [id(1), helpstring("method GetManagerName")] HRESULT GetManagerName([out,
retval] BSTR * pbstrMgrName);
        [id(2), helpstring("method OkayToPublishInfo")] HRESULT OkayToPublishInfo([in]
long lYear, [in] long lMonth, [out, retval] VARIANT_BOOL * bOkayFlag);
        [id(3), helpstring("method PeekCounter")] HRESULT PeekCounter([out, retval] long
* lCounter);
        [propget, id(4), helpstring("property InternalProperty")] HRESULT
InternalProperty([out, retval] long *pVal);
        [propput, id(4), helpstring("property InternalProperty")] HRESULT
InternalProperty([in] long newVal);
    };
    [
      uuid(C98A1A61-8840-11D0-8DD0-006052008075),
      version(1.0),
      helpstring("Atipblob 1.0 Type Library")
    ]
library ATIPBLOBLib
{
    importlib("stdole32.tlb");

    [
      uuid(F55C8EAF-87F7-11D0-8DD0-006052008075),
      helpstring("ATL_InProc_Server")
    ]
    coclass Atipblob1
    {
      [default] interface ICustomInterface2;
    };
};
```

One important point to notice is the specification of the interface as **dual**. This is saying that we'll also support the late binding of our methods in **ICustomInterface2**, and indeed, we see that **ICustomInterface2** inherits from **IDispatch** instead of **IUnknown** as in the BareBlob case. Recall our discussion in Chapter 2 on late binding. Late binding requires the server to support the **IDispatch** interface. The **IDispatch** interface contains several complex methods to obtain type library information, invoke methods by dispatch IDs, and to translate symbolic information to dispatch IDs. This was discussed at length in Chapter 2. If we were to code these methods ourselves, it would take a significant amount of time. This doesn't even include the considerable testing that would be necessary. Fortunately for us, the support by ATL for **IDispatch** makes our work trivial. It opens up a whole new world of clients to our object. For example, both Visual Basic and the Internet Explorer can now (easily) use our ActiveX control. As a rule of thumb, if possible, one should always consider making a COM class interface dual, to maximize reuse potential.

By supporting **IDispatch**, one has to be careful about the format and data types of arguments for our methods. Only certain 'automation compatible' data types may be used–this rules out any custom structures, etc. Thankfully, we've coded our sample from the beginning to use only automation compatible data types. To get a list of automation-compatible data types, simply check out the definition of the **VARIANT** union in Chapter 6, each type representable by a **VARIANT** is deemed automation-compatible. In our discussion on late binding, we learned that the **IDispatch::Invoke()** model supports setting and getting of properties, as well as invocation of methods. We can see in the IDL that ATL has assigned dispatch IDs to all of our methods and properties (from **id(1)** to **id(4)**).

The Class Definition

After examining the **.IDL** file, we're ready to take a look at the methods and the new property that ATL has generated for us. First, we examine the class definition in the **Atipblob1.h** file.

```
class ATL_NO_VTABLE CAtipblob1 :
  public CComObjectRootEx<CComMultiThreadModel>,
  public CComCoClass<CAtipblob1, &CLSID_Atipblob1>,
  public IDispatchImpl<ICustomInterface2, &IID_ICustomInterface2, &LIBID_ATIPBLOBLib>
{
public:
  CAtipblob1()
  {
    m_pUnkMarshaler = NULL;
  }

DECLARE_REGISTRY_RESOURCEID(IDR_ATIPBLOB1)
DECLARE_GET_CONTROLLING_UNKNOWN()

BEGIN_COM_MAP(CAtipblob1)
  COM_INTERFACE_ENTRY(ICustomInterface2)
  COM_INTERFACE_ENTRY(IDispatch)
  COM_INTERFACE_ENTRY_AGGREGATE(IID_IMarshal, m_pUnkMarshaler.p)
END_COM_MAP()

  HRESULT FinalConstruct()
  {
    return CoCreateFreeThreadedMarshaler(
      GetControllingUnknown(), &m_pUnkMarshaler.p);
  }

  void FinalRelease()
  {
```

```
        m_pUnkMarshaler.Release();
    }

    CComPtr<IUnknown> m_pUnkMarshaler;

// ICustomInterface2
public:
    STDMETHOD(get_InternalProperty)(/*[out, retval]*/ long *pVal);
    STDMETHOD(put_InternalProperty)(/*[in]*/ long newVal);
    STDMETHOD(PeekCounter)(/*[out, retval]*/ long * lCounter);
    STDMETHOD(OkayToPublishInfo)(/*[in]*/ long lYear, /*[in]*/ long lMonth, /*[out,
retval]*/ VARIANT_BOOL * bOkayFlag);
    STDMETHOD(GetManagerName)(/*[out, retval]*/ BSTR * pbstrMgrName);
protected:
    long m_lInternalVal;
};
```

You can see here that the ATL wizard has already created our class for us, and will also be implementing the default **IUnknown** and **IDispatch** for us. You can also see that, unlike **CBareBlob**, the base interface implementation is done through multiple inheritance rather than nested classes. **CAtipblob1** inherits from **CComCoClass<>** to obtain the default definition for class factory and aggregation mode, all externally creatable COM objects in ATL inherit from this class. **CAtipblob1** also inherits from **CComObjectRootEx<>** to receive an optimized **IUnknown** implementation which will process **QueryInterface()** calls through the **COM interface map** described below—all COM objects implemented in ATL derive from either **CComObjectRoot<>** or **CComObjectRootEx<>**. Finally, **CAtipblob1** also inherits from **IDispatchImpl<>** to get the free **IDispatch** implementation that we need to support the dual interface.

One final note about multiple inheritance here: note the use of **ATL_NO_VTABLE** optimization on the declaration of **CAtipblob1**. This is an entirely Visual C++ 5 specific optimization which tells the compiler to forget about the vtable for this class when processing the constructor, gaining speed and storage improvement. It's used typically only in classes which are to be derived from. However, it must be used very carefully (the class's constructor must not call any virtual functions), and the most derived class must not have this attribute. It may surprise you that **CAtipblob1** isn't the most derived class in the inheritance hierarchy. However, you can take my word for it that when the class factory provided by ATL creates an instance of your object, it actually creates an instance of a class derived from your object. For the curious, see the **CComObject<>** and the **CComAggObject<>** implementation in the **Atlcom.h** file.

Since we've indicated that our COM object will be aggregatable, the **DECLARE_GET_CONTROLLING_UNKNOWN()** macro will ensure that a function will be available for obtaining the controlling **IUnknown** during aggregation. In fact, **CComCoClass<>** automatically assumes that the derived class is aggregatable. If you explicitly want to make the class not aggregatable, use the **DECLARE_NOT_AGGREGATABLE()** macro, and don't use the **DECLARE_GET_COTROLLING_UNKNOWN()** macro.

Inside the class definition, we can see a **COM_INTERFACE_ENTRY()** macro with **ICustomInterface2** in it; this gives ATL the proper information to perform its **QueryInterface()** through a COM interface map. A COM interface map is an internal ATL-managed table which maps between interface IDs and the implementation member functions. We also see here, in the interface map, that the object is supporting **IDispatch**, which actually points back to **ICustomInterface2** since it's derived from **IDispatch**. Furthermore, we support the **IMarshal** interface, courtesy of the free threaded marshaller which we aggregate in this code.

We can see the complete handling of the aggregation process here with the free threaded marshaller helper object. The ATL documentation recommends this way of handling:

- Create a private **IUnknown** (**m_pUnkMarshaler** in our case) member pointer, and initialize it in the constructor of your class.

- Create the object you're aggregating in **FinalConstruct()** function of your class (keep a reference stored in **IUnknown** pointer).

- Release the object you're aggregating in the **FinalDestroy()** function of your class.

- Use the COM interface map entry of **COM_INTERFACE_ENTRY_AGGREGATE()** to expose the appropriate interface from the aggregated object.

FinalConstruct() and **FinalDestroy()** are overridable functions defined by **CComObjectRootEx<>** specifically for this purpose. ATL creates the marshaller in **FinalConstruct()** via a call to the COM runtime **CoCreateFreeThreadedMarshaler()** API, passing it as parameters to our controlling **IUnknown** and also as a pointer to receive the marshaller's **IUnknown**.

The Class Implementation

The method declarations in **Atipblob1.h** are almost identical to the **CBareBlob** case. If you look at our good old **Objbase.h** file, you'll find the definition of **STDMETHOD()** macro. The translation of:

```
STDMETHOD(GetManagerName)(BSTR * pbstrMgrName) ;
```

results in:

```
virtual HRESULT __stdcall GetManagerName(BSTR * pbstrMgrName);
```

The **DECLARE_REGISTRY_RESOURCEID()** macro is used by ATL to find the compiled script when it has to update the registry during server registration and unregistration. The **.RGS** source file is actually packed into the **.RC** file as a custom resource, which is loaded by ATL using this macro.

The class definition is now completed. We'll now proceed to implement the logic for methods and properties of our object. To do this, we'll work on the **Atipblob1.cpp** file generated by ATL. The following listing highlights the additions that we key in:

```
// Atipblob1.cpp : Implementation of CAtipblob1
#include "stdafx.h"
#include "Atipblob.h"
#include "Atipblob1.h"

/////////////////////////////////////////////////////////////////////////////
// CAtipblob1


STDMETHODIMP CAtipblob1::GetManagerName(BSTR * pbstrMgrName)
{
    *pbstrMgrName = SysAllocString(L"J. Manzini");
    return S_OK;
}

STDMETHODIMP CAtipblob1::OkayToPublishInfo(long lYear, long lMonth, VARIANT_BOOL *
bOkayFlag)
```

```
{
    if (((1Year + 1Month) % 4) == 0)
       *bOkayFlag = FALSE;
    else
       *bOkayFlag = TRUE;
    return S_OK;
}


STDMETHODIMP CAtipblob1::PeekCounter(long * 1Counter)
{
    *1Counter = _Module.GetLockCount();
    return S_OK;
}


STDMETHODIMP CAtipblob1::get_InternalProperty(long * pVal)
{
    *pVal = m_1InternalVal;
    return S_OK;
}


STDMETHODIMP CAtipblob1::put_InternalProperty(long newVal)
{
    m_1InternalVal = newVal;
    return S_OK;
}
```

Implementation of **GetManagerName()** and **OkayToPublishInfo()** has not been changed. But **PeekCounter()** needs modification to work in **CAtipblob1**. Under ATL we get our reference count from one of our inherited classes, **CComObjectRootEx**, and we get the 'instance count' from an internal function **_Module.GetLockCount()**. We have also eliminated one of the counter return values from the function as explained previously.

Notice the interesting method of implementation of our newly added property, **InternalProperty**. The function used to set the property's value must have a name which is created by adding **put_** to the property name, in our example **put_InternalProperty()**. The function used to get the property's value must be **get_** followed by the property name. This is enforced so that the **IDispatch** handling code will know, without you having to define more tables, which function to call when the **Put** or **Get** operation is invoked on a property via the **IDispatch::Invoke()** method.

Compiling

So far, we have:

- ◢ Used the ATL COM AppWizard to create a skeleton ATL project called Atipblob.

- ◢ Used the Insert ATL Object... option to activate the ATL Object Wizard to insert a Simple Component into the ATL project, specifying that it implements the **ICustomInterfac2** COM interface and that the interface should be implemented as **dual**.

- ◢ Added methods to **ICustomInterface2**, and at the same time added skeletal code in the **CAtipblob1** class to implement the interface.

- ◢ Added a new property to **ICustomInterface2**, called **InternalProperty**.

- ◢ Added our implementation to all the methods of the **CAtipblob1** class, modeling it after our earlier BareBlob implementation.

What else remains to be done for our ActiveX control? Would you believe... nothing!

Just try to build the project now. Notice how **Atipblob.dll** is created and the server registered with the system automatically.

Now, run the Object Viewer utility and examine the new ActiveX control that you've just created. Click on the All Objects folder on the left pane. Look ATL_InProc_Server Class. Click on it and notice all the registry entries (on the right-hand pane) that ATL has registered for you without any work. Double-click on the ATL_InProc_Server Class entry, this will actually instantiate a **CAtipblob1** object, and notice the interfaces that it supports. It should look like this:

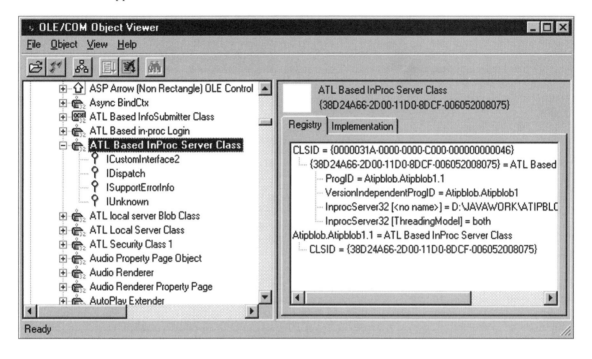

Unlike our old **CBareBlob** class, it now claims support for the **IDispatch** interface, as well as the **ICustomInterface2** that we've just defined. Also notice how aggregation really worked for us: the **IMarshal** (from the free thread marshaller helper object) is showing through as one of our own. Click on the **IDispatch** interface, and an **IDispatch** viewer will now pop up. Try to click on the View Type Info button, and notice that our methods and properties of **ICustomInterface2** showed up. Recall that we've defined **ICustomInterface2** to be **dual** in the IDL file. Furthermore, **ICustomInterface2** actually derives from **IDispatch** rather than **IUnknown**, as is the case with **ICustomInterface** in **CBareBlob**.

What the **IDispatch** viewer actually does is to find out what the **IDispatch** on the object supports directly via the **IDispatch::GetTypeInfo()** and **IDispatch::GetTypeInfoCount()** functions to get the information about the dispatch interface (in our case **ICustomInterface2**). This confirms that ATL has implemented the methods of **IDispatch** for us in our COM server.

Visual C++ 5 Native COM Support

Now, since the interface is dual, we should still be able to call it using early binding from C/C++. Let's prove it with our multithreaded tester client. Since we've 'modernized' our BareBlob object, we're going to modernize our test client, too.

To do this, we draw on the help of the newest, coolest feature of Visual C++ 5: its native support for COM client programming.

Testing Early Binding

We've seen in the last chapter how to program an early binding test client for the object. Looking back in the code, you'll discover the following:

 Dependence on a myriad of include files, especially those that define the required CLSID and interface definitions for BareBlob; for example, our former multithreaded test client had to include:

```
#include "bareblob.h"
#define IID_DEFINED
#include "bareblob_i.c
```

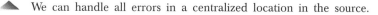 A multistep process to obtain the interface pointer to **ICustomInterface** (i.e. obtain class factory, create bareblob, query for **ICustomInterface**); for example, here is an excerpt from our previous client showing what was necessary:

```
hRes = CoGetClassObject(CLSID_CBareBlob, CLSCTX_ALL, NULL,
                        IID_IClassFactory,(void **) &pCF);
hRes = pCF->CreateInstance(NULL, IID_IUnknown, (void **) &pM);
hRes = pM->QueryInterface( IID_ICustomInterface, (void **) &pCI);
```

 Error handling code dispersed throughout the code. Just examine the source code of our previous test client and you'll see that almost half of the code deals with error conditions and handling.

 There should be careful consideration during design to ensure that reference counting rules for all instantiated objects are observed.

Now what if:

▲ We can create a COM client without having to deal with multiple include files.

▲ We create the interface that we need simply by instantiating a single C++ object.

▲ We can handle all errors in a centralized location in the source.

▲ We don't have to worry about reference counting, at all, during coding.

Seasoned COM programmers will say that we're in dreamland, and newcomers to COM client programming probably will never program any other way (and swear that COM is dead simple). Welcome to the wonderful new world of Visual C++ 5 native COM support!

The core code of our new test client will be reduced to **4** simple lines:

```
ICustomInterface2Ptr pCI(_T("Atipblob1.Atipblob11.1"));
mgrName = pCI->GetManagerName();
okFlag = pCI->OkayToPublishInfo(inYear, inMonth);
objCount = pCI->PeekCounter();
```

What are the new elements that make all this possible? Are we not still working within a C++ language?

New Features

Indeed, we're still working within the confines of the C++ language. Behind the smoke and mirrors, it's all done with:

 Several compiler/preprocessor specific new directives.

▲ A set of utility wrapper classes.

▲ Smart pointer wrapper classes for COM interfaces.

We'll look at each of these pieces in turn, and at the same time examine our revamped multithreaded tester to illustrate the points.

New Compiler Directives

Let's take a look at the most important new preprocessor directive, called the **#import** directive. In one sentence:

> **#import reads a type library and generates all the wrapper classes you need for easy COM programming.**

This is precisely what this new directive does. Let's look at it in action with our test harness client program. You can find the source code in the Atimusr project within the source code distribution.

Right at the very top of the file **Atimusr.cpp**, you'll see the **#import** directive.

```
#include <stdio.h>
#include <stdlib.h>
#include <time.h>
#include <process.h>
#include <assert.h>
#include <comdef.h>
#include <tchar.h>
#include "CRTDBG.h"

#import "Atipblob.tlb" no_namespace
```

We've seen all of the includes previously, except for **Comdef.h**. This file contains a definition of basic smart pointer support, and **BSTR** and **VARIANT** wrappers which are necessary for everything to work properly (we'll cover these in the next section).

Note that we no longer have to have the include files containing CLSIDs, interface descriptions, etc. The preprocessor, upon seeing the **#import** directive, will reverse-engineer a binary type library and generate all the headers required. Hurrah!

This also means that the type library can be embedded anywhere: in a binary TLB file, as a resource within an EXE or a DLL, etc.

The **no_namespace** attribute associated with the **#import** statement can be used to control certain characteristics associated with the reverse-engineering process. For example, in dissecting very large type libraries, it's possible for the type library to introduce symbols which are already defined in your main source code or its include files. In these cases, it's possible to send all the symbols coming from the **#import** activity into another C++ namespace. In this way, the **#import** can proceed without any name conflicts. It's also possible to selectively rename certain symbols from the **#import** process. Since our Atipblob type library is tiny, we use the **no_namespace** attribute to avoid creating any namespace. Another very useful attribute is the **raw_dispinterfaces** attribute. Without this attribute, the **#import** will create code which accesses the COM object via direct vtable interface calls. If you specify the **raw_dispinterfaces** attribute, the code generated will be using **IDispatch::Invoke()** to access the properties and methods, essentially acting as an Automation controller. See the Visual C++ documentation for other attributes for the **#import** directive.

What exactly does the **#import** directive generate? If you look under the **Debug** or **Release** directory (depending on your Visual Studio target setting), you'll find the two generated header files. They are named **.TLH** and **.TLI** respectively for Type Library Headers and Type Library Includes.

The .TLH File

The **.TLH** file is logically included with the definition (header) files, while the **.TLI** file is logically included with the source code. Here's our **.TLH** file:

```
// Created by Microsoft (R) C/C++ Compiler Version 11.00.0000 (a367badc).
//
// Debug/Atipblob.tlh
//
// C++ source equivalent of Win32 type library ..\Atipblob\Atipblob.tlb
// compiler-generated file created 02/16/97 at 22:01:17 - DO NOT EDIT!

#pragma once
#pragma pack(push, 8)

#include <comdef.h>

//
// Forward references and typedefs
//

struct /* coclass */ Atipblob1;
struct __declspec(uuid("c98a1a6e-8840-11d0-8dd0-006052008075"))
/* dual interface */ ICustomInterface2;

//
// Smart pointer typedef declarations
//
```

```
_COM_SMARTPTR_TYPEDEF(ICustomInterface2, __uuidof(ICustomInterface2));

//
// Type library items
//

struct __declspec(uuid("f55c8eaf-87f7-11d0-8dd0-006052008075"))
Atipblob1;
    // [ default ] interface ICustomInterface2

struct __declspec(uuid("c98a1a6e-8840-11d0-8dd0-006052008075"))
ICustomInterface2 : IDispatch
{
    //
    // Property data
    //

    __declspec(property(get=GetInternalProperty,put=PutInternalProperty))
    long InternalProperty;

    //
    // Wrapper methods for error-handling
    //

    _bstr_t GetManagerName ( );
    VARIANT_BOOL OkayToPublishInfo (
        long lYear,
        long lMonth );
    long PeekCounter ( );
    long GetInternalProperty ( );
    void PutInternalProperty (
        long pVal );

    //
    // Raw methods provided by interface
    //

    virtual HRESULT __stdcall raw_GetManagerName (
        BSTR * pbstrMgrName ) = 0;
    virtual HRESULT __stdcall raw_OkayToPublishInfo (
        long lYear,
        long lMonth,
        VARIANT_BOOL * bOkayFlag ) = 0;
    virtual HRESULT __stdcall raw_PeekCounter (
        long * lCounter ) = 0;
    virtual HRESULT __stdcall get_InternalProperty (
        long * pVal ) = 0;
    virtual HRESULT __stdcall put_InternalProperty (
        long pVal ) = 0;
};

//
// Wrapper method implementations
//

#include "Debug/Atipblob.tli"

#pragma pack(pop)
```

Other than a few new types which we'll cover below, this code is completely understandable. You can see the type library disassembly process here. Notice how our **ICustomInterface2** has been reverse-engineered and its member methods reassembled under a new C++ pure virtual structure. However, you will also notice that the actual calling syntax of method like **GetManagerName()** has been modified from the interface implementation to reflect the **retval** specification. And you'll note that there's a set of virtual methods with the **raw_** prefix which matches our interface methods one for one. The reason for these virtual members is that they will be used by the smart interface pointer to call the methods of the actual object. This will be more evident when we take a look at the **.TLI** file later. For now, let's look at another two new compiler keywords.

__declspec(uuid()) and __uuidof()

The **__declspec(uuid())** declaration specifier will associate a GUID with a structure or class and keep this association for later retrieval. For example, our **CAtipblob1** class is associated with its CLSID (decoded by the preprocessor) in the statement:

```
struct __declspec(uuid("f55c8eaf-87f7-11d0-8dd0-006052008075"))
Atipblob1;
```

Retrieval of the associated GUID can be performed by using the **__uuidof()** keyword on the type. For example, to retrieve the GUID from **Atipblob1**, we'll need:

```
__uuidof(Atipblob1)
```

In practice, the **__uuidof()** keyword is typically used in conjunction with smart pointer features (see the *Smart Pointers Save the Day* section later) to handle GUIDs transparently.

__declspec(property())

The **__declspec(property())** construction provides compiler shorthand for calling the 'virtual data members' of a class. These data members are virtual because they do not actually exist, but their **Set** and **Get** behaviors map to member functions of the class.

For example, in the code above, we see the following declaration:

```
__declspec(property(get=GetInternalProperty,put=PutInternalProperty))
    long InternalProperty;
```

Now, if the compiler encounters:

```
p->InternalProperty = 30;
```

the actual code generated will be:

```
p->PutInternalProperty(30);
```

Providing of course **p** points to an object derived from **ICustomInterface2** type. And the following:

```
long AVar;
AVar = p->InternalProperty;
```

will translate to:

```
long AVar;
p->GetInternalProperty(&AVar);
```

The .TLI File

Looking at the **.TLI** file generated, we see how the actual functions are implemented:

```
/ Created by Microsoft (R) C/C++ Compiler Version 11.00.0000 (a367badc).
//
// Debug/Atipblob.tli
//
// Wrapper implementations for Win32 type library ..\Atipblob\Atipblob.tlb
// compiler-generated file created 02/16/97 at 22:01:17 - DO NOT EDIT!


#pragma once

//
// interface ICustomInterface2 wrapper method implementations
//

inline _bstr_t ICustomInterface2::GetManagerName ( ) {
    BSTR _result;
    HRESULT _hr = raw_GetManagerName(&_result);
    if (FAILED(_hr)) _com_issue_errorex(_hr, this, __uuidof(this));
    return _bstr_t(_result, false);
}

inline VARIANT_BOOL ICustomInterface2::OkayToPublishInfo ( long lYear, long lMonth ) {
    VARIANT_BOOL _result;
    HRESULT _hr = raw_OkayToPublishInfo(lYear, lMonth, &_result);
    if (FAILED(_hr)) _com_issue_errorex(_hr, this, __uuidof(this));
    return _result;
}

inline long ICustomInterface2::PeekCounter ( ) {
    long _result;
    HRESULT _hr = raw_PeekCounter(&_result);
    if (FAILED(_hr)) _com_issue_errorex(_hr, this, __uuidof(this));
    return _result;
}

inline long ICustomInterface2::GetInternalProperty ( ) {
    long _result;
    HRESULT _hr = get_InternalProperty(&_result);
    if (FAILED(_hr)) _com_issue_errorex(_hr, this, __uuidof(this));
    return _result;
}

inline void ICustomInterface2::PutInternalProperty ( long pVal ) {
    HRESULT _hr = put_InternalProperty(pVal);
    if (FAILED(_hr)) _com_issue_errorex(_hr, this, __uuidof(this));
}
```

We can see above that the member functions actually wrap around the **raw_** series of direct COM interfaces calls and will raise an exception via a **_com_issue_errorex()** call to throw an exception with a **_com_error** object. The catcher of the exception can use this object's various member functions to obtain extended information about the error. If the COM object issuing the error supports **IErrorInfo** (which we've elected not to do to keep the code readable), the object itself can return extended error information, accessible through members of the **_com_error** class. This effectively translates the **HRESULT** base error handling to a structured exception based error handling. The caller to these functions can thus use a **try catch** block to put all the error handling code in a centralized location.

New Wrapper Classes

There are a couple of utility classes which ease handling of certain data types frequently used in COM. These include **_bstr_t** to wrap **BSTR** and **_variant_t** to wrap **VARIANT**. Using these wrapper types will save you a lot of unnecessary coding when working with these data types.

_bstr_t

You can use the **_bstr_t** class to create new **BSTR** objects. More useful, though, is the capability to attach an existing **BSTR** to a new **_bstr_t** object. For example, if you were passed a **BSTR** variable called **bstrInput**, the following will create a **_bstr_t** object called **newBstr** and attach it to the **BSTR** variable.

```
_bstr_t newBstr(bstrInput, FALSE);
```

This is one of many ways to construct a **_bstr_t** object. You can also use a UNICODE or ANSI string to create a **BSTR** compatible **_bstr_t** object, or you can construct a **BSTR** type variable from a **VARIANT** variable (a sort of logical casting) holding a **BSTR**.

In general, using **_bstr_t** instead of **BSTR** will make handling and conversion simpler, and eliminates the frequent calls to **SysAllocString()** family of functions (since the **_bstr_t** implementation handles all of this for us).

The code generated by the **#import** directive will use the **_bstr_t** to represent **BSTR** variables exclusively. See the Visual C++ 5 documentation on **_bstr_t** for the member functions and operators which this class supports.

_variant_t

Like the **_bstr_t** class, the **_variant_t** class makes handling of **VARIANT** variables considerably easier. You can create new **_variant_t** variables or create one based on an existing **VARIANT** variable using the constructor:

```
_variant_t newVar( inVariant, FALSE);
```

or the **Attach()** member function:

```
_variant_t newVar;
newVar.Attach(inVariant);
```

A **Detach()** member also exists to recover the **VARIANT** variable controlled by a **_variant_t** object. The underlying data in the **_variant_t** object can be extracted using a variety of extraction operators. The type can be converted (if a conversion exists) using the **ChangeType()** member function. A **Clear()** member function is provided to clear out the **_variant_t** object. A **SetString()** member function allows the setting of a **BSTR _variant_t** object when only an MBCS string is passed in.

The code generated by the **#import** directive will use the **_variant_t** to represent **VARIANT** variables exclusively. See the Visual C++ 5 documentation on **_variant_t** for the various members and operators possible with this class.

Smart Pointers Save the Day

Smart pointers are pointer objects which perform automatic lifetime management by encapsulating the operation of reference counting. Essentially the smart COM object pointer will perform the **AddRef()** and **Release()** for you so you do not have to worry about coding it.

Sounds too good to be true? Well, it is true. Smart COM object pointers work as advertised as long as all access to the underlying objects is performed through the same pointer (i.e. you or the runtime you deal with does not 'steal' the actual interface pointer from you and do its own thing for a while). In certain COM programming exercises, for example our multithreaded testing client, this is totally acceptable and is all that will be needed. In other scenarios, this may not be possible at all.

__com_ptr_t Class

The **__com_ptr_t** is a template class that encapsulates the functionality of the smart COM pointer. **IUnknown** methods such as **QueryInterface()**, **AddRef()** and **Release()** are all called automatically by the implementation. This gives the programmer apparent 'instantiate and use' flexibility.

You create a smart pointer class using the **COM_SMARTPTR_TYPEDEF()** macro. This will actually create a specialization of the **__com_ptr_t** class for the COM object you specify as a parameter. The two parameters that this macro takes are:

- The interface of the object that this pointer refers to.
- The GUID of the object.

For example, in our **.TLH** file, the **#import** preprocessor has created a smart pointer for our **ICustomInterface2** interface using:

```
_COM_SMARTPTR_TYPEDEF(ICustomInterface2, __uuidof(ICustomInterface2));
```

Here we see an actual use of the **__uuidof()** keyword in conjunction with smart pointers to retrieve the GUID (Interface ID) associated with the **ICustomInterface2** class/structure. After the execution of this macro, there will be a type called **ICustomInterface2Ptr** (note the **Ptr** postfix, this will always be the case with this macro) which when instantiated with the appropriate object's CLSID will perform instantiation and **QueryInterface()** in one simple step. Recall from the beginning of this chapter that a **typedef** of a template will not actually generate any code until the newly **typedef** type is used in a declaration.

For example, the following single line of code:

```
ICustomInterface2Ptr  pCI(__uuidof(Atipblob1));
```

will actually:

1 Call **CoGetClassObject()** on the CLSID of **Atipblob1** object to obtain a class factory.

2 Call **CreateInstance()** of the class factory to create an **Atipblob1** object.

3 Call **IUnknown::QueryInterface()** of the **Atipblob1** object to obtain an interface to **ICustomInterface2**.

4 Create a **__com_ptr_t** smart pointer object around this pointer.

5 Throw an exception with a self-describing **__com_error** object if anything should go wrong with the above.

The code 'surface area' (actual lines of code in programmer-maintained source files—i.e. not calculating any generated code that is never changed) decreases substantially between the conventional way of using C++ or C based COM programming and the use of smart pointers. Since the complexity of code design and maintenance is directly proportional to the number of lines of code, smart pointer COM programming does indeed simplify COM programming for everyone.

Multithreaded Test Client Using Smart Pointers

We now have enough background to take a look at the new multithreaded tester. You can find the listing in the Atipmusr project from the source distribution.

```
#include <stdio.h>
#include <stdlib.h>
#include <time.h>
#include <process.h>
#include <assert.h>
#include <tchar.h>
#include <comdef.h>
#include "CRTDBG.h"

#import "..\Atipblob\Atipblob.tlb" no_namespace
```

This first portion holds no surprise, as we've discussed before. Next we have a standard routine which will decipher (print to the console) a **__com_error** object thrown during a COM exception. Since our object doesn't actually support **IErrorInfo**, this will only decode error information originating from other portions of COM.

```
void dump_com_error(_com_error &e)
{
    _tprintf(_T("Oops - hit an error!\n"));
    _tprintf(_T("\a\tCode = %08lx\n"), e.Error());
    _tprintf(_T("\a\tCode meaning = %s\n"), e.ErrorMessage());
    _bstr_t bstrSource(e.Source());
    _bstr_t bstrDescription(e.Description());
    _tprintf(_T("\a\tSource = %s\n"), (LPCTSTR) bstrSource);
    _tprintf(_T("\a\tDescription = %s\n"), (LPCTSTR) bstrDescription);
}
```

The next portion of the code contains declarations and the **main()** function implementation. Nothing here has changed from the original multithreaded client; we will not repeat it in its entirety here.

```
#define MAX_THREAD  10
CRITICAL_SECTION g_Console;
#define LOCK            EnterCriticalSection(&g_Console);
#define UNLOCK          LeaveCriticalSection(&g_Console);

void AThread(LPVOID lpParam);

main()
{

    HANDLE hThread[MAX_THREAD];
...
    DeleteCriticalSection(&g_Console);
```

```
        return 0;
}
```

Finally, we arrive at the thread function where the smart pointer usage really simplifies things:

```
void AThread(LPVOID lpParam)
{

    long myNumber = *((long *) lpParam);
    HRESULT hRes;
    long  objCount, inYear, inMonth, propValue;   VARIANT_BOOL okFlag;
    _bstr_t mgrName;
```

Here, we use the **__bstr_t** type for our **mgrName**.

```
    hRes = CoInitialize(NULL);
    srand( (unsigned)time( NULL ) );
    try
    {
        ICustomInterface2Ptr pCI(__uuidof(Atipblob1));
```

This is it. After this statement, **pCI** will be pointing to **ICustomInterface2** in a newly created **Atipblob1** object (or an exception would have occurred and the thread terminated: see code at the end of the thread function).

```
        LOCK
        _tprintf(_T("T%d: Made a bare blob!\n"), myNumber);
        UNLOCK
        LOCK
        _tprintf(_T("T%d: Got its custom interface!\n"), myNumber);
        UNLOCK

        for (long i=0; i< 20; i++)
        {
            pCI->InternalProperty = rand() % 100;
```

Here we take advantage of the **__declspec(property())** on the **InternalProperty** virtual data member and set it as if it is a data member of the interface.

```
            mgrName = pCI->GetManagerName();

            inYear = 1900 + rand() %100;
            inMonth = rand() % 12 + 1;
            okFlag = pCI->OkayToPublishInfo(inYear, inMonth);
            objCount = pCI->PeekCounter();

#ifdef UNICODE
            LOCK
            _tprintf(_T("T%d: After calling GetManagerName : current manager is %s\n"),
                myNumber, mgrName );
            UNLOCK
#else
            char * tp = new char[50];
```

```
            WideCharToMultiByte(CP_ACP,0, (wchar_t *) mgrName,
                -1, tp, 50, NULL, NULL);
            LOCK
            _tprintf(_T("T%d: After calling GetManagerName : current manager is %s\n"),
                myNumber, tp);
            UNLOCK
            delete [] tp;
#endif

            LOCK
            _tprintf(_T("T%d: After calling OkToPublishInfo : Year = %d, Month = %d
Status = %s\n"),
                myNumber,   inYear, inMonth, (okFlag == TRUE) ? _T("OKAY"): _T("NOWAY"));
            UNLOCK

            propValue = pCI->InternalProperty;
            LOCK
            _tprintf(_T("T%d: Obtained InternalProperty Value = %d\n"),
                myNumber, propValue);
            UNLOCK

            LOCK
            _tprintf(_T("T%d: We now have %d object users.\n"),   myNumber,
objCount);
            UNLOCK
            Sleep(1000);  // sleep for about 1 second
        }

        LOCK
        printf("T%d, Freeing the blob now!\n", myNumber);
        UNLOCK
    }
```

The method calling and printing logic remains largely the same. Finally, we implement the exception handling by dumping out to the console a deciphered (hopefully) error message, uninitialize COM, then terminate the thread.

```
    catch (_com_error &e)
    {
        dump_com_error(e);
        CoUninitialize();
        _endthread();
    }
    CoUninitialize();
}
```

That's it. Try building the test client now and executing it. Notice how the client works exactly as our older implementation without smart pointers. Notice also how the new ATL ActiveX control behaves just like our 'from scratch' BareBlob object showing that early binding is still working. Furthermore, notice how the property retains its value after it is set, even though other threads may have set its own object's property to another value in between the **Get** and **Put** call. Since each thread sets the property to its own index number, the multiple independent instance nature of these created **CAtipblob1** objects is clearly demonstrated.

```
T2: After calling GetManagerName : current manager is J. Manzini
T2: After calling OkToPublishInfo : Year = 1985, Month = 11 Status = NOWAY
T2: Obtained InternalProperty Value = 34
T2: We now have 9 object users.
T7: After calling GetManagerName : current manager is J. Manzini
T7: After calling OkToPublishInfo : Year = 1929, Month = 5 Status = OKAY
T7: Obtained InternalProperty Value = 21
T7: We now have 9 object users.
T5: After calling GetManagerName : current manager is J. Manzini
T5: After calling OkToPublishInfo : Year = 1907, Month = 11 Status = OKAY
T5: Obtained InternalProperty Value = 88
T5: We now have 9 object users.
T4: After calling GetManagerName : current manager is J. Manzini
T4: After calling OkToPublishInfo : Year = 1919, Month = 4 Status = OKAY
T4: Obtained InternalProperty Value = 11
T4: We now have 9 object users.
T3: After calling GetManagerName : current manager is J. Manzini
T3: After calling OkToPublishInfo : Year = 1962, Month = 10 Status = NOWAY
T0: After calling GetManagerName : current manager is J. Manzini
T0: After calling OkToPublishInfo : Year = 1990, Month = 4 Status = OKAY
T3: Obtained InternalProperty Value = 27
T3: We now have 9 object users.
T0: Obtained InternalProperty Value = 87
T0: We now have 9 object users.
```

Automated Registry Manipulations

In our eagerness to test our ATL control and explore the benefits Visual C++ gives us in handling early binding we've neglected an important topic. The topic is the handling of registry updates through ATL.

With the release of ATL 1.1 and beyond, an implementation of a **Registrar** component is supplied. Using the Registrar, one can describe all the operations to be performed during the component registration and de-registration process in a text based **script** file. The benefit of this approach is clear. Instead of the raw coding using the registry APIs, we have the ability to quickly change the actions performed in the script, without having to write and test fairly tedious code again and again.

The Registrar works on a **.RGS** file. The entire file is actually 'compiled' into a custom resource. The registrar component will interpret this resource during runtime (i.e. when **DLLRegisterServer()** or **DLLUnregisterServer()** is called) and call the appropriate registry API to modify the registry.

In our **Atipblob1.h** file, the ATL generated line within the **CAtipblob1** class definition handles the mapping:

```
class ATL_NO_VTABLE CAtipblob1 :
   public CComObjectRootEx<CComMultiThreadModel>,
   public CComCoClass<CAtipblob1, &CLSID_Atipblob1>,
   public IDispatchImpl<ICustomInterface2, &IID_ICustomInterface2, &LIBID_ATIPBLOBLib>
{
public:
   CAtipblob1()
   {
```

```
        m_pUnkMarshaler = NULL;
    }
```

```
DECLARE_REGISTRY_RESOURCEID(IDR_ATIPBLOB1)
DECLARE_GET_CONTROLLING_UNKNOWN()
```

The macro translates to a static function declaration, as we can find in the **Atlcom.h** file:

```
#define DECLARE_REGISTRY_RESOURCEID(x)\
    static HRESULT WINAPI UpdateRegistry(BOOL bRegister)\
    {\
        return _Module.UpdateRegistryFromResource(x, bRegister);\
    }
```

This function is called indirectly (through another function and a mapping of the **OBJECT_ENTRY** map) through the **DllRegisterServer()** and **DllUnregisterServer()** implementations.

The **.RGS** file for our Atipblob project is listed here:

```
HKCR
{
    Atipblob1.Atipblob11.1 = s 'ATL_InProc_Server'
    {
        CLSID = s '{F55C8EAF-87F7-11D0-8DD0-006052008075}'
    }
    Atipblob1.Atipblob11 = s 'ATL_InProc_Server'
    {
        CurVer = s 'Atipblob1.Atipblob11.1'
    }
    NoRemove CLSID
    {
        ForceRemove {F55C8EAF-87F7-11D0-8DD0-006052008075} = s 'ATL_InProc_Server'
        {
            ProgID = s 'Atipblob1.Atipblob11.1'
            VersionIndependentProgID = s 'Atipblob1.Atipblob11'
            ForceRemove 'Programmable'
            InprocServer32 = s '%MODULE%'
            {
                val ThreadingModel = s 'Both'
            }
        }
    }
}
```

The syntax is actually readable and very easy to understand. Each successive level of curly braces indicates another level of subkeys. From the very top, we have **HKCR** that is shorthand for **HKEY_CLASSES_ROOT**.

Right underneath this root, we create the first subkey which is **Atipblob.Atipblob11.1** and it has a default string value of **ATL_InProc_Server**. Underneath this subkey, we have a named value called **CLSID** that has a string value of **'{F55C8EAF-87F7-11D0-8DD0-006052008075}'**.

The rest of the file follows the same pattern. Just compare this with all the code we had to write in the previous chapter and imagine having to maintain that code!

There a number of items worth mentioning here. All the keys specified in the `.RGS` file will be deleted during the unregister server phase. The deletion of a key by default is done during the unregistration process; to prevent a subkey from being deleted at unregistration time, you can use the **NoRemove** attribute before the subkey (for an example, see the **CLSID** subkey above). You don't have to mark the root key with **NoRemove**, since the registrar will not remove a root key. If you want to force the recursive deletion of a subkey prior to creation (at registration time), you can use the **Force Remove** attribute before the subkey. The ATL has done this with our **CLSID** entry. It's also possible to precede a key name with the **Delete** attribute and have the key deleted during registration time.

The **%MODULE%** macro will be replaced by the actual qualified path of the executable or DLL during execution. A value can be preceded by an **s** for a string value, or **d** for a numeric **DWORD** value in decimal; there's no provision for hex entries, simply convert to decimal. You can also create a named value, instead of a subkey and a default value, with the **val** prefix.

This Registrar component is so beautifully powerful that one may consider using it in non-ATL situations. As a matter of fact, the registrar is designed to be functionally independent from ATL. You can view its source, which is included with the ATL library, in the **Statreg.h** and **Statreg.cpp** files residing in the DevStudio\vc\atl\include directory. However, redistribution terms for the registrar are currently not clearly specified. More information on how to use the registrar can be found in the Visual C++ 5 help facility by searching for ATL Registry Component.

Back to Our Object: Sing Along with Visual Basic

We've been saying for a long time that our object is an ActiveX control, yet we haven't seen any solid proof of this. An ActiveX control, thanks to the Internet extensions of the OC96 specification from Microsoft, is any in-process COM class that implements the **IUnknown** interface. Since **Atipblob1** is definitely an in-process COM class, and we know that it implements the **IUnknown** interface, we can safely say that it is an ActiveX control. Case closed!

Stop the complaints! So I realize that it isn't one of the ActiveX controls that you're used to. Actually, at the time of writing, if you follow the new guidelines directly (and ignore the compatibility requirements), you'll be creating controls that nobody can use... yet. The sad fact is that the container and application vendors are as slow on the draw as you and me. Most container applications still expect the bloated OCXs with hundreds of user interface enhancements from the past. For now, you'll just have to trust me and Microsoft (the latter is probably an easier thing to do) that there will be a lot of containers and applications coming up shortly that will be able to make use of our '**IUnknown** only' ActiveX control.

Having said that, let's investigate what we need to do to get **Atipblob1** to work with Visual Basic 5. It turns out, at least on the system where you've been developing the ActiveX control, that this need is preempted! The control is ready to go. To enable your control in Visual Basic 5, from the Project menu, select the References... option. From the list, look for the Atipblob 1.0 Type Library reference and select it, then click OK.

Now, select the object browser from the View menu. From the top left list box, select the ATIPBLOBLib entry. Once you've selected this, you'll see the method and the internal property that we've created. Visual Basic is now ready to use the object.

We'll create a very simple program that tests out the ActiveX control. This program can be found in the **Atpipbas** directory after you've decompressed the source code from the Wrox Press web site. It consists of a sample form with three buttons and five text fields on it. Whenever a button is pressed, an object instance of **CAtipblob1** is created and its methods are called and its property set and then read back.

If you press the Late Binding Call button, late binding through **IDispatch** will be used. The following code will be executed:

```
Private Sub Command2_Click()
    Dim a As Long, b As Long, c As Long
    Dim mgr As String
    Dim flag As Boolean

    ' Late Binding Example
    Call CleanForm
    Dim AnObj As Object
    Set AnObj = New Atipblob1
    AnObj.InternalProperty = 3333
    Manager.Text = AnObj.GetManagerName()
    flag = AnObj.OkayToPublishInfo(1990 + Int(Rnd * 100 + 1), Int(Rnd * 12 + 1))
    If flag Then
        Okay.Text = "OKAY"
    Else
        Okay.Text = "NOWAY"
    End If
    Counter1.Text = Str$(AnObj.PeekCounter())
    PropOut.Text = Str$(AnObj.InternalProperty)
    Set AnObj = Nothing
End Sub
```

In this case, the **AnObj** variable is dimensioned as an **Object**. Visual Basic doesn't know anything about the object until one of its methods is called or the property is accessed. At that time, the **IDispatch::GetIDsOfNames()** method will be called to get the ID of the method or property, and then **IDispatch::Invoke()** will be called to manipulate the property or invoke the method.

If you press the Early Binding or ID Binding Call button, another routine with very similar code will be called. There's only one line in this routine that's different:

```
Private Sub Command1_Click()
    Dim a As Long, b As Long, c As Long
    Dim mgr As String
    Dim flag As Boolean

    ' Early Binding Example
    Call CleanForm
    Dim AnObj As Atipblob1
    Set AnObj = New Atipblob1
    AnObj.InternalProperty = 3333
    Manager.Text = AnObj.GetManagerName()
    flag = AnObj.OkayToPublishInfo(1990 + Int(Rnd * 100 + 1), Int(Rnd * 12 + 1))
    If flag Then
        Okay.Text = "OKAY"
    Else
        Okay.Text = "NOWAY"
    End If
    Counter1.Text = Str$(AnObj.PeekCounter())
    PropOut.Text = Str$(AnObj.InternalProperty)
    Set AnObj = Nothing
End Sub
```

In this case, we specifically point out to Visual Basic that **AnObj** will contain an object of the **CAtipblob1** variety. Since Visual Basic has access to the type library information of the **CAtipblob1** class, it already knows the methods that the **IDispatch** interface supports. It also knows: the arguments and the type of the arguments that the functions will require, their return value, and even the vtable order of the function given a pointer. Visual Basic in this case can elect to either call into **IDispatch::Invoke()** directly using the information, or call into the vtable entries directly. This has tremendous benefit in terms of improving performance (typically doubling or more), since each and every call doesn't have to go through the **IDispatch::GetIDsOfNames()** call anymore.

When you make an executable through Visual Basic with this approach, it will always use the vtable binding, giving you access to your ActiveX control with a speed equivalent to normal C++ virtual function calls. Provided that the type library information is available, Visual Basic 5 can actually take advantage of vtable binding without even making an EXE. One can imagine the possibilities of combining the best of what Visual Basic and native C++ have to offer in a complex application. As a bonus with the ActiveX control approach, the same component is reusable by a supported programming language or environment.

Let's now revisit one key statement that was made earlier. We basically said (no pun intended) that Visual Basic was able to find our ActiveX control only on the machine where the control was compiled and built. Why? It turns out that Visual Basic was able to find information regarding our control because its type library was registered with the system. Recall that a type library contains the information that we've placed into the IDL file (i.e. the interfaces, methods, properties, Interface IDs, object descriptions, etc.) in a binary form. By default, the ATL generated registration routine will register the type library and interfaces of the COM server with the system. This is done in the implementation of the **DllRegisterServer()** function inside the **Atipblob.cpp** file:

```
STDAPI DllRegisterServer(void)
{
    // registers object, typelib and all interfaces in typelib
    return _Module.RegisterServer(TRUE);
}
```

If you don't want to register the type library information, you can pass **FALSE** as a parameter into the **_Module.RegisterServer()** call. Since the build file that ATL creates for you will automatically load your DLL and execute the **DllRegisterServer()** call, the type library and interface information was entered into the registry. If you were to move the COM server (DLL) to another machine, you must remember to run **REGSVR32 /regserver ATIPBLOB.DLL** to get this information into the registry before Visual Basic will be happy. You can do this within your Setup utility if you're distributing more than a few copies.

Deploying Our ActiveX Control on a Web Page with Internet Explorer 3.01

Next, we'll try to operate our ActiveX control from a web page viewed from Internet Explorer. Later in our intranet programming, this will be performed frequently. We'll assume that we're using a WYSIWYG tool to create the web page. In our case, we'll use FrontPage 97, which supports the laying out of ActiveX controls.

The sample web page can be found in the **Atipblob\Webtest** directory of the code you will download from the Wrox website. Unlike Visual Basic, FrontPage 97 doesn't read the type libraries, registered with the registry, to come up with a list of ActiveX controls. Instead, it depends on an extra subkey under the **HKEY_CLASSES_ROOT\CLSID\{---}** entry to determine if a specific COM object is a control. Appropriately enough, the key is named **Control**. Be aware though, that this is the 'old' way that COM objects are to be identified as ActiveX controls. Microsoft is recommending a new standard based on UUIDs, called components categories, in the OC96 specifications. We'll give a synopsis of the OC96 specification in a later section. In the (hopefully near) future, more and more containers will implement this new standard. For now though, just adding the **Control** subkey to our **.RGS** file and rebuilding the project will suffice.

The new **.RGS** file now looks like this:

```
HKCR
{
   Atipblob1.Atipblob11.1 = s 'ATL_InProc_Server'
   {
      CLSID = s '{F55C8EAF-87F7-11D0-8DD0-006052008075}'
   }
   Atipblob1.Atipblob11 = s 'ATL_InProc_Server'
   {
      CurVer = s 'Atipblob1.Atipblob11.1'
   }
   NoRemove CLSID
   {
      ForceRemove {F55C8EAF-87F7-11D0-8DD0-006052008075} = s 'ATL_InProc_Server'
      {
         ProgID = s 'Atipblob1.Atipblob11.1'
         VersionIndependentProgID = s 'Atipblob1.Atipblob11'
         ForceRemove 'Programmable'
         InprocServer32 = s '%MODULE%'
         {
            val ThreadingModel = s 'Both'
         }
         Control = s ' '
      }
   }
}
```

Now, if we start up the FrontPage 97 editor, and click on the Insert menu, select the Other Components… selection, and then choose ActiveX Control…. We'll see the ATL Based InProc Server Class as a selection. Give it a name and then click the OK button.

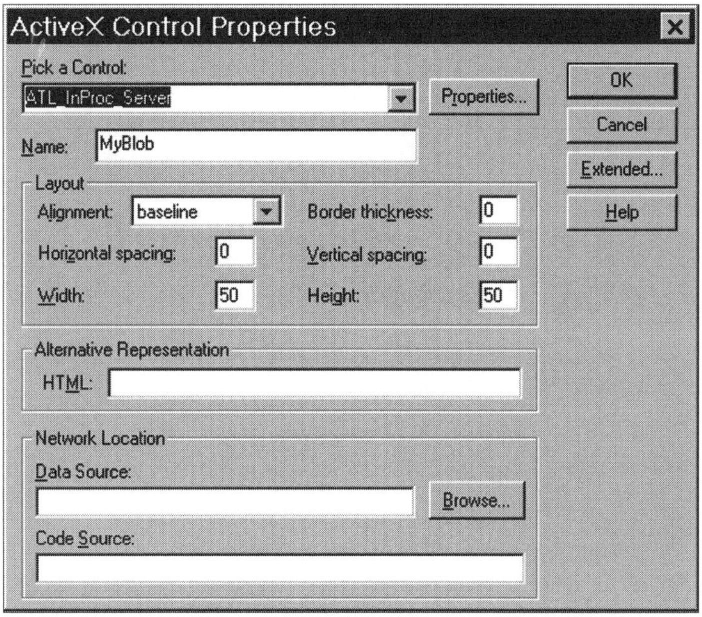

At this point, the control is embedded into the page, and you're ready to call its methods and set its property from the scripting language. The actual HTML involved in embedding the ActiveX control is shown here:

```
<p><object id="MyBlob" name="MyBlob"
classid="clsid:F55C8EAF-87F7-11D0-8DD0-006052008075"
align="baseline" border="0" width="50" height="50"></object> </p>
```

The **<OBJECT>** tag is used to insert the control on to the page. More information on this tag can be found in Appendix B.

Since our target browser is Internet Explorer 3.0, we have a choice of using either VBScript or JavaScript for scripting. For illustration purposes, we'll be using VBScript. We'll set up a web page with various HTML form controls very similar to our Visual Basic example.

Using FrontPage 97, or if you find it more comfortable you can use Notepad, you can lay out a page as follows:

FrontPage Editor - [D:\atipfp\atipblob.htm]

File Edit View Insert Format Tools Table Window Help

Normal   Times New Roman   **A** **A** **B**

abl

Test Page for the Atipblob ActiveX Control

Manager's Name:

Okay to Publish Info?

Counter:

Internal Property Value:

| Call the ActiveX Control Now! | Clear Everything |

2 seconds   NUM

You can find a 'ready-to-go' HTML file in the \Webtest directory of the source code distribution. However, you'll need to change the CLSID of the control if you created the control yourself.

The four input fields and the two buttons are HTML form elements. I used them rather than the ActiveX controls equivalent from the Microsoft Forms collection because they are far more stable when working with FrontPage 97. You can see a **FrontPage bot** (this is a markup bot which allows me to add raw HTML into the code generated) right at the top–within this bot, I have defined a VBScript procedure. The ActiveX control is embedded in the lower left-hand corner (appearing as a gray square since we don't do any UI). On the **OnClick** event of the button labeled Call the ActiveX Control Now!, I call the method and property of the **CAtipblob1** ActiveX control (called MyBlob on the page).

If you're following along using Notepad as an HTML editor, the following is the actual HTML file:

```
<!DOCTYPE HTML PUBLIC "-//IETF//DTD HTML//EN">
<html>
```

```html
<head>
<meta http-equiv="Content-Type"
content="text/html; charset=iso-8859-1">
<meta name="GENERATOR" content="Microsoft FrontPage 2.0">
<title>Atipblob Test Page</title>
</head>

<body bgcolor="#FFFFFF">

<h1><script language="VBScript"><!--
Sub CallBlob()
MyBlob.InternalProperty = 3333
Document.MyForm.Manager.value = MyBlob.GetManagerName()
randomize
inYear = rnd() * 100 + 1900
inMonth = rnd() * 12 + 1
Flag = MyBlob.OkayToPublishInfo(inYear, inMonth)
if Flag <> 0 then
 Document.MyForm.Okay.value = "OKAY"
else
 Document.MyForm.Okay.value = "NOWAY"
end if
Document.MyForm.Counter.value = MyBlob.PeekCounter()
Document.MyForm.PropOut.value = MyBlob.InternalProperty
end sub

Sub ClearForm()
Document.MyForm.Okay.value = ""
Document.MyForm.PropOut.value = ""
Document.MyForm.Counter.value = ""
Document.MyForm.Manager.value = ""
end sub

--></script> Test Page for the
Atipblob ActiveX Control</h1>

<form method="POST" name="MyForm">
    <p>Manager's Name: <input type="text" size="20"
    name="Manager"> </p>
    <p>Okay to Publish Info? <input type="text" size="20"
    name="Okay"> </p>
    <p>Counter: <input type="text" size="15" name="Counter"></p>
    <p>Internal Property Value: <input type="text" size="20"
    name="PropOut"> </p>
    <p><input type="button" name="CallBut"
    value="Call the ActiveX Control Now!" language="VBScript"
    onclick="Call ClearForm()
Call CallBlob()"> <input
    type="button" name="Clear" value="Clear Everything"
    language="VBScript" onclick="Call ClearForm()"> </p>
</form>

<p><object id="MyBlob" name="MyBlob"
classid="clsid:F55C8EAF-87F7-11D0-8DD0-006052008075"
align="baseline" border="0" width="50" height="50"></object> </p>
</body>
</html>
```

The `<Script>` tag is used to insert VBScript code into the HTML page. More information on the `<Script>` tag can be found at the end of this book. Notice in the `CallBlob()` procedure how similar the syntax is between VBScript and Visual Basic. There isn't any `Dim` or `Set` statement for object manipulation though. This is because the model of operation is quite different. With Visual Basic applications, we have the flexibility to instantiate and free the ActiveX control/COM Server whenever we want programmatically. Under the Internet Explorer, the lifetime of the ActiveX control is the lifetime of a page. When the page is in view and active, the ActiveX control is initialized and ready for action. As soon as the user moves to another page, the object instance is released and the functionality is no longer available. There's no way you can manage object lifetime programmatically using VBScript. Since you can't use the `Dim` or `Set` statements, you can't control the binding method that's used. VBScript in IE will always use the low-performance late binding. This is plainly evident during debugging since the script engine will not detect a method which doesn't belong to the object until the method is actually invoked. Microsoft has a VBScript debugger in hand with various availability options to those placing 'MS' logos on their site, etc. You should keep an eye on the MS download site and in various SDKs. In the meantime VBScript debugging can be quite frustrating. Another *big* difference between Visual Basic and VBScript is the lack of specific types for variables. Every variable in VBScript is a variant. The variant type is a monstrous union of almost all the frequently used data types, and a few of the quainter ones.

Here are some of the most common data types. The **VARTYPE** value (enumerated value) is used to signify the type of the variant. Special functions exist (and their use is strongly encouraged) that convert between variant types:

VARTYPE values	Description
VT_EMPTY	No value specified
VT_U1	unsigned 1-byte **char**
VT_I2	2-byte integer
VT_U2	unsigned 2-byte integer
VT_I4	4-byte integer
VT_U4	unsigned 4-byte integer
VT_R4	4-byte real value
VT_CY	8-byte currency number
VT_BSTR	a string in a $<$length, data$>$ format
VT_NULL	null value
VT_ERROR	an error information structure
VT_BOOL	a Boolean value (**0** or **0xFFFF**)
VT_DATE	date represented as a double-precision number
VT_DISPATCH	pointer to an object implementing **IDispatch**
VT_UNKNOWN	pointer to an object implementing **IUnknown**
VT_ARRAY	array of data of any kind

This approach makes script programming substantially easier (i.e. the engine will always try to convert types to fit whatever the programmer is doing, freeing him or her from ever worrying about type conversions). In practice, most of us already know from experience that there are many problems associated with a 'one type fits all' system. These systems frequently force us to understand and memorize a complex set of type conversion situations and rules–that can often be inconsistent.

Finally, we can test our ActiveX control on a web page. Try it out using IE 3.01. It works great!

Watching our Object Being Interrogated

You may have been a secret disbeliever back in the last chapter, when I said that Object Viewer will call **QueryInterface()** on your object for every single interface that the system knows about. Well, here's a chance to prove it once and for all. Since the ATL handles the **IUnknown** implementation automatically, the action of the underlying **QueryInterface()** method isn't visible. Yet, being able to 'trace into' a **QueryInterface()** call can often reveal the source of some complex problems. To facilitate this tracing, the ATL offers a way to debug **QueryInterface()** handling of a COM class. You can enable this facility by:

1 Running a utility program called **Findguid.exe** with the **-insert** option (i.e. **findguid -insert**).

2 In the **Stdafx.h** file, look for the following code fragment, and add a definition **#define _ATL_DEBUG_QI** before including **Atlcom.h**:

```
#include <atlbase.h>
//You may derive a class from CComModule and use it if you want to override
//something, but do not change the name of _Module
extern CComModule _Module;
```

#define _ATL_DEBUG_QI

```
#include <atlcom.h>
```

The **Findguid.exe** examines the **\HKEY_CLASSES_ROOT\Interface** tree to ensure that most of the common IIDs are defined. The key here is making sure the textual names of the common interfaces are inserted into the tree. This is the 'database' with which the trace mechanism translates an IID to the textual name of the interface.

We'll now make the modification to the Atipblob1 object and rebuild it. Select the <u>B</u>uild menu and click Start <u>D</u>ebug... <u>G</u>o, in the executable to start edit box, type in the complete path of your **Oleview.exe** (i.e. **DevStudio\vc\bin\Oleview.exe**). Once Object Viewer starts, find the ATL_InProc_Server Class entry and double-click on it. Watch the debug output window! You should see something like this:

Check this list of interfaces against **\HKEY_CLASSES_ROOT\interface** and you'll see the 'one to one' correspondence, verifying that our object was indeed viciously interrogated in order to determine which interfaces it actually supports. My poor object was interrogated a total of over 1600 times!

```
Atipblob - Microsoft Developer Studi...

File  Edit  View  Insert  Project  Debug  Tools  Window
Help

[ICustomInterface2]  [(All class members)]  [(No members - Cr

CAtipblob1 - IEnumSTATSTG - failed
CAtipblob1 - IBindCtx - failed
CAtipblob1 - IMoniker - failed
CAtipblob1 - IRunningObjectTable - failed
CAtipblob1 - IRootStorage - failed
CAtipblob1 - IMessageFilter - failed
CAtipblob1 - IStdMarshalInfo - failed
CAtipblob1 - IExternalConnection - failed
CAtipblob1 - IEnumUnknown - failed
CAtipblob1 - IEnumString - failed
CAtipblob1 - IEnumMoniker - failed
CAtipblob1 - IEnumFORMATETC - failed
CAtipblob1 - IEnumOLEVERB - failed
CAtipblob1 - IEnumSTATDATA - failed
CAtipblob1 - IPersistStream - failed
CAtipblob1 - IPersistStorage - failed
CAtipblob1 - IPersistFile - failed
CAtipblob1 - IPersist - failed
CAtipblob1 - IViewObject - failed
CAtipblob1 - IDataObject - failed
CAtipblob1 - IAdviseSink - failed
CAtipblob1 - IDataAdviseHolder - failed
CAtipblob1 - IOleAdviseHolder - failed
CAtipblob1 - IOleObject - failed
CAtipblob1 - IOleInPlaceObject - failed
CAtipblob1 - IOleWindow - failed
CAtipblob1 - IOleInPlaceUIWindow - failed
CAtipblob1 - IOleInPlaceFrame - failed
CAtipblob1 - IOleInPlaceActiveObject - faile
CAtipblob1 - IOleClientSite - failed

Find in Files 2 \ Results \ SQL Debugging \ Co
```

Ready for the Intranet Challenge

The powerful simplicity of ATL 2.1 has allowed us to cover a lot of ground in this chapter. The new native COM support of Visual C++ 5 really simplifies COM programming, reducing the amount of code we have to write to build great COM clients. We have completed the construction of our business rule ActiveX control using ATL 2.1, which allows it to be used by Visual Basic 5 and Internet Explorer immediately. We tested the control with C++, Visual Basic, and VBScript, and it worked equally well on every platform.

Now, armed with a solid understanding of COM fundamentals and a powerful tool collection like Visual C++ 5 and ATL 2.1, we're ready to tackle more intranet programming problems with an eye towards component based solutions. Along the way, we'll be covering a few more advanced COM topics, and showing how ATL and other tools can really help in constructing a highly functional intranet.

Building an Event Calendar Control

Armed with our knowledge of basic COM principles, and having created an ActiveX control first from scratch, and then using the ActiveX Template Library, we're ready to apply our knowledge to the more complex problems. The ActiveX control that we're designing in this chapter is an event calendar control. Instead of a concept demonstration piece, this is a 'near production quality' control designed for solving a complex real-world problem. This control is a miniature application that will be used on the web pages within our intranet. It will provide (display) the user interface and handle all the required user interactions. It allows the Aberdeen & Wilshire corporate calendar of events to be viewed at any time from any employee's desktop, with live data. We'll evolve the design into a completely distributed architecture where computation will be distributed over multiple machines via our intranet. Each department hosting events can keep track of their own events using whatever legacy systems and methods that already exist. As long as they provide a well-specified component interface into the system, the components making up the system can be changed or upgraded independently with no effect on others. This will illustrate how COM, and especially DCOM technology, can be used to 'wrap' dissimilar systems in a distributed intranet.

We'll cover the design, coding, and testing of this ActiveX control over two chapters. In the first chapter, we'll set the foundations for building the control. We first discuss what OLE Custom Controls (OCXs) are and how they relate to the ActiveX controls that we have been building. Next, we'll take a detailed look at a recent specification for ActiveX controls from Microsoft known as the OC96 specification. We then proceed to look at how Visual C++ 5.0 and MFC 4.21, as programming power tools, support both the older OCX model and the new OC96 specifications. Our implementation of the control will be in Visual C++ 5.0. In the last portion of the chapter, we'll begin the high level analysis and design for the Aberdeen & Wilshire calendar and conclude with an examination of the classes that make up the core logic of the control.

This will fully prepare us for the next chapter where we'll be doing some serious coding. In this later chapter, we'll look at the construction of the classes that we've designed, creating the visual ActiveX control in Visual C++, and also at testing. And we'll construct the back-end business objects (which are also a control) that will supply the visual component with the calendar event data in order to fulfill the end user's request.

Before we begin, let's clear up a likely source of confusion. It's important to realize that Microsoft's marketing department is pushing a multiyear, multimillion dollar effort in establishing a brand identity for 'ActiveX'. During this period, everything and anything that's associated with the Internet or intranet coming out of Microsoft will be labeled ActiveX. Unfortunately, this is often confusing because many of the newly labeled pieces already have well-established, accepted industry names. One good example is the OLE Control, and the OLE Control 96 technologies discussed in this chapter. Any control which has elements applicable to Internet/intranet use (and almost all OLE controls would have), Microsoft would rather have you label it as ActiveX. Since all controls covered in this book are applicable directly to intranet operations, we'll be using ActiveX controls and OCX interchangeably depending on the context. However, in the coverage of the specifications (i.e. OC96), we'll attempt to use the terminology adopted by the particular specification being examined.

Ironically, the last campaign of a similar nature undertaken by Microsoft was for 'OLE' branding of its Office suite. The effort was phenomenally successful and helped to propel Microsoft Office to the top of the chart in the Office suite category. Microsoft is aiming to repeat the success with ActiveX.

Advance Warning for Avid Readers

If you're the type of reader who likes to read chapters in a book in sequential order, please pay close attention. It's now a good time to power off your development station, and get a pot of coffee ready. This is going to be an intense chapter where we'll be condensing several complex specifications from Microsoft, and nailing down numerous advance concepts. All this in preparation for the equally intense coding chapters to follow.

We adopted this style of presentation to deliver the maximum amount of practical technology information within the limited confines of this book. If you find going through this chapter rather rough on first reading, don't worry—many of the concepts will be reinforced by actual code in later chapters. Overall, this chapter lends itself to a 'quick read' the first time through, and then serves as a reference point for later explorations.

Leveraging Market Control to Create a Product Family

First, we'll start with an introduction to visual ActiveX controls. In this introduction, we'll also examine in some detail the evolution of the de facto standards and new specifications that Microsoft is pushing through to the industry at large. At the same time, we'll note the subtle ways in which this evolution has been influenced by the emerging Internet/intranet market.

Visual Basic 3.X has created a rapidly growing component market that surprised many software visionaries, including most Microsoft executives. By arranging and orchestrating bits and pieces of code with its self-contained user interface in the form of a 'visual component', the Visual Basic programmer can rapidly create sophisticated applications out of well-tested, industrial strength components. The entire process is painlessly simple, and most construction steps are highly visual. This simplicity in application construction has attracted over 3 million programmers to the language in its five short years of existence. Unfortunately, the VBX component technology of Visual Basic 3.X was a dead-end architecture since it took advantage of many specific 16-bit Windows/Intel platform features. It was clear to Microsoft that it needed to leverage the Visual Basic 3 component market momentum and shift the developer community to an infrastructure that was less dependent on the underlying processors, and could operate in 32-bit architectures (and beyond). The fruit of this effort was called the OLE Control (or OCX) movement. By the time Visual Basic 4.0 was released, most of the VBX vendors had migrated to the new OCX architecture for their bread-and-butter components. The OCX architecture was designed to be flexible enough such that the 'hosting' application was no longer restricted to Visual Basic, but could be many other third party and Microsoft environments as well. Specifically, Microsoft has taken great pains to ensure that their primary hard-core commercial grade development environment, Visual C++, is able to take advantage of the blossoming OCX market, as well as be used in the actual construction of these OCX components.

Anatomy of an OCX

As a close cousin (and indeed the predecessor) of the ActiveX control, the original OCX has many characteristics which are similar. The most important one is that they both have methods and properties, and can source (generate) events. Methods are functions that the users of a component may invoke; this is identical in action to the functions that we created for our COM components in the early chapters. Properties are attributes of the component that the component user can change, although some may be read-only and/or hidden. In actual implementation, properties too are functions. Each property corresponds to two functions, one to 'get' the value of a property, and one to 'set' the value of a property. An OCX can also **source** (send) events because it's a visual control that supports a piece of the user interface. When certain well-specified interactions occur, the OCX can source an event to be **sinked** (received) by the hosting application, resulting in a call to a procedure within the hosting application (e.g. within a Visual Basic event handler). From this brief description of events, one can readily deduce that it maps to call back functions into the container or host of the component. This is indeed true. These functions are invoked by the component and executed by the hosting container. However, the real puzzling aspect of events at this point is how does the container know what callback functions to code ahead of time, when it doesn't know all the possible components that it will ever use? Every OCX can support a set of methods and properties, many of them also support events. Most interactions between a hosting container and an OCX component are performed through a well-defined (by Microsoft) set of COM interfaces. This was necessary because Microsoft's software (the OCX/COM support and runtimes) is standing between the hosting application and the OCX during most interactions. Obviously, this is also another flavor of Microsoft's value added in that it provides a de facto standard for the interoperation of hosting container and OCX components.

Properties of an OCX may be set or changed visually within visual programming environments such as Visual Basic. Either the design time host (e.g. Visual Basic) or the OCX itself may provide a set of property sheets for modifying the value of the properties. Once these property values are set during design time, they are **persisted** or saved as blobs into the container's image, which will be compiled into a part of the final executable. When the program is executed by the end user, these persisted properties will be restored and the OCX will come up exactly the same way the programmer has configured them.

Optionally, the container or hosting application may also provide something called **ambient properties**. Visual Basic as a host provides a comprehensive set of ambient properties. Ambient properties are properties through which the hosting environment can indicate 'preferences' or 'hints' to all the children components that it contains. Essentially, these are suggestions that the OCX should follow if it doesn't want to appear alien to the end user. For example, one ambient property may contain the suggested font for the object to use while another one may contain the suggested background color. In addition to ambient properties, if the container is a programming tool, it may optionally provide a set of **extended properties** with each embedded OCX. To the programmer using the OCX, these extended properties look like those that are implemented by the OCX. In reality, these extended properties are actually implemented by the programming tool container (support provided during runtime by the programming tool's runtime library) and are made available to the programmer together with all the properties provided by the OCX. Some typical extended properties include the **Top**, **Left**, **Width**, and **Height** properties of an OCX in Visual Basic. Since the container implements these properties for every OCX, they save the OCX implementer a significant amount of work. Other than the above distinctions, a property can be classified in other ways: as persistent (i.e. saved with the container) or transient, which is not saved but valid only while the object is instantiated. A property can also be classified as runtime only (which means it may not be available during design time), available during both runtime and design time, or design time only.

The main difference between the simple ActiveX control that we've coded and the typical OCX is that an OCX typically manages certain visual user interface elements, and interacts with the user in conjunction with its containing application. Because of this, it may also implement many more COM interfaces. All OCX/container interactions are performed through COM interfaces. The OCX may literally own a piece of screen real estate within a form that contains the OCX. During application design time, an OCX displays in a 'What You See Is What You Get' manner showing how it would look in the final application. This allows the designer to tweak its appearance incrementally without a long recompiling and testing cycle. The ActiveX controls that we've constructed so far have no user interface elements, and implement only a minimal set of COM interfaces.

Another powerful mechanism that OCX provides, and that ActiveX controls in general can have, is event sourcing. We haven't yet covered event sourcing in our ActiveX control exploration. As mentioned earlier, event sourcing allows the OCX to trigger action in the container. For example, a method in the container (or say, a Visual Basic procedure managed by the container) can be called whenever a user clicks on the visual representation of the OCX. This sort of 'reverse calling' action is implemented through a **connection points** mechanism. We'll cover connection points in more detail later on in the advanced ATL chapter (Chapter 6). For now, we can view it as a 'reversed `IDispatch`' mechanism from which the OCX can give the container a 'wish list' of COM interfaces that it (the OCX) wants the container to provide.

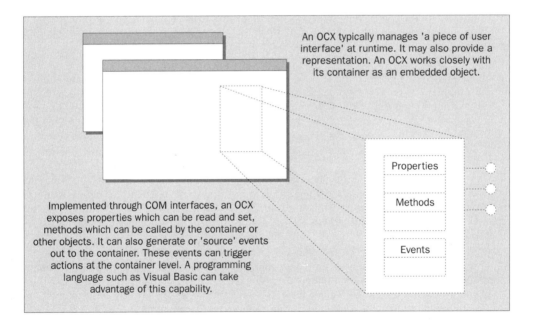

An OCX typically manages 'a piece of user interface' at runtime. It may also provide a representation. An OCX works closely with its container as an embedded object.

Implemented through COM interfaces, an OCX exposes properties which can be read and set, methods which can be called by the container or other objects. It can also generate or 'source' events out to the container. These events can trigger actions at the container level. A programming language such as Visual Basic can take advantage of this capability.

Properties

Methods

Events

The Problem with OCXs

There is only one problem with building OCXs. They are notoriously hard to build! In order to build a 'proper' OCX that can be hosted in a variety of containers, one has to create code which implements a very large set of complex COM interfaces. This assumes that the builder is be completely familiar with COM, the OCX interface specifications, as well as the style of COM support provided by the development tool or code library. Let's look at a very frequently used OCX, the 'command button with 3D look' from Visual Basic 4.0, and see what COM interfaces it implements. Here's what you'll see when you look at it through `Oleview.exe`:

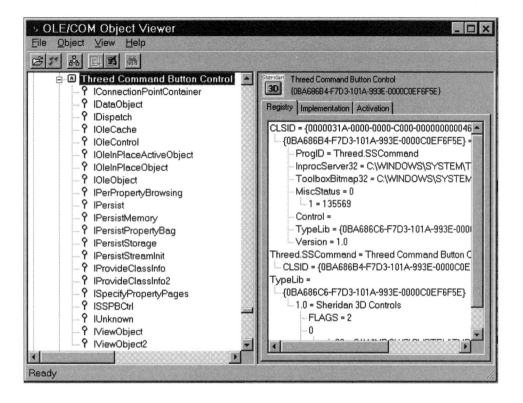

OCX Interfaces and Methods

Besides the **IUnknown**, **IDispatch**, and a custom **ISSPBCtrl** interface, the following is a list of all the other complex, yet essential interfaces (and their associated methods) implemented by this typical OCX. Remember that all this particular OCX does for a hosting application is to provide a button that the end user can click on (i.e. identical to a button control in Win32 programming). Contrast this almost 'trivial' function with the amount of work required above and beyond a simple **CreateWindow()** call, and you'll see what we mean by hard work required. We're first going to examine one by one the list of interfaces that this 'simple' button control implements. We'll provide a capsulated description for each of them. Later, we'll categorize the interfaces and try to make some sense out of them as we decode the OLE control specifications. During the description of interfaces, we'll try to give a flavor of the richness *and complexity* of Microsoft specified, required interfaces.

IConnectionPointContainer

The **IConnectionPointContainer** interface is the key to implementation of OCX event sourcing.

We'll take a raw yet extensive look at connection points implementation in Chapter 6 when we add connection points to our ATL based ActiveX controls.

Method	Description
EnumConnectionPoints()	By providing an **IConnectionPointContainer** interface, the OCX is indicating to the container that it will source events. When the **EnumConnectionPoints()** method is called, it must return an interface to an enumerator object which can be used to enumerate all the outgoing interfaces expected by the OCX.
FindConnectionPoint()	A method used in obtaining the **IConnectionPoint** interface managing a particular outgoing interface (event methods set) given an IID (interface ID) of the outgoing interface. You can also use it to determine if an OCX supports a given event.

IEnumConnectionPoints

This is a hidden interface that must be implemented by the OCX. It's an enumeration interface. An enumeration interface's sole purpose is to allow the caller to iterate through a set of items. We'll see many more examples of enumeration interfaces later, and will implement our own in Chapter 6. All enumeration interfaces have the same set of methods. In this case, we're enumerating through the set of connection points expected by an OCX.

Methods	Description
Next()	Each connection points (multiple connection points) is represented by an array of **IConnectionPoint** interfaces. The **Next()** method is used in traversing through the enumeration.
Skip()	Skips the next n items in an enumeration.
Reset()	Resets the enumeration traversal pointer back to the beginning.
Clone()	Creates another enumeration interface with the same state as the current one. Used in saving the state of an enumeration in case it will be required in the future.

IConnectionPoint

This is another interface which isn't visible from Object Viewer, but which must be implemented by the OCX. Each **IConnectionPoint** interface belongs to a connection point sub-object that manages a single outgoing interface (or event methods set).

Methods	Description
GetConnectionInterface()	**GetConnectionInterface()** will simply return the IID of the interface which is managed by the connection point.
GetConnectionPointContainer()	This method is called to obtain the associated **IConnectionPointContainer** (i.e. the **ConnectionPointContainer** object).
Advise()	The caller uses this method to pass in its own **IUnknown**, and gets back a management 'cookie' (an opaque object handle). Once the OCX receives the calling object's (usually the container) **IUnknown**, it can use it to get the outgoing inter face and the methods to call.

Methods	Description
Unadvise()	The caller calls this method to break the connection with the OCX. The management 'cookie' received during the **Advise()** call should be used in this call. Once the connection is broken, the host application can't sink any further events through this link.
EnumConnections()	Used to obtain information on all the connections currently active with this connection point sub-object.

IEnumConnections

Another enumeration interface, with the distinguishing **Next()**, **Skip()**, **Reset()**, and **Clone()** methods. This enumeration contains pointers to **CONNECTDATA** structures that give details of all the connections currently active with the associated connection point.

IDataObject

The **IDataObject** is implemented by any OLE object that needs to implement **uniform data transfer**. This allows data to be transferred between objects, from object to clipboard, from object to storage, from object to memory, etc. in a uniform way independent of the format of the data, or the data transfer medium.

Methods	Description
GetData()	The **GetData()** method is the primary data transfer method called by a consumer of data. It specifies the format that the object converts the data to, as well as the medium through which to transfer the data.
GetDataHere()	This method is almost the same as the **GetData()** method, but the caller is responsible for allocating and freeing the storage medium.
QueryGetData()	In calling this method, the caller specifies a specific format for the data to be rendered in. The data object will indicate whether it is capable of rendering the data in the specified format.
GetCanonicalFormatEtc()	This is a method used in 'normalizing' format specifications. Since the data object can't render the data in all the formats available in the entire universe, it tries its best to map each rendering request to something that it can render. You can use this method to determine if two format specifications are equivalent as far as the data object is concerned.
SetData()	Similar to **GetData()**, but transfers data in the other direction (into the data object). It also determines the ownership of the storage medium.
EnumFormatEtc()	This method returns an **IEnumFORMATETC** interface to an enumeration object. Used to discover all rendering formats supported by the data object.

Table Continued on Following Page

Methods	Description
`DAdvise()`	For callers who are interested in being notified when the data (or certain aspect of the data) managed by the data object changes. The caller passes in specification of the data, aspect, form of notification, and an **IAdviseSink** pointer. The caller gets back a management 'cookie' corresponding to the Advise link created.
`DUnadvise()`	The caller uses this method to break an Advise link by passing in the management 'cookie' corresponding to the link to be detached.
`EnumDAdvise()`	Returns an interface to an enumeration object's **IEnumSTATDATA** which can be used to discover all the Advise links currently active.

IEnumSTATDATA

An enumeration interface used in enumerating all the currently active Advise links. Again with the distinguishing **Next()**, **Skip()**, **Reset()**, and **Clone()** methods.

IEnumFORMATETC

An enumeration interface used in enumerating all the formats which the data object can render the managed data in. The **Next()**, **Skip()**, **Reset()**, and **Clone()** methods are here too.

IOleCache

This interface is provided to the caller (container) for keeping the appearance of the OCX (typically through a metafile) even when the OCX itself isn't activated. Most OCXs insist that they be activated as soon as they are visible. However, in the case of an optimized container application hosting many controls, displaying just the cached representation of the control (as of the last time it was activated) is definitely much more efficient than activating them all.

Methods	Description
`Cache()`	For the **Cache()** method, the caller passes in a format description, and the method returns a pointer to the connection which is used as a handle to the connection.
`EnumCache()`	Returns an interface to an enumeration object's **IEnumSTATDATA** which can be used to find all the cache connections active.
`InitCache()`	The caller passes in an **IDataObject** interface corresponding to a data object. The method will fill the cache with data from the data object.
`SetData()`	The caller passes in a render format and a storage medium, the method will initialize the cache with data from the storage in the format specified.
`Uncache()`	Breaks a cache connection, specified by the connection pointer.

IOleControl

The **IOleControl** interface is used in communications between container and OCXs to communicate keyboard accelerators or 'shortcuts', ambient property changes, and to throttle the flow of events.

Methods	Description
`GetControlInfo()`	The **`GetControlInfo()`** method is called by the container to obtain accelerator information from the OCX.
`OnMnemonic()`	When a corresponding mnemonic key sequence is detected by the container, this call is made to the OCX with the key information.
`OnAmbientPropertyChange()`	This method is called by the container when an ambient property of the container has changed. The **`IDispatch`** dispid of the property is passed in.
`FreezeEvents()`	A call to this method with a **`TRUE`** value indicates that the container will ignore any events sent by the OCX until it is called again with **`FALSE`**.

IOleInPlaceActiveObject

The **`IOleInPlaceActiveObject`** interface provides the 'in-place active' capability for embedded objects. An MDI model of application construction is assumed. Three parties are involved: the object itself, the document window in which the object is embedded, and the outermost frame window of the application.

Methods	Description
`EnableModeless()`	The **`EnableModeless()`** method is used to disable an object's modeless dialog display while the container displays modal dialog boxes.
`OnDocWindowActivate()`	This method is called when the document window is activated or deactivated.
`OnFrameWindowActivate()`	This method is called when the application frame window is activated or deactivated.
`ResizeBorder()`	Notifies an object that it needs to adjust its border space. This may be due to the resizing of the document or frame window. The object should resize its border and adornments (i.e. hash lines, drag handles, etc.).
`TranslateAccelerator()`	Pass down the menu acceleration keys to the in-proc object for translation.

IOleInPlaceObject

The **`IOleInPlaceObject`** interface is the workhorse interface for any object which needs to be in-place active (i.e. all visual OCXs). Typically, the caller to these methods is the immediate container of the OCX. You can find whatever methods you require that aren't found here in the **`IOleObject`** monster-interface described later.

Methods	Description
`InPlaceDeactivate()`	The `InPlaceDeactivate()` method is called by the container when the object is deactivated, and its undo state should be cleared.
`ReactivateAndUndo()`	Called to reactivate a deactivated object and to restore its state to a previously saved undo state.
`SetObjectRects()`	Notifies the object about how much of its rectangle is visible.
`UIDeactivate()`	This method is called when a `UIActive` object is being deselected. `UIActive` means that the object currently has the focus and is handling the user interactions directly.

IOleObject

`IOleObject` is a monster-interface, carrying with it all the methods supporting an embedded (or linked) object that aren't specified anywhere else. Older 'OLE object' specifications require the implementation of `IOleObject`, `IDataObject`, and `IPersistStorage` as the minimal set of interfaces to qualify a blob as an object. Some of the terminology used in describing these interfaces are a legacy from the OLE/ Document Centric computing era (prior to distributed computing). Once you've gone through this interface, you'll appreciate the *big* step Microsoft has taken by requiring an ActiveX Control to have only one required trivial interface: `IUnknown`!

Methods	Description
`Advise()`	The `Advise()` method establishes an Advise link between the calling object and the compound document object (OLE object). The caller gets back a pointer to a management token. It will be notified should the OLE object be renamed, saved, or closed.
`Close()`	This method is called when an executing object should be closed or should revert back to the loaded but not running state.
`DoVerb()`	Called when a specific **verb** is to be performed by the object due to client request. This is typically called during a complex handshake between the container and the embedded object when the user interacts with the user interface.
`EnumAdvise()`	Called to obtain an enumeration object enumerating all the Advise connections active. Used by the container to release connections prior to `Close()`.
`EnumVerbs()`	Used to obtain an enumeration object enumerating all the verbs supported by the object; it can also provide the necessary content to display a drop-down menu with the supported verbs.
`GetClientSite()`	Called to obtain the client site associated with the embedded object. This client site object is supplied by the container and manages the area of the container occupied by the embedded object's UI.
`GetClipboardData()`	Called to get an `IDataObject` representing the object itself. The caller can create a new object with the same data as the original object using the `IDataObject` interface. This can be used in drag and drop implementations across applications via the clipboard.

Methods	Description
GetExtent()	A container calls this as part of the size negotiation during initialization. The object being called must be running for this call to work. The returned rectangle should be the OCX application's preferred size.
GetMiscStatus()	Returns the miscellaneous status bitmap used to indicate particular characteristics of the OCX; this is the same as the **MiscStatus** key value in the registry for the control.
GetMoniker()	Called in object linking scenarios, this should return a Moniker (like a system name) for the object.
GetUserClassID()	Returns the CLSID of the object.
GetUserType()	Returns the OLE string representation 'AppID' of the object.
InitFromData()	This method is called when initializing a newly created data object from a data object, typically from the container or clipboard.
IsUpToDate()	Called to determine if all linked objects are up-to-date, or if the **Update()** method needs to be called.
SetClientSite()	Called by the container during initialization handshaking to supply the object with a client site that manages the screen real estate on the container display surface belonging to the OCX. Most OCXs will insist that this is called by the container even before the common **IPersist** methods are called in order to supply it (the OCX) with container ambient information. Unfortunately many containers don't follow this convention.
SetColorScheme()	Sends a recommended palette for the object to use during graphics drawing operations.
SetExtent()	Called by the container to 'dictate' a size for the embedded object to fit into. Can only be called for a running, active object.
SetHostNames()	Provides the application name and compound document name for the embedded object.
SetMoniker()	Called to provide the object with either a full moniker or the container's moniker, used in object linking situations.
Unadvise()	Breaks an active advisory link. The input parameter is the management token.
Update()	Used only for linked objects to make any linked representation up-to-date.

IPerPropertyBrowsing

The **IPerPropertyBrowsing** interface allows the access and manipulation of an object's properties through property sheets implemented by the object itself.

Methods	Description
GetDisplayString()	GetDisplayString() gives a textual descriptive name of a property given a dispid.
GetPredefinedStrings()	For a specific dispid, GetPredefinedStrings() provides a selection of textual options for the value of the dispid. Each textual option also has an associated **DWORD** token.
GetPredefinedValue()	Retrieves the **VARIANT** value associated with the **DWORD** token corresponding to a predefined string returned by the GetPredefinedStrings() method.
MapPropertyToPage()	This method returns the CLSID of the property sheet associated with a specified dispid.

IPersist

The **IPersist** interface is the base interface for **IPersistMemory**, **IPersistStorage**, and **IPersistStreamInit**.

The only method, **GetClassID()**, returns the CLSID of the object which can be persisted.

IPersistMemory

The **IPersistMemory** interface is a new optimization interface implemented by later OCXs. It allows an object to persist itself to and from fixed-size memory blocks. It also allows for initialization the first time the object is restored from the memory block. The behavior of this interface is identical to that of the **IPersistStreamInit** interface.

Methods	Description
GetSizeMax()	The GetSizeMax() method returns the size of the memory block required to persist the object.
InitNew()	This method should be used to initialize the object to a default state. If this method is called, the Load() method should not be called. For OCX, this is typically called the first time an OCX instance is created.
IsDirty()	This method should indicate whether the persistent properties of the object have changed and need to be written to the persist medium.
Load()	Initializes the object from previously persisted properties. For OCXs, this can be called many times as the form containers come and go.
Save()	Saves the object's persistent properties into the memory block supplied.

IPersistStorage

The **IPersistStorage** interface allows an object to be persisted into a compound document, within its own storage.

Methods	Description
`HandsOffStorage()`	The `HandsOffStorage()` method is called when the container wants the object to release all storage.
`InitNew()`	This method passes in an `IStorage` for a newly created object.
`IsDirty()`	Same as `IPersistMemory`.
`Load()`	Loads the persistent properties/data from a specified storage.
`Save()`	Saves the persistent properties/data to a specified storage.
`SaveCompleted()`	This method is used to notify the object that the `IStorage` may be used again if necessary after a `HandsOffStorage()` method call.

IPersistStreamInit

The interface behaves identically to the `IPersistMemory` interface covered earlier, except the object can persist to or from a stream storage provided by the host rather than memory.

Methods	Description
`GetSizeMax()`	Same as `IPersistMemory`.
`InitNew()`	Same as `IPersistMemory`.
`IsDirty()`	Same as `IPersistMemory`.
`Load()`	Same as `IPersistMemory`, except that it works with a generalized `IStream`.
`Save()`	Same as `IPersistMemory`, except that it works with a generalized `IStream`.

IPersistPropertyBag

We'll describe this interface later in the OC96 coverage.

IProvideClassInfo

This interface is used in obtaining type library information.

The solitary `GetClassInfo()` method returns an `ITypeInfo` interface for the caller to access the type library information for the object.

IProvideClassInfo2

This interface is based on `IProvideClassInfo` and extends it to cover events.

The caller to `GetGUID()` can specify the type of GUID to obtain. Currently, it's used to obtain the default event set interface ID from the OCX.

ISpecifyPropertyPages

The `ISpecifyPropertyPages` interface is used to indicate that property pages are supported by the OCX.

When called, the `GetPages()` method returns an array of CLSIDs for the property pages of the OCX.

IViewObject

The **IViewObject** interface is used to draw the object's presentation into a specified device context.

Methods	Description
Draw()	The **Draw()** method is called to draw a specified area of the object's presentation into a specified context.
Freeze()	This method is called to freeze certain aspects of an object's presentation through repeated **Draw()** methods, until **Unfreeze()** is called. The method is used typically during printing.
GetAdvise()	This method returns the most recently established advisory connection. Only one such connection is supported.
GetColorSet()	This method returns the logical palette used by the object in the **Draw()** method.
SetAdvise()	Used to connect an advise sink from the caller to the object. If the object's view is changed, this advise sink will be notified.
Unfreeze()	The method cancels the effect of the **Freeze()** method call.

IViewObject2

This interface has all the same methods as **IViewObject** but extends it with an additional **GetExtent()** method.

The **GetExtent()** method returns the size of the view object when drawn on the specified device. It offers similar functionality to the **IOleObject::GetExtent()** call except that it can be called on a loaded but not running object. In this case, the extent returned is the extent of the cached representation (i.e. metafile representation for an OCX).

The above list doesn't even include the property sheets object and associated interfaces that many OCXs need to implement. For even a trivially functioning button control, the amount of work and coding required is staggering. The message is quite clear: if one needs to implement all the above interfaces and methods for each and every OCX from scratch, OCXs wouldn't be too common!

Developing OCXs

Even though we can apply the techniques that we've covered in the COM and ATL chapters to construct all the required COM interfaces, significant time and effort would still need to be spent on implementing and testing all the interfaces and methods. To simply walk you through the code necessary to implement the above button control alone would require a book of similar size to this one. Most of this monumental work needs to be done just so that the OCX can coexist with the hosting application and run time. We haven't even started to code the actual processing logic for the OCX yet.

A tool to make the construction of OCXs easier is an obvious necessity.

A Control Development Kit (CDK), requiring OCXs to be coded in C or C++ only, not Basic, was included with the earlier Visual C++ and Visual Basic products to help developers who may want to build controls. However, building controls with this CDK requires a very steep learning curve, and the CDK isn't immediately compatible with any C++ development framework or libraries that the logic and processing part of the OCX is bound to require. To make building controls somewhat easier, the Microsoft Foundation Class (MFC) library team was given the mandate to extend their well-designed (and still small, at the time) library. The most important motivation was the significant existing base of MFC users, including users with non-Microsoft compilers such as Symantec or Watcom; and the fact that these base developers were the most likely ones to build OCXs for the general market. In time, the MFC team has done an excellent job of adapting the MFC to accommodate the construction of OCXs. For a brief moment in the history of development tools, MFC 4.0 was the only means to create OCXs relatively easily, without having to implement and maintain a large body of code.

If the world stood still forever, developers would still be happily using MFC 4.0 to program OCXs. Unfortunately (or fortunately), even before the cement had dried on the MFC 4.0 libraries, the Internet and intranet craze had taken over the world. As the world's leading software company, Microsoft really didn't have any choice but to embrace it. OCX, as it was originally conceived, is really ill-suited for general Internet consumption. But mapping Microsoft's arsenal of technologies to the Internet/intranet, you can see that OCXs map naturally to providing extended client-side custom functionality for typical 'web pages'. In combating other rival vendors (i.e. Java-based technologies from SUN), the new ActiveX controls can be downloaded with the web pages if necessary and are executed on the machine running the web browser. However, since the bandwidth available to the majority of the Internet users is limited to analog modems (typically 28.8Kbps), the amount of code downloaded is generally directly proportional to the time that the user has to wait and to the user's patience. Sadly, using MFC to create OCXs leads to the creation of controls that are relatively 'fat' in code. Furthermore, OCXs will only run happily on Intel platforms running Windows. Fat and platform-specific controls are unpopular in the Internet world.

In response to this change, and in order not to further upset the component software vendors who had just barely finished training their staff on MFC 4.0-based OCX construction, Microsoft opted for a subclassification hierarchy which will accommodate the current-day OCXs as we know them, and allow them to coexist in a world soon to be populated by newer, meaner, leaner, and more generic controls. It does this through the OLE Control 96 (or OC96) specification, and a subsequent addendum known as the 'ActiveX Control/COM Objects for the Internet'. In OC96, optimization of control size and performance is the prevailing theme. New interfaces were introduced that replaced older, bulkier interfaces and performed various optimizations. The dependency on a Windows handle, which was the very last remaining link between OCXs and the underlying Windows operating system, is now made optional. The new OC96 controls will not only be smaller and run faster, but may also be adapted to operate on a variety of operating systems or hardware platforms. Since the OC96 specification is fairly new (fourth quarter 1995 preview), there are relatively few ActiveX controls which are compliant. Microsoft started to implement support for certain OC96 features in its MFC library beginning with Visual C++ Version 4.2, which became available in late 1996.

In order to qualify as an ActiveX control in OC96, a COM object is required only to implement the **IUnknown** interface. As we've learnt in previous chapters, this makes any COM object technically an ActiveX control compliant with OC96.

The following table summarizes the OC96 specification using terms that are more familiar to us. It also highlights the items of special relevance to typical intranet application development.

Item in OC96 Specification	Mechanism to Achieve	Explanation
Handling for mouse interaction, drag and drop for inactive objects.	New **IpointerInactive** interface.	Effectively decoupling the OCX behavior from the requirement for the OCX to actually have an active Window. This allows a partially loaded, but not fully running OCX, which may be rendered through only a cached metafile on the surface of the container, to process mouse messages and drag and drop. This essentially uses a nonvisual OCX in a visual way. There can be a large performance gain since it is no longer necessary to activate and negotiate painting with every OCX on a form. Since the unmarshallable **IViewObject** isn't involved, and no windows handle is involved, it opens up the possibility of DCOM enablement in the future when high speed links are available.
Optimize drawing speed during **IViewObject::Draw()** by enabling the object to retain font, brush and pen between calls.	The **pvAspect** parameter of the **IViewObject::Draw()** can point to a **DVASPECTINFO** structure specifying the optimization desired.	This optimization speeds up rendering of forms containing many objects since each object no longer needs to select and deselect the font, brush or pen into and out of the device context. The actual cleanup may be a little harder to implement, but there's a significant performance gain.
Implementation for flicker-free activation and deactivation.	New **IOleInPlaceSiteEx** provides specific clues to the validity of an embedded object's visual presentation.	Before this enhancement, an embedded object had to repaint itself every time it was activated and have the container repaint it when deactivated. This, combined with the need for an object to be activated in order to handle mouse interaction, often makes for flickering display as objects activate and deactivate on a form. With this enhancement, the container will use **IOleInPlaceSiteEx** to redraw as necessary during activation and deactivation. If a particular OCX's display is the same whether it is activated or not, this enhancement will eliminate the additional unnecessary update.

Item in OC96 Specification	Mechanism to Achieve	Explanation
Implementation for flicker-free drawing.	New **IViewObjectEx** and **IAdviseSinkEx** interfaces.	This extension of the **IViewObject** interface provides more efficient and flicker-free drawing capabilities for nonrectangular objects and objects with transparent areas. It does so by providing for a choice of drawing algorithms without dictating a policy. New here is a 'two pass' drawing scheme where objects are drawn front to back in pass #1 and back to front in pass #2. The intention is to have the object do most of its drawing during the front-to-back pass, avoiding flickering by relying on (hopefully) speedy clipping computations. The frequently used double buffering, off-screen drawing technique is still supported.
Support for windowless ActiveX objects, including in-place activation, and support for nonrectangular objects.	New **IOleInPlaceObject Windowless** and **IOleInPlaceSite Windowless** interfaces. Also **IViewObjectEx** interface to support nonrectangular hit testing.	As we've explained previously, having each OCX consuming a window and requiring each to be active within a form is a very expensive proposition. This new specification allows you to create completely windowless visual objects. The benefit is the release of resources as there's no need to have a windows handle associated with each object. It also allows for the creation of objects that are not rectangular in nature. Essentially, the normal window message queue handling is completely replaced by interaction between container and object via COM interfaces. The real bonus is to allow the eventual support of out-of-process visual controls or even network-based visual controls over very high-speed networks. Traditionally, the user interface can only run as fast as the fastest CPU available, it is intrinsically not scaleable. With windowless objects, even the user interface can scale in terms of performance when more processor resources are added.

Table Continued on Following Page

Item in OC96 Specification	Mechanism to Achieve	Explanation
Quick activation of ActiveX controls by the container.	A new **IQuickActivate** interface.	Any control supporting **IQuickActivate** can be loaded and initialized by the container in one single COM method call. This contrasts with the conventional complex handshake required for OCXs. Essentially, the **IQuickActivate** allows for a 'batching exchange' of all information (including status information and interface pointers) between container and control and doing it all in one shot prior to control initialization.
An improved and extensible model for handling **Undo** in a component based application.	New **IOleUndoUnit**, **IOleParentUndoUnit**, **IServiceProvider**, and **IOleUndoManager** interfaces.	Introduces a centralized **Undo** manager service for tracking an application-wide undo stack across all interoperating components within the application. Individual components are responsible for creating 'undo unit' objects and submitting them to the **Undo** manager. Undo units can be nested, reflecting the nested network of interoperating components with undo states. Components or objects which have changed state in a nonundoable manner can choose to clear the undo stack of the manager when it is their turn to submit an undo object. The specification of these interfaces is conceptually very close to the services provided by the new Microsoft Transaction Server (MTS). They may be extended to embrace the MTS interfaces transparently for distributed components based applications.
Provide a mechanism for the container to manipulate and present object properties according to common groupings (categories).	New **ICatInformation** and **ICatRegister** interfaces plus the definition of standard property categories. Definition of custom categories is also allowed.	With the proliferation of complex controls sporting numerous properties, categorizing and grouping of these properties for a particular control becomes important. It will make the user experience (i.e. modifying a property visually) simpler and more pleasant. Categorization for properties is based on integer values and not UUIDs.

Item in OC96 Specification	Mechanism to Achieve	Explanation
Other miscellaneous items.	**IViewObjectEx** now supports control sizing	This allows the control to give the container 'suggested size' (or adjust the container's desired size) while the user is resizing the control.
		Coordinates specified during event method calls are now in points (not himetric) for consistency.
		IPersistPropertyBag is now formally documented for persisting an object out to a text file. This interface allows an OCX to persist in or out of its properties in textual format to a storage provided by the container. The sequence of interactions is the same as other interfaces in the **IPersist*** series of interfaces.
		Several standard dispids are defined in OC96.
		A new databinding attribute has been defined for bindable properties to control the granularity of change notifications.

Variety of Controls

With the OC96 specification in full force, and the abundance of existing OCX (minimally) compliant controls with this specification out on the market, the ActiveX control landscape is more confusing than it has ever been before. The following diagram and table attempts to summarize the variety of controls you're likely to find on your system (and in the market place).

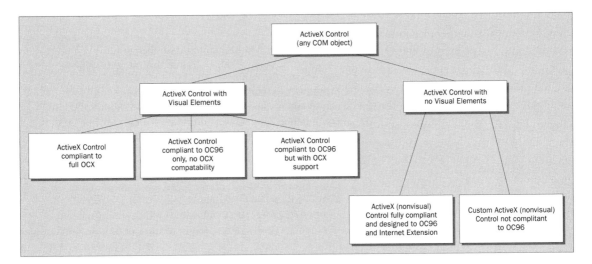

Nature of Control	Compliance with Specifications	Comments
ActiveX Control		This refers to any COM object by Microsoft's definition. Any object has to implement only **IUnknown** to be qualified as an ActiveX control.
Visual ActiveX Control		These are closer to what we typically considered to be a 'control'. They usually have a visible appearance, such as a button, list box, combo box, or a text edit. Besides managing the actual data processing or manipulation, these controls also handle their own user interface interactions.
Nonvisual ActiveX Controls		These are frequently called hidden or invisible controls. They typically don't handle any user interface interactions. Instead, they may handle data conversion, data processing, validation or business rule implementations. Without having to deal with the complex and tricky user interface handling, nonvisual ActiveX controls allow the developer to concentrate on the business problem without introducing unnecessary complexity.
Visual Control	Compliant with OCX only	Most existing OCXs fall into this category. These are typically large monolithic controls which implement all the required OCX interfaces. They are marked as a 'control' in the registry under the **HROOT\CLASSES\<CLSID>** subkeys. These OCXs work well with all currently available containers including Visual Basic 4.0, Visual C++ 5.0, Internet Explorer 3.0, and FrontPage 97.
	Compliant with OC96 only	These are futuristic controls, and are generally not available to the public except for demonstration purposes. This isn't due to complexity in implementation, but mainly due to lack of commercial containers which support the full OC96 specifications. Even the OC96 specification itself is still going through some changes as Microsoft consolidates its Internet/intranet strategy.
	Compliant with OC96 and OCX	For control developers or vendors that are committed to supporting the new OC96 standard, their control implementation generally falls into this category. These controls are typically registered under both **\HKEY\CLASSES\ROOT** as well as listed under the component categories key. New developments are embodied in the OC96 standard for the control, but OCX compatibility is maintained in order continue to sell the control today.
Nonvisual Control	Fully Compliant with OC96	Although they are nonvisual, these controls assist the container in handling and rendering the control to the end user. It does so by providing an icon and one or more component categories to allow the container to determine whether the control is one that it would like or is allowed to host.

Nature of Control	Compliance with Specifications	Comments
	Noncompliant with OC96	Essentially these controls don't exist. In order for them to be totally noncompliant with OC96, the controls will need to have no **IUnknown**, which disqualifies them from being COM objects altogether.
		A bonus is that OC96 strongly recommends that any new containers should be prepared to accommodate any ActiveX controls. Although the control may only implement one Microsoft specified interface—**IUnknown**. New OC96 compliant containers will be able to host these controls with absolutely no cooperation from the control itself. These controls can be custom controls that are very simple to create.

Creating fully OC96 complaint controls today is like dressing up and having no parties to go to. There are no robust containers that can host 'OC96 only' controls, not even from Microsoft. The situation should be much better when Internet Explorer 4.0 arrives, and a new generation of Web authoring tools beyond FrontPage 97 becomes available. The future evolution of Office 97 is also expected to fully support OC96 compliant controls. These new products will be fully OC96 compliant hosts, leading the way to enable the new generation of high performance, simpler-to-create controls.

Visual Controls of Today and Nonvisual Controls of Tomorrow

Having worked with VBXs and OCXs, it may be difficult to imagine why anyone would want to create controls that are nonvisual. With visual programming tools, it is so tempting to tightly couple the data, the application logic, and the user interface together in a monolithic component which handles all aspects related to a (or a set of) data object(s). This is certainly consistent with classical object-oriented encapsulation (i.e. an object should know how to show itself or modify itself and manage its own data). It turns out, through our evolutionary learning during the past decade of client-server and ad hoc object computing, that this 'pure' form of encapsulation isn't easily scaleable. That is, as the number of users or the size of the data collection increase, the design will break down at some point.

The distributed model of computing is based on interoperating components and takes the best from object-oriented and client-server computing, then applies this in a pragmatic way to solve the large and complex system design problems. Much of this activity is spurred on by the popularity of the Internet, which is causing the industry to redefine the term 'scaling to a very large user base or data collection size'. Under this model, the business rules are separated from the user interface and from the data management tasks. Each task is managed and encapsulated in a component (or server), and the interoperating network of components together forms an 'n-tier' client-server network that solves the problem. Careful design of solutions using this architecture will ensure scalability to very, very large user bases or data collection sizes.

In fact, we'll be designing and implementing many nonvisual ActiveX controls in our intranet implementation. They are invaluable for encapsulating business rules in software components that can be reused in a location- and even context-independent manner.

Visual C++ 5.0 and Microsoft Foundation Class 4.21

Visual C++ 5.0 is by far the most COM-friendly C++ compiler ever created. Besides the amazing native support for COM programming that we covered in Chapter 4, the ability to quickly create highly functional ActiveX controls through a reasonable amount of work makes it one of the premier tools for ActiveX control creation. Although there are other rapid development environments for creating visual ActiveX controls, such as the Visual Basic Control Creation Edition (VBCCE), Visual C++ 5.0 remains the only tool that allows the developer to have direct low-level control over all aspects of COM/ActiveX control programming. Visual C++ 5.0 also enables us to use our experience with the Visual C++ development environment and our familiarity with the Microsoft Foundation Classes library. In Visual C++ 5.0, support for ActiveX controls allows us to create useful controls that will work in today's most popular container applications without having to code all the required interfaces from scratch.

COM Interfaces That We Don't Have to Implement

MFC 4.21 makes life easy for the ActiveX control developer by providing implementations for all the required interfaces through a set of foundation classes. The developer can focus on the logic of making the ActiveX control work, and mostly avoid dealing with COM-oriented issues. As in most programming tasks, though, life isn't all that simple. A high level understanding of how and what MFC actually does is definitely worthwhile in cases where we need to do more than the standard class library provides for.

In the following section, we'll examine the MFC **COleControl** class that provides ActiveX control support and implementation. Our discussion will stay on the high level, but we'll go into enough details so that the places where customization may be performed are evident. Our approach will be COM interface-centric; we'll cover the ActiveX control interfaces (actually older OCX interfaces) one by one and point out the way that **COleControl** implements and handles them. Along the way, we'll learn about OCXs in general, and how to use MFC to implement them in specific situations.

Interfaces Supporting Object Embedding

An OCX with a visual user interface is also an embeddable OLE in-proc server which can be in-place activated. What this means is that it will have to implement a whole slew of interfaces defined for object embedding within the OLE compound document architecture. Recall our examination of the Threed button control and its (many) interfaces earlier. Let's take a look at why we needed some of these interfaces.

The hosting application for an OCX, for the purpose of discussion, will be called the container. A container can have more than one OCX embedded. The OCX, once embedded into the container's display area, can obtain the ownership of a portion of the display area. Communications between the container and the contained control are carried out solely using COM based interfaces. The container must provide one **client site** object for each embedded OCX. These sites are analogous to 'chip sockets' in the hardware world; they provide the location on the container's display and many COM based connections for the 'OCX chip' to communicate with the container application.

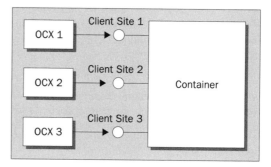

Communications between the control and the container can be broken up into two general categories:

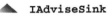 Services provided by the container to the embedded object.

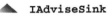 Control interfaces provided by the embedded object to the container.

Category I: Services Provided by Container to Embedded Object

In the first category, the container provides two service interfaces for this purpose:

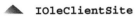 IOleClientSite

 IAdviseSink

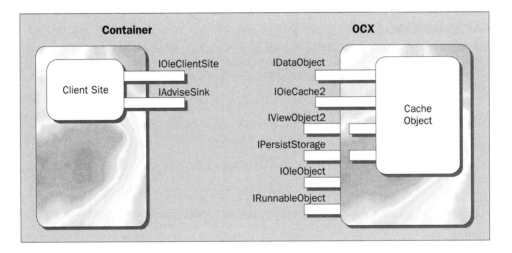

Again, one set of these interfaces is provided for each embedded OCX. They provide services to the embedded object, allowing the object to get information from, make requests or supply notification information to the container. Most of the COM interfaces defined below aren't defined specifically for OCX operations, but also for other COM object interactions. As a result, you'll frequently find that some methods of an interface may not be used by an OCX. We'll note this whenever a method is typically not used by OCXs. Taking a quick look at these interfaces, we see the following methods:

The IOleClientSite Interface

IOleClientSite Methods	Meaning
SaveObject()	Requests that the object be saved in the container's persistent storage synchronously——typically used in handling of the **Close** verb for an embedded application. Usually not applicable to OCXs.
GetMoniker()	Used in object linking to get a moniker (an object that acts as a locator for another object) corresponding to the container or of the object relative to the container. Usually not applicable to OCXs.

Table Continued on Following Page

IOleClientSite Methods	Meaning
GetContainer()	Can be called by the OCX to get a pointer to the IOleContainer interface of the container object.
ShowObject()	Request from the control that it be shown in the container.
OnShowWindow()	Notifies the container that the object is changing from visible to invisible or vice versa when the object opens a separate window to display itself. This will allow the hosting container to display a hatched area at where the object is embedded.
RequestNewObjectLayout()	Lets the container know that the object wants more or less room on the container's display.

COleControl Handling

MFC's **COleControl** class automatically takes care of all these **IOleClientSite** interface methods provided by the container. As a user of the **COleControl** class, however, you can get the pointer to the container's **IOleClientSite** directly using the **COleControl::GetClientSite()** member function, should you ever need raw access to the underlying methods.

The IAdviseSink Interface

IAdviseSink Methods	Meaning
OnDataChange()	Notifies that the name has changed. Used by data objects in uniform data transfer, typically not used by an OCX.
OnViewChange()	Lets the container know that the view has changed.
OnRename()	Notifies that the name of the object has changed. Used for linked objects, typically not by OCXs.
OnSave()	Lets the container know that the object has been saved to disk. Typically not used by OCXs.
OnClose()	Lets the container know that the object has been closed. Typically not used by OCXs.

COleControl Handling

IAdviseSink is an 'early day' version of connection points, which allows an object to send notifications to the container asynchronously whenever the object wants to. As such, it's used under various circumstances in OLE and not all the methods apply to OCXs.

The **COleControl** class again shields all of the **IAdviseSink** action from the user. However, the control redraw action is a direct consequence of the usage of the **IAdviseSink** interface. In this case, the **COleControl** detects that the display needs to be changed and invokes **IAdviseSink::OnViewChange()** on the container. Later, at a time convenient to the container, the container will invoke the control's **IViewObject::Draw()** method. The **COleControl** class will in turn call the user-implemented **COleControl::OnDraw()** or **COleControl::OnDrawMetafile()** members to actually update the control's client area. See the interaction diagram below for an illustration of this action.

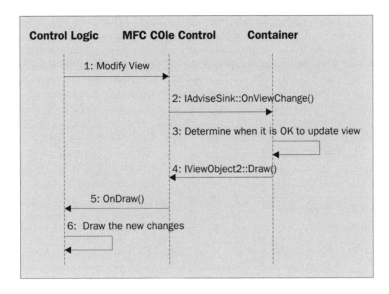

Category II: Control interfaces provided by the embedded object to the container

In this second category, the interfaces are implemented by the OCX, and used by the container. Several of the interfaces involved in object embedding are typically implemented using a default cache object provided by runtime support libraries. This means that the OCX can either use containment or delegation to implement these interfaces through the default cache object. The object can be created using the `CreateDataCache()` Win32 helper function. The interfaces implemented by the default cache object include:

- `IDataObject`
- `IPersistStorage`
- `IViewObject2`
- `IOleCache2`

What do these interfaces do and why does the container require them? In short, these interfaces provide the container with a way of displaying the control without activating it. Before we go any further, let's take a quick look at the different control states:

- Passive (on disk)
- Loaded but not activated
- In-place activated (has window, usually)
- UI activated (has focus)

An OCX can be changed between UI activated and in-place activated as the focus is shifted to and from the control by the container. In general, for efficiency purposes, it is desirable to deactivate controls as soon as possible when they're not being used.

Containers, with the potential of having many controls embedded in them, usually prefer not to do the work of bringing each control to the in-place active state unless it's necessary. That is, if the end user isn't going to be interacting with a particular control, why spend the processing time needed to create and activate the window for it? The cache object provides the container with a mechanism for saving an image (usually a metafile representation) of the control as it was last activated. The next time the control is loaded, this saved image can be retrieved and drawn into the container's display area without fully activating the control. The container will only need to activate the control when the user actually starts interacting with it (e.g. by clicking on it).

The Interfaces of the Cache Object

The following describes at a high level the purpose of each interface used in this context:

Interfaces supplied by Cache Object	Meaning
IDataObject	Used by the container to tell the object to render its representation in a specific format to a specific storage medium, or to obtain its representation from a specific medium in a specific format.
IPersistStorage	Allows the container to tell the object to 'persist in' or 'persist out' the cached images to a storage supplied by the container.
IViewObject2	Allows the container to tell the object to render its representation to a specific device. Can also be used by a container to get the set of colors used in rendering the object, to cause the object to freeze further updates to the view or to request the size of the object. This is also the interface used in passing a pointer to the container's **IAdviseSink** interface to the object.
IOleCache2	Allows the container to control caching of the object's view or data. With OCXs, this interface turns view caching on and off.

COleControl Handling

Again, the **COleControl** class creates the required cache object and implements all of the above interfaces. It also customizes the **IViewObject2** interface implementation so that it can decode the container's request and dispatch to the appropriate member functions. Specifically, the following member functions are called when **IViewObject2** methods are invoked:

The IViewObject2 Interface

IViewObject2 Method Called	COleControl Member Function Invoked
Draw()	Either **OnDraw()** or **OnDrawMetafile()** depending on the device or medium specified.
GetExtent()	OnGetViewExtent()
GetColorSet()	OnGetColorSet()

COleControl Handling

Note that the **GetExtent()** method also exists in the **IOleObject** interface; some containers may use this method instead. **COleControl** takes care of the detail for us, resulting in a **OnGetViewExtent()** call.

A rather large, yet mandatory interface implemented by an OCX is the **IOleObject** interface. We have looked at the methods of this interface earlier in this chapter.

The IOleObject Interface to COleControl Mapping

The MFC **COleControl** class implements this interface and maps certain customizable aspects to member functions. The following is a tabulation of this mapping; methods which aren't mapped are handled internally by **COleControl**:

IOleObject Method Called	COleControl Member Function Invoked
DoVerb()	OnDoVerb() and/or OnEdit()
EnumVerbs()	OnEnumVerbs()
GetClientSite()	GetClientSite()
GetUserClassID()	GetClassID()
SetClientSite()	OnSetClientSite()
SetExtent()	OnSetExtent()

The **IRunnableObject** interface is another required OCX interface that is used to control the transition of state from loaded to running and to manage the object's running state. It provides methods for getting the CLSID of the running object (which may be different from the originally requested CLSID), to lock a running object, or to deal with local server extensions. This interface is implemented and handled behind the scenes by the **COleControl** class.

Interfaces Supporting In-Place Activation User Interface

Besides being embedded in its container, an OCX can be in-place activated. This requires the implementation of two other interfaces:

  IOleInPlaceActiveObject

▲ IOleInPlaceObject

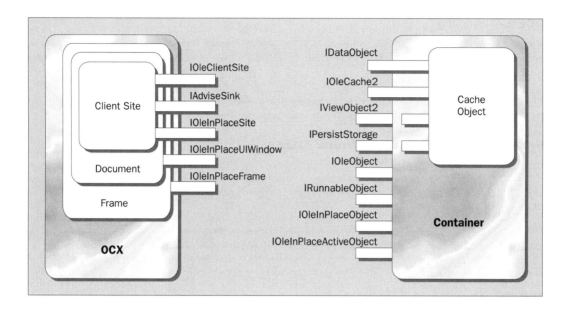

The methods of the **IOleInPlaceActiveObject** interface, derived from **IOleWindow**, have been covered previously in this chapter. The main function of this interface is for the container to notify the OCX when the frame and various document windows of the container are activated, to let the activated OCX process menu accelerator keys, or let the object know if it needs to resize itself. The **COleControl** class implements the details and maps two of the methods into corresponding member functions:

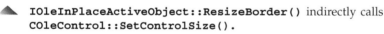

    ▲ **IOleInPlaceActiveObject::GetWindow()** maps to **CWnd::GetSafeHwnd().**

    ▲ **IOleInPlaceActiveObject::ResizeBorder()** indirectly calls
       COleControl::SetControlSize().

The **IOleInPlaceObject** interface, also derived from **IOleWindow**, allows the container to control the activation and deactivation of the OCX. It also has methods controlling how much of the OCX should be visible when activated. We covered this interface on page 13. Note that an OCX can be UI-deactivated, and plain deactivated. The difference is that transition between UI-deactivation and UI-activation should be inexpensive; nothing needs to be cleaned up by the control. Deactivation, however, should be handled with a complete cleanup by the OCX. The **COleControl** class implements the state management for activation and deactivation and maps the **IOleInPlaceObject::SetObjectRects()** to **COleControl::OnSetObjectRects().**

Though the **COleControl** class handles much of the in-place activation and UI-activation details, it does provide several hooks into the process. The following member functions are triggered during activation of an OCX:

COleControl Member	Meaning
OnGetInPlaceMenu()	Provides the container with an in-place menu for merging of menu items. This allows the menu to change depending on which control is UI-active. This is seldom used for OCXs.
OnHideToolBars()	Asks the control to hide its toolbars. Again, seldom used by OCXs.
OnShowToolBars()	Ask the control to show its toolbars. Seldom used by OCXs.

Interfaces Supporting Control-Specific Functionality

There are a set of interfaces required for OCX implementation that are above and beyond those for simple OLE embedded in-place active servers. One such interface is **IOleControl**, whose methods we've covered earlier. **IOleControl** is called by the container to notify the OCX of ambient property changes, get control information, handle mnemonics, or tell the control to stop sending events for a while. Since all of the methods are specific to OCXs, the **COleControl** class maps all of the methods from **IOleControl** into overridable functions:

IOleControl Method	COleControl Equivalent Method
GetControlInfo()	OnGetControlInfo()
OnMnemonic()	OnMnemonic()
OnAmbientPropertyChange()	OnAmbientPropertyChange()
FreezeEvents()	OnFreezeEvents()

It turns out that the **IOleClientSite** interface provided by the container is insufficient for all OCX needs. Therefore, containers actually provide an instance of **IOleControlSite** for each embedded OCX. The **IOleControlSite** is defined with the following methods:

IOleControlSite Methods	Meaning
OnControlInfoChanged()	Tells the container that the OCX's mnemonics information has changed. Mnemonics are keyboard shortcut keys which apply globally across all controls embedded in a container.
LockInPlaceActivate()	The OCX wants to be kept in-place active until further notice via the same method.
GetExtendedControl()	Allows the OCX to access the properties provided by the container's extended control implementation.
TransformCoords()	Provides a service for the OCX to transform coordinates into the container's coordinate system.
TranslateAccelerator()	Provides keyboard accelerator mapping for this OCX.
OnFocus()	Notifies the container site that the OCX has gained or lost focus.
ShowPropertyFrame()	Called by the OCX to display property pages to give the container a chance to add its own pages.

Many of these container notification/services methods are made available through member functions of the **COleControl** class. Focus handling, mnemonics mapping and property page handling are mapped into the consistent MFC model by **COleControl**. The remaining methods are mapped in the following way:

IOleControlSite Method	COleControl Equivalent
OnControlInfoChanged()	ControlInfoChanged()
LockInPlaceActivate()	LockInPlaceActivate()
GetExtendedControl()	GetExtendedControl()
TransformCoords()	TransformCoords()

Interfaces for Persistence

There are a series of **IPersist** interfaces for persisting the control's properties (and cached representation through **IPersistStorage**) to and from storage mediums. All OCXs with persistent properties will implement these. The following are three such interfaces:

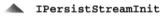 **IPersistStreamInit**

▲ **IPersistPropertyBag**

▲ **IPersistMemory**

The methods of **IPersistStreamInit** and **IPersistMemory** have been examined earlier. We discussed **IPersistPropertyBag** briefly in the OC96 coverage. The **COleControl** class maps the support of these interfaces into a handful of member functions:

COleControl Methods	Meaning
ExchangeExtent()	Used inside **DoPropExchange()** to persist or initialize an OCX's size information (usually changed in a design tool).
ExchangeStockProps()	Used inside **DoPropExchange()** to persist or initialize an OCX's stock properties.
ExchangeVersion()	Used inside **DoPropExchange()** to persist or initialize an OCX's version.
SerializeExtents()	Used to serialize the OCX's extent to a binary persistent mechanism (i.e. **IPersistStreamInit**, **IPersistMemory**, etc).
SerializeStockProps()	Used to serialize the OCX's stock properties to a binary persistent mechanism.
SerializeVersion()	Used to serialize the OCX's version to a binary persistent mechanism.
DoPropExchange()	A function to override in order to persist or initialize the properties of the OCX.
SetModifiedFlag()	Sets the modified state, indicating one or more persistent properties have been changed.
IsModified()	Determines if the OCX is in a modified state.

Essentially, all one has to do for persistent properties is to fill in the **COleControl::DoPropExchange()** function with helper **PX_** macros (we will show how to do this later in our sample). The **COleControl** class will ensure that the control properties will:

▲ Initialize properly the first time it is created with specified default values

▲ Persist in or out properly to binary sources

▲ Persist in or out properly to a property bag (i.e. for ASCII text output as in VB)

However, the above generalization also causes additional layers of code to be called even in cases where it isn't required. When performance optimization is required, the **COleControl**-derived class's **Serialize()** function should be overridden and the **COleControl::Serialize** set of functions should be used along with binary serialization of any persistent members. The regular **DoPropExchange()** implementation should be kept intact to handle non-binary persistence cases.

For the **IPersistMemory** and **IPersistStreamInit**, the container can let the OCX know when it's being persisted 'in' the very first time. With older **IPersist** interfaces, the persist operation will fail first. In these cases, the OCX's properties need to be initialized to default values. For the **COleControl** class, this is mapped to one function, **COleControl::OnResetState()**. This member resets the control to the default state. The default implementation calls **DoPropExchange()** which should suffice for most situations. However, if a default state is determined by more than just the values of persistent properties, make sure the additional steps required are taken.

Interfaces for Properties and Methods Manipulations

Two interfaces implemented by the OCX provide for properties and methods manipulations. They are:

▲ **ISpecifyPropertyPages**

▲ **IDispatch**

ISpecifyPropertyPages allows the container to enumerate the CLSIDs of the property page object that the OCX supports. The **COleControl** class implements **ISpecifyPropertyPages** internally. The user only needs to create property sheets through ClassWizard to get automatic presentation and code hookup for property pages.

The **IDispatch** interface is the dual interface which contains all the methods and properties of the OCX which can be invoked by the container. Recall that an **IDispatch** interface allows late-binding and calling of methods as well as manipulation of properties through OLE Automation using only one single known vtable interface. In addition, through supplied type library information, it's possible for the container to discover during runtime what methods and properties are supported by an OCX in a totally dynamic manner. The **COleControl** class plays no part in this case.

Interfaces for Events

Three interfaces, all implemented by **COleControl** class, provide a mechanism for the OCX to make outgoing calls into the container. These interfaces are:

 `IProvideClassInfo2`

 `IConnectionPointContainer`

`IConnectionPoint`

The supported default outgoing interface (an interface that an OCX wants the container to support) for an OCX is marked in its type library, and **IProvideClassInfo2** can give this information to the container immediately upon invocation. Once the container finds out what methods are in this outgoing interface, it constructs an **IDispatch** dynamically. This **IDispatch** is connected to the OCX via the connection point mechanism (we'll cover connection points in depth in the next chapter).

The **COleControl** class hides all this complexity from the user, and provides direct class wizard support for event firing. One only has to specify the OCX event method's parameters and their types, and ClassWizard will take care of generating the appropriate type library information, connection points handling, and a function for firing the actual event. Many common events are classified as stock events; for these events, the **COleControl** class can allow customization without the user needing to specify the parameters. The following is a table of member functions for these stock events:

COleControl Event Member	Meaning
`FireClick()`	Fires the stock click event. The default implementation fires automatically when the OCX is clicked. The OCX can override and control when it will be fired.
`FireDblClick()`	Fires the stock double-click event. The default implementation fires automatically when the OCX is double-clicked. The OCX can override and control when it will be fired.
`FireError()`	Fires the stock error event.
`FireKeyDown()`	Fires the stock key down event.
`FireKeyPress()`	Fires the stock key press event.
`FireKeyUp()`	Fires the stock key up event.
`FireMouseMove()`	Fires the stock mouse move event.
`FireMouseDown()`	Fires the stock mouse down event.
`FireMouseUp()`	Fires the stock mouse up event.
`FireReadyStateChange()`	Fires an event when the ready state of an OCX changes.

Other event-related **COleControl** member functions include:

COleControl Event Member	Meaning
`FireEvent()`	Fires a user-defined event.
`OnEventAdvise()`	Called each time the container connects or disconnects to a connection point.
`OnKeyDownEvent()`	Called after a key down event has been fired, giving access to key information.

COleControl Event Member	Meaning
OnKeyUpEvent()	Called after a key up event has been fired, giving access to key information.
OnKeyPressEvent()	Called after a key press event has been fired.

COleControl Support for OC96 Extensions

Our discussion of OC96 earlier in this chapter described the support of windowless controls, inactive objects, and optimized drawing; the **COleControl** class of MFC 4.1 has been revamped in MFC4.21 to include basic support for these new features. We'll take a brief look at this support.

Interfaces Supporting Windowless Controls

Windowless controls are supported mainly through the following interfaces:

 IOleInPlaceObjectWindowless (from the OCX)

IOleInPlaceSiteWindowless (from the container)

From the names, one can deduce that they are related to the **IOleInPlaceObject** and **IOleInPlaceSite/Ex** interfaces. In fact, they are actually vtable extensions of these interfaces; this means that they derive from these interfaces and that a pointer to one of these interfaces can serve as pointer to the other.

The following are the additional methods provided by the OCX's **IOleInPlaceObjectWindowless** interface:

IOleInPlaceObjectWindowless Methods	Meaning
OnWindowMessage()	Tunneling mechanism for the container to pass window messages for processing by the in-place active windowless OCX (see following text).
GetDropTarget()	Called by the container to let a windowless OCX participate in drag and drop.

A typical scenario starts with the OCX being in-place activated. The OCX then queries the site object for the **IOleInPlaceSiteWindowless** interface. Once the interface is obtained successfully, its **CanWindowlessActivate()** is invoked to determine if it is okay to windowless activate. On the other hand, if **IOleInPlaceSiteWindowless** isn't supported, the OCX must proceed with creating a window in the normal OCX way.

The container, by supporting **IOleInPlaceSiteWindowless**, is specially designed to activate controls windowlessly. It relies on **IOleInPlaceObject::GetWindow()** to determine when and if the OCX actually has a window at any time. The windowless object must also call **OnInPlaceActivateEx()** with the **ACTIVE_WINDOWLESS** flag bit instead of the standard **OnInPlaceActivate()** call.

Windows messages are dispatched from the container through to the windowlessly activated OCX via the appropriate method calls in the **IOleInPlaceSiteWindowless** interface. The **IOleInPlaceSiteWindowless** interface even provides an **OnDefWindowMessage()** method to serve the same function during message processing as the Win32 **DefWindowProc()** API. In essence, the entire windows message processing has been mapped to an intercomponent communications protocol between the container and the windowless OCX.

The drawing of an in-place active windowless object is still performed through **IViewObject2::Draw()**. However, the input **lprcBounds** rectangle parameter is now **NULL** to indicate the OCX is being drawn windowless; the aspect and device context properties are also handled differently. Despite this, even for a windowless OCX, a container may sometimes call **IViewObject2::Draw()** with a non-**NULL** **lprcBounds** to do drawing into a separate device context for display or printing.

Windowless OCXs can even support drag and drop. This is done by implementing an **IDropTarget** interface and passing it to the container when the container invokes the **IOleInPlaceObjectWindowless::GetDropTarget()** method. The container will then coordinate the passing through of the **IDropTarget::DragOver()** and **IDropTarget::DragEnter()** methods.

To support these new behaviors and offer customization possibilities, the **COleControl** provides hooks into each of these new methods of its implementation of the **IOleInPlaceObjectWindowless** interface:

COleControl Member	Meaning
OnWindowlessMessage()	A wrapper of **IoleInPlaceObjectWindowless::OnWindowMessage()** for the OCX to process any nonkeyboard and mouse messages. However, many of the more common messages are mapped to additional support functions; they should be used to simply program design.
GetWindowlessDropTarget()	Allows the container to obtain the OCX's **IDropTarget** interface for windowless drag and drop support.

The container supporting windowless activation (there are no known commercial containers at this point) provides a comprehensive set of services to assist in the windowless OCX presentation. The following is a listing of these methods, and the corresponding **COleControl** class member function. Notice the straightforward mapping; this thin wrapping allows for maximum customizability at this early stage of windowless OCX's heritage.

IOleInPlaceSiteWindowless (implemented by the container)	COleControl Equivalent
OnInPlaceActivateEx()	Handled internally.
OnInPlaceDeactivateEx()	Handled internally.
CanWindowlessActivate()	Handled internally.
SetCapture()	SetCapture()
GetCapture()	GetCaptrue()
SetFocus()	SetFocus()

IOleInPlaceSiteWindowless (implemented by the container)	COleControl Equivalent
GetFocus()	GetFocus()
OnDefWindowMessage()	Handled internally.
GetDC()	GetDC()
ReleaseDC()	ReleaseDC()
InvalidateRect()	Handled internally.
InvalidateRgn()	InvalidateRgn()
ScrollRect()	ScrollWindow()
AdjustRect()	Mostly handled internally, but also through ClipCaretRect().

The mapped functions in **COleControl** actually merge the windowed and windowless behaviors for the OCXs created using MFC. They override the corresponding functions provided by the **CWnd** based class and make the whole process relatively transparent to the OCX designer.

COleControl Class Member Function	Description
GetCapture()	Checks if the OCX has asked the container to capture the mouse on its behalf.
GetClientRect()	Gets the size of the client area of the windowless OCX.
ClipCaretRect()	Adjusts the size of the caret/soft-cursor. Determines how much of it needs to be redrawn.
GetDC()	Gets a device context from the container for the OCX.
GetFocus()	Checks to see if the OCX has focus logically.
InvalidateRgn()	Invalidates (and causes indirectly to be redrawn later) a region of the window less OCX's display area.
ReleaseCapture()	Releases the mouse capture for the windowless OCX (through the cooperation of the container, of course).
ReleaseDC()	Releases the DC obtained from the GetDC() function.
ScrollWindow()	Coordinates with the container to scroll the display of the OCX by a specified amount.
SetFocus()	Asks the container to get focus on behalf of the windowless OCX.
SetCapture()	Coordinates with the container to capture the mouse on the windowless OCX's behalf

An OCX designer wanting to support the handling of windowless activation should always ensure that the control flags are set properly for the **COleControl**-derived class:

```
DWORD CACtrl::GetControlFlags()
{
   return COleControl::GetControlFlags() | windowlessActivate;
}
```

Interfaces Supporting Inactive Objects

Apart from windowless controls, the **COleControl** class also provides support for the new inactive object optimized handling in OC96. We've discussed this earlier in the chapter. To recap, the idea here is that an OCX can defer the creation of windows as late as possible within a container. Meanwhile, the mouse and drag and drop detection is performed by the container and the OCX will be activated 'just in time' to handle the core interactions. In this way, controls that aren't used by the user may never need to be activated even though their container is displayed. This stands in contrast to the conventional approach of most OCXs, i.e. setting their **OLEMISC_ACTIVATEWHENVISIBLE** flag, which indicates that the control prefers to be in-place active whenever they are visible in order to process mouse messages and detect UI activation. Although a portion of this 'windowless exchange' of messages is similar to the support for windowless objects mentioned earlier, inactive objects are supported by the OCX exclusively through a new interface:

▲ **IPointerInactive**

The container and OCX interaction for inactive object support is actually quite simple. First, a new control flag, **OLEMISC_IGNOREACTIVATEWHENVISIBLE** is defined. This indicates to a container that knows about inactive object activation that the OCX supports it. Note that the **OLEMISC_ACTIVATEWHENVISIBLE** flag still needs to be set for containers that may not know about inactive object activation. An inactive object, of course, is initially displayed by the container through its cached representation. The container will call **IPointerInactive::GetPointerActivationPolicy()** upon every **WM_SETCURSOR** or **WM_MOUSEMOVE** message when the mouse is over the area occupied by the inactive object. The OCX can return the activation policy dynamically and may return a combination of **POINTERINACTIVE_ACTIVATEONENTRY** and **POINTER_DEACTIVATEONLEAVE** flags. If the **POINTERINACTIVE_ACTIVATEONENTRY** is specified, the container will immediately in-place activate the OCX and pass the same message to it once again for processing. The OCX can then process mouse messages within its own window. If the **POINTER_DEACTIVATEONLEAVE** is set as well, the object will be deactivated the moment the cursor leaves the control's display area.

Note that unlike a windowless object, an inactive object can't draw, or capture the mouse. It's restricted to giving feedback by changing the mouse cursor. If an OCX needs to provide user feedback beyond the setting of the mouse cursor, it must return **POINTERINACTIVE_ACTIVATEONENTRY** for activation policy and become activated in order to draw into its window or capture the mouse.

Since the activation policy is generated dynamically by the OCX, it can possibly indicate that it doesn't want to be in-place activated. In this case, the container will continue to forward **WM_MOUSEMOVE** messages by calling **OnInactiveMouseMove()** and **WM_SETCURSOR** messages by calling **OnInactiveSetCursor()** to the inactive OCX. The OCX can use these messages to fire events without ever having to be in-place activated. Without a supporting window, the inactive OCX can't register to be a drop target. The container determines whether to do inactive drop target support by checking to see if the OCX supports the **IPointerInactive** interface; if it does, it assumes it is a potential drop target. An inactive OCX can act as a drop target by having the container activate it as soon as something is dragged over the display area; the OCX should return **POINTERINACTIVE_ACTIVATEONDRAG** for the activation policy.

The **IPointerInactive** interface, as discussed above, contains three methods:

IPointerInactive Methods	Meaning
GetPointerActivationPolicy()	Obtains the instantaneous activation policy of the OCX. Called by the container when the mouse enters the inactive OCX display area.
OnInactiveSetCursor()	Used by the container to ask or command the object to set the mouse cursor.
OnInactiveMouseMove()	Used by the container to forward mouse move messages to the inactive object while the mouse is over the object's display area.

Again, the **COleControl** class provides member functions for handling inactive object optimization. Several member functions are used in calculating the coordinates of the inactive object's location (or the position of the mouse cursor).

COleControl Member	Meaning
GetActivationPolicy()	The container has called **IPointerInactive::GetPointerActivationPolicy()**, the OCX can supply policy flags dynamically as noted above.
OnInactiveSetCursor()	Called by the container when it receives a **WM_SETCURSOR** message and the pointer is over the inactive object.
OnInactiveMouseMove()	Called by the container when it receives a **WM_MOUSEMOVE** message and the pointer is over the inactive object.
ClientToParent()	Maps a point from the origin of inactive object to the origin of container.
GetClientOffset()	Obtains the offset of the origin of the inactive object from the origin of the container.
ParentToClient()	Maps a point from the origin of container to the origin of inactive object.

An OCX designer wanting to support inactive objects should always ensure that the control flags are set properly for the **COleControl**-derived class:

```
DWORD CACtrl::GetControlFlags()
{
    return COleControl::GetControlFlags() | pointerInactive;
}
```

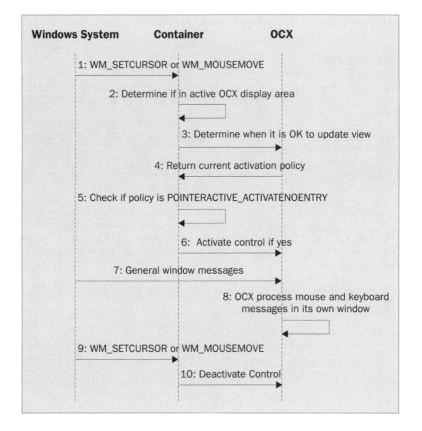

Interfaces Supporting Optimized Drawing

There are several changes defined in OC96, as we've discussed earlier, specifically for drawing optimization. The **IViewObject2::Draw()** method is now embellished with several enhancements. First, the originally **NULL pvAspect** parameter of the **Draw()** method can now contain a pointer to a **DVASPECTINFO** structure which indicates to the control that it is okay to leave font, brush, and pen selected in the device context.

Without this optimization, standard controls have to deselect and delete all the objects that they selected to draw their appearance each time. Since many controls on the same form may use the same set of font, brush and pen, this creates some undue inefficiencies. Not all containers cater for optimized drawing, so an OCX must cater for the case where optimized drawing isn't supported (the **pvAspect** parameter for **Draw()** will be **NULL**). Objects are responsible for deleting the GDI objects that they select into the device context (on an as-needed basis or based on the Least Recently Used algorithm) and the container is responsible for ensuring that the GDI objects are deselected from the device context at the end of container drawing.

The **COleControl** class has a member function which provides the OCX with knowledge of whether the container supports optimized drawing, **IsOptimizedDraw()**. This returns true if the container supports optimized drawing for the current drawing operation. Of course, this can only be valid during the execution of the **OnDraw()** or **OnDrawMetafile()** member functions.

Another optimization allows containers to skip redrawing of a control if the control has the same appearance whether it is activated or not. By eliminating the redraw when an object is activated or deactivated, flicker on the container is avoided. This involves the definition of one new interface to be supported by the container:

▲   **IOleInPlaceSiteEx**

This new interface provides a way for the container to let an object know whether it is necessary to redraw, and lets the control tell the container whether the image already on the screen is valid.

The **COleControl** class supports the calling of **IOleInPlaceSiteEx** internally, and the control user only has to modify the control flags to get automatic support:

```
DWORD CACtrl::GetControlFlags()
{
   return COleControl::GetControlFlags() | noFlickerActivate;
}
```

These past sections have provided us with a frame of reference that will allow us to confidently use the MFC **COleControl** class to implement our Aberdeen & Wilshire Calendar control (or any other OCX for that matter). The COM and OLE background will enable us to override and customize many of **COleControl**'s default handling should the need arise.

Proceeding with the Intranet Events Calendar Design

With the initial terminology and usage hurdle out of the way, we're ready to code our Calendar control. Before commencing with the code, we should take a quick look at the design requirements.

In our design, the software will consist of three main classes:

▲   **CVccalCtrl** (a user control module)

▲   **CDataMgr** (back-end data manager)

▲   **CCellMgr** (calendar cells manager)

The classes interact in the following manner:

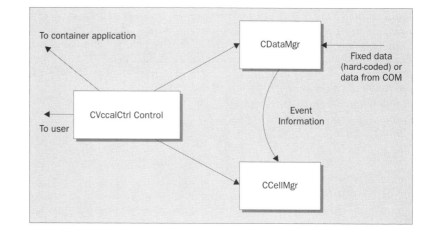

The **CVccalCtrl** is the core of the OCX that handles the display of the user interface, and input from the user. It's also the coordinator of activities between the instance of the **CDataMgr** class and an instance of the **CCellMgr** class module.

Here's a high-level design description of the code modules:

Module Name	Description
CVccalCtrl	This is the core ActiveX control, its functions include:
	▲ Coordinating the action of its **m_DataMgr** (an instance of **CDataMgr**) and **m_CellMgr** (an instance of **CCellMgr**).
	▲ Interacting with the OCX and MFC support environment for ActiveX control operations.
	▲ Drawing and managing the presentation display to the user.
	▲ Handling user interactions and displaying the required form or data.
	▲ Exposing and implementing custom properties and interfaces for the ActiveX control user.
CCellMgr	This class manages an array of calendar cells. Each cell contains coordinate information used by **CVccalCtrl** in painting the presentation display, as well as specific event information obtained from **CDataMgr**'s routine for direct access to the event data. This module provides the following functions:
	▲ Reads the value of calendar cell array elements.
	▲ Sets the value of calendar cell array elements.
	▲ Performs hit testing to determine if the user clicked on a cell.
CDataMgr	This class performs the actual data access, and hides the complexity of data access from the rest of the OCX. The class provides:
	▲ A high level logical interface to data access, hiding the actual data access mechanism.
	▲ Calendar events data to the **CVccalCtrl** class either through hard-coded data or through support from COM/DCOM objects.

One conscious design decision made was to use an array of data structures to represent the calendar cells instead of using an array of actual controls. In our design, the Calendar control paints and manages the entire canvas area. This is done mainly for efficiency. In an alternative design, one may create 42 subcontrols in a control array to represent the calendar cells. However, creating 42 subcontrols on the Calendar control would require the creation of at least another 42 windows during runtime. While the alternative design may simplify some of the coding and hit testing required, the runtime resource consumption and performance would make it an undesirable choice.

The Aberdeen & Wilshire Calendar ActiveX Control

Upon completion, the Aberdeen & Wilshire ActiveX control looks like this:

The elements on the control are designed to scale with the size of the control. The two buttons are actually native Win32 child windows that we create in our OCX. When used in Visual Basic, the calendar grid and buttons can grow and shrink as the user resizes the window. Under Internet Explorer, the size can be specified in HTML parameters for embedded objects:

```
<object id="Calendar"
    classid="clsid: DB00C004-54CE-11D0-8564-004005263AF7"
    align="baseline" border="0"
    width="500" height="300">
    <font size="2" face="ARIAL, HELVETICA"></font></object>
```

When either of the buttons is clicked, the calendar will either advance or step back a month from the currently displayed month.

Events from up to three departments can be viewed by the calendar, and each department can have up to ten events per day. When a particular department has event announcements, the calendar cell of the corresponding day will have a marking indicating the number of events from the department on that day. For example, if the Engineering department has announced two events on December 18, 1997, the calendar cell will contain E-2 in blue (color's a customizable parameter). If the user clicks on this cell, a list box of all the events available for the day, together with a header description of the event will be displayed to the user:

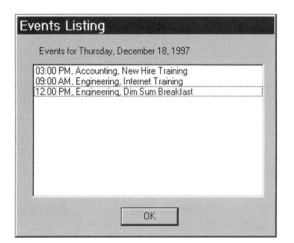

From this list box, the user may select the event that he or she is interested in by double-clicking it. Upon selection, the details of the event will be displayed:

We'll be testing the function of this ActiveX control inside the Visual C++ 5 ActiveX control test container, the Internet Explorer 3.0 as well as Visual Basic 5.

As a completely self-contained intranet mini-application, the Calendar control really doesn't need too many externally configurable parameters. This allows easy deployment of the control, and simpler overall support. While it's possible to create extremely configurable controls for more generic use using Visual C++ 5, we'll focus on applying it to our hypothetical Aberdeen & Wilshire intranet. The Calendar control will have the following properties and methods exposed to the user:

Property Name	Type	Description
`TitleFontName`	String (Default = `"Arial"`)	The typeface described by this name will be used to draw the 'Month' title of the calendar.
`TitleFontSize`	Single (Default = `10`)	This font size in points specified by this value will be used to draw the 'Month' title of the calendar.
`TitleFontBold`	Single (Default = `TRUE`)	When set to `TRUE`, the typeface of the 'Month' title will be set to bold. When set to `FALSE`, the title typeface will be set to normal.
`ButtonsVisible`	Boolean (Default = `TRUE`)	When set to `FALSE`, the two arrow buttons for advancing the month will not be drawn.

Method Prototype	Description
`void SetStartDate(Date d);`	Call this method to set the displayed month of the event calendar, and to cause the calendar to requery for all the event information across the department.
`void AdvanceMonth(Long I);`	Call this method to advance the month being displayed on the calendar. The number passed indicates the number of months to advance the calendar by, and can be either positive or negative. The number passed in will be ignored if it is greater than 12.

Our calendar ActiveX control will not generate any ActiveX events to the container.

Initially, in order to test our OCX, the `CDataMgr` access routines will be coded to access back-end COM server objects to obtain data. In this chapter, we'll be using these back-end components without going into them in any depth. In the next chapter, we'll be examining the construction of these components using some advanced ATL techniques. In addition, we'll hook up the components across a network to obtain live event data available from the individual departments using DCOM based technology. In all cases, though, we'll be artificially setting the data into the back-end components upon initialization. This frees us from having to set up real data sources for testing and demonstration purposes.

Let's take a detailed look at the two core classes that make up our Aberdeen & Wilshire Calendar control.

The CDataMgr Class

`CDataMgr` manages access to back-end event data. It provides a set of member functions that allow the calendar logic to be independent of where the data may be stored. Many of the data structures used in processing of event data are defined by this class. For sample purposes, our implementation of the event system is limited to handling up to 10 events each day from up to 3 departments. These limits can easily be changed and are defined in `DataMgr.h`:

```
#define MAX_EVENTS 10
#define MAX_DEPTS 3
```

We also define the structure of an event for the calendar cells.

```
typedef struct {
   COleDateTime DateTime;
   CString Location;
   CString Heading;
   CString Organizer;
   CString orgDept;
   CString Details;
   CString Hlink;
} CalEvent;
```

This structure matches the calendar event detail information that we may obtain from the back-end data components. Before drawing the calendar with information, the control needs to find out all the participating departments that may have events. The details of the department, including the initial character used and the color to draw the information in is kept in a structure like this:

```
typedef struct {
   CString DeptName;
   CString DeptNumber;
   BOOL CanRead;
   BOOL CanPostNew;
   CString Symbol;
   OLE_COLOR Color;
} CalDept;
```

Another data structure defined in **DataMgr.h** is the **DeptEvent** structure, which maintains the number of events a particular department may have on a particular day.

```
typedef struct {
   CalDept Dept;
   ULONG EvtCount;
   COleDateTime OnDates[MAX_EVENTS];
} DeptEvent;
```

The **CDataMgr** class provides the following high-level functions for obtaining data. The actual details of data retrieval are encapsulated completely within the **CDataMgr** class. This allows us to initially hard-code the data and eventually obtain the data through a networked DCOM link without affecting other code modules.

Member	Description
GetAnEvent()	Given a date, a department index, and an event number, this function returns full information on an event.
GetDept()	Given a department index, this function returns detailed information on the department including name, short form, color for marking the calendar, etc.
GetDeptCount()	Get the count of the number of departments currently with events information available. We support up to three departments in this version of the calendar control.
GetEventsOnDate()	Given a specific date, this function returns the number of events available for each department.

Member	Description
GrabActiveDepts()	This is a method which initializes the instance of the **CDataMgr** class with information about the departments that has events posted for the month of interest. This should always be the function called immediately after **SetEventMonth()**.
GrabEventSnapshot()	This method is used to grab event availability information for the data source across all departments. It takes a **snapshot** at the time it is called, on the number of events offered by each department. The snapshot is kept internal to the **CDataMgr** class instance. The use of this function is dependent on **SetEventMonth()** being called, setting the date of interest. It also depends on **GrabActiveDepts()** being called, setting the internal list of departments (inside **CDataMgr**) which has events postings for the month of interest.
SetEventMonth()	This method is used to set the date (a month) of the events that we're interested in. This should always be set before the **GrabActiveDepts()** is called. Otherwise, the current day and time will be used for obtaining the data. In our sample program implementation, we'll actually be filling up the back-end components with dummy data during this call.

The CCellMgr Class

The cell manager class manages the 'data' associated with the displayed calendar cells. It does not directly do any drawing of the data for the calendar. All the drawing is done by the **CVccalcCtrl** class. However, this class does manage all required data for drawing. The **OnDraw()** member of **CVccalcCtrl** class works closely with the cell manager to display calendar information.

The work is done by managing a private array of cell structures, one associated with each cell displayed on the calendar. A cell structure is defined as:

```
typedef struct {
    Attach Attachments[3];
    COleDateTime CelDate;
    CString Day;
    BOOL hasEvent;
    CString Label;
    CPoint BottomRight;
    CPoint TopLeft;
} CalCel;
```

Note that besides the values used to paint the representation of the cell, it also contains optional attachments (which aren't used in our example), the actual date represented, and the location information of the cell on the ActiveX control's client area. The location information is used by the control when the user clicks on the control. At this time, the control will check all the cells that have events to determine if the user has clicked on one of the cells.

Methods	Description
CellHitTest()	Given an index into the cell array and a client area (x,y) pair, determines if the point falls within the cell.
ClearCells()	Resets the state of the managed set of cells.
GetCellDate()	Gets the date associated with the specified cell.
GetCellEvent()	Gets the set of events associated with the day represented by the cell.
GetCellNumber()	Gets the additional label associated with the cell specified.
GetDayName()	Gets the name of the day of the week, from 0=Sun to 6=Sat.
GetDaysInMonth()	Given a month and year, gets the number of days in the month.
GetLabel()	Gets the string representation of the day represented by the cell.
GetMonthYearText()	Gets the current value of the title label for the calendar in a format similar to 'January 1998'.
InitLongNames()	Initializes data required by the cell manager.
SetCellEvent()	Sets the events array associated with a cell.
SetCorners()	Sets the coordinates that a cell occupies. This information is used in hit-testing.
SetDays()	Given a month as input, fills all the cells managed with appropriate values for displaying the calendar.
SetMonthYearText()	Sets the value of the calendar title label.

Ready to Code!

The next chapter will be an intensive coverage of the steps taken in creating the control, and analysis of the code involved in the implementation of the control. Our coding will make extensive use of the **COleControl** class in MFC 4.21 that we've covered in this chapter. We'll also be working with some advanced features of ATL and COM again to create back-end ActiveX data objects.

Visual C++ 5.0 for ActiveX Components

In this chapter and the next, we'll be coding the calendar control using the **COleControl** MFC class and Visual C++. We'll look at various ways to test the control in different containers. The control isn't very interesting by itself without some calendar event data to display. To obtain this data, we'll take a look at the design of back-end business components which supply the calendar control with vital real-time events data for display to the user. Our analysis will cover the object model presented by these back-end components. The same model can easily be incorporated into other COM-based clients, including Visual Basic and Java-based applications. In other words, these back-end components can be easily reused by front-end applications supporting a different presentation (i.e. non-calendar) to the end user. Then, in the next chapter, we'll discuss several advanced features of the ATL library, and apply them when building the back-end components. Visual C++ 5 will again be used in building these components. Finally, we'll test the entire system, including the calendar control and the business objects communicating through COM in a three-tier combination.

In our initial coverage of the Aberdeen & Wilshire calendar control's construction, we will focus on both the 'how to' aspects of creating an ActiveX control using Visual C++ 5.0 as well as some practical real-world aspects of dealing with containers and system environments during the hands-on development of an ActiveX control.

Creating the Calendar Control with Visual C++ 5.0

Visual C++ 5.0's Developer Studio, together with the ClassWizard and MFC 4.21, makes creating simple visual controls in C++ straightforward. Let's first take a look at the steps involved:

1 Create an ActiveX control project using AppWizard

2 Add properties for the ActiveX control using the ClassWizard

3 Add method for the ActiveX control using the ClassWizard

4 Add events for the ActiveX control using the ClassWizard

5 Implement the properties and methods in Visual C++

6 Implement any other support classes and logic for the control

7 Add code to the **OnDraw()** function

8 Test, test, and test the control in various containers

Creating an ActiveX Control Project Using AppWizard

Creating an ActiveX control project with AppWizard is a simple step, so we won't go into too much detail here; just create a project called Vccal. The only things we need to be aware of is to make sure that our control is activated when visible to cater for the current Internet Explorer 3.0 and Visual Basic 4 and 5 containers and we don't want it to be available in Insert Object... dialogs since, at this point, it won't be too useful for containers such as Microsoft Word or Excel. We also need to make sure that the control doesn't act as a simple frame control. A simple frame control is useful in cases where a control (say, a group box) visually contains a set of controls (say, check boxes or other buttons) which aren't ActiveX controls. Finally, we need to make sure our control isn't subclassed from any standard window controls.

Once the project is generated, you can immediately compile and use it. However, the resulting control will not be too interesting, just drawing a ellipse within the control's client area.

From the ClassView, you can see the default dispatch interface generated by the wizard, called **_DVccal**, and the default outgoing interface generated, to which clients can connect in order to be 'called back' by our control, called **_DVccalEvents**. The **_DVccal** interface, if you expand it, currently only contains the **AboutBox()** method. We'll be adding many more properties and methods shortly.

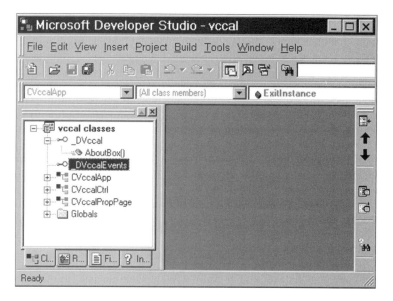

The other classes created automatically include **CVccalApp**, the default MFC application for our control, the **CVccalCtrl**, our **COleControl**-derived class where most work will be done and **CVccalPropPage** which implements a dummy properties page. We won't be creating any property pages in our example since both Visual Basic and FrontPage 97 provide their own property browser/editor for control properties.

Add Properties for the Control Using ClassWizard

With the Vccal project open, we can now start to add properties and methods to our calendar control. To add properties, we can use either the pop-up context menu for the **_DVccal** interface in the ClassView pane, or use View | ClassWizard... and go to the Automation tab to directly add to the implementation class (**CVccalCtrl** in this case):

In the Add Property dialog box, we need to add the following properties for the Calendar control:

External Name: **ButtonsVisible**
Type: BOOL
Implementation: Get/Set Methods
Get Function: **GetButtonsVisible**
Set Function: **SetButtonsVisible**
Parameter List: \<empty\>

External Name: **TitleFontBold**
Type: BOOL
Implementation: Get/Set Methods
Get Function: **GetTitleFontBold**
Set Function: **SetTitleFontBold**
Parameter List: \<empty\>

External Name: **TitleFontSize**
Type: short
Implementation: Get/Set Methods
Get Function: **GetTitleFontSize**
Set Function: **SetTitleFontSize**
Parameter List: \<empty\>

External Name: **TitleFontName**
Type: BSTR
Implementation: Get/Set Methods
Get Function: **GetTitleFontName**
Set Function: **SetTitleFontName**
Parameter List: \<empty\>

You'll notice that all of the properties are accessed through **Get** or **Set** methods instead of directly through member variables. This is always a better practice because it allows validation to be performed on the value before the property is set out of range, which may cause the OCX to enter an unstable state. The parameter list of property access methods is usually empty; the generated code will provide the appropriate parameters if specified in the list. You can look at the generated code in the class pane by expanding the **CVccalCtrl** class. For example, the **Get** and **Set** methods for the **TitleFontName** properties are:

```
BSTR CVccalCtrl::GetTitleFontName()
{
   CString strResult;
   // TODO: Add your property handler here
   return strResult.AllocSysString();
}


void CVccalCtrl::SetTitleFontName(LPCTSTR lpszNewValue)
{
   // TODO: Add your property handler here
   SetModifiedFlag();
}
```

The ClassWizard not only generates the code skeleton for the property access functions, it also automatically generates the appropriate **.ODL** file (an older variant of **.IDL**) entries for creation of type library information. For example, examining the generated **.ODL** for the above property, we find:

```
. . .
[ uuid(DB00C002-54CE-11D0-8564-004005263AF7),
    helpstring("Dispatch interface for Vccal Control"), hidden ]
dispinterface _DVccal
{
   properties:
      // NOTE - ClassWizard will maintain property information here.
      //    Use extreme caution when editing this section.
      //{{AFX_ODL_PROP(CVccalCtrl)
      [id(1)] short TitleFontSize;
      [id(2)] boolean TitleFontBold;
      [id(3)] BSTR TitleFontName;
      [id(4)] boolean ButtonsVisible;
      //}}AFX_ODL_PROP
. . .
```

The order of the properties may be different on your system, as this is the order they have been added to the interface.

Adding Methods and Events to the Calendar Control

Again, we can either right click on the default interface, **_DVccal**, in the class pane and select Add Method..., or use ClassWizard directly, to get to the Add Method dialog. For our project, we can enter in the following two methods:

External Name:	**AdvanceMonth**
Internal Name:	**AdvanceMonth**
Return Type:	VARIANT
Implementation:	Custom
Parameter List:	**inc**, long

External Name:	**SetStartDate**
Internal Name:	**SetStartDate**
Return Type:	Void
Implementation:	Custom
Parameter List:	**NewDate**, DATE

This completes the definition of the properties and methods required by the Calendar control. The appropriate member functions have been generated for the **CVccalCtrl** class, and the type library information has been generated in the **.ODL** file

Implementing the Properties and Methods in Visual C++

To implement the operation of the added property, we must create and manage the **TitleFont** font object within the **VccalCtrl** class. This is done by declaring a member variable of type pointer to **CFont**. In addition, since the user can set the size, typeface name, and weight separately, we also define member variables to hold values for these properties:

```
class CVccalCtrl : public COleControl
{
    DECLARE_DYNCREATE(CVccalCtrl)

... more member definitions
protected:
    CFont * m_TitleFont;
    CString m_TitleFontName;
    short m_TitleFontSize;
    BOOL m_TitleFontBold;
...
}
```

The actual **m_TitleFont** object is never directly accessible by the end user, but can be manipulated only through the **TitleFontName**, **TitleFontSize**, and **TitleFontBold** properties. Since **m_TitleFont** isn't an externally accessible font property, we avoid using the **CFontHolder** class; instead, we use the simple **CFont** class. Upon instantiation of the object, we initialize the **CFont**-based member to **NULL**. This is done in the constructor of the **CVccalCtrl** class:

```
CVccalCtrl::CVccalCtrl()
{
    InitializeIIDs(&IID_DVccal, &IID_DVccalEvents);

    // TODO: Initialize your control's instance data here.
    m_TitleFont = NULL;
}
```

User accessible properties must be serialized in the **DoPropExchange()** member function. Recall from last chapter that the implementation of this function is used on three distinct occasions:

1 When the control is initialized the first time after instantiation.

2 Every time the **IPersist*** interface of the control is called to do binary save or restore to/from a storage medium.

3 Every time the **IPersistPropertyBag** interface of the control is called to perform text-based persistence. This typically occurs when the control is used in Visual Basic, and the user either loads or saves a form containing the control.

To do this, we simply select the appropriate **PX_**xxx macros. Each macro will perform property exchange for a specific type. Note that since there isn't a **PX_Date** macro, we convert the **DATE** type into its string representation first before we do property exchange using a **PX_String** macro. Each use of the **PX_**xxx macro has the general form:

```
PX_<type>(pointer to exchange source,
          external name,
          member variable,
          initial value)
```

The initial value is used only when the **DoPropExchange()** member function is called during the initialization immediately after the instance is created. (Recall from the discussion in the last chapter, that this typically occurs when the **IPersistStreamInit::InitNew()** or **IPersistMemory::InitNew()** is invoked.)

```
void CVccalCtrl::DoPropExchange(CPropExchange* pPX)
{
    TRACE("CVccalCtrl::DoPropExchange\n");
    ExchangeVersion(pPX, MAKELONG(_wVerMinor, _wVerMajor));
    COleControl::DoPropExchange(pPX);

    // TODO: Call PX_ functions for each persistent custom property.
    PX_String(pPX, _T("TitleFontName"), m_TitleFontName, CString(_T("Arial")) );
    PX_Short(pPX, _T("TitleFontSize"), m_TitleFontSize, 12);
    PX_Bool(pPX, _T("TitleFontBold"), m_TitleFontBold, TRUE);
}
```

By using the **PX_** macros, a wide variety of **IPersist*** interfaces are used by our code. As a bonus, the default value specified provides the initial value for the property, which is used in initialization of the object. This means that initialization and persistence to multiple sources are all handled elegantly by one convenient set of code. Unfortunately, generality typically doesn't come without cost. The fact is, for certain initialization and/or persistence situations, all the effort spent in default initialization and/or multiple layer of functions calling simply isn't needed. This is especially true if you have a large set of properties to initialize and persist, and some of the initial value determination is nontrivial.

In cases where one wants to have individual control over the binary persistence, initialization, and property bag persistence of the ActiveX control, you can take the following approach:

▲ Override the **Serialize()** function, but don't call **COleControl::Serialize()** and perform the necessary binary persistence procedures right here

▲ Override the **OnResetState()** function, but don't call **COleControl::OnResetState()**

▲ Leave the **DoPropExchange()** function in the derived class unchanged: this will continue to be used for containers which persist to property bags

This takes care of property persistence and initialization. To actually implement the guts of the property access functions, we need to synchronize the values of the Font-related properties with the actual private **CFont** object used in drawing the title. This synchronization is performed by a single protected member function which we need to add:

```
protected:
    void InitTitleFont(CDC* pdc, CRect& inRect);
```

With this function, given a pointer to a device context and the current display rectangle for the control, it will create a **CFont** object with the attributes defined by the **m_TitleFontName**, **m_TitleFontBold**, and **m_TitleFontSize** for the device context. This **CFont** object will be later used in the **OnDraw()** member to print the title.

This function is called any time one of the font related properties is changed and the calendar control needs to be repainted. It will delete the old **CFont** object pointed to by **m_TitleFont** and create a new one with the correct attributes if necessary. Of course, if the properties haven't changed since the last time the function is called, or if the function itself is called twice within the same drawing process, there's no need to create a new **CFont** object. The following is the implementation illustrating the algorithm discussed above. Note that we maintain a pointer to a **CDC**, **m_pCachedDC**, as a private member, in order to determine if the function may be called twice during the same draw operation. This new member also needs to be initialized to **NULL** in the constructor. To create the new font according to the user specification, we use **CFont**'s **CreatePointFontIndirect()** member to create a font from the size (in absolute points), weight, and type family name specified.

```
void CVccalCtrl::InitTitleFont(CDC * pdc, CRect & inRect)
{
    TRACE("CVccalCtrl::InitTitleFont\n");
    LOGFONT tf;
    // either a new DC or someone modifying properties
    if ((pdc != m_pCachedDC) || IsModified())
    {
        CRect rcBoundsDP(&inRect);
        if (m_TitleFont != NULL)
        {
            delete m_TitleFont;
            m_TitleFont = NULL;
        }
        // Prep the DC
        m_TitleFont = new CFont();
        if (m_TitleFont != NULL)
        {
            memset((void *) &tf, 0, sizeof(tf));
            tf.lfHeight = m_TitleFontSize * 10;
            _tcscpy(tf.lfFaceName, (LPCTSTR) m_TitleFontName);
            tf.lfWeight = (m_TitleFontBold) ? FW_BOLD : FW_NORMAL;
            m_TitleFont->CreatePointFontIndirect(&tf, pdc);
        }
        m_pCachedDC = pdc;
    }
}
```

The action, therefore, which synchronizes the user-accessible properties with the actual font used in drawing the title is depicted in this interaction diagram:

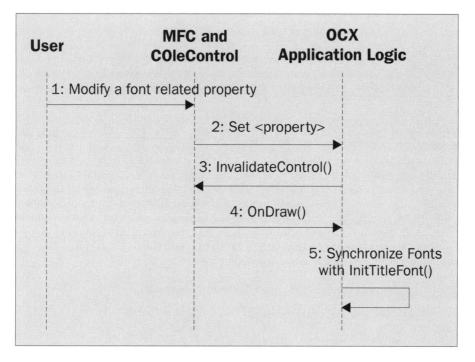

This design allows for the very straightforward implementation of the property access functions themselves. The **Get** functions simply return the member variable's value. The **Set** functions do minor validation and then set the member variable's value. **SetModifiedFlag()** is called to let **COleControl** know that some property has changed and to preserve the new state, it will be necessary to persist out the property again.

```
short CVccalCtrl::GetTitleFontSize()
{
    return  m_TitleFontSize;
}

void CVccalCtrl::SetTitleFontSize(short nNewValue)
{
    if( (nNewValue >0) && (nNewValue < 20))
    {
      m_TitleFontSize = nNewValue;
      SetModifiedFlag();
    }
}

BOOL CVccalCtrl::GetTitleFontBold()
{
    return m_TitleFontBold;
}

void CVccalCtrl::SetTitleFontBold(BOOL bNewValue)
{
    m_TitleFontBold = bNewValue;
    SetModifiedFlag();
}
```

```
BSTR CVccalCtrl::GetTitleFontName()
{
    CString strResult;
    strResult = m_TitleFontName;
    return strResult.AllocSysString();
}

void CVccalCtrl::SetTitleFontName(LPCTSTR lpszNewValue)
{
    if (_tcscmp(lpszNewValue, _T("")) != 0)
    {
        m_TitleFontName = lpszNewValue;
        SetModifiedFlag();
    }
}
```

The ButtonsVisible Property

Unlike the font-related properties, the **ButtonsVisible** property affects the two child window buttons
immediately. Just like the font-related properties, the **ButtonsVisible** property is saved in a private
member variable of the **CVccalCtrl** class called **m_ButtonsVisible**, which needs to be added to the
class. Also like the font-related properties are the access functions: **GetButtonsVisible()** and
SetButtonsVisible():

```
BOOL CVccalCtrl::GetButtonsVisible()
{
    return m_ButtonsVisible;
}

void CVccalCtrl::SetButtonsVisible(BOOL bNewValue)
{
    m_ButtonsVisible = bNewValue;
    InitializeButtonsState();
    SetModifiedFlag();
}
```

The difference here is the call to the protected method **InitializeButtonsState()**. This is done to
immediately affect the visibility of the child windows. The function changes the buttons' visibility by calling
the **ShowWindow()** member, access to which is provided through a couple of pointers we need to add to
the class:

```
...
// Implementation
protected:
    CFont * m_TitleFont;
    CString m_TitleFontName;
    short m_TitleFontSize;
    BOOL m_TitleFontBold;
    CDC* m_pCachedDC;
    BOOL m_ButtonsVisible;
    CButton* m_pLeftBut;
    CButton* m_pRightBut;

    //member functions
    void InitTitleFont(CDC * pdc, CRect & inRect);
    void InitializeButtonsState();
...
```

and initialize in the constructor:

```
CVccalCtrl::CVccalCtrl()
{
    InitializeIIDs(&IID_DVccal, &IID_DVccalEvents);
    m_TitleFont = NULL;
    m_pLeftBut = NULL;
    m_pRightBut = NULL;
}
```

The **InitializeButtonsState()** method looks like this:

```
void CVccalCtrl::InitializeButtonsState()
{
    TRACE("CVccalCtrl::InitializeButtonsStat\n");
    if (m_hWnd) // can't do it to a metafile :(
    {
        if (m_ButtonsVisible)
        {
            m_pLeftBut->ShowWindow(SW_SHOW);
            m_pRightBut->ShowWindow(SW_SHOW);
        }
        else
        {
            m_pLeftBut->ShowWindow(SW_HIDE);
            m_pRightBut->ShowWindow(SW_HIDE);
        }
    }
}
```

Note, in the above code, and frequently throughout the OCX implementation, that functions will not call manipulation functions on the window unless the window handles are valid. This is good safe practice (especially with the OC96 windowless or inactive controls), and it's also absolutely necessary in our case because we specifically use the **OnDraw()** function to implement both windows-based drawing and metafile-based drawing. During metafile-based rendering, there will be no windows created for the control.

The two child window buttons for advancing the month display demonstrate how one can use standard Windows controls inside ActiveX controls. The only trick in using child windows is that an ActiveX control is often instantiated by a container without a Window. In these cases, one must **not** create the child windows. In the last chapter, we discussed the expense associated with activating a control. In order to keep the workload down and performance up, a container may simply ask the control to draw itself without creating an actual window.

To play it safe in our implementation, we override the control's **OnCreate()** Windows message function, which is called only when a **WM_CREATE** message is received by the **COleControl** (which derives from **CWnd**) class. We know that we're getting a window here, so it is safe to create the child window most of the time. The code for this handler looks like this:

```
int CVccalCtrl::OnCreate(LPCREATESTRUCT lpCreateStruct)
{
    TRACE("CVccalCtrl::OnCreate\n");
    if (COleControl::OnCreate(lpCreateStruct) == -1)
        return -1;

    RECT rect;
    GetClientRect( &rect );
```

```
    m_pLeftBut = new CButton();
    m_pRightBut = new CButton();

    CRect tRect(rect);
    LONG unitWidth = tRect.Width()/10;
    LONG unitHeight = tRect.Height()/10;

    tRect = rect;
    tRect.DeflateRect(1 * unitWidth, 1 * unitHeight,  8 * unitWidth, 8 * unitHeight );
    m_pLeftBut->Create(_T("<<"),WS_CHILD | WS_VISIBLE, tRect ,this, IDR_LEFTBUTTON);

    tRect = rect;
    tRect.DeflateRect(8 * unitWidth, 1 * unitHeight,  1 * unitWidth, 8 * unitHeight );
    m_pRightBut->Create(_T(">>"),WS_CHILD | WS_VISIBLE, tRect ,this, IDR_RIGHTBUTTON);

    // set up the title font
    InitTitleFont(GetDC(), CRect(rect));
    return 0;
}
```

You'll need to add a couple of resource symbols to define **IDR_LEFTBUTTON** and **IDR_RIGHTBUTTON**, which can be done easily enough by viewing the resource symbols:

The child windows are destroyed only when our control window is destroyed. To do this, we implement a handler for **WM_DESTROY** message:

```
void CVccalCtrl::OnDestroy()
{
    TRACE("CVccalCtrl::OnDestroy\n");
    COleControl::OnDestroy();
    m_pLeftBut->DestroyWindow();
    delete m_pLeftBut;
```

```
      m_pLeftBut = NULL;
      m_pRightBut->DestroyWindow();
      delete m_pRightBut;
      m_pRightBut = NULL;
      delete m_TitleFont;
      m_TitleFont = NULL;
    }
```

Another problem with Windows-based child windows in general is their inability to render into a metafile. Many Windows-native controls use GDI functions which can't be encapsulated in the metafile format, making them unsuitable for metafile rendering. Since the container will call on the ActiveX control to render itself into metafiles from time to time, the ActiveX control must either:

▲ Ignore such request and not paint the child windows (but this may not be possible)

▲ Ask the child window to draw itself to the metafile, or provide the equivalent drawing code

In an ActiveX control where child windows are used extensively to provide the user interface, the first option may be unacceptable. Asking a child window to draw itself is a solution that only sometimes works, since many standard Windows controls do not draw properly when rendered into metafiles. In the worst case, the control must write code that draws the representation of the child control directly. This can be quite a tough task. Thankfully, the only child windows in our ActiveX control are the 'advance month' buttons, which are nonessential when the calendar is printed or rendered to metafiles. In this case, we adopt the simpler option, and don't draw them.

Finally, we must remember to add the property exchange code, so that the button states can be persistent:

```
void CVccalCtrl::DoPropExchange(CPropExchange* pPX)
{
  TRACE("CVccalCtrl::DoPropExchange\n");
  ExchangeVersion(pPX, MAKELONG(_wVerMinor, _wVerMajor));
  COleControl::DoPropExchange(pPX);

  // TODO: Call PX_ functions for each persistent custom property.
   PX_String(pPX, _T("TitleFontName"), m_TitleFontName, CString(_T("Arial")) );
  PX_Short(pPX, _T("TitleFontSize"), m_TitleFontSize, 12);
  PX_Bool(pPX, _T("TitleFontBold"), m_TitleFontBold, TRUE);
  PX_Bool(pPX, _T("ButtonsVisible"), m_ButtonsVisible, TRUE);
}
```

The Indispensable and Versatile COleDateTime Class

Throughout our OCX implementation, we'll use the features of **COleDateTime** class extensively. This is an extremely versatile class when dealing with information associated with dates or times. We can easily cast a **COleDateTime** variable to and from the **DATE** type typically used by COM. We use this to our advantage in the **SetStartDate()** method to assign the COM-based **DATE** type into a new protected member variable **m_CurrentDay** of **COleDateTime** by using its **=** operator:

```
void CVccalCtrl::SetStartDate(DATE NewDate)
{
    m_CurrentDay = NewDate;
}
```

A **COleDateTime** variable can also be easily transformed into a frequently used **VARIANT** data type (we'll discuss **VARIANT**s a little later). In the **DoPropExchange()** implementation, we convert **COleDateTime** to a string representation using the **Format()** member function for easier persistence, and we reconstitute the **COleDateTime** using the **ParseDateTime()** member when the string is persisted back in.

```
void CVccalCtrl::DoPropExchange(CPropExchange* pPX)
{
...
   COleDateTime tpInit(1997,1,1,0,0,1);
   CString ulInit(tpInit.Format());
   if (pPX->IsLoading())
   {
      CString ulTime("");
      PX_String(pPX, _T("CurrentDay"), ulTime, ulInit);
      m_CurrentDay.ParseDateTime(ulTime);
      InitializeButtonsState();
   }
   else
   {
      CString ulTime(m_CurrentDay.Format());
      PX_String(pPX, _T("CurrentDay"), ulTime, ulInit);
   }
}
```

Other very valuable characteristics of the **COleDateTime** class include the capability to extract the day, month and year components of the date easily. We used this extensively in the day setting routines; one example is the **SetDays()** member function of the **CCellMgr** class (which we'll cover later in the chapter):

```
void CCellMgr::SetDays(const COleDateTime &DateToSet)
{
...
   ULONG workMonth;
   COleDateTime firstDay;
   ULONG firstWeekDay;
   ULONG workYear, curDay;
   workMonth = DateToSet.GetMonth();
   workYear = DateToSet.GetYear();
   firstDay = COleDateTime(workYear, workMonth, 1,0,0,1);
   firstWeekDay = firstDay.GetDayOfWeek();
...
```

Another very useful capability of the **COleDateTime** class is date-based arithmetic operations performed in conjunction with the **COleTimeSpan** class. A **COleTimeSpan** variable can represent time as days, hours, minutes, or seconds. You can add a **COleTimeSpan** to a **COleDateTime** value to get another **COleDateTime** value. You can also subtract two **COleDateTime** values to yield a **COleTimeSpan** value. Using the **COleDateTime** class has significantly reduced the overall coding burden of our control.

Implementing Methods

The two methods supported by our ActiveX control are:

> **SetStartDate()**
>
> **AdvanceMonth()**

SetStartDate() allows the control container to move the month displayed forwards, or adjust it backwards. All that the method has to do is to set the member variable **m_CurrentDay** (used to hold the currently displayed month), and this is precisely what our implementation does:

```
void CVccalCtrl::SetStartDate(DATE NewDate)
{
    m_CurrentDay = NewDate;
}
```

The **AdvanceMonth()** function is called to adjust the displayed month by up to 12 months ahead of or 12 months prior to the current month. The action performed amounts to what happens in **SetStartDate()**, except that we do the calculation of the new date-based on the value of **m_CurrentDay**, and the input parameter indicating the number of months to adjust:

```
VARIANT CVccalCtrl::AdvanceMonth(long inc)
{
    VARIANT vaResult;
    VariantInit(&vaResult);
    if (abs(inc) <= 12)    // maximum 1 year
    {
        ULONG workMonth = m_CurrentDay.GetMonth();
        ULONG workYear = m_CurrentDay.GetYear();
        workMonth += inc;
        if (workMonth <= 0)
        {
            workYear--;
            workMonth += 12;
        }
        if (workMonth > 12)
        {
            workYear++;
            workMonth -= 12;
        }
        m_CurrentDay = COleDateTime(workYear, workMonth,1, 0,0,1);
    }
    return vaResult;
}
```

The lines above this simply calculate the new date to be displayed. We'll explain the use of **VARIANT** later in the ATL components implementation.

Note that the **AdvanceMonth()** function is exactly what is used internally when the two child window buttons are clicked by the control user. To handle clicks from these buttons, we need to code two message handlers, one for each button. Since we know from Win32 programming that a child button's message will be sent to the parent, we should be able to simply override the **WM_COMMAND** message handling. However, the entire MFC message-forwarding scheme is dependent on **WM_COMMAND** message processing, therefore we must coexist in a compliant manner by working with the message map.

In the message map definition in **VccalCtl.cpp**, we add entries (outside of the ClassWizard-managed map entries) to handle button presses from our child windows:

```
/////////////////////////////////////////////////////////////////////////////
// Message map
BEGIN_MESSAGE_MAP(CVccalCtrl, COleControl)
    //{{AFX_MSG_MAP(CVccalCtrl)
    ON_WM_CREATE()
    ON_WM_DESTROY()
    //}}AFX_MSG_MAP
    ON_BN_CLICKED(IDR_LEFTBUTTON, OnLeftButtonClicked)
    ON_BN_CLICKED(IDR_RIGHTBUTTON, OnRightButtonClicked)
```

```
      ON_OLEVERB(AFX_IDS_VERB_PROPERTIES, OnProperties)
   END_MESSAGE_MAP()
```

The **IDR_LEFTBUTTON** and **IDR_RIGHTBUTTON** are IDs for the child windows we defined earlier, and the **OnLeftButtonClicked()** and **OnRightButtonClicked()** are the two handler functions that we map to. To declare these member functions, we add the following to **VccalCtl.h**, within the **CVccalCtrl** class definition:

```
   // Message maps
   //{{AFX_MSG(CVccalCtrl)
   afx_msg int OnCreate(LPCREATESTRUCT lpCreateStruct);
   afx_msg void OnDestroy();
   //}}AFX_MSG
   afx_msg void OnRightButtonClicked();
   afx_msg void OnLeftButtonClicked();
   DECLARE_MESSAGE_MAP()
```

Finally, as we have stated before, these functions simply handle the click by calling the **AdvanceMonth()** function:

```
   void CVccalCtrl::OnLeftButtonClicked()
   {
      AdvanceMonth(-1);
   }

   void CVccalCtrl::OnRightButtonClicked()
   {
      AdvanceMonth(1);
   }
```

Implementing Any Other Support Classes and Logic for the Control

From the previous chapter, we know that there are two core classes that do a lot of work:

- **CDataMgr** which manages the back-end components and shields them from the control logic
- **CCellMgr** which manages data associated with the cells being displayed in the calendar

Of these two classes, we'll look at the **CCellMgr** class now, and reserve the discussion of the **CDataMgr** class for later. Let's start by providing some necessary definitions as well as the **CCellMgr** class declaration.

VccalConst.h contains our constants as we'll need them in files other than this one:

```
   #ifndef __VCCALCONST_H__
   #define __VCCALCONST_H__

   #define NUM_DAYS_IN_WEEK        7
   #define NUM_MONTHS_IN_YEAR      12
   #define ROWS_DISPLAYED_ON_CAL   6

   #define MAX_CELL_ATTACHMENTS    3
```

```
// capacity limits for sample prog
#define MAX_EVENTS   10
#define MAX_DEPTS    3
#endif
```

We also need some constants, and the definition of the **CalCel** type corresponding to each cell information:

```
#include "VccalConst.h"

const TCHAR numdays[] = _T("312831303130313130313031");
const TCHAR monthShortName[] = _T("JanFebMarAprMayJunJulAugSepOctNovDec");
const TCHAR dayName[] = _T("SunMonTueWedThuFriSat");
const ULONG monthShortLen = 3;
const ULONG dayNameLen = 3;

typedef struct {
   ULONG Item;
} Attach;

typedef struct {
   Attach Attachments[MAX_CELL_ATTACHMENTS];
   COleDateTime CelDate;
   CString Day;
   BOOL hasEvent;
   CString Label;
   CRect Position;
} CalCel;
```

Finally, the **CCellMgr** class declaration:

```
class CCellMgr
{
public:
   CCellMgr();
   virtual ~CCellMgr();

   void           ClearCells();
   const CString& GetCellNumber(ULONG idx);
   const CString& GetDayName(ULONG idx);
   ULONG          GetDaysInMonth(ULONG inMonth, ULONG inYear);
   const CString& GetLabel(ULONG idx);
   const CString& GetMonthYearText();
   void           SetCorners(ULONG idx, ULONG top, ULONG left, ULONG bottom, ULONG
right);
   void           SetDays(const COleDateTime &DateToSet);
   void           SetMonthYearText(const COleDateTime & inDate);

protected:
   void InitLongNames();

   CString m_MonthYearText;
   CString m_DayNames[NUM_DAYS_IN_WEEK];
   CString m_LongNames[NUM_MONTHS_IN_YEAR];
   CString m_ShortNames[NUM_MONTHS_IN_YEAR];
   ULONG m_DaysInMonth[NUM_MONTHS_IN_YEAR];
   CalCel m_Cells[NUM_DAYS_IN_WEEK * ROWS_DISPLAYED_ON_CAL];
};
```

The **CVccalCtrl** class itself has a member variable holding an instance of each of these classes:

```
...
// Implementation
protected:
    CFont * m_TitleFont;
    CString m_TitleFontName;
    short m_TitleFontSize;
    BOOL m_TitleFontBold;
    BOOL m_ButtonsVisible;
    CButton* m_pLeftBut;
    CButton* m_pRightBut;
    COleDateTime m_CurrentDay;
    CCellMgr m_CellMgr;
...
```

The cell manager is initialized each time the control's state is reset by the container, flushing out all the old cell data. Note that the timing and frequency of a call to this member is totally dependent on the container, and can vary widely between containers.

```
void CVccalCtrl::OnResetState()
{
    TRACE("CVccalCtrl::OnResetState\n");
    m_CellMgr.ClearCells();
    COleControl::OnResetState(); // Resets defaults found in DoPropExchange
}
```

The **ClearCells()** function simply dumps any data that may be in the **CalCel** array:

```
void CCellMgr::ClearCells()
{
    ULONG i;
    CalCel *tptr;
    for (i=0; i< NUM_DAYS_IN_WEEK * ROWS_DISPLAYED_ON_CAL; i++)
    {
        tptr = &m_Cells[i];
        memset((void *)tptr->Attachments,0, sizeof(tptr->Attachments));
        tptr->Day.Empty();
        tptr->hasEvent = FALSE;
        tptr->Label.Empty();
        tptr->Position.SetRectEmpty();
    }
    m_MonthYearText.Empty();
}
```

Much of the cell manager's initialization involves the initialization of constant strings and values used in painting the calendar's user interface. This initialization happens in its own constructor. This constructor is automatically executed when the parent **CVccalCtrl** is instantiated. Note that this approach to initialization allows for easy migration to resource string-based initialization, instead of constant strings as we've seen in this example. This provides us with possibilities for international localization. The generic-text mappings that are available in the include file **tchar.h** allow the use of a common source which can compile into either Unicode, single-byte or multibyte character constructs and function calls. The mappings cover data types (using, for example _**TCHAR** as a character type results in either **wchar_t**, for Unicode, or **char**, otherwise), constants and global variables (for example, _**TEOF** results in **WEOF**, for Unicode, or **EOF**, otherwise) and routine mapping (using, for example, _**ttoi()**, will result in a call to _**wtoi()**, if we compile for Unicode, or **atoi()**, otherwise).

```
CCellMgr::CCellMgr()
{
   ULONG i;
   for (i=0; i<12; i++)
   {
      m_DaysInMonth[i] = _ttoi((LPCTSTR) (CString(numdays).Mid(i*2,2)));
      m_ShortNames[i] = CString(monthShortName).Mid( i*monthShortLen,
         monthShortLen);
   }
   for (i=0; i<7; i++)
   {
      m_DayNames[i]= CString(dayName).Mid(i*dayNameLen , dayNameLen);
   }
   InitLongNames();
}
```

The `InitLongNames()` function simply sets up a static array with the long names of the month within it:

```
void CCellMgr::InitLongNames()
{
   m_LongNames[0] = _T("January");
   m_LongNames[1] = _T("February");
   m_LongNames[2] = _T("March");
   m_LongNames[3] = _T("April");
   m_LongNames[4] = _T("May");
   m_LongNames[5] = _T("June");
   m_LongNames[6] = _T("July");
   m_LongNames[7] = _T("August");
   m_LongNames[8] = _T("September");
   m_LongNames[9] = _T("October");
   m_LongNames[10] = _T("November");
   m_LongNames[11] = _T("December");
}
```

Besides the cell labels and date labels that get initialized in the constructor, the cell manager also needs the (x,y) coordinates of the cell on the display area, the actual date that the cell represents, and an array indicating the number of events happening on the day represented by the cell. These are stored in the private data members of the class.

The cell and date labels, as well as the date that the cell represents, can only be set when a date to display is decided upon, and our implementation does it in the protected `UpdateCore()` member function. This is frequently called when the control logic decides that an update of the display (if it exists) is required, i.e. whenever we change any of the properties of the control. This means that we need to add a call to this function into all our existing member functions which change a property value: all the `Set` methods (with the exception of `SetButtonsVisible()`), `AdvanceMonth()`, `SetStartDate()` and `DoPropExchange()` (but only when loading the properties).

```
void CVccalCtrl::UpdateCore()
{
   TRACE("CVccalCtrl::UpdateCore()\n");
   // set our new current day value
   m_CellMgr.SetDays(m_CurrentDay);
   if (m_pLeftBut != NULL) // we have a window
      InvalidateControl();
}
```

The **SetDays()** member of **CCellMgr**, will in turn set the cell labels and cell date values.

```cpp
void CCellMgr::SetDays(const COleDateTime &DateToSet)
{
    ULONG workMonth;
    COleDateTime firstDay;
    ULONG firstWeekDay;
    ULONG workYear, curDay;
    ULONG i,j, tpDays, pastMonth, nextMonth;
    TCHAR tpString[5];
    workMonth = DateToSet.GetMonth();
    workYear = DateToSet.GetYear();
    firstDay = COleDateTime(workYear, workMonth, 1,0,0,1);
    firstWeekDay = firstDay.GetDayOfWeek();
    ClearCells();
    SetMonthYearText(DateToSet);
    if (firstWeekDay != 1)
    {
        if (workMonth == 1)
            pastMonth = 12;
        else
            pastMonth = workMonth -1 ;
        tpDays = GetDaysInMonth(pastMonth, workYear) - firstWeekDay + 2;
        for (i=1; i<firstWeekDay; i++) // walk remainings from last mo.
        {
            _itot(tpDays, tpString, 10);
            m_Cells[i-1].Day = tpString;
            tpDays = tpDays + 1;
        }
        if (workMonth == 1)
            m_Cells[i-2].Label = m_ShortNames[11];
        else
            m_Cells[i-2].Label = m_ShortNames[workMonth -2];
    }
    i = firstWeekDay -1;
    curDay = 1;
    tpDays = GetDaysInMonth(workMonth, workYear);
    do
    {
        _itot(curDay, tpString, 10);
        m_Cells[i].Day = tpString;
        m_Cells[i].CelDate = curDay + COleDateTimeSpan(firstDay, 0, 0, 1);
        m_Cells[i].CelDate = m_Cells[i].CelDate - COleDateTimeSpan(1,0,0,1);
        i++;
        curDay++;
    } while (curDay <= tpDays);
    nextMonth = (workMonth == 12)? 1: (workMonth + 1);
    m_Cells[i].Label = m_ShortNames[nextMonth - 1];
    curDay = 1;
    for (j = i; j< NUM_DAYS_IN_WEEK * ROWS_DISPLAYED_ON_CAL; j++)
    {
        _itot(curDay, tpString, 10);
        m_Cells[j].Day = tpString;
        curDay++;
    }
} // of SetDays()
```

We use the **ClearCells()** method to clear out any old data that might be hanging around, then set the title of the control with **SetMonthYearText()**:

```
void CCellMgr::SetMonthYearText(const COleDateTime & inDate)
{
   TCHAR tpString[8];
   // Set the Month year text
   m_MonthYearText.Empty();
   m_MonthYearText = m_LongNames[inDate.GetMonth()-1] + " ";
   _itot(inDate.GetYear(), tpString, 10);
   m_MonthYearText = m_MonthYearText + tpString;
}
```

The final method used in **SetDays()** is the **GetDaysInMonth()**:

```
ULONG CCellMgr::GetDaysInMonth(ULONG inMonth, ULONG inYear)
{
   if (inMonth != 2)  // remember that inMonth is 1 based!
      return m_DaysInMonth[inMonth - 1];
   else
   { // check leap year
      if (((inYear % 4) == 0) && ((inYear % 100) != 0 || (inYear % 400) == 0))
         return 29;
      else
         return 28;
   }
}
```

The (x,y) co-ordinates maintained by the cell manager is used in hit-testing when a user clicks on the display area of the control. If the control is actually running (i.e. not in some sort of design mode, as in the case of VB or FrontPage), the **PaintGrid()** member of the **CVccalCtrl** control will initialize the cells with the appropriate coordinate values as they are being drawn.

The **PaintGrid()** function is fairly large since it has a lot to do. At a pseudocode level, it does the following:

- ▲ Calculates the margins and padding necessary, based on the input rectangle

- ▲ Draws the horizontal and vertical lines making up the grid

- ▲ During the grid drawing; it also performs the following:

   > Draws in the cell number (the day of the month) and the label (for the month prior and after the current month) by getting data from the **m_CellMgr** helper object

   > Stores the coordinates of the cells into the array managed by **m_CellMgr** for later hit-testing

- ▲ Positions the two child window buttons (if not drawing a metafile)

- ▲ Centers and draws the title using the currently selected title font and style

- ▲ Draws the short form of the days of the week above the grid columns

The calculations are straightforward and typical of any drawing routine. One liberty that we did take in coding the drawing routine is to do all calculations in **float** to avoid round off errors due to compound operations.

```cpp
void CVccalCtrl::PaintGrid(CDC * pdc, const CRect& inRect)
{
   TRACE("CVccalCtrl::PaintGrid\n");
   // do all intermediate calculations in float, elminate
   // compounding of round-offs during scaling
   float X1, Y1, X2, Y2;
   float curX, curY;
   ULONG counter;
   float cellWidth;
   float cellHeight;
   ULONG offsetY;
   float topMargin, leftMargin;
   ULONG i,j;
   float halfCellWidth, halfCellHeight;
   float xPad = 2;
   float yPad = 2;

   // calculate margins and spacing
   cellWidth = inRect.Width() / 8.0f;
   cellHeight = inRect.Height() / 8.0f;
   offsetY = long(cellHeight * 1.8); // one and half rows down

   topMargin = cellHeight / 2.0f;
   leftMargin = cellWidth / 2.0f;

   halfCellWidth = cellWidth / 2.0f;
   halfCellHeight = cellHeight /2.0f;
   // Calculate and draw vertical lines
   for( i = 0;i< 8; i++)
   {
      X1 = (i*cellWidth+leftMargin);
      Y1 = float(offsetY);
      X2 = (i * cellWidth + leftMargin);
      Y2 = (offsetY + cellHeight * 6);
      pdc->MoveTo((ULONG) X1, (ULONG) Y1);
      pdc->LineTo((ULONG) X2, (ULONG) Y2);
   }

   // Draw horizontal lines
   for (i=0; i<7; i++)
   {
      X1 = leftMargin;
      Y1 = (i *cellHeight)+offsetY;
      X2 = inRect.Width() - leftMargin;
      Y2 = (i * cellHeight) + offsetY;
      pdc->MoveTo((ULONG) X1, (ULONG) Y1);
      pdc->LineTo((ULONG) X2, (ULONG) Y2);
   }

   curX = leftMargin;
   curY = float(offsetY);
   counter = 0;
   for(i=0 ; i<6; i++)
   {
      curY = offsetY + i * cellHeight;
      for (j=0; j<7; j++)
      {
         curX = leftMargin + j * cellWidth;
```

```
                   // Print out the Cell number
                   CString tpOut = m_CellMgr.GetCellNumber(counter) + _T(" ");
                   tpOut = tpOut + m_CellMgr.GetLabel(counter);
                   // clip inside rectangle
                   CRect tmpRect(int(curX + xPad), int(curY+yPad),
                       int(curX+cellWidth -  xPad), int(curY + cellHeight - yPad));

               pdc->ExtTextOut((LONG) (curX + xPad), (LONG)(curY + yPad), ETO_CLIPPED, //
ETO_CLIPPED
                       tmpRect, tpOut, NULL);
                   //
                   // set the cell manager's cell array with coordinates values
                   m_CellMgr.SetCorners(counter, (ULONG) curY, (ULONG) curX,
                       ULONG(curY + cellHeight), ULONG(curX + cellWidth));
                   counter++;
               } // of j
        } // of i

        // Position the buttons
        float butSize = (halfCellWidth > halfCellHeight) ? halfCellHeight : halfCellWidth;
        if (m_pLeftBut != NULL)
        { // cannot move them if there are no windows
            butSize *= 1.5;
            CRect butSpace((int)leftMargin, (int)topMargin,
                int(leftMargin + butSize), int(topMargin + butSize));
            pdc->LPtoDP(butSpace);
            m_pLeftBut->MoveWindow(butSpace, TRUE);
            butSpace = CRect(int(leftMargin + 7 * cellWidth - butSize),
                (int)topMargin, int(leftMargin + 7 *cellWidth), int(topMargin + butSize));
            pdc->LPtoDP(butSpace);
            m_pRightBut->MoveWindow(butSpace, TRUE);
        }
        // center the labels
        CFont * tpFont;
        InitTitleFont(pdc, CRect(inRect));
        tpFont = pdc->SelectObject(m_TitleFont);
        float leftPad;
        CString LabelText = m_CellMgr.GetMonthYearText();
        CSize labelSize = pdc->GetTextExtent(LabelText);
        CRect boundRect;
        if (labelSize.cx > inRect.Width())
            boundRect = CRect(int(leftMargin + cellWidth),
                int(topMargin + butSize - max(labelSize.cy,0)),
                int(leftMargin + 6 * cellWidth),
                int(topMargin + butSize));
        else
        { // normal case
            leftPad = (inRect.Width()-labelSize.cx)/2.0f;
            boundRect = CRect((int)leftPad,
                int(topMargin + butSize - max(labelSize.cy,0)),
                int(inRect.Width()-leftPad),
                int(topMargin + butSize));
        }
        pdc->ExtTextOut(boundRect.left, boundRect.top, ETO_CLIPPED, //ETO_CLIPPED
            boundRect, LabelText, NULL);
        pdc->SelectObject(tpFont);
```

```
    //Paint the days of the week
    for (i = 0 ; i<7 ; i++)
    {
        TEXTMETRIC tpMetrics;
        pdc->GetTextMetrics(&tpMetrics);
        curY = offsetY - (tpMetrics.tmHeight) * 1.1f;
        curX = leftMargin + i * cellWidth;
        CRect tmpRect((int)curX, (int)curY, int(curX + cellWidth), int(curY +
cellHeight));
        pdc->ExtTextOut((LONG) (curX), (LONG)(curY), ETO_CLIPPED, //ETO_CLIPPED
            tmpRect, m_CellMgr.GetDayName(i), NULL);
    }
}
```

To output the cells properly, we need to get information from the **CCellMgr** class, namely the day number, stored in **CalCel.Label**:

```
const CString & CCellMgr::GetCellNumber(ULONG idx)
{
    return m_Cells[idx].Label;
}
```

the day of the month:

```
const CString  & CCellMgr::GetLabel(ULONG idx)
{
    return m_Cells[idx].Day;
}
```

the title for the control:

```
const CString & CCellMgr::GetMonthYearText()
{
    return m_MonthYearText;
}
```

and the day of the week:

```
const CString & CCellMgr::GetDayName(ULONG idx)
{
    return m_DayNames[idx ];
}
```

We also need to set up the **CRect** which we'll be using for hit-testing. This is done by passing the top-left and bottom-right corners of the bounding rectangle to the cell manager. These are then converted into a **CRect** and normalized:

```
void CCellMgr::SetCorners(ULONG idx, ULONG top, ULONG left, ULONG bottom, ULONG right)
{
    m_Cells[idx].Position = CRect(left, top, right, bottom);
    m_Cells[idx].Position.NormalizeRect();
}
```

We are now in a position to draw the control. The control won't have much in the way of functionality, but it's a good sanity check to make sure we have all the pieces correctly in place at this stage.

Implement the OnDraw() Function to Handle Control Drawing

We learned from the last chapter that **COleControl::OnDraw()** will be called should the control need to be re-drawn. This is where we implement all of our drawing logic. In addition, we make the simplifying assumption that the drawing we do is also good for the rendering of metafiles. Metafile rendering is required when the control is printed, or a cached representation of the control is required. For the purist reader, one can override the **OnDrawMetafile()** function, which by default calls **OnDraw()**, to better control what the metafile rendering would look like.

Before we look at **OnDraw()**, there are several rules that we must observe during control drawing:

- ▲ When we've finished, leave the device context the way it was found when we started
- ▲ Don't assume anything about the device context given
- ▲ Don't leave objects selected inside device contexts unless optimized drawing is activated
- ▲ Don't use functions requiring windows handles if drawing metafiles
- ▲ Always use the **COleControl** version of a drawing function instead of the **CWnd** one if available

The first three of these rules are good practices with any drawing code, whether associated with OCX or not. The later ones are OCX specific and are artifacts from our implementation, since we use the same function to draw into a window as well as a metafile. The last rule is a direct consequence of the newer OC96 standard for supporting windowless activation and inactive object.

We don't support optimized drawing in this sample. In order to make sure the device context is restored to the original state, we use a **SaveDC()** initially, and a **RestoreDC()** call when we finish drawing.

```
void CVccalCtrl::OnDraw(CDC* pdc, const CRect& rcBounds, const CRect& rcInvalid)
{
    TRACE("CVccalCtrl::OnDraw\n");
    ULONG savedDC = pdc->SaveDC();
...
    pdc->RestoreDC(savedDC);
}
```

The second rule, not being able to assume anything about the device context, means that we must explicitly set up the mapping mode, extents, brush, fonts, etc. which are used in the drawing. Again we perform this in the **OnDraw()** implementation:

```
void CVccalCtrl::OnDraw(CDC* pdc, const CRect& rcBounds, const CRect& rcInvalid)
{
    TRACE("CVccalCtrl::OnDraw\n");
    ULONG savedDC = pdc->SaveDC();
    CFont* pOldFont;
    pdc->SetBkMode(OPAQUE);
    pdc->FillRect(rcBounds, &CBrush(TranslateColor(AmbientBackColor())));
    CRect rcBoundsDP(rcBounds) ;
    // Convert boundaries to device points.
    pdc->LPtoDP(&rcBoundsDP) ;
    pdc->SetMapMode(MM_ANISOTROPIC) ;
    pdc->SetWindowOrg(0,0) ;
    pdc->SetWindowExt(800,600) ;
    pdc->SetViewportOrg(rcBoundsDP.left,rcBoundsDP.top) ;
```

```
    pdc->SetViewportExt(rcBoundsDP.Width(),rcBoundsDP.Height()) ;
    pdc->SetBkMode(TRANSPARENT);
    CRect Fake(0,0,800,600);
    PaintGrid(pdc, &Fake);
    pdc->RestoreDC(savedDC);
}
```

In the code above, we obtain the ambient background color from the container and use it as our background color for the calendar. We also set the extent of the control drawing area to map an 800x600 surface regardless of what shape the actual control may be resized to. This alleviates the actual drawing code from having to cope with any changing display area. The actual drawing code is performed in the **PaintGrid()** member function, which we've covered already.

Of course, make sure that you've included all the relevant header files in the source files. You should now be able to compile the control and insert it into the test container.

We now have a working control, although it only displays the month. To add department events to the calendar, we must implement the **CDataMgr** class, since it is closely associated with the back-end COM objects which make the entire system run. Therefore, let's take a look at the **CDataMgr** class and these COM objects before we proceed any further

The Object Model and the CDataMgr Class

The **CDataMgr** class actually obtains its event data through a back-end COM component. To the **CDataMgr** class, this back-end COM component is a single component exposing an 'object model' through which the **CDataMgr** class can create or manipulate objects, and obtain data. The fact that this COM component in turn uses one or more COM components to do its job is transparent to the front-end control.

In fact, the back-end COM component can be used just as readily if we were to code our front-end access through Visual Basic or Visual J++. It would present the same object model and interaction, and we can obtain the same data.

The containment and interaction relationships of objects within or 'behind' a business component is sometimes called its object model. The object model gives the user of a component a mental image of how things work behind the scenes. It serves as a visualization tool for providing documentation of how to use a set of COM interfaces exposed by the component. This may sound more complex than it actually is. Let's look at a concrete example through our project.

For the Calendar control to work in production, we want the control to go out to the network and 'pull' the event data 'live' from all the departments providing event information. We don't want to have a centralized web server or centralized database to which the individual departments submit information. Not only would this increase the cost of operating and bureaucracy, it also goes against the very nature of the intranet as a communications and enabling tool.

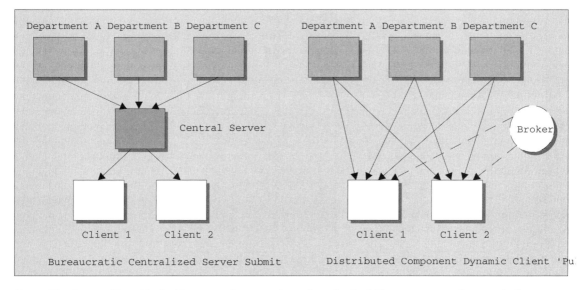

To enable this, an 'EventFinder' business object works with individual 'departments with events' objects to complete the object model. In our implementation, in order to keep the sample simple and workable even on Windows 95 machines, we've implemented these objects but haven't given them real data access capabilities. Diagrammatically, the object model looks like this:

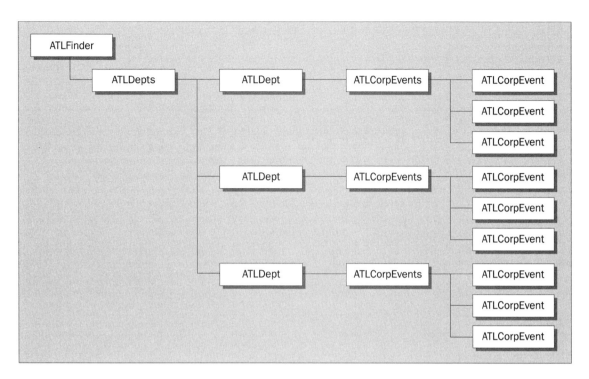

The above diagram says that the EventFinder object has a property with a value of type Depts. A Depts object is a collection of individual Dept objects. Each Dept object in turn has a property with a value of type CorpEvents. A CorpEvents object is a collection of individual CorpEvent objects. The CorpEvent object, of course, contains the details of a specific event. The following is a more detailed and specific description of the objects making up the model.

Class name	Object Represented	Description
ATLFinder	Finder for departments with events	The broker object locating all the departments with event information given a date. It keeps the collection of departments with events in an **EventfulDept** property holding a collection of department objects. This property is an instance of the **ATLDepts** class.
ATLDepts	A collection of departments	A generic collection of departments. We have added a 'secret' **Add** function to add departments for testing purposes without having to set up datasources.
ATLDept	A single department	Department containing name, symbol, and color information; also holds an instance of a **KnownEvents** property holding a collection of events.

Table Continued on Following Page

Class name	Object Represented	Description
ATLCorpEvents	Collection of events	A generic collection of events.
ATLCorpEvent	A single event	An event contains description, header, organizer, and detail information.

We can see from above that the **ATLFinder** object is the object that the Calendar control speaks directly to. It contains a (dynamic) list of departments that have events to offer. Depending on the month set by calling the **SetEventMonth()** method of the **ATLFinder** object, this list of departments may change. The property that contains this list of departments is called **EventfulDepts**. It's actually an instance of the **ATLDepts** class. Each member of this list is a department object. The department object contains the name of the department, as well as the symbol and color to be used when drawing the calendar. The most valuable member of the department object is a property called **KnownEvents**. This is actually a contained instance of the **ATLCorpEvents** class. The **KnownEvents** property is a list of known events for the specified month within the department. Each entry in this list is an instance of the **ATLCorpEvent** class. The **ATLCorpEvent** class represents the details of one particular event.

Typically, a user of this object model (one example of which is our Calendar control) will do the following:

1 Call **ATLFinder.SetEventMonth()** to set the date of the month of interest for the component

2 Access the **ATLFinder.EventfulDept** properties to get a list of all the departments with events to post during the month

3 Obtain access to a **ATLDepts** object through its COM interface

4 Iterate through the list of departments and for each department perform steps 5 to 10

5 Obtain access to a **ATLDept** object through its COM interface

6 Access the **KnownEvents** member of the department to get a list of all the events available

7 Obtain access to a **ATLCorpEvents** collection object through its COM interface

8 Iterate through the list of events performing steps 9 and 10 for each one

9 Obtain access to a **ATLCorpEvent** object through its COM interface

10 Get the event details

The diagram above shows how the entire series of interactions boils down to property access and method invocation across different objects/components. It's this simple object interaction scheme, supported by COM and OLE Automation, which will allow us to extend our application by distributing certain objects within our model.

Finally, as a visual reference point providing a much needed bird's eye view of the complete system, the following diagram presents how all of the components fit together:

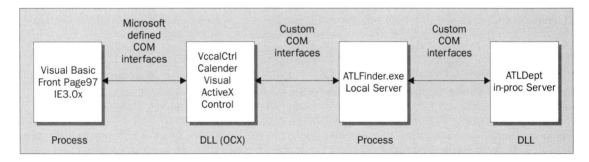

One very desirable benefit of this design is that it doesn't attempt to change the diverse operating culture within each department. Instead of introducing new systems to the legacy events filing and tracking system, that are possibly implemented on different hardware and OS platforms in each department, a project leader is only required to supply the COM interfaces used by our Calendar application. The programming language used, the system used, and the implementation details, are all invisible to the intranet developers. To ensure success, the set of defined COM interfaces provides the contract while the object model, the operating semantics documentation, and the sample code provide the contract details. In fact, by providing skeletal implementation sample code in Visual Basic, C/C++, and Java, many of the departments are able to wire up their legacy systems to this COM-based 'infrastructure' in a very short time. Some departments decided to implement a 'daily export to ASCII file' data interchange scheme, others wrote code to directly access their event data sources. Because of the higher level COM contract provided by the intranet team, each department is free to change the way they fulfill the contract at any time they choose.

About VTBL Interfaces, Disp Interfaces, and Dual Interfaces

We've been talking about how the Calendar control will interact with the **ATLFinder** object through COM interfaces, but have not elaborated on exactly how. So far, we've been building ATL-based objects that provide something called **dual interfaces**. We did this because ATL offers dual interface implementation to us with almost no work from us. A dual interface is specified in the IDL file as:

```
...
    [
        object,
        public,
        uuid(721B4F02-4D27-11D0-8564-004005263AF7),
        dual
    ]
    interface IATLFinder1 : IDispatch
    {
...
```

Other than **dual**, there are also **vtable** (vtbl) interfaces and **dispatch** (disp) interfaces. These terms will need to be explained here. First, be assured that a dual interface has the personality such that it is both a **vtable** and a **dispatch** interface. Before ATL was available, the implementation of dual interfaces was difficult. Consequently, COM objects created using MFC and Visual C++ before version 5 support either **vtable** or **dispatch** interfaces only.

VTBL interfaces, as the name suggests, depend on the existence of a virtual function table for the client to bind to. The COM interfaces that we've worked with in the earlier chapters are **vtable** interfaces. Basically, the client only needs to include the definition file of the interface. The methods of the interface are offset from the interface pointer (offset into the vtable) which can be determined at compile time. The real nice feature of VTBL interfaces is that they are extremely fast. If the COM server is an in-proc server, they execute at the same speed as a normal C++ function call. This way of accessing a COM object's interface is sometimes referred to as vtbl binding or **early binding**. The term refers to the fact that binding from the caller (client of the COM server) to the called party (the COM server) is determined early, at compile time.

The other type of interface, called a dispinterface (or dispatch interface), is actually not a physical interface type at all. That is, when we examine the binary object representing the COM server, we won't find entry points associated with the methods of the interface at all. Some may say that they are not COM interfaces, from a purist viewpoint—and they are quite right. Their history goes back to the initial growth of Visual Basic. The dispatch interface was invented so that Visual Basic programs could control and make use of the functionality contained within external applications such as Word or Excel. While normal COM vtbl interfaces would allow COM clients to control COM servers, Visual Basic, being purely interpreted in the early days, had no way of binding and making use of vtbl-based interfaces. Instead, the VB team invented one single vtbl interface, called **IDispatch**, through which it could 'tunnel' access to an unlimited number of methods. Furthermore, in an attempt to make access more transparent to the VB programmer, the specification for **IDispatch** maps access to methods of a dispinterface into two general categories:

 Property access

 Method invocation

Each property access maps to either one (for a read-only or write-only property) or more method invocations. We've seen this in our implementation of the Calendar control, in the form of **Get** and **Set** property access methods. Furthermore, since **IDispatch** uses COM underneath, it's necessary to define the types of the parameters passed ahead of time. Because of the difficulty in determining the type of the parameters passed during method invocation, all parameters of methods invoked through **IDispatch** are of the same type. This type is actually a 'mega-union' of all the types supported by Visual Basic, except for user-defined types. It's called a **VARIANT**. We'll be examining the definition of the **VARIANT** union a little later. For now, suffice it to say that the use of **VARIANT**s as parameter types split the work of conventional COM marshalling between the caller of the dispatch interface and the implementer of the dispatch interface. The caller has to format the actual parameters into the **VARIANT** structure and set its tag, signifying the actual type of the data, while the interface implementer has to examine the tag for its type, and extract the parameter.

One scenario of a client call into a dispatch interface is depicted here:

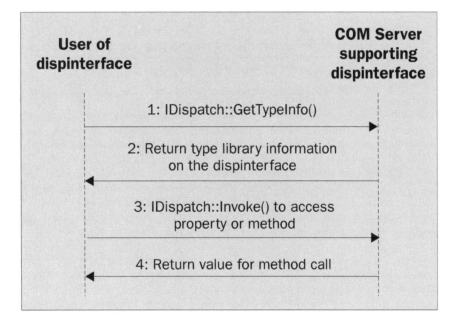

In this case, the client is interested in finding out the interface description and the dispatch IDs of the methods, properties, and parameters through the type library. After the information is obtained, the caller knows how to call **IDispatch::Invoke()** to access the methods and properties. This information can be 'compiled in' with the pseudo-executable files that interpretive languages typically provide. This is the most efficient form of binding-based on **IDispatch**, and can actually be done at 'compile time'. What happens is that steps (1) and (2) are done at compile time, and steps (3) and (4), above, are done during runtime. The latest version of Visual Basic, version 5, can take advantage of this form of binding if type library information is available for a dispatch interface.

In another scenario, the client environment doesn't study the type library information (or it isn't available). Then, the client interpretive environment has to assume that the writer of the program knows how to access the dispatch interface somehow (i.e. by reading a manual), and that the methods that they call are valid. This is the interaction:

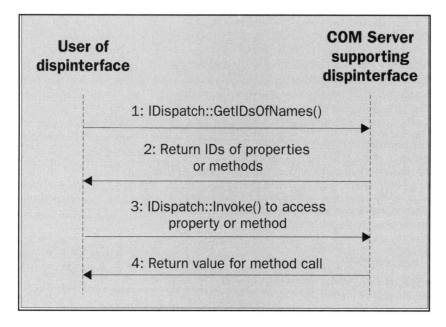

In this case, if any of the names supplied by the user's program are incorrect, it would only be discovered during runtime when the statement is executed. Furthermore, every time the statement is executed again, the same sequence of actions have to be performed again. This results in rather impaired performance but allows for maximum dynamism. This form of dispatch interface usage is called **late binding**. The binding is late because the caller doesn't even find out what it can do with the called party until the statement is actually executed. One very common form of optimization on the above is the 'caching' of the dispatch IDs once they are discovered: this avoids the extra **IDispatch::GetIDsOfNames()** call if the same property or method is invoked again. This works because the COM server providing the dispatch interface is obliged to keep the dispatch IDs the same for the lifetime of the object.

The general way of invoking methods and accessing properties through the **IDispatch** interface described above is called Automation (or OLE Automation in the past). As a result of the **VARIANT** parameter type used in Automation, automation interfaces (dispatch interfaces in most cases) can only have parameters with Visual Basic types. If you need an interface which passes a custom structure, you'll need to implement a non-automation custom vtable interface.

A dual interface, as we've said at the beginning of this section, is both a vtable interface and dispatch interface. Essentially, a dual interface has the following properties:

- It is always derived from **IDispatch**, which means it implements all four methods of **IDispatch**
- All of the methods provided are also accessible directly through vtable binding

Having constructed many COM objects, we realize that implementing the first item above requires a little work. The second item is trivial since that's what we've been doing all along: creating vtable interfaces. Now if, in implementing the first item, after determining the method called, and unpacking parameters from **VARIANT**s, we simply call one of these vtable methods—then we have the makings of a dual interface.

With Visual C++ 5.0 and ATL 2.1, all we have to do to get dual interface support is to select an option in the ATL COM Wizard. It provides support by deriving our class from the **IDispatchImpl<>** templated class:

```
class ATL_NO_VTABLE CATLFinder1 :
    public CComObjectRootEx<CComObjectThreadModel>,
    public CComCoClass<CATLFinder1, &CLSID_CATLFinder1>,
    public IDispatchImpl<IATLFinder1, &IID_IATLFinder1,
                    &LIBID_ATLFINDERLib>
{
...
};
```

ATL makes creation of dual interfaces trivial, and there's really no reason why you shouldn't create dual interfaces all the time. The only possible excuses are:

- ▲ You can't spare the minute amount of extra code generated to support a dual interface

- ▲ You know for sure that your object will only be called by clients using dispatch interfaces or vtable interfaces (this, of course, goes against the reuse spirit of component technologies anyway)

- ▲ You're lazy

Visual C++ before Version 5.0 only supported the creation of dispatch interface-based controls using MFC. However, even these controls can be retrofitted with dual interfaces by creating the vtable manually and hooking in the implementation routines. Microsoft MFC technical note 'TN065: Dual-Interface Support for OLE Automation Servers' covers this procedure if you need to convert old controls. This would be a highly unlikely activity, though, for the following reasons:

- ▲ If your control is a visual one, the OCX specification requires only dispatch interfaces, which it probably already supports.

- ▲ If your control is a nonvisual one, the chances are that you've coded it from scratch *or* using ATL. In both cases you'd have vtable interface support already.

Summary

In this chapter, we presented the design and implementation of a fully functional ActiveX control using Visual C++ and MFC. The Vccal control is the front-end part of our three-tier design and is responsible for the presentation of data acquired from the back-end COM objects. We've also presented our complete design in terms of the control and COM object interactions for the whole system. At this stage, without the implementation of the remaining COM objects to supply it with data, the front-end control isn't very impressive!

Not to worry, though! In the next chapter, we dive right into the design and implementation issues awaiting us as we implement the remaining COM objects, and then modify the front-end to access them and present the acquired data to the user.

Advanced ATL for ActiveX Components

In this chapter, we focus on the design and implementation of some core business COM objects that can be accessed by presentation components similar to the Calendar control we developed in the previous chapter, providing them with required data. We take a look at some advanced ATL issues as we apply them to the design of the back-end components.

We then modify the Calendar control we built before, in order to interact with the back-end components and complete the user interaction.

Finally, we provide a variety of testing scenarios for the complete three-tier system.

Obtaining Data

Before we can build the **CDataMgr**, though, we must construct the back-end COM objects. These are built using ATL 2.1 and Visual C++ 5.0. We'll cover their construction now.

Determining Objects, Interfaces, and Server Type

The back-end consists of two COM servers. The **Atlfinder.exe** server is a local server, and the **Atldept.dll** is an in-proc server. Construction of both servers is very similar since they both contain collections of other objects (**ATLFinder** has **EventfulDepts**, and **ATLDept** has **KnownEvents**). The construction of **Atldept.dll** is slightly more involved because it maintains data for both the 'department' objects that it represents, as well as the 'departmental event' objects. We'll look at the construction of **Atldept.dll** first. For **Atldept.dll**, we'll need to implement the following objects:

  ATLDept1, the department object

  ATLCorpEvents1, the events collection

  ATLCorpEvent1, an event object

We'll be creating an in-proc server to keep things simple. Examining the list of objects to implement, we realize that the client will only ever need to create instances of the **ATLDept1** class externally, since the **ATLCorpEvents1** and **ATLCorpEvent1** objects will be created internal to **ATLDept1**. Consequently, we should not give external clients the ability to create instances of the **ATLCorpEvents1** and **ATLCorpEvent1** classes; we can accomplish this by the appropriate specifications in the **.IDL** file. In essence, we'll only provide a **coclass** definition for the **ATLDept1** (ATL implementation of the Dept object) class. This will be explained in the *Defining the COM interface in IDL* section next.

Creating an ATL Skeletal Project

Since we've worked through several complete ATL projects already, we'll breeze through this portion to keep you from getting bored. Start a new project in Visual C++ and use the ATL COM AppWizard and call it **ATLDept**. Specify creating the above 3 objects with 1 interface each, choose advanced registry support, create an 'in-proc' DLL server, and select dual interfaces. The AppWizard will generate the skeletal code and `.IDL` file for further modifications.

Defining the COM Interfaces in IDL

Now we have to specify the properties and methods for our COM interfaces in our `.IDL` file. Let's take a look at how we define the properties and methods of the **ATLDept1** class.

```
[
    object,
    public,
    uuid(D2A1CBC2-4C5E-11D0-8564-004005263AF7),
    dual,
    helpstring("IATLDept1 Interface"),
    pointer_default(unique)
]
interface IATLDept1 : IDispatch
{
    // Name
    [propget, id(1), helpstring("property Name")]
        HRESULT Name([out, retval] BSTR *pVal);
    [propput, id(1), helpstring("property Name")]
        HRESULT Name([in] BSTR newVal);
    // Number
    [propget, id(2), helpstring("property Number")]
        HRESULT Number([out, retval] BSTR *pVal);
    [propput, id(2), helpstring("property Number")]
        HRESULT Number([in] BSTR newVal);
    // CanRead
    [propget, id(3), helpstring("property CanRead")]
        HRESULT CanRead([out, retval] BOOL *pVal);
    [propput, id(3), helpstring("property CanRead")]
        HRESULT CanRead([in] BOOL newVal);
    // CanPostNew
    [propget, id(4), helpstring("property CanPostNew")]
        HRESULT CanPostNew([out, retval] BOOL *pVal);
    [propput, id(4), helpstring("property CanPostNew")]
        HRESULT CanPostNew([in] BOOL newVal);
    // Symbol
    [propget, id(5), helpstring("property Symbol")]
        HRESULT Symbol([out, retval] BSTR *pVal);
    [propput, id(5), helpstring("property Symbol")]
        HRESULT Symbol([in] BSTR newVal);
    // Color
    [propget, id(6), helpstring("property Color")]
        HRESULT Color([out, retval] long *pVal);
    [propput, id(6), helpstring("property Color")]
        HRESULT Color([in] long newVal);
    // KnownEvents
    [propget, id(7), helpstring("property KnownEvents")]
        HRESULT KnownEvents([out, retval] VARIANT *pVal);
};
```

Notice the straightforward mapping of an automation property to a **propget** or **propput** method. The string type used is a Visual Basic compatible **BSTR** type. A Boolean type maps to **VARIANT_BOOL**. The Visual Basic **Color** type maps to a **long** value. The only tricky looking thing is the **KnownEvents** property, which was a Visual Basic compatible **ATLCorpEvents1** object reference type. Like any other complex automation type, this one also maps to a **VARIANT** type. We'll take an in-depth look at this **VARIANT** mapping a little bit later.

Note that this **IATLDept1** interface is a dual interface derived from **IDispatch**. It will also be specified as the default interface for the **ATLDept1** object, as we'll see in the declaration of the **CATLDept1** class later on. This pattern can be applied in general to automation interfaces that are compatible with Visual Basic. The default interface for an object should contain all the required methods and properties that are to be exposed to the automation client. The object, of course, may expose additional interfaces, useful to nonautomation clients.

For access to the **ATLCorpEvents1** class, we have defined an **IATLCorpEvents1** interface.

```
[
    object,
    uuid(D2A1CBC7-4C5E-11D0-8564-004005263AF7),
    dual,
    helpstring("IATLCorpEvents1 Interface"),
    pointer_default(unique)
]
interface IATLCorpEvents1 : IDispatch
{
    [propget, id(1), helpstring("Returns number of items in collection.")]
        HRESULT Count([out, retval] long *pVal);
    [id(2)]
        HRESULT Add(DATE DateTime, BSTR bstrLocation, BSTR bstrHeading,
            BSTR bstrOrganizer, BSTR bstrOrgDept, BSTR bstrDetails,
            BSTR bstrHlink);
    [id(3)] HRESULT DeleteFirst();
    [propget, id(DISPID_NEWENUM), helpstring("Returns an enumerator for the"
            "collection."), restricted]
        HRESULT _NewEnum([out, retval] LPUNKNOWN *pVal);
    [propget, id(DISPID_VALUE), helpstring("Given an index, returns an item"
            "in the collection.")]
        HRESULT Item(long Index, [out, retval] VARIANT *pVal);
};
```

The **ATLCorpEvents1** class is an automation collection class. Its implementation will be discussed in a later section. It has a function called **_NewEnum()**, which has a DISPID value of **DISPID_NEWENUM=-4**, and has a **restricted** attribute. The method is provided to enable the **For Each...Next** syntax of Visual Basic. This provides a way to work with the **ATLCorpEvents1** collection 'naturally' in scripting environments such as VBScript or VBA from Office 97. We'll talk in more detail about enumerations in a later section of this chapter.

We set the **Item()** method to be the default method by setting its DISPID to **DISPID_VALUE**. The **Item()** method is frequently designated as the default method of a collection. This allows a Visual Basic program to simply name the collection to index one of its members. For example:

```
MyDept.KnownEvents(6)
```

is equivalent to:

```
MyDept.KnownEvents.Item(6)
```

When the **Item()** method is invoked, a language like Visual Basic will expect an object reference to be returned, such as a **ATLCorpEvent1** object reference. However, we see here that the **Item()** method returns a **VARIANT**. We'll discuss **VARIANT** mapping in automation a little later on. For now, suffice it to say that most object references for Visual Basic will map to **VARIANT** when implementing interface specifications in IDL.

Finally, our **ATLCorpEvent1** class will be accessed through the **IATLCorpEvent1** interface, which is specified to be:

```
[
    object,
    uuid(D2A1CBCC-4C5E-11D0-8564-004005263AF7),
    dual,
    helpstring("IATLCorpEvent1 Interface"),
    pointer_default(unique)
]
interface IATLCorpEvent1 : IDispatch
{
    // DateTime
    [propget, id(1), helpstring("property DateTime")]
        HRESULT DateTime([out, retval] DATE *pVal);
    [propput, id(1), helpstring("property DateTime")]
        HRESULT DateTime([in] DATE newVal);
    // Location
    [propget, id(2), helpstring("property Location")]
        HRESULT Location([out, retval] BSTR *pVal);
    [propput, id(2), helpstring("property Location")]
        HRESULT Location([in] BSTR newVal);
    // Heading
    [propget, id(3), helpstring("property Heading")]
        HRESULT Heading([out, retval] BSTR *pVal);
    [propput, id(3), helpstring("property Heading")]
        HRESULT Heading([in] BSTR newVal);
    // Organizer
    [propget, id(4), helpstring("property Organizer")]
        HRESULT Organizer([out, retval] BSTR *pVal);
    [propput, id(4), helpstring("property Organizer")]
        HRESULT Organizer([in] BSTR newVal);
    // Details
    [propget, id(5), helpstring("property Details")]
        HRESULT Details([out, retval] BSTR *pVal);
    [propput, id(5), helpstring("property Details")]
        HRESULT Details([in] BSTR newVal);
    // Hlink
    [propget, id(6), helpstring("property Hlink")]
        HRESULT Hlink([out, retval] BSTR *pVal);
    [propput, id(6), helpstring("property Hlink")]
        HRESULT Hlink([in] BSTR newVal);
    // orgDept
    [propget, id(7), helpstring("property orgDept")]
        HRESULT orgDept([out, retval] BSTR *pVal);
    [propput, id(7), helpstring("property orgDept")]
        HRESULT orgDept([in] BSTR newVal);
};
```

The implementation of the **ATLCorpEvent1** class will be discussed later. Having seen the IDL declaration of **IATLDept1** and **IATLCorpEvents1**, this **IATLCorpEvent1** interface definition doesn't contain any new elements. The actual **coclass** definition, though, is quite interesting.

```
    [
      uuid(D2A1CBC0-4C5E-11D0-8564-004005263AF7),
      version(1.0),
      helpstring("ATLDept 1.0 Type Library")
    ]
    library ATLDEPTLib
    {
      importlib("stdole32.tlb");
      importlib("stdole2.tlb");

      interface IATLCorpEvents1;
      interface IATLCorpEvent1;
      interface IATLDept1;

      [
        uuid(8C80B86F-93C9-11D0-891C-004095E279DD),
        helpstring("ATLDept1 Class")
      ]
      coclass ATLDept1
      {
        [default] interface IATLDept1;
      };
    };
```

Here, we see that the type library consists of the definition of the three interfaces and one **coclass**. Only the **CATLDept1 coclass** is defined, and we specified that **IATLDept1** as its one and only default interface. What happened to the **CATLCorpEvents1** and **CATLCorpEvent1** classes?

Actually, we'll provide full implementation of these classes within our code. However, since object instances of these classes are never created externally by clients, we will not register them through the type library. When the time comes to create them, we will not go through **CoCreateObject()**, but do so directly using a facility provided by ATL. This technique provides effective encapsulation and protection for dependent objects within an object model.

Note that if you used the ATL COM App Wizard to create the **ATLCorpEvents1** and **ATLCorpEvent1** classes, it will have created **coclass** definitions in the **.IDL** file. You need to edit it so that it is identical to the one above. You must take three additional steps so that your project compiles.

First, you must remove the inheritance from the **CComCoClass** template from the class declarations of **CATLCorpEvents1** and **CATLCorpEvent1**, along with commenting out the **DECLARE_REGISTRY_RESOURCEID()**.

```
    class ATL_NO_VTABLE CATLCorpEvents1 :
        public CComObjectRootEx<CComObjectThreadModel>,
    //    public CComCoClass<CATLCorpEvents1, &CLSID_CATLCorpEvents1>,
        public IDispatchImpl<IATLCorpEvents1, &IID_IATLCorpEvents1, &LIBID_ATLDEPTLib>
    {
    ...
    // DECLARE_REGISTRY_RESOURCEID(IDR_ATLCORPEVENTS1)
    ...
    };
```

```
class ATL_NO_VTABLE CATLCorpEvent1 :
     public CComObjectRootEx<CComObjectThreadModel>,
//    public CComCoClass<CATLCorpEvent1, &CLSID_CATLCorpEvent1>,
     public IDispatchImpl<IATLCorpEvent1, &IID_IATLCorpEvent1, &LIBID_ATLDEPTLib>
{
...
// DECLARE_REGISTRY_RESOURCEID(IDR_ATLCORPEVENT1)
...
};
```

Second, you must remove the corresponding entries in the application Object Map.

```
// ATLDept.cpp : Implementation of DLL Exports.


// Note: Proxy/Stub Information
//       To build a separate proxy/stub DLL,
//       run nmake -f ATLDeptps.mk in the project directory.

#include "stdafx.h"
#include "resource.h"
#include "initguid.h"
#include "ATLDept.h"

#include "ATLDept_i.c"
#include "ATLDept1.h"
#include "ATLCorpEvents1.h"
#include "ATLCorpEvent1.h"


CComModule _Module;

BEGIN_OBJECT_MAP(ObjectMap)
    OBJECT_ENTRY(CLSID_ATLDept1, CATLDept1)
//   OBJECT_ENTRY(CLSID_ATLCorpEvents1, CATLCorpEvents1)
//   OBJECT_ENTRY(CLSID_ATLCorpEvent1, CATLCorpEvent1)
END_OBJECT_MAP()
...
```

Third, you need to remove the two **.RGS** files from the project to stop them from being registered as separate objects.

We'll explain these steps a little later on, when we talk about the **CATLCorpEvents1** and **CATLCorpEvent1** classes.

Mapping Types to VARIANT in IDL

We saw above that method parameters or return values containing object references in Visual Basic become **VARIANT** types in IDL.

The **VARIANT** is actually a tagged C **union** defined to hold a variety of different data types. The following lists the data type that a **VARIANT** can contain, and the tag value associated with it.

Type	Union Tag Value	Description
LONG	VT_I4	4 byte long value.
BYTE	VT_UI1	1 byte value.
SHORT	VT_I2	2 byte numeric value.
FLOAT	VT_R4	Four byte floating point value.
DOUBLE	VT_R8	Eight byte double precision floating point value.
VARIANT_BOOL	VT_BOOL	Boolean value, true or false.
SCODE	VT_ERROR	COM error return code.
CY	VT_CY	Fixed point currency value representing money.
DATE	VT_DATE	Absolute date time value.
BSTR	VT_BSTR	Visual Basic binary string with a preceding length value.
IUnknown *	VT_UNKNOWN	Pointer to **IUnknown** interface of a COM object.
IDispatch *	VT_DISPATCH	Pointer to the **IDispatch** interface of a COM object.
SAFEARRAY *	VT_ARRAY	Array of elements with associated locking and allocation information.
BYTE *	VT_BYREF | VT_UI1	Pointer to a byte value.
SHORT *	VT_BYREF | VT_I2	Pointer to a **short** value.
LONG *	VT_BYREF | VT_I4	Pointer to a **long** value.
FLOAT *	VT_BYREF | VT_R4	Pointer to a **float** value.
DOUBLE *	VT_BYREF | VT_R8	Pointer to a double precision value.
VARIANT_BOOL *	VT_BYREF | VT_BOOL	Pointer to a Boolean value.
SCODE *	VT_BYREF | VT_ERROR	Pointer to a COM error return code.
CY *	VT_BYREF | VT_CY	Pointer to a fixed point currency value.
DATE *	VT_BYREF | VT_DATE	Pointer to an absolute date value.
BSTR *	VT_BYREF | VT_BSTR	Pointer to a **BSTR** value
IUnknown **	VT_BYREF | VT_UNKNOWN	Pointer to an **IUnknown** pointer.
IDispatch **	VT_BYREF | VT_DISPATCH	Pointer to an **IDispatch** pointer.
SAFEARRAY **	VT_BYREF | VT_ARRAY	Pointer to an array.
VARIANT *	VT_BYREF | VT_VARIANT	Pointer to a **VARIANT** value.

Table Continued on Following Page

Type	Union Tag Value	Description
PVOID	VT_BYREF	Generic pointer.
CHAR	VT_I1	Single byte character value.
USHORT	VT_UI2	Two bytes unsigned integer.
ULONG	VT_UI4	Four bytes unsigned integer.
INT	VT_INT	Integer.
UINT	VT_UINT	Unsigned integer.
DECIMAL *	VT_BYREF | VT_DECIMAL	Pointer to a decimal value.
CHAR *	VT_BYREF | VT_I1	Pointer to a **char** value.
USHORT *	VT_BYREF | VT_UI2	Pointer to an **unsigned short** value.
ULONG *	VT_BYREF | VT_UI4	Pointer to an **unsigned long** value.
INT *	VT_BYREF | VT_INT	Pointer to an integer value.
UINT *	VT_BYREF | VT_UINT	Pointer to an unsigned integer value.

Examining this monster union, the question that springs to mind is 'Why was such a messy structure ever invented?'. The answer lies in the Visual Basic heritage of Automation that we've discussed earlier. In a nutshell, communicating objects are talking to each other via method invocations and property adjustments. These communications happen across process, machine (over a network), and virtual machine (when OLE16 talks to OLE32 on the system) boundaries. The **VARIANT** structure represents an agreement on the type of data that can be passed as arguments for the methods, and the data type that properties can have. Having this agreement allows the OS vendor to create 'automatic marshalling' code. Essentially, this means that Microsoft can create code which will guarantee that the same value passed from one object is received at the other end. This may sound trivial or stupid initially, but when one takes into account all the different representations of some common data types across different machine architectures, this is actually very useful. By defining the single magical **VARIANT** type, it allows macro language and programming tool vendors to focus on what they do best, while leaving Microsoft with the tougher problem of handling distributed object communications in a heterogeneous environment. Programming languages can be written to be completely type insensitive by making every variable a **VARIANT**, and then magically these languages can be used to script distributed components across a network.

Yes, there's definitely a cost in terms of performance, encoding and decoding variable types on the fly, and in terms of the storage size when small data types are represented by **VARIANT**s. However, with the increasing word size of modern microprocessors, and the shift from machine-specific compiled language to machine-independent interpreted language for application development, these 'problems' may eventually become nonissues.

Visual Basic, sharing its heritage with macro language such as Visual Basic for Applications, and scripting language such as VBScript, often requires the mapping of **VARIANT** compatible types to **VARIANT**s when interfacing with external code modules and/or COM based objects. This is the reason why we had to map the custom object reference (which is not **VARIANT** compatible) to a **VARIANT** containing an **IUnknown** pointer.

Implementation of the IATLDept1 Interface

With the IDL description out of the way, we're ready to code the actual methods of the interfaces. Let's take a look at the interface map entries. For the **CATLDept1** object, **IATLDept1** is the default interface, as well as the dispatch interface.

```
class ATL_NO_VTABLE CATLDept1 :
    public CComObjectRootEx<CComObjectThreadModel>,
     public CComCoClass<CATLDept1, &CLSID_CATLDept1>,
        public IDispatchImpl<IATLDept1, &IID_IATLDept1, &LIBID_ATLDEPTLib>
{
public:
    CATLDept1();

DECLARE_REGISTRY_RESOURCEID(IDR_ATLDEPT1)

BEGIN_COM_MAP(CATLDept1)
    COM_INTERFACE_ENTRY(IATLDept1)
    COM_INTERFACE_ENTRY(IDispatch)
END_COM_MAP()
. . .
```

To maintain the property values in our object, we have a set of member variables which keep the value of the properties of the object, as well as the property access methods themselves. Note how each **propget** and **propput** attribute in the IDL becomes a **get_** or **put_** member function of the class.

```
    . . .
    STDMETHOD(get_KnownEvents)(/*[out, retval]*/ VARIANT *pVal);
    STDMETHOD(get_Color)(/*[out, retval]*/ long *pVal);
    STDMETHOD(put_Color)(/*[in]*/ long newVal);
    STDMETHOD(get_Symbol)(/*[out, retval]*/ BSTR *pVal);
    STDMETHOD(put_Symbol)(/*[in]*/ BSTR newVal);
    STDMETHOD(get_CanPostNew)(/*[out, retval]*/ BOOL *pVal);
    STDMETHOD(put_CanPostNew)(/*[in]*/ BOOL newVal);
    STDMETHOD(get_CanRead)(/*[out, retval]*/ BOOL *pVal);
    STDMETHOD(put_CanRead)(/*[in]*/ BOOL newVal);
    STDMETHOD(get_Number)(/*[out, retval]*/ BSTR *pVal);
    STDMETHOD(put_Number)(/*[in]*/ BSTR newVal);
    STDMETHOD(get_Name)(/*[out, retval]*/ BSTR *pVal);
    STDMETHOD(put_Name)(/*[in]*/ BSTR newVal);
    HRESULT FinalConstruct();
    HRESULT FinalRelease();
protected:
    CComBSTR    m_bstrName;
    CComBSTR    m_bstrNumber;
    VARIANT_BOOL m_bCanPostNew;
    VARIANT_BOOL m_bCanRead;
    CComBSTR    m_bstrSymbol;
    long    m_ulColor;
    CComObject<CATLCorpEvents1>* m_pKnownEvents;
    IUnknown * m_pUnknownRansom;
};
```

Of particular interest here is the use of an ATL defined class, **CComBSTR** to handle the **BSTR** data type. This is especially convenient and saves on code. Much of the construction, copying, conversion, and release coding is performed automatically by the **CComBSTR** class.

Briefly, the ATL **CComBSTR** class includes these members:

Member	Type	Description
Attach	method	Attaches an existing **BSTR** to the object to use its method and operators.
CComBSTR	method	Constructor from a UNICODE string or an ANSI string. A copy constructor is also supplied as well as a default constructor.
Copy	method	Creates and return another copy of the represented **BSTR**.
Detach	method	Detaches a **BSTR** from the object after performing operations.
Empty	method	Frees the associated **BSTR**.
Operator BSTR	operator	Casts a **CComBSTR** object to a **BSTR**, allowing direct reference.
Operator =	operator	Allows assignment from UNICODE, ANSI, or another **CComBSTR**.
Operator &	operator	Returns a pointer to the represented **BSTR**.
Operator !	operator	Returns True if the represented **BSTR** is null, returns False otherwise.
m_str	member variable ·	The member variable containing the actual **BSTR**.

The **VARIANT_BOOL** data type, while looking especially threatening because of the mention of **VARIANT**, is actually currently defined to be a **short** value. It can thus be handled as an elementary data type. For the **m_pKnownEvents** collection member variable, we declare it as an ATL supported COM object by using:

```
CComObject<CATLCorpEvents1>* m_pKnownEvents;
```

Note the very strange declaration:

```
IUnknown * m_pUnknownRansom;
```

What's this for?

Well it turns out that we must remember an important aspect of programming COM objects using C++:

COM objects can be represented by C++ objects, but COM objects do not equal C++ objects.

The main difference lies in the lifetime management model. If a C++ object is created on the stack, it disappears when the current scope is exited. If a C++ object is allocated on the heap via a **new** call, it's deallocated when **delete** is called. A COM object, on the other hand, will die as soon as its reference count goes to zero!

This means that in order to keep an embedded COM object (the **m_pKnownEvents** property) within our **CATLDept1** object, we must always keep the COM object's reference count greater than zero. We must hold it ransom until the parent COM object terminates. This means that simply keeping

m_pKnownEvents pointer around is insufficient, and this is the reason for the **m_pUnknownRansom** pointer. This latter pointer is used to keep the embedded COM object from disappearing until we terminate.

When a COM object of the class **CATLDept1** is created, we need to create its associated **KnownEvents** COM object. The embedded object must be created by the time construction of the parent object completes, so that it can be referenced immediately. To accomplish this, we need to construct a **CATLCorpEvents1** object during the construction of the **CATLDept1** object. An ATL COM object derived from the **CComObjectRoot** ATL class can override the **FinalConstruct()** and **FinalRelease()** functions. In our case, the **CATLDept1::FinalConstruct()** function creates the **KnownEvents** object and holds it ransom by holding an **IUnknown** pointer to the object for its entire lifetime.

```
    HRESULT CATLDept1::FinalConstruct()
{
  // Create and hold ransom our contained object
  HRESULT hTmp = CComObject<CATLCorpEvents1>::CreateInstance(&m_pKnownEvents);
  _ASSERTE(SUCCEEDED(hTmp));
  // hold this object for ransom as long as we live
  m_pKnownEvents->QueryInterface(IID_IUnknown, (void **)&m_pUnknownRansom);
  return S_OK;
}
```

Note how the **CComObject<>** template class allows us to create an instance of a COM object without calling **CoCreateInstance()**. **CoCreateInstance()** would not have worked anyway in our case because the **CATLCorpEvents1** class isn't externally instantiable.

When our **CATLDept1** object is finally terminating, we free the embedded hostage by releasing its (hopefully last remaining) reference count.

```
HRESULT CATLDept1::FinalRelease()
{
    // Free Our Prisoner
    m_pUnknownRansom->Release();
    m_pKnownEvents = NULL;
    return S_OK;
}
```

Whenever a client of our **CATLDept1** object reads the **m_pKnownEvents** property, we need to set a **VARIANT** type variable as specified in the IDL file. We can see this action in the **CATLDept1::get_KnownEvents()** function. What we do here is to obtain the **IDispatch** interface of the **m_pKnownEvents** contained object, and stuff the interface pointer into the **VARIANT** passed to the function.

```
    STDMETHODIMP CATLDept1::get_KnownEvents( VARIANT* pVal)
    {
        // get the IDispatch of the embedded collection and return it
        VariantInit(pVal);
        IDispatch* pDisp;
        m_pKnownEvents->QueryInterface(IID_IDispatch, (void**)&pDisp);
        pVal->vt = VT_DISPATCH;
        pVal->pdispVal = pDisp;
        return S_OK;
    }
```

`VariantInit()` is worth mentioning. It's used to initialize variables of type **VARIANT** by setting their tag field to **VT_EMPTY**.

The rest of the implementation follows. It consists of pretty straightforward **Get**/**Put** methods for the remaining properties of **ATLDept1**.

```cpp
class ATL_NO_VTABLE CATLDept1 :
   public CComObjectRootEx<CComSingleThreadModel>,
   public CComCoClass<CATLDept1, &CLSID_ATLDept1>,
   public IDispatchImpl<IATLDept1, &IID_IATLDept1, &LIBID_ATLDEPTLib>
{
public:
   CATLDept1()
   {
      m_bstrName = "ATL Dept";
      m_bstrNumber = "34521";
      m_bCanPostNew = 1;
      m_bCanRead = 0;
      m_bstrSymbol = "X";
      m_ulColor = 0xff0000;
   }
...

STDMETHODIMP CATLDept1::get_Name(BSTR* pVal)
{
   USES_CONVERSION;
   if (pVal == NULL)
      return E_POINTER;
   *pVal = m_bstrName.Copy();
   return S_OK;
}

STDMETHODIMP CATLDept1::put_Name(BSTR newVal)
{
   USES_CONVERSION;
   m_bstrName = newVal;
   return S_OK;
}

STDMETHODIMP CATLDept1::get_Number(BSTR* pVal)
{
   USES_CONVERSION;
   if (pVal == NULL)
      return E_POINTER;
   *pVal = m_bstrNumber.Copy();
   return S_OK;
}

STDMETHODIMP CATLDept1::put_Number(BSTR newVal)
{
   USES_CONVERSION;
   m_bstrNumber = newVal;
   return S_OK;
}

STDMETHODIMP CATLDept1::get_CanRead(VARIANT_BOOL* pVal)
{
```

```
      *pVal = m_bCanRead;
      return S_OK;
   }


   STDMETHODIMP CATLDept1::put_CanRead(VARIANT_BOOL newVal)
   {
      m_bCanRead = newVal;
      return S_OK;
   }


   STDMETHODIMP CATLDept1::get_CanPostNew(VARIANT_BOOL* pVal)
   {
      *pVal = m_bCanPostNew;
      return S_OK;
   }


   STDMETHODIMP CATLDept1::put_CanPostNew(VARIANT_BOOL newVal)
   {
      m_bCanPostNew = newVal;
      return S_OK;
   }


   STDMETHODIMP CATLDept1::get_Symbol(BSTR* pVal)
   {
      USES_CONVERSION;
      if (pVal == NULL)
         return E_POINTER;
      *pVal = m_bstrSymbol.Copy();
      return S_OK;
   }


   STDMETHODIMP CATLDept1::put_Symbol(BSTR newVal)
   {
      USES_CONVERSION;
      m_bstrSymbol = newVal;
      return S_OK;
   }


   STDMETHODIMP CATLDept1::get_Color(long * pVal)
   {
      *pVal = m_ulColor;
      return S_OK;
   }


   STDMETHODIMP CATLDept1::put_Color(long newVal)
   {
      m_ulColor = newVal;
      return S_OK;
   }
```

Working with Enumerations in ATL

The **CATLCorpEvents1** class is an automation collection class. It contains a collection of **CATLCorpEvent1** objects. In this section, we'll see how an automation collection class can be implemented using ATL. During the description of the IDL, we've already seen how the **Item()** method has been assigned the **DISPID_VALUE** which makes it the default method, and how assigning the **DISPID_ENUM** to the **_NewEnum()** method has made it the method for obtaining an **IEnum** interface to a new enumerator object. The **_NewEnum()** method was also given the attribute of **restricted** to keep it hidden in most object browsers.

Besides serving as a **For Each...Next** mechanism for automation client with scripting or macro language capabilities, enumerators are frequently used in COM programming to iterate through a collection of objects in a consistent manner. By creating a new enumerator object for each enumeration, it's straightforward to implement nested enumeration of the same collection. The ability to 'clone' an enumerator during the enumeration allows the user to save a state of the enumeration, which he or she can return to later.

The **CComEnum<>** templated class takes the following arguments:

```
CComEnum<Base Interface Name, Pointer to IID of Interface, Object to Enumerate, Class
for deep Copy of Object>
```

Now, let's take a look at how the class itself is defined.

```
class ATL_NO_VTABLE CATLCorpEvents1 :
  public CComObjectRootEx<CComObjectThreadModel>,
  public IDispatchImpl<IATLCorpEvents1, &IID_IATLCorpEvents1,
                       &LIBID_ATLDEPTLib>
{
public:
  CATLCorpEvents1()  {}

BEGIN_COM_MAP(CATLCorpEvents1)
  COM_INTERFACE_ENTRY(IATLCorpEvents1)
  COM_INTERFACE_ENTRY(IDispatch)
END_COM_MAP()

public:
...
```

We can see that, unlike **CATLDept1**, it isn't subclassed from **CComCoClass**. This isn't required since the class isn't externally creatable. On the other hand, just like **CATLDept1**, we've defined the **IDispatch** interface to be the same as the **IATLCorpEvents1** interface, enabling the automation client to get at the properties and methods.

The **Count**, **Item**, and **_NewEnum** properties are read-only, and they are declared in the class definition as:

```
...
  STDMETHOD(get__NewEnum)(/*[out, retval]*/ LPUNKNOWN *pVal);
  STDMETHOD(get_Item)(long Index, /*[out, retval]*/ VARIANT *pVal);
  STDMETHOD(get_Count)(/*[out, retval]*/ long *pVal);
...
```

We have two overloaded **Add()** functions, one is the 'back-door' **Add()** that we used in the control to initialize the department with specific values from the client, the other one is an actual **Add()** for adding a new member to the collection.

```
...
  STDMETHOD(Add)(DATE DateTime, BSTR bstrLocation, BSTR bstrHeading,
      BSTR bstrOrganizer, BSTR bstrOrgDept, BSTR bstrDetails,
      BSTR bstrHlink);
    void Add(CComVariant& var) { m_VarVect.insert(m_VarVect.end(), var); }
...
```

We restricted the delete function to delete only the very first member of the collection, and named it **DeleteFirst()**.

```
    . . .
    STDMETHOD(DeleteFirst)();
    . . .
```

Internal to the class, the actual collection is implemented via a template-based vector class. This class is taken from the Standard Template Library (STL). STL is completely integrated into Visual C++ 5.0's library support. The STL is extremely handy in providing templated implementation of classical data structures (i.e. lists, vectors, hash, etc.). It allows for rapid creation of type safe and efficient data structure classes with minimal coding.

```
    . . .
    void Init(ULONG n);
protected:
    vector<CComVariant, allocator<CComVariant> > m_VarVect;
};
```

Two more steps are necessary in order to use the STL vector class. First, the necessary include file needs to be added to the **stdafx.h** file

```
#include <vector>
#if _MSC_VER>1020
using namespace std;
#endif
```

Second, since integration between ATL and STL isn't yet totally seamless, we must define two comparison operators that work on **CComVariant** types. Add the following to **ATLCorpEvents1.cpp**:

```
bool operator<(const CComVariant l, const CComVariant r)
{
    _ASSERTE(false);
    return true;
}

bool operator==(const CComVariant l, const CComVariant r)
{
    _ASSERTE(false);
    return true;
}
```

and the corresponding declarations to the **ATLCorpEvents1.h** file

```
bool operator<(const CComVariant l, const CComVariant r);
bool operator==(const CComVariant l, const CComVariant r);
```

By defining the following for **CATLCorpEvents1**, we've created an automation compatible collection:

- A **Count** property.
- An **Item** property.
- A **_NewEnum** property returning an enumerator object.

Taking a look at how each of these properties is implemented, we see:

```
STDMETHODIMP CATLCorpEvents1::get_Count(long* pVal)
{
   if (pVal == NULL)
      return E_POINTER;
   *pVal = m_VarVect.size();
   return S_OK;
}
```

The **Count** property is delegated to the **size()** member function of the STL vector class.

```
STDMETHODIMP CATLCorpEvents1::get_Item(long Index, VARIANT* pVal)
{
   if (pVal == NULL)
      return E_POINTER;
   VariantInit(pVal);
   pVal->vt = VT_UNKNOWN;
   pVal->punkVal = NULL;
   // use 1-based index, VB like
   if (((unsigned long)Index < 1) || ((unsigned long)Index > (m_VarVect.size())))
      return E_INVALIDARG;
   VariantCopy(pVal, &m_VarVect[Index-1]);
   return S_OK;
}
```

The **Item** property is implemented via an extraction from the vector, as long as the index required isn't out of range of the vector. Recall that what gets assigned into the vector is actually an **IDispatch** pointer within a **VARIANT** pointing to a **CATLEvent1** object.

The **_NewEnum** property is most interesting: it somehow has to create a new enumerator object which provides an **IEnumVariant** interface. Thanks to ATL, we have a very easy way of accomplishing this.

```
STDMETHODIMP CATLCorpEvents1::get__NewEnum(LPUNKNOWN* pVal)
{
   if (pVal == NULL)
      return E_POINTER;
   *pVal = NULL;
   typedef CComObject<CComEnum<IEnumVARIANT, &IID_IEnumVARIANT, VARIANT,
         _Copy<VARIANT> > > enumvar;
   enumvar* pEnumVar = new enumvar;
   _ASSERTE(pEnumVar);
   HRESULT hRes = pEnumVar->Init(m_VarVect.begin(), m_VarVect.end(), NULL,
         AtlFlagCopy);
   if (SUCCEEDED(hRes))
      hRes = pEnumVar->QueryInterface(IID_IEnumVARIANT, (void**)pVal);
   if (FAILED(hRes))
      delete pEnumVar;
   return hRes;
}
```

Notice that we have parameterized the **CComEnum<>** template with:

```
typedef CComObject<CComEnum<IEnumVARIANT, &IID_IEnumVARIANT, VARIANT,
      _Copy<VARIANT> > > enumvar;
```

270

The **IEnumVARIANT** is our base interface, with an IID pointer of **&IID_IEnumVARIANT**, and we want the enumeration object to enumerate **VARIANT** objects. The copy class is **_Copy<VARIANT>** as predefined by ATL. Other predefined copy classes in ATL include   **_Copy<LPOLESTR>**, **_Copy<OLEVERB>**, **_Copy<CONNECTDATA>**, and **_CopyInterface<>**.

Once an instance of the COM object represented by our enumerator class (which we have named **pEnumVar**) is created, we take advantage of the guaranteed consecutive storage property of the **vector<>** STL class, and initialize the enumerator with our vector of **VARIANT IDispatch** pointers.

```
HRESULT hRes = pEnumVar->Init(m_VarVect.begin(), m_VarVect.end(), NULL,
        AtlFlagCopy);
```

The construction of the enumerator object is now completed and we can return the **IEnumVARIANT** interface pointer to the calling automation client. The following statement sets the value of the incoming **IUnknown** pointer to the **IEnumVARIANT** interface of the newly created enumerator object.

```
hRes = pEnumVar->QueryInterface(IID_IEnumVARIANT, (void**)pVal);
```

Using the above technique, one can quickly implement automation collections or fulfill other **IEnum** requirements as they surface during COM programming. Besides the **IEnumVARIANT** interface commonly found when dealing with automation clients, there are other **IEnum** interfaces that you may encounter during COM programming. They include **IEnumUnknown**, **IEnumMoniker**, **IEnumString**, **IEnumFORMATETC**, **IEnumSTATSTG**, **IEnumSTATDATA**, and **IEnumOLEVERB**.

The remainder of the class implementation is:

```
STDMETHODIMP CATLCorpEvents1::DeleteFirst()
{
    VARIANT firstNode;

    get_Item(1, &firstNode);
    if ( firstNode.punkVal != NULL)
    {
        // free the COM object before the C++ one!
        ((IUnknown *) (firstNode.punkVal))->Release();
    }
    m_VarVect.erase(m_VarVect.begin());
    return S_OK;
}
```

Initialize by creating **n** instances of **ATLCorpEvent1** objects.

```
void CATLCorpEvents1::Init(ULONG n)
{
    for (int i=0; i<n; i++)
    {
        CComObject<CATLCorpEvent1> * pAnEvent;
        HRESULT hTmp = CComObject<CATLCorpEvent1>::CreateInstance(&pAnEvent);
        _ASSERTE(SUCCEEDED(hTmp));

        // take advantage of the friendship to do some direct
        // manipulation
        pAnEvent->m_dDateTime = 0;
        pAnEvent->m_bstrLocation = "A Location";
        pAnEvent->m_bstrHeading = "My Heading";
```

```
      pAnEvent->m_bstrOrganizer = "I'm an Orgnaizer";
      pAnEvent->m_bstrDetails = "Some Details";
      pAnEvent->m_bstrHlink = "What Link";
      pAnEvent->m_bstrOrgDept = "Super Dept";

      // get IDispatch pointer
      LPDISPATCH lpDisp = NULL;
      pAnEvent->QueryInterface(IID_IDispatch, (void**)&lpDisp);
      _ASSERTE(lpDisp);

      // create a variant and add it to the collection
      CComVariant var;
      var.vt = VT_DISPATCH;
      var.pdispVal = lpDisp;
      Add(var);
   }
}
```

The 'backdoor' **Add()** function will be presented in the next section.

Implementing the CATLCorpEvent Class

Having gone through the implementation of the **CATLDept1** class which included an embedded COM object, represented by the **m_pKnownEvents** property, and seen how the **CATLCorpEvents1** class implements an automation collection, the **CATLCorpEvent** class is relatively uninteresting. The class definition is shown here:

```
class ATL_NO_VTABLE CATLCorpEvent1 :
   public CComObjectRootEx<CComObjectThreadModel>,
   public IDispatchImpl<IATLCorpEvent1, &IID_IATLCorpEvent1,
                        &LIBID_ATLDEPTLib>
{
public:
   CATLCorpEvent1()    {}

BEGIN_COM_MAP(CATLCorpEvent1)
   COM_INTERFACE_ENTRY(IATLCorpEvent1)
   COM_INTERFACE_ENTRY(IDispatch)
END_COM_MAP()

DECLARE_NOT_AGGREGATABLE(CATLCorpEvent1)

   STDMETHOD(get_orgDept)(/*[out, retval]*/ BSTR *pVal);
   STDMETHOD(put_orgDept)(/*[in]*/ BSTR newVal);
   STDMETHOD(get_Hlink)(/*[out, retval]*/ BSTR *pVal);
   STDMETHOD(put_Hlink)(/*[in]*/ BSTR newVal);
   STDMETHOD(get_Details)(/*[out, retval]*/ BSTR *pVal);
   STDMETHOD(put_Details)(/*[in]*/ BSTR newVal);
   STDMETHOD(get_Organizer)(/*[out, retval]*/ BSTR *pVal);
   STDMETHOD(put_Organizer)(/*[in]*/ BSTR newVal);
   STDMETHOD(get_Heading)(/*[out, retval]*/ BSTR *pVal);
   STDMETHOD(put_Heading)(/*[in]*/ BSTR newVal);
   STDMETHOD(get_Location)(/*[out, retval]*/ BSTR *pVal);
   STDMETHOD(put_Location)(/*[in]*/ BSTR newVal);
   STDMETHOD(get_DateTime)(/*[out, retval]*/ DATE *pVal);
   STDMETHOD(put_DateTime)(/*[in]*/ DATE newVal);
```

```
protected:
    DATE m_dDateTime;
    CComBSTR m_bstrLocation;
    CComBSTR m_bstrHeading;
    CComBSTR m_bstrOrganizer;
    CComBSTR m_bstrDetails;
    CComBSTR m_bstrHlink;
    CComBSTR m_bstrOrgDept;
    friend class CATLCorpEvents1;
};
```

Being a leaf node in the class tree of the object model, the main purpose of this class is to contain data. All of the data is stored in the protected members. Notice that the **CATLCorpEvents1** class is made a **friend** of this class. This was done mainly for performance reasons. The **CATLCorpEvents1::Add()** backdoor function actually sets these variables directly:

```
STDMETHODIMP CATLCorpEvents1::Add(DATE DateTime, BSTR bstrLocation,
    BSTR bstrHeading, BSTR bstrOrganizer, BSTR bstrOrgDept,
    BSTR bstrDetails,   BSTR bstrHlink)
{
    CComObject<CATLCorpEvent1> * pAnEvent;
    HRESULT hTmp = CComObject<CATLCorpEvent1>::CreateInstance(&pAnEvent);
    _ASSERTE(SUCCEEDED(hTmp));
    // take advantage of the friendship to do some direct manipulation
    pAnEvent->m_dDateTime = DateTime;
    pAnEvent->m_bstrLocation = bstrLocation;
    pAnEvent->m_bstrHeading = bstrHeading;
    pAnEvent->m_bstrOrganizer = bstrOrganizer;
    pAnEvent->m_bstrDetails = bstrDetails;
    pAnEvent->m_bstrHlink = bstrHlink;
    pAnEvent->m_bstrOrgDept = bstrOrgDept;
    // get IDispatch pointer
    LPDISPATCH lpDisp = NULL;
    pAnEvent->QueryInterface(IID_IDispatch, (void**)&lpDisp);
    _ASSERTE(lpDisp);
    // create a variant and add it to the collection
    CComVariant var;
    var.vt = VT_DISPATCH;
    var.pdispVal = lpDisp;
    Add(var);
    return S_OK;
}
```

Without the **friend** statement, one would have to call the **CATLCorpEvent1::set_** functions for each of the properties to set. A significant amount of computing time would have been wasted in moving string data back and forth between memory locations. Since the **CATLCorpEvent1** is a class only creatable as internal to the **CATLDept** object, this operation is safe from external abuse.

As an aside, note again that the **IDispatch** pointer of the **CATLCorpEvent1** object is the actual item stuffed into the **VARIANT** array. This is the most direct way to provide the automation client with something to immediately access the properties and methods of the object. It is what Visual Basic will expect when accessing an automation collection.

For completion, here is the implementation of the rest of the **CATLCorpEvent1** methods. They are pretty trivial **Get**/**Set** property functions:

```
STDMETHODIMP CATLCorpEvent1::get_DateTime(DATE* pVal)
{
   *pVal = m_dDateTime;
   return S_OK;
}

STDMETHODIMP CATLCorpEvent1::put_DateTime(DATE newVal)
{
    m_dDateTime = newVal;
   return S_OK;
}

STDMETHODIMP CATLCorpEvent1::get_Location(BSTR* pVal)
{
   USES_CONVERSION;
   if (pVal == NULL)
      return E_POINTER;
   *pVal = m_bstrLocation.Copy();
   return S_OK;
}

STDMETHODIMP CATLCorpEvent1::put_Location(BSTR newVal)
{
   USES_CONVERSION;
   m_bstrLocation = newVal;
   return S_OK;
}

STDMETHODIMP CATLCorpEvent1::get_Heading(BSTR* pVal)
{
   USES_CONVERSION;
   if (pVal == NULL)
      return E_POINTER;
   *pVal = m_bstrHeading.Copy();
   return S_OK;
}

STDMETHODIMP CATLCorpEvent1::put_Heading(BSTR newVal)
{
   USES_CONVERSION;
   m_bstrHeading = newVal;
   return S_OK;
}

STDMETHODIMP CATLCorpEvent1::get_Organizer(BSTR* pVal)
{
   USES_CONVERSION;
   if (pVal == NULL)
      return E_POINTER;
   *pVal = m_bstrOrganizer.Copy();
   return S_OK;
}

STDMETHODIMP CATLCorpEvent1::put_Organizer(BSTR newVal)
{
   USES_CONVERSION;
   m_bstrOrganizer = newVal;
   return S_OK;
}
```

```
STDMETHODIMP CATLCorpEvent1::get_Details(BSTR* pVal)
{
   USES_CONVERSION;
   if (pVal == NULL)
      return E_POINTER;
   *pVal = m_bstrDetails.Copy();
   return S_OK;
}

STDMETHODIMP CATLCorpEvent1::put_Details(BSTR newVal)
{
   USES_CONVERSION;
   m_bstrDetails = newVal;
   return S_OK;
}

STDMETHODIMP CATLCorpEvent1::get_Hlink(BSTR* pVal)
{
   USES_CONVERSION;
   if (pVal == NULL)
      return E_POINTER;
   *pVal = m_bstrHlink.Copy();
   return S_OK;
}

STDMETHODIMP CATLCorpEvent1::put_Hlink(BSTR newVal)
{
   USES_CONVERSION;
   m_bstrHlink = newVal;
   return S_OK;
}

STDMETHODIMP CATLCorpEvent1::get_orgDept(BSTR* pVal)
{
   USES_CONVERSION;
   if (pVal == NULL)
      return E_POINTER;
   *pVal = m_bstrOrgDept.Copy();
   return S_OK;
}

STDMETHODIMP CATLCorpEvent1::put_orgDept(BSTR newVal)
{
   USES_CONVERSION;
   m_bstrOrgDept = newVal;
   return S_OK;
}
```

Compiling and Testing the DLL Server

You can compile the DLL server by building **ATLDept.dll** in Developer Studio. Thanks to the ATL AppWizard, the DLL will also automatically be registered in the registry via a custom build step. Remember, however, in order to install this DLL COM server on another system, you must perform the following:

1 Locate **Register.dll** from the ATL distribution and copy it to the target machine.

2 Run **regsvr32 register.dll** on the target machine.

3 Copy **ATLDept.dll** to the target machine.

4 Run **regsvr32 ATLDept.dll** on the target machine.

Forgetting to do steps 1 and 2 can easily lead to hours of frustrated debugging.

Finally, to perform a quick test of the newly created COM object server, we can again refer to the Object Viewer utility. We can try to create an instance of the **ATLDept1** object (and an invisible embedded **CATLCorpEvents1** object) by double-clicking on the **CATLDept1** entry under All Objects:

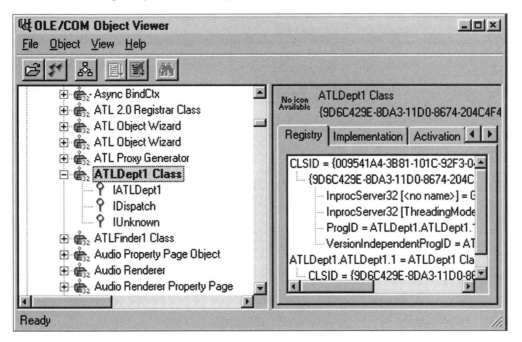

We can see the **IATLDept1** interface being supported. If we double-click on the interface, the **IDispatch** viewer can be used to view the methods and properties definition of this interface.

Implementing the ATLFinder

To implement the ATLFinder we can start by creating an ATL COM App Wizard project for a local server. We can, then, create two objects for the ATLFinder1 and ATLDepts1 classes.

Going through the same steps as with the ATLDept1 project, we need to restrict the ATLDepts1 object by:

▲ Modifying the **.IDL** file to not contain a **coclass** for **CATLDepts1**.

▲ Removing inheritance from **CComCoClass<>** .

▲ Removing the corresponding entry from the application Object Map.

▲ Removing **ATLDepts1.rgs** from the project.

▲ Removing the **DECLARE_REGISTRY_RESOURCEID()** from class.

The **.IDL** file follows. The properties and methods can be added through the ClassWizard.

```
// ATLFinder.idl : IDL source for ATLFinder.dll
//
// This file will be processed by the MIDL tool to
// produce the type library (ATLFinder.tlb) and marshalling code.
import "oaidl.idl";
import "ocidl.idl";

    [
        object,
        uuid(590AC7EF-8E6C-11D0-8677-204C4F4F5020),
        dual,
        helpstring("IATLFinder1 Interface"),
        pointer_default(unique)
    ]
    interface IATLFinder1 : IDispatch
    {
        // supports only one read-only property
        // and one method

        // Collection of departments with events
        [propget, id(1)] HRESULT EventfulDepts([out, retval]
                        VARIANT* pVal);
         // Date or Month to set
        [id(2)] HRESULT SetFindDate([in] DATE inDate);
    };
    [
        object,
        uuid(590AC7F1-8E6C-11D0-8677-204C4F4F5020),
        dual,
        helpstring("IATLDepts1 Interface"),
        pointer_default(unique)
    ]
    interface IATLDepts1 : IDispatch
    {

        [propget, id(1), helpstring("Returns number of items in collection.")]
            HRESULT Count([out, retval] long* pVal);

        [propget, id(DISPID_VALUE), helpstring("Given an index, returns an item"
            " in the collection.")]
            HRESULT Item([in] long Index, [out, retval] VARIANT* pVal);

        // Must be propget.
        [propget, restricted, id(DISPID_NEWENUM), helpstring("returns an enumerator"
            " for the collection.")]
            HRESULT _NewEnum([out, retval] LPUNKNOWN* pVal);
```

```
      [id(8)] HRESULT Add([in] BSTR bstrName,  [in] BSTR bstrNumber,
         [in] VARIANT_BOOL bCanRead, [in] VARIANT_BOOL bCanPostNew,
         [in] BSTR bstrSymbol, [in] long lColor);

      [id(9)] HRESULT DeleteFirst();
   };
...
```

Notice the similarity with the **ATLDept1.idl** file.

```
...
[
   uuid(590AC7E3-8E6C-11D0-8677-204C4F4F5020),
   version(1.0),
   helpstring("ATLFinder 1.0 Type Library")
]
library ATLFINDERLib
{
   importlib("stdole32.tlb");
   importlib("stdole2.tlb");

   interface IATLFinder1;
   interface IATLDepts1;

   [
      uuid(590AC7F0-8E6C-11D0-8677-204C4F4F5020),
      helpstring("ATLFinder1 Class")
   ]
   coclass CATLFinder1
   {
      [default] interface IATLFinder1;
   };
};
```

Here's the class declaration of the ATLFinder1 object:

```
class ATL_NO_VTABLE CATLFinder1 :
   public CComObjectRootEx<CComSingleThreadModel>,
   public CComCoClass<CATLFinder1, &CLSID_ATLFinder1>,
   public IDispatchImpl<IATLFinder1, &IID_IATLFinder1, &LIBID_ATLFINDERLib>
{
public:
   CATLFinder1()
   {
   }

DECLARE_REGISTRY_RESOURCEID(IDR_ATLFINDER1)

BEGIN_COM_MAP(CATLFinder1)
   COM_INTERFACE_ENTRY(IATLFinder1)
   COM_INTERFACE_ENTRY(IDispatch)
END_COM_MAP()

// IATLFinder1
public:
   STDMETHOD(SetFindDate)(/*[in]*/ DATE inDate);
   STDMETHOD(get_EventfulDepts)(/*[out, retval]*/ VARIANT *pVal);
```

```
    HRESULT FinalConstruct();
    HRESULT FinalRelease();

private:
    CComObject<CATLDepts1>* m_pEventfulDepts;
    IUnknown * m_pUnknownRansom;
    DATE m_dCurStartDate;
};
```

and the corresponding implementation:

```
STDMETHODIMP CATLFinder1::get_EventfulDepts(VARIANT* pVal)
{
    // get the IDispatch of the embedded collection and return it
    VariantInit(pVal);
    IDispatch* pDisp;
    m_pEventfulDepts->QueryInterface(IID_IDispatch, (void**)&pDisp);
    pVal->vt = VT_DISPATCH;
    pVal->pdispVal = pDisp;
    return S_OK;
}

// Date or Month to set
STDMETHODIMP CATLFinder1::SetFindDate(DATE inDate)
{
    m_dCurStartDate = inDate;
    return S_OK;
}

HRESULT CATLFinder1::FinalConstruct()
{
    // Create and hold ransom our contained object
    HRESULT hTmp = CComObject<CATLDepts1>::CreateInstance(&m_pEventfulDepts);
    _ASSERTE(SUCCEEDED(hTmp));
    // hold this object for ransom as long as we live
    m_pEventfulDepts->QueryInterface(IID_IUnknown, (void **)&m_pUnknownRansom);
    return S_OK;
}

HRESULT CATLFinder1::FinalRelease()
{
    // Free Our Prisoner
    m_pUnknownRansom->Release();
    m_pEventfulDepts = NULL;
    return S_OK;
}
```

Here is the class declaration for ATLDepts1:

```
class ATL_NO_VTABLE CATLDepts1 :
    public CComObjectRootEx<CComSingleThreadModel>,
    public IDispatchImpl<IATLDepts1, &IID_IATLDepts1, &LIBID_ATLFINDERLib>
{
public:
    CATLDepts1()
    {
    }
```

```
BEGIN_COM_MAP(CATLDepts1)
   COM_INTERFACE_ENTRY(IATLDepts1)
   COM_INTERFACE_ENTRY(IDispatch)
END_COM_MAP()

// IATLDepts1
public:
   STDMETHOD(get_Count)(long* retval);
   STDMETHOD(get_Item)(long Index, VARIANT* retval);
   STDMETHOD(get__NewEnum)(IUnknown** retval);
   STDMETHOD(Add)(BSTR bstrName,  BSTR bstrNumber,
      VARIANT_BOOL bCanRead,  VARIANT_BOOL bCanPostNew,
      BSTR bstrSymbol,  long lColor);
   STDMETHOD(DeleteFirst)();

   void Add(CComVariant& var);
protected:
// internal data
   vector<CComVariant, allocator<CComVariant> > m_VarVect;
};
```

And here's the implementation. Notice the similarity with the **CATLCorpEvents1** method implementation:

```
STDMETHODIMP CATLDepts1::get_Count(long* pVal)
{
   if (pVal == NULL)
      return E_POINTER;
   *pVal = m_VarVect.size();
   return S_OK;
}


STDMETHODIMP CATLDepts1::get_Item(long Index, VARIANT* pVal)
{
   if (pVal == NULL)
      return E_POINTER;
   VariantInit(pVal);
   pVal->vt = VT_UNKNOWN;
   pVal->punkVal = NULL;
   // use 1-based index, VB like
   if (((unsigned long)Index < 1) || ((unsigned long)Index > (m_VarVect.size())))
      return E_INVALIDARG;
   VariantCopy(pVal, &m_VarVect[Index-1]);
   return S_OK;
}


STDMETHODIMP CATLDepts1::DeleteFirst()
{
   // just removing the C++ object from the list
   // won't do!  although it'll work for a while.
   VARIANT firstNode;
   get_Item(1, &firstNode);
   if ( firstNode.punkVal != NULL)
   {
      // free the COM object before the C++ one!
      ((IUnknown *) (firstNode.punkVal))->Release();
   }
   m_VarVect.erase(m_VarVect.begin());
   return S_OK;
}
```

```
STDMETHODIMP CATLDepts1::Add(BSTR bstrName,  BSTR bstrNumber,
    VARIANT_BOOL bCanRead,  VARIANT_BOOL bCanPostNew,
    BSTR bstrSymbol,  long lColor)
{
    // we need to create a Dept COM object here,
    // no more luxury of it being a local C/C++
    // object
    IATLDept1 * pITmpDept;

    HRESULT hTmp = CoCreateInstance(CLSID_ATLDept1, NULL, CLSCTX_INPROC, IID_IATLDept1,
      (void**)&pITmpDept);
    _ASSERTE(SUCCEEDED(hTmp));

    // make use of the dual interface ability to
    // set the data   using C++ preferred VTBL binding
    pITmpDept->put_Name(bstrName);
    pITmpDept->put_Number(bstrNumber);
    pITmpDept->put_CanRead(bCanRead);
    pITmpDept->put_CanPostNew(bCanPostNew);
    pITmpDept->put_Symbol(bstrSymbol);
    pITmpDept->put_Color(lColor);

    // get IDispatch pointer
    LPDISPATCH lpDisp;
    lpDisp = NULL;
    pITmpDept->QueryInterface(IID_IDispatch, (void**)&lpDisp);
    _ASSERTE(lpDisp);

    // balance the reference count here from getting IUnknown
    pITmpDept->Release();

    // create a variant and add it to the collection
    CComVariant var;
    var.vt = VT_DISPATCH;
    var.pdispVal = lpDisp;
    Add(var);
    return S_OK;

}

STDMETHODIMP CATLDepts1::get__NewEnum(IUnknown** pVal)
{
    if (pVal == NULL)
        return E_POINTER;
    *pVal = NULL;
    typedef CComObject<CComEnum<IEnumVARIANT, &IID_IEnumVARIANT, VARIANT,
      _Copy<VARIANT> > > enumvar;
    enumvar* p = new enumvar;
    _ASSERTE(p);
    HRESULT hRes = p->Init(m_VarVect.begin(), m_VarVect.end(), NULL, AtlFlagCopy);
    if (SUCCEEDED(hRes))
        hRes = p->QueryInterface(IID_IEnumVARIANT, (void**)pVal);
    if (FAILED(hRes))
        delete p;
    return hRes;
}

void CATLDepts1::Add(CComVariant& var)
{
    m_VarVect.insert(m_VarVect.end(), var);
}
```

Note that we need to add to **Stdafx.h** the necessary includes for STL vector:

```
#include <vector>
#if _MSC_VER>1020
using namespace std;
#endif
```

And provide declarations and definitions for:

```
bool operator<(const CComVariant l, const CComVariant r);
bool operator==(const CComVariant l, const CComVariant r);

bool operator<(const CComVariant l, const CComVariant r)
{
    _ASSERTE(false);
    return true;
}

bool operator==(const CComVariant l, const CComVariant r)
{
    _ASSERTE(false);
    return true;
}
```

in the **ATLDepts1.h** and **ATLDepts1.cpp** files respectively. We also need the CLSIDs for ATLDept1, so include in the **ATLDepts1.cpp** the MIDL-generated **ATLDept.h** and **ATLDept_i.c** file that contains them:

```
#include "ATLDept.h"
#define IID_DEFINED
#include "ATLDept_i.c"
```

The CDataMgr Class

Switching back to the **CDataMgr** class, in the **Vccal** project, the most significant thing is that it interfaces with the **ATLFinder** COM class that supports dual interfaces. Of course, we could have simply included the **ATLFinder.h** and **ATLFinder_i.c** files (also the ones for the **IATLDepts1**, **IATLDept1**, **IATLCorpEvents1**, and **IATLCorpEvent1** interface definitions) and have the **CDataMgr** access these interfaces via vtable invocation as usual. This early binding would actually be a higher performance way of accessing the **ATLFinder** server.

However, to make life more interesting, and to demonstrate how Visual C++ 5.0 can easily also make use of dispatch interface support, we'll code **CDataMgr** so that it will only use **IDispatch** late binding to access the **ATLFinder** object.

This turns out to be much easier than you might imagine. The key thing is that you must have the type library information available. If you do have the type library for the interfaces available for a set of dispatch interfaces that you'd like to use with a Visual C++ project, then the task is simplified to running ClassWizard through it.

For our purposes, we have the **ATLFinder.tlb** type library available from the ATLFinder project and the **ATLDept.tlb** type library available from the ATLDept project. To have ClassWizard generate wrapper classes for us:

1 Invoke ClassWizard.

2 Click on the Add Class... button and select From a type library...

3 Select the **ATLFinder.tlb** file (or **ATLDept.tlb**).

After you have run ClassWizard through both type library files, you should notice that there are several new classes defined in the class pane. You should see the following new classes:

Class Name	Description
IATLFinder1	Wrapper for accessing the **IATLFinder** dual interface.
IATLDepts1	Wrapper for accessing the **IATLDepts** dual interface, required for using the **EventfulDepts** property of **IATLFinder**.
IATLDept1	Wrapper for accessing the **IATLDept** dual interface, required for accessing the properties of a department object.
IATLCorpEvents1	Wrapper for accessing the **IATLCorpEvents1** dual interface, required for using the **KnownEvents** property of **IATLDept1**.
IATLCorpEvent1	Wrapper for accessing the **IATLCorpEvent1** dual interface, required for accessing the properties of an event object.

If you examine the code in any one of the above classes, you'll find that they actually wrap the **IDispatch::Invoke()** call that is required to access the interface. The **Get** and **Set** operation of each property is wrapped, as well as every method defined by the interface. You'll also discover that the C++ wrapper uses the most efficient form of late binding. That is, it examines the type library information and compiles in all the required dispatch IDs.

Before we proceed with the **CDataMgr** class itself, let's take a look at some necessary declarations:

```
#include "atlfinder.h"    // Created by ClassView
#include "atldept.h"

#include "VCCalConst.h"

typedef struct {
   COleDateTime DateTime;
   CString Location;
   CString Heading;
   CString Organizer;
   CString orgDept;
   CString Details;
   CString Hlink;
} CalEvent;
```

CalEvent encapsulates information about a calendar event.

```
typedef struct {
   CString DeptName;
   CString DeptNumber;
   BOOL CanRead;
   BOOL CanPostNew;
   CString Symbol;
   OLE_COLOR Color;
} CalDept;
```

CalDept encapsulates information about a department posting events.

```
typedef struct {
   CalDept Dept;
   ULONG EvtCount;
   COleDateTime OnDates[MAX_EVENTS];
} DeptEvent;
```

DeptEvent associates a department with an events count and an array of dates on which the events fall. We're now ready to take a look at the **CDataMgr** class:

```
class CDataMgr
{
public:
   CDataMgr();
   virtual ~CDataMgr();

   BOOL CreateFinder();
   void GetAnEvent(const COleDateTime & inDate, ULONG inDept,
                   ULONG idx, CalEvent & anEvent);
   const CalDept & GetDept(ULONG idx);
   ULONG GetDeptCount();
```

```
    BOOL GetEventsOnDate(const COleDateTime & inDate, ULONG * EvtCount);
    ULONG GetEventsInMonth(const COleDateTime & inDate, ULONG inDept);
    void GrabActiveDepts();
    BOOL InfoAvail();
    void ResetState();
    void ReleaseFinder();
    void SetEventMonth(const COleDateTime & inMonth);
protected:
    BOOL        m_InfoAvail;
    IATLFinder1 m_MyFinder;
    ULONG      m_OurMaxDept;
    DeptEvent      m_DeptEventList[MAX_DEPTS];
};
```

Our **CDataMgr** class has its own **ATLFinder** object, which we needed to add to the class declaration:

```
class CDataMgr
{
...
protected:
    BOOL m_InfoAvail;
    IATLFinder1 m_MyFinder;
...
```

The actual **ATLFinder** object is created in the **CreateFinder()** member function. As we will see, this function is called by the **CVccalCtrl** class during its initialization only if the control is running in user mode.

```
BOOL CDataMgr::CreateFinder()
{
    // create the object and get its IDispatch
    return m_MyFinder.CreateDispatch("ATLFinder1.ATLFinder.1");
}
```

Simply by calling **IATLFinder1**'s **CreateDispatch()** member with the desired CLSID, the wrapper class takes care of the **CoCreateInstance()** call and query interface for the default **IDispatch** interface of the server, and stores it inside the **IATLFinder1** object. How's that for work saving!

Since we're dealing with a COM object which stays alive if there are still outstanding references, we must remember to release the COM object. We supply code for release in the **ReleaseDispatch()** member function. This is called by **CVccalCtrl** class when the Calendar control's window is destroyed.

```
void CDataMgr::ReleaseFinder()
{
    // free our ATLFinder object
    m_MyFinder.ReleaseDispatch();
}
```

Many of the **CDataMgr**'s member functions make use of these wrapper classes. The style of programming is more closely associated with those of a typical Visual Basic program rather than C++. Instead of going through all of them in detail, let's look at a case when we iterate through the **EventfulDepts** properties of **IATLFinder1** to obtain an individual **IATLDept** object. This is done in the **GrabActiveDepts()** member function. If you're following along creating your own project, the following implementation of **GrabActiveDepts()** will compile only if you added the properties of the **IATLCorpEvents1** and **IATLCorpEvent1** through the ClassWizard. If you just copied the **.IDL** file, you'll need to add the appropriate **Get**/**Set** member function declarations and definitions. We'll cover these in a later section.

```
void CDataMgr::GrabActiveDepts()
{
   TRACE("CDataMgr::GrabActiveDepts\n");
   ULONG i, j, evtCount;
   // we simply obtains the count and fill the list in one shot
   IATLDepts1 tmp_Depts((m_MyFinder.GetEventfulDepts()).pdispVal );
   m_OurMaxDept = tmp_Depts.GetCount();
   . . .
```

In this first part shown above, we create an **IATLDepts1** object called **tmp_Depts** based on the **GetEventfulDepts()** value. This is the value of the **EventfulDepts** property and is a **VARIANT**. We take advantage of our knowledge that it is a pointer to an **IDispatch** interface by accessing the **pdispVal** member directly. Next, we invoke the **IATLDepts1::GetCount()** method to obtain the current number of active departments.

```
   . . .
   IATLDept1 tpDept;
   IATLCorpEvents1 tpEvents;
   IATLCorpEvent1 tpEvent;

   for (i=1; i <= m_OurMaxDept; i++)
   {
      tpDept.AttachDispatch( (tmp_Depts.GetItem(i)).pdispVal);
      m_DeptEventList[i-1].Dept.DeptName = tpDept.GetName();
      m_DeptEventList[i-1].Dept.DeptNumber = tpDept.GetNumber();
      m_DeptEventList[i-1].Dept.CanRead = tpDept.GetCanRead();
      m_DeptEventList[i-1].Dept.CanPostNew = tpDept.GetCanPostNew();
      m_DeptEventList[i-1].Dept.Symbol = tpDept.GetSymbol();
      m_DeptEventList[i-1].Dept.Color = tpDept.GetColor();
   . . .
```

In the above segment, we first declare some temporary wrapper objects to hold **IATLDept1**, **IATLCorpEvents1**, and **IATLCorpEvent1** dispatch pointers. Next, we iterate through all the departments, and for each one we attach the **IATLDept1** wrapper object to it, then we extract the value of the properties and copy them to our internally maintained **m_DeptEventList[]** data structure.

```
   . . .
   tpEvents.AttachDispatch((tpDept.GetKnownEvents()).pdispVal);
   evtCount = m_DeptEventList[i-1].EvtCount = tpEvents.GetCount();
   for (j=1; j<=evtCount; j++)
   {
      tpEvent.AttachDispatch((tpEvents.GetItem(j)).pdispVal);
      m_DeptEventList[i-1].OnDates[j-1] = COleDateTime(tpEvent.GetDateTime());
      tpEvent.ReleaseDispatch();
      tpEvent.DetachDispatch();
   }
   . . .
```

Then, we access the **IATLDept::KnownEvents** property and iterate through it. For each of the events, we attach the temporary **IATLEvent** object called **tpEvent** to it, and use it to copy the event's date to the **OnDates[]** member of the **m_DeptEventList[]** structure. Note that we need to **ReleaseDispatch()** which does a COM based release, and a detach before the same temporary class can be used again.

```
. . .
        tpDept.ReleaseDispatch();
        tpDept.DetachDispatch();
        tpEvents.ReleaseDispatch();
        tpEvents.DetachDispatch();
    }
    m_InfoAvail = TRUE;
}
```

In this last segment, we release the **IATLDept** and **ICorpEvents** temporary wrapper objects so they too can be reused again in the loop. Before we return, we set a flag that indicates that back-end object information is now available.

For completeness, here are the remaining member functions of the **CDataMgr** class. Examining them, you'll see very similar coding; this is generally true when we're dealing with back-end COM servers with dispinterfaces using Visual C++.

```
CDataMgr::CDataMgr():m_InfoAvail(FALSE) {}

CDataMgr::~CDataMgr() {}

ULONG CDataMgr::GetDeptCount()
{
    return m_OurMaxDept;
}

const CalDept & CDataMgr::GetDept(ULONG idx)
{
    return m_DeptEventList[idx].Dept;
}

ULONG CDataMgr::GetEventsInMonth(const COleDateTime & inDate, ULONG inDept)
{
    return m_DeptEventList[inDept].EvtCount;
}

void CDataMgr::ResetState()
{
    m_InfoAvail = FALSE;
}

BOOL CDataMgr::InfoAvail()
{
    return m_InfoAvail;
}
```

GetEventsOnDate() returns in its out parameter, the number of events available on the date specified.

```
BOOL CDataMgr::GetEventsOnDate(const COleDateTime & inDate, ULONG * EvtCount)
{
    ULONG i,j, counter;
    BOOL hasEvent;
    DeptEvent * tpEvt;
    hasEvent = FALSE;
    counter = 0;
```

```
        for (i=0; i< m_OurMaxDept; i++)
        {
           EvtCount[i]=0;
           tpEvt = &m_DeptEventList[i];
           for (j=0; j< tpEvt->EvtCount; j++)
           {
              if ((tpEvt->OnDates[j].GetDay()==inDate.GetDay()) &&
                  (tpEvt->OnDates[j].GetMonth() == inDate.GetMonth()))
              {
                 EvtCount[i] ++;
                 hasEvent = TRUE;
              }
           }
        }
        return hasEvent;
}
```

GetAnEvent() returns an event, given a date, a department and an event index. It uses similar constructs to **GrabActiveDepts()**.

```
    void CDataMgr::GetAnEvent(const COleDateTime & inDate, ULONG inDept,
                 ULONG idx, CalEvent & anEvent)
{
    TRACE("CDataMgr::GetAnEvent\n");

    //Given a date, a department, and an event index, get the event
    //
    // Get it from the actual dept object instead, date is redundant
    IATLDepts1 tmp_Depts((m_MyFinder.GetEventfulDepts()).pdispVal );

    IATLDept1 tpDept((tmp_Depts.GetItem(inDept + 1)).pdispVal);
    IATLCorpEvents1 tpEvents((tpDept.GetKnownEvents()).pdispVal);
    IATLCorpEvent1 tpEvent((tpEvents.GetItem(idx + 1)).pdispVal);
    anEvent.DateTime = COleDateTime(tpEvent.GetDateTime());
    anEvent.Details = tpEvent.GetDetails();
    anEvent.Heading = tpEvent.GetHeading();
    anEvent.Hlink = tpEvent.GetHlink();
    anEvent.Location = tpEvent.GetLocation();
    anEvent.Organizer = tpEvent.GetOrganizer();
    anEvent.orgDept = tpEvent.GetOrgDept();

    // let destructor of the COleDispatchDriver object clean up
}
```

Finishing off the Control

We now have all the pieces in place to finish off our control. First we have to add an instance of the **CDataMgr** class to our project. Then we need to update the drawing code so that events are actually shown on the days that they occur. Finally, we need some way of displaying the event information to the user.

Adding CDataMgr

The most obvious change to make to our code is to create a instance of **CDataMgr** either statically or dynamically. As there only ever needs to be one instance of the **CDataMgr** class for the **Vccal** control (the actually dynamic information being handled by the back-end COM objects), this is what we'll do:

```
class CVccalCtrl : public COleControl
{
...
// Implementation
protected:
    CFont * m_TitleFont;
    CString m_TitleFontName;
    short m_TitleFontSize;
    BOOL m_TitleFontBold;
    BOOL m_ButtonsVisible;
    CButton* m_pLeftBut;
    CButton* m_pRightBut;
    COleDateTime m_CurrentDay;
    CCellMgr m_CellMgr;
    CDataMgr m_DataMgr;
...
```

We now have to add some supporting code to deal with obtaining data from the back-end COM objects, and releasing the objects as necessary. The first, obvious place this is going to happen is in the destructor. We need to release the object so that it can unload itself from memory. This is simply a case of calling the **ReleaseFinder()** method of **CDataMgr**:

```
CVccalCtrl::~ CVccalCtrl()
{
    // let the finder object go!
    m_DataMgr.ReleaseFinder();
}
```

Of course, before we've finished with the data manager, we need to have used it. There are various circumstances where data will have changed and we need to re-initialize the information. Therefore, it's fairly obvious that we should wrap up the initialization code into a single function, and this is what we do:

```
void CVccalCtrl::InitializeBackEnd()
{
    TRACE("CVccalCtrl::InitializeBackEnd\n");
    if (AmbientUserMode())
    {
        m_DataMgr.SetEventMonth(m_CurrentDay);
        m_DataMgr.GrabActiveDepts();
    }
}
```

We check to make sure that we're in user mode rather than design mode before setting up the data manager. Okay, so where exactly do we use this function? Well, starting from the top, we need to use it in the **DoPropExchange()** function:

```
void CVccalCtrl::DoPropExchange(CPropExchange* pPX)
{
...
   COleDateTime tpInit(1997,1,1,0,0,1);
   CString ulInit(tpInit.Format());
   if (pPX->IsLoading())
   {
      CString ulTime("");
      PX_String(pPX, _T("CurrentDay"), ulTime, ulInit);
      m_CurrentDay.ParseDateTime(ulTime);
      InitializeButtonsState();
      InitializeBackEnd();
      UpdateCore();
   }
   else
   {
      CString ulTime(m_CurrentDay.Format());
      PX_String(pPX, _T("CurrentDay"), ulTime, ulInit);
   }
}
```

Another obvious place is in the **AdvanceMonth()** method:

```
VARIANT CVccalCtrl::AdvanceMonth(long inc)
{
   VARIANT vaResult;
   VariantInit(&vaResult);
   if (abs(inc) <= 12)    // maximum 1 year
   {
      ULONG workMonth = m_CurrentDay.GetMonth();
      ULONG workYear = m_CurrentDay.GetYear();
      workMonth += inc;
      if (workMonth <= 0)
      {
         workYear--;
         workMonth = 12;
      }
      if (workMonth > 12)
      {
         workYear++;
         workMonth -= 12;
      }
      m_CurrentDay = COleDateTime(workYear, workMonth,1, 0,0,1);
      InitializeBackEnd();
      UpdateCore();
   }
   return vaResult;
}
```

SetStartDate() also manipulates the date, so needs to cause the data manager to refresh the information:

```
void CVccalCtrl::SetStartDate(DATE NewDate)
{
   m_CurrentDay = NewDate;
   InitializeBackEnd();
   UpdateCore();
}
```

The final function (apart from **PaintGrid()**) in which we need to initialize the data manager is the message handler for those containers which decided to be nice and honour **OLEMISC_SETCLIENTSITEFIRST**. The **OnSetClientSite()** should then look like this:

```
void CVcCalc1Ctrl::OnSetClientSite()
{
   TRACE("CVccalCtrl::OnSetClientSite\n");
   // if we are not in design mode, then create
   // the ATLFinder object in our CellMgr
   if ( m_ambientDispDriver.m_lpDispatch  &&  AmbientUserMode() )
   {
      m_DataMgr.CreateFinder();
      InitializeBackEnd();
   }
   COleControl::OnSetClientSite();
}
```

Notice that in this function we actually cause the data manager to create the **ATLFinder** object.

Painting the Control

Having the data in the manager allows us to add the code to the **PaintGrid()** function to indicate to the user that events are available for them to look at on that day.

```
void CVcCalc1Ctrl::PaintGrid(CDC * pdc, const CRect& inRect)
{
...
   curX = leftMargin;
   curY = offsetY;
   counter = 0;
   for(i=0 ; i<6; i++)
   {
      curY = offsetY + i * cellHeight;
      for (j=0; j<7; j++)
      {
         curX = leftMargin + j * cellWidth;

         // Print out the Cell number
         CString tpOut = m_CellMgr.GetCellNumber(counter) + _T(" ");
         tpOut = tpOut + m_CellMgr.GetLabel(counter);
         // clip inside rectangle
         CRect tmpRect((curX + xPad), (curY+yPad),
            (curX+cellWidth -  xPad), (curY + cellHeight - yPad));

         pdc->ExtTextOut((LONG) (curX + xPad), (LONG)(curY + yPad), ETO_CLIPPED, //
ETO_CLIPPED
         tmpRect, tpOut, NULL);
         //
         // set the cell manager's cell array with co-ordinates values
         m_CellMgr.SetCorners(counter, (ULONG) curY, (ULONG) curX,
            (ULONG) curY + cellHeight, (ULONG) curX + cellWidth);
```

We ensure we're in user mode and that the back end has been initialized:

```
                // avoid doing any backend operations during design mode
                if ( AmbientUserMode() )
                {
                    if (!m_DataMgr.InfoAvail())  // VB5 doesn't do @ setclientsite
                    {
                        m_DataMgr.CreateFinder();
                        InitializeBackEnd();
                    }
                    // paint in events indications
                    float cellX = curX + cellWidth / 20;
                    float cellY = curY + cellHeight / 2;
                    ULONG countMax = m_DataMgr.GetDeptCount();
                    ULONG* MyDeptEvtCount = new ULONG[countMax];

                    // check if something is happening on this day
                    if (m_DataMgr.GetEventsOnDate( m_CellMgr.GetCellDate(counter),
                        MyDeptEvtCount))
                    {
                        m_CellMgr.SetCellEvent(counter, TRUE);
```

If there are events happening on this day, corresponding to the current cell, we iterate through all departments, creating a text string formed by the symbol for the department, followed by the number of events by that department on this day. The strings are drawn beside each other within the confines of the cell area.

```
                    for (ULONG countDept = 0; countDept < countMax; countDept++)
                    {
                        if (MyDeptEvtCount[countDept] != 0)
                        {
                            TCHAR tpString[8];
                            _itot(MyDeptEvtCount[countDept], tpString, 10);
                            CString ab(m_DataMgr.GetDept(countDept).Symbol +
                                _T("-"));
                            ab = ab + tpString;
                            ab = ab + _T(" ");
                            // draw the text in
                            CPen tPen;
                            COLORREF oldColor = pdc->SetTextColor(
                            m_DataMgr.GetDept(countDept).Color);
                            CRect boundRect(cellX, cellY, curX+cellWidth,
                                cellY + cellHeight/2);
                            pdc->ExtTextOut(cellX, cellY, ETO_CLIPPED, //ETO_CLIPPED
                                boundRect, ab, NULL);
                            // move the current position over
                            curX += (pdc->GetTextExtent(ab)).cx;
                            cellX = curX + cellWidth / 20;
                            pdc->SetTextColor(oldColor);

                        } // of if
                    } // of for loop
                }// of if GetEventsOnDate()
                delete [] MyDeptEvtCount;
            } // of if UserMode
        counter++;
    } // of j
} // of i
...
}
```

We also implement **OnAmbientPropertyChange()** so that client changes are affected immediately in the control.

```
void CVccalCtrl::OnAmbientPropertyChange(DISPID dispid)
{
    InitializeBackEnd();
    UpdateCore();
    COleControl::OnAmbientPropertyChange(dispid);
}
```

Supporting Dialog Boxes

Our data is in and we've indicated to the user that the information is available for them to view, we just have to actually show the event details. If you remember back to our design, we're going to use dialog boxes to show the data. If a user double-clicks on one of the days with events, a dialog appears with a list of events for that day. Selecting from the list opens a second dialog with the details.

The actual hit-testing is done when the control receives a mouse click on its display area when it's running in the user mode. In this case, we simply check all the cells that have events to see if the mouse point falls into one such cell. For this purpose, we create a handler for the **WM_LBUTTONUP** windows message for the control:

```
void CVccalCtrl::OnLButtonUp(UINT nFlags, CPoint point)
{
    ULONG i;
    if ((m_hWnd) && ( m_ambientDispDriver.m_lpDispatch && AmbientUserMode() ))
    {
        CDC * pdc = GetDC();
        CRect rcBoundsDP;
        GetClientRect(&rcBoundsDP);

        pdc->SetMapMode(MM_ANISOTROPIC) ;
        pdc->SetWindowOrg(0,0) ;
        pdc->SetWindowExt(800,600) ;
        pdc->SetViewportOrg(rcBoundsDP.left,rcBoundsDP.top) ;
        pdc->SetViewportExt(rcBoundsDP.Width(),rcBoundsDP.Height()) ;
        CPoint tppoint(point);
        pdc->DPtoLP(&tppoint);

        for (i=0; i< NUM_DAYS_IN_WEEK * ROWS_DISPLAYED_ON_CAL; i++)
            if (m_CellMgr.GetCellEvent(i))
            {
                if (m_CellMgr.CellHitTest(i, tppoint.x, tppoint.y))
                {
                    m_pDlgEvtLst->m_DateToShow = m_CellMgr.GetCellDate(i);
                    PreModalDialog();
                    m_pDlgEvtLst->DoModal();
                    PostModalDialog();
                }
            }
        ReleaseDC(pdc);
    }
    COleControl::OnLButtonUp(nFlags, point);
}
```

We have introduced three functions of the **CCellMgr** class here: **GetCellEvent()**, **CellHitTest()** and **GetCellDate()**. To start with **GetCellEvent()** simply returns a Boolean indicating whether that particular cell has an events associated with it by returning the **hasEvent** member of the **CalCel** structure:

```
BOOL CCellMgr::GetCellEvent(ULONG idx)
{
    return m_Cells[idx].hasEvent;
}
```

which has be set with a call to **SetCellEvent()**:

```
void CCellMgr::SetCellEvent(ULONG idx, BOOL hasEvent)
{
    m_Cells[idx].hasEvent = hasEvent;
}
```

The **GetCellDate()** function returns the date that corresponds to the indicated cell.

```
COleDateTime & CCellMgr::GetCellDate(ULONG idx)
{
    return m_Cells[idx].CelDate;
}
```

The **CellHitTest()** function is another simple function checking to see if the passed coordinates fall within the cells stored rectangle:

```
BOOL CCellMgr::CellHitTest(ULONG idx, LONG x, LONG y)
{
    return  m_Cells[idx].Position.PtInRect( CPoint( x,y ) );
}
```

When a hit-test is successful, it means that the user has clicked into a cell that has events, while the control is running. In this case, we actually want to pop up a dialog box for the user to select an event that will be happening on that day. After this selection, we'll display the events detail directly in yet another modal dialog box. We see from the hit-test code above how the **m_pDlgEvtLst** member is used to present the selection list dialog. Note the bracketing **PreModalDialog()** and **PostModalDialog()** call while invoking **DoModal()** on m_DlgEvtLst. This is necessary to ensure that modal behavior can be achieved in all containers regardless of how many other controls may be managed by the container.

The two dialog classes are created using the Resource Editor and the ClassWizard. First, we used the Resource Editor to add the two dialog resources. We painted these dialogs using the Dialog Editor. Here's the essential part of the **.RC** file:

```
IDD_EVENTLIST DIALOG DISCARDABLE  0, 0, 222, 154
STYLE DS_MODALFRAME | WS_POPUP | WS_CAPTION
CAPTION "Events Listing"
FONT 8, "MS Sans Serif"
BEGIN
    DEFPUSHBUTTON     "OK",IDOK,90,133,50,14
    LISTBOX           IDC_LIST1,13,22,200,103,LBS_NOINTEGRALHEIGHT |
                      LBS_NOSEL | WS_VSCROLL | WS_TABSTOP
    LTEXT             "Static",IDC_LABEL,19,8,184,11
END
```

```
IDD_EVENTDETAIL DIALOG DISCARDABLE  0, 0, 224, 159
STYLE DS_MODALFRAME | WS_POPUP | WS_CAPTION
CAPTION "Event Details"
FONT 8, "MS Sans Serif"
BEGIN
    DEFPUSHBUTTON    "OK",IDOK,94,138,50,14
    LISTBOX          IDC_LIST1,7,7,210,124,NOT LBS_NOTIFY |
                     LBS_NOINTEGRALHEIGHT | WS_VSCROLL | WS_TABSTOP
END
```

If you decide to copy this code into **Vccal.rc** *rather than creating the dialogs from within Developer Studio, you'll need to add the following resource symbols first:* **IDD_EVENTLIST**, **IDD_EVENTDETAIL**, **IDC_LIST1** *and* **IDC_LABEL**.

Next, we started ClassWizard by right clicking on the dialog. ClassWizard will then ask whether you want to generate a class for the dialog box. We created the following classes in this fashion:

CDlgEvLst

COneEvt

These are relatively simple dialog boxes whose sole purpose in life is to display the calendar event information. The first class **CDlgEvLst**, will display a dialog with a listbox and a button. When the user double-clicks on an item on the listbox, the **CDlgEvLst** handler will create an instance of a **COneEvt** class displaying the details.

Here's the **CDlgEvLst** class declaration:

```
...
typedef struct {
    ULONG Dept;
    ULONG Event;
protected:
    ULONG m_workDeptCount;
} ListShadow;

///////////////////////////////////////////////////////////////////////////
// CDlgEvLst dialog

class CDlgEvLst : public CDialog
{
// Construction
public:
    CDlgEvLst(CWnd* pParent = NULL);   // standard constructor

// Dialog Data
    //{{AFX_DATA(CDlgEvLst)
    enum { IDD = IDD_DIALOG1 };
    //}}AFX_DATA


// Overrides
    // ClassWizard generated virtual function overrides
    //{{AFX_VIRTUAL(CDlgEvLst)
    protected:
    virtual void DoDataExchange(CDataExchange* pDX);   // DDX/DDV support
    //}}AFX_VIRTUAL
```

```
   // Implementation
public:
   COleDateTime m_DateToShow;
   void FillEvents(COleDateTime & inDate);
protected:
   COneEvt * m_DlgEvt;
   ListShadow m_Shadow[MAX_DEPTS * MAX_EVENTS];
   CalEvent m_workList[MAX_DEPTS][MAX_EVENTS];
   ULONG m_workEvents[MAX_EVENTS];

   // Generated message map functions
   //{{AFX_MSG(CDlgEvLst)
   afx_msg void OnDblclkList1();
   virtual BOOL OnInitDialog();
   afx_msg int OnCreate(LPCREATESTRUCT lpCreateStruct);
   afx_msg void OnDestroy();
   //}}AFX_MSG
   DECLARE_MESSAGE_MAP()
};
```

The containment relationship is straightforward: **CVccalCtrl** contains a pointer to an instance of
CDlgEvLst (**m_pDlgEvtLst**), and the instance of **CDlgEvLst** contains a pointer to an instance of
COneEvt (**m_DlgEvt**).

```
   // Implementation
protected:
   CFont * m_TitleFont;
   CString m_TitleFontName;
   short m_TitleFontSize;
   BOOL m_TitleFontBold;
   BOOL m_ButtonsVisible;
   CButton* m_pLeftBut;
   CButton* m_pRightBut;
   COleDateTime m_CurrentDay;
   CDataMgr m_DataMgr;
   CCellMgr m_CellMgr;
   CDlgEvLst* m_pDlgEvtLst;
```

And within the **CDlgEvLst** class:

```
class CDlgEvLst : public CDialog
{
...
// Implementation
protected:
   COneEvt * m_DlgEvt;
...
```

Notice that we're only declaring a pointer to the dialog classes, not the class itself as a member. This is
done so that the dialog boxes don't have to be instantiated if the control itself is instantiated without a
window. As a matter of fact, **m_pDlgEvtLst** will only be non-**NULL** if the control has a window, in this
case the member is initialized in the **CVccalCtrl::OnCreate()** function:

```
int CVccalCtrl::OnCreate(LPCREATESTRUCT lpCreateStruct)
{
   TRACE("CVccalCtrl::OnCreate\n");
```

```
   if (COleControl::OnCreate(lpCreateStruct) == -1)
      return -1;
...
   m_pRightBut->Create(_T(">>"),WS_CHILD | WS_VISIBLE,
      tRect ,this, 101);
   m_pDlgEvtLst = new CDlgEvLst(this);
   // set up the title font
   InitTitleFont(GetDC(), CRect(rect));
   return 0;
}
```

And removed in the **CVccalCtrl::OnDestroy()**:

```
void CVccalCtrl::OnDestroy()
{
   TRACE("CVccalCtrl::OnDestroy\n");
   COleControl::OnDestroy();
   m_pLeftBut->DestroyWindow();
   delete m_pLeftBut;
   m_pLeftBut = NULL;
   m_pRightBut->DestroyWindow();
   delete m_pRightBut;
   m_pRightBut = NULL;
   delete m_TitleFont;
   m_TitleFont = NULL;
   delete m_pDlgEvtLst;
   m_pDlgEvtLst = NULL;
}
```

In a similar fashion, the **CDlgEvLst::m_DlgEvt** is instantiated in the **OnCreate()** member of the **CDlgEvLst** class:

```
int CDlgEvLst::OnCreate(LPCREATESTRUCT lpCreateStruct)
{
   if (CDialog::OnCreate(lpCreateStruct) == -1)
      return -1;
   m_DlgEvt = new COneEvt(this);
   return 0;
}
```

And is released in the **OnDestroy()** method:

```
void CDlgEvLst::OnDestroy()
{
   CDialog::OnDestroy();
   delete m_DlgEvt;
   m_DlgEvt = NULL;
}
```

Time for the declaration of the **COneEvt** class:

```
class COneEvt : public CDialog
{
// Construction
public:
   COneEvt(CWnd* pParent = NULL);   // standard constructor
```

```
// Dialog Data
   //{{AFX_DATA(COneEvt)
   enum { IDD = IDD_DIALOG2 };
      // NOTE: the ClassWizard will add data members here
   //}}AFX_DATA


// Overrides
   // ClassWizard generated virtual function overrides
   //{{AFX_VIRTUAL(COneEvt)
   protected:
   virtual void DoDataExchange(CDataExchange* pDX);    // DDX/DDV support
   //}}AFX_VIRTUAL

// Implementation
protected:
   CalEvent * m_pEvent;
   void FillDetails();
   friend class CDlgEvLst;

   // Generated message map functions
   //{{AFX_MSG(COneEvt)
   virtual BOOL OnInitDialog();
   //}}AFX_MSG
   DECLARE_MESSAGE_MAP()
};
```

How is the information to be displayed transferred into the dialog boxes? In the case of the **CDlgEvLst** class, it has a public member variable **m_DateToShow** that is set to the required date before the dialog is displayed. Recall that the sequence to display the dialog from our hit test code, in method **CVccalCtrl::OnLButtonUp()**, was this:

```
if (m_CellMgr.CellHitTest(i, tppoint.x, tppoint.y))
{
   m_pDlgEvtLst->m_DateToShow = m_CellMgr.GetCellDate(i);
   PreModalDialog();
   m_pDlgEvtLst->DoModal();
   PostModalDialog();
}
```

When **DoModal()** is called, and the actual dialog is displayed, the **OnInitDialog()** member function of **CDlgEvLst** will be called. This member is the one actually responsible for filling up the listbox with events by calling the **FillEvents()** member function:

```
BOOL CDlgEvLst::OnInitDialog()
{
   CDialog::OnInitDialog();
   FillEvents(m_DateToShow);
   return TRUE;
}
```

The **FillEvents()** function uses the **m_DataMgr** member of the **CVccalCtrl** class to gain access to the back-end data. To do this, we need to make the **CDlgEvLst** class a friend of **CVccalCtrl**. **FillEvents()** actually obtains a pointer to the **CVccalCtrl** object by accessing its **m_pParentWnd** member.

```cpp
void CDlgEvLst::FillEvents(COleDateTime & inDate)
{
    CListBox * pMyList;
    CStatic * pLabel;
    CVccalCtrl * pCtl;
    pMyList = (CListBox *) GetDlgItem(IDC_LIST1);
    pLabel = (CStatic *) GetDlgItem(IDC_LABEL);
    pCtl = (CVccalCtrl *) m_pParentWnd;
    ULONG i,j,listCount,evInMonth;
    listCount = 0;
    ULONG workDeptCount = pCtl->m_DataMgr.GetDeptCount();
    pMyList->ResetContent();
    CString caption("Events for " + inDate.Format("%A, %B %d, %Y"));
    pLabel->SetWindowText(caption);
    // the following should always be true anyway
    if (pCtl->m_DataMgr.GetEventsOnDate(inDate, m_workEvents))
    {
        for (i=0; i< workDeptCount; i++)
        {
            if (m_workEvents[i] != 0)
            {
                evInMonth = pCtl->m_DataMgr.GetEventsInMonth(inDate, i);
                for (j=0; j<evInMonth; j++)
                {
                    pCtl->m_DataMgr.GetAnEvent(inDate, i,j, m_workList[i][j]);
                    // *** update to do date check
                    if ((inDate.GetDay() == m_workList[i][j].DateTime.GetDay())
                     && (inDate.GetMonth() ==
                        m_workList[i][j].DateTime.GetMonth()) )
                    {
                        CString inLine(m_workList[i][j].DateTime.Format("%I:%M %p"));
                        inLine += ", ";
                        inLine += pCtl->m_DataMgr.GetDept(i).DeptName;
                        inLine += ", ";
                        inLine += m_workList[i][j].Heading;
                        pMyList->AddString(inLine);
                        m_Shadow[listCount].Dept = i;
                        m_Shadow[listCount].Event = j;
                        listCount++;
                    } // of if day mach
                }// of for j
            } // of if workevent != 0
        } // of for i
    } // of EventsOnDate
}
```

The **FillEvents()** function fills up the list box with all the events happening on the day selected (we'll cover the data manager class later). It also keeps around the events information and a shadow list which maps the listbox selection back to an array of events data structure. When the user actually selects an event in the listbox, the **CDlgEvLst** class handles the double-click event, initializes the data of the **COneEvt** member, and instantiates the dialog:

```cpp
void CDlgEvLst::OnDblclkList1()
{
    CListBox * pMyList;
    pMyList = (CListBox *) GetDlgItem(IDC_LIST1);
```

```
            ULONG idx = pMyList->GetCurSel();
        m_DlgEvt->m_pEvent = &(m_workList[m_Shadow[idx].Dept][m_Shadow[idx].Event]);
        m_DlgEvt->DoModal();
    }
```

We can see above that the **m_DlgEvt** dialog box has a public **m_pEvent** variable which we can set pointing to one of the event references we've stored internal to the **CDlgEvLst** class during **FillEvents()**. The **COneEvt** based class will then create the dialog box when **DoModal()** is called. The **OnInitDialog()** of the **COneEvt** class calls a **FillDetails()** member function, and it is this function which fills the **COneEvt**'s listbox with the event details:

```
BOOL COneEvt::OnInitDialog()
{
    CDialog::OnInitDialog();
    FillDetails();

    return TRUE;  // return TRUE unless you set the focus to a control
                  // EXCEPTION: OCX Property Pages should return FALSE
}
```

```
void COneEvt::FillDetails()
{
    CListBox * pMyList = (CListBox *) GetDlgItem(IDC_LIST1);
    pMyList->ResetContent();
    CString inLine(_T("Date:          "));
    inLine        += m_pEvent->DateTime.Format("%B %d, %Y");
    pMyList->AddString(inLine);
    inLine.Empty();
    inLine        = _T("Time:          ");
    inLine        += m_pEvent->DateTime.Format("%I:%M %p");
    pMyList->AddString(inLine);
    inLine.Empty();
    inLine         = _T("Location:      ");
    inLine        += m_pEvent->Location;
    pMyList->AddString(inLine);
    inLine.Empty();
    inLine         = _T("Event:         ");
    inLine        += m_pEvent->Heading;
    pMyList->AddString(inLine);
    inLine.Empty();
    inLine         = _T("Organizer:     ");
    inLine        += m_pEvent->Heading;
    inLine        += ", ";
    inLine        += m_pEvent->orgDept;
    pMyList->AddString(inLine);
    inLine.Empty();
    inLine         = _T("Description:   ");
    pMyList->AddString(inLine);
    inLine.Empty();
    inLine        = m_pEvent->Details;
    pMyList->AddString(inLine);
}
```

Initializing with Data

Finally, in order to have some data to actually show up when testing our control, here is the function that populates the back-end objects.

Note that we use 1-based enumeration when dealing with VB-compatible ActiveX controls.

```cpp
void CDataMgr::SetEventMonth(const COleDateTime & inMonth)
{
    TRACE("CDataMgr::SetEventMonth\n");

    ULONG workMonth, workYear, i, j;
    COleDateTime workDate, tmpDate;
    IATLDept1 mydept;
    workMonth = inMonth.GetMonth();
    workYear = inMonth.GetYear();
    workDate = COleDateTime(workYear, workMonth, 1, 0,0,1);

    IATLDepts1 tmp_Depts((m_MyFinder.GetEventfulDepts()).pdispVal );
    if (tmp_Depts.GetCount()== 0)
    {
        tmp_Depts.Add(_T("Accounting"), _T("23240"), TRUE, FALSE,
            _T("A") , RGB(255,0,0));
        tmp_Depts.Add(_T("Engineering"), _T("21204"), TRUE, FALSE,
            _T("E"), RGB(0,0,255));
    }
    m_MyFinder.SetFindDate((DATE) inMonth);
    //  delete all items in event list first
    ULONG tpCount = tmp_Depts.GetCount();
    IATLDept1 tpDept;
    IATLCorpEvents1 tpEvents;
    for (i=1; i<= tpCount; i++)
    {
        tpDept.AttachDispatch((tmp_Depts.GetItem(i)).pdispVal);
        tpEvents.AttachDispatch((tpDept.GetKnownEvents()).pdispVal);
        ULONG innerCount = tpEvents.GetCount();
        for (j=0; j< innerCount; j++)
            tpEvents.DeleteFirst();
        tpDept.ReleaseDispatch();
        tpEvents.ReleaseDispatch();
        tpDept.DetachDispatch();
        tpEvents.DetachDispatch();
    }
    // fill them up again
    tpDept.AttachDispatch((tmp_Depts.GetItem(1)).pdispVal);
    tpEvents.AttachDispatch((tpDept.GetKnownEvents()).pdispVal);
    tmpDate = workDate + COleDateTimeSpan(5,14,30,1);
    tpEvents.Add((DATE) tmpDate, _T("Toronto Campus"),
        _T("Super Christmas Celebration"),
        _T("Ray Neveda"), _T("Armanda"),
        _T("everybody welcomed to this terrific party"),
        _T("http://www.anw.com/events"));
```

```
        tmpDate = workDate + COleDateTimeSpan(17,15,0,1);
        tpEvents.Add((DATE) tmpDate, _T("San Jose Site"),
           _T("New Hire Training"), _T("Ray Neveda"),
           _T("Armanda"),
           _T("See your training calendar for more details"),
           _T("http://www.anw.com/events"));
        tpDept.ReleaseDispatch();
        tpEvents.ReleaseDispatch();
        tpDept.DetachDispatch();
        tpEvents.DetachDispatch();

        tpDept.AttachDispatch((tmp_Depts.GetItem(2)).pdispVal);
        tpEvents.AttachDispatch((tpDept.GetKnownEvents()).pdispVal);
        tmpDate = workDate + COleDateTimeSpan(5,10,0,1);
        tpEvents.Add((DATE) tmpDate, _T("Toronto Campus"),
           _T("United Way Kickoff"), _T("Jack Lateman"),
           _T("Toledo"),
           _T("Come donate to this great charity."),
           _T("http://www.anw.com/events"));

        tmpDate = workDate + COleDateTimeSpan(8,19,30,1);
        tpEvents.Add((DATE) tmpDate, _T("Toronto Campus"),
           _T("Farewell Dinner for John Monroe"),
           _T("Jack Lateman"), _T("Toledo"),
           _T("Sorry to see John go after 40 years of service."),
           _T("http://www.anw.com/events"));

        tmpDate = workDate + COleDateTimeSpan(17,9,0,1);
        tpEvents.Add((DATE) tmpDate, _T("Toronto Campus"),
           _T("Internet Training"), _T("Jack Lateman"), _T("Toledo"),
           _T("Free to all employees, take advantage of it!"),
           _T("http://www.anw.com/events"));

        tmpDate = workDate + COleDateTimeSpan(17,12,0,1);
        tpEvents.Add((DATE) tmpDate, _T("Toronto Campus"),
           _T("Dim Sum Breakfast"), _T("Joanne Rogers"),
           _T("Support"), _T("Dare to try something new?"),
           _T("http://www.anw.com/events"));

        tmpDate = workDate + COleDateTimeSpan(20,16,0,1);
        tpEvents.Add((DATE) tmpDate, _T("Toronto Campus"),
           _T("Hammer the IBM370 Fest"), _T("Joanne Rogers"),
           _T("Support"),
           _T("$5 for each punch with a sledgehammer on the retired  370, proceed goes"
               " to United Way."),
           _T("http://www.anw.com/events"));
    }
```

That's the lot!

The control, once you've sorted out the headers, will compile. The next stage is to make sure our control is robust.

Testing the Control

At this final step of the process, we've completed all the logic involved in the ActiveX control, and should be ready to compile and test the code using various containers.

Unit Testing the Calendar Control in the ActiveX Control Test Container

After ensuring that both the ATLDept and ATLFinder back-end COM components can be started up, we're ready to test our entire system consisting of the ActiveX control, and the back-end COM components. With our configuration, it actually consists of:

- One ActiveX control instance.
- One ATLFinder object instance.
- Two ATLDept object instances.

The first container that we'll be testing in is the ActiveX Control Test Container that comes installed with Visual C++ 5.0. This very useful test container allows you to adjust the properties of the control as well as the container, and observe how the control will respond to it.

Notice that it comes up initially in user mode. We know this is the case because the events data summary is displayed. Click on the advance month buttons and watch it work. Click on one of the squares with events and get the event details.

Now change the Ambient user mode to false. Notice that now the events detail is not displayed. In fact the `Atlfinder.dll` local server is also not started.

Other tests you can perform with the Calendar control using the test container include:

Binary persistence through IPersistStorage
UI activate the control
select File | Save to Substorage
select Edit | Delete All to remove the control
select File | Load to recreate the control from saved storage image

Binary persistence through IPersistStream
UI activate the control
select File | Save to Stream
select Edit | Delete All to remove the control
select File | Load to recreate the control from saved stream

Property bag persistence through IPersistPropertyBag
UI activate the control
select File | Save Property Set
select Edit | Delete All to remove the control
select File | Load Property Set to recreate the control

Set the properties
Select View | Properties...
Change TitleFontName to Times
Change TitleFontSize to 18

Change TitleFontBold to 0 (-1 is TRUE, 0 is FALSE)
Change ButtonsVisible to -1 and then back to 0

Invoke the Methods
Select Edit | Invoke Methods...
Invoke AdvanceMonth with inc=2

Test Drawing
Select Edit | Draw Metafile

There are many other possible tests, but the above list gives a feel for the comprehensive testing that is possible using the test container. Until we actually test with a real commercial container, though, it is hard to weed out those nasty bugs that only surface when the end-user tries it.

Testing the Calendar Control in VB

To give the externally accessible properties and methods a good test, we've designed the form in a Visual Basic project to test each of them. You can find the Visual Basic 5 test sample in the **\Vb\Test\Vccal** directory of the source code. Simply open the **Vccaltest.mdp** file. In general, it's good practice to create such a form for a visual ActiveX control and fully test the specified functionality of the control before releasing it for general deployment. Our test form in VB looks like this:

The fictitious event data populated in the calendar can be viewed by clicking on a cell with an events indicator. The **AdvanceMonth()** method can be tested by clicking on one of the buttons to advance the date by one month or back one month. The **ButtonsVisible** property can be

tested by clicking on the Hide Buttons checkbox. Available fonts can be selected, together with the desired size and weight, and then applied to the title by clicking the Apply Title button. To get the test harness filled up with the correct default values, we initialize the calendar and test controls during the **Form_Initialize** event:

```
Private Sub Form_Initialize()
  Dim i As Long
  ACalendar1.SetStartDate (#1/1/98#)
  For i = 1 To Screen.FontCount
     FontList.AddItem Screen.Fonts(i)
  Next i
  FontList.Text = ACalendar1.TitleFontName
  SizeEdit.Text = Mid$(Str(ACalendar1.TitleFontSize), 2)
```

```
        If ACalendar1.TitleFontBold Then
            BoldCheck.Value = 1
        Else
            BoldCheck.Value = 0
        End If
    End Sub
```

You can put Visual Basic 5 back to design mode to do more testing. Notice that the control doesn't display the event data. Bring up the properties of the control, and notice how our custom properties such as **ButtonsVisible**, **TitleFontName**, etc. are merged with the extended properties provided by Visual Basic itself.

Testing Under Internet Explorer 3.0

To ensure that the control can be utilized in the same way on a web page over the intranet, we'll create a web page to perform similar testing of the control. The page is as follows:

```html
<!DOCTYPE HTML PUBLIC "-//IETF//DTD HTML//EN">
<html>

<head>
<meta http-equiv="Content-Type" content="text/html; charset=iso-8859-1">
<meta name="GENERATOR" content="Microsoft FrontPage 2.0">
<title>Intranet Calendar Test Page</title>
</head>

<body bgcolor="#FFFFFF" link="#0033CC">
<div align="center"><center>

<table border="0" cellpadding="0" cellspacing="0">
    <tr>
        <td align="center" valign="top"><font color="#660033"
        size="2" face="ARIAL, HELVETICA">Aberdeen and Wilshire</font><font
        size="2" face="ARIAL, HELVETICA"><br>
        </font><font color="#660033" size="5"
        face="ARIAL, HELVETICA"><b>Intranet Calendar Control Test</b></font></td>
        <td align="center" valign="top"> </td>
    </tr>
</table>
</center></div><div align="center"><center>

<table border="1">
    <tr>
        <td><object id="ACal" name="ACal"
        classid="clsid:DB00C004-54CE-11D0-8564-004005263AF7"
        align="middle" border="0" width="406" height="243"
        font="Arial"><param name="_ExtentX" value="10583"><param
        name="_ExtentY" value="7938"><param name="TitleFontSize"
        value="14.25"></object> </td>
    </tr>
</table>
</center></div>

<form method="POST">
    <p align="center"><input type="button" name="B2" value="-1"
    language="VBScript" onclick="ACal.AdvanceMonth(-1)"> <input
    type="button" name="B3" value="+1" language="VBScript"
    onclick="ACal.AdvanceMonth(1)"> <input type="button"
    name="HideBut" value="Hide Buttons" language="VBScript"
    onclick="ACal.ButtonsVisible = False"> <input type="button"
    name="ShowBut" value="Show Buttons" language="VBScript"
    onclick="ACal.ButtonsVisible = True"> </p>
    <p align="center"><input type="button" name="B7"
    value="Times Roman" language="VBScript"
    onclick="ACal.TitleFontName = 'Times New Roman'"> <input
    type="button" name="B8" value="Set Font to Arial"
    language="VBScript" onclick="ACal.TitleFontName = 'Arial'"> </p>
</form>
</body>
</html>
```

When creating the above page, make sure you include the correct CLSID of the control you've been building.

We've We've tried to set up a test page as close to the VB test page as possible. Due to limitations in the VBScript language, the page can't be identical. For example, there's no easy way to enumerate the fonts available on the system using the VBScript language. Instead, we've created two push buttons that will toggle between the Times New Roman and the Arial font to show that the **TitleFontName** property is functional on the control.

Try out the test page; try the control's advance month buttons; and try clicking on a cell with events to view them. Notice that the intrinsic functions for interacting with the user, retrieving events data, and displaying them are identical regardless of what container is hosting the control. Next, try the +1 and -1 buttons and note that they work like the native buttons. Click Hide Buttons to see the buttons disappear, and then Show Buttons to show them again. Click either Times Roman or Set Font to Arial to change the title font.

Testing Under FrontPage 97

The web page above was created using the FrontPage 97 editor. To test the control under FrontPage 97, do the following:

1 Create a new blank page.

2 Insert an ActiveX control and select the Aberdeen and Wilshire ActiveX Calendar.

3 Right click the control and select properties to display its property.

Notice that the FrontPage 97 editor itself brings up the control in User Mode, but protects it from user interaction. When you select it to set the control properties, however, a new instance of the control would be created in design mode. Again, just as in Visual Basic, you can see the custom properties that we implemented mixed with the runtime properties provided by FrontPage.

This concludes our testing with different containers. Of course, your testing should use all the containers that your intranet users may use.

Just How Much Has VC5 and MFC Done For Us?

To gain an appreciation of how many interfaces required by a Visual ActiveX Control are actually implemented for us by the VC5 and MFC, we can take a look at the COM object from Object Viewer. This is what you'll see:

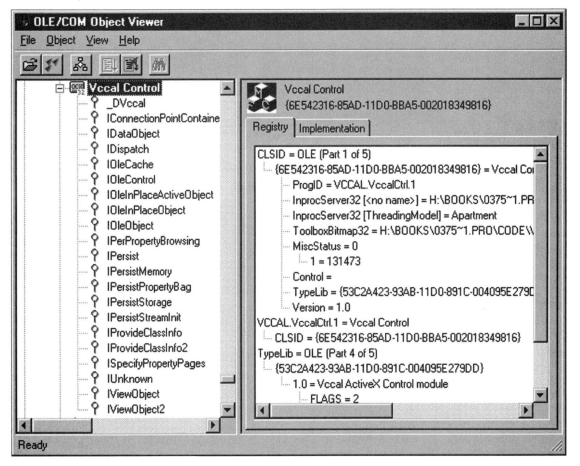

The interfaces implemented included:

_DVcCalc1	IConnectionPointContainer	IDataObject
IDispatch	IOleCache	IOleControl
IOleInPlaceActiveObject	IOleInPlaceObject	IOleInPlaceObjectWindowless
IOleObject	IPersistMemory	IPersistPropertyBag
IPerPropertyBrowsing	IPersist	IProvideClassInfo
IPersistStorage	IPersistStreamInit	ISpecifyPropertyPages
IQuickActivate	IProvideClassInfo2	IViewObject
IViewObject2	IUnknown	IViewObjectEx

That's a total of 24 interfaces (and many hidden support ones)! The saving in effort here is quite clear. To implement all these interfaces from scratch and still be able to focus on the main objectives of the control–data display, interaction handling, and data retrieval–would easily require the effort of a small development team.

Complexity Shouldn't Triumph

This may be an appropriate point to reiterate one vital difference between programming with objects through COM interfaces specified by Microsoft, and those which are defined in a custom fashion. Custom interface COM programming is far easier! To be fair to Microsoft, when we define custom interfaces, we don't have to solve problems in a very generic sense, and we don't have to worry about legacy compatibility issues. We can define COM interfaces to specifically suit our needs, and make them as efficient as we want them to be.

In our intranet design in this book, we've adopted a strategy where we reduce our programming complexity by isolating the interfacing boundaries with Microsoft specified COM interfaces. For example, in this chapter, we used VC5 and MFC to create the user interface handling portion of our Event Calendar intranet application, effectively isolating the complex OC96 interface requirements from the back-end ActiveX components which operate through simple custom interfaces. This design strategy enhances the overall ease of implementation, maintenance, and reuse.

In conclusion, the following diagram illustrates the various interfacing scenarios and the correlation with the level of complexity. The final message is: most of what we cover in this book are intranet design and programming techniques which are more straightforward and simpler than the effort required to become an expert in control mechanics.

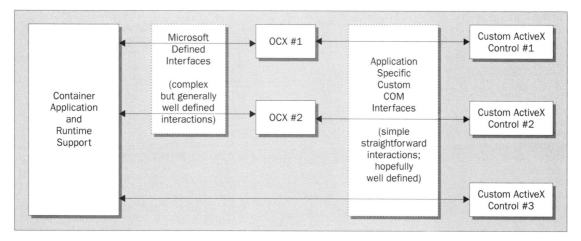

Stay Tuned for the Next Surgery

Up to this point, all of the ActiveX controls and back-end COM objects have been running on the same machine. There's no networking or distributed computing involved, but simple interactive component based computing. We have a visual ActiveX control interacting with an external hierarchy of objects provided by COM servers.

The ability to separate the event finder server from the ActiveX Calendar control across two machines is just the very beginning. In the next chapter, we'll take a more in-depth look at DCOM and what it is good for, and what its limitations are. The next step of the evolution will take us to distributing the in-proc ATLDept set of objects as well. We'll be working with a 3+ machines configuration, observing the action of fully distributed communicating components.

For Aberdeen & Wilshire, deploying our ATL components across multiple machines will allow us to locate the events finder server on a universally accessible and high performance server. The individual departmental implementation of the 'Dept' interfaces will be distributed throughout the intranet. Each department will be responsible for providing a relatively up-to-date view of the available events in their departments through these interfaces. Users hitting the web page containing the Calendar control will be able to retrieve the latest event information across all departments in this distributed object system.

Distributed Objects With DCOM

We're about to experience one of the major benefits of designing component objects based on COM technology. Our objects will become network-ready without any extra work! We'll make this happen in this chapter. We'll also take a more in-depth look at the technology behind this magic: DCOM (or Distributed COM). We'll investigate how DCOM provides an object-based communications service to both DCOM-aware and legacy COM-only objects. We'll attempt to answer the question: why DCOM? We'll examine a couple of the nuts-and-bolts technologies beneath the DCOM covers that may affect us when creating DCOM based applications. And we'll briefly examine the question of security, just enough to understand some of the security fences that our ActiveX control has to jump over during a typical deployment situation, leaving most of the details for Chapter 9. Penultimately, we'll take a cold, hard look at some of the shortcomings of creating distributed component-based applications using today's technology. Coverage will be given to some upcoming technologies that Microsoft is working with to overcome some of these difficulties.

Putting some of our new knowledge to work, we will DCOM-enable our ATL based Dept object server. We'll walk through a step-by-step experiment configuring a network with three machines and testing our Aberdeen & Wilshire Calendar application with cooperating components running on the network of machines.

Distributed COM

> DCOM is just COM with a longer wire.

This is a perfect way to describe how DCOM provides extension to basic COM that we have grown to know and love. By examining how COM operates when a client interacts with object instances served through a local `.EXE` server, we'll be able to see how DCOM actually does its job.

Obtaining DCOM

At the time of writing, DCOM is a standard part of the Windows NT 4.0 distribution, but is an add-on for Windows 95. DCOM for Windows 95 is expected to be included as a standard system component of the next major release of the Windows 95 operating system.

A copy of the released version of DCOM for Windows 95 is also included on the Visual C++ 5 Professional Edition CD.

You can download the latest version of DCOM for Windows 95 over the Internet at the following URL:

http://www.microsoft.com/oledev/olemkt/oledcom/dcom95.htm

A utility that you'll need to configure DCOM for Windows 95 is called the DCOM Configuration, and can also be downloaded from the same URL.

Even if you've installed Windows NT 4.0 release distribution, it's important that you have applied the latest Service Pack for the operating system. As of the time of writing, Service Pack 2 for Windows NT 4.0 is available. This Service Pack brings the DCOM component and related libraries up to the same level as the DCOM for Windows 95 release. You can find the Service Pack at the URL:

http://www.microsoft.com/ntserversupport/Default-SL.HTM

To bring your development environment up to the same level as these DCOM products, you'll need the Win32 SDK Update for Windows NT 4.0 Service Pack 2. This update is delivered as a standard part of the Microsoft Developer's Network subscription CD, the April 97 edition or later. It can also be downloaded at the following URL:

http://www.microsoft.com/msdownload/platformsdk/sp2sdk.htm

Once you have all the above pieces assembled together and installed on your system, you're ready to explore the capabilities of DCOM by following through the code samples. Let's first look at the installation process for DCOM for Windows 95.

Installing DCOM

Installing DCOM for Windows 95 is quite straightforward, simply click on the **Dcom95.exe** distribution executable and it will start (and complete) the installation on your system. You'll need to reboot the system once. During installation, DCOM for Windows 95 will backup all the system files that it replaces. Your system can be restored to the original condition should you wish to uninstall DCOM for Windows 95. This can be done through the Add/Remove Programs applet within the control panel. There exists no known reason why you may want to remove it. However, as with most system upgrades, it's possible that some yet untested application software may not work properly with it.

After installation, the only directly user accessible application is a configuration utility called **Dcomcnfg.exe**. You can try running it, but you may get the following message depending on how your computer is configured on the network.

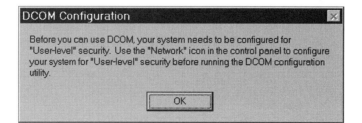

`Dcomcnfg.exe` is coded in a way that it will not start if user authentication against a Windows NT Server is not configured for your system. This isn't actually a requirement for the proper operation of DCOM for Windows 95, and the restriction may be lifted in a future version of the `Dcomcnfg.exe` utility (watch the URL in the last section for the latest version).

DCOM for Windows 95 also installs two other system EXEs: `Rpcss.exe` and `Dllhost.exe`. `Rpcss.exe` is the DCOM enhanced System Control Manager; the `Dllhost.exe` utility surrogate which allows in-proc COM servers to be executed out-of-process or remotely across the network. We'll take a look at `Dllhost.exe` a little later on.

DCOM Enabling Our ActiveX Controls: A Preview

Before digging into the more technical aspects of DCOM, we'll now get our hands wet with a quick demonstration. We'll reserve a more complex scenario involving three machines for the last section of the chapter. Since our ActiveX control and the back-end objects are already communicating across processes (the Calendar control running inside the Visual Basic or Test Container process and the Finder object running inside `Atlfinder.exe`), it should be an easy matter to make them run across machine boundaries over the network. In fact, it's quite simple, with the help of DCOM.

First, we'll need machines connected over a TCP/IP network with DCOM enabled. The previous section has described how DCOM for Windows 95 may be obtained, as well as the installation procedure. In our example, we'll be using DCOM for Windows 95. This choice is made since Windows 95 machines are easier to locate in most cases than Windows NT based machines. However, all of what we cover should be equally applicable to Windows NT 4.0 systems as well.

Preparing the Network

The following are instructions to follow in preparing the network for DCOM testing. Depending on the type of network that the Windows 95 machines are on, the setup procedures are slightly different. If you have machines belonging to an NT Server administered domain, follow the *For NT Server Administered Domains* instructions. If you have Windows 95 machines connected peer-to-peer (or any other Windows 95 network configuration), follow the *For Peer-to-Peer Windows 95 Networks* instructions.

For NT Server Administered Domains

The following instructions are for readers who have machines connected to an NT Server Administered Domain. Readers with standalone peer-to-peer networks consisting of Windows 95 machines do not have to perform the following steps.

Assuming that DCOM for Windows 95 has been properly installed on both machines, we must ensure that both machines have printer and file sharing enabled (this allows the system to 'listen' for RPC requests), and that user based security is enabled with both machines authenticating against the same domain server. This can be done by clicking on the network icon in the control panel.

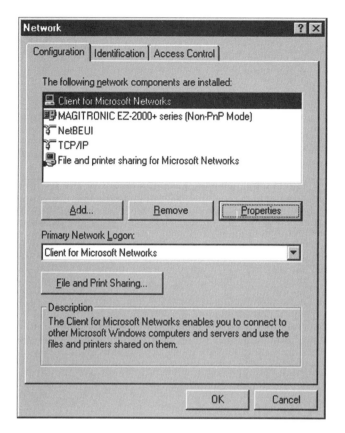

Select the Client for Microsoft Networks networking component, and click the Properties... button. You can now select the Log on to Windows NT domain option and enter in the name of the NT domain that you'll use. Of course, you need to ensure that your user ID and password have been setup with NT domain in order to log on for our experimentation.

After you make this change, the system may request the location of a Windows 95 CD, and finally the system will ask you to restart Windows 95.

The system will now authenticate against the NT domain when you log on to the system. However, we still need to enable user level sharing, and this is where we converge with the instructions for those without Windows NT Domains.

For Peer-to-Peer Windows 95 Networks

DCOM for Windows 95 (Release 1.0) defaults to relaxed security upon installation on peer-to-peer Windows 95 networks. This allows operation of DCOM without specifically configuring any security parameters.

Start Control Panel and click on the Network icon. Instead of selecting properties, click on the File and Print Sharing... button. You'll see this dialog:

If the I want to be able to give others access to my files option is already selected, you're all set. Just Cancel out of the operation and go on to the next step.

If it isn't yet selected, then select it and go through the Windows 95 CD-Rom check and reboot one more time. After this reboot, you'll be all setup for DCOM under Windows 95.

Now we must make sure that the machine can accept remote DCOM calls from clients. This is done by setting the following registry key:

`\HKEY_LOCAL_MACHINE\SOFTWARE\Microsoft\OLE\EnableRemoteConnect = 'Y'`

This key isn't set by default. You'll need to restart the machine again if you change the value of this key.

Another key you'll find at this location is:

`\HKEY_LOCAL_MACHINE\SOFTWARE\Microsoft\OLE\EnableDCOM = 'Y'`

This key is set to **Y** by default, and can be turned off if you should ever want to disable DCOM operations altogether on this machine; however, it would be cleaner to uninstall DCOM for Windows 95 from the machine if you want to do this permanently.

A somewhat easier way to change the value of the key is through the Object Viewer application. If you start `Oleview.exe` and select File | System Configuration, you'll get the following dialog box:

If you check or uncheck these boxes, the **Oleview.exe** program will handle the setting and resetting of the registry keys for you automatically. It will also remind you to reboot should you change any of these values. Object Viewer provides a much safer and friendlier way to the registry settings. If you should run Object Viewer under Windows NT, you'll find the ability to configure the default security blanket for the system as well when you select this option.

Repeat these steps on the other machine.

Installing the Software Components

Now, we're ready to move the **Atldept.dll** and **Atlfinder.exe** over to the remote machine that we'll call the server machine. On the 'server' machine, make sure that the network is prepared, including the activation of printer and file sharing, activation of the user level shares, and the enabling of DCOM connections if necessary. Having done this, create a **C:\Test** directory on the 'server' machine and copy the following files into the directory:

- ▲ **Atldept.dll**

- ▲ **Atlfinder.exe**

- ▲ **atl.dll** (from the ATL 2.1 distribution or your system directory)

- ▲ **Regsvr32.exe** (from **DevStudio\vc\bin** directory)

Now change directory to **C:\Test** and type in the following:

REGSVR32 ATL.DLL
REGSVR32 ATLDEPT.DLL
ATLFINDER /RegServer

Each of these operations should complete successfully. Now install Object Viewer and start it up. Check under the All Objects list and find ATLFinder1 Class and ATLDept1 class. Double-click each one to ensure that you can create an instance of each class. Release the instances.

Finally, on the 'server' machine, type in **ATLFINDER /Server**. This will start the **Atlfinder.exe** COM server listening for incoming COM requests. DCOM for Windows 95 doesn't support remote server launching. Therefore, all remote servers must be started manually. If you have a Windows NT 4.0 system, however, you'll not need to manually enter the above command. **Atlfinder.exe** will be automatically launched on-demand under Windows NT DCOM.

Now the 'server' machine is completely configured for operations. Go back to the 'client' machine. I assume that this machine has been properly configured as specified above, and that you've logged on with the same user ID as on the 'server' machine. Now, start up Object Viewer and click on the ATLFinder1 Class under All Objects. On the right-hand pane, you'll see a set of tabs. Click on the Implementation tab. Click on Local Server and you should see a path to the **Atlfinder.exe** on your system. Remove this path and leave the edit box empty. This effectively removes the content of the **LocalServer32** key from the registry. Now, we need to tell the 'client' machine that the **ATLFinder1** class is to be instantiated remotely. To do this, click on the Activation tab, click on the Launch As Interactive User and key in the IP address of the 'server' machine.

```
┌─────────────────────────────────────────────────────────┐
│  No icon    ATLFinder1 Class                             │
│  Available  {721B4F06-4D27-11D0-8564-004005263AF7}       │
│  ┌──────────┬────────────────┬──────────────┐            │
│  │ Registry │ Implementation │  Activation  │            │
│  │          └────────────────┘              └────────────│
│  │   ☐ Enable "At Storage" Activation                    │
│  │   ☑ Launch as Interactive User                        │
│  │   Remote Machine Name: │47.149.128.51          │      │
│  │                                                        │
│  │                                                        │
│  └────────────────────────────────────────────────────── │
└─────────────────────────────────────────────────────────┘
```

Now go back to the left-hand pane and click on the ATLFinder1 Class entry to instantiate an object. If this is successful (it may take a little while), you'll see the interfaces listed and you'll have successfully instantiated an object across the network.

> **Important note: DCOM for Windows 95 is supposed to automatically start a program named Rpcss.exe when a connection is made to the object. However, this doesn't always work. If you have problems connecting to the object try running Rpcss.exe on the 'server' before you attempt to connect.**

To put the entire scenario to work now, open **TestPage.htm** from the last chapter. After a moment the calendar should start and display all the events. Try selecting a cell with events to get the details. Notice the response. Next, try changing months: notice again the significantly slower response. The ActiveX control is now working over the TCP/IP network via DCOM. The exact same interaction is happening across machine boundaries.

The significant note to make here is that we haven't specifically programmed any DCOM server or DCOM client. The binary code hasn't actually changed at all. It's the same in-proc **Atldept.dll** server, the same **Atlfinder.exe** local server, and the same ActiveX control. All we did was some external configuration, and our COM objects started to communicate with each other over the network. This is significant because it shows the fact that:

> **DCOM is COM**

Almost all legacy COM applications (ones designed with no consideration for DCOM) can be configured to work with DCOM. Of course, new 'from-scratch' applications can take specific advantage of the new features available in DCOM by programming directly to it or—more importantly—being designed specifically for it. We'll have a further discussion on these topics in a later section.

The following diagram depicts the interaction between the ActiveX control and the remote DCOM server components.

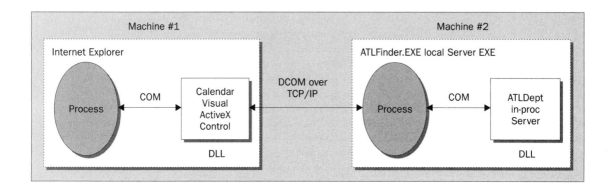

Making Calls Across Processes

Let's now take a closer look at how the DCOM magic works. When a client creates an object instance supported by a local `.EXE` server, this is what happens:

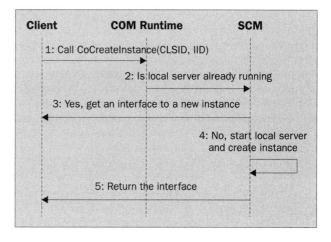

1 The client calls `CoCreateInstance()` on a CLSID supported by a local server.

2 The DCOM runtime working together with the SCM (Service Control Manager), determines if the requested local server is already running and can be connected to. The SCM is a part of the OS on Windows NT.

3 If the local server is already running and can be connected to, the client is provided with a pointer to an interface proxy (more on this later).

4 If no connectable instance of the class requested exists, a new instance of the object is created by launching the local server if necessary.

5 An interface proxy representing the requested interface from the newly created object is returned to the client.

The SCM is a process whose sole purpose in life is to locate implementations or specific instances of requested COM classes. Because of this, it's a close friend of the system registry where all the CLSIDs to implementation mappings are kept persistently. This SCM is typically named **Rpcss.exe** on Windows 95 and Windows NT systems.

Once a client is connected to an instance of a COM class, it holds an interface pointer to an interface proxy. With this interface proxy, the client may obtain other interface pointers (using **QueryInterface()** –recall that all interfaces must implement **IUnknown::QueryInterface()**) or call methods of the interface directly). When such methods are invoked, the COM runtime must send all the arguments for the method from the client process to the local server process. This requires the use of a type of interprocess communications supported by the underlying operating system. In the case of COM, the mechanism used is Distributed Computing Environment Remote Procedure Calls (DCE RPC). DCE RPC has several nice features:

- ▲ It works in the same way across processes on the same machine or across machines on a network.

- ▲ It handles procedure calls and parameter passing across two machines with dissimilar hardware architectures and operating systems.

- ▲ It provides security support that allows the identity of the client process to be passed over to the server.

- ▲ It's basically network transport protocol independent, being currently able to work over TCP, UDP, IPX/SPX or Named Pipes.

- ▲ It's a time-tested mechanism widely deployed in both Windows NT system design and UNIX based network programming.

COM and DCOM leverage heavily on these capabilities.

Note: COM actually will attempt to use lightweight RPC (LRPC) whenever possible when the two communicating objects/components are residing on the same machine and OS. LRPC is a Microsoft proprietary variant of RPC which has the exact same calling syntax as DCE RPC runtime (thus the seamless interchangeability) but is optimized to reduce data copying and eliminate access to the networking code altogether.

When we put the RPC layer into the picture during a method invocation, the situation becomes a bit more complex. Namely, the call is now 'cross-process' or 'cross-machine'. The actual call is delivered to an object within the current process called an Interface Proxy. The following diagram shows the activities that will occur

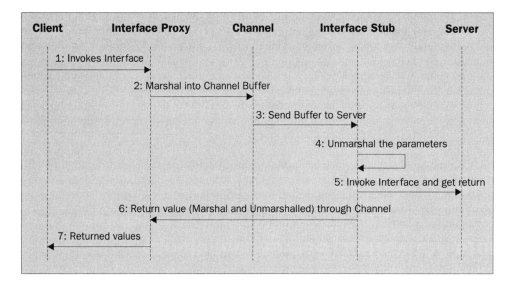

1 The client invokes the interface through the interface proxy.

2 The interface proxy marshals the parameters into a buffer provided by a **channel**. The channel is supplied by the RPC runtime system and is an abstraction above the different transports. The channel can be operating on shared memory spanning two processes on the same machine, or could be operating over a network protocol stack across two machines. It can be viewed as a virtual tunnel connecting the two communicating processes (regardless of their location). Data going into the tunnel (marshaled) on Process A will come out the same way (unmarshaled) from the other end of the tunnel on Process B. Loosely speaking, marshaling means packing the data into the channel's buffer in a well-defined format (for DCE RPC, this well defined format is called the Network Data Representation or NDR). NDR is an agreed format to transmit different data types between dissimilar machines so that the same data can be reconstructed exactly at the destination machine).

3 The channel forwards the data to the server.

4 An interface stub on the server receives the buffer from the channel and unmarshals the data from the buffer .

5 The interface stub calls the associated interface on the server object.

6 The interface stub sends return values back to the interface proxy.

7 The interface proxy returns the values to the client.

Note that there are many more subtleties associated with the marshaling action than the simple description implies. For example, if a pointer to a data item is marshaled across two processes, just sending the value of the pointer itself is useless since the receiver lives in a totally separate process/addressing space. Instead, the actual data item itself must be sent across the wire and a pointer to it reconstructed within the receiver process in order for the marshaling to work.

Now is a good time to find out what the interface proxies and stubs are. Under the COM model, they are actually small COM objects. The code for these objects was created automatically when we ran our original IDL (interface description language) through the MIDL compiler. Based on the data type of the method arguments and return values, the MIDL compiler creates these marshalling proxy/stub pairs for communicating between processes. One pair of proxy/stub classes is created for each interface. If you look back in Chapter 7 where we created a local server called **ATLFinder.EXE**, you'll find a file called **ATLFINDERPS.MK.** You can actually perform:

```
NMAKE -F ATLFINDERPS.MK
```

in a DOS box to create and register the proxy/stub for marshalling of the interfaces supported by the **ATLFinder.EXE** local server. To satisfy your curiosity, look in your Chapter 7 working directory for the **ATLFinder.EXE** project and find the **ATLFinder_p.c** file to see what MIDL generated proxy/stub code physically looks like.

So far we've focused on the conceptual view of providing proxy and stub code for interface method invocation across processes, and indeed it was the way that it was done for a period of time. With DCOM, though, Microsoft has introduced automatic type-library based marshaling. Automatic type-library marshaling actually builds these proxy and stub objects *on the fly* from type library information obtained on an interface. What we see here is actually a reuse of the marshaling technology Microsoft had been using for OLE Automation. As long as the data type that needs to be marshaled is compatible with OLE Automation (which essentially means all the data types that a **VARIANT** can hold), you don't even need the MIDL generated proxy/stub code.

Calling COM Methods Between Machines

Now that we have a basic understanding of how an interface method call is transmitted across two communicating processes on the same machine or across a network, the next logical question is: how is the object on the destination created in the first place? Simply put, the SCM will locate or create the object instance across the network whenever necessary (if there are no object instances which can service the call, the SCM will launch the required object server on the remote machine, subjected to security constraints detailed in the next chapter). In the case where the caller and called party are both on the same machine under the same OS, the channel is typically working over shared memory and LRPC will be used. In the case where the caller and called party are on different machines over a network, the channel uses the DCE RPC over a layer of network software called the protocol stack (usually TCP/IP but IPX and NETBEUI are also supported by RPC on Windows platforms).

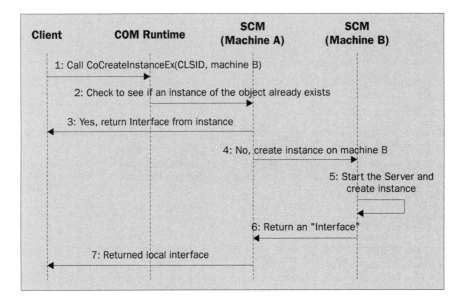

Of course, there's low level sanity checking and connection management work that DCOM must do because of the added network connection. All this work, though, is completely hidden from you as an application developer and you can develop components without worrying about where they may be executed.

The Premise of DCOM: Why DCOM?

Now, back to discussions on a higher level. We, as technical professionals, are often asked to justify or support strategic decisions through analysis and/or case studies. If such a decision involves the question 'Why DCOM?', we have a dilemma. DCOM, being an extremely young technology, will not have too many substantial or particularly compelling case studies that one can draw from. Instead, the decision may have to be made based on initial testing and more casual 'feature-set' analysis.

Here we'll provide a list of salient 'selling points' for DCOM that can be used when building a case for DCOM. Beware, portions of what follows may read more like sales pitches than sound technical punches.

The Object-Oriented Hype

The object-oriented gold rush of the early 1990s has been eclipsed by the painful discovery of the difficulties involved when putting the methods into practice. Full adoption of the object-oriented culture entails revolutionary changes throughout the life cycle of a product, from OO Analysis/Planning to OO Design, to OO Programming, through to OO environment for software maintenance and support. The exposure to such culture, for most people, is limited to the utilization of object-oriented programming languages and development environments. The C++ language has became the most popular ambassador of object-oriented design and development techniques. Unfortunately, much of its popularity comes from the fact that it attempts to be backward compatible with the most popular system (and microcomputer applications) programming language of all time: C. This compatibility has provided many 'backdoors' in programming which break all rules of object-oriented software design. While discipline in software design works well in small object-oriented projects working in C++, industry case studies have shown that the practice inevitably breaks down in very large projects involving multiple programming teams. One key problem cited is the inability to reuse C++ classes effectively across projects without having access to the underlying source code. Many of the promises made by the object-oriented pundits remained undeliverable in the era of object-oriented C++ software development.

Another very real limitation is that unless the entire system is object-oriented, it becomes very difficult to manage the 'boundaries' between the pieces on a system that are and aren't object-oriented. After all, a simple computing language can only give an 'illusion' of object-orientation without an underlying object-oriented runtime operating system, or data access support. Without these supports, some sort of 'mapping' has to be performed to work with the underlying subsystem if it isn't object-oriented. Because an alternative method of access is available which isn't object-oriented, such a system typically requires very involved maintenance and is subjected to easy corruption. There were valiant attempts in the industry to address this problem by making the complete system object-oriented, most notable are the Next operating system, the SmallTalk programming language and programming/runtime environment, and many of the object databases. In each case, by having total control over the entire operating environment, some of the higher level benefits of object-oriented design based on inheritance and polymorphism can be realized. While there are a significant number of people following and adopting the approaches of these systems, their 'revolutionary' nature has kept them from many of the largest corporate installations.

Dream of Code Reuse

As we've said before, the promise of code reuse is somewhat realized in reuse of class libraries within in-house small projects. In the larger 'shrink wrap' software market, the postulated 'uninhibited world-wide' market for class libraries never materialized. It turns out that class libraries delivered without source code are very hard to use and debug. Delivering class libraries with source code still gives the seriously business-minded software vendor heartaches because of the potential for unauthorized plagiarism.

While the leading edge fraction of the industry are trying various 'silver bullet' object-oriented solutions, and failing, various standards organization and industry groups (i.e. OMG, DCE, Open Group, the COM camp within Microsoft) are taking a step-by-step approach by evolving the current operating system and supporting services towards an object-oriented style of computing. The current result from these working groups is a computing model based on distributed objects, or components. Almost all of the abstract concepts preached by the object-oriented evangelists are deployed in creating reusable software components that can interoperate over heterogeneous networks of computers.

Regardless of what architectural appeal a new methodology may have, the business community will not usually commit to it wholesale unless there exists compelling business reasons for them to do so. The overwhelming driving force towards a component model of computing is simple economics. In the ideal world of component based applications building, pieces of prefabricated and tested code can be assembled together to create applications. The same pieces of code can be reused in other contexts to build alternative applications. In this world, software components only have to be written once, drastically saving the time and effort required for 'reinventing the wheel' for each individual project. If it sounds familiar, this is the exact same promise almost a decade back that had brought the object-oriented design and development into vogue. What, then, makes it different ten years later?

The key here is the slow emergence and development of a simple yet effective supporting infrastructure that can actually make it work. One term that is often used to describe these 'piece of functionality' components is a **Software IC** or **Software Integrated Circuit**. The analogy drawn upon here is the silicon chip in hardware design that encapsulates a fixed piece of functionality and works with other chips to create functional electronic devices. Take the example of a microprocessor chip. By itself, it's not very interesting, and it can do very little for the end-user. However, when it's put into a design where it can communicate via a bus to memory chips and input/output chips, we end up with a highly functional computer system. It's this 'bus' which has been missing for our 10-year-old Software ICs. In the hardware example, the electronic bus interconnecting the microprocessor, memory, and input/output chips has well defined electrical and timing specifications, and documented protocols for how the connected devices will be interoperating. In our software example, COM and DCOM (and also CORBA, dominant in the UNIX world) provides such a bus for object cooperation.

Compelling Business Reasons

Some other compelling business reasons why an infrastructure like COM and DCOM may finally be able to deliver on the component based computing promise include:

(disclaimer: intense sales pitch coming up)

- ▲ Preservation of existing investment: current software can be 'wrapped' and participate in the DCOM component computing world regardless of its current implementation platform.

- ▲ Autonomy through distributed business-rule components, allowing components encapsulating business-rules to reside and be maintained by the authority group which decides and implements them.

- ▲ Efficient and effective use of low-cost commodity computing resources; many mainframe or mini-class solutions can be migrated to fault-tolerant clusters of inexpensive microcomputers, greatly reducing deployment and maintenance costs.

- ▲ Potentially unlimited scalability for server solutions: ongoing developments in DCOM and related support services will soon enable very large server systems which can handle very large databases (up to a terabyte) and very high transaction rates (up to a million transactions per day). In a recent industry summit, Microsoft's Bill Gates has made a commitment to deliver this in 1997.

- ▲ Enable distributed workflow computing: a choice of scripting languages is available for creating workflow applications orchestrating the action of various business-rule components over a network using DCOM.

- ▲ Lower cost of development and support: the platform and language independence provided by DCOM enable an organization to use existing programming and design expertise, say in COBOL or BASIC, to develop and maintain reusable software components. (MicroFocus COBOL can create native COM components!)

- ▲ Delivery over diverse heterogeneous environments: the support of DCOM over both TCP/IP, IPX/SPX and many other transports, coupled with the implementation of DCOM on UNIX, Macs, and other systems allows deployment of DCOM over existing network and computing resources without additional investment.

- ▲ 'Riding the power curve': the ability to leverage the currently available commodity microprocessor based technologies and apply them to new or legacy problems that formerly required very expensive dedicated or niche computing equipment.

- ▲ DCOM can work securely through an intranet, the public Internet, or over virtual private networks enabled through the Internet today making objects location-independent.

Dealing with Legacy Applications

We've seen how regular COM objects can be made to work across a network using DCOM simply by altering a registry configuration. This is done by design to allow the crop of existing COM components to participate in the DCOM world immediately. You don't even need to recompile these components to make them work across the network. Specifically, the following registry keys are essential in letting the SCM know that the server is located on another machine:

```
\HKEY_CLASSES_ROOT\AppID\<the object's CLSID>\RemoteServerName =
    "ip address of server node"
\HKEY_CLASSES_ROOT\AppID\<the object's CLSID>\RunAs =
    "Interactive User"
```

These settings will make the SCM look for the remote class on the server node, and run with the security principal and identity of the current user

In addition, we need to make sure that the following keys in the registry are removed:

```
\HKEY_CLASSES_ROOT\CLSID\<the object's CLSID>\InProcServer32
\HKEY_CLASSES_ROOT\CLSID\<the object's CLSID>\LocalServer32
```

otherwise the SCM will use either the in-proc or local server versions of the object to create the instance of the object, as the mechanism is more efficient.

This approach works well when only one externally created class can be created by the remote executable. In the case where there are multiple classes corresponding to the same remote executable, we'll need to create a registry key called **AppID** at each **\HKEY_CLASSES_ROOT\CLSID\<the object's CLSID>** entry. The **AppID** key should contain a GUID that refers back to the entry under **\HKEY_CLASSES_ROOT\AppID\<GUID>**. For example:

```
\HKEY_CLASSES_ROOT\CLSID\{A023F6A0-F4C1-11CE-8EAF-00608C85E107}\AppID =
{208D2C60-3AEA-1069-A2D7-08002B30309D}
\HKEY_CLASSES_ROOT\CLSID\{B10CBD8E-F9B6-11CF-9B38-0080AD11B667}\AppID =
{208D2C60-3AEA-1069-A2D7-08002B30309D}

\HKEY_CLASSES_ROOT\AppID\{208D2C60-3AEA-1069-A2D7-
08002B30309D}\RemoteServerName = "192.168.0.1"
\HKEY_CLASSES_ROOT\AppID\{208D2C60-3AEA-1069-A2D7-08002B30309D}\RunAs =
    "Interactive User"
```

In this example, we can see that objects with CLSIDs **{A023F6A0-F4C1-11CE-8EAF-00608C85E107}** and **{B10CBD8E-F9B6-11CF-9B38-0080AD11B667}** can both be created using a server on the node **192.168.0.1**. The SCM will use this information to decide where to go and create instances for these two classes.

We're running as the **Interactive User** (under DCOM for Windows 95, there exists really no other choice) in these cases in order to avoid complications due to security constraints on Windows NT based systems. Interactive User means the user who is currently logged on at the particular PC. Under Windows 95, all currently active processes 'belong' to the system that is currently logged on. Adopting this simple approach to security allows us to focus our effort on development and testing. As long as we're logged on as the same user on all machines containing clients and servers to be tested, DCOM will be able to connect and execute. For production, however, we must plan our security strategy carefully using DCOM's security blanket mechanism. This will be the subject matter of Chapter 9.

Some Changes for DCOM-Aware objects

While 'normal' COM objects can plug-and-play in the DCOM world, it's certainly possible to create DCOM-aware objects that can take advantage of some new features that DCOM offers. We'll now take a look at some of the new APIs and security oriented COM interfaces available for DCOM and how we may be able to take advantage of them.

CoCreateInstanceEx()

First, we have a **CoCreateInstanceEx()** call to specifically create an object instance on a remote machine, and also optimize on the performance of the **QueryInterface()** mechanism across the network by handling multiple **QueryInterface()** operations during the **CoCreateInstanceEx()** call (utilizing only one network round-trip). The prototype is shown here:

```
HRESULT CoCreateInstanceEx( REFCLSID  rclsid,
                            IUnknown *  punkOuter,
                            DWORD * dwClsCtx,
                            COSERVERINFO* pServerInfo,
                            ULONG   cmq,
                            MULTI_QI  rgmqResults   );
```

The parameters are explained below:

Function Parameters	Description
REFCLSID rclsid	The CLSID of the COM class from which the object instance is to be created.
IUnknown * punkOuter	If **NULL**, indicate that the object is not being aggregated. If non-**NULL**, the object being created is part of an aggregate. Note that out-of-process aggregation isn't supported in the currently available version of DCOM. **CoCreateInstanceEx()** is guaranteed to return **CLASS_E_NOAGGREGATION** if a non-**NULL** value is passed, and the instance to be created is remote.
DWORD * dwClsCtx	A value from the CLSCTX (execution context) enumeration, it can be: **CLSCTX_INPROC_SERVER, CLSCTX_INPROC_HANDLER, CLSCTX_LOCAL_SERVER, CLSCTX_REMOTE_SERVER, CLSCTX_SERVER** or **CLSCTX_ALL** Note that the last three values include **CLTSCTX_REMOTE_SERVER**, which means that they will also allow creation of a remote instance. Recall that it's still possible to create a remote server by external registry configuration, potentially overriding the use of this parameter by the client.

Function Parameters	Description

COSERVERINFO *
pServerInfo
	Pointer to a **COSERVERINFO** structure that specifies the machine on which to create the object instance. The **COSERVERINFO** structure is defined to be:
	
	``
	typedef struct _COSERVERINFO
	{
	    DWORD dwReserved1;
	    LPWSTR pwszName;
	    COAUTHINFO __RPC_FAR *pAuthInfo;
	    DWORD dwReserved2;
	} COSERVERINFO;
	``
	
	The **pwszName** should be pointing to a wide string containing the server's name. When using DCOM over TCP/IP, this can contain the IP address of the node, or a DNS name such as **WWW2.ABC.COM**. Otherwise, a UNC name such as **\\MACHINE** is allowed. The **COAUTHINFO** member contains a security blanket definition (see Chapter 9) structure:
	
	``
	typedef struct _COAUTHINFO
	{
	    DWORD dwAuthnSvc;
	    DWORD dwAuthzSvc;
	    LPWSTR pwszServerPrincName;
	    DWORD dwAuthnLevel;
	    DWORD dwImpersonationLevel;
	    COAUTHIDENTITY __RPC_FAR *pAuthIdentityData;
	    DWORD dwCapabilities;
	} COAUTHINFO;
	``
	
	In most cases, when an NT Domain server is used to authenticate a user (using NTLMSSP), this member of the **COSERVERINFO** should be set to **NULL** rather than a pointer to **COAUTHINFO**. We'll cover security in more detail in Chapter 9.
	
	If this parameter, **COSERVERINFO**, is **NULL**, the SCM will be asked to do its job to determine how to create an instance of the class by examining the registry.

ULONG cmq	The number of the **MULTI_QI** structures being passed in as the **rgmqResults** parameter. Combined with **rgmqResults**, this parameter allows the DCOM runtime to save network round-trips by specifying multiple **QueryInterface()** calls to perform on the object immediately after creation. This must be at least 1 (i.e. you must get at least one interface for the remote object, otherwise why create it?).

Table Continued on Following Page

Function Parameters	Description
MULTI_QI rgmqResults	Contains an array of **MUTLI_QI** structures, which is defined as:

```
typedef struct _MULTI_QI
{
    const IID*    pIID;
    IUnknown *    pItf;
    HRESULT       hr;
} MULTI_QI;
```

Upon calling, the **pIID** portion contains a pointer to the IID of each interface to **QueryInterface()** for. Upon call return, the **pItf** member will contain the interface pointer requested if the **hr** member is **S_OK**. If the **hr** member for a specified interface is **E_NOINTERFACE**, the **pItf** member is invalid, and the object doesn't support the interface requested.

The possible return values from **CoCreateInstanceEx()** are:

Return Code	Description
S_OK	The object instance was created successfully.
E_INVALIDARG	One or more arguments passed in were invalid.
E_NOINTERFACE	None of the specified interfaces in the **rqmqResults** was available from the object.
CO_S_NOTALLINTERFACES	Not all of the specified interfaces in the **rqmqResults** were available, but at least one entry contains a valid interface.

CoInitializeSecurity()

A new **CoInitializeSecurity()** call allows a process to set a default security blanket. A security blanket is a suite of security parameters specifying the level of security required. A negotiation process takes place when a client connects to a server, when the system matches the security levels specified by the client to make sure it is at the same level or higher than those specified in the server's security blanket. More discussion of security and the **CoInitializeSecurity()** will be presented in Chapter 9. Typically, the **CoInitializeSecurity()** call is made after a call to **CoInitializeEx()**. If a process doesn't call **CoInitializeSecurity()**, COM will actually make the call on the process's behalf, using the defaults found in the registry (under the **AppID** key). This is how legacy non-DCOM aware components get to play along with DCOM-aware components, without having to worry about security.

Again, we'll discuss other DCOM related security interfaces, including the **IClientSecurity**, **IServerSecurity**, and **IAccessControl** interfaces (together with their associated helper functions) in Chapter 9.

New CoRegisterPSClsid() API

This API function is used to temporarily register the CLSID of a proxy/stub class server associated with a specified interface. The normal behavior for COM is to read the proxy/stub server information from the **HKEY_CLASSES_ROOT\Interface\{interface ID}** registry key. However, in certain cases, the object wishing to replace the proxy may not have write-access to the registry. This is frequently true under the Windows NT where the access security level of the running object may not be sufficient to modify the registry. `CoRegisterPSClsid()` is useful in these situations. In addition, it is an all around preferred way to specify a specific proxy/stub code for an interface without affecting the registry settings. For example, if you would like the system to use a network-optimized, custom-coded marshalling scheme rather than the system default automatic type library marshaling.

The scope of the temporary assignment will last until the termination of the process or until `CoRegisterPSClsid()` is called again. If the proxy/stub objects aren't yet registered with the system, `CoRegisterClassObject()` should be called to register the CLSIDs before calling `CoRegisterPSClsid()`.

The `CoRegisterPSClsid()` has the following prototype:

```
WINOLEAPI CoRegisterPSClsid( REFIID riid,
                             REFCLSID rclsid );
```

It has the following parameters:

Parameter Name	Description
`REFIID riid`	A pointer to the interface ID of the interface that the proxy/stub code is to be associated with.
`REFCLSID rclsid`	A pointer to the CLSID representing the proxy/stub code for marshaling the `riid` interface.

`CoRegisterPSClsid()` may return:

Return Value	Description
`S_OK`	Mapping of proxy/stub code to interface successful.
`E_INVALIDARG`	A parameter is invalid.
`E_OUTOFMEMORY`	The runtime ran out of memory while executing the API call.

This concludes our coverage of new interfaces and APIs associated with DCOM. None of these new features are required for COM objects to participate in a distributed environment. But DCOM-aware objects that make use of these features can gain better control over the way DCOM performs remote instantiation, client and server security checking, as well as marshaling.

Remote Activation (Server Launching)

One major difference between DCOM for Windows 95 and Windows NT DCOM is the ability to automatically launch (or activate) a remote server to create object instances. Providing that the client has the required security blanket, server launching/activation is automatic on Windows NT. On Windows 95, it isn't possible to automatically launch a server. Instead, COM servers must be launched manually in Windows 95 before they may be used remotely.

This difference can be attributed to the lack of support for network or multiuser security under Windows 95. Under Windows 95, every process runs as the current user and there's no way to circumvent this. The only authentication level accepted is 'connect' under Windows 95 (once again, more on this in Chapter 9), this means that separation between accessible resources for concurrently executing servers is nonexistent and that impersonation isn't possible. From a security perspective, all currently running processes on a Windows 95 system are executing under a single user account. The bottom line is that COM servers running concurrently on Windows 95 can't provide privacy or resource protection features. This is a rather sad affair, and renders Windows NT the preferred server platform for DCOM objects.

Typelib and Registrations

Registration of type library information is mandatory for classes that are to be used by automation clients. You should register your type library if you want the object that you've created, whether it's local or remote, to be usable by VBScript and JAVAScript in Internet Explorer, and Visual Basic as well as Java.

Recall from Chapter 2 that type libraries are maintained in **.TLB** files generated by the MIDL compiler from the project's **.IDL** file. But, ATL also combines the type library information with the generated executable (either **.EXE** or **.DLL**). When we do a **regsvr32 <name>.DLL** or a **<name>.EXE / RegServer**, the type library registration is also performed automatically.

Let's look into the registry and see where these type libraries are actually located. In general, a type library can be located under:

\HKEY_CLASSES_ROOT\TYPELIB\{Type library's UUID}

Taking our ATLFinder local server as an example, we find the following registry values:

Matching this with the **Atlfinder.idl** that we've created in Chapter 7, we can see the correspondence.

```
[
    uuid(721B4F00-4D27-11D0-8564-004005263AF7),
    version(1.0),
```

```
      helpstring("ATLFinder 1.0 Type Library")
]
library ATLFINDERLib
{
... skipped interface and coclass definitions
};
```

The GUID of the type library is used as the main key under **\HKEY_CLASSES_ROOT\TYPELIB**. Then a subkey containing **<MajorVersion.MinorVersion>** has a default value that is the name or 'helpstring' attribute in the IDL file. Under this subkey, there can be a **FLAGS** subkey. This subkey can contain a unary ORed combination of the following values:

FLAGS value	Description
1	Restricted–no user tools should display or use this type library.
2	Control–the type library contains descriptions of controls. Tools which examine nonvisual objects should skip this library.
4	Hidden–this library should not be displayed to the users, but can be used by controls.

The actual location of the type library information, in this case the **Atlfinder.exe** file with the TLB information merged in as a custom resource, can be found under a subkey with **0\win32**. The **0** subkey is there mainly for historical reasons. Older OLE implementations had no means of deleting a type library entry programmatically, so the numeric index is used to keep track of older versions of the type library.

The **HELPDIR** subkey specifies the path to the **.HLP** file associated with this type library. If a type library is published for commercial or production purposes, a context index can be associated with a help file for each item in the type library to give more information to the end user as they browse the type library.

Shipping Components Across the Intranet

Building applications out of reusable distributed components is a great idea. Keeping such an application up-to-date with respect of new versions of the application as a whole, and to the varying new versions of the components used in the application isn't a trivial task. One new technology introduced by Microsoft along with its ActiveX push, which addresses this problem, is a system for automated code download and installation.

Conventional software upgrades produce major headaches for MIS departments, involving coordinated install, update schedules and user training sessions. It's easy to see the tremendous effort and cost associated with each build of a widely used piece of software.

It simply will not work in the componentized world.

Imagine an average component-based application using directly and indirectly about 50 to 60 classes of component objects. Just imagine two revisions for each component class each year, and you end up with 120 software upgrades a year or approximately 10 each month. We must look for an automated and reliable way of upgrading components.

Automated Application Download and Install

Though not explicitly designed for COM or DCOM, the automated code download feature solves our problem nicely. This features allows ActiveX controls (COM servers) to be downloaded from a centralized location, installed, and activated on an end-user machine when a web page containing the control is reached. As an additional feature, if the ActiveX control is already installed on the user's machine, but is of an older version, the support system will download and replace the control with the newer version. This behavior is almost exactly what we want. Paired with the code download technology is digital signature/code signing technology from Microsoft. This allows the receiver of the downloaded component to be sure of the integrity of the code during the download process, and the authenticity of the original source of the code. However, this technology is less relevant in the isolated intranet environment.

In a typical usage on a web page, an ActiveX control object is embedded in the following manner with the **<OBJECT>** tag.

```
<OBJECT
   ID="MyCalendar"
   CLASSID="clsid:99B42120-6EC7-11CF-A6C7-00AA00A57DD2"
   CODEBASE="http://objectstore.aw.com/controls/vbsamp/vbcalctl.ocx#Version=1,0,0,121"
   TYPE="application/x-oleobject"
   WIDTH=150
   HEIGHT=60
   VSPACE=0
   ALIGN=left
>
```

The key attributes for version control and download are the **CLASSID** and **CODEBASE** entries. The **CLASSID** entry contains the CLSID of the control to download, and the **CODEBASE** entry contains the location for downloading the code if necessary, as well as a version number consisting of four parts. The first two parts are the two words making up the most significant double word of the version number (typically the major version number), and the last two parts are two words making up the lower double word of the version number (usually the minor version number). The new control will be downloaded if it hasn't been installed in the local machine and/or if the version number of the code on the local machine is older than the one required.

Under the hood, the browser (in this case IE3.0) uses a new API call to accomplish its task. The API is generally available, and we may use it to create centrally stored, version controlled component code for automatic distribution and version management. The name of this new API function is **CoGetClassObjectFromURL()**, and is equivalent to **CoGetClassObject()**, which relies solely on the SCM to check the information in the local registry.

CoGetClassObjectFromURL()

Like **CoGetClassObject()**, this function will return a class factory interface for a specified CLSID. The object instance will be created if it's already installed locally. If necessary, this routine will also download and install the code from the specified URL. If the URL points to an uncompressed **.OCX**, **.DLL**, (**.CLASS** for Java) or **.EXE** file, the component is registered locally after download and the object factory instance will be created. If the URL points to a **.INF** file, the instruction within the **.INF** file will be followed to either download more URL based files, or install and download more components. If the URL is a compressed **.CAB** file, the file is decompressed and authenticated (via call to **WinVerifyTrust()**) with its embedded digital signature; the decompressed contents are then treated as if they are freshly downloaded COM servers or an **.INF** file as described above. This API is server agnostic, it will work with any web servers, not just the Microsoft IIS.

It's also possible to call without a specified CLSID, in this case, the content type parameter determines the CLSID of the executable to use in interpreting or displaying the specific MIME type. The MIME type to CLSID mapping is kept in the local registry directly under the key:

`\HKEY_CLASSES_ROOT\MIME\Database\ContentType`

Using the MIME type feature is a way for the system to associate a specific default executable to deal with a specific multimedia data type. For example, if the content is a music file in MIDI **.MID** format, the associated executable may be the Media Player applet.

The call prototype for **CoGetClassObjectFromURL()** is:

```
STDAPI CoGetClassObjectFromURL( REFCLSID rclsid,
                                LPCWSTR szCodeURL,
                                DWORD dwFileVersionMS,
                                DWORD dwFileVersionLS,
                                LPCWSTR szContentTYPE,
                                LPBINDCTX pBindCtx,
                                DWORD dwClsContext,
                                LPVOID pvReserved,
                                REFIID riid,
                                VOID **ppv ) ;
```

Parameter	Description
`rclsid`	A pointer to the CLSID of the object instance to be created. It can contain **NULL**, in which case the **szContentTYPE** will be used to determine what to instantiate.
`szCodeURL`	A wide-string indicating the URL of the code for the COM object. As mentioned above, it can be a **.CAB**, **.INF**, **.OCX**, **.DLL**, **.CLASS** or **.EXE** file.
`dwFileVersionMS`	The most significant word of the version number (usually the major version number).
`dwFileVersionLS`	The least significant word of the version number (usually the minor version number).
`szContentType`	A wide-string containing the MIME content type description string. It's used to determine the CLSID to instantiate in cases where the **rclsid** parameter contains **NULL**. For example, **szContentType** may contain **audio/x-wav** which will cause the sound recorder applet to be instantiated.
`pBindCtx`	Pointer to a bind context that is passed in. Note that if the client is interested in receiving status information during the download (i.e. if the link is slow), a callback should be registered with the bind context. We'll explain what a bind context is later on in this section.
`dwClsContext`	A value from the **CLSCTX** enumeration specifying the execution context of the object (i.e. **CLSCTX_INPROC_SERVER**, **CLSCTX_INPROC_HANDLER**, or **CLSCTX_LOCAL_SERVER**).
`pvReserved`	Set this to **NULL**.

Table Continued on Following Page

Parameter	Description
`riid`	Pointer to the IID of the initial interface to ask for, almost always `IClassFactory`.
`ppv`	An output value, a pointer to an interface pointer which will be set to point at the requested interface from the new object instance.

The possible return values from `CoGetClassObjectFromURL()` are:

Return Value	Description
`S_OK`	The `ppv` return value now contains the requested interface.
`E_NOINTERFACE`	Cannot obtain the requested interface.
`REGDB_E_READREGDB`	Error encountered when accessing the registry.
`CO_E_ERRORINDLL`	The `.DLL` or `.EXE` image has problems.
`CO_E_APPDIDNTREG`	The local server was started but it did not register any class objects.
`E_ACCESSDENIED`	General access failure.
`MK_S_ASYNCHRONOUS`	Asynchronous completion. If the client has registered a callback, it will be called to update status.

Asynchronous and URL Monikers

We'll now explain the `pBindCtx` parameter and the `E_PENDING` return value. These parameters are supporting the **asynchronous** nature of the `CoGetClassObjectFromURL()` call. Under the hood, the `CoGetClassObjectFromURL()` call makes use of a COM facility called a **URL Moniker** to do its magic. The URL Moniker is actually an instance of a concept known as an **Asynchronous Moniker** defined by the Internet Addendum to the OC96 specifications. The following is the conceptual inheritance tree.

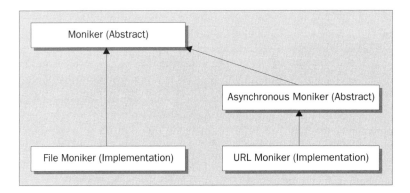

First, we must give a quick explanation of what a Moniker implements is. Monikers are essentially 'smart name objects' in COM. Any COM object that the `IMoniker` interface is deemed a Moniker. The unique property of a Moniker (usually a relatively small object) is that it knows how to find the object that it names. It also completely hides from the client how it goes about finding the object. By 'binding' to a Moniker, we magically get the object that it names. Monikers provide a level of indirection between the client of an object and the object itself. This level of indirection provides unlimited extensibility because the Moniker isn't obliged to follow any standard rules or protocols when it goes about its binding operation. In the old days, Monikers were used almost exclusively for OLE linking operations. In this context, embedding means to embed an entire object into a document while linking means embedding a Moniker (much smaller object) into the document. It's easy to throw Monikers into compound documents (or any arbitrary file) because **IMoniker** is derived from **IPersistStream**, which supports serialization of the Moniker to memory, disk, or even across a network.

Asynchronous Monikers are a relatively new breed introduced to solve the problems produced by operations over a slow Internet link. Unlike its age-old parent, the binding operation on an Asynchronous Moniker can take as long as it wants. Meanwhile, the client invoking the binding operation gets freed to do other things right away. If the client registers a callback function with the Asynchronous Moniker, the Moniker will report back status information as it's performing the binding operation.

A URL Moniker is a specific implementation of an Asynchronous Moniker. We know how it does its magic. Since a URL Moniker is a name (URL in this case) that knows how to find the object that it represents (i.e. an ActiveX control stored on the web server), we can deduce that the URL Moniker will be using HTTP to fetch the object over the network. And this is indeed how it's done. Of course, if the URL should be **ftp://ftp.abwil.com/objects/atldept.dll**, then alternative protocols would be used (again, transparent to the client since the Moniker performs all the magic). Since the going rate for asynchronous modems is 28.8Kbps, we can quickly understand why a URL Moniker must be asynchronous. We certainly don't want to hold the client (and thus the application) in a frozen blocked state while a URL Moniker is finishing its magical binding effort.

The current implementation of URL Monikers uses standard Win32 Internet APIs (formerly called WinINET) to access the actual resources, this allows security proxies to work transparently underneath.

It's quite easy to see that our **CoGetClassObjectFromURL()** call is using URL Monikers underneath to do its dirty work. This is where the **BindCtx** requirement comes from. A bind context is just a small COM object that's passed into a Moniker during a bind operation. It functions as a client-supplied instance-identification 'scratch pad'. While not always necessary, you may want to receive status feedback during the asynchronous process, and then there's substantially more work to be done. You can easily create a bind context by making the **CreateBindCtx()** call. The interface that you grab a bind context object by is, not surprisingly, called **IBindCtx**. The **IBindCtx** interface comprises 13 methods altogether, including the three required by **IUnknown**. We aren't actually interested in any of these methods. There exists a (new!) helper function, called **RegisterBindStatusCallback()**, which will do our callback registration for us. The usage of **RegisterBindStatusCallback()** is:

```
HRESULT RegisterBindStatusCallback( IBindCtx *pbc,
                                    IBindStatusCallback *pbsc,
                                    IBindStatusCallback **ppbscPrevious,
                                    DWORD dwReserved );
```

The parameters required are:

Parameter	Description
pbc	Pointer to the **IBindCtx** of our bind context object.
pbsc	Pointer to an **IBindStatusCallback** of a bind status callback object to be registered. We'll discuss how to create this later.
PpbscPrevious	An output parameter which will be filled with a pointer to the previously registered **IBindStatusCallback** instance.
dwReserved	Set this to **0**.

The possible return values for **RegisterBindStatusCallback()** are:

Return Value	Description
S_OK	The operation has completed successfully.
E_INVALIDARG	An argument passed was invalid.
E_OUTOFMEMORY	The operation can't be performed because memory was exhausted during its execution.

The use of the function is straightforward, except for the **IBindStatusCallback** pointer that we need. Typically, the **ppbscPrevious** returned will be **NULL** since it will be the first **IBindStatusCallback** that we register for this bind context. Once we've registered an **IBindStatusCallback** with a bind context, it would last until it's revoked by **RevokeBindStatusCallback()**, displaced by a new one through another **RegisterBindStatusCallback()** call, or the bind context itself is destroyed.

The **IBindStatusCallback** pointer should be pointing to an interface that the client (or an object that the client controls) would implement. The **IBindStatusCallback** interface consists of a total of 11 methods, including the three **IUnknown** methods. These methods are:

IBindStatusCallBack Method Name	Description
QueryInterface()	Standard **IUnknown** requirement. Make sure that a query for **ICodeInstall** will return the client's **ICodeInstall** interface (see below).
AddRef()	Standard **IUnknown** requirement.
Release()	Standard **IUnknown** requirement.
GetBindInfo()	Called by the Moniker to get binding information.
OnStartBinding()	A chance for the client to tell the Moniker which events/ callback the client is interested in. Also provides the client with an **IBinding** interface for the client to control downloading.
GetPriority()	Obtains the priority of this binding operation.
OnProgress()	Reports progress to the client.

`IBindStatusCallBack` Method Name	Description
`OnDataAvailable()`	Reports the incremental availability of data.
`OnObjectAvailable()`	The requested object interface pointer is passed to the client.
`OnLowResource()`	The Moniker reports a low resource condition during the bind.
`OnStopBinding()`	Notification that the binding operation has completed, and returns error code if any.

It's safe to return **E_NOTIMPL** for the **GetPriority()**, and **OnDataAvailable()** members in most cases.

If we're supporting automatic installation of a component (i.e. through registry update or an **.INF** file), we must also implement the **ICodeInstall** interface The Moniker willdo a **QueryInterface()** on **IBindStatusCallback** for **ICodeInstall**. The **ICodeInstall** interface has a total of only 5 methods. The client must implement this interface.

`ICodeInstall` Method Name	Description
`QueryInterface()`	Standard **IUnknown** requirement.
`AddRef()`	Standard **IUnknown** requirement.
`Release()`	Standard **IUnknown** requirement.
`NeedVerificationUI()`	Called when the server needs to display a verification window. The client should supply a parent window in this case.
`OnCodeInstallProblem()`	Called when server encounters code installation problem (i.e. out of disk space). The client may attempt to correct the situation by prompting the user accordingly.

By supporting a callback in our bind context for the asynchronous (URL) moniker, we gain a lot of control over the display of status during the binding process, as well as the ability to customize system-displayed UI and handle error conditions during the code installation process.

There exists also an asynchronous moniker specific function, called **CreateAsyncBindCtx()** whichcombines the function of **RegisterBindStatusCallback()** and **CreateBindCtx()** into one convenient call.

```
HRESULT CreateAsyncBindCtx( DWORD dwReserved,
                            IBindStatusCallback *pbsc,
                            IEnumFORMATETC *penumfmtetc,
                            IBindCtx **ppbc );
```

The parameters required are:

Parameter	Description
dwReserved	Must be zero.
pbsc	Pointer to an **IBindStatusCallback** of a bind status callback object to be registered.
penumfmtetc	Pointer to an **IEnumFORMATETC** of an enumerator object for format negotiation during binding, should be set to **NULL** for URL moniker binding through the **CoGetClassObjectFromURL()** call.
ppbc	Pointer to hold the **IBindCtx** pointer for the newly created bind context object.

The possible return values for **CreateAsyncBindCtx()** are:

Return Value	Description
S_OK	The operation has completed successfully.
E_INVALIDARG	An argument passed was invalid.
E_OUTOFMEMORY	The operation can't be performed because memory was exhausted during its execution.

An Applied Example: The 'Downloader' Control

Let's put some of these interfaces and APIs to work. We'll create an ActiveX control that you can use to download and install components over the intranet. We'll be encapsulating in an ATL based component all of the APIs and interfaces we've described above. Through COM based code reuse, we can avoid the required elaborate coding each time we need the download and install functionality. The implementation of the control is skeletal in nature, in order to keep things simple. The reader can easily modify and enhance the control for specific situations.

The ILoadlate Interface

Our completed component will support an **ILoadlate** interface. This is a dual interface that we've defined. The methods for this interface are:

ILoadlate Method Name	Description
QueryInterface()	Standard **IUnknown** requirement.
AddRef()	Standard **IUnknown** requirement.
Release()	Standard **IUnknown** requirement.
GetFactory([out, retval] LPUNKNOWN* itf)	Called after the download and installation is completed in order to obtain the **IClassFactory** interface from the newly downloaded (and instantiated) object.
GetLatest([in] BSTR bstrCLSID, [in] BSTR bstrURL)	Called to start the code download, install, and object creation process. **bstrCLSID** should contain the string representation of the CLSID of the object; **bstrURL** should contain the URL to download the object from.

`ILoadlate` Method Name	Description
`PollResult([out] long * current, [out] long * max, [out,retval] BSTR * bstrStatus)`	Called periodically during download to get the current status of the download. `bstrStatus` is a status message indicating the current progress. `current` may contain the number of bytes downloaded and `max` may contain the number of bytes of the object being downloaded (this depends on the server and the URL used).

This is the only interface that our ActiveX control will provide. Essentially, it encapsulates all the calls necessary for code download and installation, and it also changes the 'callback' model that the `CoGetClassObjectFromURL()` calls to an easier-to-use polling model for the client.

Coding the Downloader Control

Use the Visual C++5 ATL COM AppWizard to create a new DLL based project. In the project, use the ATL Object Wizard to put a Simple COM object into the project. Call this object **CLoadlate**, call the interface **ILoadlate**, select Apartment model threading and create dual interfaces.

When the basic code generation is completed, add the three methods according to the **ILoadlate** interface description earlier in this section.

Next, add the implementation for these methods:

```
STDMETHODIMP CLoadlate::PollResult( long * current, long * max, BSTR * bstrStatus)
{
    *bstrStatus = SysAllocString(m_bstrStatus);
    *current = m_lLoaded;
    *max = m_lTotal;
    return S_OK;
}
```

The implementation of **ILoadlate::PollResult()** simply copies the value of a set of member variables to the return values. We'll see how these variables get updated later.

The **ILoadlate::GetFactory()** implementation is:

```
STDMETHODIMP CLoadlate::GetFactory(LPUNKNOWN * ift)
{
    *ift = m_myFactory;
    return S_OK;
}
```

Again, we assume that the caller will be calling after the download/binding is completed. We simply copy the member variable's value to the return value.

Most of the work is done in the **ILoadlate::GetLatest()** implementation:

```
STDMETHODIMP CLoadlate::GetLatest(BSTR bstrCLSID, BSTR bstrURL)
{
    HRESULT hr;

    hr = CLSIDFromString(bstrCLSID, &m_clsid);
    if (FAILED(hr))
        return S_FALSE;
```

Here, we recover the CLSID from its string representation. This will be used later in the **CoGetClassObjectFromURL()** call. We'll store it in the **m_clsid** member variable for now.

```
m_bstrUrl = bstrURL;
m_pbsc = new CBindStatusCallback(this);
if (m_pbsc == NULL)
    return S_FALSE;
```

We then save the value of the URL in the **m_bstrUrl** variable, and create a **CBindStatusCallback()** object (which implements the **IBindStatusCallback** interface), storing a pointer to it in the **m_pbsc** member variable.

```
hr = CreateAsyncBindCtx(0, m_pbsc,NULL, &m_pbc);
if (FAILED(hr))
    return S_FALSE;
```

Next, we create a bind context object by calling **CreateAsyncBindCtx()** using the **CBindStatusCallback** object we created earlier. The resulting bind context is assigned to a **m_pbc** member variable (of the point-to-**IBindCtx** type). Finally, we're ready to call **CoGetClassObjectFromURL()**.

```
LPUNKNOWN tpInf;

hr = CoGetClassObjectFromURL(m_clsid,
    m_bstrUrl,
    0xffffffff,
    0xffffffff,
    NULL,
    m_pbc,
    CLSCTX_INPROC_SERVER,
    NULL, IID_IClassFactory,
    (void * *)&tpInf);

if (!FAILED(hr))
    m_myFactory = tpInf;

return hr;
}
```

Note that we used **0xffffffff** for both version numbers to ensure that the control will download the latest version of the requested object. The reader may customize this for actual deployment. When called successfully, this call will return **MK_S_ASYNCHRONOUS** which indicates that the download and install will be taking place asynchronously.

We used a few member variables in the code above without declaring them. Now we must add these variables to the **CLoadlate** class. Add the following variables and make them all public.

```
WCHAR                   m_bstrStatus[100];
CComBSTR                m_bstrUrl;
IUnknown*               m_myFactory;
long                    m_lLoaded;
long                    m_lTotal;
uuid_t                  m_clsid;
IBindCtx*               m_pbc;
IBindStatusCallback*    m_pbsc;
```

This completes our **CLoadlate** class. However, we see above that we must also define the **CBindStatusCallback** class. This class is defined in the **.H** file as:

```
class CLoadlate;

class CBindStatusCallback : public IBindStatusCallback
{
public:
    // IUnknown methods
    STDMETHODIMP     QueryInterface(REFIID riid,void ** ppv);
    STDMETHODIMP_(ULONG)   AddRef()    { return m_cRef++; }
    STDMETHODIMP_(ULONG)   Release()   { if (--m_cRef == 0) { delete this; return 0;
                                 } return m_cRef; }

    // IBindStatusCallback methods
    STDMETHODIMP     OnStartBinding(DWORD dwReserved, IBinding* pbinding);
    STDMETHODIMP     GetPriority(LONG* pnPriority);
    STDMETHODIMP     OnLowResource(DWORD dwReserved);
    STDMETHODIMP     OnProgress(ULONG ulProgress, ULONG ulProgressMax, ULONG
                         ulStatusCode, LPCWSTR pwzStatusText);
    STDMETHODIMP     OnStopBinding(HRESULT hrResult, LPCWSTR szError);
    STDMETHODIMP     GetBindInfo(DWORD* pgrfBINDF, BINDINFO* pbindinfo);
    STDMETHODIMP     OnDataAvailable(DWORD grfBSCF, DWORD dwSize, FORMATETC *pfmtetc,
                         STGMEDIUM* pstgmed);
    STDMETHODIMP     OnObjectAvailable(REFIID riid, IUnknown* punk);

    // constructors/destructors
    CBindStatusCallback(CLoadlate * pLate);
    ~CBindStatusCallback();

    // data members
    CLoadlate      * m_ptrLate;
    DWORD            m_cRef;
    IBinding*        m_pbinding;
    CCodeInstall   * m_CodeInstall;
};
```

Note: If you use the New Class... menu option to add this and the following class, then you need to add a generic class derived from the interface. Then in the .CPP file you'll find a #define for new to DEBUG_NEW. This needs to be removed as it's for MFC projects only.

We can see that this class implements the **IBindStatusCallback** interface through its member functions. It also has a member which holds a pointer to the **CLoadlate** class which instantiates it (in order to update the member variables of the **CLoadlate** class during status call back). It also has the **m_pbinding** member to hold an **IBinding** interface during the binding process. Since we need to support installation, there's also a **CCodeInstall** object reference (we'll describe this class later).

The implementation of this class (in the **.CPP** file) is simple. The constructor initializes member variables, and the destructor does nothing.

```
CBindStatusCallback::CBindStatusCallback(CLoadlate * pLate):m_ptrLate(pLate)
{
    m_ptrLate->m_lLoaded = 0;
```

```
        m_ptrLate->m_lTotal = 0;
        m_ptrLate->m_myFactory = NULL;
        m_cRef = 1;
        m_pbinding = NULL;
    } // CBindStatusCallback
```

```
    CBindStatusCallback::~CBindStatusCallback()
    {
    } // ~CBindSt
```

Several functions return trivially with **E_NOTIMPL**:

```
    STDMETHODIMP CBindStatusCallback::GetPriority(LONG* pnPriority)
    {
        return E_NOTIMPL;
    }
    STDMETHODIMP CBindStatusCallback::OnLowResource(DWORD dwReserved)
    {
        return E_NOTIMPL;
    }
    STDMETHODIMP CBindStatusCallback::OnDataAvailable(DWORD grfBSCF, DWORD dwSize,
        FORMATETC* pfmtetc, STGMEDIUM* pstgmed)
    {
        return E_NOTIMPL;
    }
```

In **QueryInterface()**, we handle request for our own **IBindStatusCallback**, as well as **ICodeInstall** since we support installation.

```
    STDMETHODIMP CBindStatusCallback::QueryInterface(REFIID riid, void** ppv)
    {
        *ppv = NULL;
        if (riid==IID_ICodeInstall)
        {
            m_CodeInstall = new CCodeInstall();
            *ppv = (ICodeInstall *) m_CodeInstall;
            m_CodeInstall->AddRef();
            return S_OK;
        }
        if (riid==IID_IUnknown || riid==IID_IBindStatusCallback)
        {
            *ppv = this;
            AddRef();
            return S_OK;
        }
        return E_NOINTERFACE;
    }
```

Notice that above we create a new **CCodeInstall** object if the query interface for **ICodeInstall** is called.

Before download (binding) begins, the **GetBin()** member will be called by the system to determine how to bind. We set the flags to indicate an asynchronous bind/download, and that the newest version should be fetched.

```
STDMETHODIMP CBindStatusCallback::GetBindInfo(DWORD* pgrfBINDF, BINDINFO* pbindInfo)
{
   *pgrfBINDF = BINDF_ASYNCHRONOUS
      | BINDF_ASYNCSTORAGE |BINDF_GETNEWESTVERSION ;
   return S_OK;
}
```

When download (binding) begins, the **OnStartBinding()** member will be called by the system. We're obliged to grab hold of a binding object at this time:

```
STDMETHODIMP CBindStatusCallback::OnStartBinding(DWORD dwReserved, IBinding* pbinding)
{
   if (m_pbinding != NULL)
      m_pbinding->Release();
   m_pbinding = pbinding;
   if (m_pbinding != NULL)
   {
      m_pbinding->AddRef();
   }
   return S_OK;
}
```

During the binding/download, the **OnProgress()** member will be called regularly. We take this opportunity to update the status variables of the **CLoadlate** class.

```
STDMETHODIMP CBindStatusCallback::OnProgress(ULONG ulProgress, ULONG ulProgressMax,
      ULONG ulStatusCode, LPCWSTR szStatusText)
{
   wcscpy(m_ptrLate->m_bstrStatus, szStatusText);
   m_ptrLate->m_lLoaded = ulProgress;
   m_ptrLate->m_lTotal = ulProgressMax;
   return S_OK;
}
```

When the binding/download is completed, the **OnStopBinding()** method is called. Here we release the binding object we seized earlier in **OnStartBinding()**. We also signify to our client that the binding is completed by setting the **m_bstrStatus** of the **CLateload** member to **"DONE!"**.

```
STDMETHODIMP CBindStatusCallback::OnStopBinding(HRESULT hrStatus, LPCWSTR pszError)
{
   wcscpy(m_ptrLate->m_bstrStatus, L"DONE!");
   if (m_pbinding)
   {
    m_pbinding->Release();
    m_pbinding = NULL;
   }

   return S_OK;
}
```

When installation is completed and the requested **IClassFactory** interface is available, the **OnObjectAvailable()** member will be called. Here, we simply assign the pointer to our member variable, ready for the client to fetch.

```
STDMETHODIMP CBindStatusCallback::OnObjectAvailable(REFIID riid, IUnknown* punk)
{
    m_ptrLate->m_myFactory = punk;
    return S_OK;
}
```

This is all that's required for the **CBindStatusCallback** class to implement the
IBindStatusCallback. Next, we'll examine the **ICodeInstall** interface (and the **CCodeInstall**
class) that we'll need. The **CCodeInstall** class is defined in the **.H** file as:

```
class CCodeInstall:public ICodeInstall
{
public:
    // IUnknown methods
    STDMETHODIMP       QueryInterface(REFIID riid,void ** ppv);
    STDMETHODIMP_(ULONG)    AddRef()    { return m_cRef++; }
    STDMETHODIMP_(ULONG)    Release()   { if (--m_cRef == 0) { delete this; return 0; }
        return m_cRef; }
    STDMETHODIMP       GetWindow(REFGUID ab, HWND *pwnd);
    STDMETHODIMP       OnCodeInstallProblem(ULONG ulStatus, LPCWSTR szDest, LPCWSTR szSrc,
        DWORD dwRes);
    CCodeInstall();
    ~CCodeInstall();
protected:
    DWORD              m_cRef;
};
```

ICodeInstall only has two new member functions. In the **.CPP** file, constructor and destructor are implemented trivially.

```
CCodeInstall::CCodeInstall():m_cRef(1)
{
}

CCodeInstall::~CCodeInstall()
{
}
```

ICodeInstall::QueryInterface() is also implemented in a standard fashion.

```
STDMETHODIMP CCodeInstall::QueryInterface(REFIID riid, void** ppv)
{
    *ppv = NULL;
    if (riid==IID_IUnknown || riid==IID_ICodeInstall)
    {
        *ppv = this;
        AddRef();
        return S_OK;
    }
    return E_NOINTERFACE;
}
```

ICodeInstall::GetWindow() asks for a parent window to display some user interface. We return **NULL**
which indicates that the desktop window should be used.

```
STDMETHODIMP CCodeInstall::GetWindow(REFGUID ab, HWND *pwnd)
{
    *pwnd = NULL;
    return S_OK;
}
```

To implement **ICodeInstall::OnCodeInstallProblem()**, we return **S_OK** for all the reported problems which we would ignore, and return **E_ABORT** for all other problems (e.g. out of disk space).

```
STDMETHODIMP CCodeInstall::OnCodeInstallProblem(ULONG ulStatus, LPCWSTR szDest,
    LPCWSTR szSrc, DWORD dwRes)
{
    switch(ulStatus)
    {
    case CIP_OLDER_VERSION_EXISTS:
    case CIP_NAME_CONFLICT:
    case CIP_TRUST_VERIFICATION_COMPONENT_MISSING:
    case CIP_NEWER_VERSION_EXISTS:
        return S_OK;
    default:
        return E_ABORT;
    }
}
```

Finally, we need to include the definitions for the two interfaces we're implementing as well as linking in the relevant library. The best place to add the required header is in **StdAfx.h**:

```
...
#include <atlbase.h>
//You may derive a class from CComModule and use it if you want to override
//something, but do not change the name of _Module
extern CComModule _Module;
#include <atlcom.h>
#include <urlmon.h>
...
```

In the Link tab of the Project Setting dialog, you need to add **Urlmon.lib** to the list of library modules:

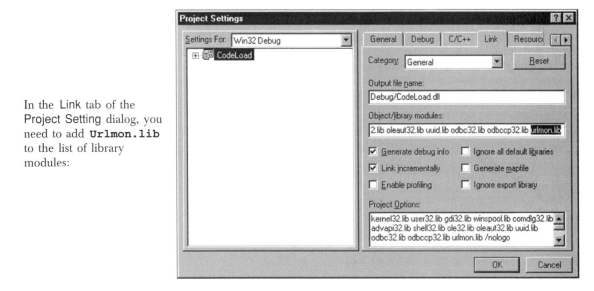

This completes our implementation of the 'downloader' control. You can now compile, link, and register the control.

Coding the Test Client

Typically, a client of this object will:

1 Call `ILoadlate::GetLatest()` with information for the object to download and install. This call will return immediately while the download and installation occurs asynchronously.

2 Handle user interface or perform other tasks, while intermittently calling the `ILoadlate::PollResult()` looking for a status string of **"DONE!"**. It can also update the user on the progress of the download if desired.

3 After `ILoadlate::PollResult()` returns **"DONE!"** for status, call `ILoadlate::GetFactory()` to obtain the class factory interface of the object.

4 Use the class factory to create the object, and release the class factory.

5 Proceed to use the newly created object.

Let's follow these five steps and quickly code our test client. First, create a new Win32 application project in Visual C++ 5. We called ours 'lotestw'. Create a blank C++ source file in the project and start entering the code:

```
#include <assert.h>
#include <comdef.h>
#include "resource.h"

#import "codeload.tlb" no_namespace
#import "atldept.tlb" no_namespace
```

Here, we're using the native COM support of the Visual C++ 5 compiler again. In the two **#import** directives, we obtain the type information (and smart pointer definitions) for our **Atldept.dll**, as well as the type information from our new 'downloader' ActiveX control. Next, we have a few constant declarations.

```
const char szURLofObject[] = "http://PENTIUM1/ATLDEPT.DLL";
const unsigned TIMER_DURATION = 200; // refresh every 200 ms
const int TIMER_ID = 1001;
```

Since the **ILoadlate** interface supports polling, we'll be creating a Windows timer to activate our polling during the download. **TIMER_DURATION** is the interval time between each pool, the **TIMER_ID** is used to identify the timer in Win32 API calls. Next, we define a custom Windows message. This message is posted by the timer handler after receiving **"DONE!"** from the control; the handler for this message will get the **IClassFactory** interface and create an object from it.

```
#define   WM_CUSTOM1   WM_USER+100
```

The next section is the COM exception handling required by the native COM support. We aren't going to implement the details here, but you're free to do so.

```
void dump_com_error(_com_error &e)
{
// handle error intelligently in here
}
```

The **WinMain()** function is quite straightforward:

```
int WINAPI WinMain(HINSTANCE hinst, HINSTANCE hinstPrev, LPSTR szCmdLine,
    int nCmdShow)
{
  HRESULT  hr;
  hr = CoInitialize(NULL);
  if (FAILED(hr))
     return hr;
  DialogBox(hinst, MAKEINTRESOURCE(IDD_DIALOG1), HWND_DESKTOP, (FARPROC)&DialogProc);
  CoUninitialize();
  return 0;
}
```

In the above code, we simply call **CoInitialize()**, create a dialog box, then call **CoUninitialize()** and quit. Making the desktop window the parent for the dialog box means we don't need to create any window in **WinMain()** (however, **CoInitialize()** will actually create a hidden window).

Let's take a look at the dialog box; create this using the resource editor in Visual C++ 5 and name it **IDD_DIALOG1** (the default).

Use the default dialog generated by the resource editor, and change the text of the OK button to Install Object Asynchronously and the Cancel button to Exit. Create a read-only edit and name it **IDC_EDIT1**.

Now, we're ready to examine our dialog procedure, where all of the testing logic resides. If you're keying in the code, make sure this goes before the **WinMain()** in the file.

```
BOOL CALLBACK DialogProc(HWND hwndDlg, UINT message, WPARAM wParam, LPARAM lParam)
{
    static ILoadlatePtr  pIC;
    long current, max;
    BSTR bstrStatus;
```

We declare a smart pointer to our **ILoadlate** interface as static, so we would not recreate the object on every message. **Current**, **max**, and **bstrStatus** are to hold the results from

`ILoadlate::PollResult()` for reporting to the end user. Next, we're into the message decoding loop portion:

```
switch(message)
{
case WM_INITDIALOG:
   try
   {
      pIC.CreateInstance("Loadlate.Loadlate.1");
   }
   catch (_com_error &e)
   {
      dump_com_error(e);
   }
   break;
```

In the **WM_INITDIALOG** message (sent only once after the creation of dialog box), we instantiate a 'downloader' control, and obtain the **ILoadlate** interface through the smart pointer using the **CreateInstance()** member.

```
case WM_TIMER:
   {
      bstrStatus = pIC->PollResult(&current, &max);
      char    sz[255];
      if(bstrStatus!=NULL)
         WideCharToMultiByte(CP_ACP, 0, bstrStatus,-1, sz, 255, 0,0);
      char    msg[100];
      wsprintf(msg,"Loading: %s %d of %d ", sz, current, max);
      SetWindowText(GetDlgItem(hwndDlg,IDC_EDIT1), msg);
      if (wcscmp(bstrStatus, L"DONE!") == 0)
      {
         KillTimer(hwndDlg, TIMER_ID);
         PostMessage(hwndDlg, WM_CUSTOM1, 0, 0);
      }
   }
   break;
```

The next message handled here is the timer message. We call the **ILoadlate::PollResult()** method through the smart pointer **pIC** and then fill the edit box in the dialog with the status. We convert the string from wide character **BSTR** to MBCS in order to format the output using **wsprintf()**. If the download is completed, we stop the timer messages and then post our custom message **WM_CUSTOM1**.

```
case WM_CUSTOM1:
   {
      HRESULT hr;
      IClassFactory * tpF = (IClassFactory *) pIC->GetFactory();
      IUnknown * tp2;
      tpF->CreateInstance(NULL, IID_IUnknown, (void **) &tp2);
      if (!FAILED(hr))
         SetWindowText(GetDlgItem(hwndDlg, IDC_EDIT1), "Object Created!");
      else
         SetWindowText(GetDlgItem(hwndDlg, IDC_EDIT1), "Cannot create obj!");
      tpF->Release();
      tp2->Release();
   }
   break;
```

Handling of the **WM_CUSTOM1** message is straightforward. At this time, the download has been completed. We obtain the **IClassFactory** interface by calling **ILoadlate::GetFactory()** through the smart pointer. We then use **IClassFactory::CreateInstance()** to create an instance of the ATLDept object. If this is successful, we print the message Object Created! in the dialog box. In any case, we release the class factory and the object before returning.

We come now to the button handling messages:

```
case WM_COMMAND:
    {
        switch (LOWORD(wParam))
        {
        case IDOK:
            {
                _bstr_t bstrUrl(szURLofObject);
                _bstr_t bstrStatus;
                try
                {
                    LPOLESTR  ab;
                    CLSID myID = __uuidof(ATLDept1);

                    StringFromCLSID(myID, &ab);
                    _bstr_t bstrProgID(ab);

                    pIC->GetLatest(bstrProgID, bstrUrl);
                }
                catch (_com_error &e)
                {
                    dump_com_error(e);
                };
                SetTimer(hwndDlg, TIMER_ID, TIMER_DURATION, NULL);
            }
            break;
```

When the Install Object Asynchronously button (OK button) is pressed, we call **ILoadlate::GetLatest()**. This is done by calling **StringFromCLSID()** on the CLSID of the ATLDept object that we want to create to get a **BSTR** parameter. We also start the timer for refreshing the status edit box during the download.

```
        case IDCANCEL:
            pIC.Release();
            EndDialog(hwndDlg,0);
            return 1;
            }
            break;
        }
    }
    return 0;
}
```

Finally, if the user presses the Exit button, we release the interface encapsulated within our smart pointer and exit from the application.

This is all the code required to download and install the ATLDept object. Thanks to the 'downloader' control and its **ILoadlate** interface, the code for this client is very simple and uncluttered.

You can now compile the test program. Make sure that you have updated the URL embedded in the test program so that it points to your own web server.

Testing the Downloader Control

The following is the procedure for testing the 'downloader' control with the test program.

1 Unregister the current ATLDept1 object by going to the directory where **Atldept.dll** resides, and perform a **REGSVR32 /U ATLDEPT.DLL**.

2 Use **Oleview.exe** to ensure that the ATLDept1 object no longer shows up (i.e. removed from the registry).

3 Copy **Atldept.dll** to the location of the URL. In our case, we have it at **C:\Webshare\Wwwroot\Atldept.dll**. The Personal Web Server for Windows 95 is set to point to the directory **\Webshare\Wwwroot** as the root directory. Our URL is **http://PENTIUM1/ATLDEPT.DLL**.

4 Make sure your web server is working properly.

5 Start the test program, **Lotestw.exe**.

6 Press the Install Object Asynchronously button.

If everything is working properly, you should start to see the status appearing in the read-only edit of the dialog box. You should also see or hear some disk activity. It will report the download progress (but this probably won't be for too long since **Atldept.dll** is so small in size). After the download, the following security dialog will pop up asking if it's all right to install a component:

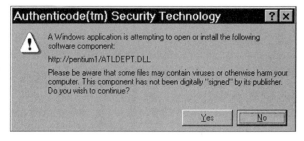

If you click Yes, the installation will complete, and you should see the Object Created! message in the dialog. This indicates a successful object creation using **CoGetClassObjectFromURL()** call.

To convince yourself, use the **Oleview.exe** program to see that now the ATLDept1 class is registered again. Click on the class entry to create an instance and notice that it is now working.

If you like to repeat the test, you must first remove the newly registered DLL.

1 Go to the `\Windows\Occache` directory.

2 Do a `REGSVR32 /U ATLDEPT.DLL` to remove the registry entries.

3 Delete `Atldept.dll` to remove the downloaded DLL.

4 Restart the test program and try download/install again.

The 'downloader' ActiveX control substantially simplifies the calls to perform automated code download and install. It can also be called from C++ or other clients (i.e. Visual Basic). While the Internet Explorer itself provides automation capability similar to the 'downloader' control, the control provides the function with a significantly smaller code and runtime memory footprint.

Problems Still Unsolved: The Missing Links

Despite all the flexibility that distributed component computing will bring us, there are vital missing pieces in the COM/DCOM puzzle that will prevent the immediate widespread deployment of the technology. This has little impact on self-contained project development environments, such as our Aberdeen & Wilshire intranet. However, these shortcomings do surface as problems that we must solve in an ad hoc manner on a per-project basis unless they are addressed by the system vendor. We'll examine several of these 'missing links' in this section.

Making it Simple: Hide the Details

The discussion we had in the previous section on the `CoGetObjectClassFromURL()` call, leading to URL Monikers, bind contexts and callback objects certainly wasn't for the faint of heart. And as long as the building of COM/DCOM based applications requires a high level of expertise, there will continue to be very few applications in circulation. The requirement here is to hide the details and make things as simple as possible. Witness that there are very few truly OLE-compliant applications on the general market despite the fact that OLE technology has been available for the past 6 years. The complexity and difficulties in dealing with the technology have created an artificial barrier to adoption.

A high priority for Microsoft's ActiveX initiative is the goal of making it simple for the developer. This is accomplished by hiding the complexity as much as possible from the end user and general programmers. With support of COM/DCOM by Visual Basic, VBA, VBScript and Java available (mainly through OLE automation), users and programmers can start experimenting with DCOM without having to go through the steep learning curves. The first generation of these COM/DCOM capable tools is just becoming available. In the future, we can look forward to enhanced ease of use/programming that ought to put things like IDL files, type library registrations, and direct registry editing behind us once and for all.

On the server end, the new Active Server Platform architecture will eventually allow for the creation of powerful, high performance, scalable server applications without being an operating system guru.

Finding Objects: Location Service

In a world full of objects, locating the object that you need to get a job done could be a tough problem. Depending on the application, the need to locate a specific instance of an object in a department or even throughout the enterprise may frequently arise. The need to find all the departments that have events posted for a given month is a good example. We bypassed the problem by creating our own **EventsFinder** class.

If the underlying system offers an object location service, however, the problem can be solved easily. Having a global location service will also enable effective pooling of computing resources. In this case, a component based application would consult the location service each time it needs to instantiate a server object to do some work, and the service can pick the component instance which is running on the 'most available' machine or based on certain pre-set criteria.

Part of this problem can be solved today using File Monikers and their **BindToObject()** capability (as with URL Monikers that we examined earlier, you can use File Monikers to reunite an object instance with its persistent data, assuming that the data is saved on disk as a file). Another part will be resolved with the introduction of a global 'class store' in future releases of Windows NT. The availability of a global directory service in the future will further unify the location and naming of all network and local resources, providing yet another step in the right direction.

What is still missing, though, is the ability to support the equivalence of a 'global running objects table' across an administrative domain, an intranet, or the entire Internet. The problem is very complex and requires tracking of a very large set of highly dynamic data items. Until a general solution becomes available, each project requiring such a service must reinvent the wheel in an ad hoc manner.

Transforming Chaos into Order: Transaction Service

A typical distributed application consists of computations, each requiring coordination of software components functioning across a network of computers. Each computation being coordinated may require a different mix of components residing on different machines. The pure software coordination problem is by itself a daunting task. Even if we manage to write perfect code and all the components reside on the same machine, the combination and permutation of lower level software failures, system hardware failures, reaching resource limits, etc. can create a very large number of 'error states' that our computing system can fall foul of. Now compound the effect with a distributed computing system where network failure, delays, and system availability contribute further to increase the possible error conditions.

Even though you have probably voiced this complaint to yourself already while walking through the Aberdeen & Wilshire code samples, I'll just repeat it here. There's no error handling code! Besides the normal excuse of 'the error handling code complicates the sample', I must admit that writing error handling code for DCOM applications is a science in its own right.

The problem is that the very same component may be running either locally or remotely, and the computational requirement for each case of reuse is not predictable at component design time (i.e. does this component work by itself, or does it feed into other components at every input/output junction?). Even if you know that your application spans, say, 6 computers in a network and uses a total of 30 components during its lifetime, writing a good application requires you to identify and recover from a tremendous combination of complex failure states. It's very hard to be sure that a system will detect or catch all software/hardware failure scenarios. It's easy to predict, though, that a distributed system consisting of a large number of software components will occasionally fail.

Learning from the Internet phenomenon (users on the Internet are notoriously famous for tolerating alpha or beta-software which contains many errors) maybe we should just ignore network errors and go on. While acceptable when casually surfing for interesting information on the web, it's definitely not an acceptable practice in the business world. What we need is a facility, or a service, which will enable us to greatly simplify the handling of errors, and greatly reduce the permutation of failure possibilities.

One implementation of such a service is called a transaction service. Microsoft's version of it is called the Microsoft Transaction Server. A transaction service for distributed components will allow the application writer to adopt a very simple view of error handling. A piece of work performed either by a component in isolation or by a large network of distributed components, can have only one of two outcomes. It either completed or failed. If the operation has failed, the state of the system is guaranteed to be the same as before the attempt to perform the piece of work. While the distributed system is carrying out its piece of work, the intermediate changes to the state of the system aren't visible to other concurrently computing system(s) until a success or failure state for the entire piece of work is reached. Note how this greatly simplifies failure cases. There may have been a million different reasons why a piece of work failed, but the application designer doesn't have to deal with them.

With this simple premise, the work of application design is reduced to transforming the application logic into an orchestration of a set of concurrent transactions. Each transaction can contain multiple computational steps involving many distributed components, and it can also include other nested transactions. A successful transaction is completed by a **commit** action, and an unsuccessful transaction is completed by a **rollback** action. A commit sends the system of distributed objects on to the next predictable state while a rollback reverts the system back to a previously stable state. In between transactions, while the system of distributed objects is computing, it may go through an unpredictable series of state changes including partial or complete software/network failure. None of these state changes, however, will be visible outside of the system. The other concurrently executing systems will only see a state change when a successful commit is performed on a transaction.

Before the availability of a robust and reliable transaction service, design presentations for component based distributed applications are full of frantic hand-waving and crossed fingers among the architects and engineers. Notice that the design of an application using a transactional model of computing is significantly different from designing, say, for a C++ or Java implementation. We require a new way of thinking about the problem.

Working in an Asynchronous World: Queuing Transport

We live in a highly asynchronous world. Just when you start to make that all-important business call to your supplier in Switzerland, he left the office and took the family out to dinner. Meanwhile, you end up with his voice-mail, so you leave him a message which he'll answer when he's next at his desk.

This scenario repeats itself in all shapes and forms millions of times per day around the world. Many business procedures involve the flow of work from one individual to another, each processing or adding value to the work in progress. Unfortunately, not every individual involved is connected to the networked system all the time. Therefore, there's a need to reliably queue the work while it's being relayed from one processing stop to another.

The flow of work from one agent to another is called **workflow** and many business procedures can be automated with workflow based systems. Fitting into the distributed computing perspective, the work performed by each agent can be considered a subtransaction, while the entire workflow itself can be considered as a single large transaction. In cases where a workflow consists of many subworkflows, this can be nested even further.

Now, without the availability of a reliable queuing mechanism, asynchronous workflow can't participate in the transaction world. This is because the typical delay between the processing steps of the workflow may be in terms of hours, days, or even weeks. Any mechanism of network sanity detection would consider such time delays as a network failure, and will cause the transaction-in-progress to fail, resulting in a rollback.

With the introduction of reliable queuing mechanisms, you can introduce the concept of a very long transaction in terms of duration, and computational integrity can be guaranteed. This is an absolute necessity in the handling of business procedure workflow.

One side benefit of having a reliable queuing mechanism in a distributed system is the ability to use it as an alternative transport. For example, imagine a world where DCOM is transmitted over a reliable queuing transport. This means that a link between inter-operating components can be broken, yet the request will be persistently queued at the source until the link is recovered minutes, hours, or even days later. At that time, the interaction between the components can continue. With the highly interactive nature of DCOM today (freshly evolved from OLE-centric, UI-focused COM), it's hard to imagine the practical implication of this ability. However, given time, as more and more transactional applications are delivered based on DCOM technology, the reliable queuing mechanism will become indispensable.

The Microsoft version of this queuing mechanism is code-named 'Falcon' and will become a fundamental enabler for the future world of robust DCOM based component computing.

Ensuring Uptime: Clustering of Redundant Inexpensive Computers

Transaction allowservices us to focus on the business problem and be more independent of failure scenarios. Reliable queuing allows component interactions to survive network and hardware failures.

The assumption in these statements is that the system will occasionally fail. To address the issue of general system reliability, to enable the high-availability, 24 hours-a-day, 7 days-a-week operation required of the distributed computing world, one promising technology is the clustering of inexpensive computers.

By pooling together the resources of a cluster of 'identical' computers, connected via some high bandwidth (i.e. fibre channel, ATM, etc.) means one can construct a 'virtual' system where the components (hardware and software) are fault tolerant. In fact, all hardware components will fail eventually. However, by making available duplicate sets of hardware components in this 'clustered' environment, a hardware failure can be switched, or **failed over**, to a backup piece of hardware transparently to the client. By classifying running software processes as another failable resource, it's possible to fail these over as well. In this manner, fault tolerance can be achieved in this cluster (which looks to the rest of the network as one computing machine).

As work performed by computing systems become more and more componentized, this clustering of computing resources can also be used in the scaling of computational throughput. For example, the same fail over for software processes can be used in load balancing where the executing process is transferred on to a machine within a cluster that is the least busy. The ultimate objective of such a load balancer would be to ensure that every computing resource on the cluster is loaded evenly. This results in high throughput for the cluster.

Traditionally, high availability, fault tolerance, transactional service, reliable queuing and unrestricted throughput scaling are the domain of mainframe or highly proprietary minicomputers. With the amazing computational power afforded by commodity microprocessors, the ability to productively apply these advanced concepts to inexpensive and widely available hardware presents a very interesting and potentially lucrative business opportunity.

Hands on DCOM: Wiring Components Across Three Machines

Let's take our DCOM experimentation with our ActiveX Calendar application to the final stage and distribute the computing load over three (or more) machines. This will allow us to get our hands wet working with the DCOM facilities provided by Windows 95 and the Windows NT system. The same technique can easily apply to any multitiered intranet applications that you may build employing DCOM technology.

While this book has dealt mainly with software development and techniques thus far, the following section will feel more like a description of a laboratory exercise. In general, any description for testing of DCOM applications will involve describing the network topology, machine profiles and the staging scenario.

What we'll be attempting to do is set out in this diagram:

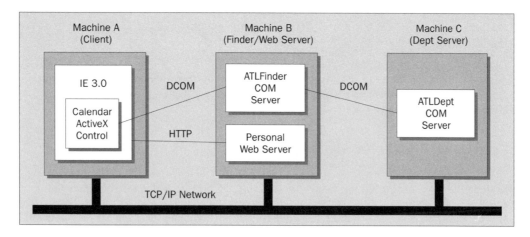

There are three machines in this configuration. They are all connected via a TCP/IP Ethernet LAN. Machine A is our client machine running the Calendar control embedded on a web page. Our web server is residing on machine B. Machine B is also where the ATLFinder COM object is run. Machine C is the host for a departmental server. The ATLDept object on machine C supports the **IATLDept**, **ICorpEvents**, and **ICorpEvent** interfaces with the object (and interaction) model that we covered in the last chapter.

All our clients and servers are running under Windows95 in the hope that the configuration can be easily duplicated by the reader for experimentation purposes. Another reason is the relatively simple security model that DCOM for Windows 95 supports. This allows us to focus on setting up DCOM without getting caught up in security issues. Remember that since a built-in, operating system based security infrastructure is nonexistent in Windows 95, DCOM based servers all run as the currently logged on interactive user. What this means is that provided we're logged on to all the machines as the same user when we're doing the staging, there'll be no security issues whatsoever. In Chapter 9, we'll be examining the finer-grained control over DCOM security that a Windows NT platform can offer.

We'll assume all four machines are setup for DCOM as described in the *DCOM Enabling our ActiveX Control: A Preview* section of this chapter. The following will only cover setup procedures which are customized for each machine involved in the experiment.

Setting up Machine A (the Client Machine)

Machine A is the client machine with the following software configuration:

▲   Windows 95 with Service Pack 1

▲   DCOM for Windows 95

▲   Internet Explorer 3.01

On this machine, we'll set up the Aberdeen & Wilshire Calendar ActiveX control. This will require the pre-installation of the **Vccalc1.ocx** control and required associated files on the client station.

To pre-install the **Vccalc1.ocx** file on machine A, you may use the following procedure:

1 Copy the **Regsvr32.exe** program over to **\Windows\System** directory if it's not already there.

2 Copy the **Vccalc1.ocx** file to the **\Windows\System** directory.

3 Copy the support files for **Vccalc1.ocx** to the **\Windows\System** directory (these files can be determined by running **DUMPBIN/IMPORTS VCCALC.OCX**); you'll also need **Mfc42d.dll**, **Mfco42d.dll**, and **Msvcrtd.dll**.

4 Run **regsvr32 VCCALC1.OCX** on the control.

The next thing that you need to do on machine A is set up DCOM class linkage. We know that **Vccalc1.ocx** will instantiate an ATLFinder object during its operation, therefore we'll need to pre-wire this class (through its class ID) to a remote machine. Recall that we could have indeed hard-coded this into **ATLFinder.exe** using **CoCreateInstanceEx()**, but we'll take advantage of DCOM support for legacy applications in our experiment.

The easiest way to do this, again, is with the assistance of the indispensable **Oleview.exe** utility. Follow these steps:

1 Copy the ATL support DLL, **atl.dll**, over to **\Windows\System** directory.

2 Run **regsvr32 atl.dll**.

3 Copy the **ATLFinder.exe** file over to a temporary directory.

4 Run **ATLFinder /RegServer** to create the registry entries.

5 Remove the **ATLFinder.exe**.

Running **ATLFinder.exe** will prepare the registry with information about the ATLFinder object. The actual **ATLFinder.exe** isn't required on this node, so we remove it after it's completed the job of setting up the registry entries. While ATLFinder adjusted the registry, it also inserted the location of the **.EXE** file under the **\HKEY_CLASSES_ROOT\<clsid>\LocalServer32** key. We need to remove this and point it at the remote machine B. Start up **Oleview.exe**. Select All Objects on the left pane, and find the ATLFinder1 Class entry and select it. On the right pane, select the Implementation tab. Select the Local Server subtab, and clear out the Path to Implementation edit. This will clear up the associated registry key. Next, select the Activation tab. The pane will look like this:

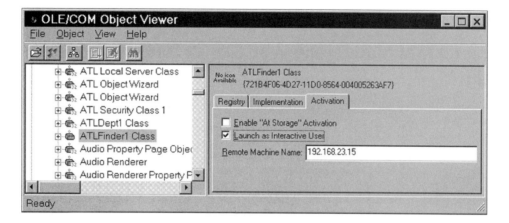

Select the Launch as Interactive User check box and enter in the IP address of machine B in the Remote Machine Name edit. This tells the DCOM runtime to find a server for the ATLFinder1 class on the remote machine. When DCOM tries to launch the server remotely, the identity used will be that of the currently logged on user in Windows 95.

The Enable 'At Storage' Activation setting is specifically used in ActiveX document and/or Moniker binding scenarios where the desired operation is to 'start the object server on the node wherever the persistent data file of the object instance is stored'. This can be a powerful, albeit confusing, mechanism for starting object servers remotely. Essentially, it will allow for the activation of a DCOM object server remotely if the client has a pathname (e.g. **\\System5\User\Doe\Mper.dat**) to a file containing the persistent data used by the class (in this case, the server will be started on the **\\System5** machine). The network filesystem is used as a type of persistent object instance store, and a UNC pathname is used to access and reactivate persisted object instances.

> In actual deployment and production scenarios, performing the above setup on every client machine would be impossible. The ideal situation is to have the entire procedure automated when the user reaches a web page containing the **Vccall.ocx**. Our earlier discussion of automated code download and installation is a perfect solution for this problem. Thankfully, Microsoft has built the call to the **CoGetClassObjectFromURL()** helper API into the Internet Explorer, saving us a tremendous amount pain. To deploy using automatic code download and installation, in this case, boils down to the creation of a **.CAB** file bundling everything together.

A .CAB file contains a compressed archive of one or more files. If the archives contains a .INF file, it will be used as the setup script to install the software component after it's downloaded. The WinVerifyTrust() facility is automatically called to allow the user to deny installation.

Bear in mind, however, even if a .CAB file is used, that DCOM for Windows 95 will still need to be installed at each client workstation before our Vccall.ocx page would work properly.

Setting up Machine B (the Web Server and Finder Service machine)

This is the server machine, and it has the following software configuration:

- ▲ Windows 95 with Service Pack 1
- ▲ DCOM for Windows 95
- ▲ Microsoft Personal Web Server for Windows 95

On this machine, machine B, we'll set up the **ATLFinder.exe** COM server class, and we will set pointers to the **ATLDept.dll** class that will be residing on machine C. To prepare the machine for serving ATLFinder objects, perform the following steps:

1 Copy **Regsvr32.exe** into **\Windows\System** directory if it's not already there.

2 Copy the ATL support DLL, **atl.dll**, over to **\Windows\System** directory.

3 Run **regsvr32 atl.dll**.

4 Copy the **ATLFinder.exe** file over to a working directory.

5 Run **ATLFinder /RegServer** to create the registry entries.

This is all that's needed for ATLFinder. In order to create the link to the required ATLDept objects, we need to do the following:

1 Copy the **ATLDept.dll** file over to the working directory.

2 Run **regsvr32 ATLDept.DLL**.

3 Remove the **ATLDept.dll** file.

4 Start `Oleview.exe`, select ATLDept1 Class on the left pane, and the Implementation tab on the right pane.

5 Select the Inproc Server tab and remove the Path to Implementation content.

6 Select the Activation tab on the right pane, click the Launch as Interactive User check box, and enter in the IP address of machine C into the Remote Machine Name edit.

This machine is now ready to support calls to ATLFinder1 classes and remote calls to ATLDept1 classes. Before moving on to set up machine C, it's a good idea to test the setup between machine A and machine B. To do this, we again acquire the assistance of `Oleview.exe`:

1 Start the ATLFinder server on machine B by typing **ATLFinder /Server** at the command line.

2 Start `Oleview.exe` on machine A.

3 Find the ATLFinder1 Class entry on the left pane and double-click on it.

If everything is setup correctly, after a little delay, you should see ATLFinder being expanded on the left pane with all its interfaces exposed. The ATLFinder1 Class entry is also in bold to indicate that an instance has been created successfully.

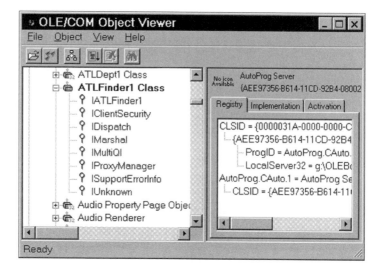

Using Object Viewer, you can then select the Object menu and Release Instance to release the selected instance.

This concludes and confirms the setup of machine B.

In actual deployment, under certain design circumstances, one may need to install the middle tier server components (such as ATLFinder) repeatedly on different systems. In these cases, of course, the Setup toolkit that comes with Visual C++ 5.0 may be used to create a setup script which can perform all of the above for us when the server object is installed on the system.

Setting up Machine C, the Departmental Server

This machine represents a departmental server, and it has the following software configuration:

▲ Windows 95 with Service Pack 1

▲ DCOM for Windows 95

Setting up this machine is rather similar to the setup of machine B. However, since the **ATLDept.dll** is a DLL, we can't simply start it listening for calls as we did with **ATLFinder.exe** on machine B.

To install **ATLDept.dll** on this machine, follow these steps:

1 Copy **Regsvr32.exe** into **\Windows\System** directory if it's not already there.

2 Copy the ATL support DLL, **atl.dll**, over to **\Windows\System** directory.

3 Run **regsvr32 atl.dll**.

4 Copy the **ATLDept.dll** file over to the working directory.

5 Run **regsvr32 ATLDept.dll**.

This is all that's necessary for this machine since it isn't accessing any remote server.

To make sure everything is running okay, start Object Viewer on machine C. In the left-hand pane, select ATLDept1 Class, double-click it to instantiate it. If you have a problem instantiating ATLDept locally, backtrack over the steps and correct any errors.

Once you can instantiate it locally, it's time to try it on machine B. First, however, since Windows 95 offers no remote launching facility (due to security issues), you need to start the server.

Running an In-Proc Server Remotely

We can't just run ATLDept since it's a DLL. Instead we use a surrogate provided by DCOM. This is a program called **Dllhost.exe** and is installed by default in your **\Windows\System** directory during installation of DCOM for Windows 95. The operation of the surrogate process is quite straightforward: it simply creates a process space for the DLL server to execute in. It aggregates all of the DLL's interfaces and exposes them to any remote clients.

The command line syntax for invoking the surrogate is:

```
DLLHOST <clsid>
```

For example, we can host the **ATLDept.dll** by specifying the class id of the ATLDept class. (Note: one easy way to get the class id is to use Object Viewer, select the class and choose the Object menu, selecting the Copy CLSID to the clipboard option).

```
DLLHOST {D2A1CBC6-4C5E-11D0-8564-004005263AF7}
```

This will start the surrogate process waiting for DCOM calls on behalf of the **ATLDept.dll** server. If you examine the Implementation tab of the right pane of the Object Viewer display with the Inproc Server tab selected, you'll also see a space for specifying the surrogate process:

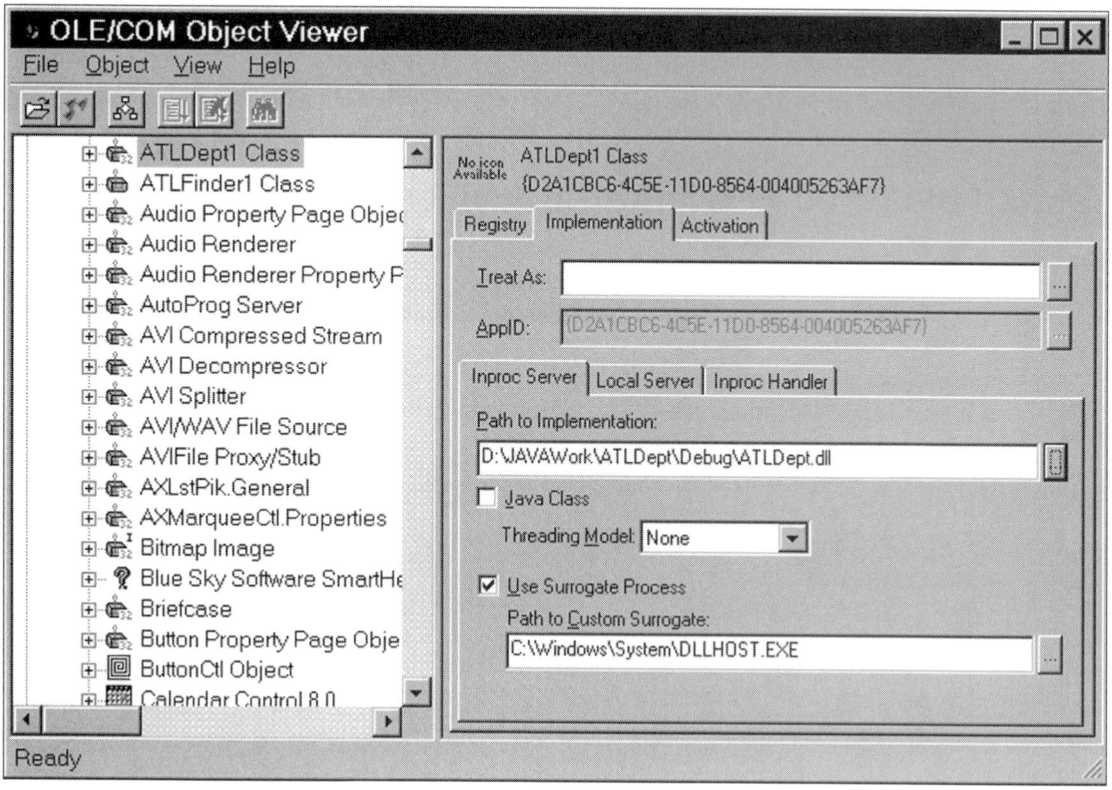

The entry here is rather useless under Windows 95. Under Windows NT, if you specify an entry here, the 'automatic launching' service can launch the **Dllhost.exe** surrogate with the **ATLDept.dll** whenever a client call is received remotely. On the other hand, starting such a surrogate must be performed manually on Windows 95. What's more interesting, if you were to instantiate ATLDept from Object Viewer, it would simply call the in-proc server directly without going through the expensive surrogate process.

Testing the Remote Instantiation of ATLDept

It would be a good time now to test the remote ATLDept class instantiation from machine B. To do this, perform the following steps:

1 Run **DLLHOST {D2A1CBC6-4C5E-11D0-8564-004005263AF7}** on machine C.

2 Use **Pview95.exe** (supplied with Visual C++ 5.0) to verify that **Dllhost** is running.

3 Start Object Viewer on machine B, select ATLDept1 class on the left pane, double-click on the entry to create an instance on machine C.

Once this is successful, you have completed the setup required for machine C. Now we are ready to attempt testing the three machines together.

As in the case of machine B, if you find that you need to repeatedly perform server installation during actual deployment, it would be wise to spend the extra effort on creating a setup script for the server.

Testing the Three Networked Machines

Just to make sure that everything is still in order:

- Run **Pview95.exe** on machine B to ensure that the **Atlfinder.exe** server is still running. If it isn't, restart with **ATLFinder /Server**.

- Run **Pview95.exe** on machine C to ensure that the **Dllhost.exe** surrogate is still running. If it isn't, restart with **DLLHOST {D2A1CBC6-4C5E-11D0-8564-004005263AF7}**.

Finally, start Internet Explorer 3.01 on machine A, and enter in the following URL:

http://<Machine B's name or IP>/TestPage.htm

This, of course, assumes that you've placed the **TestPage.htm** file at the root of the web supported by machine B's Personal Web Server.

As the web page loads, you'll see the Calendar control activate (albeit quite slowly). Try clicking on a cell to select the event list and get the event details. Remember that the control coding has to initialize the ATLDept objects on machine C from machine A with dummy data across the network.

Notice how the entire application still functions as it did when it was standalone. The only difference is the slower network based operation.

Testing DCOM with Windows NT 4.0

If you'll be carrying out testing on Windows NT 4.0 systems rather than Windows 95 systems, the following will be helpful in isolating some of the differences between the DCOM support on the two platforms. Some major differences between the two support platforms are:

- Windows NT 4.0 has full launch and access security support (see Chapter 9 for more discussion on this topic).

- Windows NT 4.0 offers automatic launch service.

- Besides in-proc and local servers, Windows NT 4.0 also supports COM servers executing in the form of a native NT Service.

Make sure that you have Service Pack 2 installed on your system.

Dcomcnfg.exe on Windows NT 4.0 will allow you to adjust the registry entries and security permissions, etc. You can continue to use **Oleview.exe** in the Windows NT environment.

For our casual testing, we would like to disable the security and permission checking support. You can do this by setting the default values:

> Default Authentication Level = None
> Default Impersonation Level = Anonymous

This puts the system at the same level of accessibility as the Windows 95 machines.

One would never operate production systems in this state. However, a viable security policy requires careful planning before deployment. Again, see Chapter 9 for an in-depth discussion of security issues when working with Windows NT security in general, and DCOM security in particular.

Summary

In this chapter, we've introduced DCOM as COM with a longer wire. We looked at DCOM on Windows NT 4.0 and DCOM for Windows 95, and covered how we can obtain the software as well as the installation process. We demonstrated how ordinary COM objects can be made to interact over the network with simple registry changes.

Lifting the covers, we took a brief look at how DCOM works. We also covered several changes and additions in APIs that are associated with DCOM. To satisfy situations where we may need to justify DCOM, we provided a top 10 of reasons for deploying DCOM.

Not all is rosy, though. DCOM had some definite limitations, and we discussed how Microsoft intends to address them.

Distributed component systems are of no use if there's no way to distribute the components' code when necessary. We looked at the automated code download and installation technology provided through the complex **CoGetClassObjectFromURL()** call. We saw how this technology can help in maintaining an updated version of a component based application. To send the concept home, we've even created a 'downloader' ActiveX control to encapsulate the complex call.

Finally, in the last part of the chapter, we went back to the Aberdeen and Wilshire Calendar control example and step by step showed how to distribute the application over three machines.

All the while, we've avoided the complex issue of security in our network and software setup. This is a very important topic and it's the subject of the next chapter.

CHAPTER 9

Security

Overview

We've gone through most of this book looking at ActiveX, COM, DCOM and component software, all the time avoiding the issue of security. This is not because security is a less important topic. Security is of paramount importance, and can't be treated lightly in a 'by the way' fashion within sections embedded in other chapters. With this is mind, we've opted to focus on it in its own independent chapter and thereby do it some justice.

Moreover, the sheer complexity of security concerns means they don't mix easily with other technical subjects that require their own focus. And the implementation of security measures in a distributed computing environment isn't simple. The situation is further aggravated by the set of new terminologies and jargon that the security industry employs. In this chapter, we'll demystify many of the concepts, and discover the available APIs, system objects, and built-in system features which facilitate the implementation of secure distributed computing systems.

On the other side of the coin, we'll see the roadblocks, harassment, and trepidation that an ActiveX component has to live and deal with in order to carry out its chores in a secured environment.

The branches of security that we'll be focusing on are those related to distributed component computing (i.e. COM and DCOM security), as well as web server extension security (i.e. IIS and ISAPI security).

The Need for Network Security

From the beginning in the history of multiuser computing, there was always a need to protect and secure information or resources of one user from access by another. Security violations can be intentional or unintentional, vicious or benign; in all cases, it's highly undesirable and best prevented, if at all possible. Now that networking machines and sharing of resources and information becomes enterprise-wide (in the intranet) and global (in the Internet), the need for sound and robust security measures is more important than ever before.

The security industry is a relatively 'fear' driven one, and deservedly so. The sensational cases that occasionally surface, with employees or demonic individuals bringing down entire enterprises through electronic attack or espionage, is enough to drive any executive into committing major resources to prevention measures.

There are many reasons why you should secure a web server or distributed software components in an intranet environment. Most of them revolve around the previously mentioned need to protect the information and/or resources belonging to one party against access or tampering from other unauthorized parties. In order to carry this out, one typically has to provide means for:

▲ Restricting access

▲ Providing positive identification and authentication

▲ Ensuring data integrity (i.e. against embedding of a virus into a program, or data tampering during network transmission)

▲ Ensuring privacy (i.e. against 'secret peeks' into unauthorized data)

We'll briefly explain these terminologies and see how they all fit together.

Restricting Access

Let's try to clarify the definition of **access**. Access is the ability of the **accessing entity** of an object to interact with the object. Object in this sense doesn't refer to an ActiveX object or a COM object, but rather any logical or physical entity in the computing environment. The accessing entity isn't necessarily a person sat at a keyboard, but could quite easily be another object (for example, an ActiveX component running as an unattended service).

There are different types of access too. Broadly speaking, they are: view, read, change, delete and execute. Viewing means that the accessing entity is aware of the object in question, but can't do anything with it. Reading allows the accessing entity to view the contents of the objects, but not change that content. Change means that the contents can be updated, while delete means the object can be deleted by the accessing entity. Finally, there's execute. Execute is possibly the most 'dangerous' as the object may have access to other objects that the **accessing entity** normally has no **access rights** to.

Access rights

There's a need to assign different levels of access to objects in a system. **Access rights** is the mechanism by which security-conscious operating systems (for example, Windows NT) follow in order to achieve this. Access rights specify what the accessing entity has the right to do with the object. Objects in the system have an associated list of access rights that specifies which accessing entities have which rights.

This brings us to the issue of how to ensure that the accessing entity is who they claim to be, so that they can be allowed to exercise the rights they may have. That is, the accessing entity must be **authenticated**.

Identification and Authentication

In most computer systems that support security mechanisms, the notion of a **user** or **account** associates the accessing entity with certain access rights to the objects managed by the system. Any programs, then, that run on such systems, run 'on behalf of', or 'in the context of' a user or an account.

The security issue that arises immediately is that of ensuring that when an entity presents to the system its credentials purporting that it is user 'A', there's a mechanism to indeed verify that it is, or it is not, 'A'.

Authentication is the mechanism of ensuring or verifying the identity of the entities requiring access to a computer system and is based on the secure exchange of identity information.

Integrity

Integrity effectively means ensuring that data or communications are 'unaltered'. In the context of security, integrity doesn't cover alteration of data or interactions because of nonmalicious, unintentional errors. Taking care of those is the job of error recovery on a local or network scale. Instead, integrity means ensuring that data or communications aren't tampered with. For example:

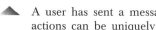 A user has accessed certain system resources. Preserving integrity means that they can't claim that they didn't. History can't be rewritten. Support for auditing the exercising of access rights ensures this.

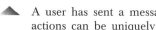 A user has sent a message. Preserving integrity means that they can't claim it wasn't them; actions can be uniquely attributed to the entity that initiated them. Signatures are valid. The technical name for this issue is **nonrepudiation**.

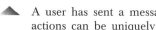 A user sends data, that gets modified en route to the receiving party. Preserving integrity means that the modification can't go unnoticed. You can't change somebody else's letter with impunity! 'Message tampering' activities are detected.

In this context, even authentication can be construed as an aspect of integrity. It preserves the integrity of presenting an identity.

Privacy

Let's define **privacy**: it's the right to disallow access to one's private data or to one's communications with another party.

If there are no 'third parties', i.e. in a totally isolated system, this requirement is vacuously true.

In reality, however, the world is much more interesting than that and does consist of more than single entities. In addition to setting access rights for known users, the need to use insecure communications channels may mean that you have eavesdroppers who can gain access to the information passing between trusted users without the need to impersonate one of the users.

The fundamental mechanism that provides solutions to the issue of privacy is **encryption**, a process of transforming the data to be protected into some form that only the trusted parties have the ability to interpret.

Fitting the Pieces Together

The following table shows all these elements fit together in a typical security implementation.

Security Issue	Security mechanism
Controlled access	Access rights, identities
Right for privacy	Encryption
Integrity	Authentication

In the following pages, we'll be examining the security implementation of Windows NT and Windows 95 in the context of ActiveX components and distributed computing in an intranet environment. We'll be revisiting each of the above security elements as appropriate and showing how you can implement and reuse them.

ActiveX and Windows NT Server Network

Thankfully, when dealing with ActiveX based technology in a Windows NT Server network, there is a lot that can be done. The Windows NT Server product is designed from the conceptual stage to provide a secure computing environment.

Security isn't something that can be added to an operating system as an afterthought. It has to be designed into the core of the system from day one. In particular, it was designed to meet the so-called C2 security guidelines set out by the U.S. government. Even though being certified for compliance with the C2 guidelines may be required only for deployment in government organizations, the enhanced security that compliant systems offer is very important for businesses at large as well.

The main requirements for C2 compliance are:

▲ *User identification and authentication.* The system requires the users to prove their identity before they are allowed access.

▲ *Auditing.* User actions, and object access can be logged by the system.

▲ *Discretionary access control.* Objects on the system have owners who can grant or restrict at various levels access to the resources.

▲ *Object reuse.* The system guarantees that discarded or deleted objects are not accessible by other entities. This holds true, for example, for deleted files, deallocated memory, etc.

▲ *System integrity.* The system protects resources that belong to one entity from being read or written to by other entities. For example, the memory that's been allocated to a process isn't accessible by other processes.

The C2 guidelines refer to standalone systems only, and are published in an orange book aptly called the *Orange Book.* Guidelines for networking aspects of security are covered in the *Red Book.*

NT 3.51 received C2 certification in September 1996. NT 4.0 is undergoing networking and C2 certification at the time of writing.

With such robust security support in place, network software, application software, and distributed components (really networked application software pieces) can leverage off these system features to extend the secure computing environment. We'll see how this is done throughout the rest of the chapter.

Where We Need Security in an Intranet

Other than controlling and administering access to the individual machines in an intranet (this is the function of a network operating system), we may want to restrict access to certain intranet-accessible information to only a selected group of users. For example, we may want everybody to be able to access the general Accounting Department web server, but we only want people in the Accounting Department to access a draft annual report which is linked to from the home page.

Controlled Access to Web Pages

In many ways, this type of protection is very similar to the access control that's supplied by the network operating system like Windows NT Server. What's different, though, is that the user may not be currently 'logged in' to the network serving the page. He or she may be totally remote, may not be using an ActiveX-enabled browser, and may even be running on a Macintosh computer. Yet, we still want to be able to enforce the same access control.

It's easy enough to protect specific web pages or other files from casual access. Simply use the file manager and put an explicit access control attribute on it (assuming you're in a secured installation using the NTFS file system). This, however, will prevent **all** users from accessing the protected pages, including the users who you have explicitly given permissions to access.

Thinking through the situation, whatever the solution may be, the web server must somehow obtain the capability to identify who the user is at the other end of the connection (sitting behind the browser) in order for it to work. This, of course, boils down to the ability for the server to authenticate a remote user accessing the web server. How would such authentication be performed, though? Even if we obtain the true identity of the user somehow, what if the network hosting the web server doesn't know about the user at all (i.e. there's no account information on the user)? In our example, consider the case where Joe Belmont of Accounting is trying to access the secured draft report (which he has access rights to) from Italy over a modem using a Unix machine at a trade show. We'll take a look at ways in which this authentication can be done today in the next section. This will give us an insight into the security problems faced by the IIS and ISAPI applications.

Secure Intranet Interactions

Ensuring orderly controlled access, data integrity and user privacy in an Intranet environment requires careful analysis of the access scenarios and access patterns that a typical user of an intranet application (or Active web site) may undergo. Designed too tightly, the user may end up with an impression of a highly restrictive, and rather frustrating (i.e. repeated requests for password and user IDs) experience. Designed too loosely, the system/application may be subjected to security abuse and vicious attacks.

Before we look at how to secure IIS, ISAPI and DCOM, let's look at the state-of-the-art with respect to security in the 'normal' web page access scenario. This access pattern is fundamental to our later discussions.

Basically, we're talking about the scenario we've described in the previous section. We need to authenticate a remote user accessing a web server in order to restrict access to certain web pages. We'll look at three specific cases and see how the problem is solved. The first case will be the general case where both the browser and the server may not be a Microsoft product. The second and third cases feature a Microsoft browser and a Microsoft server, but one over the public Internet and the other over a private intranet. As we'll soon realize, even though everything looks very similar above the surface, major differences in security implementation exist under the covers.

A Non-Microsoft Scenario

If you've surfed the Internet at all, you've probably encountered sites or web pages which require a password and user ID. When such a page is reached, the browser would pop up a little password entry dialog box. The interesting thing here is that there seems to be something built into the browser-server combination that provides this authentication capability. Yet, if you were to look into the documentation for the browser (and sometimes even from the server), you may be surprised to find that this capability is often not well described. At any rate, there seems to be no standard way to follow for authenticating a remote user using a random browser and server combination. How exactly is this done?

The secret, it turns out, lies in the transmitted HTTP packet's header information.

The scenario which leads to the triggering of the pop-up on the browser is as follow:

1 The client clicked on a link on the browser display which attempts to access some protected resource

2 The browser, having no way to tell a requested resource is protected, formats a normal HTTP request packet and transmit it to the server asking for the resource

3 The server attempts to access the resource and faces an 'access denied' situation

4 The server sends an access denied HTTP response packet back to the client, but in the header indicates the authentication schemes that the server will support in the order of preference

5 The browser receives the 'access denied' packet, and looks into the header to find the authentication schemes supported by the server and matches it against what it would support

6 If the lowest common denominator between the browser and server authentication support is basic authentication, the browser will pop-up the dialog box asking the user for a user ID and password

7 The user keys in the user ID and password

8 The browser retries the request packet, this time including the desired authentication method, the user ID, and Base64-encoded (totally unsecured) password in the header

9 The server receives the request packet with authentication information, impersonates the client if authentication is successful, and accesses the protected resource on behalf of the remote user

10 The server sends the contents of the requested resource back to the browser which promptly displays it

We should notice a few distinguishing points about the above scenario:

- Nothing about it is specific to Microsoft or ActiveX: the situation can be handled with any browser supporting basic authentication, and any server running on any operating system which supports authentication capabilities

- If the user were to access a series of protected pages, the above scenario would repeat itself, asking the user to repeatedly enter his or her user ID and password

The password of the user is sent over the wire with minimal encoding, leaving it vulnerable to potential interception

The form of authentication detailed above is called **basic authentication** and is the most widely used one over the Internet, since most browser, web server, and operating system combinations will support it.

Internet Explorer with IIS over an Intranet

Now let's switch some details of the previous scenario. We're on a private intranet that is controlled under one Windows NT domain (see the next section coverage of Windows NT security); the IIS 3.0 server is running on a departmental server machine. We're accessing the IIS server from a Windows 95 client logged on as an Accounting department user, and running Internet Explorer 3.01.

Picking up from Step 4 above, we now have a greatly improved situation:

4 The server sends an access denied HTTP response packet back to the client, but in the header indicates the authentication schemes that the server will support, in the order of preference. At the top of the list is NTLM challenge/response authentication (see next section for details).

5 IE 3.01 receives the 'access denied' packet, and looks into the header to find the authentication schemes supported by the server and matches it against what it would support. It likes the NTLM challenge/response authentication because it supports it.

6 IE 3.01 will actually initiate the challenge/response authentication process by informing the NTLMSP. The user will not be asked for the user ID and password, because IE 3.01 can cause it to be passed to NTLMSP (the user ID and password is cached by the system as long as the user remains logged on).

7 NTLM-based challenge/response authentication takes place over the network across the two nodes using a proprietary (non-HTTP) protocol. See the next section for details of how NTLM challenge/response works.

8 The challenge/response sequence terminates with the server impersonating the client if authentication is successful, and retries the access to the protected resource on behalf of the remote user.

9 The server sends the contents of the requested resource back to the browser which promptly displays it.

Note the great improvement of this scenario over the previous one:

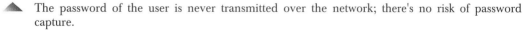 The password of the user is never transmitted over the network; there's no risk of password capture.

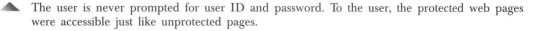 The user is never prompted for user ID and password. To the user, the protected web pages were accessible just like unprotected pages.

This improvement certainly makes intranet surfing (and intranet resource access control) much simpler to manage. However, there's one potential drawback: everything is from Microsoft, from the desktop OS to the network OS, from the desktop browser to the web server.

Internet Explorer with IIS over the Internet

Finally, let's take a look at the situation if the previous scenario took place over the Internet instead. Here, we still have everything from Microsoft. However, since the user logged on is authorized against a domain that's separate and unconnected from the server machine. One can't enjoy the cached user ID and password capability.

In this case, the IE 3.0 and IIS combination will still try the NTLM challenge/response sequence first using the cached user ID and password at the client end, but this attempt will fail (because the user is unknown to the server domain). IE 3.0 will then pop up a dialog box prompting the user for an ID and password. Next, IE 3.0 will reattempt the NTLM challenge/response authentication using this new set of user ID and password.

Since the user will enter a user ID and password which can be authenticated in the IIS's domain, this will succeed and the server will reply with the protected data. From this point on, if the server requests any further authentication, IE 3.0 will use the user-entered user ID and password to authenticate the request.

The end result is somewhere between the transparent, all-Microsoft intranet situation, and the any-browser/any-server situation:

▲ The user's password is never transmitted over the wire

▲ The user only has to enter his or her user ID and password once for the entire session, accessing multiple protected objects

Best Method for Secured Intranet

We see above a gamut of ways in which a web browser and server combination would react in a secured environment. It's interesting to observe that a fully homogeneous Microsoft installation in the intranet scenario can make security control completely transparent to the end user. This is obviously done by design rather than by accident, and is often a consideration when IS departments consider new intranet implementations.

Basic Windows NT Security

Before bravely diving into the specifics of IIS, ISAPI and DCOM security, it's essential that we give a brief coverage to basic Windows NT security. This is the security framework upon which all IIS, ISAPI and DCOM security implementations are built. An understanding of the basic framework will go along way in ensuring that our later discussions can proceed without hindrance.

The Security Model

The security model prescribed by the Windows (and Active) platform is a client-server one. The model is pervasive in that a network need not be involved; we can be talking about client and server processes running on the same machine. In this situation, the partitioning is between the application space that the client is running in and the (usually) kernel mode protected space that the server is running in.

Under this model, clients should only access objects through servers. They should never access objects directly. This means that access to files, devices, other servers, etc., must be arbitrated and 'passed through' by an intermediary server.

Servers, on the other hand, must manage the access of the object and enforce access control. This can be done by the server through assistance from the operating system, or the server may decide to 'roll its own' access control mechanism. Specifically, under Windows NT, it's typical that servers don't actually maintain and verify access rights directly. To make life simpler (and more secure) for server writers, servers are requested to impersonate the identity of the client, and attempt access to objects under such impersonation. In this way, unauthorized access would be prevented by the operating system without the server maintaining elaborate access verification schemes.

Windows NT provides such an impersonation capability for server applications through Win32 APIs.

The Elements of Security: Domains, Users, SIDs, and SDs

From the operating system point of view, everything creatable on Windows NT is securable. By 'creatable' we mean any object (excuse our overloaded usage of the word object here again) that either the system can create or the programmer may create using programmatic means. This includes the standard files and devices, but also applies to processes, threads, and even more mundane things like a semaphore, a piece of shared memory, or a registry key. By 'securable' we mean that specific access rights can be associated with it, and those rights can be verified by the OS when the object is accessed.

The implementation for such security handling is buried deep, deep in the kernel space. Essentially, every new object created gets a handle which can have a security descriptor associated with it. We'll talk about the composition of this security descriptor in a section coming up soon.

Domains

A domain is an administrative grouping of networked machines (and all the users plus resources associated with these machines). The domain controller machine in a domain stores and authenticates all users in the domain for network resource access. This means that the user and password database is stored and managed by the domain controller machine. Windows NT domain implementation allows for a Primary Domain Controller and a Backup Domain Controller. The Backup Domain Controller sits on the network and gets a replication of all modifications and changes to the Primary Domain Controller. If and when the Primary Domain Controller should go out of commission, the Backup Domain Controller can take over as the Primary Domain Controller, ensuring continued network operation. Note that it isn't currently possible to perform any administrative operations on the Backup Domain Controller while the Primary Domain Controller is still alive and operating.

For proper secured operations, every machine within a domain should authenticate user IDs and passwords against its domain controller.

For every large installation, it's possible to organize multiple domains in one or more 'trusted relationship'. This basically allows all users in one domain to access resources on another (access rights are still checked, of course). Operationally, a domain controller will authenticate a user against a trusted domain should it fail to authenticate the user locally. This allows for a degree of separation between the functions of user-account administration and shared resource management.

Authentication Authority

Each and every time a user on a secured Windows network is authenticated, three pieces of information are required. The authentication authority (i.e. the domain which the user belongs to), the user ID, and the password. For example:

> UserID: WRXDOMAIN\JULIAN
> Password: xyzzy

indicates that the authentication authority is the domain controller of WRXDOMAIN, the user ID is JULIAN, and the password is xyzzy.

If the authentication authority isn't explicitly named, it will always default to the local authentication authority. This means the local registration database on a non-domain controller Windows machine, and the domain registration database on a domain controller machine.

Users and Groups

To make administration and assignments of access rights somewhat easier, Windows NT Server-based networking allows the assignment of users to groups. A user is considered a 'member' of a group if the group is defined to be containing the user. Access rights can then be assigned to the object, allowing or denying access to a group instead of spelling out all its members.

Groups which contain purely users from a single domain are called **global groups**; these groups are assigned and tracked on the Domain Controller. Groups which are administered local to a machine are called **local groups** and can contain users on the local machine, users from trusted domains, or global groups.

Security Identifier

Each user on a secured Windows network has an account, the account contains information such as password, groups that the user belongs to, profile-specific items, hours allowed to logon, etc. It also contains something called a **Security ID** (or SID). An SID uniquely identifies the user in both 'space and time'. What this means is that no two SIDs generated will ever be the same due to the generation algorithm. It contains information which can be used to uniquely locate the user's account information on a registration database. Notice that a group can also have its own SID.

Security Descriptors

As mentioned earlier, every elementary operating system object created by the operating system can be associated with a Security Descriptor. This descriptor contains the following important pieces:

Information Contained	Meaning
Owner	Owner of the object, qualified by authentication authority.
Group	Group that the owner belongs to, qualified by authentication authority.
Discretionary Access Control List (DACL)	A set of access rights set by owner or administrator.
System Access Control List	A set of access rights set by the system for system operations.

The discretionary ACL can be used to specifically allow or deny access to the object by certain user and/or groups. The OS provides set and query operations to this descriptor. It also provides APIs to assist in manipulation of access lists, perform access checking, or assist in generating operating system based audits.

Let's now take a look at what Access Control Lists (ACLs) are.

Access Control Lists

An access control list consists of zero or more Access Control Entries (ACEs). Each ACE will contain:

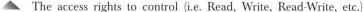

- ▲ The type of entry—either an **ACCESS_ALLOWED_ACE_TYPE** or an **ACCESS_DENY_ACE_TYPE**
- ▲ The access rights to control (i.e. Read, Write, Read-Write, etc.)
- ▲ The user or group (global or local) as represented by its SID

The access control list within a security descriptor that can be changed by applications or users programmatically is called the discretionary access control list (DACL). All SDs and the associated ACLs are stored in compact binary form.

It's interesting to note that an object which has an SD with a DACL containing no ACE entry is deemed to be explicitly inaccessible to everyone, while an object that has an SD with no DACL (i.e. set to **NULL**) is accessible by everyone.

Historically, programmatic modification of ACLs has been a very complex procedure requiring painstakingly careful coding (and testing since you can easily lock up a machine or a domain with faulty ACL modification code). The recent release of Windows NT 4.0 Service Pack 2 has fixed this problem through the implementation of a well-tested body of code in the form of a reusable COM based software component! This provides an interface called **IAccessControl** which ActiveX/COM programmers can readily reuse in situations requiring modifications to ACLs.

Security Access Tokens

ACLs are associated with static objects such as files, devices, and users. For dynamic objects in the operating system (things that come and go relatively quickly), such as processes and threads, they have associated with them something called a security access token. It's this security access token which enables a server to impersonate a client after authentication. Among other information, the security access token contains the following very important information:

- ▲ The user SID, used in matching against ACLs.
- ▲ The SID of the groups that the user belongs to, used in matching against ACLs.
- ▲ The default ACL for creating new objects.
- ▲ Default owner SID for creating new objects.
- ▲ Special token privileges, such as reboot, settime, logout, etc. These are used in very special cases only.

Since it's always servers (or threads) which actually access protected resources, it's important that threads can carry with them a context for security. The security access token is such a context.

A thread of execution assumes an alternative personality (i.e. impersonates others) by switching security access tokens. The same thread can later revert back to itself by switching back to the base process's security access token.

Client Credential

Client credential refers to the set of user ID and password information maintained by a server on behalf of a calling client. This is often required, in addition to an impersonation token, to access networked resources on other networked nodes.

SSPI and NTLMSP Authentication

We've been talking about authentication thus far as if it just magically happens between the client seeking authentication and the server performing the authentication. If the client simply sends the textual user ID and password over the network to the server, the system can't be totally secure because other nodes on the network can easily capture the user ID and password, and wreak havoc on the server with this information.

Since so much of the Windows security implementation rests on dependably robust and secure authentication, the above simple scenario can't be depended upon for proper authentication.

Instead, Microsoft has designed an elaborate architecture for handling authentication. This architecture allows the actual method of authentication to be abstracted away from the user using the authentication service. As a side benefit, it allows arbitrary extensibility through the 'plug-in' of new authentication providers. This architecture is frequently referred to as the Security Service Provider Interface (SSPI).

The following diagram shows how the SSPI fits in with the rest of the security implementation.

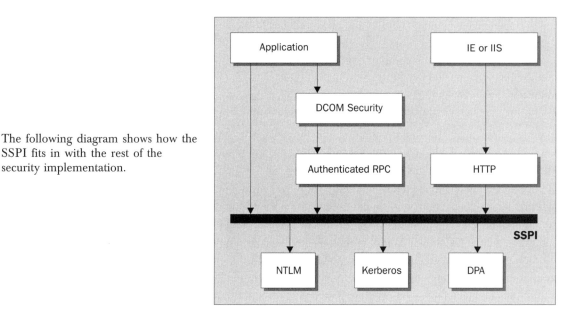

The architecture clearly separates the user of the security services from the provider of the services, and allows newer service providers to 'plug-in' and function with existing application using the SSPI services.

While the architecture is indeed elegant, the only easily usable default security provider for Windows NT 4.0 is the NTLM security provider (or NTLMSP). As a bonus, the client portion of the NTLM security provider is also implemented on Windows 95 so that Windows 95 client workstation can participate in the network.

Since this is all we've got today, it may be worthwhile to understand how NTLM works. The key element here is that the user's password is never transmitted across the wire during authentication. This is both NTLM's strong point (for security) and its weakness. We'll cover the weakness part later, but first let's see how authentication can be performed without sending the password over the wire. When a client application supplies the authentication authority, user ID, and password triplet to the client portion of the NTLMSP, the following happens:

1 The client NTLMSP sends the domain, user, and machine information to the server NTLMSP

2 The server NTLMSP uses this information to generate a unique challenge sequence (of binary bits)

3 The client NTLMSP receives this sequence and encrypts the sequence using the user's password as a key, this forms the response

4 The client NTLMSP sends the encrypted response to the server NTLMSP

5 The server NTLMSP calls the authentication authority with the user ID, the challenge sequence and the response sequence

6 The authentication authority uses the password associated with the user ID to encrypt the challenge sequence and verify it against the response sequence, authenticating the user in the process

7 If successful, the authentication is completed, and the server NTLMSP will allow the server to impersonate the client

So far so good: only an encrypted response is sent across the wire, but not the actual password. However, since the server actually never receives the password, the server will have no way of using the password to access other resources that user would have access to. Specifically, these may be network resources (i.e. files, databases, etc.) that the user would normally be able to access. This is one weakness of NTLMSP, significantly reducing the possible tasks which the server can perform on behalf of the client.

It's anticipated that the Kerberos security provider will be available with Windows NT 5.0 in the future. It's based on a mature public standard originated from MIT called MIT Kerberos V5 and endorsed by the Internet Engineering Task Force for interoperability. This new security provider is expected to provide improved performance, scalability and flexibility over the NTLM implementation. Most important of all, it will eliminate the problem we've cited with the NTLM provider.

NTFS

The NT File System format (called NTFS), although not new, is an essential piece of the Windows NT security puzzle. While NT supports alternative file format for hard disk, such as FAT and HPFS, one must make use of NTFS to enable a fully secured system. Besides offering higher performance and less fragmentation with large disks, it is the only NT-supported disk format which allows ACLs to be associated and stored with files and folders. This capability is vital to the proper operation of a secured Windows network.

As a bonus, NTFS also supports optional journalizing of all disk transactions, allowing the file system to be totally recoverable against disk failures.

Authenticated RPC

Take a careful look at the diagram in the previous section, and you'll notice a box called 'Authenticated RPC' under the 'DCOM Security' box. This implies that authenticated RPC, whatever it is, is the foundation upon which DCOM security is built on. It would be wise, then, for us to take a look at what authenticated RPC is about.

> *You'll frequently see the mention of Secure RPC as well. They actually refer to the same thing. Secure RPC can be viewed as where authenticated RPC is heading in the near future.*

We've learned that DCOM (or COM for that matter) is based on RPC (or LRPC) as the interprocess communications mechanism. We also learnt that RPC can operate over a variety of network transports, including TCP/IP, IPX and named pipes. The named pipe protocol has provided authenticated connections across networks long before the arrival of RPC. Unfortunately, other TCP/IP or IPX based protocols don't offer such features.

By building in code which will call the SSPI service, and bundle additional security information 'on-the-wire' in the runtime implementation of RPC, Microsoft has created authenticated RPC which can operate over all transports supported by the raw RPC implementation.

This can be viewed as a layer of software on top of RPC (but since it's implemented in the RPC runtime code, it can be treated just as a variant of RPC) which provides a secured channel for intermachine procedure calls. The specification for Secure RPC has five levels of security:

Security Level	Meaning
NONE (1)	This is regular RPC with no security ramification.
CONNECT (2)	Authenticate the client connection during the connection phase (i.e. when the initial TCP/IP socket is established under TCP/IP).
CALL (3)	Authenticate the request for each and every interface call.
INTEGRITY (4)	Authenticate and verify that the request packets received have not been modified.
PRIVACY (5)	Perform all of the above **and** encrypt the data packets for transmission of the wire.

Obviously, level 5 security would be very CPU-intensive when performed on a packet level. For performance reasons only the CONNECT level of security is implemented on Windows 95 clients. The symmetric connection nature of RPC requires both ends of an RPC connection to be at the same security level. This means that most applications or software components must work on the CONNECT level of security, or below, if it is ever to accommodate Windows 95 clients.

So far, Windows NT appears to be more secure than Windows 95. We have always been saying '...but Windows 95 cannot do this...' or '...except for Windows 95 because...'. Is Windows 95 really a security 'wimp'? You bet your CDROMs! Let's take a good look at what's missing.

Windows NT versus Windows 95

It's important to realize that Windows 95 plays a purely 'client' role in the overall Windows network security picture. This was necessary to fulfill several other nonsecurity related design objectives:

- To be 100% compatibile with 16-bit Windows 3.1 applications
- To require a very small memory and disk footprint, lowering the cost of platforms required to run it
- To run with excellent performance even in low-end processors and configurations
- To be easy to configure and use

Unfortunately, every one of these objectives runs against the goals and requirements of a fully secured system. Not to mention that the heritage evolution for Windows 95 (from DOS to Windows 3.1 to Windows 95) is one with a desktop focus, and had little consideration for security.

Security Features in Windows 95

There are various provisions made with Windows 95 for it to be 'compatible' with Windows NT system APIs. What this means is that applications that are written to be secure (using the various security APIs) will run fine under Windows 95. However, almost all of these APIs simply call empty stubs that do nothing and let the application carry on with its chores.

The client side of all network based security measures are implemented. For example, a Windows 95 client can participate in authenticated RPC exchange with a server over any network transport (secured RPC link with full encryption isn't yet supported). A Windows 95 machine can securely authenticate against a Windows NT domain controller (using the SSPI and the NTLM security provider) without transmitting the password over the wire. It's important to note, though, that such logons are valid only for further network based resource access (i.e. access through servers as per Windows security model); access to local resources on the Windows 95 workstation doesn't conform to the Windows NT security model and is essentially unsecured.

The Client for Microsoft Network component of Windows 95 enables something called **User Level Resource Sharing**. Sharing of resources (printers, directories, disk volumes, but not files) can be specified on a user-by-user basis, with custom permissions. The actual authentication of the user in this case will be performed by a authentication authority such as a Windows NT domain controller.

This is saying, if all you ever do after logon is to access network drives and interact with distributed remote software components on a secured server, then you'll be operating in a secured environment. If you start using the local disk on the Windows 95 workstation and working with locally executing application, then there's no security protection.

In summary, Windows 95 is a secure client partner in the Windows security model, it isn't a secure desktop platform.

What Is Not There

Almost everything that makes Windows NT secure is missing from Windows 95.

System enforced secured access to system resources is nonexistent on Windows 95. Not only does it not support the NTFS securable file system, anyone with an access to a Windows 95 workstation can access all the files and data (and devices) residing on the workstation.

Specifically, the following is true:

- No ACLs are maintained with system resources, files, etc.; nothing is protected by the OS

- User login and authentication is done via unsecured databases in either standalone or peer-to-peer configurations (i.e. the system is not part of a Windows NT domain or the user does not logon using a domain qualified user id)

- All processes running on an entire Windows 95 machine are considered to be in the context of the currently logged on user

- There's no documented way to run a process on a Windows 95 system with no current user logon (if you disable logon and/or press cancel on the logon box, the 'default user' will own the current session)

- No hardware-enforced isolation between running processes, leaving system corruption as a definite possibility after an application crash (this is a major blow to the robustness requirement of any typical server platforms)

In any case, gaining physical access to a Windows 95 workstation means gaining complete access to all the data contained on that workstation. There are tricky ways of configuring Windows 95 so that it looks as though the system is secure; but there are a variety of methods to thwart every one of such attempts. This fact alone is driving many corporations to switch to its secured elder brother: the Windows NT Workstation operating system.

In fact, Windows NT Workstation is a fully-fledged Windows NT operating system, with full security implementation, but specially configured and tuned for interactive workstation operation (and leaving out most server-specific functionality to maintain a smaller memory footprint, as well as creating a market differentiation).

What Is Possible

Just because the Windows 95 operating system doesn't enforce security on behalf of its applications doesn't mean that the operating system can't be used for secured computing. First, as a client accessing networked servers, Windows 95 has all the bells and whistles built in to maintain security. Second, it's possible to build a secure server infrastructure on top of the unsecured operating system, and implement what is missing from the underlying OS (and some vendors have done so: WebSite Server from O'Reilly; FastTrack Server from Netscape).

Another nontrivial example of a security infrastructure implementation is Microsoft's own User Level Resource Sharing that we mentioned earlier. It provides an 'ACL-like' capability for controlling access to resources down to a directory level (not file level), but only when such resources are accessed through the server application. Most of these application-level security infrastructures are proprietary in implementation. In our discussions to follow, however, we'll view Windows 95—without enhancement—as a capable secured client platform but an unsecured server platform.

IIS and ISAPI Security

This section focuses on the security issues that surround the usage of IIS and the implementation of ISAPI based extensions, of both filters and applications types. The rules are the same whether the extensions are part of the system (i.e. Active Server Pages, the Internet Data Connector) or ones that you and I write (i.e. our samples in the Server Extensions chapter).

IIS is a process running on the Windows NT operating system, and we learnt earlier that every process has a Security Access Token containing the security context under which the threads in the process would run by default. For the IIS, this is a very powerful **system user**. This particular user has access to almost everything on the local system, but no access whatsoever to networked resources.

Due to the tremendous power that the system user has, we couldn't possibly expect the IIS to use the system user's context when serving web pages or running ISAPI extensions. And, of course, it doesn't. Instead, when servicing a user request to access web pages and other server resources, the working thread(s) are operating under impersonation (via a change of the Security Access Token) in the security context of a local user account. This account could be a 'default' one that can be set during IIS setup, or a user account specified by the requesting browser when submitting the request.

All the security problems that arise during access through IIS revolve around the proper matching of the access rights of the requesting user, the user account under which IIS executes the request, and the rights associated with the resources that are accessed during the processing of the request.

The exact security context that will be used depends on the HTTP requests that the IIS receives and the setting of the Authentication Options in the Internet Service Manager configuration. The WWW service of IIS can be set to one or more of the following authentication options:

- Allow Anonymous
- Basic
- Windows NT Challenge/Response

Let's look at each of these options.

Anonymous Authentication

If the Allow Anonymous option is set, IIS will choose to use Anonymous Access wherever the headers of the HTTP request being served doesn't contain user ID and password information.

Under Anonymous Access, all access to web pages and resources are done under impersonation of the default anonymous user account. This account is created and setup during IIS installation.

The account, by default, is named after the server machine as follows:

IUSR_<machinename>

It's given a random password and permissions to 'log on locally'. This allows the IIS threads executing requests of an anonymous user to access resources on the local server machine, but not venture out into the local network. This user will also be made a member of the local Guest group. This setting allows the anonymous account to access most of the 'public' contents on a server machine.

Note that, if IIS is installed on a primary domain controller, then the anonymous user account is added to the domain account database. You can use this technique to extend the visibility of the anonymous account. For example, all other servers in the Windows NT domain can now 'publish' information which can be accessed by the IIS anonymous user.

If you have a very large domain with multiple IISs installed on several domain controllers, it's often more convenient to change all the anonymous access accounts to use the same user ID and passwords. This makes it simple to set the ACLs for anonymous serving of 'public' contents throughout the entire enterprise. One can change the anonymous access account information on the Internet Service Manager configuration utility at each IIS installation.

Basic Authentication

If the Basic authentication option is set on the Internet Service Manager configuration, the IIS will honor authenticated access for HTTP requests that contain user ID and password information.

As we've discussed before, most browsers don't automatically include user ID and password information with HTTP requests. Instead, this will only happen if access is denied when the server attempts to access a page or resource. At this time, a request denied HTTP response is sent back to the browser, with a list of authentication methods supported by the server in preferred order. Now, if the server indicated that it would prefer Basic HTTP Authentication, the browser (if capable) will honor it by popping up a dialog box requesting the user ID and password from the user. Only after the user has entered the user ID and password will the browser actually send an HTTP request that contains user ID and password information in its header.

Basic HTTP Authentication involves sending the user ID information (potentially containing an authentication authority–WRDOMAIN\JULIAN), and the password over the wire using simple Base64 encoding. This is equivalent to sending the password in clear text, and is inherently insecure. Ironically, this is also (currently) the most powerful form of authentication available for the IIS. It's powerful because the server actually obtains full credentials including the password of the user. With this information, the server can access all the resources that the original user can access, including network based resources which require passwords for access.

Windows NT Challenge/Response Authentication

If the Windows NT Challenge/Response authentication option is set on the Internet Service Manager configuration, the IIS will honor authenticated browser-initiated NTLM-based authentication.

> *We've covered this scenario in the* Secure Intranet Interaction *section before.*

Recall that the NTLM protocol is secure in that the user's password is never transmitted over the network. This also makes the authentication significantly weaker because the server doesn't have the complete credentials of the user. It can only access local resources under impersonation with NTLM authentication.

Regardless of the authentication method you use, the appropriate permissions must be carefully set to all directories or files accessible through IIS, taking care to protect any sensitive contents. For complete safety, if IIS is to be used for disseminating public information, no sensitive data should be stored on the same machine. This is particularly important if you can't guarantee the correct behavior (from a security standpoint) of any and all extensions and scripts running on the system. Recall that IIS by default runs under the system user security context with complete access to all local resources. A badly coded server extension may accidentally allow access to local files which the requester would otherwise have no access to. However, the extension will not be able to accidentally access nonlocal resources. To prevent this from happening, an ISAPI extension must take certain steps in order to ensure that it doesn't grant requesting users more rights than they are entitled to.

ISAPI Applications Security Issues

IIS offers FTP, Gopher and HTTP server capabilities, each running as an NT service. An NT service is a running process that is, potentially, started at system startup and may be running while users log on and off the machine. It appears to be part of the system services. As a process, it must run in the security context of some NT user account. Depending on the type of the service, the account may be a generic, privileged system account, or a specific account with particular rights. We know from the previous section that IIS runs under the almighty system user account. For other services, like some of the Microsoft BackOffice servers (Exchange or SQL), it's recommended that they are installed and run under a separate 'service' account to which the 'log on as service' privilege is added. In general, this is a good idea for these other servers since you then have finer control over the access rights of your services by just adding or removing membership to appropriate groups.

Unlike the other BackOffice servers, the 'normal mode' of operation of the IIS involves the access of server-based, operating-system-managed resources on behalf of remote client requests. We already know that the IIS accomplishes this securely through impersonation.

Let's now take a look at how this impersonation happens and what APIs are available under NT in order to exercise finer control on the thread's access rights.

By default, under NT, a newly created thread inherits the security context of its parent process. Access rights to resources accessed by the thread are checked against the process account. In a typical server like the IIS, the server process may have created a pool of worker threads to which it parcels out each request for servicing. Each worker thread services a request, perhaps producing a response to be sent back to the client and then is ready to process the next client request that has been queued. Now, each client request may require access to data (files or objects) that are accessible only to its corresponding user account. Since the server must access data on behalf of a variety of users, with different access rights, two avenues are open:

 The server process runs as a super-privileged account (with full access rights to all the user's resources)

 The server process 'impersonates' each client before accessing any resources on its behalf

The first method is very dangerous! A bug in the server process, or a rogue request (depending on how general the request is and what checks and balances have been implemented) may allow an unauthorized user access to somebody else's private data. This method is also inconsistent with the Windows NT security model that we have discussed previously.

Fortunately, Win32 provides a number of API calls that support the second method allowing us much finer control over who accesses what.

The basic principle at work here, one that system components of NT adhere to, too, is this corollary of the general security model:

> **Before accessing system resources on behalf of a user, assume the identity of that user.**

In this way, the server thread has exactly the same access rights as a process started by the logged on client (well, almost, since the impersonated user may not have access to networked resources). These rights are stored with the thread specific Security Access Token. These rights are checked against the ACL for the resources in question by the NT security reference monitor and access is granted or denied. Thus security decisions are kept centralized and protected within the NT executive, deep inside the kernel. The access model is also simplified since all access is reduced to the level of a process instantiated by a logged on user.

Let's look at some of the relevant functions from the security API before we go through an example of how we can use this from within our ISAPI extensions. The security API is large and complex and outside the scope of this chapter—the following subset, however, is sufficient to solve the problem at hand.

```
BOOL OpenThreadToken( HANDLE ThreadHandle,
                      DWORD DesiredAccess,
                      BOOL OpenAsSelf,
                      PHANDLE pTokenHandle );
```

OpenThreadToken() opens the Security Access Token associated with the thread identified by the thread handle. As we've discussed before, this access token encapsulates the security context of the current thread, or its parent process, and can be potentially modified and then used in order to change the security context of a running thread–either the same one, or another one. This token is the key to 'impersonation'. The function returns **TRUE** on success.

Let's take a look at the parameters:

Parameter	Meaning
ThreadHandle	This is a handle to the thread for which we want to get the security information. This implies that the calling thread must have permissions to inquire about the **ThreadHandle** thread.
	Thread handles are returned by the **CreateThread()** call that creates a new thread. A running thread may get at its handle by invoking **GetCurrentThread()**.
	(Actually **GetCurrentThread()** returns a 'pseudohandle' that the thread can use to specify itself wherever a thread handle is required. If a proper thread handle is required, e.g. to pass to other threads to refer to the current thread, then **DuplicateHandle()** must be invoked on the pseudohandle.)
DesiredAccess	This specifies an access mask with the requested types of access to the thread access token. As any other object in the system, the access token has a discretionary access control list (DACL) against which the **DesiredAccess** is checked.
OpenAsSelf	This is an important parameter. If set to **TRUE**, the access check to decide whether access to the thread token will be granted or not, is done against the security context of the calling process. If the value is **FALSE**, the access check is against the calling thread security context.
	In other words, if the thread belongs to a server process running under a privileged account, passing **TRUE** will perform the check against the privileged account, while a **FALSE** will result in a check against the current security context of the thread. If the thread is already impersonating a user account with fewer privileges, the check may fail.

Parameter	Meaning
PTokenHandle	This is a pointer to a handle. If the call is successful, it will be set to a handle to an open access token to the thread. When the token is no longer necessary, the handle should be closed with **CloseHandle()**.
	The access rights implied by the token depend on the **DesiredAccess** parameter; that is, it may not encapsulate the complete set of rights for the thread.

Here are some of the most important values for the **DesiredAccess** parameter

DesiredAccess Value	Meaning
TOKEN_ADJUST_PRIVILEGES	Required to change the privileges specified in the access token.
TOKEN_DUPLICATE	Required in order to duplicate an access token.
TOKEN_QUERY	Required in order to inquire about the contents of an access token.
TOKEN_IMPERSONATE	Required in order to get an access token that can then be used by a process or thread to impersonate the user with the rights that the access token represents.

An almost identical function is available in order to capture the access token of a process:

```
BOOL OpenProcessToken( HANDLE ProcessHandle,
                       DWORD DesiredAccess,
                       PHANDLE pTokenHandle );
```

If we now want to modify the privileges associated with the token, for example, in order to enable a the thread or process to perform a system shutdown, we must use the **AdjustTokenPrivileges()** function. Note that the function can't add new privileges to the access token but only enable or disable existing privileges.

The main parameters are the token handle in question, an array of the new privileges we want (we can specify whether we want them enabled or disabled), and a pointer to an array to set to the current set of privileges (so that we can revert to it after we're done).

```
BOOL AdjustTokenPrivileges( HANDLE TokenHandle,
                            BOOL DisableAllPrivileges,
                            PTOKEN_PRIVILEGES NewPriv,
                            DWORD PreviousBufferLen,
                            PTOKEN_PRIVILEGES PreviousPriv,
                            PDWORD RequirdPreviousBufferLen );
```

Parameter	Meaning
`TokenHandle`	Handle to the access token to be modified.
`DisableAllPrivileges`	If set to **TRUE**, all privileges are revoked.
`NewPriv`	Pointer to a **TOKEN_PRIVILEGES** structure. This contains a counter and an array of **LUID_AND_ATTRIBUTES** structures. Each one of these contains just two members: a locally unique identifier (LUID) for the privilege and a Boolean flag to be set to **TRUE** if the privilege should be enabled and to **FALSE** otherwise.
`PreviousBufferLen`	The size of the buffer passed in the **PreviousPriv** argument.
	The calling code must have allocated an array large enough to hold the **PreviousPriv TOKEN_PRIVILEGES** structure, if we want to keep hold of the current privileges before they get modified. If the size isn't sufficient, the last argument is set to the required buffer size and the call fails.
`PreviousPriv`	If not set to **NULL**, it should point to an allocated buffer of size **PreviousBufferLen**
`RequirdPreviousBufferLen`	Set to the size of the required buffer pointed to by **PreviousPriv** that can hold the current privileges.

The function will return **TRUE** if it has managed to modify at least some of the requested privileges.

Let's go now through an example where the thread in question must set the system time. Since this is a privileged operation, the thread must first attempt to adjust its privileges to include the **SE_SYSTEMTIME_NAME** privilege, change the time and then revert back to disabling the privilege.

```
HANDLE       hToken;      // handle to thread token
TOKEN_PRIVILEGES    tp;        // structure to hold the privileges array

// Get the current thread access token
if ( !OpenThreadToken( GetCurrentThread(),      // current thread handle
        TOKEN_ADJUST_PRIVILEGES   // we want to modify the access token privileges
        |  TOKEN_QUERY,      // ask for the existing privileges
        TRUE,   // access check against the process
        & hToken) )
    // error handling
```

We now need to get the LUID for the system time change privilege. A privilege has a well-known name, an LUID (which is unique on one machine while the system is up–but not necessarily between reboots) and a display string that is meaningful to the end user (in this case, for example, it could be 'Change system time'). We need to look up the LUID for this session, given the text string representing the well-known privilege name. The LUID is assigned to the first **LUID_AND_ATTRIBUTES** array of the token privilege structure.

```
LookupPrivilegeValue( NULL,       // system name - NULL for the local system
    SE_SHUTDOWN_NAME,   // string with privilege in question
    & tp.Privileges[0].Luid );      // pointer to 64-bit LUID
```

Enable the privilege in the token privilege structure.

```
tp.PrivilegeCount = 1;
tp.Privileges [0].Attributes = SE_PRIVILEGE_ENABLED;
```

We're now ready to attempt to adjust our thread privileges. For this example, we won't be interested in the current privilege set.

```
AdjustTokenPrivileges( hToken,    // token handle
    FALSE,         // do not disable all
    & tp,          // new token privilege structure
    0,        // not interested in current structure
    NULL,         // same here
    NULL );        // same here
```

Now we check whether all requested modifications have taken place. Checking whether the return value is **TRUE** isn't enough, since the function will succeed even for partial modifications. We need to invoke **GetLastError()** which will return **ERROR_SUCCESS** if all modifications succeeded and **ERROR_NOT_ALL_ASSIGNED** otherwise.

```
if ( GetLastError() != ERROR_SUCCESS )
   // handle error
```

The coast is clear! Let's change the system time!

```
SYSTEMTIME   t;

GetSystemTime( &t );
t.wHour += 1;   // add one hour to current time!
if ( ! SetSystemTime( &t ) )
   // handle error
```

We now need to disable the change system time privilege to bring things back to the default state.

```
tp.Privileges[0].Attributes =  0;   // disable it
AdjustTokenPrivileges( hToken,   // token handle
    FALSE,         // do not disable all
    & tp,          // token privilege structure reverting to original state
    0,        // not interested in current structure
    NULL,         // same here
    NULL );        // same here

if ( GetLastError() != ERROR_SUCCESS )
   // handle error
```

Let's move on now to the core subject of impersonation.

Impersonation

IIS takes certain steps towards security by handling most of the requirements for simple ISAPI applications. Before a request thread is used to invoke an ISAPI application, IIS sets the thread to impersonate the client that submitted the request. Remember that the client must been locally authenticated, either against client-supplied credentials or the anonymous access account. Impersonating the client does two things: it protects resources that the client doesn't have the right to access and potentially allows for network access (by default, the system account is a local account and can't access network resources–network access is only possible when HTTP Basic authentication is used, not when NTLM authentication is used).

However, not all of the extensions are invoked through an impersonated thread. Here's a table showing which entry points to an ISAPI application or filter are called in which security context:

Exported functions	Impersonated (client)	Non-impersonated (system)
GetExtensionVersion()		✓
HttpExtensionProc()	✓	
TerminateExtension()		✓
GetFilterVersion()		✓
HttpFilterProc() (except for some notifications)		✓
TerminateFilter()		✓

It's obvious that if we want protected access to resources, we must in some way 'cache' the access token from an impersonated call (from the above table **HttpExtensionProc()** is the prime candidate) and use it when necessary, let's say from **TerminateExtension()**.

Even invoking **HttpExtensionProc()** by an impersonating thread may not be sufficient. Consider an ISAPI application that must handle requests that do take some amount of time to complete. In this case, the extension must not take up a request thread by staying in **HttpExtensionProc()** until the call completes. Request threads are scarce resources. Instead, the right architecture calls for setting up a pool of worker threads that are dealt stored requests from a queue. The main purpose of **HttpExtensionProc()** in this case is to queue the incoming request (that is the extension control block) and return with status **HSE_STATUS_PENDING**. When a worker thread finishes with the request later, it returns through the control block's **ServerSupportFunction()** with **HSE_REQ_DONE_WITH_SESSION** so that IIS can free the resources tied up to the request.

The big problem from the standpoint of security is: how can the worker thread acquire the security context of the client? The request thread is long gone by the time the worker thread gets ready to handle the request.

The answer lies in the access token of the request thread. **HttpExtensionProc()** is invoked by the request thread. Along with storing the extension control block with the incoming request, it can acquire the access token of the calling thread and store it with the request. When the request thread gets to handle the request, it can use the access token in order to impersonate the client.

Let's first examine the relevant Win32 API functions before we delve into the code.

```
BOOL ImpersonateLoggedOnUser( HANDLE hToken );
```

where **hToken** is an access token that represents the logged-on user. The token may have been returned by a call to, among others, **LogonUser()**, **OpenProcessToken()** or **OpenThreadToken()**. It could be either a primary token (produced by the NT executive) or an impersonation token, acquired from an impersonating thread.

The calling thread needs no special privileges in order to successfully invoke this function. Upon success, with a nonzero return code, the calling thread will continue running in the security context of the access token **hToken**. The impersonation lasts until either the thread exits or it invokes the function **RevertToSelf()**.

```
BOOL RevertToSelf( VOID );
```

Upon success, the function returns **TRUE** and terminates the impersonation of a client.

Let's go back, now, to the worker pool example we mentioned before. We need to keep track of an extension control block along with an impersonation token for each request. We'll skip the code for storing each request's data to an appropriate data structure as well as the synchronization code necessary to allow multithreaded access to it.

```
struct  Request
{
    EXTENSION_CONTROL_BLOCK *   lpEcb;        // from request
    HANDLE              hImpToken;   // impersonation token of calling thread
};

// add a request to a list
BOOL AddRequest( const Request& req );

// get a request from the list
Request* GetRequest( void );
```

For simplicity, in the code snippets below we'll deal with one worker thread.

```
// worker thread handle
HANDLE   worker;
```

In the worker pool situation we mentioned above, the first entry point in the extension DLL is **DllMain()**. It's a good place to create our worker threads, but not as good a place to terminate them. The threads should be terminated in the **TerminateExtension()** call. Since the threads are created before any requests have arrived, they inherit the security context of the parent process–that's the local system account that IIS is running under.

```
BOOL WINAPI DllMain( HANDLE hInst,  ULONG reason_for_call,  LPVOID  reserved)
{
    switch (reason_for_call)
    {
        DWORD   threadId;

        case DLL_PROCESS_ATTACH:
            worker = CreateThread (
                    NULL,   // the thread gets the default security descriptor
                    0,      // default stack size - same as main thread
                    (LPTHREAD_START_ROUTINE ) DoWork,  // thread function ptr
                    NULL,      // argument to thread function
```

```
                    0,       // creation flags - 0 means thread runs immediately
                &threadId );   // thread identifier
        break;

    case DLL_PROCESS_DETACH:
        // cleanup
        break;
    }
}
```

When `HttpExtensionProc()` is invoked it should acquire the access token of the calling thread and store it in the list along with the control block:

```
DWORD HttpExtensionProc( LPEXTENSION_CONTROL_BLOCK lpEcb )
{
    Request*  pReq = new Request;
    if (pReq)
    {
        // get the thread access token
        if ( ! OpenThreadToken( GetCurrentThread() ,
            TOKEN_QUERY | TOKEN_IMPERSONATE,
            TRUE,
            & pReq->hImpToken ) )
        {
            // handle error
        }
        pReq->lpEcb = lpEcb;

        // add to list
        AddRequest( *pReq );

        // instruct IIS to hold on to request resources
        return HSE_STATUS_PENDING;
    }
    else
        // handle error

}
```

The worker thread would effectively wait on a synchronization object to signal that work was added to the list. It would then get a request from the list, impersonate the request client, do the actual work and revert back to its previous security context. We're now done with the request, and we can inform IIS that this is the case.

We should also not forget to close the handle to the impersonation token: otherwise, the resource will remain open until the process exits. Perhaps this doesn't seem a terrible waste and might not be a great concern if your process takes a few milliseconds to run. Memory leaks, however, are of considerable concern for the stability of IIS (under which the extension runs) which in a production environment may stay up for days on end, processing millions of requests. You should employ every means at your disposal to ensure that IIS extensions are as free from memory-related bugs as possible.

```
DWORD  WINAPI   DoWork( LPVOID parm )
{
    // wait until there is work to do
    ...
```

```
    // get a request from the queue
    Request*    pReq = GetRequest();
    if ( pReq )
    {
        // impersonate client
        ImpersonateLoggedOnUser( pReq->hImpToken );

        // do the actual work
        ...

        // revert to previous security context
        RevertToSelf();

        // notify IIS we are done
        pReq->lpEcb->ServerSupportFunction( pReq->lpEcb->ConnID,
                HSE_REQ_DONE_WITH_SESSION,
                NULL,
                NULL,
                NULL );
        // close token handle
        CloseHandle( pReq->hImpToken );

        // free request
        delete pReq;
    }
    ...
}
```

This concludes our coverage of security issues and techniques related to IIS and ISAPI applications. The basic principals are very straightforward and simple; incorporating them into the design and coding them requires careful planning and meticulous attention to details.

DCOM Security

Now let's look at security issues which are specific to DCOM operations and programming.

We've seen in the 'Authenticated RPC' section that the DCOM security implementation is based on Authenticated RPC. Authenticated RPC uses the security support providers that are available through the Win32 Security Support Provider Interface (SSPI). At this time, Authenticated RPC uses the NTLMSSP exclusively.

Security can be configured externally, that is, without either the client or the server having to include security-specific code. This is suitable for both legacy and simple COM applications. If the security needs of the application are more sophisticated, a variety of functions and interfaces are available to both clients and servers to configure security programmatically, as we'll see shortly.

DCOM Security Blankets

The set of services and parameters that can be configured in order to specify the security settings for a DCOM component is called the 'security blanket'. This is essentially a packaging of security parameters. By bundling security parameters in a package, the negotiation process between the client and the server can be made 'network efficient'. Instead of negotiating each parameter across the network with multiple round trips, only a single round trip is required to complete the negotiation. We'll see how this is possible in the next section.

The parameters contained in the security blanket include:

Parameter	Meaning
Authentication service	The SSPI to use for authentication, e.g. NTLM.
Authentication level	The degree to which to authenticate the access to the object and ensure the privacy of the communications over the connection. These are identical to the security levels of Authenticated RPC.
Server principle	The user security context under which the COM server is running.
Impersonation level	The degree of 'similarity' to the client being impersonated which the COM server is allowed during its execution. For example, it is possible to restrict the COM server to only query rights to security information, but not actually impersonate the client.
Authentication identity	The identification of the client, as seen by the server. Usually a user name.

Security Blanket Negotiation

During a security blanket negotiation, the client supplies a security blanket which indicates the maximum level of security that the client can support. When the server receives this security blanket, it matches it against what it would accept. The server decides the minimum level of security which it will accept. If the client's security blanket levels are all above the ones expected by the client, the negotiation succeeds, otherwise negotiation fails.

This approach reduces network traffic down to a single round trip. This low overhead allows security negotiation on a very fine-grain level. For example, security negotiation can be performed on a 'per remote interface instance' level.

DCOM Security Categories

The following security categories are important in DCOM:

Category	Meaning
Access security	Specifying which clients have the right to connect with a running object. Clients might not have the right to launch a server but might be allowed to connect to one if it is already running.
Launch (activation) security	Specifying which clients can start the execution of the server process on the remote machine.

Category	Meaning
Call security	This essentially allows for security blanket negotiation on a 'per interface instance' level. More precisely, it enables the client to set the security blanket for each server interface proxy object which allows the server to check the security blanket per call when it arrives.
	It is important to have call level security in DCOM. After a successful launch, the client might pass a remote interface pointer (actually a proxy) to another unauthorized client. If security isn't provided on a per call level, the system can be compromised.

Security Level Configuration

Let's see now how we can configure the system for launch and call security. These activities can be performed through the **Dcomcnfg.exe** tool that provides a user-friendly interface to modifying the corresponding registry entries. If, like me, editing ACLs in binary in the registry editor isn't your idea of fun, then **Dcomcnfg** is indispensable!

Launch Security

Launch security is automatically applied by the COM runtime when a server application is started due to a remote object creation request. After the request has been received from a client, the COM runtime obtains all the necessary security parameters from the registry if the creating process didn't specifically specify security parameters.

There are two default activation settings in the registry that have machine-wide effect. They are both named values under the same key.

```
HKEY_LOCAL_MACHINE\Software\Microsoft\OLE
  EnableDCOM = <value>
```

The value is a string (**REG_SZ**) and can be a **Y** or an **N**. A value of **Y** enables remote activation of COM servers on this machine, any other value disables it. Even when remote activation is disabled, local activation is still allowed and is governed by the specific permissions in the **LaunchPermission** key of each class and the default settings in the **DefaultLaunchPermission** key.

```
HKEY_LOCAL_MACHINE\Software\Microsoft\OLE
  DefaultLaunchPermission = <value>
```

The **DefaultLaunchPermission** value is of type **REG_BINARY** and consists of a binary ACL of the principals (accounts or groups) that can have launch classes on this system. The value can be overridden by specifying a **LaunchPermission** value in the registry for a particular COM object. By default, the following principals are given 'allow launch' permissions:

 Administrators—the administrator group

 System—the local system-privileged account

 Interactive—corresponding to the user currently logged in at the console

On a per-class basis, security configuration settings are stored as a set of named values under the following key:

```
HKEY_LOCAL_MACHINE\Software\Classes\AppID\
  {AppID_value}\
    <named_value> = <value>
```

For a class, the **AppID_value** is a GUID that appears, as a string, under the **AppID** named value under the CLSID key of the class. The string **{AppID_value}** is used as a subkey under **...\Classes\AppID**.

For an executable, the **AppID_value** is the name of the module (e.g. **myapp.exe**). Under the **{myapp.exe}** key there's a **REG_SZ** named value **AppID** with the AppID associated with the executable.

The launch permissions are set in the named value **LaunchPermission**. The type and content of the value is the same as in the **DefaultLaunchPermission**. Other named values under the same key are:

- ▲ **AccessPermission** specifying permissions to access running instances of the class. It's used only if the client doesn't call **CoInitializeSecurity()**.

- ▲ **RunAs** specifying that the server should run with the security context of the specified user.

- ▲ **LocalService** specifying that the server is a Windows NT service.

- ▲ **ServiceParameters** specifying the parameters to be passed to the service on invocation.

- ▲ **RemoteServerName** specifying the remote machine on which the server will be activated by default, if the client hasn't programmatically requested otherwise (by specifying, for example, a **COSERVERINFO** parameter to **CoCreateInstanceEx()**).

You can change the default settings through the **Dcomcnfg** utility.

The procedure is similar for setting the security parameters of a specific application.

Other than configuring DCOM security parameters through registry editing, it's also possible to have fine-grain control over these parameters using programmatic means. Let's examine some of the Win32 APIs and COM object interfaces associated with DCOM security control.

DCOM Security API

We've covered the **CoCreateInstanceEx()** in Chapter 8. The new **COSERVERINFO** parameter allows us to specify a remote machine on which to create the new object instance. The support for multiple **QueryInterface()** calls in a single round trip keeps everything fast and efficient.

CoCreateInstanceEx() and Client Security Blanket

If we take a look at the **COSERVERINFO** structure again, there's a member of the structure that we didn't cover at any length. It was the **COAUTHINFO** structure which is the actual client security blanket.

```
typedef struct _COSERVERINFO
{
    DWORD    dwReserverd1;
    LPWSTR   pwszName;
    COAUTHINFO*   pAuthInfo;
    DWORD    dwReserved2;
} COSERVERINFO;
```

pAuthInfo is the security blanket which gets passed through the COM runtime to the server for negotiation. It's instructive to look at the details of the structure since some fields will be identical to the one for the **CoInitializeSecurity()** call that we'll be covering later. You can find this definition in **Wtypes.h**:

```
typedef struct _COAUTHINFO
{
    DWORD         dwAuthnSvc;
    DWORD         dwAuthzSvc;
    LPWSTR        pwszServerPrincName;
    DWORD         dwAuthnLevel;
    DWORD         dwImpersonationLevel;
    COAUTHIDENTITY *  pAuthIdentityData;
    DWORD         dwCapabilities;
} COAUTHINFO;
```

dwAuthnSvc signifies the authentication service. It's a value from the enumeration **RPC_C_AUTHN_**xxx:

dwAuthnSvc Value	Meaning
RPC_C_AUTHN_DCE_PRIVATE	DCE private key authentication.
RPC_C_AUTHN_DCE_PUBLIC	DCE public key authentication.
RPC_C_AUTHN_DEC_PUBLIC	DEC public key authentication.
RPC_C_AUTHN_DEFAULT	The system default authentication service. NT 4.0 defaults to DCE private key authentication.
RPC_C_AUTHN_WINNT	The NTLM Security Support Provider. Except for the default and this one, these services do not currently have native NT 4.0 support.
RPC_C_AUTHN_NONE	No authentication.

dwAuthzSvc signifies the authorization service. In other words, what should the server use in order to check the access rights it should have on behalf of the client. The values are from the **RPC_C_AUTHZ_**xxx enumeration:

dwAuthzSvr Value	Meaning
RPC_C_AUTHZ_NONE	Server performs no authorization.
RPC_C_AUTHZ_NAME	Server performs authorization using the client's name.
RPC_C_AUTHZ_DCE	Server performs authorization using the client's DCE privileges.

pwszServerPrincName points to a wide character string indicating the principal name to use on the server with the authentication name. If the service chosen is **RPC_C_AUTHN_WINNT**, the value should be **NULL**.

dwAuthnLevel specifies the level of authentication required ranging from once when connecting, to packet-level authentication and encryption.

DwAuthnLevel Value	Meaning
RPC_C_AUTHN_LEVEL_NONE	No authentication.
RPC_C_AUTHN_LEVEL_CONNECT	Authenticates only when client establishes a connection.
RPC_C_AUTHN_LEVEL_CALL	Authenticates at the beginning of each remote procedure call.
RPC_C_AUTHN_LEVEL_PKT	Authenticates origin of all data. Used by datagram trans ports.
RPC_C_AUTHN_LEVEL_PKT_INTEGRITY	Authenticates origin and integrity of data.
RPC_C_AUTHN_LEVEL_PKT_PRIVACY	Authenticates origin and integrity of data and encrypts remote procedure call arguments.

dwImpersonationLevel specifies the impersonation level. Corresponds to the levels of impersonation specified in NT 4.0

DwImpersonationLevel Value	Meaning
RPC_C_IMP_LEVEL_ANONYMOUS	The server doesn't get any information about the client identification and doesn't attempt to impersonate the client.
RPC_C_IMP_LEVEL_IDENTIFY	The server can get security information about the client–for example, security identifiers and privileges–but it can't impersonate the client. The significance of this is that the server can make decisions about whether the client has the right to access resources, however, it can't use system resources or access objects 'as the client'.
RPC_C_IMP_LEVEL_IMPERSONATE	The server can impersonate the client's security context. Note that this is valid **only** on the server's local systems. It is **not** supported on remote systems. In other words, the server can't access resources over the network as if it were the client.
RPC_C_IMP_LEVEL_DELEGATE	This level allows the server to impersonate the client over a network. It isn't currently supported by the default SSPs on NT 4.0. It will, however, be supported by the Kerberos SSP which will be an integral part of the Distributed Security Services in the next major release of NT.

pAuthIdentityData: specific to the authentication service. Usually left as **NULL**.

dwCapabilities: extra capabilities to be defined.

The CoIntializeSecurity() Call

If the client or server calls **CoInitializeSecurity()**, the default security blanket for the process is set. It has be called only once per process. If a DCOM client or server doesn't call **CoInitializeSecurity()**, the COM runtime will use the configured default security blanket in the registry. The call is typically made immediately after a call to **CoInitializeEx()**. The security blanket parameter for the **COSERVERINFO** parameter of the **CoCreateInstanceEx()** call can be used to override the **CoInitializeSecurity()** settings on a per-class basis. Let's examine the calling syntax of the **CoInitializeSecurity()** API:

```
HRESULT CoInitializeSecurity( PSECURITY_DESCRIPTOR pSecDesc,
                              LONG cAuthSvc,
                              SOLE_AUTHENTICATION_SERVICE* asAuthSvc,
                              void* pReserved1,
                              DWORD dwAuthnLevel,
                              DWORD dwImpLevel,
                              void* pReserved2,
                              DWORD dwCapabilities,
                              void* pReserved3 );
```

Parameter	Meaning
PsecDesc	The pointer to the **SECURITY_DESCRIPTOR** In the first argument, if not **NULL**–in which case all callers are allowed–specifies which principals are allowed to communicate with the process and which are disallowed.
CauthSvc	This is the size of the array **asAuthSvc**. If **0** is passed, no authentication service is registered. **-1** signals COM to choose on its own which service to use.
AsAuthSvc	Specifies an array of structures each containing a principal name as well as an authentication and authorization service ID. These are the initial values used. The actual services to be used for each connection are negotiated and may be different.
dwAuthnLevel	Default authentication level for proxies. The available values are as in the **CoCreateInstanceEx()** call.
dwImpLevel	Default impersonation level for proxies. The available values are as in the **CoCreateInstanceEx()** call.

IClientSecurity for Call Security Control

If the client calls **CoInitializeSecurity()**, the security values for authentication and authorization for the process are set. If a fine-grain security control is required on the calls to individual interfaces, the client can achieve this by invoking security functions on each of the interface proxies. The main security interface to achieve this on the client side is **IClientSecurity**. You can obtain it by doing a **QueryInterface()** on an interface from the remote object for **IID_IClientSecurity**. In reality, since every remote object method invocation goes through a proxy managed by a proxy manager (who actually aggregates the proxy object), the proxy manager will intercept and provide this interface.

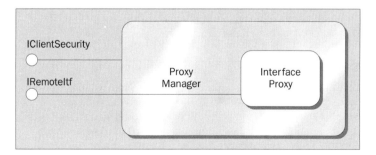

Once the **IClientSecurity** interface is obtained, the client can change the security blanket for this single proxy instance by first using the **IClientSecurity::CopyProxy()** method to create a new instance of the proxy, and then using the **IClientSecurity::SetBlanket()** method of the interface to alter the blanket. It's important to make a copy of the proxy before setting its security blanket to avoid contention with other portions of the process that may be setting the security blanket to other values.

There are wrapper functions available which call the **IClientSecurity** methods, these include **CoSetProxyBlanket()**, **CoQueryProxyBlanket()**, and **CoCopyProxy()**.

Clients can call **CoQueryProxyBlanket()** to inquire about the existing security blanket on a proxy, **CoSetProxyBlanket()** to set a new security blanket on a proxy, and **CoCopyProxy()** to obtain a proxy copy on which a security blanket can be set without contention.

IServerSecurity Interface

On the server side, the server is to obtain the parameters contained in the client's security blanket for this interface and perform manipulation based on these parameters (such as impersonating the client). The main interface for this purpose is the **IServerSecurity**. This interface also provides control over the security level while executing on behalf of the client. To obtain this interface, which is actually provided by a call context object inside the stub, the server must make a **CoGetCallContext()** call.

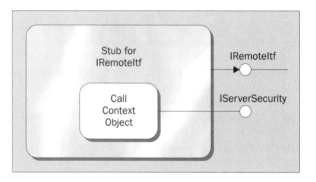

Once the **IServerSecurity** interface is obtained, the server has the option to:

▲ Get specific security level information from the blanket by making the **IServerSecurity::QueryBlanket()** method call

▲ Impersonate the client's security level and identification while carrying out resource access by making the **IServerSecurity::ImpersonateClient()** and **IServerSecurity::RevertToSelf()** method calls

▲ Determine if the server thread is currently impersonating the client using the **IServerSecurity::IsImpersonating()** method call

As with the **IClientSecurity** interface, there are wrapper APIs including **CoQueryClientBlanket()**, **CoImpersonateClient()** and **CoRevertToSelf(),** making the use of the **IServerSecurity** interface somewhat simpler.

Client-Side Proxy Copying

Occasionally, a client may want to ensure a specific security blanket is set on a particular interface when presented to the server for security negotiation. Directly changing the security blanket on the default proxy (returned by initial **QueryInterface()** call) will affect all other users of the proxy who may have different security requirements. The way out of the predicament is to make a private copy of the proxy on which to set the desired security blanket.

Beware, however: proxy copies are special in that a **QueryInterface()** on a proxy copy will return a pointer to an interface on the original proxy, with the original's security blanket.

CoCopyProxy() encapsulates several steps. It does a **QueryInterface()** on the original proxy for **IID_IClientSecurity**, invoking **IClientSecurity::CoCopyProxy()** on it and then releasing it.

```
HRESULT CoCopyProxy( IUnknown* pProxy, // original
                     IUnknown** ppCopy ); // pointer to copy pointer
```

The client can now set the security blanket by doing, for example:

```
IUnknown pCopy;  // copy proxy

CoCopyProxy( pProxy, &pCopy );
CoSetProxyBlanket( pCopy,
          RPC_C_AUTHN_WINNT,
          RPC_C_AUTHZ_NONE,
          L"HOST",
          RPC_C_AUTHN_LEVEL_CONNECT,
          RPC_C_IMP_LEVEL_IMPERSONATE,
          NULL,
          0);
// use the proxy
...
pCopy->Release();
```

Here's the exact declaration:

```
HRESULT CoSetProxyBlanket( IUnknown* pProxy,
                           DWORD dwAuthnSvc,
                           DWORD dwAuthzSvc,
                           OLECHAR* pServerPrincName,
                           DWORD dwAuthnLevel,
                           DWORD dwImpLevel,
                           RPC_AUTH_IDENTITY_HANDLE* pAuthInfo,
                           DWORD dwCapabilities );
```

We've seen most of the arguments before!

Parameter	Meaning
Pproxy	Pointer to a copy proxy on which this blanket will be set.
DwAuthnSvc	An **RPC_C_AUTHN**_xxx value.
DwAuthzSvc	An **RPC_C_AUTHZ**_xxx value.
PserverPrincName	A wide character string with server's principal name to be used for authentication.
DwAuthnLevel	An **RPC_C_AUTHN_LEVEL**_xxx value.
DwImpLevel	An **RPC_C_IMP_LEVEL**_xxx value.
PAuthInfo	Authentication service specific. **NULL** for default.
DwCapabilities	Extra capabilities for the proxy. Not defined.

Working with IServerSecurity

The server obtains the **IServerSecurity** interface by invoking **CoGetCallContext()**. This is the only easy way for the server to work with successfully negotiated security parameters from the client.

```
IServerSecurity*    pSS;
CoGetCallContext( IID_IServerSecurity, (void **)&pSS );
```

To get more information on the security blanket from the client, the server may invoke:

```
HRESULT CoQueryClientBlanket( DWORD* pAuthnSvc,
                              DWORD* pAuthzSvc,
                              OLECHAR** pServerPrincName,
                              DWORD* pAuthnLevel,
                              DWORD* pImpLevel,
                              RPC_AUTHZ_HANDLE* pPrivs,
                              DWORD* pCapabilities );
```

One of the interesting new fields here is the **pPrivs** (the type is really a **void ****) which is set to point to a Unicode string identifying the client. The caller must not modify the string in any way. The default NTLM security provider will return an **Domain\\User** value.

In order to access resources with the client's security context, the server can impersonate the client of this call and then revert to its own security context when done. You can use the wrapper functions for the **IServerSecurity** interface for this:

```
CoImpersonateClient();
//access resources
 . . .
CoRevertToSelf();
```

Summary

In this chapter, we've given the vast topic of security a fair shake. We began by examining what security means in the intranet context. Narrowing it down to interactions between a web browser and a web server, we examined the specifics of where security measures should be implemented. We found that authentication of the client is a big and essential issue in intranet security. While simple on the surface, this is a complex task underneath and no standard implementation exists today. However, an all-Microsoft solution in an intranet environment can provide a secured environment with security features which can be transparent to an authorized end-user.

Laying the foundation for a more in-depth coverage of security, we examined all the fundamentals of Windows NT security. We covered the basic client/server security model, and stressed the importance of impersonation. We discovered the built-in and designed-in nature of Windows NT security and resolved the definitions of many security-specific terminologies.

We finally extend our discussion of security to the bigger picture of IIS, ISAPI Server Extensions, and DCOM distributed software components. Authentication is vital to proper IIS operations; we learnt about the anonymous user account created by IIS, and saw the importance of impersonation when accessing protected resources. ISAPI server extensions must work in harmony with the IIS and Windows NT security philosophy. This means the implementer must be careful not to grant the client process more access rights than it has. It also means a judicial use of impersonation wherever system resources are accessed.

In our DCOM security coverage, we examined the DCOM security blanket which significantly optimizes the security negotiation process. We discussed Access Security, Launch Security, and Call Security. The importance of fine-grain security control was stressed during our discussion, and we concluded with a comprehensive discussion of the APIs and COM interfaces available for both client and servers to set, discover, and manipulate security parameters.

The message is clear in this chapter. Security in the intranet context, or the distributed component computing context, is a nontrivial matter. A functional, secure computing environment requires careful planning and design. The Windows NT security model gives a solid and robust foundation upon which we can build more elaborate security schemes appropriate for our intranet project, using many of the new Win32 API and COM interfaces available.

Fitting ActiveX to the Intranet

Congratulations, you've finally arrived at the end of the book.

During this short journey, we've immersed ourselves in ActiveX technology and philosophy within the intranet context. In review, we have:

- Analyzed Microsoft's Internet/intranet strategy centered around ActiveX, and seen how the client and server side technologies fit together

- Discussed the issue of intranet definition, and how the intranet will benefit from the rapid innovation occurring in the Internet world

- Covered COM fundamentals, and shown how ATL can be used to build COM servers rapidly

- Discussed how to activate an intranet, and created several fully visual ActiveX controls using Visual C++ 5.0 and MFC 4.21

- Examined the anatomy of an ActiveX control, and discussed how the OC96 specification affects its definition; we've seen how MFC 4.21 provides support for creating ActiveX controls that are compliant with the OC96 specification

- Discussed advanced COM concepts such as Automation, enumeration, and early versus late binding

- Explored DCOM as a natural extension of basic COM

- Examined how you can manage code download and installation across the network for ActiveX controls

- Created and staged a DCOM-based ActiveX control which worked in a three-tiered configuration across three machines

- Examined the security infrastructure provided by Windows NT Server, and seen how it applies to ActiveX technologies through COM and DCOM influences

While far from comprehensive, we hope that the coverage has given you an overall sense of what ActiveX is all about. There should be enough coverage in the selected application areas for the working professional to start ActiveX-based intranet design and coding activities while exploring the subject matter further.

In this final chapter, we'll briefly review our Aberdeen & Wilshire solution. Not all is rosy with our design; we'll now take a look at a couple of caveats involved when designing distributed systems. We'll also examine some hard issues involved when deploying an intranet in a typical corporate environment. Just before we conclude with a 'where shall we go from here?', we'll recap what makes Visual C++ 5.0 such a great tool for ActiveX programming and how we, as seasoned Visual C++ programmers, may take maximum advantage of these features. Finally, we conclude with an open-ended glance towards the next decade of exciting software evolution.

Aberdeen & Wilshire Solution Reviewed

Throughout this book, we've 'Activated' the Aberdeen & Wilshire web site using a collection of ActiveX-based intranet technologies. Along the way, we've gained some hands-on experience and became familiar with the following fundamental ActiveX technological pieces:

- Component Object Model (COM)
- Active Template Library 2.1 (ATL)
- OLE Control 96 Specifications and Internet Extension (OC96)
- Distributed COM (DCOM)
- Security issues as they apply to these technologies
- Visual C++ 5.0 and MFC enhancements to make it all easier

Many of these technologies may be classified into architectural layers.

The Events Calendar

A static version of the Events Calendar would be very uninteresting. To find events for a specific department requires navigating through many layers of interlinked static HTML pages. All information, including date-related links, are in prefabricated HTML files.

Events information must be submitted weekly (and ahead of time) to the web page maintenance crew in order to be placed into the intranet events calendar. The web site maintenance crew is responsible for laying out and updating the events information on all these static web pages.

The new solution embeds the ActiveX control on the Events Calendar page. The presentation is a very familiar metaphor of a calendar. At a glance, the user can determine the departments that have events posted for a particular month. The user can click on a date and obtain events details without leaving the web page.

The entire calendar system is on-line, with the actual departments handling the supply of events information. This increases the timeliness and correctness of the information and eliminates unnecessary delays.

Layer	Technologies
The Fundamental Layer	COM and DCOM (others: OLE-DS, OLE-DB, MTS, FALCON)
The Application Layer	ActiveX Controls
The Tools Layer	MFC, ATL

The fundamental technology layer is the slowest to evolve, and most resilient to change. Much of what COM is about today was designed over 5 years ago and has been implemented incrementally through the various version of Windows and OLE. The upper layers are more prone to change and obsolescence. They can change quite dynamically depending on customer reception and marketing requirements.

Taking the Events Calendar, we can see how ActiveX controls improves the situation for us.

How Has the System Improved?

Through the deployment of ActiveX technologies, we have:

Increased User Interactivity

The interaction with the end user is enhanced. Users are able to get more done with less navigation and less 'clicking around' in general. All intranet users experience shorter paths to the desired information.

Made Operation More Efficient

The model of information delivery which involved an intermediary (i.e. the Employee Directory Publishing Group; or the web page layout team for the Events Calendar) was improved by eliminating that intermediary.

Unlike the static pages, the employee directory is now maintained only at one central site. There's no longer a need to publish and maintain separately a large set of computer generated web pages on a periodic basis. This eliminated the tedious work that was carried out by the Employee Directory Publishing Group.

The calendar update process is now completely distributed. Each department providing events information is responsible for providing the `IATLDept` COM interface into the information system. As long as they honor this agreement, their events are automatically available for general user-perusal on the intranet.

Shifted Assets from Process to Technology

In a static site, a heavily process-based operation is evident. Events must be submitted weekly, web pages must be generated and custom edited, etc. With our final system, much of the process has been encapsulated in the automated application or eliminated altogether. This shifts the long-term asset base from the process itself to a technology base (the intranet software). A technology base asset is resilient to high staff turnover situations.

Caveats of Distributed Solutions

Seldom do we get something for nothing. In addition to the coding and design required to 'Activate' the web pages, there are some new subtle problems which are introduced into the new systems. These problems are typical systems problems encountered in migration from a centralized control environment to a distributed environment.

One such problem is the 'shared update' problem.

Let's illustrate an instance of this problem with our Aberdeen & Wilshire Calendar ActiveX control and the associated back-end COM data objects.

The Problem with Our Calendar

Recall that the calendar ActiveX control queries the ATLFinder object for the departments which have events, and then queries each department for the events that it has to offer. Now suppose that the data at the departments is actually updated 'live' while many people may be simultaneously accessing the event data.

What if, after ATLFinder has reported that the accounting department has three events on December 1, 1997, someone else from the accounting department then adds another event?

The ActiveX control has shown the user that there are 3 events available, but when the control goes to get the events details as the user clicks on the cell, there'll be 4 events available. What if, instead of someone adding an event, he or she has deleted one instead? What if all were deleted? The list goes on and on. The only way to eliminate these problems is to somehow restrict when changes can take place. If changes can only take place when nobody is accessing the system, everything will be fine.

Of course, complying with such restrictions may or may not be feasible, depending on the individual case. Another solution is to buffer the change, and only reflect the change when there will be no impact to the system. If you think this is starting to sound like transaction processing, you're absolutely right. Live updates to data can be performed without affecting simultaneous readers if both the reads and writes are encapsulated within a transaction. Transaction processing will allow the ActiveX control to get consistent data from the ATLFinder and ATLDept COM objects; it will also allow the events information update (writer) of the system to provide a consistent all-or-nothing image to the simultaneous read clients.

Beware of Systems with Distributed Updates

We'll have to solve the distributed update problem in cases where data from multiple related distributed data sources must be read and updated at the same time. In multiprocessing systems, this problem is solved by selectively locking the related data resources, ensuring only one executing context can have access to the resources at a given time. In distributed systems, this will almost always require transaction processing to solve the access problem, ensuring that each simultaneously executing entity always has a consistent non-corrupted view of the available data. In both cases, the design and testing requirements are going to be nontrivial.

Centralized Control Problem Never Goes Away

Just as it will always be easier to code single threaded programs than multithreaded ones, it will always be easier to design centralized solutions than distributed solutions. If you have only a single centralized database, the design problem will be significantly simpler than the distributed Events Calendar problem.

The only guideline here is to consider mapping your problem into a centralized control problem if at all possible. It's entirely legitimate and legal to deploy a logically centralized system using distributed computing technology such as DCOM.

For scalability and performance reasons, there may be no alternative but to make the data access logically distributed. In these cases, the Microsoft Transaction Server provides various facilities through its integration with the Active Platform (in particular the Active Server Pages) which may make the problem easier by solving some of the tougher problems in a generic fashion for your application.

Network Traffic and Interface Factoring

Without exception, given a problem with conflicting constraints, certain design tradeoffs have to be made. Dual interfaces allow access to COM objects via either **IDispatch** or vtable binding; most designers will design their vtable interfaces to be Automation-compliant in order to enjoy the best of all worlds. These objects can be accessed by scripting and macro languages such as VB Script, VBA, JAVAScript; rapid development environments such as Visual Basic 5 and Visual J++; and professional tools like Visual C++. And all in the most efficient calling manner. Unfortunately, in order to enjoy these benefits, the parameters passed in the methods and the data types of the properties allowed are limited to 'Automation' compatible types. The list of 'Automation'-compatible types is the same as the list of types that a **VARIANT** can assume.

In most cases, this doesn't pose any problem. However, in some situations, it may be more efficient to pass parameters using custom defined data structures instead of Automation data types. This approach sacrifices compatibility with Automation for gain in efficiency when exchanging data over the network.

In the future, Automation may be extended to support more complex data structures. Until then, the interface designer is forced to select between the widest range of compatibility and the highest performance. Of course, nothing would prevent an object from defining the Automation-compatible set of interfaces, plus an additional set of vtable compatible interfaces which transfer data via custom interfaces with user-defined data structures. The additional development required for the redundant capability may be justified in certain projects.

ActiveX Intranet Deployment Issues

With the downsizing trends and reduced IT budgets of the late 1990s, individuals involved in the design and deployment of intranet technologies have to deal with a set of tough issues which may not have been problems previously. The following is a quick coverage of the most common deployment issues one is most likely to encounter when activating an intranet.

The only fundamental assumption we've made, and a realistic one at that, is that the intranet engineer or consultant wasn't allowed to dispose of all the old system equipment and software; nor was he allowed to purchase a completely new hardware system to implement the intranet function. In rare cases where the intranet implementation is to be built completely from scratch for a brand-new organization, or an organization which has no computing history, some of the following may not apply.

Dealing with Legacy Systems

When dealing with legacy systems which are currently functioning perfectly, the most popular MIS strategies for introducing intranet technologies can be summed up as:

 Evolution, not revolution

 Coexistence, not replacement

 Embrace and extend, not displace

Not only are these points savvy political advice in most organizations, they also make the most business sense. 'Why fix it if it isn't broken?'

By coexisting with a proven legacy system, it will provide an opportune testing ground for the newer technology to prove itself as a more cost-effective alternative for the long term.

To coexist with hardware or software subsystems which are foreign to PC hardware (for example, mainframe or minicomputers), the best initial step is to provide a COM-based wrapping for external access. The actual implementation of the COM server can use whatever means to communicate with the legacy system (e.g. perhaps through Microsoft's SNA Server product). Once this wrapping is in place, it will allow the data from the legacy system to be accessed from the external system and/or allow the legacy system to participate in interacting with the component world.

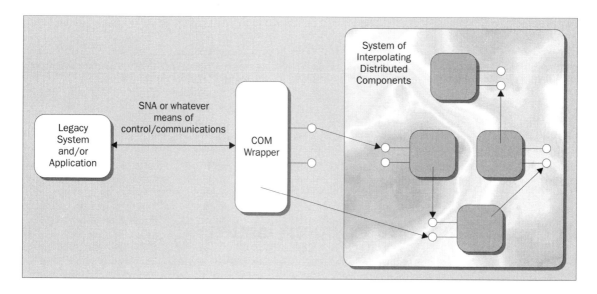

This is typically the way banking systems are interfaced to the Internet for 'online banking' applications. While this approach may first appear to be 'kludgy' to any object-oriented purists or distributed computing enthusiasts, it actually represents the most acceptable way to introduce intranet and distributed component technology to a legacy system. It also bears the best 'shortest time to observable benefits' when compared with other more aggressive alternatives.

In due time, the ability to interface to the component world should prove itself to be invaluable within the organization. In a search for more efficient and potentially lower cost operations, a second phase of the project may involve re-implementing certain performance-sensitive interfacing portions of the legacy system/application using PC hardware and ActiveX technology. This will be an opportune time to examine the legacy system as a whole, and plan out a longer-term strategy to migrate the system to robust PC-based hardware and component technology.

By phasing in the change over a significant period of time, each step displacing a small portion of the legacy solution, one can embrace the new component and distributed computing technologies without taking the culture shock, deployment risk, and instability associated with radical displacement alternatives.

Version Control for Distributed Components

Intranet users reaching a web page with an embedded ActiveX control, such as the Event Calendar control, run a distributed application which consists of a client portion (the OCX itself), and a server portion (the ATLFinder object). If your intranet consists of many such pages, each with its own set of client controls and supporting software, version control can become a problematic issue very quickly.

If we don't want the support hotline swamped with calls on why a certain web page doesn't work, then we must carefully plan for version control during deployment. One of the greatest helps in this area is the facility provided by Internet Explorer 3.01 for code download and installation. To embed an object (e.g. an ActiveX control) in an HTML page, the following tag is used:

```
<OBJECT ID="VcEmpDir11" WIDTH=399 HEIGHT=301
    CODEBASE=http://ocxmaster.abwil.com/Vccal.ocx#Version=0,1,0,1
    CLASSID="CLSID:4129D886-6256-11D0-9EE6-006052008075">
<PARAM NAME="_ExtentX" VALUE="10530">
    <PARAM NAME="_ExtentY" VALUE="7964">
    <PARAM NAME="_StockProps" VALUE="0">
</OBJECT>
```

The above HTML fragment will embed the Events Calendar control into a web page. The **CODEBASE** attribute specifies where the binary OCX is to be found. The component is downloaded from this location if and only if:

▲ The component is not available locally

or

▲ The copy of the component available is of an older version

By implementing the **CODEBASE** tag above, and keeping the latest up-to-date version of the OCX in a centralized server (**ocxmaster.abwil.com** in the above example) we can ensure that all users will be updated with the latest copy of the required OCX when they reach one of the intranet pages utilizing the ActiveX control.

Instead of pointing directly to an OCX file, the **CODEBASE** attribute can also point to a **.CAB** file. The **.CAB** file can contain compressed archives of multiple executables, libraries, and/or an installation **.INF** file. If an **.INF** file exists in the **.CAB** file, it will be used to install the OCX after the system de-archives the **.CAB** file and certifies its integrity.

Conventional means of installation and software tracking, such as facilities provided by the Microsoft System Management Server, can also be used in addition to or in lieu of the above described mechanism for version tracking of ActiveX control and intranet applications.

Supporting Heterogeneous Networks

If all machines in every organization were running Windows 95 or Windows NT, life would be very simple and Microsoft would be omnipresent. Fortunately (or unfortunately), most organizations are populated by islands of irregularly configured PCs, Macs, UNIX workstations, and assorted legacy machines. Developing an intranet effectively in a highly heterogeneous environment requires very careful analysis of the requirements and available resources.

Statistically speaking, the chances are that a majority of the network is either already on a PC or will be moving to PC technology shortly (since it's currently the most cost-effective platform for business computing). If this is the case, the ideal strategy would be to design the intranet with ActiveX-enabled pages which will 'degrade gracefully' for access from platforms which don't support ActiveX technologies.

This will allow a majority of the intranet users to enjoy the enhanced interactivity that the ActiveX interface offers while still permitting the non-Windows platforms to enjoy the benefits of the intranet.

With time, more and more platforms will be able to support ActiveX technologies. Microsoft has already made available versions of COM and the Internet Explorer for the Macintosh. DCOM for various flavors of UNIX will be available shortly from Software AG.

You should note, though, that even without ActiveX client support (for example, a Netscape browser on a Silicon Graphics workstation), server-based ActiveX technologies can be utilized for component-based intranet computing. Active Server Pages (ASP) allows controls to be used on the server to generate standard HTML that can be read on any browser.

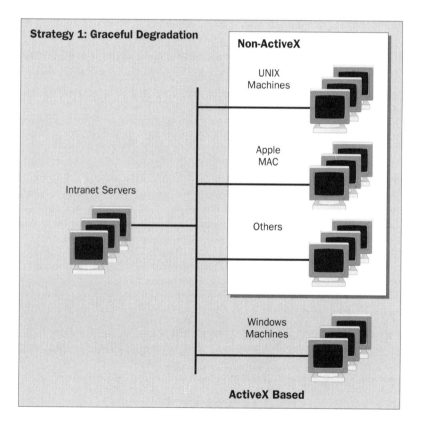

In some situations, it may be easier (or even required) to partition the intranet into an ActiveX capable portion and a non-ActiveX capable portion. To avoid doing everything twice in such a situation, the design should attempt to reuse as much server-based data and computing resources as possible.

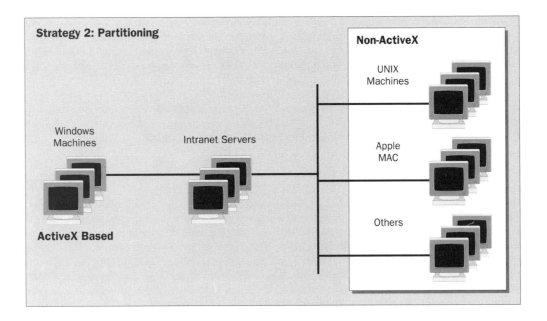

The following table lists some of the technologies that we've covered in this book, and how they may or may not apply to the various popular client computing platforms.

Technology/Product	Windows 95/NT	Apple MAC	UNIX Workstation	Others
Internet Explorer	Yes	Yes	No	No
VBScript	Yes	Yes	No	No
JAVAScript	Yes	via Netscape	via Netscape	via Netscape
ActiveX Control (visual)	Yes	soon	No	No
ActiveX Control (nonvisual)	Yes	Yes	soon (Software AG)	soon (Software AG)
IIS with ASP	Yes	Yes	Yes	Yes
ADC	Yes	No	No	No
OLE-DS	Yes	No	Interoperate	Interoperate
COM/DCOM	Yes	Yes (COM)	soon (Software AG)	soon (Software AG)

Working with All Network Transports

TCP/IP is the universal networking protocol for Internet and intranet operations. All machines on one or more TCP/IP networks may be connected together with routers to form larger networks statically or dynamically. Intranets may have segments of network which may or may not be running TCP/IP for various reasons. If these segments are using IPX/SPX (Novell-based) or NETBIOS, it's possible to design intranet solutions for these segments of network using DCOM technology. Note that it's also possible to configure the network to run TCP/IP alongside these protocols on the same network card. If it's absolutely impossible to provide TCP/IP (perhaps due to machine or physical network constraints), it may still be possible to implement the intranet applications. Without TCP/IP, it won't be possible to provide web browser type services which rely on HTTP running over TCP/IP.

Instead, custom applets may be constructed which will start the intranet application. For example, to provide the Events Calendar for a machine on a NETBIOS only segment, we can create a small Visual Basic application which simply has a form with the ActiveX control embedded.

Use and Reuse of Expertise

Intranet designers and consultants aren't usually hired to wreak havoc in an organization. So that one doesn't disturb the harmonious order of things, one must be ready to use the expertise and human resources available in the implementation plans of the intranet. Training will be necessary, but a planned and gradual transition will have a much better chance of succeeding for the long term.

In any case, one has to be ready to deal with a variety of designers fluent in structured design, COBOL programmers, BASIC programmers, etc. Fortunately, there's enough room in the contemporary component-based computing tool sets to accommodate everybody.

The focus should be to use the expertise of these individuals in the construction of the intranet immediately. At the same time, training for Internet- and intranet-based technology should commence. Bear in mind the following table of possible scenarios for using expertise:

Existing Expertise	Expertise Reuse	Training Plan
Structural Design Experts	An individual component (for example, a business rule component) can be structurally designed internally —all that's needed is a COM-based outer wrapper (this can be done by the consultant independently).	Train immediately in object-oriented design, special focus on component technology and distributed computing.
COBOL Programmers	MicroFocus COBOL can be used to build COM servers directly. This is the fastest and most rewarding way to give a taste of component-based computing.	Training in component technology and distributed computing. Additional training in Visual Basic or Java.
BASIC or FORTRAN Programmers	Use Visual Basic 5 to design and develop ActiveX controls, both server- and client-side, immediately.	Additional training in VB5. Training in component technology (COM) and distributed computing.
SmallTalk or other OO Environment Programmers	Design and prototype in Visual J++ to create ActiveX components or Java applets immediately.	Additional training in Visual J++. Training in COM and DCOM.
C Programmers	Create business rule-based ActiveX components using C-based framework immediately.	Training in object-oriented design and C++. Training in COM and DCOM. Training in Win32 programming if not already fluent.

Existing Expertise	Expertise Reuse	Training Plan
Web Master and HTML Designer	Create pages incorporating new IE3 features and embedded ActiveX controls immediately.	No training necessary, just familiarization with IE3 specifics.

With the wide scope of distributed component computing, enabled by ActiveX technologies, no one in the organization needs to be left out of the excitement of building a new intranet. Involving existing staff and crews in building the new infrastructure benefits all parties; their experience with the local culture and domain expertise will provide invaluable contributions to the project, on top of the applicable expertise that they have to offer.

Protecting Against Changes In Object/Component Technology

Predicting which company and what particular technology may be popular next year is akin to predicting a shift in the weather. Nobody knows for sure what will happen. In this unforgiving environment, how can one MIS manager or consultant attain the confidence to recommend a Microsoft specific solution, a COM-based solution, or a PC-based solution?

It isn't as tough as it may sound. First, our only assumption: with the increasing global competition and shifting international business culture, the motto 'do more with less' will stay with us for the foreseeable future. Given this urgency to be more effective and efficient, software development from scratch for each project will not be a viable or competitive alternative. The only software technology which offers proven and effective software reuse, without sacrificing flexibility, has been component-based technology. This makes component-based software reuse a sure thing. From a hardware perspective, the emergence of extremely powerful commodity (low priced) PC platforms, and availability of new fault-tolerant clustering technology for these platforms, will make them a sure thing too.

However, given component-based software reuse, we still have a couple of viable vehicles. There's ActiveX/COM and OpenDoc/CORBA. If all you will ever deal with is Microsoft-based desktops and servers, the choice is clear and simple. If you have UNIX-based legacy systems, very large system requirements, mainframe connections, then OpenDoc/CORBA is an alternative.

The best strategy to deal with this situation is to design the components and architecture such that it is as independent as possible from the final deployment technology. This is actually quite possible, given the tremendous similarity between ActiveX/COM and OpenDoc/CORBA. There'll always be some 'edge' glue code which must be coded in a vehicle specific manner; minimizing this glue will ensure that the core logic will remain and be reusable should the trend of the day change.

Given the market share of Microsoft on both the desktop and applications server market, ActiveX/COM is actually a very safe bet. The increasing availability of COM/DCOM implementation on UNIX, mainframe and mini-computer platforms, and the delivery of DCOM technology and products will further push Microsoft to deliver actual working code for this critical area in a timely manner.

One additional, relatively new language that's worth serious consideration is Java. Business rule components developed in Java can be made to adapt easily to either COM or CORBA. Not only is it an ideal development language and environment for reusable software components, the intense competition between various vendors of compiler and development environments will ensure a succession of great products for years to come.

Visual C++ 5.0, the Power Programmer's Tool for Intranet ActiveX

To reap the best that ActiveX has to offer, there's no need to switch development environment or language. Visual C++ 5.0 remains the ideal programming tool for ActiveX development. The rich heritage of evolution behind Visual C++ 5.0 and its associated MFC 4.21 library guarantees a lead time that would make it difficult for other tools and platforms to catch up. The wide adoption and licensing for the MFC library also guarantees wide third party tool and add-on support for the library.

How friendly is Visual C+ 5.0 to intranet and ActiveX development? Well, let's list the ways:

MFC and Wizards for Building OCX and Visually Oriented ActiveX Controls Painlessly

We've seen how easy it was to create powerful, functional, and lightweight visual ActiveX controls using the MFC and Wizards. ActiveX controls can be fabricated which draw their own user interface completely, or make use of an assortment of native Windows controls and ActiveX controls to carry out their own operations. MFC support means we have access to many, many interfaces which are implemented by tested MFC code without us having to rewrite the tedious code.

Support for OC96 Optimization Simplifies Windowless or Nonrectangular Controls

New support in MFC for the OC96 optimizations makes support for these implementations (almost) as easy as clicking a checkbox in the ActiveX Control Wizard. Support for optimized drawing, windowless activation and inactive control in the **COleControl** class makes implementation of the new interfaces and functionality straightforward.

Support for Internet Extension of OC96

Visual C++ 5.0 and MFC 4.21 also support the Internet extension of the OC96 specifications. Asynchronous download of properties and code is made possible through support for URL Monikers within the MFC class hierarchy. The new **CPathProperty** can be used to retrieve URL-based properties which will load incrementally in an asynchronous manner. This feature is extremely useful when large properties (i.e. a graphics file) are loaded across a slow-link network (e.g. the Internet).

Native Client Support for 'Low Surface Area' Applications with No 'Code-Bloat'

Visual C++ 5.0 now supports smart pointers which are system types **_com_ptr_t**, **_variant_t**, and **_bstr_t**. Through the use of these types, plus new **#import** and **_declspec** constructs, it's possible to write COM client code with very small code sizes. The model of operation is quite elegant. Client COM code can be written which treats COM objects as almost native 'built-in' C/C++ types. This is in stark contrast to typical C based or C++ based COM code which consists of a large number of include files, wrapper classes, prototypes, etc. Furthermore, the implementation of a smart pointer makes it unnecessary to call **AddRef()** and **Release()** on interfaces as long as all your interface manipulations are performed through the smart pointer type. Smart pointers handle vtable interfaces with the same ease as Automation interfaces. Internally generated wrapper class code is hidden from the programmer. For all intents and purposes, the compiler appears to know about and support COM objects natively.

MFC and Wizard-Based Automation Support, as Easy as Calling C++ Library Functions

The ClassWizard automatically generates wrapper classes for automation interfaces based on type library information. Once these wrapper classes are generated, invoking a method or accessing a property through Automation interfaces is exactly the same as calling regular C++ library functions. These wrappers make the traditionally tedious procedure of making an **IDispatch** call extremely simple.

ATL 2.1 to Create 'Lean-and-Mean' COM Servers in Any Form: In-Proc, Local, or NT Service

ATL is a completely separate, template-based class library for building very light COM servers. ATL-based ActiveX controls can even be free from C runtime routines. MFC-based controls simply can't be compared with ATL. Though MFC is great for constructing visual ActiveX controls, because of its default implementation and support for many required interfaces, the ATL provides minimal support for visual controls. ATL is ideal for creating custom, nonvisual, ActiveX controls which are light and can be used in both server and client context. ATL ActiveX controls can be in-proc server, local server, or an NT service. All threading models are supported including apartment, free threaded, and both.

Simple Dual Interface Support

ATL-based COM servers can support dual interface simply by clicking a box during the generation of the skeleton code. Even MFC-based Automation interfaces created by the ActiveX Control Wizard can be retrofitted to support dual interfaces.

Use Data Source and Data-Aware ActiveX Controls in Creating New Controls

The professional version of Visual C++ 5.0 comes with the Remote Data Control, which you can use to bind other data-aware controls in a form for access to a SQL Server 6.5 data source. The technique of combining ActiveX controls in the building of an ActiveX control greatly simplifies the creation of controls which access data. All the control drawing, update code, together with all the data access and management code, are reused from prefabricated components. The ActiveX control implementer simply provides the glue code and the constituent ActiveX controls take care of the rest.

Create Your Own Data-Aware Controls Bound to Data Source for ADC or RDO Operation Today

MFC 4.21 comes with the addition of several new member functions to the **CWnd** class, which provide support for data binding with data source controls. These include the Remote Data Control and the Advanced Data Control. With these new member functions, it's possible to write a control which binds to remote data. For example, you can create a bar graph control which fluctuates with the change in value of a specific database field.

A Powerful Language Tool to 'Tap' into the ActiveX Client/Platform Stack at Any Level

With Visual C++, it's possible to program ActiveX features at as low a level as raw Win32 API, or at as high a level as some MFC abstract implementations. There's no restriction on what one can do, what one can override, or what one can modify. The raw access capability gives peace-of-mind that one can optimize or hand-tune code to be as efficient as possible, without some uncontrollable runtime getting in the way.

Go Down to the Protocol Level

Visual C++ allows the programming of intranet application on top of the raw WinINET API (Internet extension to Win32), but also support WinINET programming through a set of thin MFC wrapper classes. If an intranet application requires direct use of HTTP, Gopher or FTP protocols, WinINET allows full flexibility in operating with these protocols.

MFC-Based DocObject Support

Creating a DocObject server is as simple as marking a checkbox during the code generation of the AppWizard. DocObject allows applications (which can save a document to disk) to provide in-place activation capability in a web browser or the Microsoft Office Binder application. The DocObject document can be the target of a hyperlink, in which case documents can be linked to from a web page. For example, a page on the intranet may refer to a custom report which may link to a DocObject whose server is a custom application written by you.

Although not required, most DocObjects make use of compound documents for storage, and can be activated 'at storage'. As a matter of fact, one can create a DCOM server that supports DocObjects for the sole purpose of controlled remote activation. In this case, if we want to run an instance of MyObject (which produces **.M5** files) on the node **\\AWNODE**, we can create a File Moniker to **\\AWNODE\MyDoc.M5** and bind to it. If the MyObject class actually has no persistent data, the compound file can remain empty besides the identifying CLSID for the server.

The Ultimate Flexibility in Code Reuse

Code reuse can be realized on a multilevel basis when using Visual C++. Notice that each level of code reuse has a different scope and is more suitable for code reuse under specific contexts.

Source/Language Level Code Reuse

This is very simple—the subroutine level code reuse.

In addition, Visual C++ also supports macro level code reuse through the macro preprocessor. For example, MFC makes use of many macros to handle its message map mechanism.

Visual C++ 5.0 also supports template-level code reuse. As a matter of fact, both the Active Template Library and the Standard Template Library are a set of highly useful utility template classes to facilitate code reuse. Both ATL and STL are included as standard features of Visual C++ 5.0.

Binary/Link Level Code Reuse

Binary libraries in `.LIB` files can be reused during the linking phase of compilation. Code reused in this manner is linked into the executable code. It's also possible to reuse code at the link level through dynamically linked libraries. This is the popular DLL scheme where the code is maintained in shared libraries and not linked into the executable. Instead, the executable will load an image of the library at runtime in order to make use of its service.

Binary/Component Level Code Reuse

Of course, component level code reuse is what this book is all about. With the facilities provided by Visual C++, COM-based code reuse is as natural as source-level or link-level code reuse. Visual C++ code can be bundled in a self-contained COM server and be reused across environments by Visual Basic and Visual J++, or across networks by a UNIX-based client.

The Great Rewards

As professional Visual C++ developers, we've never been at a more fortunate juncture. The time and investment we've vested into the ramp-up of C++, Windows, and MFC now pays off real dividends when we can whip up high-demand, efficient, production-quality ActiveX controls using Visual C++ 5.0 in record time. The code libraries and routines that we've painstakingly built during our careers can now be wrapped in the COM wrapping and be readily reused in a whole new world of distributed component computing, or simply inside ActiveX controls for an entirely new market.

As alternative development platforms for ActiveX controls, such as Visual Basic 5.0 or Visual J++ proliferate, so will the demand for tight, efficient, and powerful libraries and components to facilitate access to the native capability of the hosting operating system. These libraries and components represent new development and product opportunities for Visual C++ veterans. No matter what the doomsayers chant, or how many programmer defections to Java the statistics may show, the fundamental fact remains that as long as the core operating system and support libraries continue to be created in C/C++, the demand for Visual C++ expertise will continue to rise.

Microsoft: Friend or Foe?

Any analysts or designers working in the industry for a decade or more will realize that the evolution of popular computing is largely independent of exactly which corporation may be ruling the day. It's entirely analogous to a country in financial or internal crisis, in which case the actual politician elected becomes more of an actor on the stage. Regardless of whichever party may be elected, the same set of critical decisions will be made in the same way. The delivery will be different, but the end result will be the same.

The software industry as a whole is powered by the collective of creative individual talents working within it. A large portion of this talent pool will move to different environments depending on the available opportunities. Independent of the corporations which they may be employed in at the current time, the long-term evolution of computing follows a relatively stable, predictable evolutionary path.

Adopting this viewpoint, what Microsoft may be attempting to do with ActiveX today is in essence no different to what UNIX vendors may have done with the TCP/IP suite and OpenDoc/CORBA if they had the majority platform today.

The Big "Who's On Next?" Question

What we're saying here is that the answer to the 'Who's on next?' question isn't important at all. Whoever it may be, whenever it may be, the time for truly distributed computing and component-based code reuse has come, and these technologies are here to stay.

There are turbulent times ahead, some might say; but it really depends upon how you want to see it: if you're a journalist looking for a sensational story for next month's column then yes, turbulent times may well be coming. For the rest of us, most of us who have suffered through the slings and arrows of DOS, UNIX, and now the Windows family, life goes on as usual. The facts remains, as the computing world plunges into distributed computing and component-based code reuse, that:

 Microsoft's COM technology is the most accessible, immediately deployable, large-scale tested alternative available today.

If software components are carefully designed and crafted, such that the dependence on the 'ActiveX bandwagon' is kept to the interfacing mechanics (as in adopting only the COM portion of the ActiveX model), then these components will easily weather the test of time and shifting component standards.

It really doesn't matter if Microsoft should lose favor with the world tomorrow (which, according to accumulated business wisdom, it is indeed hard to see): the investment in design, problem solving, and even coding, can be completely preserved.

Component-Based Computing for the Next Millennium

From client-server to multi-tiered component-based computing, from a centralized time-shared systems to the completely distributed systems, computing technologies go through cyclic swings of trendy architectures. Whether the computing platforms of tomorrow will be client-fat/server-thin or client-thin/server-fat actually matters less than the press sometimes makes out. The bottom line is that truly distributed, component-based computing is finally here. Its arrival heralds a new era of computing, where the network adds great value to a wave of new applications which will, in time, take full advantage of the amazing connectivity. The manifestation of this phenomenon within the enterprise is what we've come to recognize as the intranet. We are, indeed, at the very infancy of distributed component-based computing. What is yet to come will both amaze us and provide us with invaluable new services for the corporate communications infrastructure.

The evolution of office computing has closely followed the evolution of general computing. Mainframes and minicomputers gave way to microcomputers. Centralized timesharing systems gave way to powerful networked workstations. The popularity of the Internet has catapulted component technologies and multitiered and distributed computing into the forefront, quickly eclipsing the popularity of traditional client-server designs.

In this appendix we look at the motivation behind distributed interactive applications. These applications may include, for example, interdepartmental communications and information publishing using applied Internet technologies. We'll introduce the concept of an intranet, and describe why it will inevitably become a very important conduit for the ongoing evolution of office automation and interdepartmental communications. We showcase the tremendous leverage possible by harnessing the critical mass achieved on the Internet, and applying the leading edge technologies back in the higher speed, lower security risk environment of the office intranet. We'll also cover typical intranet (network-LAN/WAN) topologies.

Aberdeen & Wilshire's web site will be available online over the Internet for experimentation and feedback from readers. To try out the site for yourself, simply point your browser to:

`http://www.abwil.com/`

Evolution from Client-Server

To set the background for our discussions, I'll briefly recap the history of business computing and networking.

An Historical Perspective

If you've lived through the early computing days of the 60s and early 70s, you'll be familiar with the completely centralized style of computing offered by mainframe computers. Since the cost of these early machines was considerable, computing was typically done non-interactively. 'Jobs' for the computers were created by programmers, and submitted in a batch by operators into the central computer for processing. This was usually done via magnetic tape or punched cards. Due to this centralization, management of computing assets (both software and hardware) was simple.

The 70s brought with them the minicomputers which an individual business or division could own and operate in house. The typical computing style was through 'dumb terminals' connecting to the minicomputer. The connection was usually made through a proprietary communications link or through some form of point-to-point networking technology. Each user 'time-shared' the computing power of the minicomputer. The flexible UNIX operating system came into vogue during this decade. This phase of computing evolution also saw the decentralization of control over computing resources and computing assets. Departments and/or subsidiaries which could afford their own minicomputer started to accumulate and acquire assets specific to their needs and business activities. Corporate-wide management of computing assets became increasingly difficult. However, since the 'bread and butter' business information was still typically stored in headquarter mainframes there was, on the face of it, no urgent need to 'straighten out the situation'.

The 80s heralded in the decade of the PC revolution. First came the 'super-micro' replacement for the minicomputer. It ran the same UNIX (or other multiuser) operating system, but cost much less. It was a kind of 'el-cheapo' mini. Timeshared interaction through inexpensive serial connections to dumb terminals was still the main style of operation. However, as PCs became more widely available and economical, they quickly supplanted the dumb terminals. Users could run a terminal emulator program as an application on their PC, and connect to the 'time share' server over the serial link and/or a network. When not connected via terminal emulation, the PC could still be used to run a variety of office applications. These office applications either were not formerly available, or they were available only through a restrictive, text based, terminal emulation interface.

Marketplace critical mass on the PC was achieved in the mid-80s. An unbelievable proliferation of practical PC software, reflective of the tremendous pent-up creative energy in the developer community, swamped the software market. Soon, office users found that they could do more on their PC outside of terminal emulation sessions, than they could within them. With a powerful computer on every corporate desktop, the volume and variety of computing and data management functions and operations grew exponentially. To add fuel to the fire, an auxiliary market of low cost Local Area Networking hardware exploded, and there were expertly pitched promises of cost-effective sharing of expensive peripherals and a bright future for 'group collaborative software'. Irresistibly, the corporate world embraced LANs and the 'groupware' vision. Soon, they were all connected up in one way or another. Corporate-wide management of computing assets, and control of computing resources, suddenly became a nightmare. This was the decade of the bloated MIS departments, struggling to control and make sense of the diversity of 'islands of computers', 'islands of technology' and 'islands of knowledge' built up independently within the organization.

If you can't beat them, join them. The MIS awakening of the early 90s reflected this sentiment precisely. The decentralization of corporate MIS functions became inevitable. The catchphrase often heard among management consultants during the late 80s and early 90s was 'client-server'. This terminology chimes nicely of compromise and coexistence: the 'client' on the PCs that the satellite departments love so much, and the 'server' on the adorable mainframe that belongs to the MIS bigwigs. Ironically, panicking MIS directors had created a booming market for management consultants, and there were simply too many conflicting schools of thought as to the exact meaning of 'client-server'.

The continual increase in PC computational power also didn't help in this regard. Soon it appeared that the 'client' sitting on the corporate desktop was more powerful than the heavily loaded server that it relied on for service. Meanwhile, many of the promised benefits of the local area networks were being delivered by the application software vendors. Users were sharing disks, CD-Roms, printers, modems, and doing group scheduling right on their desktop PCs. Mainframes were relegated to the archiving of consolidated business data, batch processing of high volume data and execution of complex or badly designed legacy business software too costly to recode for other computing platforms. The MIS function itself within an enterprise had also started to become more distributed and less centralized. The former middle level MIS personnel were finding themselves at unemployment line-ups in droves during the harsh and cruel restructuring and downsizing exercise of the mid 1990s.

Rise of the Internet

While all this was going on within the business enterprise, things weren't standing still outside of the business circle. What's most significant to us is the tremendous rise in popularity of the Internet. In one sentence, the Internet is the wholesale civilian deployment of network technologies and network infrastructure originally developed for defense and scientific use. Without rehashing the obvious, the Internet can be viewed as the computer network which links all Internet users together. For the brief moment in time when you dial into your ISP (Internet Service Provider), you become one node on this giant network. Typically, any node on the network can communicate to any other node. This gives a bewildering array of possible interactions and application opportunities akin to the colorful and complex human world behind the PC terminals.

Client-server pundits claim credit for the client-server nature of many Internet applications. In reality, the fabric of the Internet goes significantly further than anything the client-server following could have planned for. Some of them may have a client-server like architecture, while others are more peer to peer in nature. Starting off with a tested suite of applications from its TCP/IP origin, Internet users immediately enjoy email, newsgroup discussions, information retrieval through Gopher or the World Wide Web, file transfer through FTP, information search through WAIS, etc. On top of these traditional applications, more and more exciting new ones are being invented by the day. We now have audio and video broadcast, information push technologies, interactive shopping and commerce technologies, interactive gaming, online magazines, video and audio phone and conferencing technologies, with many, many more to come.

What Is an Intranet?

According to business analysts, the use of the public Internet reached critical mass during the mid-1990s. What this means is that there will be a replay of the tremendous growth, creativity, and opportunities explosion we witnessed during the PC revolution of the 80s. This movement will be felt by the population at large, and not just the corporate world. A tremendous number of innovative developments in the area of entertainment, electronic commerce, and information publishing are already taking place. What's important to us is that there will be opportunity to use the new tools, leverage the creativity, and harness much of the exciting new hardware and software technologies for practical use within our business computing world.

This is one very important dimension of an intranet:

> **An intranet harnesses the technologies of the Internet for productive use within the corporate computing network.**

Here's an attempt at a definition:

> **An intranet is the network and the communication paths which connect all the computing devices together, on a permanent, temporary or roaming (dynamic) basis, within a company; and the application software which make use of these connections.**
>
> **This can include existing email, news or bulletin systems. The network definition is not restricted to data communications but also communications by voice, or by video.**
>
> **The intranet offers end-users immediate and ubiquitous access to timely business-relevant information (from almost anywhere, not just through some custom applications). It provides a more approachable and accessible way to access the intellectual assets of a company.**

Of course, there isn't a commonly agreed upon definition for an intranet because it's still a rapidly evolving entity: it's one of the fastest growth areas in the computer industry at the moment. The large, enthusiastic Internet community is providing the world's largest beta site to put new and promising software and technology through its paces. Adopting tested and proven technologies (and some exciting new ones) from the Internet world, the intranet gives the good old corporate network a brand new lease of life, and a rather dynamic one at that.

Reality of a Competitive Marketplace

Along with the aggressive restructuring and downsizing of companies, in response to a more competitive global business environment, the mainstream IS strategy of the early 1990s has shifted from obtaining business value from proprietary technology to one of buying the most cost-effective off-the-shelf solution; and from sizable investment in in-house expertise to massive outsourcing of nonvital functions. In this new business climate, the deployment of existing, widely available, inexpensive, and effective technologies to solve business problems has become a way of life.

The prevailing mentality during this era is 'Why build if you can buy?', reflecting the significant cost involved in building and sustaining custom-built solutions. The intranet and the availability of prepackaged solutions is a match made in heaven. The innovative momentum of the Internet supplies the intranet designer with a virtually unlimited supply of new technologies for solving specific business problems: anything from completely built and tested, ready-to-customize solution frameworks, to individual generically reusable software components. The wholesale participation in this arena from major software vendors such as Microsoft, IBM/Lotus, Netscape, ORACLE, etc. endorses this cost-effective problem-solving approach.

Characteristics of the Intranet

Given that global connectivity and uninhibited interaction characterizes the Internet, what characterizes the intranet? We now know that, physically, the intranet is simply the same network that was installed in the department during the late 80s networking boom, so what makes it different today?

The simple answer is: the software that's available.

While the vendors who were selling networking hardware and providing networking operating systems were making incremental progress developing their proprietary solutions, great progress was made on the open standards based Internet. The most important developments were the gradual standardization and wide scale deployment of several fundamental protocols. Mainly emanating from the TCP/IP suite, the fundamental protocols included SMTP (mail), NNTP (news), FTP (file transfer), TELNET (remote terminal access), GOPHER (text based information access), and of course HTTP (web).

Once these protocols were agreed upon, they provided a standard way for one computer to talk to another regardless of their hardware, operating system, or configuration. These standards provided a solid platform for software developers to start creating the groupware products that they had promised back in the 80s.

Another major contributor to the making of the intranet's 'personality' is Moore's law of hardware doubling processing power every 18 months, coupled with the maturing of the memory manufacturing process (dramatically reducing memory pricing). This provided powerful platforms upon which software with rich interactions can be developed, placing unprecedented processing and storage power at the client access station. Unlike the character-oriented, manually navigated system typical of the original early days (70s and 80s) Internet, today's intranet boasts applications which provide powerful point-and-click, drag-and-drop graphical interfaces (and very soon intelligent agents and speech recognition), dramatically changing the way we carry out network computing tasks.

Leveraging Technology from the Internet

Many of the existing and proven Internet based technologies can be applied immediately within an enterprise network context without any complex adaptations. For example, an SMTP/POP based email system from the Internet can serve as a corporate email system; FTP servers can be set up for remote retrieval of files from repositories; a set of discussion forums can be set up on a Internet news server; and of course, web pages may be created and information disseminated using an Internet web server. The server and client software required to implement most of these services can be downloaded directly from the Internet.

Most of the core elements of these TCP/IP services have been tested on the Internet for well over a decade on a world-wide basis, and provide a robust foundation to build business solutions upon. In some situations, simple deployment of prefabricated Internet servers within the enterprise network is sufficient. However, in most cases, a significant amount of configuration and customization will be necessary to meet business requirements more precisely. The end user of the corporate Intranet will need to work directly with an application which solves his or her problem, instead of trying to learn how to use a set of Internet utilities. While presenting an application-specific interface to the user, the customized intranet applications could be using all the Internet protocols and services behind the scenes to get the job done.

Along with the great leverage we can obtain from existing and emerging Internet technology, an intranet can combine the best from the Internet with portions of the workhorse legacy client-server systems already existing in the enterprise network to create the most cost-effective solution.

Physical Network Requirements

To leverage on the available Internet technologies fully, an existing corporate network must have the following fundamental qualities in order to build a corporate intranet:

- The network should be TCP/IP capable (NETBIOS and Novell based networks can be retrofitted to coexist with TCP/IP)

- Departmental networks should be interconnected to the enterprise network through a Wide Area Network or leased lines

- Storage (files, etc.) and computing (database, mail) servers should be available via this enterprise network

- The network should be ubiquitously available to all corporate users (i.e. every corporate PC should be able to access resources on the enterprise network), including (potentially) remote access telecommuters

The following diagram illustrates a typical corporate network that meets these criteria.

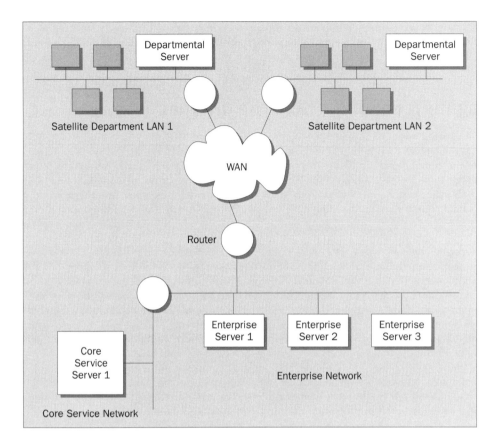

The two departmental LANs are connected to the enterprise network at the headquarters through the Wide Area Network (WAN). Each of the two departmental LANs hosts its own server. Any PC on the satellite LAN in this configuration has access to all of the servers on the departmental and enterprise network. This is true with the exception of the Core Service Servers on the Core Service Network. Servers on this network are accessible directly only by machines which are physically on the enterprise network. Controlled data access from the satellite networks can be provided if the enterprise servers on the enterprise network make requests to Core Service Servers on behalf of the satellite client.

Internet versus Intranet

Now that we know what the Internet and intranet have in common, let's take a look at how they differ.

Predictability of Topology

In the enterprise, the topology of the network is typically well planned and completely predictable. Even in cases where islands of individual LANs have built up, it can be connected to form a controlled, predictable intranet. On the Internet, other than the core backbone conduit carrying the traffic across countries and continents, the rest of the network topology is in a constant flux.

A lot more engineering and planned growth can be done in a network with relatively predictable topology, usage, and traffic requirements (like an intranet) rather than a completely unpredictable and dynamic network (like the Internet).

Network Robustness and Dependability

By design, you can make an intranet arbitrarily robust and dependable. You can accomplish this through physical redundant replication of services across servers that are geographically separated, and redundant allocation of network paths to vital resources. While this sort of planning is possible on a site-by-site basis over the Internet, robustness and dependability in terms of services over the Internet is much more of an art than a science. It's worthwhile mentioning, though, that TCP/IP (underlying the Internet) as a network routing protocol is itself quite robust when it comes to a large dispersed network surviving a major disaster in geographically isolated areas.

Access Security

Security is a top concern on the Internet. The fact that every computer on the Internet is connected to every other one gives the criminally minded a fertile field to exploit. Couple this with the typical scenario of naïve users accessing the Internet using a general purpose PC containing vital and essential business or personal information, and you have thousands of security disaster stories waiting to happen.

The corporate intranet, being a more planned and controlled environment isolated from the public Internet, is less of a security concern. Security is still an issue within the enterprise, however, to guard against leakage of trade secrets and damage sustained from disgruntled employees. Regardless, the intranet usually isn't subjected to the security threats possible over the public Internet. There's also more funding commitment and administrative effort to deter and install measures against such threats.

Speed of Access

Most users access the Internet through relatively slow analog modems having 28.8, 33.6, or 57.6Kbps transfer rate. Even if the cable modems or ISDN become commonplace in the future, the typical Internet access rate will still be limited to one or two hundred kilobits per second. Most corporate users, however, access the intranet through 10Mbps or higher LAN-based connections. The high speed access available for the intranet makes the size of program or data file transferred during an interactive session less important, and provides a viable platform for the deployment of multimedia messaging and conferencing.

Scope of Access

The Internet connects all the individuals of the world, inside and outside of the enterprise. The intranet connects the organization/enterprise and all the individuals within it. It's also possible to build links (gateways) between intranets to link suppliers with their customers, etc. However, the intranet is usually restricted to individuals belonging to the organization/enterprise.

What Can I Do with an Intranet?

Since an intranet is usually formed from an existing corporate network, the functionality and features of a typical intranet can be roughly divided into two areas:

 Legacy functionality/features

 Enhanced and new functionality/features

The following sections explore these two general areas of intranet functions further. Almost all intranets in existence will embrace the legacy functions, while the enhanced and new functionality are selectively deployed by the MIS department.

Legacy Intranet Functionality

These are the traditional capabilities and features that we've adopted LAN and client-server for. They include:

- File sharing between users
- Printer and other device sharing across the network
- Email
- Custom legacy client-server applications (i.e. database server applications)

These are existing applications that were working fine before the intranet was introduced and will continue to be used until a more functional or attractive intranet alternative becomes available.

Enhanced and New Intranet Features

These are new capabilities and features that are available only upon the introduction of the intranet. In general, they provide more instantaneous and richer interaction between the information source and the user of the information.

Enhanced Email

Traditional email is limited to text based messaging. The enhancements provided by multimedia messaging standards provide the capability to send and receive messages and attachments in pictures, voice/audio, and video. While the availability of voice and video mail may be constrained by the current hardware, the capability to send web-based links, pointers to documents on the intranet, or securely encrypted messages is available immediately.

On-Demand Information Retrieval via Web-Based Navigation

Once the majority of departments have published relevant information using web technology over the intranet, a new intranet user will be able to reap the benefit of 'information at the finger tip'. Surfing through the intranet, the user will gain knowledge of the company's mission, organization, its people, the services that it provides, plus specific information pertaining to individual departments. For the employee to gain the same information without the intranet would have required substantial investment in time and research.

Free-Form Discussion Groups

The Internet newsgroup technology is a tested and proven effective way to leverage the intellectual resources of a collective group (such as a corporation). Through the strategic deployment and management of a mixture of free-formed and moderated forums, an organization can benefit from the productive exchange of information and ideas between employees without exposing the forum technology to potential abuse.

Instant Information Publishing

Taking advantage of the web paradigm, information in the form of new web pages can be made available to other users in the intranet (in either a controlled access, or uncontrolled manner) instantaneously.

Rapid Development and Deployment of Custom Applications Based on Component Technology

New 'software component' based application building tools are being introduced by major software vendors. These tools and components are built to be intranet friendly from day one. Even complex business applications may be constructed from a combination of web page design, software scripting, reuse and development of distributed software components. The exact nature of these new applications may be diversified, but what they have in common is that they all provide user interface through the 'universal client' or browser, and they all leverage the ubiquitous connectivity provided by the corporate intranet.

Alternative Point-to-Point and Multipoint Communications

An online chat program can allow two parties to converse in real time over the intranet. This can be an effective way to supplement normal telephone conversations. With the new 'shared whiteboards', 'application sharing', and network-meeting technologies from vendors such as Microsoft, Netscape, and Intel, it's possible to share the working desktop, including a document and/or application directly over the intranet. This encourages frequent interchange of ideas, and effectively eliminates the need for some face-to-face meetings, reducing costs both in terms of travel expense and time lost. This same technology also allows team collaboration, regardless of geographical location, for running projects across the intranet.

The above general categories barely scratch the surface of the possibilities enabled by an intranet. What we're interested in is the fifth point made above: the rapid development and deployment of custom applications based on component technology. COM and ActiveX form just such a component technology, and they are the subject of this book.

However, in general, the Internet can provide a means of interaction between departments and/or individuals which can be more flexible (live or queued), more traceable (logging and journalizing), and accessible (right from every desktop). Typically, any established processes and procedures which require interaction between individuals and involve the circulation of forms or documents can be further streamlined by deployment of intranet based technologies.

How Does an Intranet Work?

The simplest way to find out how an intranet works is to examine the interacting software components operating on a typical intranet. On the desktop, we have a simple to use 'universal client'. This client talks to a network of multitiered, inter-operating servers to get a particular job done.

The client, in its present day manifestation, is usually a web browser. We know that web browsers are typically easy to use and available for almost any client platform. The only requirement of this universal client is that it speaks one language (HTTP) and translates information in one format (HTML). In an intranet environment, this isn't strictly true, as we can control the client used within the corporation. This allows us to support other protocols if necessary. Generally though, we would still use HTML as our basic information format. The job of this translation and formatting is often relegated to the 'first tier server', which is usually a web server (HTTP server).

The action of the HTTP server is twofold: it can be servicing client requests by accessing a file system (or sending requests to a file server) and retrieving static HTML pages; it can also be accessing one of its extensions to communicate with 'second tier' servers to obtain the required data. In turn, these 'second tier' servers may contact 'third tier' servers for data or services. Conceptually, our intranet interactions may look like this:

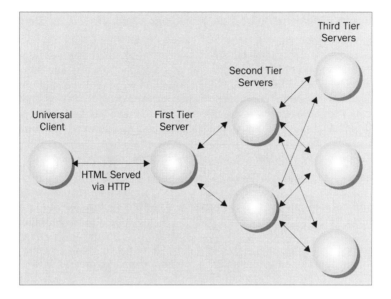

Through the collaborating network of multitiered back-end servers, almost all conventional data entry, access, manipulation, and update tasks can be accomplished. The user needs to learn only the user interface provided by the universal client in order to access all the rich contents and resources available through the back-end servers. Roughly translated, the user needs to know only how to surf the Web. This represents a pragmatic and natural extension of the more limited and poorly defined client-server models of the early 90s.

A notable exception to the above decomposition are the popular suites of office applications. These are typically represented by monolithic, feature-laden word processors, spreadsheets and presentation programs. To accommodate these applications during the transition to the distributed model, the universal client will 'host' the monolithic application within its own frame. This allows the end user to remain in the familiar environment of the universal client and continue to work using the 'soon to become legacy' office automation tools that they've grown accustomed to.

Intranet and Internet Linkage

Despite the separate worlds that the intranet and the Internet each live in, almost all intranet implementations will sooner or later require some means of accessing the external Internet. There are many common business situations where access to the Internet will be vital. Timely news, competitive information research, keeping in touch with customers, etc., can all be used to justify the need for a connection to the external Internet. Since the hardware (PC), the networking (a TCP/IP network), and the software (the browser and tools, etc.) are already on every desktop for accessing the intranet, it becomes a simple matter to provide a connection out to the Internet world… or so it seems. Unfortunately, due to the two way nature of TCP/IP networking, the solution is not so simple. If you were to allow internal intranet access out to the Internet, you would be exposing the entire corporate intranet to the perils of the Internet. This is a highly undesirable situation.

The solution, if you must link the intranet to the Internet, is through expertly configured firewalls and associated isolation techniques. A firewall works by acting as a middleman and passing through specific requests from the intranet to the Internet, while filtering the incoming traffic from the Internet. Typical firewall implementations are protocol specific, having knowledge of what constitutes a legal and illegal (and therefore potentially vicious) exchange. There are many excellent journal articles and books written on the subject of firewalls, and we won't repeat the material here.

Intranet design engineers face many challenges of a diverse nature in their work. One of the most difficult tasks is one of network topology analysis and traffic planning. We'll get a glimpse below of how it is intimately tied to the problem of provisioning firewall servers on a corporate intranet.

Intranet to Internet Gateways

Two common questions, which often come up during intranet/Internet linkage planning sessions, are:

 How can we provide intranet access to the Internet in a secure way?

 How can we provide secure and controlled access to the intranet from the Internet to our mobile/telecommuting workforce?

To see how we would plan the intranet/Internet linkage, let's look at an intranet with the following topology:

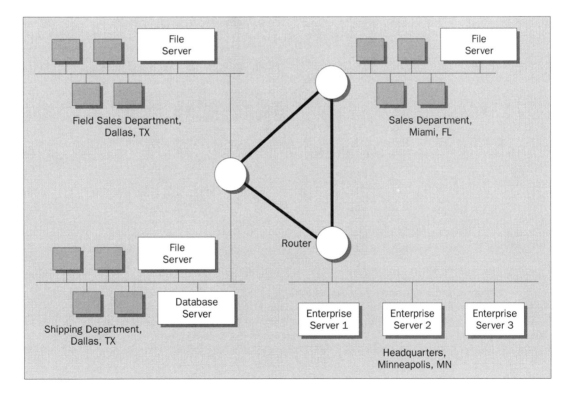

In this topology, we have one headquarters and two satellite offices representing three different departments within the corporation: a field sales department and shipping department in Dallas, a sales department in Miami, and the central headquarters in Minneapolis. Each department has its own LAN, including file servers. The shipping department also has a database server. A set of inventory and billing applications run against the database server. Routers connect the LANs between the satellite office and the headquarters through leased lines. In addition, the field sales departments are connected together via another router/leased line combination.

To provide access from the intranet to the Internet, we will install a proxy/firewall server. In the first situation depicted below, only one Internet firewall exists, and all accesses to the Internet must be made through this firewall. This solution provides a high degree of control over the security aspects of the intranet. However, it can be costly if traffic to access the Internet is high, since everyone accessing the Internet from the satellite offices must be sending traffic over the expensive Wide Area Network. If Internet access traffic is sufficiently high, it may even obstruct the flow of business critical data through the same router/Wide Area Network.

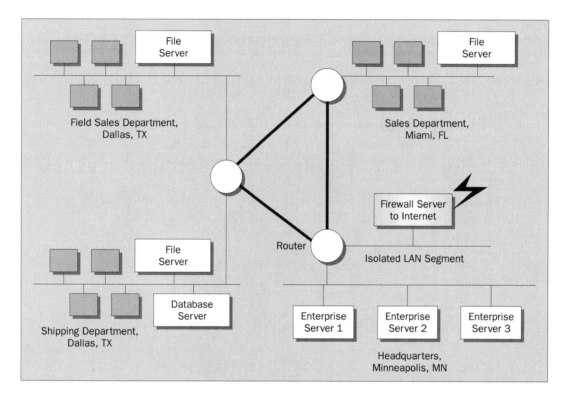

To improve typical access bandwidth, we eliminate the leased line problem by providing an Internet access gateway/firewall at each satellite office. See the next diagram for the new configuration. While this alleviates the leased line logjam, it does pose potential security problems. The administrator at each of the satellite office firewalls is counted on to provide the same level of security as the central headquarters administrator.

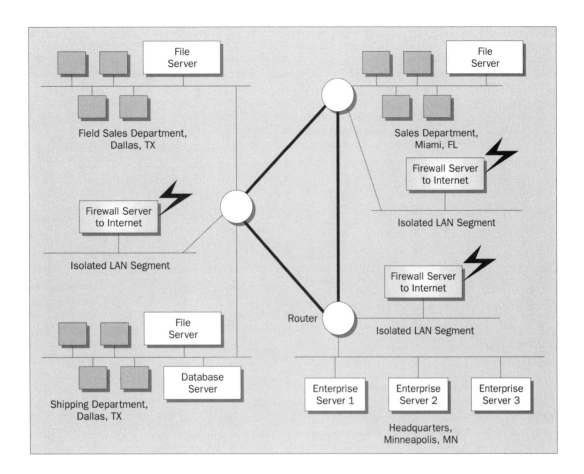

From the analysis of the two scenarios above, we can conclude that there exists no 'one best way' to add an Internet Firewall/Gateway to an intranet. The most appropriate solution will be determined by the specifics of each case.

Extending the Intranet through the Internet: Virtual Private Networks

Historically, the inter-LAN connections are typically handled through leased lines. The advantage of leased line is that they are always available. The disadvantage is that they can be costly and you're charged even if you do not use the line all the time. Other alternative means of connection include a dial-up version of the leased line situation (circuit switched network), as well as a usage-sensitive packet based public data network. With the packet based networks, the data is placed into packets and measured to determine the cost of service. You're paying for only the 'bandwidth' you actually use. Connections to different end-points need not be pre-registered or ordered ahead of time, since each packet can be addressed to a different end-point on the network.

With Windows NT 4.0, this situation has changed, as you can actually implement your own secure Virtual Private Network (VPN) over the Internet at very low cost. This capability is known as PPTP (Point-to-Point Tunneling Protocol). The idea is quite simple: given two end-points connected to the Internet, you encrypt **all** the traffic going between them and tunnel it through the Internet. Since the Point-to-Point Protocol

(PPP) can carry multiple network protocols across a connection, this is equivalent to placing a segment of the traditional network over the Internet (thus the tunneling aspect). Windows NT implementation of PPTP extends the conventional Remote Access Service (RAS) over long distances through the Internet. With the eventual support of routing over RAS, PPTP can give many of the benefits associated with conventional leased line at relatively low cost. In effect, you can obtain a virtual private network by simply paying for the 'unlimited connection' rate to your ISP at both ends of the network. The only potential drawback is the unpredictability of bandwidth availability over the Internet. However, unless one is dealing with time critical applications, a slight delay in data transmission isn't normally a concern.

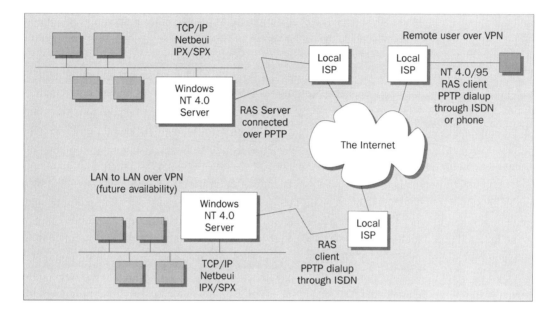

Intranet Benefits

Having examined the concept of an intranet and how it works, we'll now discuss how an intranet can benefit an organization and the individuals within the organization. The points noted below can serve as a useful starting place in the justification or rationalization phase of the intranet planning process. Since we can't anticipate the exact detail of your specific plans, the salient points are kept to a generic yet pragmatically applicable level.

Benefits for the Enterprise

The benefits of an intranet can be broken down into short-term and long-term ones. The short-term benefits, which we can realize almost immediately, are:

Improved Internal Communications

Email and voice mail have gone a long way to improve internal corporate communications. Intranet technology adds to this the ability to participate in discussion groups, collaborate using text, share whiteboards, and audio and video conferencing capabilities. The increased accessibility of corporate information 'right on the desktop' helps substantially in eliminating misunderstanding in corporate communications frequently attributed to a lack of timely knowledge about the state of business affairs.

Better Information Sharing

Maintaining the entire knowledge and information assets of a corporation in an online-accessible format helps to educate employees, reduce redundant queries, avoid 'reinventing the wheel', and give everyone a better sense of the why, where, what and how of everyday company operations. Given the amount of information buried in legacy storage media or technologies, this goal may not be quickly achievable in some organizations. Nevertheless, any additional degree of information sharing will yield the above tangible results.

For the longer term, some achievable benefits may be:

Quicker Reaction to Change

Success in many businesses depends on the ability of an organization to react quickly to change. The larger an organization is, the harder it is to make quick (yet wise) moves. By having an intranet to assist in synchronizing the goals, directions, strategies and ideals of an organization, it will stand a better chance of being able to react quickly and consistently to changing conditions.

Improved manageability of Computing Resources and Assets

Manageability is a feature that is currently being worked on by major intranet software vendors. It picks up from where the Internet's SNMP (Simple Network Management Protocol) left off. In the next few years, we'll see a succession of new server and operating system enhancements that will substantially reduce the management costs for intranet PCs.

Improved Employee Morale

Direct feedback from employees at the lowest level often reveals problems long before the troublesome news can filter through the hierarchy associated with conventional bureaucracy. The intranet provides a medium over which these feedback loops can take place when necessary. Any directional or strategic statements can be issued by the highest level of management and be immediately available for perusal and interpretation for all employees. This provides the best possible means of precise communications, eliminating many of the misunderstandings that may result when important mission statements are mixed with biased interpretations.

Improved Automation, Reduced Operation Cost

Once the supplier and consumer of information (and complex paper forms) have a taste of what the intranet can do for paperless publishing, many of the conventional paper based publications and processes will be automatically streamlined. This is especially true if the intranet launch is synchronized with a corporate wide intranet education campaign, alerting the new intranet users to the tools and facilities available to make information publishing easier than word processing.

Reduced In-house Development and Maintenance Costs

This is a natural consequence of an intranet. By definition, an intranet leverages component technologies. Almost every major intranet software product vendor is now preaching new models of distributed, component based application building. These new models of application creation will dramatically shorten development time, reduce costs, and deliver the true value of software reuse. The intranet application builder will be able to select the 'best of the breed' from a large base of software component vendors.

Why Use an Intranet for Client-Server Solutions?

Traditional business problems can often be solved by the in-house development of conventional client-server based solutions. So what are the benefits of building it on web based intranet technologies?

Widely Available Skilled Professional Pool

This is already here. One can hire experts in Internet and/or intranet technologies readily worldwide. Thanks to the standards-based nature of intranet technologies, hiring and replacing skilled professionals will be significantly easier when compared to the former, proprietary world of in-house development.

Simpler to Solve Complex Problems

Delivering on the promise of distributed components-based computing, intranet applications will make the solution of complex business problems easier than ever before. New software will have to be written only for the pieces of the problem that no existing software component addresses.

Easier to Adopt to Changing Requirements and Conditions

The style of component based application development uses a mixture of scripting, drag and drop placement/design, and custom component configuration to create an easy-to-modify, and easy-to-maintain solution framework. In most cases, should any application requirements or conditions change, then only the script or component configuration need to be altered for the application.

Tough System Problems are Left to be Solved by Experts

New server side platforms (such as the Active Server Platform) enable creation of complex highly scalable, transaction based intranet applications when necessary. This can be done without having operating system and design gurus to do the development. Provided the guidelines for the platform are followed, the designer of the application (server) platform will take care of all the 'tough' issues.

System Based on Widely Available Commodity Components

This is an inherent characteristic of component based computing. Proprietary large-scale development of MIS systems has become a thing of the past.

Accommodates Remote Access, Facilitates Telecommuting

The Remote Access Service plugs-and-plays gracefully with any intranet installation, allowing a telecommuting user to access the intranet securely over any dial-up or ISDN line.

A Compatible, Yet Extensible and Upgradable Communication Infrastructure

The network operating system and hardware market has completed its 'shake-out' phase, and is now mature and stable. An Ethernet based solution allows legacy networks to coexist with the TCP/IP based intranet. The network can be arbitrarily extended using commodity routers and wide area connections. All of the network equipment can be upgraded from 10 MB Ethernet to 100MB Ethernet and beyond.

Overall Development Cost Reduction and Faster Concept to Deployment Time

More opportunities for code reuse means reduced overall development costs. The drag-and-drop friendly development typically used in component based application design can act as a catalyst for rapid application development (RAD), significantly shortening the concept-to-deployment time.

Benefits to Individuals

Depending on an individual's role, the popularity of intranet applications and systems will provide benefits in different areas. In this section, we'll also look at smaller businesses which may adopt a very local intranet (i.e. for a single office location), as well as entrepreneurs who may be developing software for sale into the intranet or component software market. Here are some examples:

Business	Benefits
Managers/Small Business Owners	New and more accessible tools to communicate, better, faster. Can streamline processes to run organization more efficiently and effectively. Better control over flow and distribution of information. Faster reaction to external changes. Better communications with employees or customers. Natural extension to include customers as part of intranet. Improved employee satisfaction through interactive feedback. Easier to gauge opinion or readiness for change. Easier utilization of human and computing resources.
MIS Designers/ Programmers	New component technologies for intranets provide more functionality for less work than conventional development tools. The focus is on bigger problems and interactions. Many pre-fabricated components/subsystems/solutions to choose from. Can address 'tough' problems with more ease. Communications, scalability, etc. More effective management of turmoil caused by ever changing requirements. Acquisition of a more universally applicable set of skills than those offered through proprietary solutions.
System Programmers /ISVs/Entrepreneurs	Much larger market (worldwide, Internet and intranet) for your application, component, or tool. Brand new business opportunities in areas not yet exploited. Significant opportunities in making the old stuff work while folding in the new.

Some Caveats

The real total cost of deployment may be an issue. The old adage says 'If it ain't broke, don't fix it.' If a system exists which does the job, there may be little justification for replacing it with an intranet solution. This is especially true in situations where a large investment has been made in equipment or software that is incompatible with web based intranet technology. An evaluation of deployment cost must be objective, and take into account training and maintenance costs.

You shouldn't adopt intranet based technology simply because it's 'cool'. You must perform a proper business analysis to ascertain that there is long term strategic business value before proceeding with the investment.

Vendor Alternatives

This book is about Microsoft's ActiveX technology and how it can be applied productively in the corporate intranet. Are there other non-Microsoft alternatives?

Certainly there are. As a matter of fact, most of the Internet, where many of the intranet technologies came from, is still living on UNIX servers. What that means is that there are many time-tested, robust, UNIX based solutions out there.

If you're working in an IBM or Novell based shop, these vendors provide their own family of intranet technologies upon which you can base your design.

For intranet infrastructure and foundation software, Microsoft's formidable rival, Netscape, has a whole range of products and vertical solution frameworks for you to choose from.

However, despite all these choices, if you're using Microsoft operating systems and using Microsoft Office products on your desktop PCs, adopting another vendor's solution means that you may need to wait for the vendor to 'play catch up' if you need to track the latest available alternatives. If you don't want to gamble with mix-and-match, patch-and-splice solutions in a fast moving technology area, the Microsoft solution fares quite well in the 'peace of mind' department, even though it may not be as mature as some of the competitive offerings.

Planning and Building an Intranet

Despite popular belief, running and operating an intranet is not the simple matter of being a web master. In almost all situations, the long term operation and maintenance of an intranet is a cooperative effort of multiple departments and experts from multiple disciplines. Typically, you need to take the following steps to establish a corporate intranet:

- ▲ Justify and obtain approval and blessing of high level management
- ▲ Obtain commitment of resources for a 'pilot project' and agreement for long term support
- ▲ Plan contents with high level representatives of various branches and departments
- ▲ Develop procedures and processes to update the contents continually, and maintain, and operate the intranet
- ▲ Appoint a technology advisory council to evaluate and adopt new Internet technology into the intranet should they provide a strategic business advantage
- ▲ Plan hardware, topologies, and bandwidth with operations and telecommunications staff
- ▲ Coordinate regional/departmental server setup, deployment and assignment of regional/departmental webmasters
- ▲ Set up the required software and communications infrastructure

- Develop and create the necessary code, contents, and pages (these two steps can be planned in phases)

- Kick off meeting with all involved staff, and establish regular intranet staff meetings or teleconferences

- Pre-launch and test with the live network configuration before enabling end user access

- Advertise implementation and notify end-users, and organize training on 'how to access'

It's true that one can find various case studies which deviate from this linear approach to intranet deployment. However, closer examination of such case studies will usually reveal the 'early adopter' nature of the circumstance. For long term, sustained, smooth operations of the corporate intranet, the formalized approach is required because of the significant team effort required for a successful intranet implementation.

In many situations, you may need to factor in some way of measuring the effectiveness of the intranet implementation. You may also need to devise some metrics to contrast the ways specific interactive flows operated before and after the intranet implementation. These metrics may be subjective (for example, a user satisfaction survey), or objective (such as business transaction efficiency, and usage rate for a specific application). This may necessitate the formation of a subgroup to evaluate the effectiveness of the intranet. You can use web server access logs and data reduction tools to quantify or substantiate the conclusions.

As you can see, there are many nontechnical issues that must be addressed. From now on, though, we'll be taking a technocrat's view to focus on some of the exciting enabling intranet technologies.

To Be Continued

Just as the winds of change have carried corporate computing from the mainframe to minicomputers to today's super powerful microcomputers, we're seeing the proprietary client-server ways of yesteryear giving way to the new distributed computing model enabled by the modern corporate intranet.

An intranet, we surmise, is simply the deployment of existing and new Internet based technology within a corporate network. The proliferation and global popularity of the Internet has focused tremendous creative and engineering energy on the rapid development of new and exciting Internet based technologies and products. Many of these new products are applicable to both the Internet and the intranet.

An implementation of an intranet leverages the 'off-the-shelf' technologies available for the Internet, and adds in enough custom interface development to make it easy for the business oriented user. Based on either a universal client (the web browser) or a custom application, and making extensive use of prefabricated, reusable software components, the new distributed model of intranet computing fits perfectly with the 'buy instead of build whenever possible' trend of modern companies.

Isolated intranets are inherently safe from vicious external tempering. Unfortunately, there are many business reasons for interconnecting the Internet to an intranet. One must proceed with caution in this area. Inevitably you'll need to deploy some firewall technology: the exact configuration and best deployment strategy is completely topology and situation dependent.

If upper management isn't already sold on the idea (from the tremendous return on investment reported in the popular computing press), justifying the implementation of an intranet will be relatively easy. We looked at a very large list of benefits that an organization with an intranet can enjoy. We also tabulated the benefits for individuals with specific IS roles in the enterprise.

HTML Reference

APPENDIX B

Here we give a full listing of all the tags and their attributes. We have also marked which tags and attributes are part of the HTML 2.0 and HTML 3.2 standards, and which are supported by the two leading browsers: Internet Explorer 3.0 and Netscape Navigator 3.0.

The following key explains the icons used to indicate browser support for the tags.

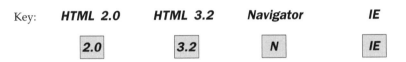

Key: **HTML 2.0**   **HTML 3.2**   *Navigator*   IE
       `2.0`   `3.2`   `N`   `IE`

A complete reference to these tags can be found in Instant HTML also published by Wrox Press.

`<!-- -->`   `2.0` `3.2` `N` `IE`
Allows authors to add comments to code.

`!DOCTYPE`   `2.0` `3.2` `N` `IE`
Defines the document type. Required by all HTML documents.

`A`   `2.0` `3.2` `N` `IE`
Used to insert an anchor, which can be either a local reference point or a hyperlink to another URL.

Attributes	HTML 2.0	HTML 3.2	Navigator 3.0	IE 3.0
`HREF=url`	✓	✓	✓	✓
`NAME=name`	✓	✓	✓	✓
`TITLE=name`	x	✓	x	x
`TARGET=window`	x	x	✓	✓

Notes: The **REL** and **REV** attributes are not well-defined and should not be used.

`ADDRESS`   `2.0` `3.2` `N` `IE`
Indicates an address. The address is typically displayed in italics.

APPLET   `3.2` `N` `IE`

Inserts an applet.

Attributes	HTML 2.0	HTML 3.2	Navigator 3.0	IE 3.0
`ALIGN=left│right│top│texttop│middle│` `absmiddle│baseline│bottom│absbottom`	x	✓	✓	✓
`ALT=alternativetext`	x	✓	✓	✓
`CODE=appletname`	x	✓	✓	✓
`CODEBASE=url`	x	✓	✓	✓
`HEIGHT=n`	x	✓	✓	✓
`HSPACE=n`	x	✓	x	✓
`NAME=name`	x	✓	x	✓
`VSPACE=n`	x	✓	x	✓
`WIDTH=n`	x	✓	✓	✓

AREA   `3.2` `N` `IE`

Defines a client-side imagemap area.

Attributes	HTML 2.0	HTML 3.2	Navigator 3.0	IE 3.0
`ALT=alternativetext`	x	✓	✓	x
`COORDS=coords`	x	✓	✓	✓
`HREF=url`	x	✓	✓	✓
`NOHREF`	x	✓	✓	✓
`SHAPE=RECT│CIRCLE│POLY`	x	✓	✓	✓
`TARGET="window"│_blank│_parent│_self│_top`	x	x	✓	✓

Notes: Internet Explorer also supports the values **RECTANGLE**, **CIRC**, and **POLYGON** for **SHAPE**.

B   `2.0` `3.2` `N` `IE`

Emboldens text.

BASE

Base URL–defines the original location of the document. It is not normally necessary to include this tag. May be used only in **HEAD** section.

Attributes	HTML 2.0	HTML 3.2	Navigator 3.0	IE 3.0
`HREF=url`	✓	✓	✓	✓
`TARGET="window"|_blank|_parent|_self|_top`	x	x	✓	✓

BASEFONT

Defines font size over a range of text.

Attributes	HTML 2.0	HTML 3.2	Navigator 3.0	IE 3.0
`COLOR`	x	x	x	✓
`FACE`	x	x	x	✓
`SIZE=1|2|3|4|5|6|7`	x	x	✓	✓

BGSOUND

Plays a background sound.

Attributes	HTML 2.0	HTML 3.2	Navigator 3.0	IE 3.0
`LOOP`	x	x	x	✓
`SRC=url`	x	x	x	✓

BIG

Changes the physical rendering of the font to one size larger.

BLINK

Defines text that will blink on and off.

BLOCKQUOTE

Formats a quote–typically by indentation.

BODY   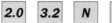

Contains the main part of the HTML document.

Attributes	HTML 2.0	HTML 3.2	Navigator 3.0	IE 3.0
`ALINK="#rrggbb"`	x	✓	✓	x
`BACKGROUND=url`	x	✓	x	✓
`BGCOLOR="#rrggbb"`	x	✓	✓	✓
`LINK="#rrggbb"`	x	✓	✓	✓
`TEXT="#rrggbb"`	x	✓	✓	✓
`VLINK="#rrggbb"`	x	✓	✓	✓
`BGPROPERTIES=fixed`	x	x	x	✓
`LEFTMARGIN=n`	x	x	x	✓
`TOPMARGIN=n`	x	x	x	✓

BR   ▢2.0 ▢3.2 ▢N ▢IE

Line break.

Attributes	HTML 2.0	HTML 3.2	Navigator 3.0	IE 3.0
`CLEAR=left|right|all`	x	✓	✓	✓

CAPTION   ▢3.2 ▢N ▢IE

Puts a title above a table.

Attributes	HTML 2.0	HTML 3.2	Navigator 3.0	IE 3.0
`ALIGN=top|bottom|left|right`	x	✓	✓	✓

Notes: Netscape Navigator does not support the **left** and **right** values for the **ALIGN** attribute.

CENTER

Centers text or graphic.

CITE   `2.0` `3.2` `N` `IE`

Indicates a citation, generally displaying the text in italics.

CODE   `2.0` `3.2` `N` `IE`

Renders text in a font resembling computer code.

COL   `3.2` `IE`

Defines column width and properties for a table.

Attributes	HTML 2.0	HTML 3.2	Navigator 3.0	IE 3.0
`ALIGN=left|right|center`	x	x	x	✓
`SPAN=n`	x	x	x	✓

COLGROUP   `3.2` `IE`

Defines properties for a group of columns in a table.

Attributes	HTML 2.0	HTML 3.2	Navigator 3.0	IE 3.0
`ALIGN=left|right|center`	x	x	x	✓
`SPAN=n`	x	x	x	✓

DD   `2.0` `3.2` `N` `IE`

Definition description. Used in definition lists with `<DT>` to define the term.

DFN   `3.2` `N` `IE`

Indicates the first instance of a term or important word.

DIR   `2.0` `3.2` `N` `IE`

Defines a directory list by indenting the text.

DIV　　　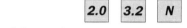

Defines a block division of the `<BODY>`.

Attributes	HTML 2.0	HTML 3.2	Navigator 3.0	IE 3.0
`ALIGN=left|right|center`	x	✓	✓	✓
`NOWRAP`	x	x	x	x
`CLEAR=left|right|all`	x	x	x	x

DL　　　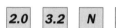

Defines a definition list.

DT　　　2.0　3.2　N　IE

Defines a definition term. Used with definition lists.

EM　　　2.0　3.2　N　IE

Emphasized text–usually italic.

EMBED　　　N　IE

Defines an embedded object in an HTML document.

Attributes	HTML 2.0	HTML 3.2	Navigator 3.0	IE 3.0
`HEIGHT=n`	x	x	✓	✓
`NAME=name`	x	x	✓	✓
`PALETTE=foreground|background`	x	x	x	✓
`SRC=url`	x	x	✓	✓
`WIDTH=n`	x	x	✓	✓

FONT

Changes font properties.

Attributes	HTML 2.0	HTML 3.2	Navigator 3.0	IE 3.0
COLOR="#rrggbb"	x	✓	✓	✓
FACE=typeface	x	x	✓	✓
SIZE=1|2|3|4|5|6|7	x	✓	✓	✓

FORM

Defines part of the document as a user fill-out form.

Attributes	HTML 2.0	HTML 3.2	Navigator 3.0	IE 3.0
ACTION=url	✓	✓	✓	✓
ENCTYPE=enc_method	✓	✓	✓	✓
METHOD=get|post	✓	✓	✓	✓
TARGET="window"|_blank|_parent|_self|_top	x	x	✓	✓

FRAME

Defines a single frame in a frameset.

Attributes	HTML 2.0	HTML 3.2	Navigator 3.0	IE 3.0
ALIGN=top|bottom|left|center|right	x	x	✓	✓
FRAMEBORDER=0|1	x	x	x	✓
MARGINHEIGHT=n	x	x	✓	✓
MARGINWIDTH=n	x	x	✓	✓
NAME=name	x	x	✓	✓
NORESIZE	x	x	✓	✓
SCROLLING=yes|no|auto	x	x	✓	✓
SRC=url	x	x	✓	✓

FRAMESET

Defines the main container for a frame.

Attributes	HTML 2.0	HTML 3.2	Navigator 3.0	IE 3.0
COLS=colswidth	x	x	✓	✓
FRAMEBORDER=1|0	x	x	✓	✓
FRAMESPACING=n	x	x	x	✓
ROWS=rowsheight	x	x	✓	✓

HEAD

Contains information about the document itself. Can include the following tags: **TITLE**, **META**, **BASE**, **ISINDEX**, **LINK**, **SCRIPT**, **STYLE**.

Hn

Defines a heading, can be one of **<H1>**, **<H2>**, **<H3>**, **<H4>**, **<H5>**, **<H6>** where **<H1>** is the largest and **<H6>** is the smallest.

Attributes	HTML 2.0	HTML 3.2	Navigator 3.0	IE 3.0
ALIGN=left|right|center	x	✓	✓	✓

HR

Defines a horizontal rule.

Attributes	HTML 2.0	HTML 3.2	Navigator 3.0	IE 3.0
ALIGN=left|right|center	x	✓	✓	✓
NOSHADE	x	✓	✓	✓
SIZE=n	x	✓	✓	✓
WIDTH=width	x	✓	✓	✓
COLOR="#rrggbb"	x	x	x	✓

HTML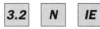

Signals the start and end of an HTML document.

I   2.0 3.2 N IE

Defines italic text.

IFRAME   IE

Defines a 'floating' frame within a document.

Attributes	HTML 2.0	HTML 3.2	Navigator 3.0	IE 3.0
`ALIGN=top|middle|bottom|left|right`	x	x	x	✓
`FRAMEBORDER=0|1`	x	x	x	✓
`HEIGHT=n`	x	x	x	✓
`MARGINHEIGHT=n`	x	x	x	✓
`MARGINWIDTH=n`	x	x	x	✓
`NAME=name`	x	x	x	✓
`NORESIZE`	x	x	x	✓
`SCROLLING=yes|no|auto`	x	x	x	✓
`SRC=url`	x	x	x	✓
`WIDTH`	x	x	x	✓

IMG   2.0 3.2 N IE

Defines an inline image.

Attributes	HTML 2.0	HTML 3.2	Navigator 3.0	IE 3.0
`ALIGN=top|middle|bottom|left|right`	✓	✓	✓	✓
`ALT=alternativetext`	✓	✓	✓	✓
`BORDER=n`	x	✓	✓	✓
`HEIGHT=n`	x	✓	✓	✓

Table Continued on Following Page

455

Attributes	HTML 2.0	HTML 3.2	Navigator 3.0	IE 3.0
HSPACE=n	x	✓	✓	✓
ISMAP	✓	✓	✓	✓
SRC=url	✓	✓	✓	✓
USEMAP=mapname	x	✓	✓	✓
VSPACE=n	x	✓	✓	✓
WIDTH=n	x	✓	✓	✓
CONTROLS	x	x	x	✓
DYNSRC	x	x	x	✓
LOOP	x	x	x	✓
START	x	x	x	✓
LOWSRC	x	x	✓	x

INPUT   `2.0` `3.2` `N` `IE`

Defines a user input box.

Attributes	HTML 2.0	HTML 3.2	Navigator 3.0	IE 3.0
ALIGN=top|middle|bottom	✓	✓	✓	✓
CHECKED	✓	✓	✓	✓
MAXLENGTH=n	✓	✓	✓	✓
NAME=name	✓	✓	✓	✓
SIZE=n	✓	✓	✓	✓
SRC=url	✓	✓	✓	✓
TYPE=checkbox|hidden|image|password|radio| reset|submit|text	✓	✓	✓	✓
VALUE=value	✓	✓	✓	✓

ISINDEX

Defines a text input field for entering a query.

Attributes	HTML 2.0	HTML 3.2	Navigator 3.0	IE 3.0
`ACTION=url`	X	X	✓	✓
`PROMPT=message`	✓	✓	✓	✓

KBD

Indicates typed text. Useful for instruction manuals, etc.

LH 3.2 N IE

Defines a list heading in any type of list.

LI 3.2 N IE

Defines a list item in any type of list other than a definition list.

Attributes	HTML 2.0	HTML 3.2	Navigator 3.0	IE 3.0
`TYPE=A|a|I|i|1`	✓	✓	✓	✓
`VALUE=n`	✓	✓	✓	✓

Note: Netscape Navigator also supports `TYPE=disc|square|circle` for use with unordered lists.

LINK 3.2 IE

Defines the current document's relationship with other documents.

Attributes	HTML 2.0	HTML 3.2	Navigator 3.0	IE 3.0
`REL=`	x	✓	✓	✓
`HREF=url`	x	✓	✓	✓
`REV=`	x	✓	✓	✓
`TITLE=`	x	✓	✓	✓

MAP

Defines the different regions of a client-side imagemap.

Attributes	HTML 2.0	HTML 3.2	Navigator 3.0	IE 3.0
NAME=mapname	x	✓	✓	✓

MARQUEE   IE

Sets a scrolling marquee.

Attributes	HTML 2.0	HTML 3.2	Navigator 3.0	IE 3.0
ALIGN=top|middle|bottom	x	x	x	✓
BEHAVIOR=scroll|slide|alternate	x	x	x	✓
BGCOLOR="#rrggbb"	x	x	x	✓
DIRECTION=left|right	x	x	x	✓
HEIGHT=n	x	x	x	✓
HSPACE=n	x	x	x	✓
LOOP=n	x	x	x	✓
SCROLLAMOUNT=n	x	x	x	✓
SCROLLDELAY=n	x	x	x	✓
VSPACE=n	x	x	x	✓
WIDTH=n	x	x	x	✓

MENU

Defines a menu list.

META

Describes the content of a document.

Attributes	HTML 2.0	HTML 3.2	Navigator 3.0	IE 3.0
CONTENT=	✓	✓	✓	✓
HTTP-EQUIV	x	✓	✓	✓
NAME	x	✓	✓	✓
URL=document url	x	x	x	✓

NOBR   N   IE

Prevents a line of text breaking.

NOFRAMES   N   IE

Allows for backward compatibility with non-frame-compliant browsers.

OBJECT   IE

Inserts an object.

Attributes	HTML 2.0	HTML 3.2	Navigator 3.0	IE 3.0
ALIGN=baseline|center|left|middle|right| textbottom|textmiddle|texttop	x	x	x	✓
BORDER=n	x	x	x	✓
CLASSID=url	x	x	x	✓
CODEBASE	x	x	x	✓
CODETYPE=codetype	x	x	x	✓
DATA=url	x	x	x	✓
DECLARE	x	x	x	✓
HEIGHT=n	x	x	x	✓
HSPACE=n	x	x	x	✓
NAME=url	x	x	x	✓
SHAPES	x	x	x	✓
STANDBY=message	x	x	x	✓
TYPE=type	x	x	x	✓

Table Continued on Following Page

Attributes	HTML 2.0	HTML 3.2	Navigator 3.0	IE 3.0
USEMAP=url	x	x	x	✓
VSPACE=n	x	x	x	✓
WIDTH=n	x	x	x	✓

OL

Defines an ordered list.

Attributes	HTML 2.0	HTML 3.2	Navigator 3.0	IE 3.0
COMPACT	x	✓	✓	x
START=n	x	✓	✓	✓
TYPE=1|A|a|I|i	x	✓	✓	✓

OPTION   `3.2` `IE`

Used within the `<SELECT>` tag to present the user with a number of options.

Attributes	HTML 2.0	HTML 3.2	Navigator 3.0	IE 3.0
SELECTED	x	✓	✓	✓
PLAIN	x	✓	✓	✓
VALUE	x	✓	✓	✓
DISABLED	x	✓	✓	✓

P   `2.0` `3.2` `N` `IE`

Defines a paragraph.

Attributes	HTML 2.0	HTML 3.2	Navigator 3.0	IE 3.0
ALIGN=left|right|center	x	✓	✓	✓

PARAM   **3.2**   **N**   **IE**

Defines parameters for a Java applet.

Attributes	HTML 2.0	HTML 3.2	Navigator 3.0	IE 3.0
`NAME=name`	x	✓	✓	✓
`VALUE=value`	x	✓	✓	✓
`VALUETYPE=Data|Ref|Object`	x	x	x	✓
`TYPE=InternetMediaType`	x	x	x	✓

PRE   **2.0**   **3.2**   **N**   **IE**

Preformatted text. Renders text exactly how it is typed, i.e. carriage returns, styles, etc., *will* be recognized.

Attributes	HTML 2.0	HTML 3.2	Navigator 3.0	IE 3.0
`WIDTH`	x	✓	✓	x

S   **3.2**   **N**   **IE**

Strikethrough. Renders the text as deleted (crossed out).

SAMP   **3.2**   **N**   **IE**

Sample output.

SCRIPT   **3.2**   **N**   **IE**

Inserts a script.

Attributes	HTML 2.0	HTML 3.2	Navigator 3.0	IE 3.0
`LANGUAGE=VBScript|JavaScript`	x	✓	Note	✓

Note: Netscape Navigator 3.0 only supports JavaScript.

SELECT

Defines the default selection in a list.

Attributes	HTML 2.0	HTML 3.2	Navigator 3.0	IE 3.0
MULTIPLE	x	x	✓	✓
NAME=name	✓	✓	✓	✓
SIZE=n	x	x	✓	✓

SMALL

Changes the physical rendering of a font to one size smaller.

SPAN

Defines localized style information, e.g. margin width.

Attributes	HTML 2.0	HTML 3.2	Navigator 3.0	IE 3.0
STYLE=Style	x	x	x	✓

STRIKE

Strikethrough. Renders the text as deleted or crossed out.

STRONG   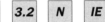

Strong emphasis–usually bold.

STYLE

Reserved for future use with style sheets.

SUB

Subscript.

SUP

Superscript.

TABLE

Defines a series of columns and rows to form a table.

Attributes	HTML 2.0	HTML 3.2	Navigator 3.0	IE 3.0
ALIGN= left|right|center	x	✓	✓	✓
VALIGN	x	✓	x	x
BORDER=n	x	✓	✓	✓
WIDTH=n	x	✓	✓	✓
CELLSPACING=n	x	✓	✓	✓
CELLPADDING=n	x	✓	✓	✓
FRAME=void|above|below|hsides|lhs|rhs|vsides|box|border	x	✓	x	✓
RULES=none|groups|rows|cols|all	x	✓	x	✓
BACKGROUND=url	x	x	x	✓
BGCOLOR="#rrggbb"	x	x	✓	✓
COLS=n	x	✓	x	✓
BORDERCOLOR="#rrggbb"	x	x	x	✓
BORDERCOLORDARK="#rrggbb"	x	x	x	✓
BORDERCOLORLIGHT="#rrggbb"	x	x	x	✓

Notes: ALIGN, CHAR, CHAROFF, and **VALIGN** are common to all cell alignments, and may be inherited from enclosing elements.

The **CENTER** value for the **ALIGN** attribute is not supported by Netscape Navigator 3.0 or Internet Explorer 3.0.

TBODY

Defines the table body.

TD

Marks the start point for table data.

Attributes	HTML 2.0	HTML 3.2	Navigator 3.0	IE 3.0
ALIGN=left|right|center	x	✓	✓	✓
ASIX	x	✓	x	x
AXES	x	✓	x	x
COLSPAN=n	x	✓	✓	✓
ROWSPAN=n	x	✓	✓	✓
NOWRAP	x	✓	✓	✓
WIDTH=n	x	Note	✓	x
BACKGROUND	x	x	x	✓
BGCOLOR="#rrggbb"	x	x	✓	✓
BORDERCOLOR="#rrggbb"	x	x	x	✓
BORDERCOLORDARK="#rrggbb"	x	x	x	✓
BORDERCOLORLIGHT="#rrggbb"	x	x	x	✓
VALIGN=top|middle|bottom|baseline	x	✓	✓	✓

The **WIDTH** attribute is not in HTML 3.2, but support is recommended for backward compatibility. Use the **WIDTH** attribute for **COL** instead.

TEXTFLOW

Replacement for text in applet. May be inserted inside **<APPLET>** tag.

TEXTAREA

Defines a text area inside a **FORM** element.

Attributes	HTML 2.0	HTML 3.2	Navigator 3.0	IE 3.0
NAME=name	✓	✓	✓	✓
ROWS=n	✓	✓	✓	✓

Table Continued on Following Page

Attributes	HTML 2.0	HTML 3.2	Navigator 3.0	IE 3.0
`COLS=n`	✓	✓	✓	✓
`WRAP=off|virtual|physical`	x	x	✓	x

TFOOT

Defines a table footer.

TH

Defines names for columns and rows.

Attributes	HTML 2.0	HTML 3.2	Navigator 3.0	IE 3.0
`ALIGN=left|center|right`	x	✓	✓	✓
`AXIS`	x	✓	x	x
`AXES`	x	✓	x	x
`COLSPAN`	x	✓	✓	✓
`ROWSPAN`	x	✓	✓	✓
`WIDTH=n`	x	Note	✓	x
`NOWRAP`	x	✓	✓	✓
`BACKGROUND`	x	x	x	✓
`BGCOLOR="#rrggbb"`	x	x	✓	✓
`BORDERCOLOR="#rrggbb"`	x	x	x	✓
`BORDERCOLORDARK="#rrggbb"`	x	x	x	✓
`BORDERCOLORLIGHT="#rrggbb"`	x	x	x	✓
`VALIGN=n`	x	✓	✓	✓

The **WIDTH** attribute is not in HTML 3.2, but support is recommended for backward compatibility. Use the **WIDTH** attribute for **COL** instead.

THEAD

Defines a table header.

TITLE

Defines the title of the document. Required by all HTML documents.

TR

Defines the start of a table row.

Attributes	HTML 2.0	HTML 3.2	Navigator 3.0	IE 3.0
ALIGN=left|right|center	x	✓	✓	✓
CHAR	x	✓	x	x
CHAROFF	x	✓	x	x
BACKGROUND	x	x	x	✓
BGCOLOR="#rrggbb"	x	x	✓	✓
BORDERCOLOR="#rrggbb"	x	x	x	✓
BORDERCOLORDARK="#rrggbb"	x	x	x	✓
BORDERCOLORLIGHT="#rrggbb"	x	x	x	✓
VALIGN=top|middle|bottom|baseline	x	✓	✓	✓

TT

Renders text in fixed width, typewriter style font.

U

Underlines text. Not widely supported at present, and not recommended, as could cause confusion with hyperlinks, which also normally appear underlined.

UL

Defines an unordered, usually bulleted list.

Attributes	HTML 2.0	HTML 3.2	Navigator 3.0	IE 3.0
COMPACT	x	✓	✓	x
TYPE=disc|circle|square	x	✓	✓	x

VAR

Indicates a variable.

WBR

Defines the word to break and wrap to the next line. Often used with `<NOBR>`

INDEX

Instant HTML Programmers Reference

Author: Steve Wright
ISBN: 1861000766
Price: $15.00 C$21.00 £13.99

This book is a fast paced guide to the latest version of the HTML language, including the extensions to the standards added by Netscape and Microsoft. Aimed at programmers, it assumes a basic knowledge of the Internet. It starts by looking at the basics of HTML including document structure, formatting tags, inserting hyperlinks and images and image mapping, and then moves on to cover more advanced issues such as tables, frames, creating forms to interact with users, animation, incorporating scripts (such as JavaScript) into HTML documents, and style sheets.

The book includes a full list of all the HTML tags, organised by category for easy reference.

Instant VBScript

Authors: Alex Homer, Darren Gill
ISBN: 1861000448
Price: $25.00 C$35.00 £22.99

This is the guide for programmers who already know HTML and another programming language and want to waste no time getting up to speed. This book takes developers right into the code, straight from the beginning of Chapter 1. The first object is to get the programmer to create their own 'reactive' web pages as quickly as possible while introducing the most important HTML and ActiveX controls. This new knowledge is quickly incorporated into more complex examples with a complete sample site built early in the book.

As Internet Explorer is the browser that introduced VBScript, we also take a detailed look at how to use VBScript to access different objects within the browser. We create our own tools to help us with the development of applications, in particular a debugging tool to aid error-trapping. Information is provided on how to build your own controls and sign them to secure Internet download. Finally we take a look at server side scripting and how with VBScript you can get the clients and server communicating freely. The book is supported by our web site which contains all of the examples in the book in an easily executable form.

Professional Web Site Optimization

Authors: Ware, Barker, Slothouber
and Gross
ISBN: 186100074x
Price: $40.00 C$56.00 £36.99

OK, you've installed your web server, and it's working fine
and you've even got people interested in visiting your site -
too many people, in fact. The real challenge is just starting
you need to make it run faster, better and more flexibly.

This is the book for every webmaster who needs to improve
site performance. You could just buy that new T-1 you've had
your eye on, but what if the problem is really in your disk controller? Or
maybe it's the way you've designed your pages or the ISP you're using.

The book covers web server optimization for all major platforms and includes coverage of LAN
performance, ISP performance, basic limits imposed by the nature of HTTP, IP and TCP. We also
cover field-proven methods to improve static & dynamic page content from database access and
the mysteries of graphic file manipulation and tuning.

If you've got the choice between spending fifteen thousand on a new line, or two hundred dollars
in new hardware plus the cost of this book, which decision would your boss prefer?

Professional Visual C++ ISAPI Programming

Author: Michael Tracy
ISBN: 1861000664
Price: $40.00 C$56.00 £36.99

This is a working developer's guide to customizing Microsoft's
Internet Information Server, which is now an integrated and
free addition to the NT4.0 platform. This is essential reading
for real-world web site development and expects readers to
already be competent C++ and C programmers. Although all
techniques in the book are workable under various C++
compilers, users of Visual C++ 4.1 will benefit from the ISAPI
extensions supplied in its AppWizard.

This book covers extension and filter programming in depth. There is a walk through the API
structure but not a reference to endless calls. Instead, we illustrate the key specifications with
example programs.

HTTP and HTML instructions are issued as an appendix. We introduce extensions by mimicking
popular CGI scripts and there's a specific chapter on controlling cookies. With filters we are not
just re-running generic web code - these are leading-edge filter methods specifically designed for
the IIS API.

Beginning Visual Basic 5

Author: Peter Wright

ISBN: 1861000081

Price: $29.95 C$41.95 £27.49

The third edition of the best selling Beginner's Guide to Visual Basic is the most comprehensive guide for the complete beginner to Visual Basic 5. Peter Wright's unique style and humour have long been a favourite with beginners and, because the book has just the one author, you can be sure that the text has a consistent voice and flow.

As with all Wrox Beginning guides, every topic is illustrated with a Try It Out, where each new concept is accompanied by a focused example and explanatory text. This way, you get to create an example program that demonstrates some theory, and then you get to examine the code behind it in detail.

Peter starts with a lightning tour of the Visual Basic 5 environment, before moving on to the creation of a Visual Basic 5 program. Critical concepts such as events, properties and methods are given the attention they deserve. You'll find yourself starting with basics, such as "What is a control and how does VB5 use them?", but you'll quickly be able to move on to more complex topics such as graphics, object-oriented programming, control creation and creating databases. By the end of the book, you'll be able to build your own application from scratch, with very impressive results.

Instant VB5 ActiveX Control Creation

Authors: Alex Homer, Stephen Jakab
and Darren Gill

ISBN: 1861000235

Price: $29.95 C$41.95 £27.99

Aimed at experienced Visual Basic programmers who want to be able to create their own controls using the freely downloadable Visual Basic 5 CCE, this book takes you from an overview of VB5 CCE, right up to how to create your own, highly customized controls. It explains in detail how to create different types of control, including sub-classed, aggregate and owner-draw controls, and also includes coverage of the issues you need to be aware of when distributing your controls.

Instant ActiveX Web Database Programming

Authors: Alex Homer, Stephen Jakab
and Darren Gill
ISBN: 1861000464
Price: $29.95 C$41.95 £27.99

This book describes practical techniques for publishing database information on the web or intranet. Aimed at web developers who want to improve their sites by adding live data, and at programmers who want to create functional business applications for the Internet or intranet, the book covers IDC, OLEISAPI, dbWeb, Index Server and Active Server Pages. It also takes a look at the security issues you need to consider when publishing database information on the Internet.

Visual C++ 4 MasterClass

Authors: Various   ISBN: 1874416443
Price: $49.95 C$69.95 £46.99

The book starts by covering software design issues related to programming with MFC, providing tips and techniques for creating great MFC extensions. This is followed by an analysis of porting issues when moving your applications from 16 to 32 bits.

The next section shows how you can use COM/OLE in the real world. This begins with an examination of COM technologies and the foundations of OLE (aggregation, uniform data transfer, drag and drop and so on) and is followed by a look at extending standard MFC OLE Document clients and servers to make use of database storage.

The third section of the book concentrates on making use of, and extending, the features that Windows 95 first brought to the public, including the 32-bit common controls, and the new style shell. You'll see how to make use of all the new features including appbars, file viewers, shortcuts, and property sheets.

The fourth section of the book provides a detailed look at multimedia and games programming, making use of Windows multimedia services and the facilities provided by the Game SDK (DirectX).

The final section covers 'net programming, whether it's for the Internet or the intranet. You'll see how to make the most of named pipes, mailslots, NetBIOS and WinSock before seeing how to create the corporate intranet system of your dreams using WinINet and ActiveX technology.

Beginning Linux Programming

Authors: Neil Matthew, Richard Stones
ISBN: 187441680
Price: $36.95 C$51.95 £33.99

The book is unique in that it teaches UNIX programming in a simple and structured way, using Linux and its associated and freely available development tools as the main platform. Assuming familiarity with the UNIX environment and a basic knowledge of C, the book teaches you how to put together UNIX applications that make the most of your time, your OS and your machine's capabilities.

Having introduced the programming environment and basic tools, the authors turn their attention initially on shell programming. The chapters then concentrate on programming UNIX with C, showing you how to work with files, access the UNIX environment, input and output data using terminals and curses, and manage data. After another round with development and debugging tools, the book discusses processes and signals, pipes and other IPC mechanisms, culminating with a chapter on sockets. Programming the X-Window system is introduced with Tcl/Tk and Java. Finally, the book covers programming for the Internet using HTML and CGI.

The book aims to discuss UNIX programming as described in the relevant POSIX and X/Open specifications, so the code is tested with that in mind. All the source code from the book is available under the terms of the Gnu Public License from the Wrox web site.

Professional SQL Server 6.5 Admin

Authors: Various   ISBN: 1874416494
Price: $44.95 C$62.95 £41.49

This book is not a tutorial in the complete product, but is for those who need to become either professionally competent in preparation for Microsoft exams or those DBAs needing real-world advice to do their job better. It assumes knowledge of databases and wastes no time on getting novices up to speed on the basics of data structure and using a database server in a Client-Server arena.

The book covers everything from installation and configuration right through to the actual managing of the server. There are whole chapters devoted to essential administrative issues such as transaction management and locking, replication, security, monitoring of the system and database backup and recovery. We've used proven techniques to bring robust code and script that will increase your ability to troubleshoot your database structure and improve its performance. Finally, we have looked very carefully at the new features in 6.5, such as the Web Assistant and Distributed Transaction Controller (DTC) and provided you with key practical examples. Where possible, throughout the book we have described a DBA solution in Transact SQL, Visual Basic and the Enterprise Manager.

Wrox Press
http://www.wrox.com/

Beginning Java 1.1

Author: Ivor Horton
ISBN: 1861000278
Price: $36.00 C$50.40 £32.99
Available May 97

If you've enjoyed this book, you'll get a lot from Ivor's new book, Beginning Java.

Beginning Java teaches Java 1.1 from scratch, taking in all the fundamental features of the Java language, along with practical applications of Java's extensive class libraries. While it assumes some little familiarity with general programming concepts, Ivor takes time to cover the basics of the language in depth. He assumes no knowledge of object-oriented programming.

Ivor first introduces the essential bits of Java without which no program will run. Then he covers how Java handles data, and the syntax it uses to make decisions and control program flow. The essentials of object-oriented programming with Java are covered, and these concepts are reinforced throughout the book. Chapters on exceptions, threads and I/O follow, before Ivor turns to Java's graphics support and applet ability. Finally the book looks at JDBC and RMI, two additions to the Java 1.1 language which allow Java programs to communicate with databases and other Java programs.

Beginning Visual C++ 5

Author: Ivor Horton ISBN: 1861000081
Price: $39.95 C$55.95 £36.99

Visual Basic is a great tool for generating applications quickly and easily, but if you really want to create fast, tight programs using the latest technologies, Visual C++ is the only way to go.

Ivor Horton's Beginning Visual C++ 5 is for anyone who wants to learn C++ and Windows programming with Visual C++ 5 and MFC, and the combination of the programming discipline you've learned from this book and Ivor's relaxed and informal teaching style will make it even easier for you to succeed in taming structured programming and writing real Windows applications.

The book begins with a fast-paced but comprehensive tutorial to the C++ language. You'll then go on to learn about object orientation with C++ and how this relates to Windows programming, culminating with the design and implementation of a sizable class-based C++ application. The next part of the book walks you through creating Windows applications using MFC, including sections on output to the screen and printer, how to program menus, toolbars and dialogs, and how to respond to a user's actions. The final few chapters comprise an introduction COM and examples of how to create ActiveX controls using both MFC and the Active Template Library (ATL).

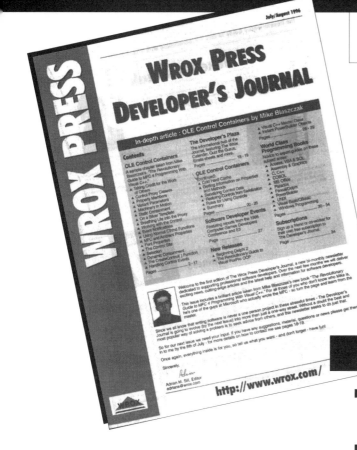

'Ever thought about writing a book'

Have you ever thought to yourself "I could do better than that"? Well, here's your chance to prove it! Wrox Press are continually looking for new authors and contributors and it doesn't matter if you've never been published before.

Interested?

contact John Franklin at Wrox Press, 30 Lincoln Road, Birmingham, B27 6PA, UK.

e-mail johnf@wrox.com